WOMEN'S LIBERATION!

▲

▲

WOMEN'S
LIBERATION!

*Feminist Writings That Inspired a Revolution
& Still Can*

▼

Edited by
Alix Kates Shulman and Honor Moore

A LIBRARY OF AMERICA *Special Publication*

Contents

1980–1991

Acronyms

AFDC	Aid to Families with Dependent Children
CARASA	Committee for Abortion Rights and against Sterilization Abuse
CORE	Congress of Racial Equality
CR	Consciousness Raising
EEOC	Equal Employment Opportunity Commission
ERA	Equal Rights Amendment
FACT	Feminist Anti-Censorship Taskforce
FAP	Family Assistance Plan
GAI	Guaranteed Adequate Income
ILGWU	International Ladies' Garment Workers' Union
LAPD	Los Angeles Police Department
NAACP	National Association for the Advancement of Colored People
NARAL	National Association for the Repeal of Abortion Laws; changed to National Abortion Rights Action League after 1973 Supreme Court's *Roe v. Wade* decision legalizing abortion
NBFO	National Black Feminist Organization
NOW	National Organization for Women
NWRO	National Welfare Rights Organization
NYRF	New York Radical Feminists
NYRW	New York Radical Women
SCUM	Society for Cutting Up Men
SDS	Students for a Democratic Society
SNCC	Student Non-Violent Coordinating Committee
U.S. PROS	U.S. PROstitutes Collective
WAP	Women Against Pornography
WITCH	Women's International Terrorist Conspiracy from Hell; various other, temporary meanings

Introduction

DURING THE 1960s, '70s, and '80s, feminist activism—richly diverse both in the women involved and in its aims, tone, and strategies—exploded in the United States and around the world, forever changing society by expanding the rights, opportunities, and identities available to women. And at the center of everything that the women's liberation movement achieved was the writing that both forged and propelled it, writing that continues to inspire, challenge, educate, and even offend.

Yet, by the mid-1980s, despite occasional victories, the feminist movement had become so distorted and vilified that the tag "feminist" was rejected by many women who had welcomed the changes in their lives the movement produced. At the end of World War II—and even as recently as 1970, as detailed by Gene Boyer in her essay, excerpted in this volume, "Are Woman Equal Under the Law?"—a husband's forcing sex on his wife was not legally considered rape. In some states, unless there was a title establishing the wife's ownership, all her purchases belonged to her husband, even if bought entirely with her own earnings, and a married woman could not make a contract or obtain a credit card without her husband's signature. In many states a mother who daily lifted and carried her toddler could be barred from any job that required lifting more than twenty-five pounds, or, in California, ten. Newspaper employment ads were segregated by sex, and sometimes also by race. There were no policewomen or female firefighters and hardly any women broadcasters—female voices were considered too "shrill." In fact, any job that required authority was in practice off limits to women: most law and medical schools had female quotas, and women were excluded from the clergy of most religions. Women made on average fifty-nine cents for every dollar a man made for similar work, with the largest gender pay gap for women of color. All hurricanes bore female names, women being considered the creators of chaos, and in 1970 a prominent physician famously declared on TV that women were unfit for high office due to "raging hormonal imbalances of the lunar cycle."

▲▼

The revolution began quietly in 1946, when a French philosopher in her thirties named Simone de Beauvoir began to write about what it meant to be a woman. When her book *Le Deuxième Sexe* (*The Second Sex*), which criticized all Western thought for positioning woman as Other and man as default, was published in France in 1949, it became a sensation, and, given its stance on religion and sexuality, was banned by the Vatican.

When *The Second Sex: Woman as Other* was published in the U.S. in 1953, it had a profound effect, influencing many of the women who would go on to create the American feminist movement. One of them was Betty Friedan, then a freelance writer for women's magazines, who surveyed her Smith College class at their fifteenth reunion and found that an overwhelming number had a common set of complaints, ranging from the vague to the desperate. To their shared malaise she gave the appellation "the problem that has no name." *The Feminine Mystique*, published in February 1963, the first chapter of which opens this book, quickly became a best seller. Friedan based her conclusions, which included the need for married women to work outside the home, on her sample of white educated housewives. Though she did not take up the concerns of women, both white and of color, who already had outside jobs and whose paychecks were essential to a family's survival, the book's revelations of discrimination against all women reverberated through the culture.

Like *The Second Sex*, *The Feminine Mystique* was a call to action, but no movement yet existed. This changed in 1966, during the Third National Conference of Commissions on the Status of Women in Washington, D.C., which was attended by Friedan. The network of state commissions had been created five years earlier by President John F. Kennedy to document the barriers that limited women's full participation in American life. The initial report of the commissions, published in 1963, endorsed women's legal equality, and sex—what is now called gender—was included in Title VII of the Civil Rights Act of 1964 as one of the bases for which employment discrimination was prohibited. The Equal Employment Opportunity Commission (EEOC) was established as Title VII's enforcement arm, but although nearly a third of the almost two thousand complaints filed during the EEOC's first year concerned sex discrimination, those complaints were seldom acted upon. Anger at this injustice led twenty-eight conference attendees, meeting in Friedan's hotel room in June 1966, to plan a civil rights organization "to bring women into full participation in the mainstream of American society now, assuming all the privileges and responsibilities thereof in truly equal partnership with men."

The result was the National Organization for Women (NOW), the first grassroots organization of the movement that has been written into history as the second wave of feminism. (The nineteenth-century women's rights movement, which won the women's suffrage amendment in 1920, is known as the first wave.) NOW's first organizing conference was held in Washington, D.C., four months later. The forty-nine members in attendance—five of whom have writings in this volume: Friedan, Gene Boyer, Mary O. Eastwood, and civil rights activists Pauli Murray and Shirley Chisholm—hammered out a platform focused on ending legal discrimination in employment, education, and reproductive rights. NOW grew rapidly and today has hundreds of thousands of members, female and male, in more than five hundred chapters nationwide.

Soon after its founding, NOW would feel pressure from an emerging movement of radical women activists to broaden its concerns. That movement, which named itself women's liberation, had its own history, goals, and style that differed from those of NOW. Its members, many of them young veterans of the civil rights, antiwar, and student movements, began to extend the radical social analyses they had learned in those movements to the situation of women. Some organized women's caucuses within their civil rights and New Left organizations, such as the Student Non-Violent Coordinating Committee (SNCC) and the Young Lords Party (both represented in this volume); but others, after presenting their ideas to dismissive or contemptuous male comrades, decided their cause required an independent women's movement. Unlike women's rights activists (also sometimes called moderate, reformist, or liberal feminists) who created traditional organizations like NOW and the National Women's Political Caucus with officers, bylaws, and chapters, radical feminists came together in small, autonomous, women-only groups that rejected formal structure and focused on exposing the deep-rooted attitudes of sexism and misogyny and challenging everyday humiliations and injustices.

In Chicago, in 1967, a small band of radical feminists established The Westside Group, widely considered the country's first radical feminist group. When its cofounder, a twenty-two-year-old art student named Shulamith Firestone, moved to New York City later that year, she helped organize New York Radical Women, the first group in that city. Soon small groups were forming in cities, in towns, and on campuses all over the country—from Boston, New York, and Gainesville, to Chicago, Detroit, Iowa City, and Madison, to Seattle, Berkeley, and Los Angeles. By the early 1970s, radical feminists of diverse identities, ethnicities, races, classes, and sexualities had organized into groups— mainly of like rather than mixed membership—of Black feminists, lesbian feminists, socialist feminists, separatist feminists, high school feminists, as well as collectives devoted to a particular feminist activity, such as providing safe, though illegal, abortions; publishing a journal or books; opening a gallery or bookstore; opposing racism; practicing women's self-defense; teaching vaginal self-examination; and starting a day care center or a battered women's shelter.

From among the thousands of varied groups, we have included in this book pieces by New York Radical Women, the Black Women's Liberation Group of Mt. Vernon, WITCH, The Feminists, Redstockings, Radicalesbians, La Raza, the Boston Women's Health Collective, The Combahee River Collective, Wages against Housework, and U.S. PROStitutes Collective, several of which are pictured in our photo insert.

In some cities, umbrella organizations like The Chicago Women's Liberation Union or the Boston area's Bread and Roses gathered autonomous groups into loose coalitions. Frequently groups divided or split apart—resulting in the proliferation of new ideas and new organizations, and sometimes anger or heartbreak. Yet despite their many differences, radical feminists shared the overarching goal of creating a mass women's liberation movement to transform power relations between the sexes and thus revolutionize society.

Having grown up in a society in which female subordination in nearly every aspect of life was not only taken for granted but so normal as to be often invisible, radical feminists embraced as their foremost task convincing women of their oppression as women—and the need for a women's liberation movement. This was accomplished through two major organizing methods: the technique of consciousness-raising (CR), by which women in small groups gained understanding of their subjugation through shared personal testimony—described in Kathie Sarachild's article on CR in this volume—and women's liberation writings, a creative ferment of ideas proliferated via feminist newspapers, journals, conferences, and radio programs on radical stations. For many, recognition of a need for change was instantaneous—an experience Jane O'Reilly named a click! moment in her 1972 article "The Housewife's Moment of Truth," included here. A mounting sense of purpose aroused excitement, commitment, and sometimes such feelings of rebirth that some women, rejecting patronymics, renamed themselves: Elana Dykewoman, Laura X, and Judy Chicago, whose name change proclamation we include in our photo insert.

Under the slogans "the personal is political" (discussed by Carol Hanisch in her article "The Personal Is Political") and "sisterhood is powerful," women in small groups, in many thousands of living rooms, kitchens, and newly opened women's centers throughout the country, practiced CR by describing their maltreatment and exploitation in a range of ordinary experiences concerning sex, race, class, family, jobs, housework, health care, childcare, and more. Speaking for the first time of forbidden truths or private humiliations—as would women in the #MeToo movement decades later—they discovered that feelings they thought unique were widely shared: resentment at being judged by their looks, at having to fake orgasms, at being overlooked, silenced, and patronized. In 1969, CR went public in a Greenwich Village church, when the radical feminist group Redstockings presented the movement's first public speakout—on the subject of abortion—to be followed in subsequent years by other groups' speakouts on rape and sexual harassment, which ended taboos and opened vital national conversations. It was after reading about the first rape speakout that I, Honor, joined my first CR group in Manhattan.

At the same time, from the mid-1960s on, beginning with Valerie Solanas's notorious *SCUM Manifesto*, excerpted here, there was a great outpouring of feminist writing, from incitements to action, group manifestos, and visionary analyses to seething satires, passionate polemics, and the burgeoning of feminist poetry, fiction, plays, film, and visual arts. Before photocopier technology and the Internet, these writings circulated as mimeographed pamphlets piled onto literature tables at every feminist gathering, and in the new feminist newsletters and journals springing up across the country, such as Chicago's *Voice of the Women's Liberation Movement* and *The Lavender Woman*, Washington D.C.'s *off our backs*, Denver's *Big Mama Rag*, Iowa City's *Ain't I a Woman?*, Seattle's *Lilith*, Baltimore's *Women: A Journal of Liberation*, Boston's *No More Fun & Games*, New York's *Aphra*, *Triple Jeopardy*, and *Notes from the First Year*, and the San Francisco Bay Area's *Tooth and Nail*, *It Ain't Me Babe*, and *Mother Lode*.

In 1970, the first anthologies of these writings were issued by mainstream publishers and reached an eager mass audience: *Sisterhood Is Powerful*, *The Black Woman*, *Voices of Women's Liberation*, *Women's Liberation: A Blueprint for the Future*. Also that year, two scathing book-length radical feminist manifestos, *The Dialectic of Sex* by Shulamith Firestone and *Sexual Politics* by Kate Millett, both excerpted here, swept the nation and the best-seller lists.

On August 26, 1970—fifty years to the day after the suffrage amendment was adopted and two years after the small, now iconic Miss America protest garnered national media attention for women's liberation (see photo insert), and which I, Alix, helped to plan and gleefully attended—the movement held its first mass demonstration. A huge march, organized by NOW as a Women's Strike for Equality, urged women not to go to work or do housework that day ("Don't iron while the strike is hot!"). Some fifty thousand feminists, individually and in more than seventy groups—with names like Revolutionary Childcare Collective, the Lesbian Food Conspiracy, Black Women's Liberation, Women Artists in Revolution, and Half of Brooklyn, representing both the radical and moderate branches of the movement—paraded together in triumph down New York's Fifth Avenue (see photo insert). Demonstrators carried signs expressing the day's spirit and demands: "Free Universal Childcare," "I Am Not a Barbie Doll," "Free Abortion on Demand," "Liberté

Egalité Sororité," "Equal Pay for Equal Work." In Boston, Syracuse, Pittsburgh, Detroit, Minneapolis, St. Louis, San Francisco, and Los Angeles "sister marches" were held, drawing between one hundred and five thousand demonstrators. The movement had entered the mainstream.

The new movement encompassed a culturally, ideologically, and racially diverse multitude of activists and visionaries and a cadre of daring writers and theorists who would reevaluate nearly every aspect of women's lives and so thoroughly open new avenues of opportunity that it would seem to subsequent generations they had always been there. The movement that began by addressing "a problem that has no name" had become a movement that named with impunity, bringing into being new ideas and opportunities. Among the new terms were sexism, sexual harassment, marital rape, date rape, wife battering, sisterhood, double and triple jeopardy (early designations of what came to be called intersectionality), womanism, and women's liberation. The ninety pieces in this volume trace that movement's arc.

The week of the August 26, 1970, strike and marches, the mass newsweekly magazine *Time* profiled author Kate Millett and put on its cover her portrait by Alice Neel. Meanwhile, at *Newsweek,* the other mass-circulation newsweekly, forty-six women, many of them researchers who had no opportunities for advancement, let alone bylines—though their qualifications were usually equal to those of the male writers they assisted—were preparing to file an EEOC Title VII suit for sex discrimination. They shrewdly filed their suit on the very day *Newsweek* published "Women in Revolt," a cover story about the new movement, for which the male editors had hired a freelance female writer. In 1973 the magazine settled the suit.

Frustrated at their marginalization by the mainstream media, another group of women journalists and editors launched, in January 1972, a national feminist monthly magazine they named *Ms.* for the honorific that conceals—as "Mr." does—marital status. A year later, two young feminists, Kirsten Grimstad and Susan Rennie, hit the road to gather information on the panorama of the new women's culture for a pair of books titled *The New Woman's Survival Catalog* (1973) and *The New Woman's Survival Sourcebook* (1975), which spread news of women-run services and resources available in towns and cities all over the country. In one locale, a discretely situated lesbian bar was repurposed as a venue for feminist poetry readings and theatre performances; in another, feminists took over an old-line sexist radical newspaper. Playwrights, fed-up actresses, and women directors who couldn't get hired started women's theatre groups, and women singers and musicians started festivals and record labels.

These guidebooks are snapshots of the scope and reach of feminism at the time, including women's centers, women's restaurants, bookstores, schools, communes, and other enterprises that catered to women, including, in Kansas City, a feminist hotel. Many of them would vanish within a few years, but some, like the Feminist Press, the Boston Women's Health Collective, and a national network of battered women's shelters and rape crisis centers, endured, sometimes evolving into nonprofit institutions.

──────── ▲▼ ────────

While the media described every argument among feminists as a fatal division or a catfight, with hindsight one can see a movement that was wildly diverse and alive, arguing over differences of tactics, sensibility, interpretation, and ideology. In our book such arguments are explored or passionately waged by, among others, Dana Densmore, Lucinda Cisler, Ti-Grace Atkinson, Barbara Smith, Ellen Willis, bell hooks, and Ann Snitow. And, from the mid-1970s on, the addition of new, very personal writings enhanced feminist literature, including the work of Alice Walker, Michele Wallace, Maxine Hong Kingston, Adrienne Rich, Sonia Johnson, Jo Freeman, Sonia Sanchez, and Joan Nestle, all represented here.

Yet, even as feminism continued to change U.S. society, by the late 1970s a powerful conservative backlash against feminism was gaining force, driven by opposition to abortion, homosexuality, and the proposed Equal Rights Amendment (ERA) to the U.S. Constitution, which states, simply: "Equality of rights under the law shall not be denied or abridged by the United States or by any State on account of sex."

Conservative and religious anti-feminism gained a critical success when, four years after the Supreme Court legalized abortion in *Roe v. Wade* (1973), Congress passed the 1977 Hyde Amendment, which forbade the use of federal funds for almost all abortions, greatly restricting poor women's access and strengthening the anti-abortion pro-life movement. In another conservative triumph, a growing anti-ERA movement, led by Phyllis Schlafly and supported by the insurance industry and other businesses, focused on lobbying state legislatures to defeat it, predicting that the amendment's passage would cause women to be drafted into the military, make all public bathrooms unisex, and undermine family values. Though the ERA had easily passed in Congress in 1972 and was ratified by thirty-five of the required thirty-eight states by the deadline in 1979, so strong was this resistance that even after a three-year deadline extension, not one more state ratified it, and five conservative state legislatures rescinded their prior ratification. By then, most of the small, unstructured early women's liberation groups that had done so much to change women's lives and deepen American awareness of sexist oppression had disbanded, and the name "women's liberation movement" was being replaced by the tamer "women's movement," as lamented in Anne Forer's article "Sex and Women's Liberation," included here.

Despite these setbacks, feminist organizing and writing continued to expand the scope of activism and thinking, particularly among women of color and their allies. The Combahee River Collective of Black lesbian women was founded in 1977, CARASA (the Committee for Abortion Rights and Against Sterilization Abuse) in 1979, and Kitchen Table: Women of Color Press in 1980 (see photo insert). *This Bridge Called My Back,* the influential anthology of writings by radical women of color, was published in 1981, followed, in 1983, by both *A Gathering of Spirit,* the first anthology of indigenous women's writings edited by an indigenous woman, and *Home Girls: A Black Feminist Anthology.* From *Bridge,* we have excerpted essays by Gloria Anzaldúa, Cherríe Moraga, Rosario Morales, and Mitsuye Yamada, and from *Spirit,* pieces by Beth Brant, Paula Gunn Allen, and Kate Shanley.

In 1975, Congress had funded a National Conference for Women, with delegates elected from every state, including a minority of anti-feminists; it was held in Houston, Texas, in 1977 (see photo insert), and passed a wish list of twenty-six resolutions in areas from rape to reproductive freedom and education to sexual preference and welfare rights. But after 1980, when Ronald Reagan rode a conservative wave into the presidency, government support for feminist efforts halted, including funding for many grassroots women's cultural organizations. From then on, the movement was forced to divert its energies to defending its gains from escalating right-wing attacks, and internal divisions that had long simmered became insurmountable. The notorious "sex wars" of the late 1970s and 1980s—represented in this volume with pieces by Susan Jacoby, Andrea Dworkin, Catharine MacKinnon, Paula Webster, Sarah Wynter, and Rachel West—reached a crisis at the 1982 Barnard Conference on Sexuality, which Women Against Pornography (WAP) picketed and where feminist factions battled over the ever-fraught issues of pornography and the nature and practice of sexuality itself.

Facing relentless backlash by political and religious conservatives, popular culture, and the media—as detailed in our final selection, from Susan Faludi's best-selling *Backlash* (1991)—many feminist activists turned their focus to single issues, such as equal pay for equal work or violence against women or abortion rights. Coalitions of large grassroots organizations led by NOW marshaled hundreds of thousands to march for reproductive rights in the capital in 1989 and 1992 and more than a million in 2004. Yet, despite continuing progress in areas like women's employment and education, each single issue became ever harder to view as part of the overarching vision of women's freedom and a transformed society that had powered early women's liberation.

Women writers and artists who had been inspired or influenced by feminism persisted, although sometimes muting directly feminist content. Other feminists found in university women's studies departments, as discussed by Catharine R. Stimpson in "The New Feminism and Women's Studies," a haven and opportunity to pursue feminist scholarship. But throughout the 1980s and subsequent decades, as the backlash demonized feminism as the cause, rather than the solution, of women's discontent, and the mainstream media stopped covering feminism unless the news undercut feminist achievement, the mass women's liberation movement, which had so profoundly changed American society, stagnated. When archconservative Clarence Thomas was confirmed to the Supreme Court in 1991 despite law professor Anita Hill's compelling televised allegations of sexual harassment, the movement's impotence was evident. By then, in place of claiming "feminist" as a proud sobriquet, many women who appreciated the movement's accomplishments volunteered, "I'm not a feminist, but—," a bafflingly paradoxical disclaimer.

———————— ▲▼ ————————

Two decades into the twenty-first century, in an increasingly polarized society with vast, widening disparities between rich and poor, a new, multifaceted, and intersectional feminist activism has swept the country and the world. The label "feminist" is once again embraced; millions of women and men march in protest against the misogyny, racism, and xenophobia of a mostly white male ruling class; even the media that shunned feminism for decades now reports on it seriously. Today's feminist movement is the daughter of the radical women's liberation movement that was formed and fashioned from the writings collected in this volume, writings now urgently needed.

Starting in the 1970s and through the 1980s, feminist writing greatly expanded, from those early mimeographed manifestos to entire books devoted to exploring new subjects or old subjects through a new feminist lens: books on the psychology of women, motherhood, women's history, sexuality, religion, rape, sexual harassment, and pornography—all excerpted in this volume—as well as many moving memoirs, novels, and books of poetry. In fact, the literature of women's liberation was so vast and varied that this collection must be considered only a sampler; other editors might have made different selections.

Yet, having seen how frequently the second wave has been mischaracterized as a monolithic white women's movement, and often as a merely reformist or even elitist one as well, we are grateful for this opportunity to demonstrate in the writings collected here the falsity of those diminishments, as we know first-hand from our lifetimes in the movement. This collection, unlike many others, shows not only the movement's great diversity of race, class, and ethnicity, with writings by African American, Latina, Asian American, American Indian, and white women, but also diversity of politics, emphases, styles, interests, sexual practice, aesthetics, and vision. As with Frances M. Beal's 1969 essay "Double Jeopardy" and the 1977 Combahee River Collective's discussion of "inter-locking oppressions," the theme of intersectionality is frequently articulated in these pieces, though the term was not coined until 1989, by feminist legal scholar Kimberlé Crenshaw.

For myself, Alix, as coeditor of this collection I view the opportunity to correct these stereotypes and misconceptions as the culmination of a lifetime steeped both in the literature of feminism, as reader, writer, and teacher, and also in radical activism: weaning my second child in order to travel to the 1963 March on Washington, where Martin Luther King, Jr., declared his dream; then attending, in late 1967, my first meeting of New York's earliest women's liberation group, New York Radical Women; then, with our long-lived social action group Take Back the Future, organizing demonstrations well into the twenty-first century; and right on up to today's pandemic-endangered protest marches for racial justice and gay pride, which, because of my advanced age, I join by chanting from my open window as they pass by. Not least, I've wel-comed the chance to put to more than personal use my extensive, treasured library of now historic—though too often publicly forgotten—feminist writ-ings, here remembered and redeployed.

I, Honor, made my first public feminist gesture by inviting poets Adrienne Rich and Sonia Sanchez (both included in this volume) to read in a Manhat-tan poetry series. Soon I was helping to organize group readings by women poets; Alix attended these, and we soon got to know each other. My activism, different from hers, proceeded in teaching women's poetry-writing workshops where I witnessed the growing feminist awareness of fledgling writers of all ages who had not been part of the movement. When my first play, reviewed brilliantly enough out of town, moved to Broadway only to be shuttered after one night by a phalanx of white male reviewers, I responded by editing an anthology of plays by women.

We began this anthology when it seemed certain Hillary Clinton would be elected president. Another heartbreak, I thought, despairing. And then came the massive 2017 Women's Marches, soon followed by the revelations of sexual harassment and sexual assault that exploded in the #MeToo movement, which had been launched in 2006 by African American activist Tarana Burke. An encounter with a young woman thrilled by a 2010 women's group reading from *Poems from the Women's Movement,* which I edited for Library of America, reminded me of my ignorance, as a young feminist, of the women's suffrage movement. "That was awesome," she said. "We have to start a revolution." She knew nothing of the movement that had so informed my life. With this anthology, we offer a new generation of revolutionary feminists access to what our movement would have called their *herstory.*

We have arranged the ninety entries chronologically to reveal the movement's development, recognizing that our choice to end in 1991 is somewhat arbitrary, since women's liberation writings continue to be published to this day. It is with regret that we, a novelist and a poet who participated in the movement and in the creation of its literature ourselves, have had to exclude for reasons of space the vibrant feminist fiction, poetry, and drama that stirred a generation, as well as major consequential essays too long to include in full and impossible for us to excerpt. Nor have we included academic writing, which, while expanding the scope of feminist thought, is addressed mainly to scholars.

———— ▲▼ ————

We hope that today's readers may discover in the women's liberation writings of the 1960s, '70s, and '80s paths imagined but not taken, cautionary reflections, insightful analyses, creative actions, damaging mistakes, and, most of all, inspiration.

Alix Kates Shulman and Honor Moore
August 2020

WOMEN'S LIBERATION!

1963–1969

BETTY FRIEDAN

(from) *The Feminine Mystique*
The Problem That Has No Name

Betty Friedan (1921–2006) first encountered feminism reading Simone de Beauvoir's *The Second Sex*. Four years later, pursuing an intuition, she distributed a questionnaire at her fifteenth Smith College reunion asking classmates about their lives. Their near-unanimous discontent matched hers; she planned to explore that discontent in a magazine piece but ended up writing a book. Boldly argued and thoroughly researched, *The Feminine Mystique* (1963) identified, analyzed, and attacked myths and beliefs that bound women to an ideology—a "mystique"—of which they were largely unconscious. While Friedan's sample centered on the educated and well-off—leaving out women of color and women who worked out of necessity rather than for fulfillment—her book was the fuse that ignited a massive movement that reached women in every corner of American life. Here is the opening chapter, "The Problem That Has No Name."

THE PROBLEM lay buried, unspoken, for many years in the minds of American women. It was a strange stirring, a sense of dissatisfaction, a yearning that women suffered in the middle of the twentieth century in the United States. Each suburban wife struggled with it alone. As she made the beds, shopped for groceries, matched slipcover material, ate peanut butter sandwiches with her children, chauffeured Cub Scouts and Brownies, lay beside her husband at night—she was afraid to ask even of herself the silent question—"Is this all?"

For over fifteen years there was no word of this yearning in the millions of words written about women, for women, in all the columns, books and articles by experts telling women their role was to seek fulfillment as wives and mothers. Over and over women heard in voices of tradition and of Freudian sophistication that they could desire no greater destiny than to glory in their own femininity. Experts told them how to catch a man and keep him, how to breastfeed children and handle their toilet training, how to cope with sibling rivalry and adolescent rebellion; how to buy a dishwasher, bake bread, cook gourmet snails, and build a swimming pool with their own hands; how to dress, look, and act more feminine and make marriage more exciting; how to keep their husbands from dying young and their sons from growing into delinquents. They were taught to pity the neurotic, unfeminine, unhappy women who wanted to be poets or physicists or presidents. They learned that truly feminine women do not want careers, higher education, political rights—the independence and the opportunities that the old-fashioned feminists fought for. Some women, in their forties and fifties, still remembered painfully giving up those dreams, but most of the younger women no longer even thought about them. A thousand expert voices applauded their femininity, their adjustment, their new maturity. All they had to do was devote their lives from earliest girlhood to finding a husband and bearing children.

By the end of the nineteen-fifties, the average marriage age of women in America dropped to 20, and was still dropping, into the teens. Fourteen million girls were engaged by 17. The proportion of women attending college in comparison with men dropped from 47 per cent in 1920 to 35 per cent in 1958. A century earlier, women had fought for higher education; now girls went to college to get a husband. By the mid-fifties, 60 per cent dropped out of college to marry, or because they were afraid too much education would be a marriage bar. Colleges built dormitories for "married students," but the students were almost always the husbands. A new degree was instituted for the wives—"Ph.T." (Putting Husband Through).

Then American girls began getting married in high school. And the women's magazines, deploring the unhappy statistics about these young marriages, urged that courses on marriage, and marriage counselors, be installed in the high schools. Girls started going steady at twelve and thirteen, in junior high. Manufacturers put out brassieres with false bosoms of foam rubber for little girls of ten. And an advertisement for a child's dress, sizes 3–6x, in the *New York Times* in the fall of 1960, said: "She Too Can Join the Man-Trap Set."

By the end of the fifties, the United States birthrate was overtaking India's. The birth-control movement, renamed Planned Parenthood, was asked to find a method whereby women who had been advised that a third or fourth baby would be born dead or defective might have it anyhow. Statisticians were especially astounded at the fantastic increase in the number of babies among college women. Where once they had two children, now they had four, five, six. Women who had once wanted careers were now making careers out of having babies. So rejoiced *Life* magazine in a 1956 paean to the movement of American women back to the home.

In a New York hospital, a woman had a nervous breakdown when she found she could not breastfeed her baby. In other hospitals, women dying of cancer refused a drug which research had proved might save their lives: its side effects were said to be unfeminine. "If I have only one life, let me live it as a blonde," a larger-than-life-sized picture of a pretty, vacuous woman proclaimed from newspaper, magazine, and drugstore ads. And across America, three out of every ten women dyed their hair blonde. They ate a chalk called Metrecal, instead of food, to shrink to the size of the thin young models. Department-store buyers reported that American women, since 1939, had become three and four sizes smaller. "Women are out to fit the clothes, instead of vice-versa," one buyer said.

Interior decorators were designing kitchens with mosaic murals and original paintings, for kitchens were once again the center of women's lives. Home sewing became a million-dollar industry. Many women no longer left their homes, except to shop, chauffeur their children, or attend a social engagement with their husbands. Girls were growing up in America without ever having jobs outside the home. In the late fifties, a sociological phenomenon was suddenly remarked: a third of American women now worked, but most were no longer young and very few were pursuing careers. They were married women who held part-time jobs, selling or secretarial, to put their husbands through school, their sons through college, or to help pay the mortgage. Or they were widows supporting families. Fewer and fewer women were entering professional work. The shortages in the nursing, social work, and teaching professions caused crises in almost every American city. Concerned over the Soviet Union's lead in the space race, scientists noted that America's greatest source of unused brainpower was women. But girls would not study physics: it was "unfeminine." A girl refused a science fellowship at Johns Hopkins to take a job in a real-estate office. All she wanted, she said, was what every other American girl wanted—to get married, have four children and live in a nice house in a nice suburb.

The suburban housewife—she was the dream image of the young American women and the envy, it was said, of women all over the world. The American housewife—freed by science and labor-saving appliances from the drudgery, the dangers of childbirth and the illnesses of her grandmother. She was healthy, beautiful, educated, concerned only about her husband, her children, her home. She had found true feminine fulfillment. As a housewife and mother, she was respected as a full and equal partner to man in his world. She was free to choose automobiles, clothes, appliances, supermarkets; she had everything that women ever dreamed of.

In the fifteen years after World War II, this mystique of feminine fulfillment became the cherished and self-perpetuating core of contemporary American culture. Millions of women lived their lives in the image of those pretty pictures of the American suburban housewife, kissing their husbands goodbye in front of the picture window, depositing their stationwagonsful of children at school, and smiling as they ran the new electric waxer over the spotless kitchen floor. They baked their own bread, sewed their own and their children's clothes, kept their new washing machines and dryers running all day. They changed the sheets on the beds twice a week instead of once, took the rug-hooking class in adult education, and pitied their poor frustrated mothers, who had dreamed of having a career. Their only dream was to be perfect wives and mothers; their highest ambition to have five children and a beautiful house, their only fight to get and keep their husbands. They had no thought for the unfeminine problems of the world outside the home; they wanted the men to make the major decisions. They gloried in their role as women, and wrote proudly on the census blank: "Occupation: housewife."

For over fifteen years, the words written for women, and the words women used when they talked to each other, while their husbands sat on the other side of the room and talked shop or politics or septic tanks, were about problems with their children, or how to keep their husbands happy, or improve their children's school, or cook chicken or make slipcovers. Nobody argued whether women were inferior or superior to men; they were simply different. Words like "emancipation" and "career" sounded strange and embarrassing; no one had used them for years. When a Frenchwoman named Simone de Beauvoir wrote a book called *The Second Sex*, an American critic commented that she obviously "didn't know what life was all about," and besides, she was talking about French women. The "woman problem" in America no longer existed.

If a woman had a problem in the 1950's and 1960's, she knew that something must be wrong with her marriage, or with herself. Other women were satisfied with their lives, she thought. What kind of a woman was she if she did not feel this mysterious fulfillment waxing the kitchen floor? She was so ashamed to admit her dissatisfaction that she never knew how many other women shared it. If she tried to tell her husband, he didn't understand what she was talking about. She did not really understand it herself. For over fifteen years women in America found it harder to talk about this problem than about sex. Even the psychoanalysts had no name for it. When a woman went to a psychiatrist for help, as many women did, she would say, "I'm so ashamed," or "I must be hopelessly neurotic." "I don't know what's wrong with women today," a suburban psychiatrist said uneasily. "I only know something is wrong because most of my patients happen to be women. And their problem isn't sexual." Most women with this problem did not go to see a psychoanalyst, however. "There's nothing wrong really," they kept telling themselves. "There isn't any problem."

But on an April morning in 1959, I heard a mother of four, having coffee with four other mothers in a suburban development fifteen miles from New York, say in a tone of quiet desperation, "the problem." And the others knew, without words, that she was not talking about a problem with her husband, or her children, or her home. Suddenly they realized they all shared the same problem, the problem that has no name. They began, hesitantly, to talk about it. Later, after they had picked up their children at nursery school and taken them home to nap, two of the women cried, in sheer relief, just to know they were not alone.

Gradually I came to realize that the problem that has no name was shared by countless women in America. As a magazine writer I often interviewed women about problems with their children, or their marriages, or their houses, or their communities. But after a while I began to recognize the telltale signs of this other problem. I saw the same signs in suburban ranch houses and split-levels on Long Island and in New Jersey and Westchester County; in colonial houses in a small Massachusetts town; on patios in Memphis; in suburban and city apartments; in living rooms in the Midwest. Sometimes I sensed the problem, not as a reporter, but as a suburban housewife, for during this time I was also bringing up my own three children in Rockland County, New York. I heard echoes of the problem in college dormitories and semi-private maternity wards, at PTA meetings and luncheons of the League of Women Voters, at suburban cocktail parties, in station wagons waiting for trains, and in snatches of conversation overheard at Schrafft's. The groping words I heard from other women, on quiet afternoons when children were at school or on quiet evenings when husbands worked late, I think I understood first as a woman long before I understood their larger social and psychological implications.

Just what was this problem that has no name? What were the words women used when they tried to express it? Sometimes a woman would say "I feel empty somehow . . . incomplete." Or she would say, "I feel as if I don't exist." Sometimes she blotted out the feeling with a tranquilizer. Sometimes she thought the problem was with her husband, or her children, or that what she really needed was to redecorate her house, or move to a better neighborhood, or have an affair, or another baby. Sometimes, she went to a doctor with symptoms she could hardly describe: "A tired feeling . . . I get so angry with the children it scares me . . . I feel like crying without any reason." (A Cleveland doctor called it "the housewife's syndrome.") A number of women told me about great bleeding blisters that break out on their hands and arms. "I call it the housewife's blight," said a family doctor in Pennsylvania. "I see it so often lately in these young women with four, five and six children who bury themselves in their dishpans. But it isn't caused by detergent and it isn't cured by cortisone."

Sometimes a woman would tell me that the feeling gets so strong she runs out of the house and walks through the streets. Or she stays inside her house and cries. Or her children tell her a joke, and she doesn't laugh because she doesn't hear it. I talked to women who had spent years on the analyst's couch, working out their "adjustment to the feminine role," their blocks to "fulfillment as a wife and mother." But the desperate tone in these women's voices, and the look in their eyes, was the same as the tone and the look of other women, who were sure they had no problem, even though they did have a strange feeling of desperation.

A mother of four who left college at nineteen to get married told me:

> I've tried everything women are supposed to do—hobbies, gardening, pickling, canning, being very social with my neighbors, joining committees, running PTA teas. I can do it all, and I like it, but it doesn't leave you anything to think about—any feeling of who you are. I never had any career ambitions. All I wanted was to get married and have four children. I love the kids and Bob and my home. There's no problem you can even put a name to. But I'm desperate. I begin to feel I have no personality. I'm a server of food and a putter-on of pants and a bedmaker, somebody who can be called on when you want something. But who am I?

A twenty-three-year-old mother in blue jeans said:

> I ask myself why I'm so dissatisfied. I've got my health, fine children, a lovely new home, enough money. My husband has a real future as an electronics engineer. He doesn't have any of these feelings. He says maybe I need a vacation, let's go to New York for a weekend. But that isn't it. I always had this idea we should do everything together. I can't sit down and read a book alone. If the children are napping and I have one hour to myself I just walk through the house waiting for them to wake up. I don't make a move until I know where the rest of the crowd is going. It's as if ever since you were a little girl, there's always been somebody or something that will take care of your life: your parents, or college, or falling in love, or having a child, or moving to a new house. Then you wake up one morning and there's nothing to look forward to.

A young wife in a Long Island development said:

> I seem to sleep so much. I don't know why I should be so tired. This house isn't nearly so hard to clean as the cold-water flat we had when I was working. The children are at school all day. It's not the work. I just don't feel alive.

In 1960, the problem that has no name burst like a boil through the image of the happy American housewife. In the television commercials the pretty housewives still beamed over their foaming dishpans and *Time's* cover story on "The Suburban Wife, an American Phenomenon" protested: "Having too good a time . . . to believe that they should be unhappy." But the actual unhappiness of the American housewife was suddenly being reported—from the *New York Times* and *Newsweek* to *Good Housekeeping* and CBS Television ("The Trapped Housewife"), although almost everybody who talked about it found some superficial reason to dismiss it. It was attributed to incompetent appliance repairmen (*New York Times*), or the distances children must be chauffeured in the suburbs (*Time*), or too much PTA (*Redbook*). Some said it was the old problem—education: more and more women had education, which naturally made them unhappy in their role as housewives. "The road from Freud to Frigidaire, from Sophocles to Spock, has turned out to be a bumpy one," reported the *New York Times* (June 28, 1960). "Many young women—certainly not all—whose education plunged them into a world of ideas feel stifled in their homes. They find their routine lives out of joint with their training. Like shut-ins, they feel left out. In the last year, the problem of the educated housewife has provided the meat of dozens of speeches made by troubled presidents of women's colleges who maintain, in the face of complaints, that sixteen years of academic training is realistic preparation for wifehood and motherhood."

There was much sympathy for the educated housewife. ("Like a two-headed schizophrenic . . . once she wrote a paper on the Graveyard poets; now she writes notes to the milkman. Once she determined the boiling point of sulphuric acid; now she determines her boiling point with the overdue repairman. . . . The housewife often is reduced to screams and tears. . . . No one, it seems, is appreciative, least of all herself, of the kind of person she becomes in the process of turning from poetess into shrew.")

Home economists suggested more realistic preparation for housewives, such as high-school workshops in home appliances. College educators suggested more discussion groups on home management and the family, to prepare women for the adjustment to domestic life. A spate of articles appeared in the mass magazines offering "Fifty-eight Ways to Make Your Marriage More Exciting." No month went by without a new book by a psychiatrist or sexologist offering technical advice on finding greater fulfillment through sex.

A male humorist joked in *Harper's Bazaar* (July, 1960) that the problem could be solved by taking away woman's right to vote. ("In the pre–19th Amendment era, the American woman was placid, sheltered and sure of her role in American society. She left all the political decisions to her husband and he, in turn, left all the family decisions to her. Today a woman has to make both the family *and* the political decisions, and it's too much for her.")

A number of educators suggested seriously that women no longer be admitted to the four-year colleges and universities: in the growing college crisis, the education which girls could not use as housewives was more urgently needed than ever by boys to do the work of the atomic age.

The problem was also dismissed with drastic solutions no one could take seriously. (A woman writer proposed in *Harper's* that women be drafted for compulsory service as nurses' aides and baby-sitters.) And it was smoothed over with the age-old panaceas: "love is their answer," "the only answer is inner help," "the secret of completeness—children," "a private means of intellectual fulfillment," "to cure this toothache of the spirit—the simple formula of handing one's self and one's will over to God."[1]

The problem was dismissed by telling the housewife she doesn't realize how lucky she is—her own boss, no time clock, no junior executive gunning for her job. What if she isn't happy—does she think men are happy in this world? Does she really, secretly, still want to be a man? Doesn't she know yet how lucky she is to be a woman?

The problem was also, and finally, dismissed by shrugging that there are no solutions: this is what being a woman means, and what is wrong with American women that they can't accept their role gracefully? As *Newsweek* put it (March 7, 1960):

> She is dissatisfied with a lot that women of other lands can only dream of. Her discontent is deep, pervasive, and impervious to the superficial remedies which are offered at every hand. . . . An army of professional explorers have already charted the major sources of trouble. . . . From the beginning of time, the female cycle has defined and confined woman's role. As Freud was credited with saying: "Anatomy is destiny." Though no group of women has ever pushed these natural restrictions as far as the American wife, it seems that she still cannot accept them with good grace. . . . A

young mother with a beautiful family, charm, talent and brains is apt to dismiss her role apologetically. "What do I do?" you hear her say. "Why nothing. I'm just a housewife." A good education, it seems, has given this paragon among women an understanding of the value of everything except her own worth . . .

And so she must accept the fact that "American women's unhappiness is merely the most recently won of women's rights," and adjust and say with the happy housewife found by *Newsweek*: "We ought to salute the wonderful freedom we all have and be proud of our lives today. I have had college and I've worked, but being a housewife is the most rewarding and satisfying role. . . . My mother was never included in my father's business affairs . . . she couldn't get out of the house and away from us children. But I am an equal to my husband; I can go along with him on business trips and to social business affairs."

The alternative offered was a choice that few women would contemplate. In the sympathetic words of the *New York Times*: "All admit to being deeply frustrated at times by the lack of privacy, the physical burden, the routine of family life, the confinement of it. However, none would give up her home and family if she had the choice to make again." *Redbook* commented: "Few women would want to thumb their noses at husbands, children and community and go off on their own. Those who do may be talented individuals, but they rarely are successful women."

The year American women's discontent boiled over, it was also reported (*Look*) that the more than 21,000,000 American women who are single, widowed, or divorced do not cease even after fifty their frenzied, desperate search for a man. And the search begins early—for seventy per cent of all American women now marry before they are twenty-four. A pretty twenty-five-year-old secretary took thirty-five different jobs in six months in the futile hope of finding a husband. Women were moving from one political club to another, taking evening courses in accounting or sailing, learning to play golf or ski, joining a number of churches in succession, going to bars alone, in their ceaseless search for a man.

Of the growing thousands of women currently getting private psychiatric help in the United States, the married ones were reported dissatisfied with their marriages, the unmarried ones suffering from anxiety and, finally, depression. Strangely, a number of psychiatrists stated that, in their experience, unmarried women patients were happier than married ones. So the door of all those pretty suburban houses opened a crack to permit a glimpse of uncounted thousands of American housewives who suffered alone from a problem that suddenly everyone was talking about, and beginning to take for granted, as one of those unreal problems in American life that can never be solved—like the hydrogen bomb. By 1962 the plight of the trapped American housewife had become a national parlor game. Whole issues of magazines, newspaper columns, books learned and frivolous, educational conferences and television panels were devoted to the problem.

Even so, most men, and some women, still did not know that this problem was real. But those who had faced it honestly knew that all the superficial remedies, the sympathetic advice, the scolding words and the cheering words were somehow drowning the problem in unreality. A bitter laugh was beginning to be heard from American women. They were admired, envied, pitied, theorized over until they were sick of it, offered drastic solutions or silly choices that no one could take seriously. They got all kinds of advice from the growing armies of marriage and child-guidance counselors, psychotherapists, and armchair psychologists, on how to adjust to their role as housewives. No other road to fulfillment was offered to American women in the middle of the twentieth century. Most adjusted to their role and suffered or ignored the problem that has no name. It can be less painful, for a woman, not to hear the strange, dissatisfied voice stirring within her.

It is no longer possible to ignore that voice, to dismiss the desperation of so many American women. This is not what being a woman means, no matter what the experts say. For human suffering there is a reason; perhaps the reason has not been found because the right questions have not been asked, or pressed far enough. I do not accept the answer that there is no problem because American women have luxuries that women in other times and lands never dreamed of; part of the strange newness of the problem is that it cannot be understood in terms of the age-old material problems of man: poverty, sickness, hunger, cold. The women who suffer this problem have a hunger that food cannot fill. It persists in women whose husbands are struggling internes and law clerks, or prosperous doctors and lawyers; in wives of workers and executives who make $5,000 a year or $50,000. It is not caused by lack of material advantages; it may not even be felt by women preoccupied with desperate problems of hunger, poverty or illness. And women who think it will be solved by more money, a bigger house, a second car, moving to a better suburb, often discover it gets worse.

It is no longer possible today to blame the problem on loss of femininity: to say that education and independence and equality with men have made American women unfeminine. I have heard so many women try to deny this dissatisfied voice within themselves because it does not fit the pretty picture of femininity the experts have given them. I think, in fact, that this is the first clue to the mystery: the problem cannot be understood in the generally accepted terms by which scientists have studied women, doctors have treated them, counselors have advised them, and writers have written about them. Women who suffer this problem, in whom this voice is stirring, have lived their whole lives in the pursuit of feminine fulfillment. They are not career women (although career women may have other problems); they are women whose greatest ambition has been marriage and children. For the oldest of these women, these daughters of the American middle class, no other dream was possible. The ones in their forties and fifties who once had other dreams gave them up and threw themselves joyously into life as housewives. For the youngest, the new wives and mothers, this was the only dream. They are the ones who quit high school and college to marry, or marked time in some job in which they had no real interest until they married. These women are very "feminine" in the usual sense, and yet they still suffer the problem.

Are the women who finished college, the women who once had dreams beyond housewifery, the ones who suffer the most? According to the experts they are, but listen to these four women:

> My days are all busy, and dull, too. All I ever do is mess around. I get up at eight—I make breakfast, so I do the dishes, have lunch, do some more dishes and some laundry and cleaning in the afternoon. Then it's supper dishes and I get to sit down a few minutes before the children have to be sent to bed. . . . That's all there is to my day. It's just like any other wife's day. Humdrum. The biggest time, I am chasing kids.

> Ye Gods, what do I do with my time? Well, I get up at six. I get my son dressed and then give him breakfast. After that I wash dishes and bathe and feed the baby. Then I get lunch and while the children nap, I sew or mend or iron and do all the other things I can't get done before noon. Then I cook supper for the family and my husband watches TV while I do the dishes. After I get the children to bed, I set my hair and then I go to bed.

> The problem is always being the children's mommy, or the minister's wife and never being myself.

> A film made of any typical morning in my house would look like an old Marx Brothers' comedy. I wash the dishes, rush the older

children off to school, dash out in the yard to cultivate the chrysanthemums, run back in to make a phone call about a committee meeting, help the youngest child build a blockhouse, spend fifteen minutes skimming the newspapers so I can be well-informed, then scamper down to the washing machines where my thrice-weekly laundry includes enough clothes to keep a primitive village going for an entire year. By noon I'm ready for a padded cell. Very little of what I've done has been really necessary or important. Outside pressures lash me through the day. Yet I look upon myself as one of the more relaxed housewives in the neighborhood. Many of my friends are even more frantic. In the past sixty years we have come full circle and the American housewife is once again trapped in a squirrel cage. If the cage is now a modern plate-glass-and-broadloom ranch house or a convenient modern apartment, the situation is no less painful than when her grandmother sat over an embroidery hoop in her gilt-and-plush parlor and muttered angrily about women's rights.

The first two women never went to college. They live in developments in Levittown, New Jersey, and Tacoma, Washington, and were interviewed by a team of sociologists studying workingmen's wives.[2] The third, a minister's wife, wrote on the fifteenth reunion questionnaire of her college that she never had any career ambitions, but wishes now she had.[3] The fourth, who has a Ph.D. in anthropology, is today a Nebraska housewife with three children.[4] Their words seem to indicate that housewives of all educational levels suffer the same feeling of desperation.

The fact is that no one today is muttering angrily about "women's rights," even though more and more women have gone to college. In a recent study of all the classes that have graduated from Barnard College,[5] a significant minority of earlier graduates blamed their education for making them want "rights," later classes blamed their education for giving them career dreams, but recent graduates blamed the college for making them feel it was not enough simply to be a housewife and mother; they did not want to feel guilty if they did not read books or take part in community activities. But if education is not the cause of the problem, the fact that education somehow festers in these women may be a clue.

If the secret of feminine fulfillment is having children, never have so many women, with the freedom to choose, had so many children, in so few years, so willingly. If the answer is love, never have women searched for love with such determination. And yet there is a growing suspicion that the problem may not be sexual, though it must somehow be related to sex. I have heard from many doctors evidence of new sexual problems between man and wife—sexual hunger in wives so great their husbands cannot satisfy it. "We have made woman a sex creature," said a psychiatrist at the Margaret Sanger marriage counseling clinic. "She has no identity except as a wife and mother. She does not know who she is herself. She waits all day for her husband to come home at night to make her feel alive. And now it is the husband who is not interested. It is terrible for the women, to lie there, night after night, waiting for her husband to make her feel alive." Why is there such a market for books and articles offering sexual advice? The kind of sexual orgasm which Kinsey found in statistical plenitude in the recent generations of American women does not seem to make this problem go away.

On the contrary, new neuroses are being seen among women—and problems as yet unnamed as neuroses—which Freud and his followers did not predict, with physical symptoms, anxieties, and defense mechanisms equal to those caused by sexual repression. And strange new problems are being reported in the growing generations of children whose mothers were always there, driving them around, helping them with their homework—an inability to endure pain or discipline or pursue any self-sustained goal of any sort, a devastating boredom with life. Educators are increasingly uneasy about the dependence, the lack of self-reliance, of the boys and girls who are entering college today. "We fight a continual battle to make our students assume manhood," said a Columbia dean.

A White House conference was held on the physical and muscular deterioration of American children: were they being over-nurtured? Sociologists noted the astounding organization of suburban children's lives: the lessons, parties, entertainments, play and study groups organized for them. A suburban housewife in Portland, Oregon, wondered why the children "need" Brownies and Boy Scouts out here. "This is not the slums. The kids out here have the great outdoors. I think people are so bored, they organize the children, and then try to hook everyone else on it. And the poor kids have no time left just to lie on their beds and daydream."

Can the problem that has no name be somehow related to the domestic routine of the housewife? When a woman tries to put the problem into words, she often merely describes the daily life she leads. What is there in this recital of comfortable domestic detail that could possibly cause such a feeling of desperation? Is she trapped simply by the enormous demands of her role as modern housewife: wife, mistress, mother, nurse, consumer, cook, chauffeur; expert on interior decoration, child care, appliance repair, furniture refinishing, nutrition, and education? Her day is fragmented as she rushes from dishwasher to washing machine to telephone to dryer to station wagon to supermarket, and delivers Johnny to the Little League field, takes Janey to dancing class, gets the lawnmower fixed and meets the 6:45. She can never spend more than 15 minutes on any one thing; she has no time to read books, only magazines; even if she had time, she has lost the power to concentrate. At the end of the day, she is so terribly tired that sometimes her husband has to take over and put the children to bed.

This terrible tiredness took so many women to doctors in the 1950's that one decided to investigate it. He found, surprisingly, that his patients suffering from "housewife's fatigue" slept more than an adult needed to sleep—as much as ten hours a day—and that the actual energy they expended on housework did not tax their capacity. The real problem must be something else, he decided—perhaps boredom. Some doctors told their women patients they must get out of the house for a day, treat themselves to a movie in town. Others prescribed tranquilizers. Many suburban housewives were taking tranquilizers like cough drops. "You wake up in the morning, and you feel as if there's no point in going on another day like this. So you take a tranquilizer because it makes you not care so much that it's pointless."

It is easy to see the concrete details that trap the suburban housewife, the continual demands on her time. But the chains that bind her in her trap are chains in her own mind and spirit. They are chains made up of mistaken ideas and misinterpreted facts, of incomplete truths and unreal choices. They are not easily seen and not easily shaken off.

How can any woman see the whole truth within the bounds of her own life? How can she believe that voice inside herself, when it denies the conventional, accepted truths by which she has been living? And yet the women I have talked to, who are finally listening to that inner voice, seem in some incredible way to be groping through to a truth that has defied the experts.

I think the experts in a great many fields have been holding pieces of that truth under their microscopes for a long time without realizing it. I found pieces of it in certain new research and theoretical developments in psychological, social and biological science whose implications for women seem never to have been examined. I found many clues by talking to suburban doctors, gynecologists, obstetricians, child-guidance clinicians, pediatricians, high-school guidance counselors, college professors, marriage counselors, psychiatrists and ministers—questioning them not on their theories, but on their actual experience in treating American women. I became aware of a growing body of evidence, much of which has not been reported publicly because it does not fit current modes of thought about women—evidence which throws into question the standards of feminine normality, feminine adjustment, feminine fulfillment, and feminine maturity by which most women are still trying to live.

I began to see in a strange new light the American return to early marriage and the large families that are causing the population explosion; the recent movement to natural childbirth and breastfeeding; suburban conformity, and the new neuroses, character pathologies and sexual problems being reported by the doctors. I began to see new dimensions to old problems that have long been taken for granted among women: menstrual difficulties, sexual frigidity, promiscuity, pregnancy fears, childbirth depression, the high incidence of emotional breakdown and suicide among women in their twenties and thirties, the menopause crises, the so-called passivity and immaturity of American men, the discrepancy between women's tested intellectual abilities in childhood and their adult achievement, the changing incidence of adult sexual orgasm in American women, and persistent problems in psychotherapy and in women's education.

If I am right, the problem that has no name stirring in the minds of so many American women today is not a matter of loss of femininity or too much education, or the demands of domesticity. It is far more important than anyone recognizes. It is the key to these other new and old problems which have been torturing women and their husbands and children, and puzzling their doctors and educators for years. It may well be the key to our future as a nation and a culture. We can no longer ignore that voice within women that says: "I want something more than my husband and my children and my home."

---

1. See the Seventy-fifth Anniversary Issue of *Good Housekeeping*, May, 1960, "The Gift of Self," a symposium by Margaret Mead, Jessamyn West, *et al.*

2. Lee Rainwater, Richard P. Coleman, and Gerald Handel, *Workingman's Wife*, New York, 1959.

3. Betty Friedan, "If One Generation Can Ever Tell Another," *Smith Alumnae Quarterly*, Northampton, Mass., Winter, 1961. I first became aware of "the problem that has no name" and its possible relationship to what I finally called "the feminine mystique" in 1957, when I prepared an intensive questionnaire and conducted a survey of my own Smith College classmates fifteen years after graduation. This questionnaire was later used by alumnae classes of Radcliffe and other women's colleges with similar results.

4. Jhan and June Robbins, "Why Young Mothers Feel Trapped," *Redbook*, September, 1960.

5. Marian Freda Poverman, "Alumnae on Parade," *Barnard Alumnae Magazine*, July, 1957.

CASEY HAYDEN AND MARY KING

Sex and Caste: A Kind of Memo

Casey Hayden (born 1937) and Mary King (born 1940) were white volunteer activists and staff members of the Student Non-Violent Coordinating Committee (SNCC), one of the principal organizations struggling for racial equality in postwar America. In 1965, galvanized by Beauvoir's *The Second Sex*, they privately circulated among other women activists a memo criticizing women's subordinate place in society and in *the movement*. (As the radical women's movement did not yet exist, they were referring to the larger civil rights and antiwar communities of the New Left.) In 1966 they published this expanded version in the left-wing magazine *Liberation*. While it was written well before women's liberation groups began to form and expresses doubt "that we could start a movement based on anything as distant to general American thought as a sex-caste system," it is widely considered a founding document of radical feminism.

November 18, 1965

WE'VE TALKED a lot, to each other and to some of you, about our own and other women's problems in trying to live in our personal lives and in our work as independent and creative people. In these conversations we've found what seems to be recurrent ideas or themes. Maybe we can look at these things many of us perceive, often as a result of insights learned from the movement:

▸ Sex and caste: There seem to be many parallels that can be drawn between treatment of Negroes and treatment of women in our society as a whole. But in particular, women we've talked to who work in the movement seem to be caught up in a common-law caste system that operates, sometimes subtly, forcing them to work around or outside hierarchical structures of power which may exclude them. Women seem to be placed in the same position of assumed subordination in personal situations too. It is a caste system which, at its worst, uses and exploits women.

This is complicated by several facts, among them: 1) The caste system is not institutionalized by law (women have the right to vote, to sue for divorce, etc.); 2) Women can't withdraw from the situation (a la nationalism) or overthrow it; 3) There are biological differences (even though those biological differences are usually discussed or accepted without taking present and future technology into account so we probably can't be sure what these differences mean). Many people who are very hip to the implications of the racial caste system, even people in the movement, don't seem to be able to see the sexual caste system and if the question is raised they respond with: "That's the way it's supposed to be. There are biological differences." Or with other statements which recall a white segregationist confronted with integration.

▶ Women and problems of work: The caste system perspective dictates the roles assigned to women in the movement, and certainly even more to women outside the movement. Within the movement, questions arise in situations ranging from relationships of women organizers to men in the community, to who cleans the freedom house, to who holds leadership positions, to who does secretarial work, and who acts as spokesman for groups. Other problems arise between women with varying degrees of awareness of themselves as being as capable as men but held back from full participation, or between women who see themselves as needing more control of their work than other women demand. And there are problems with relationships between white women and black women.

▶ Women and personal relations with men: Having learned from the movement to think radically about the personal worth and abilities of people whose role in society had gone unchallenged before, a lot of women in the movement have begun trying to apply those lessons to their own relations with men. Each of us probably has her own story of the various results, and of the internal struggle occasioned by trying to break out of very deeply learned fears, needs, and self-perceptions, and of what happens when we try to replace them with concepts of people and freedom learned from the movement and organizing.

▶ Institutions: Nearly everyone has real questions about those institutions which shape perspectives on men and women: marriage, child rearing patterns, women's (and men's) magazines, etc. People are beginning to think about and even to experiment with new forms in these areas.

▶ Men's reactions to the questions raised here: A very few men seem to feel, when they hear conversations involving these problems, that they have a right to be present and participate in them, since they are so deeply involved. At the same time, very few men can respond non-defensively, since the whole idea is either beyond their comprehension or threatens and exposes them. The usual response is laughter. That inability to see the whole issue as serious, as the strait-jacketing of both sexes, and as societally determined often shapes our own response so that we learn to think in their terms about ourselves and to feel silly rather than trust our inner feelings. The problems we're listing here, and what others have said about them, are therefore largely drawn from conversations among women only—and that difficulty in establishing dialogue with men is a recurring theme among people we've talked to.

▶ Lack of community for discussion: Nobody is writing, or organizing or talking publicly about women, in any way that reflects the problems that various women in the movement come across and which we've tried to touch above. Consider this quote from an article in the centennial issue of *The Nation*:

> However equally we consider men and women, the work plans for husbands and wives cannot be given equal weight. A woman should not aim for "a second-level career" because she is a *woman*; from girlhood on she should recognize that, if she is also going to be a wife and mother, she will not be able to give as much to her work as she would if single. That is, she should not feel that she cannot aspire to directing the laboratory simply because she is a woman, but rather because she is also a wife and mother; as such, her work as a lab technician (or the equivalent in another field) should bring both satisfaction and the knowledge that, through it, she is fulfilling an additional role, making an additional contribution.

And that's about as deep as the analysis goes publicly, which is not nearly so deep as we've heard many of you go in chance conversations.

The reason we want to try to open up dialogue is mostly subjective. Working in the movement often intensifies personal problems, especially if we start trying to apply things we're learning there to our personal lives. Perhaps we can start to talk with each other more openly than in the past and create a community of support for each other so we can deal with ourselves and others with integrity and can therefore keep working.

Objectively, the chances seem nil that we could start a movement based on anything as distant to general American thought as a sex-caste system. Therefore, most of us will probably want to work full time on problems such as war, poverty, race. The very fact that the country can't face, much less deal with, the questions we're raising means that the movement is one place to look for some relief. Real efforts at dialogue within the movement and with whatever liberal groups, community women, or students might listen are justified. That is, all the problems between men and women and all the problems of women functioning in society as equal human beings are among the most basic that people face. We've talked in the movement about trying to build a society which would see basic human problems (which are now seen as private troubles), as public problems and would try to shape institutions to meet human needs rather than shaping people to meet the needs of those with power. To raise questions like those above illustrates very directly that society hasn't dealt with some of its deepest problems and opens discussion of why that is so. (In one sense, it is a radicalizing question that can take people beyond legalistic solutions into areas of personal and institutional change.) The second objective reason we'd like to see discussion begin is that we've learned a great deal in the movement and perhaps this is one area where a determined attempt to apply ideas we've learned there can produce some new alternatives.

PAULI MURRAY AND MARY O. EASTWOOD

(from) Jane Crow and the Law: Sex Discrimination and Title VII

Feminist activists and lawyers Pauli Murray (1910–1985) and Mary O. Eastwood (1930–2015) were among the cofounders of the National Organization for Women (NOW) in 1966. Murray, a towering figure in women's rights law, was also a civil rights activist, teacher, author, poet, and, at age sixty-six would become the first African American woman ordained as an Episcopal priest. In 1940, she was arrested for refusing to give up her seat on a segregated bus—fifteen years before Rosa Parks's arrest. After encountering sex discrimination in college, Murray coined the term "Jane Crow" by analogy to Jim Crow. Murray and Eastwood's 1965 article "Jane Crow and the Law: Sex Discrimination and Title VII" was credited by future Supreme Court justice Ruth Bader Ginsburg with the legal theories Ginsburg successfully used in the 1970s to advance women's rights. Presented here are the landmark article's first and final sections.

ANTIFEMINISM AND RACISM

NEGROES HAVE successfully invoked the protection of the Constitution against race discrimination; the enactment of the Civil Rights Act of 1964 was achieved primarily because of the evils of race discrimination. We think that sex discrimination can be better understood if compared with race discrimination and that recognition of the similarities of the two problems can be helpful in improving and clarifying the legal status of women.

Discriminatory attitudes toward women are strikingly parallel to those regarding Negroes. Women have experienced both subtle and explicit forms of discrimination comparable to the inequalities imposed upon minorities.[1]

---

1. Thirty years ago, Blanche Crozier pointed out this parallel:

> Not only are race and sex entirely comparable classes, but there are no others like them. They are large, permanent, unchangeable, natural classes. No other kind of class is susceptible to implications of innate inferiority. Aliens, for instance, are essentially a temporary class, like an age class. Only permanent and natural classes are open

Contemporary scholars have been impressed by the interrelation of these two problems in the United States, whether their point of departure has been a study of women or of racial theories. In *The Second Sex*, Simone de Beauvoir makes frequent reference to the position of American Negroes.[2] In *An American Dilemma*, Gunnar Myrdal noted that the similarity of the two problems was not accidental, but originated in the paternalistic order of society.[3] "From the very beginning," Dr. Myrdal observed, "the fight in America for the liberation of the Negro slaves was closely coordinated with the fight for women's emancipation. . . . The women's movement got much of its public support by reason of its affiliation with the Abolitionist movement."[4]

The myths built up to perpetuate the inferior status of women and of Negroes were almost identical, Dr. Myrdal found:

> As in the Negro problem, most men have accepted as self-evident, until recently, the doctrine that women had inferior endowments in most of those respects which carry prestige, power, and advantages in society, but that they were, at the same time, superior in some other respects. The arguments, when arguments were used, have been about the same: smaller brains, scarcity of geniuses and so on. The study of women's intelligence and personality has had broadly the same history as the one we record for Negroes. As in the case of the Negro, women themselves have often been brought to believe in their inferiority of endowment. As the Negro was awarded his "place" in society, so there was a "woman's place." In both cases the rationalization was strongly believed that men, in confining them to this place, did not act against the true interest of the subordinate groups. The myth of the "contented woman," who did not want to have suffrage or other civil rights and equal opportunities, had the same social function as the myth of the "contented Negro."[5]

to those deep, traditional implications which become attached to classes regardless of the actual qualities of the members of the class. This is the only kind of class prejudice which can be reached by laws aimed not toward guarding against the unjust effect of the prejudice in the particular case but toward a general upholding of the dignity and equality, the legal status, of the class.

Crozier, *Constitutionality of Discrimination Based on Sex*, 15 B.U.L. Rev. 723, 727–28 (1935).
2. de Beauvoir, *The Second Sex* 116, 297–98, 331, 714–15 (5th ed. Parshley transl. 1964).
3. Myrdal, *An American Dilemma* 1075 (2d ed. 1962).
4. *Ibid.*
5. *Id.* at 1077.

Similarly, Ashley Montagu, in his study, *Man's Most Dangerous Myth: The Fallacy of Race*, documents the parallel between antifeminism and race prejudice:

> In connection with the modern form of race prejudice it is of inter-est to recall that almost every one of the arguments used by the rac-ists to "prove" the inferiority of one or another so-called "race" was not so long ago used by the antifeminists to "prove" the inferiority of the female as compared with the male. In the case of these sexual prejudices one generation has been sufficient in which to discover how completely spurious and erroneous virtually every one of these arguments and assertions are.[6]

The myths essentially "deny a particular group equality of opportunity and then assert that because that group has not achieved as much as the groups enjoying complete freedom of opportunity it is obviously inferior and can never do as well."[7] Moreover, Dr. Montagu finds the same underlying motives at work in antifeminism as in racism, "namely, fear, jealousy, feelings of inse-curity, fear of economic competition, guilt feelings and the like."[8]

These findings indicate that, in matters of discrimination, the problems of women are not as unique as has been generally assumed.[9] That manifestations of racial prejudice have been more brutal than the more subtle manifestations of prejudice by reason of sex in no way diminishes the force of the equally obvious fact that the rights of women and the rights of Negroes are only dif-ferent phases of the fundamental and indivisible issue of human rights.

The United Nations Charter and the Universal Declaration of Human Rights both stress respect for human rights and fundamental freedoms for all persons without distinction as to race, sex, language, or religion.[10] Until the enactment of the Civil Rights Act of 1964, "sex" generally had not been included with "race, color, religion and national origin" in federal laws and regulations designed to eliminate discrimination. As a practical matter, "civil rights" had become equated with Negro rights, which created bitter opposi-tion and divisions. The most serious discrimination against both women and

6. Montagu, *Man's Most Dangerous Myth: The Fallacy of Race* 181 (4th ed. 1964).
7. *Id.* at 182.
8. *Id.* at 184.
9. Hacker, *Women As a Minority Group*, 30 Social Forces 60, 65 (1951). The author lists a number of similarities in the status of Negroes and the status of women.
10. See U.N. Charter preamble; art. 1, para. 3; art. 8; art. 13, para. 1; art. 55; and art. 76; and the Universal Declaration of Human Rights preamble; art. 2; and art. 16, para. 1.

Negroes today is in the field of employment. The addition of "sex" to Title VII of the Civil Rights Act, making it possible for a second large group of the population to invoke its protection against discrimination in employment, represents an important step toward implementation of our commitment to human rights.

―――――――――――

CONCLUSION

According women equality of rights under the Constitution and equal employment opportunity, through positive implementation of Title VII of the Civil Rights Act of 1964, would not likely result in any immediate, drastic change in the pattern of women's employment. But great scientific and social changes have already taken place,[11] such as longer life span, smaller families, and lower infant death rate, with the result that motherhood consumes smaller proportions of women's lives. Thus, the effects of sex discrimination are felt by more women today.

The recent increase in activity concerning the status of women indicates that we are gradually coming to recognize that the proper role of the law is not to protect women by restrictions and confinement, but to protect both sexes from discrimination.

We are entering the age of human rights. In the United States, perhaps our most important concerns are with the rights to vote and to representative government and with equal rights to education and employment. Hopefully, our economy will outgrow concepts of class competition, such as Negro v. white, youth v. age, or male v. female, and, at least in matters of employment, standards of merit and individual quality will control rather than prejudice.

11. See Ware, *Women Today: Trends and Issues in the United States* (1963).

VALERIE SOLANAS

(from) *SCUM Manifesto*

The *SCUM Manifesto* is Valerie Solanas's jolting and polarizing self-published 1967 broadside calling for women "to overthrow the government, eliminate the money system, . . . and destroy the male sex." In it, Solanas (1936–1988), a Manhattan playwright, expresses some of the pure, unfiltered rage that fueled the nascent feminist movement. Through hyperbolic wit and scathing social commentary, the mock manifesto for SCUM, an organization of female revolutionaries sometimes called the Society for Cutting Up Men, delivers a searing, at times hilarious, indictment of patriarchy. Described by critics as, variously, Swiftian satire, utopian fantasy, parody, and a feminist call to arms, it inspired radical groups from Boston's Cell 16 to New York's The Feminists, while scandalizing other feminists, including some from the recently formed NOW. Though in popular memory Solanas's 1968 shooting of Andy Warhol has eclipsed her writing, the *SCUM Manifesto* remains a feminist classic. This excerpt comprises the opening pages.

L IFE IN this society being, at best, an utter bore and no aspect of society being at all relevant to women, there remains to civic-minded, responsible, thrill-seeking females only to overthrow the government, eliminate the money system, institute complete automation and destroy the male sex.

It is now technically possible to reproduce without the aid of males (or, for that matter, females) and to produce only females. We must begin immediately to do so. The male is a biological accident: the y (male) gene is an incomplete x (female) gene, that is, has an incomplete set of chromosomes. In other words, the male is an incomplete female, a walking abortion, aborted at the gene stage. To be male is to be deficient, emotionally limited; maleness is a deficiency disease and males are emotional cripples.

The male is completely egocentric, trapped inside himself, incapable of empathizing or identifying with others, of love, friendship, affection or tenderness. He is a completely isolated unit, incapable of rapport with anyone. His responses are entirely visceral, not cerebral; his intelligence is a mere tool in the service of his drives and needs; he is incapable of mental passion, mental interaction; he can't relate to anything other than his own physical sensations. He is a half dead, unresponsive lump, incapable of giving or receiving pleasure or happiness; consequently, he is at best an utter bore, an inoffensive blob, since only those capable of absorption in others can be charming. He is trapped in a twilight zone halfway between humans and apes, and is far worse off than the apes because, unlike the apes, he is capable of a large array of negative feelings—hate, jealousy, contempt, disgust, guilt, shame, doubt—and, moreover he is *aware* of what he is and isn't.

Although completely physical, the male is unfit even for stud service. Even assuming mechanical proficiency, which few men have, he is, first of all, incapable of zestfully, lustfully, tearing off a piece, but is instead eaten up with guilt, shame, fear and insecurity, feelings rooted in male nature, which the most enlightened training can only minimize; second, the physical feeling he attains is next to nothing; and, third, he is not empathizing with his partner, but is obsessed with how he's doing, turning in an A performance, doing a good plumbing job. To call a man an animal is to flatter him; he's a machine, a walking dildo. It's often said that men use women. Use them for what? Surely not pleasure.

Eaten up with guilt, shame, fears and insecurities and obtaining, if he's lucky, a barely perceptible physical feeling, the male is, nonetheless, obsessed with screwing; he'll swim a river of snot, wade nostril-deep through a mile of vomit, if he thinks there'll be a friendly pussy awaiting him. He'll screw a woman he despises, any snaggle-toothed hag, and, furthermore, pay for the opportunity. Why? Relieving physical tension isn't the answer, as masturbation suffices for that. It's not ego satisfaction; that doesn't explain screwing corpses and babies.

Completely egocentric, unable to relate, empathize or identify, and filled with a vast, pervasive, diffuse sexuality, the male is psychically passive. He hates his passivity, so he projects it onto women, defines the male as active, then sets out to prove that he is ("prove he's a Man"). His main means of attempting to prove it is screwing (Big Man with a Big Dick tearing off a Big Piece). Since he's attempting to prove an error, he must "prove" it again and again. Screwing, then, is a desperate, compulsive attempt to prove he's not passive, not a woman; but he *is* passive and *does* want to be a woman.

Being an incomplete female, the male spends his life attempting to complete himself, to become female. He attempts to do this by constantly seeking out, fraternizing with and trying to live through and fuse with the female, and by claiming as his own all female characteristics—emotional strength and independence, forcefulness, dynamism, decisiveness, coolness, objectivity, assertiveness, courage, integrity, vitality, intensity, depth of character, grooviness, etc.—and projecting onto women all male traits—vanity, frivolity, triviality, weakness, etc. It should be said, though, that the male has one glaring area of superiority over the female—public relations. (He has done a brilliant job of convincing millions of women that men are women and women are men.) The male claim that females find fulfillment through motherhood and sexuality reflects what males think they'd find fulfilling if they were female.

Women, in other words, don't have penis envy; men have pussy envy. When the male accepts his passivity, defines himself as a woman (males as well as females think men are women and women are men), and becomes a transvestite he loses his desire to screw (or to do anything else, for that matter; he fulfills himself as a drag queen) and gets his cock chopped off. He then achieves a continuous diffuse sexual feeling from "being a woman." Screwing is, for a man, a defense against his desire to be female. Sex is itself a sublimation.

The male, because of his obsession to compensate for not being female combined with his inability to relate and to feel compassion, has made of the world a shitpile. He is responsible for:

War: The male's normal method of compensation for not being female, namely, getting his Big Gun off, is grossly inadequate, as he can get it off only a very limited number of times; so he gets it off on a really massive scale, and proves to the entire world that he's a "Man". Since he has no compassion or ability to empathize or identify, proving his manhood is worth an endless number of lives, including his own—his own life being worthless, he would rather go out in a blaze of glory than plod grimly on for fifty more years.

Niceness, Politeness and "Dignity": Every man, deep down, knows he's a worthless piece of shit. Overwhelmed by a sense of animalism and deeply ashamed of it; wanting, not to express himself, but to hide from others his total physicality, total egocentricity, the hate and contempt he feels for other men, and to hide from himself the hate and contempt he suspects other men feel for him; having a crudely constructed nervous system that is easily upset by the least display of emotion or feeling, the male tries to enforce a "social" code that ensures a perfect blandness, unsullied by the slightest trace of feeling or upsetting opinion. He uses terms like "copulate", "sexual congress", "have relations with" (to men, "*sexual* relations" is a redundancy), overlaid with stilted manners; the suit on the chimp.

Money, Marriage and Prostitution, Work and Prevention of an Automated Society: There is no human reason for money or for anyone to work. All non-creative jobs (practically all jobs now being done) could have been automated long ago, and in a moneyless society everyone can have as much of the best of everything as she wants. But there are non-human, male reasons for maintaining the money-work system:

1. Pussy. Despising his highly inadequate self, overcome with intense anxiety and a deep, profound loneliness when by his empty self, desperate to attach himself to any female in dim hopes of completing himself, in the mystical belief that by touching gold he'll turn to gold, the male craves the continuous companionship of women. The company of the lowest female is preferable to his own or that of other men, who serve only to remind him of his repulsiveness. But females, unless very young or very sick, must be coerced or bribed into male company.

2. Supply the non-relating male with the delusion of usefulness, and enable him to try to justify his existence by digging holes and filling them up. Leisure time horrifies the male, who will have nothing to do but contemplate his grotesque self. Unable to relate or to love, the male must work. Females crave absorbing, emotionally satisfying, meaningful activity, but lacking the opportunity or ability for this, they prefer to idle and waste away their time in ways of their own choosing—sleeping, shopping, bowling, shooting pool, playing cards and other games, breeding, reading, walking around, daydreaming, eating, playing with themselves, popping pills, going to the movies, getting analyzed, traveling, raising dogs and cats, lolling on the beach, swimming, watching T.V., listening to music, decorating their houses, gardening, sewing, nightclubbing, dancing, visiting, "improving their minds" (taking courses), and absorbing "culture" (lectures, plays, concerts, "arty" movies). Therefore, many females would, even assuming complete economic equality between the sexes, prefer living with males or peddling their asses on the street, thus having most of their time for themselves, to spending many hours of their days doing boring, stultifying, non-creative work for somebody else, functioning as less than animals, as machines, or, at best—if able to get a "good" job— co-managing the shitpile. What will liberate women, therefore, from male control is the total elimination of the money-work system, not the attainment of economic equality with men within it.

3. Power and control. Unmasterful in his personal relations with women, the male attains to general masterfulness by the manipulation of money and of everything and everybody controlled by money, in other words, of everything and everybody.

4. Love substitute. Unable to give love or affection, the male gives money. It makes him feel motherly. The mother gives milk; he gives bread. He is the Breadwinner.

5. Provides the male with a goal. Incapable of enjoying the moment, the male needs something to look forward to, and money provides him with an eternal, never-ending goal: Just think what you could do with 80 trillion dollars—Invest it! And in three years' time you'd have 300 trillion dollars!!!

6. Provides the basis for the male's major opportunity to control and manipulate—fatherhood.

Fatherhood and Mental Illness (fear, cowardice, timidity, humility, insecurity, passivity): Mother wants what's best for her kids; Daddy only wants what's best for Daddy, that is peace and quiet, pandering to his delusion of dignity ("respect"), a good reflection on himself (status) and the opportunity to control and manipulate, or, if he's an "enlightened" father, to "give guidance". His daughter, in addition, he wants sexually—he gives her *hand* in marriage; the other part is for him. Daddy, unlike Mother, can never give in to his kids, as he must, at all costs, preserve his delusion of decisiveness, forcefulness, always-rightness and strength. Never getting one's way leads to lack of self-confidence in one's ability to cope with the world and to a passive acceptance of the status quo. Mother loves her kids, although she sometimes gets angry, but anger blows over quickly and even while it exists, doesn't preclude love and basic acceptance. Emotionally diseased Daddy doesn't love his kids; he approves of them—if they're "good", that is, if they're nice, "respectful", obedient, subservient to his will, quiet and not given to unseemly displays of temper that would be most upsetting to Daddy's easily disturbed male nervous system—in other words, if they're passive vegetables. If they're not "good", he doesn't get angry—not if he's a modern, "civilized" father (the old-fashioned ranting, raving brute is preferable, as he is so ridiculous he can be easily despised)—but rather expresses disapproval, a state that, unlike anger, endures and precludes a basic acceptance, leaving the kid with a feeling of worthlessness and a lifelong obsession with being approved of; the result is fear of independent thought, as this leads to unconventional, disapproved of opinions and way of life.

For the kid to want Daddy's approval it must respect Daddy, and, being garbage, Daddy can make sure that he is respected only by remaining aloof, by distantness, by acting on the precept "familiarity breeds contempt", which is, of course, true, if one is contemptible. By being distant and aloof, he is able to remain unknown, mysterious, and, thereby, to inspire fear ("respect").

Disapproval of emotional "scenes" leads to fear of strong emotion, fear of one's own anger and hatred, and to a fear of facing reality, as facing it leads at first to anger and hatred. Fear of anger and hatred combined with a lack of self-confidence in one's ability to cope with and change the world, or even to affect in the slightest way one's own destiny, leads to a mindless belief that the world and most people in it are nice and that the most banal, trivial amusements are great fun and deeply pleasurable.

The effect of fatherhood on males, specifically, is to make them "Men", that is, highly defensive of all impulses to passivity, faggotry, and of desires to be female. Every boy wants to imitate his mother, be her, fuse with her, but Daddy forbids this; *he* is the mother; *he* gets to fuse with her. So he tells the boy, sometimes directly, sometimes indirectly, to not be a sissy, to act like a "Man". The boy, scared shitless of and "respecting" his father, complies, and becomes just like Daddy, that model of "Man"-hood, the all-American ideal— the well-behaved heterosexual dullard.

The effect of fatherhood on females is to make them male—dependent, passive, domestic, animalistic, nice, insecure, approval and security seekers, cowardly, humble, "respectful" of authorities and men, closed, not fully responsive, half dead, trivial, dull, conventional, flattened out and thoroughly contemptible. Daddy's Girl, always tense and fearful, uncool, unanalytical, lacking objectivity, appraises Daddy, and thereafter, other men, against a background of fear ("respect") and is not only unable to see the empty shell behind the aloof façade, but accepts the male definition of himself as superior, as a female, and of herself, as inferior, as a male, which, thanks to Daddy, she really is.

It is the increase of fatherhood, resulting from the increased and more widespread affluence that fatherhood needs in order to thrive, that has caused the general increase of mindlessness and the decline of women in the United States since the 1920s. The close association of affluence with fatherhood has led, for the most part, to only the wrong girls, namely, the "privileged" middle-class girls, getting "educated".

The effect of fathers, in sum, has been to corrode the world with maleness. The male has a negative Midas Touch—everything he touches turns to shit.

Incapable of a positive state of happiness, which is the only thing that can justify one's existence, the male is, at best, relaxed, comfortable, neutral, and this condition is extremely short-lived, as boredom, a negative state, soon sets in; he is, therefore, doomed to an existence of suffering relieved only by occasional, fleeting stretches of restfulness, which state he can achieve only at the expense of some female. The male is, by his very nature, a leech, an emotional parasite and, therefore, not ethically entitled to live, as no one has the right to live at someone else's expense.

Just as humans have a prior right to existence over dogs by virtue of being more highly evolved and having a superior consciousness, so women have a prior right to existence over men. The elimination of any male is, therefore, a righteous and good act, an act highly beneficial to women as well as an act of mercy.

However, this moral issue will eventually be rendered academic by the fact that the male is gradually eliminating himself. In addition to engaging in the time-honored and classical wars and race riots, men are more and more either becoming fags or are obliterating themselves through drugs. The female, whether she likes it or not, will eventually take complete charge, if for no other reason than that she will have to—the male, for practical purposes, won't exist.

Accelerating this trend is the fact that more and more males are acquiring enlightened self-interest; they're realizing more and more that the female interest is *their* interest, that they can live only through the female and that the more the female is encouraged to live, to fulfill herself, to be a female and not a male, the more nearly *he* lives; he's coming to see that it's easier and more satisfactory to live through her than to try to *become* her and usurp her qualities, claim them as his own, push the female down and claim she's a male. The fag, who accepts his maleness, that is, his passivity and total sexuality, his femininity, is also best served by women being truly female, as it would then be easier for him to be male, feminine. If men were wise they would seek to become really female, would do intensive biological research that would lead to men, by means of operations on the brain and nervous system, being able to be transformed in psyche, as well as body, into women.

Whether to continue to use females for reproduction or to reproduce in the laboratory will also become academic: what will happen when every female, twelve and over, is routinely taking the Pill and there are no longer any accidents? How many women will deliberately allow themselves to get pregnant? No, Virginia, women don't just adore being brood mares, despite what the mass of robot, brainwashed women will say. Should a certain percentage of women be set aside by force to serve as brood mares for the species? Obviously, this will not do. The answer is laboratory reproduction of babies.

As for the issue of whether or not to continue to reproduce males, it doesn't follow that because the male, like disease, has always existed among us that he should continue to exist. When genetic control is possible—and it soon will be—it goes without saying that we should produce only whole, complete beings, not physical defects or deficiencies, including emotional deficiencies, such as maleness. Just as the deliberate production of blind people would be highly immoral, so would be the deliberate production of emotional cripples.

Why produce even females? Why should there be future generations? What is their purpose? When aging and death are eliminated, why continue to reproduce? Even if they are not eliminated, why reproduce? Why should we care what happens when we're dead? Why should we care that there is no younger generation to succeed us?

Eventually the natural course of events, of social evolution, will lead to total female control of the world and, subsequently, to the cessation of the production of males and, ultimately, to the cessation of the production of females.

But SCUM is impatient; SCUM is not consoled by the thought that future generations will thrive; SCUM wants to grab some swinging living for itself. And, if a large majority of women were SCUM, they could acquire complete control of this country within a few weeks simply by withdrawing from the labor force, thereby paralyzing the entire nation. Additional measures, any one of which would be sufficient to completely disrupt the economy and everything else, would be for women to declare themselves off the money system, stop buying, just loot and simply refuse to obey all laws they don't care to obey. The police force, National Guard, Army, Navy and Marines combined couldn't squelch a rebellion of over half the population, particularly when it's made up of people they are utterly helpless without.

If all women simply left men, refused to have anything to do with any of them—ever, all men, the government, and the national economy would collapse completely. Even without leaving men, women who are aware of the extent of their superiority to and power over men, could acquire complete control over everything within a few weeks, could effect a total submission of males to females. In a sane society the male would trot along obediently after the female. The male is docile and easily led, easily subjected to the domination of any female who cares to dominate him. The male, in fact, wants desperately to be led by females, wants Mama in charge, wants to abandon himself to her care. But this is not a sane society, and most women are not even dimly aware of where they're at in relation to men.

The conflict, therefore, is not between females and males, but between SCUM—dominant, secure, self-confident, nasty, violent, selfish, independent, proud, thrill-seeking, free-wheeling, arrogant females, who consider themselves fit to rule the universe, who have free-wheeled to the limits of this "society" and are ready to wheel on to something far beyond what it has to offer—and nice, passive, accepting, "cultivated", polite, dignified, subdued, dependent, scared, mindless, insecure, approval-seeking Daddy's Girls, who can't cope with the unknown, who want to continue to wallow in the sewer that is, at least, familiar, who want to hang back with the apes, who feel secure only with Big Daddy standing by, with a big, strong man to lean on and with a fat, hairy face in the White House, who are too cowardly to face up to the hideous reality of what a man is, what Daddy is, who have cast their lot with the swine, who have adapted themselves to animalism, feel superficially comfortable with it and know no other way of "life", who have reduced their minds, thoughts and sights to the male level, who, lacking sense, imagination and wit can have value only in a male "society", who can have a place in the sun, or, rather, in the slime, only as soothers, ego boosters, relaxers and breed-ers, who are dismissed as inconsequents by other females, who project their deficiencies, their maleness, onto all females and see the female as a worm.

But SCUM is too impatient to hope and wait for the de-brainwashing of millions of assholes. Why should the swinging females continue to plod dis-mally along with the dull male ones? Why should the fates of the groovy and the creepy be intertwined? Why should the active and imaginative consult the passive and dull on social policy? Why should the independent be confined to the sewer along with the dependent who need Daddy to cling to?

A small handful of SCUM can take over the country within a year by sys-tematically fucking up the system, selectively destroying property, and murder:

SCUM will become members of the unwork force, the fuck-up force; they will get jobs of various kinds and unwork. For example, SCUM salesgirls will not charge for merchandise; SCUM telephone operators will not charge for calls; SCUM office and factory workers, in addition to fucking up their work, will secretly destroy equipment. SCUM will unwork at a job until fired, then get a new job to unwork at.

SCUM will forcibly relieve bus drivers, cab drivers and subway token sellers of their jobs and run busses and cabs and dispense free tokens to the public.

SCUM will destroy all useless and harmful objects—cars, store windows, "Great Art", etc.

Eventually SCUM will take over the airwaves—radio and T.V. networks—by forcibly relieving of their jobs all radio and T.V. employees who would impede SCUM's entry into the broadcasting studios.

SCUM will couple-bust—barge into mixed (male-female) couples, wher-ever they are, and bust them up.

SCUM will kill all men who are not in the Men's Auxiliary of SCUM. Men in the Men's Auxiliary are those men who are working diligently to eliminate themselves, men who, regardless of their motives, do good, men who are playing ball with SCUM. A few examples of the men in the Men's Auxiliary are: men who kill men; biological scientists who are working on constructive programs, as opposed to biological warfare; journalists, writers, editors, pub-lishers and producers who disseminate and promote ideas that will lead to the achievement of SCUM's goals; faggots who, by their shimmering, flaming example, encourage other men to de-man themselves and thereby make them-selves relatively inoffensive; men who consistently give things away—money, things, services; men who tell it like it is (so far not one ever has), who put women straight, who reveal the truth about themselves, who give the mindless male females correct sentences to parrot, who tell them a woman's primary goal in life should be to squash the male sex (to aid men in this endeavor

SCUM will conduct Turd Sessions, at which every male present will give a speech beginning with the sentence: "I am a turd, a lowly, abject turd," then proceed to list all the ways in which he is. His reward for so doing will be the opportunity to fraternize after the session for a whole, solid hour with the SCUM who will be present. Nice, clean-living male women will be invited to the sessions to help clarify any doubts and misunderstandings they may have about the male sex); makers and promoters of sex books and movies, etc., who are hastening the day when all that will be shown on the screen will be Suck and Fuck (males, like the rats following the Pied Piper, will be lured by Pussy to their doom, will be overcome and submerged by and will eventually drown in the passive flesh that they are); drug pushers and advocates, who are hastening the dropping out of men.

Being in the Men's Auxiliary is a necessary but not a sufficient condition for making SCUM's escape list; it's not enough to do good; to save their worthless asses men must also avoid evil. A few examples of the most obnoxious or harmful types are: rapists, politicians and all who are in their service (campaigners, members of political parties, etc.); lousy singers and musicians; Chairmen of Boards; Breadwinners; landlords; owners of greasy spoons and restaurants that play Musak; "Great Artists"; cheap pikers; cops; tycoons; scientists working on death and destruction programs or for private industry (practically all scientists); liars and phonies; disc jockeys; men who intrude themselves in the slightest way on any strange female; real estate men; stock brokers; men who speak when they have nothing to say; men who loiter idly on the street and mar the landscape with their presence; double dealers; flim-flam artists; litterbugs; plagiarizers; men who in the slightest way harm any female; all men in the advertising industry; dishonest writers, journalists, editors, publishers, etc.; censors on both the public and private level; all members of the armed forces, including draftees (LBJ and McNamara give orders, but servicemen carry them out) and particularly pilots (if the Bomb drops, LBJ won't drop it; a pilot will). In the case of a man whose behavior falls into both the good and bad categories, an overall subjective evaluation of him will be made to determine if his behavior is, in the balance, good or bad.

BEVERLY JONES AND JUDITH BROWN

(from) Toward a Female Liberation Movement, Part I

This influential 1968 pamphlet from the newly formed Gainesville Women's Liberation—widely known as "The Florida Paper"—was written by two southern white
New Left civil rights activists. Part I, by psychologist Beverly Jones (born 1927),
presents the case for a separate mass women's liberation movement. (Part II,
by future lawyer Judith Brown [1941–1991], outlines a theoretical framework for
accomplishing this.) In this excerpt from Part I, Jones argues for the futility of working within such male-run radical organizations as Students for a Democratic Society (SDS), in which Jones and Brown had been active, since even radical men
when challenged on sexism fight to "keep things the way they are." With its grim
psychological portraits of women's constricted lives under male supremacy—first,
of students desperate for husbands; then, in this excerpt, of subjugated wives—the
paper stirred women to join the new movement.

4. RADICAL WOMEN DO NOT REALLY
UNDERSTAND THE DESPERATE CONDITIONS
OF WOMEN IN GENERAL—BECAUSE SO FEW ARE
MARRIED, OR IF MARRIED HAVE NO CHILDREN

No ONE would think to judge a marriage by its first hundred days. To
be sure there are cases of sexual trauma, of sudden and violent misunderstandings, but in general all is happiness; the girl has finally made it, the
past is but a bad dream. All good things are about to come to her. And then
reality sets in. It can be held off a little as long as they are both students and
particularly if they have money, but sooner or later it becomes entrenched. The
man moves to ensure his position of power and dominance.

There are several more or less standard pieces of armament used in this
assault upon wives, but the biggest gun is generally the threat of divorce or
abandonment. With a plucky woman a man may actually feel it necessary to
openly and repeatedly toy with this weapon, but usually it is sufficient simply
to keep it in the house undercover somewhere. We all know the bit, we have

heard it and all the others I am about to mention on television marital comedies and in night club jokes; it is supposed to be funny.

The husband says to the wife who is about to go somewhere that doesn't meet with his approval, "If you do, you need never come back." Or later, when the process is more complete and she is reduced to frequent outbreaks of begging, he slams his way out of the house claiming that she is trying to destroy him, that he can no longer take these endless, senseless scenes; that "this isn't a marriage, it's a meat grinder." Or he may simply lay down the law that God damn it, her first responsibility is to her family and he will not permit or tolerate something or other. Or if she wants to maintain the marriage she is simply going to have to accommodate herself.

There are thousands of variations on this theme and it is really very clever the way male society creates for women this pre-marital hell so that some man can save her from it and control her ever after by the threat of throwing her back. Degrading her further, the final crisis is usually averted or postponed by a tearful reconciliation in which the wife apologizes for her shortcomings, namely the sparks of initiative still left to her.

The other crude and often open weapon that a man uses to control his wife is the threat of force or force itself. Though this weapon is not necessarily used in conjunction with the one described above, it presupposes that a woman is more frightened of returning to an unmarried state than she is of being beaten about one way or another. How can one elaborate on such a threat? At a minimum it begins by a man's paling or flushing, clenching his fists at his sides or gritting his teeth, perhaps making lurching but controlled motions or wild threatening ones while he states his case. In this circumstance it is difficult for a woman to pursue the argument which is bringing about the reaction, usually an argument for more freedom, respect, or equality in the marital situation. And of course, the conciliation of this scene, even if he has beat her, may require his apology, but also hers, for provoking him. After a while the conditioning becomes so strong that a slight change of color on his part, or a slight stiffening of stance, nothing observable to an outsider, suffices to quiet her or keep her in line. She turns off or detours mechanically, like a robot, not even herself aware of the change, or only momentarily and almost subliminally.

But these are gross and vulgar techniques. There are many more subtle and intricate which in the long run are even more devastating. Take for instance the ploy of keeping women from recognizing their intelligence by not talking to them in public, which we mentioned earlier. After marriage this technique is extended and used on a woman in her own home.

At breakfast a woman speaks to her husband over or through the morning paper, which he clutches firmly in his hands. Incidentally, he reserves the right to see the paper first and to read the sections in order of his preference. The assumption is, of course, that he has a more vested interest in world affairs and a superior intelligence with which to grasp the relevance of daily news. The Women's Section of the paper is called that, not only because it contains the totality of what men want women to be concerned with, but also because it is the only section permitted to women at certain times of the day.

I can almost hear you demur. Now she has gone too far. What super-sensitivity to interpret the morning paper routine as a deliberate put-down. After all, a woman has the whole day to read the paper and a man must get to work. I put it to you that this same situation exists when they both work or when the wife works and the husband is still a student, assuming he gets up for breakfast, and on Sundays. What we are describing here is pure self-indulgence. A minor and common, though none the less enjoyable, exercise in power. A flexing of the male prerogative.

Perhaps the best tip-off to the real meaning of the daily paper act comes when a housewife attempts to solve the problem by subscribing to two papers. This is almost invariably met with resistance on the part of the man as being an unnecessary and frivolous expense, never mind whether they can afford it. And if his resistance doesn't actually forestall the second subscription he attempts to monopolize the front sections of both papers! This is quite a complicated routine, but, assuming the papers are not identical, it can be done and justified.

However, we were talking about conversation and noted that it was replaced by the paper in the morning. In the evening men attempt to escape through more papers, returning to work, working at home, reading, watching television, going to meetings, etc. But eventually they have to handle the problem some other way because their wives are desperate for conversation, for verbal interchange. To understand this desperation you have to remember that women before marriage have on the whole only superficial, competitive, and selfish relationships with each other. Should one of them have a genuine relationship it is more likely with a male than a female. After marriage a woman stops courting her old unmarried or married female side-kicks. They have served their purpose, to tide her over. And there is the fear, often well founded, that these females will view her marriage less as a sacrament than a challenge, that they will stalk her husband as fair game, that they will outshine her, or in some other way lead to the disruption of her marriage.

Her husband will not tolerate the hanging around of any past male friends, and that leaves the woman isolated. When, as so often happens, after a few years husband and wife move because he has graduated, entered service, or changed jobs, her isolation is complete. Now all ties are broken. Her husband is her only contact with the outside world, aside, of course, from those more or less perfunctory contacts she has at work, if she works.

So she is desperate to talk with her husband because she must talk with *someone* and he is all she has. To tell the truth a woman doesn't really understand the almost biologic substructure to her desperation. She sees it in psychological terms. She thinks that if her husband doesn't talk to her he doesn't love her or doesn't respect her. She may even feel that this disrespect on his part is causing her to lose her own self-respect (a fair assumption since he is her only referent). She may also feel cheated and trapped because she understood that in return for all she did for him in marriage she was to be allowed to live vicariously, and she cannot do that if he will not share his life.

What she does not understand is that she cannot go on thinking coherently without expressing those thoughts and having them accepted, rejected, or qualified in some manner. This kind of feed-back is essential to the healthy functioning of the human mind. That is why solitary confinement is so devastating. It is society's third-rung "legal deterrent," ranking just below capital punishment and forced wakefulness, or other forms of torture that lead to death.

This kind of verbal isolation, this refusal to hear a woman, causes her thought process to turn in upon itself, to deteriorate, degenerate, to become disassociated from reality. Never intellectually or emotionally secure in the first place, she feels herself slipping beyond the pale. She keeps pounding at the door.

And what is her husband's response. He understands in some crude way what is happening to her, what he is doing to her, but he is so power-oriented that he cannot stop. Above all, men must remain in control; it's either him or her. The worse she becomes the more convinced he is the coin must not be turned. And from thence springs anew his fear of women, like his fear of blacks.

We tend to forget that witches were burned in our own country not too long ago, in those heroic days before the founding fathers. That each day somewhere in our country women are raped or killed just for kicks or out of some perverted sense of retribution. And we never even consider the ten thousand innocent women annually murdered by men who refuse to legalize abortion. The fear and hatred must be deep indeed to take such vengeance.

But back to the husband. We all know that marriage is far from solitary confinement for a woman. Of course, the husband talks to her. The questions are, how often, what does he say, and how does he say it? He parries this plea for conversation, which he understands thoroughly, until bedtime or near it and then exhausted and exasperated he slaps down his book or papers, or snaps off the TV, or flings his shoe to the floor if he is undressing and turns to his wife, saying, "Oh, for Christ sake, what is it you want to talk about?"

Now he has just used all of his big guns. He has showed temper which threatens violence. He has showed an exasperated patience which threatens eventual divorce. He has been insulting and purposely misunderstanding. Since she is not burning with any specific comments, since she is now frightened, hurt, angry, and thoroughly miserable, what is she to say? I'll tell you what she does say: "Forget it. Just forget it. If that's the way you are going to respond I don't want to talk with you anyway."

This may bring on another explosion from him, frightening her still further. He may say something stupid like, "You're crazy, just crazy. All day long you keep telling me you've got to talk to me. O.K., you want to talk to me, talk. I'm listening. I'm not reading. I'm not working. I'm not watching TV. I'm listening."

He waits sixty silent seconds while the wife struggles for composure and then he stands up and announces that he is going to bed. To rub salt in the wound, he falls to sleep blissfully and instantly.

Or, playing the part of both cops in the jailhouse interrogation scene he may, after the first explosion, switch roles. In this double-take he becomes the calm and considerate husband, remorseful, apologizing, and imploring her to continue, assuring her he is interested in anything she has to say, knowing full well the limitations of what she can say under the circumstances. Predictably, done in by the tender tone, she falls in with the plot and confesses. She confesses her loneliness, her dependence, her mental agony, and they discuss *her* problem. Her problem, as though it were some genetic defect, some personal shortcoming, some inscrutable psychosis. Now he can comfort her, avowing how he understands how she must feel, he only wished there were something he could do to help.

This kind of situation if continued in unrelieved manner has extreme consequences. Generally the marriage partners sense this and stop short of the brink. The husband, after all, is trying to protect and bolster his frail ego, not drive his wife insane or force her suicide. He wants in the home to be able to hide from his own inner doubts, his own sense of shame, failure, and meaninglessness. He wants to shed the endless humiliation of endless days parading as a man in the male world. Pretending a power, control, and understanding he does not have.

All he asks of his wife, aside from hours of menial work, is that she not see him as he sees himself. That she not challenge him but admire and desire him, soothe and distract him. In short, make him feel like the kind of guy he'd like to be in the kind of world he thinks exists. _____

And by this time the wife asks little more really than the opportunity to play that role. She probably never aspired to more, to an equalitarian or reality-oriented relationship. It is just that she cannot do her thing if it is laid out so baldly; if she is to be denied all self-respect, all self-development, all help and encouragement from her husband.

So generally the couple stops short of the brink. Sometimes, paradoxically enough, by escalating the conflict so that it ends in divorce, but generally by some accommodation. The husband encourages the wife to make some girl friends, take night courses, or have children. And sooner or later, if she can, she has children. Assuming the husband has agreed to the event, the wife's pregnancy does abate or deflect the drift of their marriage, for a while anyway.

The pregnancy presents to the world visible proof of the husband's masculinity, potency. This visible proof shores up the basic substructure of his ego, the floor beyond which he cannot now fall. Pathetically his stock goes up in society, in his own eyes. He is a man. He is grateful to his wife and treats her, at least during the first pregnancy, with increased tenderness and respect. He pats her tummy and makes noises about mystic occurrences. And since pregnancy is not a male thing and he is a man, since this is cooperation, not competition, he can even make out that he feels her role is pretty special.

The wife is grateful. Her husband loves her. She is suffused with happiness and pride. There is at last something on her side of the division of labor which her husband views with respect, and delight of delights, with perhaps a twinge of jealousy.

Of course, it can't last. After nine months the child is bound to be born. And there we are back at the starting gate. Generally speaking, giving birth must be like a bad trip with the added feature of prolonged physical exhaustion.

Sometimes it takes a year to regain one's full strength after a messy caesarian. Sometimes women develop post-parturational psychosis in the hospital. More commonly, after they have been home awhile they develop a transient but recurring state called the "Tired Mother Syndrome." In its severe form it is, or resembles, a psychosis. Women with this syndrome complain of being utterly exhausted, irritable, unable to concentrate. They may wander about somewhat aimlessly, they may have physical pains. They are depressed, anxious, sometimes paranoid, and they cry a lot.

Sound familiar? Despite the name one doesn't have to be a mother to experience the ailment. Many young wives without children do experience it, particularly those who, without an education themselves, are working their husband's way through college. That is to say, wives who hold down a dull eight or nine hour a day job, then come home, straighten, cook, clean, run down to the laundry, dash to the grocery store, iron their own clothes plus their husband's shirts and jeans, sew for themselves, put up their hair, and more often than not type their husband's papers, correct his spelling and grammar, pay the bills, screw on command, and write the in-laws. I've even known wives who on top of this load do term papers or laboratory work for their husbands. Of course, it's insanity. What else could such self-denial be called? Love?

Is it any wonder that a woman in this circumstance is tired? Is it any wonder that she responds with irritability when she returns home at night to find her student husband, after a day or half day at home, drinking beer and shooting the bull with his cronies, the ring still in the bathtub, his dishes undone, his clothes where he dropped them the night before, even his specific little chores like taking out the garbage unaccomplished?

Is it any wonder that she is tempted to scream when at the very moment she has gotten rid of the company, plowed through some of the mess, and is standing in a tiny kitchen over a hot stove, her husband begins to make sexual advances? He naively expects that these advances will fill her with passion, melting all anger, and result not only in her forgetting and forgiving but in gratitude and renewed love. Ever hear the expression, "A woman loves the man who satisfies her"? Some men find that delusion comforting. A couple of screws and the slate is wiped clean. Who needs to pay for servants or buy his wife a washing machine when he has a cock?

No More Miss America!

New York Radical Women (NYRW), organized in the autumn of 1967 by Shulamith Firestone and Pam Allen, was the first women's liberation organization in New York City. At the suggestion of member Carol Hanisch, NYRW proposed the annual Miss America Pageant in Atlantic City for the movement's first national demonstration. This leaflet was distributed to announce it. On September 7, 1968, protesters on the boardwalk tossed bras, brooms, and other "instruments of female torture" into a Freedom Trash Can (contrary to legend, they burned no bras), while inside the convention hall others unfurled a banner from the balcony proclaiming WOMEN'S LIBERATION—disrupting the pageant and bringing the fledgling movement international media attention. In 1969, after its weekly meetings grew unwieldy, NYRW dissolved, splitting off into smaller consciousness-raising groups, including WITCH, Redstockings, and New York Radical Feminists (NYRF), each of which quickly spun off yet more groups. NYRW published the groundbreaking journal *Notes from the First Year, Second Year,* and *Third Year.*

O N SEPTEMBER 7TH in Atlantic City, the Annual Miss America Pageant will again crown "your ideal." But this year, reality will liberate the contest auction-block in the guise of "genyooine" de-plasticized, breathing women. Women's Liberation Groups, black women, high-school and college women, women's peace groups, women's welfare and social-work groups, women's job-equality groups, pro–birth control and pro-abortion groups— women of every political persuasion—all are invited to join us in a day-long boardwalk-theater event, starting at 1:00 p.m. on the Boardwalk in front of Atlantic City's Convention Hall. We will protest the image of Miss America, an image that oppresses women in every area in which it purports to represent us. There will be: Picket Lines; Guerrilla Theater; Leafleting; Lobbying Visits to the contestants urging our sisters to reject the Pageant Farce and join us; a huge Freedom Trash Can (into which we will throw bras, girdles, curlers, false eyelashes, wigs, and representative issues of *Cosmopolitan, Ladies' Home Journal, Family Circle,* etc.—bring any such woman-garbage you have around the house); we will also announce a Boycott of all those commercial products related to the Pageant, and the day will end with a Women's Liberation rally at midnight when Miss America is crowned on live television. Lots of other surprises are being planned (come and add your own!) but we do not plan heavy disruptive tactics and so do not expect a bad police scene. It should be a groovy day on the Boardwalk in the sun with our sisters. In case of arrests, however, we plan to reject all male authority and demand to be busted by policewomen only. (In Atlantic City, women cops are not permitted to make arrests—dig that!)

Male chauvinist-reactionaries on this issue had best stay away, nor are male liberals welcome in the demonstrations. But sympathetic men can donate money as well as cars and drivers.

Male reporters will be refused interviews. We reject patronizing reportage. *Only newswomen will be recognized.*

THE TEN POINTS WE PROTEST:

1. *The Degrading Mindless-Boob-Girlie Symbol.* The Pageant contestants epitomize the roles we are all forced to play as women. The parade down the runway blares the metaphor of the 4-H Club county fair, where the nervous animals are judged for teeth, fleece, etc., and where the best "specimen" gets the blue ribbon. So are women in our society forced daily to compete for male approval, enslaved by ludicrous "beauty" standards we ourselves are conditioned to take seriously.

2. *Racism with Roses.* Since its inception in 1921, the Pageant has not had one Black finalist, and this has not been for a lack of test-case contestants. There has never been a Puerto Rican, Alaskan, Hawaiian, or Mexican-American winner. Nor has there ever been a *true* Miss America—an American Indian.

3. *Miss America as Military Death Mascot.* The highlight of her reign each year is a cheerleader-tour of American troops abroad—last year she went to Vietnam to pep-talk our husbands, fathers, sons and boyfriends into dying and killing with a better spirit. She personifies the "unstained patriotic American womanhood our boys are fighting for." The Living Bra and the Dead Soldier. We refuse to be used as Mascots for Murder.

4. *The Consumer Con-Game.* Miss America is a walking commercial for the Pageant's sponsors. Wind her up and she plugs your product on promotion tours and TV—all in an "honest, objective" endorsement. What a shill.

5. *Competition Rigged and Unrigged.* We deplore the encouragement of an American myth that oppresses men as well as women: the win-or-you're-worthless competitive disease. The "beauty contest" creates only one winner to be "used" and forty-nine losers who are "useless."

6. *The Woman as Pop Culture Obsolescent Theme.* Spindle, mutilate, and then discard tomorrow. What is so ignored as last year's Miss America? This only reflects the gospel of our society, according to Saint Male: women must be young, juicy, malleable—hence age discrimination and the cult of youth. And we women are brainwashed into believing this ourselves!

7. *The Unbeatable Madonna-Whore Combination.* Miss America and Playboy's centerfold are sisters over the skin. To win approval, we must be both sexy and wholesome, delicate but able to cope, demure yet titillatingly bitchy. Deviation of any sort brings, we are told, disaster: "You won't get a man!!"

8. *The Irrelevant Crown on the Throne of Mediocrity.* Miss America represents what women are supposed to be: unoffensive, bland, apolitical. If you are tall, short, over or under what weight The Man prescribes you should be, forget it. Personality, articulateness, intelligence, commitment—unwise. Conformity is the key to the crown—and, by extension, to success in our society.

9. *Miss America as Dream Equivalent To—?* In this reputedly democratic society, where every little boy supposedly can grow up to be President, what can every little girl hope to grow to be? Miss America. That's where it's at. Real power to control our own lives is restricted to men, while women get patronizing pseudo-power, an ermine cloak and a bunch of flowers; men are judged by their actions, women by their appearance.

10. *Miss America as Big Sister Watching You.* The Pageant exercises Thought Control, attempts to sear the Image onto our minds, to further make women oppressed and men oppressors; to enslave us all the more in high-heeled, low-status roles; to inculcate false values in young girls; to use women as beasts of buying; to seduce us to prostitute ourselves before our own oppression.

NO MORE MISS AMERICA

BLACK WOMEN'S LIBERATION GROUP OF MT. VERNON, NEW YORK

Statement on Birth Control

Women of color comprised an important part of the second wave feminist movement, including as prominent founders and leaders of NOW. From the late 1960s on, some of the most active women's liberation groups springing up across the country were formed by women of color—like the Mt. Vernon Group, also known as the Pat Robinson Group or "The Damned." Self-identified as poor women, they first organized in 1960 in response to a community teen pregnancy crisis. Their writings, published in various New Left and early women's liberation journals, were composed collectively, and their advocacy of self-determination for Black women and reproductive and abortion rights is foundational in the history of Black feminism. The fierce tone of this September 11, 1968, "Statement on Birth Control" characterized many early women's liberation writings.

September 11, 1968

Dear Brothers:

Poor black sisters decide for themselves whether to have a baby or not to have a baby. If we take the pills or practise birth control in other ways, it's because of poor black men.

Now here's how it is. Poor black men won't support their families, won't stick by their women—all they think about is the street, dope and liquor, women, a piece of ass, and their cars. That's all that counts. Poor black women would be fools to sit up in the house with a whole lot of children and eventually go crazy, sick, heartbroken, no place to go, no sign of affection—nothing. Middle-class white men have always done this to their women—only more sophisticated like.

So when whitey put out the pill and poor black sisters spread the word, we saw how simple it was not to be a fool for men any more (politically we would say men could no longer exploit us sexually or for money and leave the babies with us to bring up). That was the first step in our waking up!

Black women have always been told by black men that we were black, ugly, evil, bitches and whores—in other words we were the real niggers in this society—oppressed by whites, male and female, and the black man, too.

Now a lot of the black brothers are into a new bag. Black women are being asked by militant black brothers not to practise birth control because it is a form of whitey committing genocide on black people. Well, true enough, but it takes two to practise genocide and black women are able to decide for themselves, just like poor people all over the world, whether they will submit to genocide. For us, birth control is freedom to fight genocide of black women and children.

Like the Vietnamese have decided to fight genocide, the South American poor are beginning to fight back, and the African poor will fight back, too. Poor black women in the U.S. have to fight back out of our own experience of oppression. Having too many babies stops us from supporting our children, teaching them the truth or stopping the brainwashing as you say, and fighting black men who still want to use and exploit us.

But we don't think you are going to understand us because you are a bunch of little middle-class people and we are poor black women. The middle class never understands the poor because they always need to use them as you want to use poor black women's children to gain power for yourself. You'll run the black community with your kind of black power—you on top!

Mount Vernon, N.Y.

Patricia Haden—welfare recipient
Sue Rudolph—housewife
Joyce Hoyt—domestic
Priscilla Leake—housewife

Rita Van Lew—welfare recipient
Catherine Hoyt—grandmother
Patricia Robinson—housewife and
psychotherapist

and others who read it, agreed with it, but did not help to compose.

DANA DENSMORE

On Celibacy

Dana Densmore (born 1945), cofounder with Roxanne Dunbar-Ortiz of the Boston area's militant feminist separatist group Cell 16 (1968–73), published "On Celibacy" in the first issue of the group's journal *No More Fun and Games* in October 1968. Cell 16 advocated independence from men, including sexual independence. Rejecting lesbian separatism as withdrawal from political engagement, Densmore proposes here the extreme—and at the time shocking—tactic of celibacy. Densmore, along with Cell 16 member Jayne West, also championed and taught women's self-defense through karate.

ONE HANGUP to liberation is a supposed "need" for sex. It is something that must be refuted, coped with, demythified, or the cause of female liberation is doomed.

Already we see girls, thoroughly liberated in their own heads, understanding their oppression with terrible clarity trying, deliberately and a trace hysterically, to make themselves attractive to men, men for whom they have no respect, men they may even hate, because of "a basic sexual-emotional need."

Sex is not essential to life, as eating is. Some people go through their whole lives without engaging in it at all, including fine, warm, happy people. It is a myth that this makes one bitter, shriveled up, twisted.

The big stigma of life-long virginity is on women anyway, created by men because woman's purpose in life is biological and if she doesn't fulfill that she's warped and unnatural and "must be all cobwebs inside."

Men are suspected at worst of being self-centered or afraid of sex, but do not carry any stigma of being unnatural. A man's life is taken as a whole on its merits. He was busy, it may be thought, dedicated, a great man who couldn't spare the time and energy for demanding relationships with women.

The guerillas don't screw. They eat, when they can, but they don't screw. They have important things to do, things that require all their energy.

Every one of us must have noticed occasions when he was very involved in something, fighting, working, thinking, writing, involved to the extent that eating was haphazard, sleeping deliberately cheated. But the first thing that goes is sex. It's inconvenient, time-consuming, energy-draining, and irrelevant.

We are programmed to crave sex. It sells consumer goods. It gives a lift and promises a spark of individual self-assertion in a dull and routinized world. It is a means to power (the only means they have) for women.

It is also, conversely, a means of power for men, exercized over women, because her sexual desire is directed to men.

Few women ever are actually satisfied, of course, but they blame the particular man and nurse the myth that they can be satisfied and that this nirvana is one which a man and only a man can bring her.

Moreover, sexual freedom is the first freedom a woman is awarded and she thinks it is very important because it's all she has; compared to the dullness and restrictiveness of the rest of her life it glows very brightly.

But we must come to realize that sex is actually a minor need, blown out of proportion, misunderstood (usually what passes for sexual need is actually desire to be stroked, desire for recognition or love, desire to conquer, humiliate or wield power, or desire to communicate).

We must come to realize that we don't need sex, that celibacy is not a dragon but even a state that could be desirable, in many cases preferable to sex. How repugnant it really is, after all, to make love to a man who despises you, who fears you and wants to hold you down! Doesn't screwing in an atmosphere devoid of respect get pretty grim? Why bother? You don't need it.

Erotic energy is just life energy and is quickly worked off if you are doing interesting, absorbing things. Love and affection and recognition can easily be found in comrades, a more honest and open love that loves you for yourself and not for how docile and cute and sexy and ego-building you are, a love in which you are always subject, never merely object, always active, never merely relative. And if despite all this genital tensions persist you can still masturbate. Isn't that a lot easier anyway?

This is a call not for celibacy but for an acceptance of celibacy as an honorable alternative, one preferable to the degradation of most male-female sexual relationships. But it is only when we accept the idea of celibacy completely that we will ever be able to liberate ourselves.

Until we accept it completely, until we say "I control my own body and I don't need any insolent male with an overbearing presumptuous prick to come and clean out my pipes" they will always have over us the devastating threat of withdrawing their sexual attentions and worse, the threat of our ceasing even to be sexually attractive.

And that devastating rejection is absolutely inevitable. If you are serious and men realize it they will cease being attracted to you.

If you don't play the game, the role, you are not a woman and they will NOT be attracted. You will be sexless and worse, unnatural and threatening.

You will be feared and despised and viciously maligned, all by men you know perfectly well you could charm utterly and wrap around your finger just by falling into the female role, even by men who have worshipped you in the past.

How is that possible? Obviously, because they never were worshipping you. That's the bitter truth, and you'd better catch on now.

Whenever they're nice to us, it isn't us they're being nice to but their own solipsistic creations, the versions of us they manufacture for their own amusement and pleasure and purposes. How presumptuous it is of us to accept the love and admiration, to crave it even, as if it were meant for us!

It's their female ideal they adore and they will be resentful and angry if you mar that image and will turn against you to a man if you try to destroy it.

Unless you accept the idea that you don't need them, don't need sex from them, it will be utterly impossible for you to carry through, it will be absolutely necessary to lead a double life, pretending with men to be something other than what you know you are. The strain of this would be unimaginable and could end in any number of disastrous ways.

You, who have had such heady power to charm and arouse and win men's total admiration and respect, must be willing to give it up. You must be willing that they cease to be attracted to you, even find you repulsive, that they cease to respect you, even despise you, that they cease to admire you, even find you unnatural and warped and perverted sexually.

These men who were so tenderly protective will try to destroy you, to stab you in the back, to use any underhanded means to get back at you for posing this threat to them. You have done them the incalculable offense of not deferring to their sex, of daring to be yourself (putting your needs ahead of his), of stepping out of your role, of rejecting the phony sexual differentiations that make each of them feel like a man.

If you don't act like a woman he doesn't see himself as a man, since his sexual identity depends on the differences, and so he feels actually castrated. Expect no love, no desire, no mercy from this man.

You have to be prepared, then, to be not just unattractive but actually sexually repulsive to most men, perhaps including all the men you currently admire.

We've spent many years learning to be appealing to men, to all men, whether we are specifically interested in them or not. We dress, we walk, we laugh, we talk, we move our hands and our heads, we sit, we speak, all in a way carefully cultivated to be feminine and charming.

We need to be thought charming and appealing even by men who bore us or repulse us, by strangers who may be trying to pick us up; we have a horror of appearing vulgar and repulsive even to the most nauseating creep. The creeps must all be brushed off gracefully, in a way that leaves their egos intact and consequently leaves them with a friendly impression of us.

It's so important that our image be favorable, we are willing to put up with the fact that it is false, distorted, that we are being loved for our weaknesses, or for qualities we don't have at all, and our strengths are denied or ridiculed.

If we are going to be liberated we must reject the false image that makes men love us, and this will make men cease to love us.

Unless we can accept this we will crumble under the first look of fear and disgust; or certainly under the first such look from a man we love and admire.

Ultimately, of course, we will cease to love and admire such men. We will have contempt for men who show that they cannot love us for ourselves, men whose egos demand and require falsehoods.

It will be a less friendly world, but there will be no unrequited longing. What we're really after is to be loved for ourselves and if that's impossible, why should we care about love at all? Friends and enemies will be clearly lined up, and the friends will be real friends and the enemies unable to hide behind phony benevolence—nor will we have to toady to them.

An end to this constant remaking of ourselves according to what the male ego demands! Let us be ourselves and good riddance to those who are then repulsed by us!

ANNE KOEDT

The Myth of the Vaginal Orgasm

Though by 1968 the "sexual revolution" was in full swing and birth control increasingly available, cultural norms based on theories of Freud and others still asserted that the perfect woman was passive in sex. Drawing on the work of such contemporary sexologists as Alfred C. Kinsey, Albert Ellis, and Masters and Johnson, Anne Koedt (born 1941) denounced this expectation as another aspect of women's oppression. In the piece included here—published in *Notes from the First Year* (1968), expanded in 1970, and widely circulated in pamphlet form—Koedt declared that the female orgasm was a source of revolutionary energy, and that the clitoris rendered a woman sexually independent. Empowered with this knowledge, she might enjoy sex with a man, but also with herself or with another woman.

WHENEVER FEMALE orgasm and frigidity are discussed, a false distinction is made between the vaginal and the clitoral orgasm. Frigidity has generally been defined by men as the failure of women to have vaginal orgasms. Actually the vagina is not a highly sensitive area and is not constructed to achieve orgasm. It is the clitoris which is the center of sexual sensitivity and which is the female equivalent of the penis.

I think this explains a great many things: First of all, the fact that the so-called frigidity rate among women is phenomenally high. Rather than tracing female frigidity to the false assumptions about female anatomy, our "experts" have declared frigidity a psychological problem of women. Those women who complained about it were recommended psychiatrists, so that they might discover their "problem"—diagnosed generally as a failure to adjust to their role as women.

The facts of female anatomy and sexual response tell a different story. Although there are many areas for sexual arousal, there is only one area for sexual climax; that area is the clitoris. All orgasms are extensions of sensation from this area. Since the clitoris is not necessarily stimulated sufficiently in the conventional sexual positions, we are left "frigid."

Aside from physical stimulation, which is the common cause of orgasm for most people, there is also stimulation through primarily mental processes. Some women, for example, may achieve orgasm through sexual fantasies, or through fetishes. However, while the stimulation may be psychological, the orgasm manifests itself physically. Thus, while the cause is psychological, the *effect* is still physical, and the orgasm necessarily takes place in the sexual organ equipped for sexual climax—the clitoris. The orgasm experience may also differ in degree of intensity—some more localized, and some more diffuse and sensitive. But they are all clitoral orgasms.

All this leads to some interesting questions about conventional sex and our role in it. Men have orgasms essentially by friction with the vagina, not the clitoral area, which is external and not able to cause friction the way penetration does. Women have thus been defined sexually in terms of what pleases men; our own biology has not been properly analyzed. Instead, we are fed the myth of the liberated woman and her vaginal orgasm—an orgasm which in fact does not exist.

What we must do is redefine our sexuality. We must discard the "normal" concepts of sex and create new guidelines which take into account mutual sexual enjoyment. While the idea of mutual enjoyment is liberally applauded in marriage manuals, it is not followed to its logical conclusion. We must begin to demand that if certain sexual positions now defined as "standard" are not mutually conducive to orgasm, they no longer be defined as standard. New techniques must be used or devised which transform this particular aspect of our current sexual exploitation.

Freud—A Father of the Vaginal Orgasm

Freud contended that the clitoral orgasm was adolescent, and that upon puberty, when women began having intercourse with men, women should transfer the center of orgasm to the vagina. The vagina, it was assumed, was able to produce a parallel, but more mature, orgasm than the clitoris. Much work was done to elaborate on this theory, but little was done to challenge the basic assumptions.

To fully appreciate this incredible invention, perhaps Freud's general attitude about women should first be recalled. Mary Ellmann, in *Thinking About Women*, summed it up this way:

> Everything in Freud's patronizing and fearful attitude toward women follows from their lack of a penis, but it is only in his essay *The Psychology of Women* that Freud makes explicit . . . the deprecations of women which are implicit in his work. He then prescribes

for them the abandonment of the life of the mind, which will inter-fere with their sexual function. When the psychoanalyzed patient is male, the analyst sets himself the task of developing the man's capacities; but with women patients, the job is to resign them to the limits of their sexuality. As Mr. Rieff puts it: For Freud, "Analysis cannot encourage in women new energies for success and achieve-ment, but only teach them the lesson of rational resignation."

It was Freud's feelings about women's secondary and inferior relationship to men that formed the basis for his theories on female sexuality.

Once having laid down the law about the nature of our sexuality, Freud not so strangely discovered a tremendous problem of frigidity in women. His recommended cure for a woman who was frigid was psychiatric care. She was suffering from failure to mentally adjust to her "natural" role as a woman. Frank S. Caprio, a contemporary follower of these ideas, states:

> . . . whenever a woman is incapable of achieving an orgasm via coitus, provided the husband is an adequate partner, and prefers clitoral stimulation to any other form of sexual activity, she can be regarded as suffering from frigidity and requires psychiatric assis-tance. (*The Sexually Adequate Female*, p. 64.)

The explanation given was that women were envious of men—"renunciation of womanhood." Thus it was diagnosed as an anti-male phenomenon.

It is important to emphasize that Freud did not base his theory upon a study of woman's anatomy, but rather upon his assumptions of woman as an inferior appendage to man, and her consequent social and psychological role. In their attempts to deal with the ensuing problem of mass frigidity, Freudians embarked on elaborate mental gymnastics. Marie Bonaparte, in *Female Sex-uality*, goes so far as to suggest surgery to help women back on their rightful path. Having discovered a strange connection between the non-frigid woman and the location of the clitoris near the vagina,

> it then occurred to me that where, in certain women, this gap was excessive, and clitoridal fixation obdurate, a clitoridal-vaginal rec-onciliation might be effected by surgical means, which would then benefit the normal erotic function. Professor Halban, of Vienna, as much a biologist as surgeon, became interested in the problem and worked out a simple operative technique. In this, the suspen-

sory ligament of the clitoris was severed and the clitoris secured to the underlying structures, thus fixing it in a lower position, with eventual reduction of the labia minora. (p. 148.)

But the severest damage was not in the area of surgery, where Freudians ran around absurdly trying to change female anatomy to fit their basic assumptions. The worst damage was done to the mental health of women, who either suffered silently with self-blame, or flocked to psychiatrists looking desperately for the hidden and terrible repression that had kept from them their vaginal destiny.

LACK OF EVIDENCE

One may perhaps at first claim that these are unknown and unexplored areas, but upon closer examination this is certainly not true today, nor was it true even in the past. For example, men have known that women suffered from frigidity often during intercourse. So the problem was there. Also, there is much specific evidence. Men knew that the clitoris was and is the essential organ for masturbation, whether in children or adult women. So obviously women made it clear where *they* thought their sexuality was located. Men also seem suspiciously aware of the clitoral powers during "foreplay," when they want to arouse women and produce the necessary lubrication for penetration. Foreplay is a concept created for male purposes, but works to the disadvantage of many women, since as soon as the woman is aroused the man changes to vaginal stimulation, leaving her both aroused and unsatisfied.

It has also been known that women need no anesthesia inside the vagina during surgery, thus pointing to the fact that the vagina is in fact not a highly sensitive area.

Today, with extensive knowledge of anatomy, with Kelly, Kinsey, and Masters and Johnson, to mention just a few sources, there is no ignorance on the subject. There are, however, social reasons why this knowledge has not been popularized. We are living in a male society which has not sought change in women's role.

ANATOMICAL EVIDENCE

Rather than starting with what women *ought* to feel, it would seem logical to start out with the anatomical facts regarding the clitoris and vagina.

The Clitoris is a small equivalent of the penis, except for the fact that the urethra does not go through it as in the man's penis. Its erection is similar to the male erection, and the head of the clitoris has the same type of structure and function as the head of the penis. G. Lombard Kelly, in *Sexual Feeling in Married Men and Women*, says:

> The head of the clitoris is also composed of erectile tissue, and it possesses a very sensitive epithelium or surface covering, supplied with special nerve endings called genital corpuscles, which are peculiarly adapted for sensory stimulation that under proper mental conditions terminates in the sexual orgasm. No other part of the female generative tract has such corpuscles. (Pocketbooks; p. 35.)

The clitoris has no other function than that of sexual pleasure.

The Vagina—Its functions are related to the reproductive function. Principally, 1) menstruation, 2) receive penis, 3) hold semen, and 4) birth passage. The interior of the vagina, which according to the defenders of the vaginally caused orgasm is the center and producer of the orgasm, is:

> like nearly all other internal body structures, poorly supplied with end organs of touch. The internal entodermal origin of the lining of the vagina makes it similar in this respect to the rectum and other parts of the digestive tract. (Kinsey, *Sexual Behavior in the Human Female*, p. 580.)

The degree of insensitivity inside the vagina is so high that "Among the women who were tested in our gynecologic sample, less than 14% were at all conscious that they had been touched." (Kinsey, p. 580.)

Even the importance of the vagina as an *erotic* center (as opposed to an orgasmic center) has been found to be minor.

Other Areas—Labia minora and the vestibule of the vagina. These two sensitive areas may trigger off a clitoral orgasm. Because they can be effectively stimulated during "normal" coitus, though infrequently, this kind of stimulation is incorrectly thought to be vaginal orgasm. However, it is important to distinguish between areas which can stimulate the clitoris, incapable of producing the orgasm themselves, and the clitoris:

> Regardless of what means of excitation is used to bring the individual to the state of sexual climax, the sensation is perceived by the genital corpuscles and is localized where they are situated: in the head of the clitoris or penis. (Kelly, p. 49.)

Psychologically Stimulated Orgasm—Aside from the above mentioned direct and indirect stimulations of the clitoris, there is a third way an orgasm may be triggered. This is through mental (cortical) stimulation, where the imagination stimulates the brain, which in turn stimulates the genital corpuscles of the glans to set off an orgasm.

WOMEN WHO SAY THEY HAVE VAGINAL ORGASMS

Confusion—Because of the lack of knowledge of their own anatomy, some women accept the idea that an orgasm felt during "normal" intercourse was vaginally caused. This confusion is caused by a combination of two factors. One, failing to locate the center of the orgasm, and two, by a desire to fit her experience to the male-defined idea of sexual normalcy. Considering that women know little about their anatomy, it is easy to be confused.

Deception—The vast majority of women who pretend vaginal orgasm to their men are faking it to "get the job." In a new best-selling Danish book, *I Accuse*, Mette Ejlersen specifically deals with this common problem, which she calls the "sex comedy." This comedy has many causes. First of all, the man brings a great deal of pressure to bear on the woman, because he considers his ability as a lover at stake. So as not to offend his ego, the woman will comply with the prescribed role and go through simulated ecstasy. In some of the other Danish women mentioned, women who were left frigid were turned off to sex, and pretended vaginal orgasm to hurry up the sex act. Others admitted that they had faked vaginal orgasm to catch a man. In one case, the woman pretended vaginal orgasm to get him to leave his first wife, who admitted being vaginally frigid. Later she was forced to continue the deception, since obviously she couldn't tell him to stimulate her clitorally.

Many more women were simply afraid to establish their right to equal enjoyment, seeing the sexual act as being primarily for the man's benefit, and any pleasure that the woman got as an added extra.

Other women, with just enough ego to reject the man's idea that they needed psychiatric care, refused to admit their frigidity. They wouldn't accept self-blame, but they didn't know how to solve the problem, not knowing the physiological facts about themselves. So they were left in a peculiar limbo.

Again, perhaps one of the most infuriating and damaging results of this whole charade has been that women who were perfectly healthy sexually were taught that they were not. So in addition to being sexually deprived, these women were told to blame themselves when they deserved no blame. Looking for a cure to a problem that has none can lead a woman on an endless path of self-hatred and insecurity. For she is told by her analyst that not even in her one role allowed in a male society—the role of a woman—is she successful. She is put on the defensive, with phony data as evidence that she'd better try to be even more feminine, think more feminine, and reject her envy of men. That is, shuffle even harder, baby.

Why Men Maintain the Myth

1. *Sexual Penetration Is Preferred*—The best physical stimulant for the penis is the woman's vagina. It supplies the necessary friction and lubrication. From a strictly technical point of view this position offers the best physical conditions, even though the man may try other positions for variation.

2. *The Invisible Woman*—One of the elements of male chauvinism is the refusal or inability to see women as total, separate human beings. Rather, men have chosen to define women only in terms of how they benefited men's lives. Sexually, a woman was not seen as an individual wanting to share equally in the sexual act, any more than she was seen as a person with independent desires when she did anything else in society. Thus, it was easy to make up what was convenient about women; for on top of that, society has been a function of male interests, and women were not organized to form even a vocal opposition to the male experts.

3. *The Penis as Epitome of Masculinity*—Men define their lives primarily in terms of masculinity. It is a universal form of ego-boosting. That is, in every society, however homogenous (i.e., with the absence of racial, ethnic, or major economic differences) there is always a group, women, to oppress.

The essence of male chauvinism is in the psychological superiority men exercise over women. This kind of superior-inferior definition of self, rather than positive definition based upon one's own achievements and development, has of course chained victim and oppressor both. But by far the most brutalized of the two is the victim.

An analogy is racism, where the white racist compensates for his feelings of unworthiness by creating an image of the black man (it is primarily a male struggle) as biologically inferior to him. Because of his position in a white male power structure, the white man can socially enforce this mythical division.

To the extent that men try to rationalize and justify male superiority through physical differentiation, masculinity may be symbolized by being the *most* muscular, the most hairy; having the the deepest voice, and the biggest penis. Women, on the other hand, are approved of (i.e., called feminine) if they are weak, petite; shave their legs; have high soft voices.

Since the clitoris is almost identical to the penis, one finds a great deal of evidence of men in various societies trying to either ignore the clitoris and emphasize the vagina (as did Freud), or, as in some places in the Mideast, actually performing clitoridectomy. Freud saw this ancient and still practiced custom as a way of further "feminizing" the female by removing this cardinal vestige of her masculinity. It should be noted also that a big clitoris is considered ugly and masculine. Some cultures engage in the practice of pouring a chemical on the clitoris to make it shrivel up into "proper" size.

It seems clear to me that men in fact fear the clitoris as a threat to masculinity.

4. *Sexually Expendable Male*—Men fear that they will become sexually expendable if the clitoris is substituted for the vagina as the center of pleasure for women. Actually this has a great deal of validity if one considers *only* the anatomy. The position of the penis inside the vagina, while perfect for reproduction, does not necessarily stimulate an orgasm in women because the clitoris is located externally and higher up. Women must rely upon indirect stimulation in the "normal" position.

Lesbian sexuality could make an excellent case, based upon anatomical data, for the irrelevancy of the male organ. Albert Ellis says something to the effect that a man without a penis can make a woman an excellent lover.

Considering that the vagina is very desirable from a man's point of view, purely on physical grounds, one begins to see the dilemma for men. And it forces us as well to discard many "physical" arguments explaining why women go to bed with men. What is left, it seems to me, are primarily psychological reasons why women select men at the exclusion of women as sexual partners.

5. *Control of Women*—One reason given to explain the Mideastern practice of clitoridectomy is that it will keep the women from straying. By removing the sexual organ capable of orgasm, it must be assumed that her sexual drive will diminish. Considering how men look upon their women as property, particularly in very backward nations, we should begin to consider a great deal more why it is not in men's interest to have women totally free sexually. The double standard, as practiced for example in Latin America, is set up to keep the woman as total property of the husband, while he is free to have affairs as he wishes.

6. *Lesbianism and Bisexuality*—Aside from the strictly anatomical reasons why women might equally seek other women as lovers, there is a fear on men's part that women will seek the company of other women on a full, human basis. The recognition of clitoral orgasm as fact would threaten the heterosexual *institution*. For it would indicate that sexual pleasure was obtainable from either men *or* women, thus making heterosexuality not an absolute, but an option. It would thus open up the whole question of *human* sexual relationships beyond the confines of the present male-female role system.

Books Mentioned in This Essay

Sexual Behavior in the Human Female, Alfred C. Kinsey, Pocketbooks, 1953.
Female Sexuality, Marie Bonaparte, Grove Press, 1953.
Sex Without Guilt, Albert Ellis, Grove Press, 1958 and 1965.
Sexual Feelings in Married Men and Women, G. Lombard Kelly, Pocketbooks, 1951 and 1965.
I Accuse (Jeg Anklager), Mette Ejlersen, Chr. Erichsens Forlag (Danish), 1968.
The Sexually Adequate Female, Frank S. Caprio, Fawcett Gold Medal Books, 1953 and 1966.
Thinking About Women, Mary Ellmann; Harcourt, Brace & World, 1968.
Human Sexual Response, Masters and Johnson; Little, Brown, 1966.

MARY ELLMANN

(from) Phallic Criticism

Critic Mary Ellmann's *Thinking About Women* (1968) is one of the earliest books of second wave feminist literary criticism. In chapter-length essays, this witty exposé of literary misogyny dissects various strategies, conceits, and contradictions used by male writers and critics to denigrate women authors and their work. In one chapter, Ellmann (1921–1989) reveals the absurdity of analogies of sexual or reproductive activity to mental activity and works of art; in another she lays bare many of the stigmatizing female stereotypes (e.g., passivity, instability, irrationality) male critics have used in characterizing women's writing. In the chapter excerpted here, "Phallic Criticism," Ellmann exposes male critics' preoccupation with femininity and what is now called gender in responding to women's writing.

THE DISCUSSION of women's books by men will arrive punctually at the point of preoccupation, which is the fact of femininity. Books by women are treated as though they themselves were women, and criticism embarks, at its happiest, upon an intellectual measuring of busts and hips. Of course, this preoccupation has its engaging and compensatory sides.* Like such minor physical disorders as shingles and mumps, it often seems (whether or not it *feels* to the critic) comical as well as distressing. Then too, whatever intellectual risks this criticism runs, one of them is not abstraction. Any sexual reference, even in the most dryasdust context, shares the power which any reference to food has, of provoking fresh and immediate interest. As lunch

---

*It has an unnerving side as well, though this appears less often in criticism, I think, than in fiction or poetry. For example, James Dickey's poem "Falling" expresses an extraordinary concern with the underwear of a woman who has fallen out of an airplane. While this woman, a stewardess, was in the airplane, her girdle obscured, to the observation of even the most alert passenger, her mesial groove. The effect was, as the poem recalls, "monobuttocked." As the woman falls, however, she undresses and "passes her palms" over her legs, her breasts, and "deeply between her thighs." Beneath her, "widowed farmers" are soon to wake with futile (and irrelevant?) erections. She lands on her back in a field, naked, and dies. The sensation of the poem is necrophilic: it mourns a vagina rather than a person crashing to the ground.

can be mentioned every day without boring those who are hungry, the critic can always return to heterosexual (and, increasingly, to homosexual) relations and opinions with certainty of being read.

Admittedly, everyone is amused by the skillful wrapping of a book, like a negligee, about an author. Stanley Kauffmann opened a review of Françoise Sagan's *La Chamade* with this simile:

> Poor old Françoise Sagan. Just one more old-fashioned old-timer, bypassed in the rush for the latest literary vogue and for youth. Superficially, her career in America resembles the lifespan of those medieval beauties who flowered at 14, were deflowered at 15, were old at 30 and crones at 40.*

A superior instance of the mode—the play, for example, between *flowered* and *deflowered* is neat. And quite probably, of course, women might enjoy discussing men's books in similar terms. Some such emulative project would be diverting for a book season or two, if it were possible to persuade conventional journals to print its equivalent remarks. From a review of a new novel by the popular French novelist, François Sagan:

> Poor old François Sagan. . . . Superficially, his career in America resembles the life-span of those medieval troubadours who masturbated at 14, copulated at 15, were impotent at 30 and prostate cases at 40.

Somehow or other, No. It is not that male sexual histories, in themselves, are not potentially funny—even though they seem to be thought perceptibly less so than female sexual histories. It is rather that the literal fact of masculinity, unlike femininity, does not impose an erogenic form upon all aspects of the person's career.

I do not mean to suggest, however, that this imposition necessarily results in injustice. (Stanley Kauffmann went on to be more than just, *merciful* to Françoise Sagan.) In fact, it sometimes issues in fulsome praise. Excess occurs when the critic, like Dr. Johnson congratulating the dog who walked like a man, is impressed that the woman has—not so much written well, as written at all. But unfortunately, benign as this upright-pooch predisposition can be in the estimate of indifferent work, it can also infect the praise of work which deserves (what has to be called) asexual approval. In this case, enthusiasm

*Stanley Kauffmann, "Toujours Tristesse," *New Republic*, October 29, 1966, p. 2.

issues in an explanation of the ways in which the work is free of what the critic ordinarily dislikes in the work of a woman. He had despaired of ever seeing a birdhouse built by a woman; now *here* is a birdhouse built by a woman. Pleasure may mount even to an admission of male envy of the work examined: an exceptionally sturdy birdhouse at that! In *Commentary*, Warren Coffey has expressed his belief that "a man would give his right arm to have written Flannery O'Connor's 'Good Country People.'"* And here, not only the sentiment but the confidence with which the cliché is wielded, is distinctly phallic. It is as though, merely by thinking about Flannery O'Connor or Mrs. Gaskell or Harriet Beecher Stowe, the critic experienced acute sensations of his own liberty. The more he considers a feeble, cautious and timid existence, the more devil-may-care he seems to himself. This exhilaration then issues, rather tamely, in a daring to be commonplace.

And curiously, it often issues in expressions of contempt for delicate men as well. In this piece, for example, Flannery O'Connor is praised not only as a woman writer who writes as well as a man might wish to write, but also as a woman writer who succeeds in being less feminine than some men. She is less "girlish" than Truman Capote or Tennessee Williams.† In effect, once the critic's attention is trained, like Sweeney's, upon the Female Temperament, he invariably sideswipes at effeminacy in the male as well. The basic distinction becomes nonliterary: it is less between the book under review and other books, than between the critic and other persons who seem to him, regrettably, less masculine than he is. The assumption of the piece is that no higher praise of a woman's work exists than that such a critic should like it or think that other men will like it. The same ploy can also be executed in reverse. Norman Mailer, for example, is pleased to think that Joseph Heller's *Catch-22* is a man's book to read, a book which merely "puzzles" women. Women cannot comprehend male books, men cannot tolerate female books. The working rule is simple, basic: there must always be two literatures like two public toilets, one for Men and one for Women.

Sometimes it seems that no achievement can override this division. When Marianne Moore received the Poetry Society of America's Gold Medal for Poetry, she received as well Robert Lowell's encomium, "She is the best woman poet in English." The late Langston Hughes added, "I consider her the most

---

*Warren Coffey, *Commentary*, November 1965, p. 98.

†Though Tennessee Williams is cited here to enhance Flannery O'Connor's virtues, he is just as easily cited to prove other women's defects. For example, Dr. Karl Stern has resorted to Williams and Edward Albee as witnesses to the modern prevalence of the Castrating Woman. (*Barat Review*, January 1967, p. 46.) Naturally, in this context, both playwrights assume a status of unqualified virility.

famous Negro woman poet in America," and others would have enjoyed "the best blue-eyed woman poet."* Lowell has also praised Sylvia Plath's last book of poems, *Ariel*. His foreword begins:

> In these poems, written in the last months of her life and often rushed out at the rate of two or three a day, Sylvia Plath becomes herself, becomes something imaginary, newly, wildly and subtly created—hardly a person at all, or a woman, certainly not another "poetess," but one of those super-real, hypnotic, great classical heroines. The character is feminine, rather than female, though almost everything we customarily think of as feminine is turned on its head. The voice is now coolly amused, witty, now sour, now fanciful, girlish, charming, now sinking to the strident rasp of the vampire—a Dido, Phaedra, or Medea, who can laugh at herself as "cow-heavy and floral in my Victorian nightgown."

A little cloudburst, a short heavy rain of sexual references. The word *poetess*, whose gender killed it long ago, is exhumed—to be denied. Equivalently, a critic of W. H. Auden would be at pains, first of all, to deny that Auden is a poetaster. But *poetess* is only part of the general pelting away at the single fact that Sylvia Plath belonged to a sex (that inescapable membership) and that her sex was not male—*woman, heroines, feminine, female, girlish, fanciful, charming, Dido, Phaedra, Medea. Vampire*, too. And it would of course be this line, "Cow-heavy and floral in my Victorian nightgown," which seizes attention first and evokes the surprised pleasure of realizing that Sylvia Plath "can laugh at herself." Self-mockery, particularly sexual self-mockery, is not expected in a woman, and it is irresistible in the criticism of women to describe what was expected: the actual seems to exist only in relation to the preconceived.

Lowell's distinction between *feminine* and *female* is difficult, though less difficult than a distinction between *masculine* and *male* would be—say, in an introduction to Blake's *Songs of Innocence*. What helps us with the first is our all knowing, for some time now, that femaleness is a congenital fault, rather like eczema or Original Sin. An indicative denunciation, made in 1889: "They

---

*Miss Moore's femininity leaves her vulnerable even to the imagination of John Berryman:

> *Fancy a lark with Sappho,*
> *a tumble in the bushes with Miss Moore,*
> *a spoon with Emily, while Charlotte glare.*
> *Miss Bishop's too noble-O.*

("Four Dream Songs," *Atlantic*, February 1968, p. 68.)

are no ladies. The only word good enough for them is the word of oppro-brium—females." But fortunately, some women can be saved. By good man-ners, they are translated from females into ladies; and by talent, into feminine creatures (or even into "classical heroines"). And we are entirely accustomed to this generic mobility on their part: the individual is assumed into the sex and loses all but typical meaning within it. The emphasis is finally maca-bre, as though women wrote with breasts instead of pens—in which event it would be remarkable, as Lowell feels that it is, if one of them achieved ironic detachment.

When the subject of the work by a woman is also women (as it often has to be, since everyone has to eat what's in the cupboard), its critical treatment is still more aberrant. Like less specialized men, critics seem to fluctuate between attraction and surfeit. An obsessive concern with femininity shifts, at any moment, into a sense of being confined or suffocated by it. In the second condition, a distaste for books *before they are read* is not uncommon, as in Norman Mailer's unsolicited confession of not having been able to read Vir-ginia Woolf, or in Anthony Burgess's inhibitory "impression of high-waisted dresses and genteel parsonage flirtation"* in Jane Austen's novels. More luckily, the work may be patronized by mild minds already persuaded that the human temperament combines traits of both sexes and that even masculine natures may respond, through their subterranean femininity, to the thoroughly fem-inine book.

A similar indulgence is fostered by any association, however tenuous, which the critic forms between the woman writer and some previous student of his own.† Now that almost everyone who writes teaches too, the incidence of this association is fairly high. Robert Lowell remembers that Sylvia Plath once audited a class of his at Boston University:

> She was never a student of mine, but for a couple of months seven
> years ago, she used to drop in on my poetry seminar at Boston Uni-
> versity. I see her dim against the bright sky of a high window, view-
> less unless one cared to look down on the city outskirts' defeated
> yellow brick and square concrete pillbox filling stations. She was
> willowy, long-waisted, sharp-elbowed, nervous, giggly, gracious—a
> brilliant tense presence embarrassed by restraint. Her humility and
> willingness to accept what was admired seemed at times to give her

New York Times Book Review, December 4, 1966, p. 1.
†For the especial amicability of this sexual relationship, see "The Student," p. 119.

an air of maddening docility that hid her unfashionable patience and boldness.*

It is not easy, of course, to write about a person whom one knew only slightly in the past. The strain is felt here, for example, in the gratuitous street scene from the classroom window. And in general, there is a sense of a physical recollection emended by a much later intellectual and poetic impression. The "brilliant tense presence" of the final poetry is affixed, generously enough, to the original figure of a young girl. The "maddening docility" too must have been a sexual enlargement, now reduced to an "air" of docility, since again the poems demonstrate the artistic (rather than "feminine") union of "patience and boldness." (Elsewhere they are, according to Lowell, "modest" poems too, they are uniquely "modest" *and* "bold.") But then the poet Anne Sexton's recollections, which originate in the same poetry seminar, make no reference to elbows or giggles or docility. Miss Sexton seems to have seen even at that time a woman entirely congruous with her later work. After class, the two used to drink together—at the Ritz bar, some distance away from those "concrete pillbox filling stations"—and conduct workmanlike discussions of suicidal techniques:

> *But suicides have a special language.*
> *Like carpenters they want to know* which tools.
> *They never ask* why build.
>
> ("Wanting to Die")†

Lowell seems honestly caught between two ways of comprehending what exists outside the self. And certainly there is nothing of the stag posture about his remarks, no pretense of writing only for other men about women. All critics are of course secretly aware that no literary audience, except perhaps in Yemen, is any longer restricted to men. The man's-man tone is a deliberate archaism, coy and even flirtatious, like wearing spats. No one doubts that some silent misogyny may be dark and deep, but written misogyny is now generally a kind of chaffing, and not frightfully clever, gambit. For the critic in this style, the writer whose work is most easily related to established stereotypes of femininity is, oddly, the most welcome. What-to-say then flows effortlessly from the stereotypes themselves. The word *feminine* alone, like a grimace, expresses a displeasure which is not less certain for its being undefined. In a

---

*Foreword to Sylvia Plath's *Ariel*, p. xi.
†Anne Sexton, "The barfly ought to sing," *Tri-Quarterly*, Fall 1966, p. 90.

review of Fawn Brodie's biography of Sir Richard Burton, *The Devil Drives*, Josh Greenfeld remarked on the "feminine biographer's attachment to subject," and suggested that this quality (*or else* a "scholarly objectivity") prevented Mrs. Brodie's conceding Burton's homosexuality.* So her book is either too subjective or too objective: we will never know which.

But the same word can be turned upon men too. John Weightman has remarked that Genet's criminals cannot play male and female effectively because "a convicted criminal, however potent, has been classified as an object, and therefore feminized, by society."† An admirably simple social equation: a man in prison amounts to a woman. Similarly, *feminine* functions as an eight-letter word in the notorious Woodrow Wilson biography by Freud and William Bullitt. At one heated point, Clemenceau calls Wilson feminine, Wilson calls Clemenceau feminine, then both Freud and Bullitt call Wilson feminine again. The word means that all four men thoroughly dislike each other. It is also sufficient for Norman Mailer to say that Herbert Gold reminds him "of nothing so much as a woman writer,"‡ and for Richard Gilman to consign Philip Roth to the "ladies' magazine" level."§ In fact, chapters of *When She Was Good* were first published, and seemed to settle in snugly, at the *haut bourgeois* level of *Harper's* and the *Atlantic*. But, except perhaps in the *Daily Worker*, the consciousness of class is less insistent than that of sex: the phrase "ladies' magazine" is one of those which refuses not to be written once a month.¶

But at heart most of these "the-ladies-bless-them" comments are as cheerful and offhand as they are predictable. When contempt, like anything else, has an assigned route to follow, and when it is accustomed to its course, it can proceed happily. This is evident, for example, in Norman Mailer's lively, even jocular, essay on the deplorable faults of Mary McCarthy's *The Group*. What

---

Book Week, May 28, 1967, p. 2. Mrs. Brodie had still more trouble in the *Times Literary Supplement* (January 11, 1968, p. 32), where her nationality as well as her sex was at fault: "So immense is this gulf, so inalienably remote are the societies that produced biographer and subject, *so difficult is it, even now, for a woman to get beneath a man's skin*, that only some imaginative genius could really have succeeded in the task Mrs. Brodie so boldly undertook." [My italics.]

†*New York Review of Books*, August 24, 1967, p. 8.

‡*Advertisements for Myself*, p. 435.

§Richard Gilman, "Let's Lynch Lucy," *New Republic*, June 24, 1967, p. 19.

¶The phrase is at least sociologically interesting: it suggests the impossibility of remarking that some bad novel is fit for the "men's magazine." For fiction, there is none. At the same level of intelligence and cultivation, women evidently prefer stories (*McCall's, Redbook, The Ladies' Home Journal*, etc.) and men prefer facts (or quasi-facts) and photographs (*Time, Life, Look, Dude, Gent*, etc.). *Playboy* is exceptional in presupposing an eclectic male audience (does it exist?) for both photographs *and* fiction.

accounts for these high spirits, except the fact that Mailer rejoices in what he spanks so loudly? The pleasure lies in Mary McCarthy's having capitulated, as it seems to Mailer, having at last written what he can securely and triumphantly call a female novel.* Not that Mailer's treatment of *The Group*, even in these familiar terms, is not still remarkable—even frightening, and that is a rare treat in criticism. One does not expect a disdain for feminine concerns, which is entirely commonplace, to mount to cloacal loathing. Mary McCarthy has soiled an abstraction, a genre, the novel-yet-to-be: "Yes, Mary deposited a load on the premise, and it has to be washed all over again, this little long-lived existential premise."†

But few rise to that kind of washing-up with Mailer's alacrity. In most critics, revulsion is an under-developed area. What rouses a much more interesting hostility in many is the work which does not conform to sexual preconception. That is, if feminine concerns can be found, they are conventionally rebuked; but their absence is shocking. While all women's writing should presumably strive for a supra-feminine condition, it is profoundly distrusted for achieving it. So for all Anthony Burgess's resistance to Jane Austen, he is still less pleased by George Eliot ("The male impersonation is wholly successful") or by Ivy Compton-Burnett ("A big sexless nemesic force"). Similarly, he cannot leave alone what strikes him as the contradiction between Brigid Brophy's appearance and her writing.‡ His review of her book of essays, *Don't Never Forget*, opens in this sprightly manner:

---

*A female novel, Mailer indicates, is one which deals with the superficial details of women's lives instead of their lower depths. Such a book is at once tedious and cowardly. On the other hand, Joseph Heller's *Catch-22* is a book for men (rather than a male novel) which deals with the superficial details of men's lives. It speaks, according to Mailer, to the man who "prefers to become interested in quick proportions and contradictions; in the practical surface of things." Both novels, then, are tedious but the first is a disgrace while the second has "a vast appeal." Obviously, it all depends on which practical surface of things the commentator himself is glued to.

† *Cannibals and Christians*, p. 138.

‡ Burgess has also furnished this country, in a "Letter from London" (*Hudson Review*, Spring 1967), the following couplet:

> People who read Brigid Brophy
> Should contend for the Krafft-Ebing Trophy.

In fact, he seems unfailingly exhilarated by Miss Brophy's faults, thrilled by them as Norman Mailer is by Mary McCarthy's. Burgess's most recent agitation was a review of *Fifty Works of English Literature We Could Do Without* (by Miss Brophy, Michael Levey and Charles Osborne): "The authors are now rubbing themselves in an ecstacy of the kind granted only to Exclusive Brethren." (*Encounter*, August 1967, p. 71.)

An American professor friend of mine, formerly an admirer of Miss Brophy's work, could no longer think of her as an author once he'd seen her in the flesh. "That girl was made for love," he would growl. Various writers who have smarted from her critical attentions might find it hard to agree.*

It is as though Elizabeth Hardwick, asked to review William Manchester's *Death of a President*, was obliged to refuse, growling, "That man was made for love." The same notion of an irreconcilable difference between the nature of woman and the mind of man prompts the hermaphroditic fallacy according to which one half the person, separating from the other half, produces a book by binary fission. So Mary McCarthy has been complimented, though not by Norman Mailer, on her "masculine mind" while, through the ages, poor Virgil has never been complimented on his "effeminacy." (Western criticism begins with this same tedious distinction—between manly Homer and womanish Virgil.) At the same time, while sentiment is a disadvantage, the alternative of feminine coolness is found still more disagreeable. Mary McCarthy used to be too *formidable*, Jean Stafford has sometimes been *clinical*, and others (going down, down) are *perverse, petulant, catty, waspish*.

The point is that comment upon Violette Leduc, who is not directly assertive, will be slurring; but the slur hardens into resentment of those writers who seem to endorse the same standards of restraint and reason which the critic presumably endorses. If for nothing else, for her tolerance of Sade, Simone de Beauvoir must be referred to (scathingly!) as "the lady," and then even her qualifications of tolerance must be described as a reluctance "to give herself unreservedly" to Sade.† Similarly, it is possible that much of the voluble male distaste for Jane Austen is based, not upon her military limitations (her infamous failure to discuss the Napoleonic Wars), but upon her antipathetic detachment. So a determined counteremphasis was first placed by her relatives, and has been continued since by most of her critics, upon her allegiance to domestic ideals—when, in fact, she is read only for her mockery of them.

What seems to be wanted, insisted upon, is the critic's conception of women expressed in his conception of feminine terms—that is, a confirmation of the one sex's opinions by the imagination of the other, a difficult request which can seldom be gratified. It is perhaps this request which explains Louis

*_Manchester Guardian Weekly_, November 24, 1966, p. 11. There is, incidentally, An American Professor who exists only in the minds of English journalists. The _Times Literary Supplement_ would be halved without him.
†Leslie Schaeffer, _New Republic_, August 19, 1967, p. 28.

Auchincloss's erratic view of Mary McCarthy in his *Pioneers and Caretakers*. Suddenly she is sister to Ellen Glasgow and Sarah Orne Jewett, as one of our feminine "caretakers of the culture," a guise in which few other readers can easily recognize her. But if one's thesis is sexual, the attachment of women to the past and the incapacity of women for "the clean sweep," then Mary McCarthy only seems to hate a few present things and actually loves many past things. One might as well argue that it was Swift's finding babies so sweet that made him think of eating them for dinner.

WITCH

Leaflet

Founded in New York City on Halloween 1968, WITCH (Women's International Terrorist Conspiracy from Hell), a spin-off of New York Radical Women, used street theater to call out sexism and inequality. Refuting the stereotype of feminists as "humorless," WITCH embodied the irreverent, high-spirited fun of the early women's liberation movement with playful "zap actions" such as marching through New York's financial district dressed as witches to place a hex on Wall Street. Soon, autonomous WITCH "covens" surfaced in many U.S. cities, from Boston to San Francisco. A University of Chicago coven hexed the Sociology Department with hair and fingernail clippings to protest a popular feminist professor's dismissal; a Washington D.C. coven hexed the presidential inauguration. WITCH groups continued zapping into the early 1970s, assigning the WITCH acronym new meanings to suit the action, e.g., Women Incensed at Telephone Company Harassment. This 1968 New York leaflet displays the roguish WITCH style.

For Rebellion Is As The Sin Of Witchcraft . . .

—*I Samuel*, 15:23

New York Covens

WITCH is an all-women Everything. It's theater, revolution, magic, terror, joy, garlic flowers, spells. It's an awareness that witches and gypsies were the original guerrillas and resistance fighters against oppression—particularly the oppression of women—down through the ages. Witches have always been women who dared to be: groovy, courageous, aggressive, intelligent, nonconformist, explorative, curious, independent, sexually liberated, revolutionary. (This possibly explains why nine million of them have been burned.) Witches were the first Friendly Heads and Dealers, the first birth-control practitioners and abortionists, the first alchemists (turn dross into gold and you devalue the whole idea of money!). They bowed to no man, being the living remnants of the oldest culture of all—one in which men and women were equal sharers in a truly cooperative society, before the death-dealing sexual, economic, and spiritual repression of the Imperialist Phallic Society took over and began to destroy nature and human society.

WITCH lives and laughs in every woman. She is the free part of each of us, beneath the shy smiles, the acquiescence to absurd male domination, the make-up or flesh-suffocating clothing our sick society demands. There is no "joining" WITCH. If you are a woman and dare to look within yourself, you are a Witch. You make your own rules. You are free and beautiful. You can be invisible or evident in how you choose to make your witch-self known. You can form your own Coven of sister Witches (thirteen is a cozy number for a group) and do your own actions.

Whatever is repressive, solely male-oriented, greedy, puritanical, authoritarian—those are your targets. Your weapons are theater, satire, explosions, magic, herbs, music, costumes, cameras, masks, chants, stickers, stencils and paint, films, tambourines, bricks, brooms, guns, voodoo dolls, cats, candles, bells, chalk, nail clippings, hand grenades, poison rings, fuses, tape recorders, incense—your own boundless beautiful imagination. Your power comes from your own self as a woman, and it is activated by working in concert with your sisters. The power of the Coven is more than the sum of its individual members, because it is *together*.

You are pledged to free our brothers from oppression and stereotyped sexual roles (whether they like it or not) as well as ourselves. You are a Witch by saying aloud, "I am a Witch" three times, and *thinking about that*. You are a Witch by being female, untamed, angry, joyous, and immortal.

MARY ANN WEATHERS

An Argument for Black Women's Liberation as a Revolutionary Force

An early text of Black feminism, this piece by Mary Ann Weathers, an original member of the Boston-area militant feminist group Cell 16, presents to the Black liberation movement reasons to embrace women's liberation as well. The essay dismisses the idea of male superiority as "the master's prattle," and argues that, while the oppression of minority and poor women is "tripled," *all* women are subject to oppression, and therefore women's liberation should be used to unite "the entire revolutionary movement consisting of women, men, and children." It was first published in Cell 16's journal *No More Fun and Games* in February 1969.

"NOBODY CAN FIGHT your battles for you; you have to do it yourself." This will be the premise used for the time being for stating the case for Black women's liberation, although certainly it is the least significant. Black women, at least the Black women I have come in contact with in the movement, have been expending all their energies in "liberating" Black men (if you yourself are not free, how can you "liberate" someone else?). Consequently, the movement has practically come to a standstill. Not entirely due however to wasted energies but adhering to basic false concepts rather than revolutionary principles and at this stage of the game we should understand that if it is not revolutionary it is false.

We have found that Women's Liberation is an extremely emotional issue, as well as an explosive one. Black men are still parroting the master's prattle about male superiority. This now brings us to a very pertinent question: How can we seriously discuss reclaiming our African Heritage—cultural living modes which clearly refute not only patriarchy and matriarchy, but our entire family structure as we know it. African tribes live communally where households let alone heads of households are non-existent.

It is really disgusting to hear Black women talk about giving Black men their manhood—or allowing them to get it. This is degrading to other Black women and thoroughly insulting to Black men (or at least it should be).

How can someone "give" one something as personal as one's adulthood? That's precisely like asking the beast for your freedom. We also chew the fat about standing behind our men. This forces me to the question: Are we women or leaning posts and props? It sounds as if we are saying if we come out from behind him, he'll fall down. To me, these are clearly maternal statements and should be closely examined.

Women's Liberation should be considered as a strategy for an eventual tie-up with the entire revolutionary movement consisting of women, men, and children. We are now speaking of real revolution (armed). If you can not accept this fact purely and without problems examine your reactions closely. We are playing to win and so are they. Viet Nam is simply a matter of time and geography.

Another matter to be discussed is the liberation of children from a sick slave culture. Although we don't like to see it, we are still operating within the confines of the slave culture. Black women use their children for their own selfish needs of worth and love. We try to live our lives which are too oppressing to bear through our children and thereby destroy them in the process. Obviously the much acclaimed plaudit of the love of the Black mother has some discrepancies. If we allow ourselves to run from the truth we run the risk of spending another 400 years in self destruction. Assuming of course the beast would tolerate us that long, and we know he wouldn't.

Women have fought with men and we have died with men in every revolution, more timely in Cuba, Algeria, China, and now in Viet Nam. If you notice, it is a woman heading the "Peace Talks" in Paris for the NLF. What is wrong with Black women? We are clearly the most oppressed and degraded minority in the world, let alone the country. Why can't we rightfully claim our place in the world?

Realizing fully what is being said, you should be warned that the opposition for liberation will come from everyplace, particularly from other women and from Black men. Don't allow yourselves to be intimidated any longer with this nonsense about the "Matriarchy" of Black women. Black women are not matriarchs but we have been forced to live in abandonment and been used and abused. The myth of the matriarchy must stop and we must not allow ourselves to be sledgehammered by it any longer—not if we are serious about change and ridding ourselves of the wickedness of this alien culture. Let it be clearly understood that Black women's liberation is not anti-male; any such sentiment or interpretation as such can not be tolerated. It must be taken clearly for what it is—pro-human for all peoples.

The potential for such a movement is boundless. Where as in the past only certain types of Black people have been attracted to the movement—younger people, radicals, and militants. The very poor, the middle class, older people and women have not become aware or have not been able to translate their awareness into action. Women's liberation offers such a channel for these energies.

Even though middle-class Black women may not have suffered the brutal supression of poor Black people, they most certainly have felt the scourge of the male superiority oriented society as women, and would be more prone to help in alleviating some of the conditions of our more oppressed sisters by teaching, raising awareness and consciousness, verbalizing the ills of women and this society, helping to establish communes.

Older women have a wealth of information and experience to offer and would be instrumental in closing the communications gap between the generations. To be Black and to tolerate this jive about discounting people over 30 is madness.

Poor women have knowledge to teach us all. Who else in this society sees more and is more realistic about ourselves and this society and about the faults that lie within our own people than our poor women? Who else could profit and benefit from a communal setting that could be established than these sisters? We must let the sisters know that we are capable and some of us already do love them. We women must begin to unabashedly learn to use the word "love" for one another. We must stop the petty jealousies, the violence that we Black women have for so long perpetrated on one another about fighting over this man or the other. (Black men should have better sense than to encourage this kind of destructive behavior.) We must turn to ourselves and one another for strength and solace. Just think for a moment what it would be like if we got together and internalized our own 24 hour a day communal centers knowing our children would be safe and loved constantly. Not to mention what it would do for everyone's egos especially the children. Women should not have to be enslaved by this society's concept of motherhood through their children, and then the kids suffer through a mother's resentment of it by beatings, punishment, and rigid discipline. All one has to do is look at the statistics of Black women who are rapidly filling the beast's mental institutions to know that the time for innovation and change and creative thinking is here. We cannot sit on our behinds waiting for someone else to do it for us. We must save ourselves.

We do not have to look at ourselves as someone's personal sex objects, maids, baby sitters, domestics and the like in exchange for a man's attention. Men hold this power, along with that of the breadwinner over our heads for these services and that's all it is—servitude. In return we torture him, and fill him with insecurities about his manhood, and literally force him to "cat" and "mess around" bringing in all sorts of conflicts. This is not the way really human people live. This is whitey's thing. And we play the game with as much proficiency as he does.

If we are going to bring about a better world, where best to begin than with ourselves? We must rid ourselves of our own hang-ups, before we can begin to talk about the rest of the world and we mean the world and nothing short of just that (Let's not kid ourselves). We will be in a position soon of having to hook up with the rest of the oppressed peoples of the world who are involved in liberation just as we are, and we had better be ready to act.

All women suffer oppression, even white women, particularly poor white women, and especially Indian, Mexican, Puerto Rican, Oriental and Black American women whose oppression is tripled by any of the above mentioned. But we do have females' oppression in common. This means that we can begin to talk to other women with this common factor and start building links with them and thereby build and transform the revolutionary force we are now beginning to amass. This is what Dr. King was doing. We can no longer allow ourselves to be duped by the guise of racism. Any time the White man admits to something you know he is trying to cover something else up. We are all being exploited, even the white middle class, by the few people in control of this entire world. And to keep the real issue clouded, he keeps us at one another's throats with this racism jive. Although, Whites are most certainly racist, we must understand that they have been programmed to think in these patterns to divert their attention. If they are busy fighting us, then they have no time to question the policies of the war being run by this government. With the way the elections went down it is clear that they are as powerless as the rest of us. Make no question about it, folks, this fool knows what he is doing. This man is playing the death game for money and power, not because he doesn't like us. He could care less one way or the other. But think for a moment if we all go together and just walked on out. Who would fight his wars, who would run his police state, who would work his factories, who would buy his products?

We women must start this thing rolling.

TI-GRACE ATKINSON

(from) *Radical Feminism*

A philosopher, feminist theorist, and frequent dissenting voice within the women's movement, Ti-Grace Atkinson (born 1938) was radicalized as an undergraduate by reading Beauvoir's *The Second Sex*. At Beauvoir's suggestion, Atkinson joined NOW in 1966, becoming president of its New York City chapter. However, finding NOW insufficiently radical, she resigned in 1968 to found the women-only group called the October 17th Movement, named for its founding date, but soon restyled The Feminists (see pp. 92–93 in this volume). Her essays critique such "institutions" as marriage, heterosexual intercourse, motherhood, prostitution, and love. Written specifically for young women, *Radical Feminism*, excerpted here, was issued as a pamphlet by The Feminists in May 1969.

ALMANINA BARBOUR, a black militant woman in Philadelphia, once pointed out to me: "the women's movement is the first in history with a war on and no enemy." I winced. It was an obvious criticism. I fumbled about in my mind for an answer: surely the enemy must have been defined at some time. Otherwise, what had we been shooting at for the last couple of years? into the air? Only two responses came to me, although in looking for those two I realized that it was a question carefully avoided. The first and by far the most frequent answer was "society". The second, infrequently and always furtively, was "men". If "society" is the enemy, what could that mean? If women are being oppressed, there's only one group left over to be doing the oppressing: men. Then why call them "society"? Could "society" mean the "institutions" that oppress women? But institutions must be maintained, and the same question arises: by whom? The answer to "who is the enemy?" is so obvious that the interesting issue quickly becomes "why has it been avoided?" The master might tolerate many reforms in slavery but none that would threaten his essential role as master. Women have known this, and since "men" and "society" are in effect synonymous, they have feared confronting him. Without this confrontation and a detailed understanding of what *his* battle strategy has been that has kept us so successfully pinned down, the "women's movement" is worse than useless: it invites backlash from men, and no progress for women.

———— ▲▼ ————

There has never been a feminist analysis. While discontent among women and the attempt to resolve this discontent have often implied that women form a class, no political or *causal* class analysis has followed. To rephrase my last point, the persecution of women has never been taken as the starting point for a political analysis of society.

Considering that the last massing of discontent among women continued some 70 years (1850–1920) and spread the world and that the recent accumulation of grievances began some three years ago here in America, the lack of a structural understanding of the problem is at first sight incomprehensible. It is the understanding of the *reasons* for this devastating omission and of the *implications* of the problem that forces one to "radical feminism".

Women who have tried to solve their problems as a class have proposed not solutions but dilemmas. The traditional feminists want equal rights for women with men. But on what grounds? If women serve a different *function* from men in society, wouldn't this necessarily affect women's "rights"? For example, do *all* women have the "right" not to bear children? Traditional feminism is caught in the dilemma of demanding equal treatment for unequal functions, because it is unwilling to challenge political (functional) classification by sex. Radical women, on the other hand, grasp that women as a group somehow fit into a political analysis of society, but err in refusing to explore the significance of the fact that women form a class, the uniqueness of this class, and the implications of this description to the system of political classes. Both traditional feminists and radical women have evaded questioning any part of their *raison d'être*: women are a class, and the terms that make up that initial assumption must be examined.

The feminist dilemma is that it is as women—or "females"—that women are persecuted, just as it was as slaves—or "blacks"—that slaves were persecuted in America: in order to improve their condition, those individuals who are today defined as women must eradicate their own definition. Women must, in a sense, commit suicide, and the journey from womanhood to a society of individuals is hazardous. The feminist dilemma is that we have the most to do, and the least to do it with; we must create, as no other group in history has been forced to do, from the very beginning.

The "battle of the sexes" is a commonplace, both over time and distance. But it is an inaccurate description of what has been happening. A "battle" implies some balance of powers, whereas when one side suffers all the losses, such as in raids (often referred to as the "rape" of an area), that is called a *massacre*. Women have been massacred as human beings over history, and this destiny is entailed by their definition. As women begin massing together, they take the first step from *being* massacred to *engaging in* battle (resistance) and, hopefully, eventually to negotiations—in the *very* far future—and peace.

CAROL HANISCH

The Personal Is Political

The concerns of women's liberation activists were often disparaged in the male-dominated New Left political movements as trivial, diversionary, or merely personal, and the favored information-gathering technique of consciousness raising (see pages 238–241 in this volume), involving examining personal experience and feelings, was deprecated as "therapy" rather than a political tool. Carol Hanisch (born 1942), a founding member of New York Radical Women, wrote "The Personal Is Political" in 1969 to counter these views. In a later introduction to this oft-reprinted essay, Hanisch wrote, "they belittled us no end for bringing our so-called 'personal problems' into the public arena—especially 'all those body issues' like sex, appearance, and abortion," along with demands that men share housework and childcare. After publication in *Notes from the Second Year* (1970), the essay's title became an international byword, a shorthand for a key principle of radical feminism.

FOR THIS paper I want to stick pretty close to an aspect of the Left debate commonly talked about—namely "therapy" vs. "therapy and politics." Another name for it is "personal" vs. "political" and it has other names, I suspect, as it has developed across the country. I haven't gotten over to visit the New Orleans group yet, but I have been participating in groups in New York and Gainesville for more than a year. Both of these groups have been called "therapy" and "personal" groups by women who consider themselves "more political." So I must speak about so-called therapy groups from my own experience.

The very word "therapy" is obviously a misnomer if carried to its logical conclusion. Therapy assumes that someone is sick and that there is a cure, e.g., a personal solution. I am greatly offended that I or any other woman is thought to *need* therapy in the first place. Women are messed over, not messed up! We need to change the objective conditions, not adjust to them. Therapy is adjusting to your bad personal alternative.

We have not done much trying to solve immediate personal problems of women in the group. We've mostly picked topics by two methods: In a small group it is possible for us to take turns bringing questions to the meeting (like, Which do/did you prefer, a girl or a boy baby or no children, and why? What happens to your relationship if your man makes more money than you? Less than you?). Then we go around the room answering the questions from our personal experiences. Everybody talks that way. At the end of the meeting we try to sum up and generalize from what's been said and make connections.

I believe at this point, and maybe for a long time to come, that these analytical sessions are a form of political action. I do not go to these sessions because I need or want to talk about my "personal problems." In fact, I would rather not. As a movement woman, I've been pressured to be strong, selfless, other-oriented, sacrificing, and in general pretty much in control of my own life. To admit to the problems in my life is to be deemed weak. So I want to be a strong woman, in movement terms, and not admit I have any real problems that I can't find a personal solution to (except those directly related to the capitalist system). It is at this point a political action to tell it like it is, to say what I really believe about my life instead of what I've always been told to say.

So the reason I participate in these meetings is not to solve any personal problem. One of the first things we discover in these groups is that personal problems are political problems. There are no personal solutions at this time. There is only collective action for a collective solution. I went, and I continue to go to these meetings because I have gotten a political understanding which all my reading, all my "political discussions," all my "political action," all my four-odd years in the movement never gave me. I've been forced to take off the rose-colored glasses and face the awful truth about how grim my life really is as a woman. I am getting a gut understanding of everything as opposed to the esoteric, intellectual understandings and *noblesse oblige* feelings I had in "other people's" struggles.

This is not to deny that these sessions have at least two aspects that are therapeutic. I prefer to call even this aspect "political therapy" as opposed to personal therapy. The most important is getting rid of self-blame. Can you imagine what would happen if women, blacks, and workers (my definition of worker is anyone who *has* to work for a living as opposed to those who don't. All women are workers) would stop blaming ourselves for our sad situations? It seems to me the whole country needs that kind of political therapy. That is what the black movement is doing in its own way. We shall do it in ours. We are only starting to stop blaming ourselves.

We also feel like we are thinking for ourselves for the first time in our lives. As the cartoon in *Lilith* puts it, "I'm changing. My mind is growing muscles." Those who believe that Marx, Lenin, Engels, Mao, and Ho have the only and last "good word" on the subject and that women have nothing more to add will, of course, find these groups a waste of time.

The groups that I have been in have also not gotten into "alternative life-styles" or what it means to be a "liberated" woman. We came early to the conclusion that all alternatives are bad under present conditions. Whether we live with or without a man, communally or in couples or alone, are married or unmarried, live with other women, go for free love, celibacy or lesbianism, or any combination, there are only good and bad things about each bad situation. There is no "more liberated" way; there are only bad alternatives.

This is part of one of the most important theories we are beginning to artic-ulate. We call it "the pro-woman line." What it says basically is that women are really neat people. The bad things that are said about us as women are either myths (women are stupid), tactics women use to struggle individually (women are bitches), or are actually things that we want to carry into the new society and want men to share too (women are sensitive, emotional). Women as oppressed people act out of necessity (*act* dumb in the presence of men), not out of choice. Women have developed great shuffling techniques for their own survival (look pretty and giggle to get or keep a job or man) which should be used when necessary until such time as the power of unity can take its place. Women are smart not to struggle alone (as are blacks and workers). It is no worse to be in the home than in the rat race of the job world. They are both bad. Women, like blacks, workers, must stop blaming ourselves for our "failures."

It took us some ten months to get to the point where we could articulate these things and relate them to the lives of every woman. It's important from the standpoint of what kind of action we are going to do. When our group first started, going by majority opinion, we would have been out in the streets demonstrating against marriage, against having babies, for free love, against women who wore makeup, against housewives, for equality without recogni-tion of biological differences, and god knows what else. Now we see all these things as what we call "personal solutionary." Many of the actions taken by "action" groups have been along these lines. The women who did the anti-woman stuff at the Miss America Pageant were the ones who were screaming for action without theory. The members of one group want to set up a private day care center without any real analysis of what could be done to make it better for little girls, much less any analysis of how that center hastens the revolution.

That is not to say, of course, that we shouldn't do action. There may be some very good reasons why women in the group don't want to do anything at the moment. One reason that I often have is that this thing is so important to me that I want to be very sure that we're doing it the best way we know how, and that it is a "right" action that I feel sure about. I refuse to go out and "produce" for the movement. We had a lot of conflict in our New York group about whether or not to do action. When the Miss America Protest was proposed there was no question but that we wanted to do it. I think it was because we all saw how it related to *our* lives. We *felt* it was a good action. There were things wrong with the action; but the basic idea was there.

This has been my experience in groups that are accused of being "therapy" or "personal." Perhaps certain groups may well be attempting to do therapy. Maybe the answer is not to put down the method of analyzing from personal experiences in favor of immediate action, but to figure out what can be done to make it work. Some of us started to write a handbook about this at one time and never got past the outline. We are working on it again, and hope to have it out in a month at the latest.

It's true we all need to learn how to better draw conclusions from the experiences and feelings we talk about and how to draw all kinds of connections. Some of us haven't done a very good job of communicating them to others.

One more thing: I think we must listen to what so-called apolitical women have to say—not so we can do a better job of organizing them but because together we *are* a mass movement. I think we who work full-time in the movement tend to become very narrow. What is happening now is that when non-movement women disagree with us, we assume it's because they are "apolitical," not because there might be something wrong with *our* thinking. Women have left the movement in droves. The obvious reasons are that we are tired of being sex slaves and doing shitwork for men whose hypocrisy is so blatant in their political stance of liberation for everybody (else). But there is really a lot more to it than that. I can't quite articulate it yet. I think "apolitical" women are not in the movement for very good reasons, and as long as we say "you have to think like us and live like us to join the charmed circle," we will fail. What I am trying to say is that there are things in the consciousness of "apolitical" women (I find them very political) that are as valid as any political consciousness we think we have. We should figure out why many women don't want to do action. Maybe there is something wrong with the action or something wrong with why we are doing the action or maybe the analysis of why the action is necessary is not clear enough in our minds.

PAT MAINARDI

The Politics of Housework

Mimeographed copies of this trenchant essay circulated widely through the wom-
en's liberation movement in 1969 before being featured in several 1970 feminist
anthologies. Pat Mainardi (born 1942), an artist and early member of the radical
feminist group Redstockings, used housework, something typically dismissed as
a trivial matter, as an example of the idea that "the personal is political," a phrase
coined by feminist Carol Hanisch (see pp. 82–85 in this volume) that quickly
became a powerful women's liberation slogan. In the decades since Mainardi's
provocative exposé, the question of who-does-the-housework has remained con-
tentious, and the answer has proven, despite much attention, stubbornly resistant
to change.

Though women do not complain of the power of husbands, each complains of her own husband, or of the husbands of her friends. It is the
same in all other cases of servitude, at least in the commencement of the
emancipatory movement. The serfs did not at first complain of the power
of the lords, but only of their tyranny.

—John Stuart Mill,
On the Subjection of Women

L IBERATED WOMEN—very different from Women's Liberation! The first
signals all kinds of goodies, to warm the hearts (not to mention other
parts) of the most radical men. The other signals—HOUSEWORK. The first
brings sex without marriage, sex before marriage, cozy housekeeping arrangements ("I'm living with this chick") and the self-content of knowing that
you're not the kind of man who wants a doormat instead of a woman. That will
come later. After all, who wants that old commodity anymore, the Standard
American Housewife, all husband, home and kids. The New Commodity, the
Liberated Woman, has sex a lot and has a Career, preferably something that
can be fitted in with the household chores—like dancing, pottery, or painting.

On the other hand is Women's Liberation—and housework. What? You say this is all trivial? Wonderful! That's what I thought. It seemed perfectly reasonable. We both had careers, both had to work a couple of days a week to earn enough to live on, so why shouldn't we share the housework? So I suggested it to my mate and he agreed—most men are too hip to turn you down flat. You're right, he said. It's only fair.

Then an interesting thing happened. I can only explain it by stating that we women have been brainwashed more than even we can imagine. Probably too many years of seeing television women in ecstasy over their shiny waxed floors or breaking down over their dirty shirt collars. Men have no such conditioning. They recognize the essential fact of housework right from the very beginning. Which is that it stinks.

Here's my list of dirty chores: buying groceries, carting them home and putting them away; cooking meals and washing dishes and pots; doing the laundry, digging out the place when things get out of control; washing floors. The list could go on but the sheer necessities are bad enough. All of us have to do these things, or get someone else to do them for us. The longer my husband contemplated these chores, the more repulsed he became, and so proceeded the change from the normally sweet considerate Dr. Jekyll into the crafty Mr. Hyde who would stop at nothing to avoid the horrors of housework. As he felt himself backed into a corner laden with dirty dishes, brooms, mops and reeking garbage, his front teeth grew longer and pointier, his fingernails haggled and his eyes grew wild. Housework trivial? Not on your life! Just try to share the burden.

So ensued a dialogue that's been going on for several years. Here are some of the high points:

▶ "I don't mind sharing the housework, but I don't do it very well. We should each do the things we're best at." MEANING: Unfortunately I'm no good at things like washing dishes or cooking. What I do best is a little light carpentry, changing light bulbs, moving furniture (how often do *you* move furniture?). ALSO MEANING: Historically the lower classes (black men and us) have had hundreds of years' experience doing menial jobs. It would be a waste of manpower to train someone else to do them now. ALSO MEANING: I don't like the dull stupid boring jobs, so you should do them.

▶ "I don't mind sharing the work, but you'll have to show me how to do it." MEANING: I ask a lot of questions and you'll have to show me everything every time I do it because I don't remember so good. Also don't try to sit down and read while I'M doing my jobs because I'm going to annoy hell out of you until it's easier to do them yourself.

▶ "We used to be so happy!" (Said whenever it was his turn to do something.) MEANING: I used to be so happy. MEANING: Life without housework is bliss. No quarrel here. Perfect Agreement.

▶ "We have different standards, and why should I have to work to your standards? That's unfair." MEANING: If I begin to get bugged by the dirt and crap I will say, "This place sure is a sty" or "How can anyone live like this?" and wait for your reaction. I know that all women have a sore called "Guilt over a messy house" or "Household work is ultimately my responsibility." I know that men have caused that sore—if anyone visits and the place *is* a sty, they're not going to leave and say, "He sure is a lousy housekeeper." You'll take the rap in any case. I can outwait you. ALSO MEANING: I can provoke innumerable scenes over the housework issue. Eventually doing all the housework yourself will be less painful to you than trying to get me to do half. Or I'll suggest we get a maid. She will do my share of the work. You will do yours. It's women's work.

▶ "I've got nothing against sharing the housework, but you can't make me do it on your schedule. MEANING: Passive resistance. I'll do it when I damned well please, if at all. If my job is doing dishes, it's easier to do them once a week. If taking out laundry, once a month. If washing the floors, once a year. If you don't like it, do it yourself oftener, and then I won't do it at all.

▶ "I hate it more than you. You don't mind it so much." MEANING: Housework is garbage work. It's the worst crap I've ever done. It's degrading and humiliating for someone of *my* intelligence to do it. But for someone of *your* intelligence . . . .

▶ "Housework is too trivial to even talk about." MEANING: It's even more trivial to do. Housework is beneath my status. My purpose in life is to deal with matters of significance. Yours is to deal with matters of insignificance. You should do the housework.

▶ "This problem of housework is not a man-woman problem. In any relationship between two people one is going to have a stronger personality and dominate. MEANING: That stronger personality had better be *me*.

▶ "In animal societies, wolves, for example, the top animal is usually a male even where he is not chosen for brute strength but on the basis of cunning and intelligence. Isn't that interesting?" MEANING: I have historical, psychological, anthropological and biological justification for keeping you down. How can you ask the top wolf to be equal?

▶ "Women's Liberation isn't really a political movement." MEANING: The Revolution is coming too close to home. ALSO MEANING: I am only interested in how I am oppressed, not how I oppress others. Therefore the war, the draft and the university are political. Women's Liberation is not.

▶ "Man's accomplishments have always depended on getting help from other people, mostly women. What great man would have accomplished what he did if he had to do his own housework?" MEANING: Oppression is built into the system and I, as the white American male, receive the benefits of this system. I don't want to give them up.

——————— ▲▼ ———————

Participatory democracy begins at home. If you are planning to implement your politics, there are certain things to remember:

1. He *is* feeling it more than you. He's losing some leisure and you're gaining it. The measure of your oppression is his resistance.

2. A great many American men are not accustomed to doing monotonous repetitive work which never issues in any lasting, let alone important, achievement. This is why they would rather repair a cabinet than wash dishes. If human endeavors are like a pyramid with man's highest achievements at the top, then keeping oneself alive is at the bottom. Men have always had servants (us) to take care of this bottom strata of life while they have confined their efforts to the rarefied upper regions. It is thus ironic when they ask of women—where are your great painters, statesmen, etc. Mme Matisse ran a millinery shop so he could paint. Mrs. Martin Luther King kept his house and raised his babies.

3. It is a traumatizing experience for someone who has always thought of himself as being against any oppression or exploitation of one human being by another to realize that in his daily life he has been accepting and implementing (and benefiting from) this exploitation; that his rationalization is little different from that of the racist who says "Black people don't feel pain" (women don't mind doing the shitwork); and that the oldest form of oppression in history has been the oppression of 50% of the population by the other 50%.

4. Arm yourself with some knowledge of the psychology of oppressed peoples everywhere, and a few facts about the animal kingdom. I admit playing top wolf or who runs the gorillas is silly but as a last resort men bring it up all the time. Talk about bees. If you feel really hostile bring up the sex life of spiders. They have sex. She bites off his head.

The psychology of oppressed peoples is not silly. Jews, immigrants, black men and all women have employed the same psychological mechanisms to survive: admiring the oppressor, glorifying the oppressor, wanting to be like the oppressor, wanting the oppressor to like them, mostly because the oppressor held all the power.

5. In a sense, all men everywhere are slightly schizoid—divorced from the reality of maintaining life. This makes it easier for them to play games with

it. It is almost a cliché that women feel greater grief at sending a son off to a war or losing him to that war because they bore him, suckled him, and raised him. The men who foment those wars did none of those things and have a more superficial estimate of the worth of human life. One hour a day is a low estimate of the amount of time one has to spend "keeping" oneself. By foisting this off on others, man has seven hours a week—one working day more to play with his mind and not his human needs. Over the course of generations it is easy to see whence evolved the horrifying abstractions of modern life.

6. With the death of each form of oppression, life changes and new forms evolve. English aristocrats at the turn of the century were horrified at the idea of enfranchising working men—were sure that it signalled the death of civilization and a return to barbarism. Some working men were even deceived by this line. Similarly with the minimum wage, abolition of slavery, and female suffrage. Life changes but it goes on. Don't fall for any line about the death of everything if men take a turn at the dishes. They will imply that you are holding back the Revolution (their Revolution). But you are advancing it (your Revolution).

7. Keep checking up. Periodically consider who's actually *doing* the jobs. These things have a way of backsliding so that a year later once again the woman is doing everything. After a year make a list of jobs the man has rarely if ever done. You will find cleaning pots, toilets, refrigerators and ovens high on the list. Use time sheets if necessary. He will accuse you of being petty. He is above that sort of thing (housework). Bear in mind what the worst jobs are, namely, the ones that have to be done every day or several times a day. Also the ones that are dirty—it's more pleasant to pick up books, newspapers, etc., than to wash dishes. Alternate the bad jobs. It's the daily grind that gets you down. Also make sure that you don't have the responsibility for the housework with occasional help from him. "I'll cook dinner for you tonight" implies it's really your job and isn't he a nice guy to do some of it for you.

8. Most men had a rich and rewarding bachelor life during which they did not starve or become encrusted with crud or buried under the litter. There is a taboo that says women mustn't strain themselves in the presence of men—we haul around 50 lbs of groceries if we have to but aren't allowed to open a jar if there is someone around to do it for us. The reverse side of the coin is that men aren't supposed to be able to take care of themselves without a woman. Both are excuses for making women do the housework.

9. Beware of the double whammy. He won't do the little things he always did because you're now a "Liberated Woman," right? Of course he won't do anything else either. . . .

I was just finishing this when my husband came in and asked what I was doing. Writing a paper on housework. Housework? he said. *Housework?* Oh my god how trivial can you get. A paper on housework.

LITTLE POLITICS OF HOUSEWORK QUIZ

1. The lowest job in the army, used as punishment is *a) working 9–5 b) kitchen duty (K.P.).*

2. When a man lives with his family, his *a) father b) mother* does his housework.

3. When he lives with a woman, *a) he b) she* does the housework.

4. *a) His son b) His daughter* learns in preschool how much fun it is to iron daddy's handkerchief.

5. From the *New York Times*, 9/21/69: "Former Greek Official George Mylonas pays the penalty for differing with the ruling junta in Athens by performing household chores on the island of Amorgos where he lives in forced exile" (with hilarious photo of a miserable Mylonas carrying his own water). What the *Times* means is that he ought to have *a) indoor plumbing b) a maid.*

6. Dr. Spock said (*Redbook*, 3/69) "Biologically and temperamentally I believe, women were made to be concerned first and foremost with child care, husband care, and home care." Think about *a) who made us b) why? c) what is the effect on their lives d) what is the effect on our lives?*

7. From *Time*, 1/5/70, "Like their American counterparts, many housing project housewives are said to suffer from neurosis. And for the first time in Japanese history, many young husbands today complain of being henpecked. Their wives are beginning to demand detailed explanations when they don't come home straight from work and some Japanese males nowadays are even compelled to do housework." According to *Time*, women become neurotic *a) when they are forced to do the maintenance work for the male caste all day every day of their lives* or *b) when they no longer want to do the maintenance work for the male caste all day every day of their lives.*

Women: Do You Know The Facts About Marriage?

The Feminists—founded by renegade members of NOW and originally called the October 17th Movement—was an all-women radical feminist group active in New York City from 1968 to 1973. Considering both marriage and heterosexual intercourse institutions of male oppression, The Feminists limited to one-third of its membership women who lived with men. In September 1969 the group picketed the New York City Marriage License Bureau, where they distributed this pamphlet.

DO YOU KNOW THAT RAPE IS LEGAL IN MARRIAGE?

According to law, *sex* is the purpose of marriage. You have to have sexual intercourse in order to have a valid marriage.

DO YOU KNOW THAT LOVE AND AFFECTION ARE NOT REQUIRED IN MARRIAGE?

If you can't have sex with your husband, he can get a divorce or annulment. If he doesn't love you, that's *not* grounds for divorce.

DO YOU KNOW THAT YOU ARE YOUR HUSBAND'S PRISONER?

You have to live with him wherever *he* pleases. If he decides to move someplace else, either you go with him or he can charge you with desertion, get a divorce and, according to law, you deserve nothing because *you're the guilty party*. And that's if *he* were the one who moved!

DO YOU KNOW THAT, ACCORDING TO THE UNITED NATIONS, MARRIAGE IS A "SLAVERY-LIKE PRACTICE"?

According to the marriage contract, your husband is entitled to more household services from you than he would be from a live-in maid. So, why aren't you getting paid? Under law, you're entitled only to "bed and board."

When you got married, did you know these facts? If you didn't know, what did you *think* you were consenting to? But these are the *laws*. If you *had* known the terms, would you have signed the contract?

Do You Resent This Fraud?

All the discriminatory practices against women are patterned and rationalized by this slavery-like practice. We can't destroy the inequities between men and women until we destroy marriage. *We must free ourselves. And marriage is the place to begin.*

THE FEMINISTS
- v -
THE MARRIAGE LICENSE BUREAU OF THE CITY OF NEW YORK

WHEREAS it is common knowledge that women believe the conditions of the marriage contract to be positive and reciprocal feelings between the two parties (known as "love and affection"); and

WHEREAS the marriage contract in fact legalizes and institutionalizes the rape of women and the bondage of women, both their internal (reproductive) and external (domestic labor) functions; and

WHEREAS the marriage contract, known as "license", fails to list the terms of that contract, a failure which would automatically nullify the validity of any other important contract

THEREFORE, WE, THE FEMINISTS, do hereby charge the city of New York and all those offices and agents aiding and abetting the institution of marriage, such as the Marriage License Bureau, of fraud with malicious intent against the women of this city.

September 23, 1969

FRANCES M. BEAL

Double Jeopardy: To Be Black and Female

This classic essay by Frances M. Beal (born 1940) was issued as a pamphlet in 1969 and revised for two 1970 feminist collections, *The Black Woman* and *Sisterhood Is Powerful*. Beal presents a complex analysis of the economic, reproductive, and psychological exploitation of Black women in America through racism, sexism, and capitalism, insisting that white feminist groups must become anti-imperialist and antiracist. In 1968 Beal had been a founding member of the Black Women's Liberation Committee of the Student Non-Violent Coordinating Committee (SNCC). By 1970 she was a leader of the Third World Women's Alliance ("third world" being an inclusive term for people of color in use at the time), whose bimonthly newsletter displayed the intersectional title *Triple Jeopardy* over the banner "Racism, Imperialism, Sexism."

I N ATTEMPTING to analyze the situation of the black woman in America, one crashes abruptly into a solid wall of grave misconceptions, outright distortions of fact, and defensive attitudes on the part of many. The System of capitalism (and its afterbirth—racism) under which we all live, has attempted by many devious ways and means to destroy the humanity of all people, and particularly the humanity of black people. This has meant an outrageous assault on every black man, woman, and child who resides in the United States.

In keeping with its goal of destroying the black race's will to resist its subjugation, capitalism found it necessary to create a situation where the black man found it impossible to find meaningful or productive employment. More often than not, he couldn't find work of any kind. And the black woman, likewise, was manipulated by the System, economically exploited and physically assaulted. She could often find work in the white man's kitchen, however, and sometimes became the sole breadwinner of the family. This predicament has led to many psychological problems on the part of both man and woman and has contributed to the turmoil in the black family structure.

Unfortunately, neither the black man nor the black woman understood the true nature of the forces working upon them. Many black women tended to accept the capitalist evaluation of manhood and womanhood and believed, in fact, that black men were shiftless and lazy; otherwise they would get a job and support their families as they ought to. Personal relationships between black men and women were thus torn asunder and one result has been the separation of man from wife, mother from child, etc.

America has defined the roles to which each individual should subscribe. It has defined "manhood" in terms of its own interests and "femininity" likewise. Therefore, an individual who has a good job, makes a lot of money, and drives a Cadillac is a real "man," and conversely, an individual who is lacking in these "qualities" is less of a man. The advertising media in this country continuously informs the American male of his need for indispensable signs of his virility— the brand of cigarettes that cowboys prefer, the whisky that has a masculine tang, or the label of the jock strap that athletes wear.

The ideal model that is projected for a woman is to be surrounded by hypocritical homage and estranged from all real work, spending idle hours primping and preening, obsessed with conspicuous consumption, and limiting life's functions to simply a sex role. We unqualitatively reject these respective models. A woman who stays at home, caring for children and the house, leads an extremely sterile existence. She must lead her entire life as a satellite to her mate. He goes out into society and brings back a little piece of the world for her. His interests and his understanding of the world become her own and she cannot develop herself as an individual, having been reduced to only a biological function. This kind of woman leads a parasitic existence that can aptly be described as "legalized prostitution."

Furthermore, it is idle dreaming to think of black women simply caring for their homes and children like the middle-class white model. Most black women have to work to help house, feed, and clothe their families. Black women make up a substantial percentage of the black working force and this is true for the poorest black family as well as the so-called "middle-class" family.

Black women were never afforded any such phony luxuries. Though we have been browbeaten with this white image, the reality of the degrading and dehumanizing jobs that were relegated to us quickly dissipated this mirage of womanhood. The following excerpts from a speech that Sojourner Truth made at a Women's Rights Convention in the nineteenth century show us how misleading and incomplete a life this model represents for us:

> . . . Well, chilern whar dar is so much racket dar must be something out o'kilter. I tink dat 'twixt de niggers of de Souf and de women at de Norf all a talkin' 'bout rights, de white men will be in a fix pretty soon. But what's all dis here talkin' 'bout? Dat man ober

dar say dat women needs to be helped into carriages, and lifted ober ditches, and to have de best place every whar. Nobody ever help me into carriages, or ober mud puddles, or gives me any best places . . . and ar'nt I a woman? Look at me! Look at my arm! . . . I have plowed, and planted, and gathered into barns, and no man could head me—and ar'nt I a woman? I could work as much as a man (when I could get it), and bear de lash as well—and ar'nt I a woman? I have borne five chilern and I seen 'em mos' all sold off into slavery, and when I cried out with a mother's grief, none but Jesus heard—and ar'nt I a woman?

Unfortunately, there seems to be some confusion in the Movement today as to who has been oppressing whom. Since the advent of Black Power, the black male has exerted a more prominent leadership role in our struggle for justice in this country. He sees the System for what it really is, for the most part, but where he rejects its values and mores on many issues, when it comes to women, he seems to take his guidelines from the pages of the *Ladies' Home Journal.* Certain black men are maintaining that they have been castrated by society but that black women somehow escaped this persecution and even contributed to this emasculation.

Let me state here and now that the black woman in America can justly be described as a "slave of a slave." When the black man in America was reduced to such an abject state, the black woman had no protector and was used and is still being used in some cases as the scapegoat for the evils that this horrendous System has perpetrated on black men. Her physical image has been maliciously maligned; she has been sexually assaulted and abused by the white colonizer; she has suffered the worse kind of economic exploitation, having been forced to serve as the white woman's maid and wet nurse for white offspring while her own children were starving and neglected. It is the depth of degradation to be socially manipulated, physically raped, used to undermine your own household—and to be powerless to reverse this syndrome.

It is true that our husbands, fathers, brothers, and sons have been emasculated, lynched, and brutalized. They have suffered from the cruellest assault of mankind that the world has ever known. However, it is a gross distortion of fact to state that black women have oppressed black men. The capitalist System found it expedient to oppress them and proceeded to do so without consultation or the signing of any agreements with black women.

It must also be pointed out at this time, that black women are not resentful of the rise to power of black men. We welcome it. We see in it the eventual liberation of all black people from this oppressive System of capitalism. Nevertheless, this does not mean that you have to negate one for the other. This kind of thinking is a product of miseducation; that it's either X or it's Y. It is fallacious reasoning that in order for the black man to be strong, the black woman has to be weak.

Those who are exerting their "manhood" by telling black women to step back into a submissive role are assuming a counterrevolutionary position. Black women likewise have been abused by the System and we must begin talking about the elimination of all kinds of oppression. If we are talking about building a strong nation, capable of throwing off the yoke of capitalist oppression, then we are talking about the total involvement of every man, woman, and child, each with a highly developed political consciousness. We need our whole army out there dealing with the enemy, and not half an army.

There are also some black women who feel that there is no more productive role in life than having and raising children. This attitude often reflects the conditioning of the society in which we live and is adopted from a bourgeois white model. Some young sisters who have never had to maintain a household and accept the confining role which this entails, tend to romanticize (along with the help of a number of brothers) this role of housewife and mother. Black women who have had to endure this kind of function are less apt to have these utopian visions. Those who project in an intellectual manner how great and rewarding this role will be and who feel that the most important thing that they can contribute to the black nation is children, are doing themselves a great injustice. This line of reasoning completely negates the contributions that black women have historically made to our struggle for liberation. These black women include Sojourner Truth, Harriet Tubman, Mary McLeod Bethune, and Fannie Lou Hamer, to name but a few.

We live in a highly industrialized society and every member of the black nation must be as academically and technologically developed as possible. To wage a revolution, we need competent teachers, doctors, nurses, electronics experts, chemists, biologists, physicists, political scientists, and so on and so forth. Black women sitting at home reading bedtime stories to their children are just not going to make it.

ECONOMIC EXPLOITATION OF BLACK WOMEN

The economic System of capitalism finds it expedient to reduce women to a state of enslavement. They oftentimes serve as a scapegoat for the evils of this system. Much in the same way that the poor white cracker of the South, who is equally victimized, looks down upon blacks and contributes to the oppression of blacks—so, by giving to men a false feeling of superiority (at least in their own home or in their relationships with women)—the oppression of women acts as an escape valve for capitalism. Men may be cruelly exploited and subjected to all sorts of dehumanizing tactics on the part of the ruling class, but they have someone who is below them—at least they're not women.

Women also represent a surplus labor supply, the control of which is absolutely necessary to the profitable functioning of capitalism. Women are consistently exploited by the System. They are often paid less for the same work that men do and jobs that are specifically relegated to women are lowpaying and without the possibility of advancement. Statistics from the Women's Bureau of the United States Department of Labor show that in 1967, the wage scale for white women was even below that of black men; and the wage scale for non-white women was the lowest of all:

White Males	$6704
Non-White Males	4277
White Females	3991
Non-White Females	2861

Those industries that employ mainly black women are the most exploitative in the country. The hospital workers are a good example of this oppression; the garment workers in New York City provide us with another view of this economic slavery. The International Ladies Garment Workers Union (ILGWU) whose overwhelming membership consists of black and Puerto Rican women has a leadership that is nearly all lily-white and male. This leadership has been working in collusion with the ruling class and has completely sold its soul to the corporate structure.

To add insult to injury, ILGWU has invested heavily in business enterprises in racist, apartheid South Africa—with union funds. Not only does this bought-off leadership contribute to our continued exploitation in this country by not truly representing the best interests of its membership, but it audaciously uses funds that black and Puerto Rican women have provided to support the economy of a vicious government that is engaged in the exploitation and murder of our black brothers and sisters in our motherland, Africa.

The entire labor movement in the United States has suffered as a result of the superexploitation of black workers and women. The unions have historically been racist and male chauvinistic. They have upheld racism in this country and have failed to fight the white-skin privileges of white workers. They have failed to struggle against inequities in the hiring and pay of women workers. There has been virtually no struggle against either the racism of the white worker or the economic exploitation of the working woman, two factors which have consistently impeded the advancement of the real struggle against the ruling class.

The racist, chauvinistic, and manipulative use of black workers and women, especially black women, has been a severe cancer on the American labor scene. It therefore becomes essential for those who understand the workings of capitalism and imperialism to realize that the exploitation of black people and women works to everyone's disadvantage and that the liberation of these two minority groups is a stepping stone to the liberation of all oppressed people in this country and around the world.

BEDROOM POLITICS

I have briefly discussed the economic and psychological manipulation of black women, but perhaps the most outlandish act of oppression in modern times is the current campaign to promote sterilization of non-white women, in an attempt to maintain the population and power imbalance between the white "haves" and the non-white "have nots."

These tactics are but another example of the many devious schemes that the ruling class elite attempts to perpetrate on the black population in order to keep itself in control. It has recently come to our attention that a massive campaign for so-called "birth control" is presently being promoted not only in the underdeveloped non-white areas of the world, but also in black communities here in the United States. However, what the authorities in charge of these programs refer to as "birth control" is in fact nothing but a method of outright surgical genocide.

The United States has been sponsoring sterilization clinics in non-white countries, especially in India where already some three million young men and boys in and around New Delhi have been sterilized in makeshift operating rooms set up by the American Peace Corps workers. Under these circumstances, it is understandable why certain countries view the Peace Corps not as a benevolent project, not as evidence of America's concern for underdeveloped areas, but rather as a threat to their very existence. This program could more aptly be named the "Death Corps."

The vasectomy, which is performed on males and takes only six or seven minutes, is a relatively simple operation. The sterilization of a woman, on the other hand, is admittedly major surgery. This operation, (salpingectomy) must be performed in a hospital under general anesthesia.* This method of "birth control" is a common procedure in Puerto Rico. Puerto Rico has long been

*Salpingectomy: through an abdominal incision, the surgeon cuts both fallopian tubes and

used by the colonialist exploiter, the United States, as a huge experimental laboratory for medical research before allowing certain practices to be imported and used here. When the birth-control pill was first being perfected, it was tried out on Puerto Rican women and selected black women (poor), as if they were guinea pigs to see what its effect would be and how efficient the Pill was.

The salpingectomy has now become the commonest operation in Puerto Rico, commoner than an appendectomy or a tonsilectomy. It is so widespread that it is referred to simply as *la operación*. *On the Island, 20 percent of the women between the ages of fifteen and forty-five have already been sterilized.*

And now, as previously occurred with the Pill, this method has been imported into the United States. These sterilization clinics are cropping up around the country in the black and Puerto Rican communities. These so-called "Maternity Clinics," specifically outfitted to purge black women or men of their reproductive possibilities, are appearing more and more in hospitals and clinics across the country.

A number of organizations have recently been formed to popularize the idea of sterilization, such as The Association for Voluntary Sterilization, and the Human Betterment (!!!?) Association for Voluntary Sterilization, Inc., which has its headquarters in New York City. Front Royal, Virginia, has one such "Maternity Clinic" in Warren Memorial Hospital. The tactics used in the clinic in Fauquier County, Virginia, where poor and helpless black mothers and young girls are pressured into undergoing sterilization, are certainly not confined to that clinic alone.

Threatened with the cut-off of relief funds, some black welfare women have been forced to undergo this sterilization procedure in exchange for a continuation of welfare benefits. Mt. Sinai Hospital in New York City performs these operations on its ward patients whenever it can convince the women to undergo this surgery. Mississippi and some of the other Southern states are notorious for this act. Black women are often afraid to permit any kind of necessary surgery because they know from bitter experience that they are more likely than not to come out without their insides. (Both salpingectomies and hysterectomies are performed.)

We condemn this use of the black woman as a medical testing ground for the white middle class. Reports of the ill effects, including deaths, from the use of the birth-control pill only started to come to light when the white privileged class began to be affected. These outrageous Nazi-like procedures on the part of medical researchers are but another manifestation of the totally amoral and

---

ties off the separated ends, after which there is no way for the egg to pass from the ovary to the womb.

brutal behavior that the capitalist System perpetrates on black women. The sterilization experiments carried on in concentration camps some twenty-five years ago have been denounced the world over, but no one seems to get upset by the repetition of these same racist practices today in the United States of America—land of the free and home of the brave.

The rigid laws concerning abortions in this country are another means of subjugation and, indirectly, of outright murder. Rich white women somehow manage to obtain these operations with little or no difficulty. It is the poor black and Puerto Rican woman who is at the mercy of the local butcher. Statistics show us that the non-white death rate at the hands of the unqualified abortionist is substantially higher than for white women. Nearly half of the childbearing deaths in New York City are attributed to abortion alone and out of these, 79 percent are among non-whites and Puerto Rican women.

We are not saying that black women should not practice birth control. Black women have the right and the responsibility to determine when it is in *the interest of the struggle to have children or not to have them and this right must not be relinquished to anyone.* It is also her right and responsibility to determine when it is in *her own best interests* to have children, how many she will have, and how far apart. The lack of the availability of safe birth-control methods, the forced sterilization practices, and the inability to obtain legal abortions are all symptoms of a sick society that jeopardizes the health of black women (and thereby the entire black race) in its attempt to control the very life processes of human beings. This is a symptom of a society that is attempting to bring economic and political factors into the privacy of the bedchamber. The elimination of these horrendous conditions will free black women for full participation in the revolution, and thereafter in the building of the new society.

RELATIONSHIP TO WHITE MOVEMENT

Much has been written recently about the white women's liberation movement in the United States and the question arises whether there are any parallels between this struggle and the movement on the part of black women for total emancipation. While there are certain comparisons that one can make because we both live under the same exploitative System, there are certain differences, some of which are quite basic.

The white woman's movement is far from being monolithic. Any white woman's group that does not have an anti-imperialist and antiracist ideology has absolutely nothing in common with the black woman's struggle. In fact, some groups come to the incorrect conclusion that their oppression is due simply to male chauvinism. They therefore have an extremely antimale tone to their dissertations. Black people are engaged in a life-and-death struggle and the main emphasis of black women must be to combat the capitalist, racist exploitation of black people. While it is true that male chauvinism has become institutionalized in American society, one must always look for the main enemy—the fundamental cause of the female condition.

Another major differentiation is that the white women's movement is basically middle class. Very few of these women suffer the extreme economic exploitation that most black women are subjected to day by day. This is the factor that is most crucial for us. It is not an intellectual persecution alone; it is not an intellectual outburst for us; it is quite real. We as black women have got to deal with the problems that the black masses deal with, for our problems in reality are one and the same.

If the white groups do not realize that they are in fact fighting capitalism and racism, we do not have common bonds. If they do not realize that the reasons for their condition lie in the System and not simply that men get a vicarious pleasure out of "consuming their bodies for exploitative reasons" (this kind of reasoning seems to be quite prevalent in certain white women's groups), then we cannot unite with them around common grievances or even discuss these groups in a serious manner because they're completely irrelevant to the black struggle.

THE NEW WORLD

The black community and black women especially must begin raising questions about the kind of society we wish to see established. We must note the ways in which capitalism oppresses us and then move to create institutions that will eliminate these destructive influences.

The new world that we are attempting to create must destroy oppression of any type. The value of this new system will be determined by the status of the person who was low man on the totem pole. Unless women in any enslaved nation are completely liberated, the change cannot really be called a revolution. If the black woman has to retreat to the position she occupied before the armed struggle, the whole movement and the whole struggle will have retreated in terms of truly freeing the colonized population.

A people's revolution that engages the participation of every member of the community, including man, woman, and child, brings about a certain transformation in the participants as a result of this participation. Once you have caught a glimpse of freedom or experienced a bit of self-determination, you can't go back to old routines that were established under the racist, capitalist regime. We must begin to understand that a revolution entails not only the willingness to lay our lives on the firing line and get killed. In some ways, this is an easy commitment to make. To die for the revolution is a one-shot deal; to live for the revolution means taking on the more difficult commitment of changing our day-to-day life patterns.

This will mean changing the routines that we have established as a result of living in a totally corrupting society. It means changing how you relate to your wife, your husband, your parents, and your co-workers. If we are going to liberate ourselves as a people, it must be recognized that black women have very specific problems that have to be spoken to. We must be liberated along with the rest of the population. We cannot wait to start working on those problems until that great day in the future when the revolution, somehow, miraculously, is accomplished.

To assign women the role of housekeeper and mother while men go forth into battle is a highly questionable doctrine for a revolutionary to maintain. Each individual must develop a high political consciousness in order to under- stand how this System enslaves us all and what actions we must take to bring about its total destruction. Those who consider themselves revolutionary must begin to deal with other revolutionaries as equals. And, so far as I know, rev- olutionaries are not determined by sex.

Old people, young people, men, and women must take part in the struggle. To relegate women to purely supportive roles or purely cultural considerations is dangerous doctrine to project. Unless black men who are preparing them- selves for armed struggle understand that the society which we are trying to create is one in which the oppression of *all* members of that society is elimi- nated, then the revolution will have failed in its avowed purpose.

Given the mutual commitment of black men and black women alike to the liberation of our people and other oppressed peoples around the world, the total involvement of each individual is necessary. A revolutionary has the responsibility of not only toppling those who are now in a position of power, but creating new institutions that will eliminate all forms of oppression. We must begin to rewrite our understanding of traditional personal relationships between man and woman.

All the resources that the black community can muster up must be chan- neled into the struggle. Black women must take an active part in bringing about the kind of society where our children, our loved ones, and each citizen can grow up and live as decent human beings, free from the pressures of racism and capitalist exploitation.

ROXANNE DUNBAR-ORTIZ AND LISA LEGHORN

The Man's Problem

Roxanne Dunbar-Ortiz (born 1939), a founder of Boston's militant radical feminist group Cell 16, and fellow member Lisa Leghorn (born 1951) published this article, presented here in full, in the group's journal *No More Fun and Games* in November 1969. In it they promote separation from men "who are not consciously working for female liberation," thus distinguishing Cell 16's brand of militant separatism from the positions of other radical groups, like Redstockings, which advocated political and personal engagement with men, and lesbian feminists whose avowed separatism Dunbar-Ortiz and Leghorn considered merely "personal" rather than a political response to the oppression of women by men.

MALE SUPREMACY reigns in the United States and Europe. The disease still exists in socialist countries despite a philosophy to the contrary. Men are the oppressors of women in private and public situations. Where men are oppressed, they are oppressed by other men. They fill all the political power positions in this corrupt system. Women form a lower caste in a still rigid caste system, and their economic situation has worsened rather than improved in the past decade (just as it has for black people). Most women come from the working class in the lowest positions in the labor force, or they are domestic servants and mistresses for males (husbands) who possess property, among which property women are counted and highly valued. Like a black person who has "made it," a woman who has "made it" is subject to the same social and economic humiliations as the commonest woman if she leaves the small protective kingdom of her triumph (usually the family). A woman alone on the street or in a public place is fair game for any man, for being the property of none, she becomes the property of all or any.

No man plays a passive role in the oppression of females. The caste system could not function another day unless men vigorously acted out their oppressive roles, took their rewards for granted and stomped on women. Men not only support the caste system; they are terrified of losing any part of it. A bare rumbling from women is exaggerated to the scale of an army of castrating amazons. Men are threatened by women speaking about their freedom just as the racists fear the freedom of black people. To the man, in the absence of social and economic power, woman's freedom literally means his *loss* of freedom. For his only justification for existence lies in his *being a man*, which means possessing the right to oppress a woman (in the family) and feel superior to women in general.

The history and training of the male develops in him a serious deficiency. But it is difficult to comprehend for one who is not programmed in that way (women and black people in this society). The deficiency can be termed "weakness," "false consciousness," "stupidity" or "paranoia." There are many terms which indicate that men are debilitated and diseased by their training as men (as opposed to the idea that men are *oppressed* by their programming to the man's role). Many men go insane from the aggressiveness which is trained into them. Almost all acts of violence committed in this society are by men. Women are not the sole receptors of the violence, but they are now the only group of people who do not believe they have the right to defend themselves.

Females or black people who are programmed to a similar aggressiveness are as thoroughly diseased and maddened as males in those roles. So neither racial inferiority nor male genes can account for the white man's sickness.

We must pose the question: "How then does one deal with madness?" Obviously, the person who is the object of aggressive energy, as women are for men, cannot be the therapist. Every action of a woman is a threat to a man. Men are obsessed with their fears of the female—especially *femaleness* in themselves. Men also have the peculiar problem of dealing with their fears of being tainted with the "blood" of the lower caste, since all males are born of women.

The insane rationale of men's reactions to the slightest objections of women to accept the identities forced upon them (wife, mother, lover, whore, etc.) is the result of their dependence on the inferior role of women for thousands of years. The oppressor is threatened by any hint that women could be regarded equally or even prove superior to him. He responds frantically, fearing the loss of his strength-giving identity. If he is forced to consider the equality of the oppressed he must deal not only with the fact that he is the same as her, but also with his history of oppressing an equal.

There are men who do not appear to be the vicious oppressors of women. Yet any man who is not working consciously to change the unequal relationship of men and women is opposing the interests of women. He is just as guilty as the more blatantly violent man and is actually a great deal more insidious.

Analysis of the man's problem is necessary for women to develop good consciousness, but action is another problem. One thing is certain: Proximity to the male cannot effect cure. The disease is social and must be dealt with politically. We cannot "work out" the problem with a man or men, nor can we transfer the problem to an all female situation. That would mean simply finding comfort there and then returning to our cages. Homosexuality is again no more than a personal "solution."

We should deal with the problem in material terms, not in fantasy terms. Our attitude should lead us to separation from men who are not consciously working for female liberation, not to sectarianism in an all female movement; isolation (desertion) of males, not hate invective; self-defense, not shaming and begging men to stop being brutes (they love being considered brutes). Hatred and resentment for men are not sufficient to give women lasting energy to fight. Yet they are probably inevitable results of increasing awareness of what men have done and do to us. Recognition of the SOCIAL nature of the oppression of females is our first step to consciousness. It might seem that such recognition would free individual men of the burden of guilt. But in fact it makes continued subjugation impossible for the woman. She will begin to fight back and the man will have to confront HIS problem.

VIVIAN GORNICK

(from) The Next Great Moment in History Is Theirs

In November 1969, on her first day on staff at the *Village Voice*, the iconic left-wing New York City weekly of politics and culture, Vivian Gornick (born 1935) was sent to cover (in the words of the paper's founding editors, Edwin Fancher and Dan Wolf) "all these women who call themselves liberationist chicks." While in the resulting piece, excerpted here, she refers to feminists in the third person in keeping with journalistic objectivity, one feels the pulse of individual discovery in Gornick's prose. Her conversion came, she would later write, "as a kind of explosion" leading to "moments of perfect clarifying calm when the thing, as it were, was grasped whole."

A T THE very center of all human life is energy, psychic energy. It is the force of that energy that drives us, that surges continually up in us, that must repeatedly spend and renew itself in us, that must perpetually be reaching for something beyond itself in order to satisfy its own insatiable appetite. It is the imperative of that energy that has determined man's characteristic interest, problem solving. The modern ecologist attests to that driving need by demonstrating that in a time when all the real problems are solved, man makes up new ones in order to go on solving. He must have work, work that he considers real and serious, or he will die, he will simply shrivel up and die. That is the one certain characteristic of human beings. And it is the one characteristic, above all others, that the accidentally dominant white male asserts is not necessary to more than half the members of the race—that is, the female of the species. This assertion is, quite simply, a lie. Nothing more, nothing less. A lie. That energy is alive in every woman in the world. It lies trapped and dormant like a growing tumor, and at its center there is despair, hot, deep, wordless.

It is amazing to me that I have just written these words. To think that one hundred years after Nora slammed the door, and in a civilization and a century utterly converted to the fundamental insights of that exasperating genius Sigmund Freud, women could still be raised to believe that their basic makeup is determined not by the needs of their egos but by their peculiar childbearing properties and their so-called unique capacity for loving. No man worth his salt does not wish to be a husband and father; yet no man is raised to be a husband and father and no man would ever conceive of those relationships as instruments of his prime function in life. Yet every woman is raised, still, to believe that the fulfillment of these relationships is her prime function in life and, what's more, her instinctive choice.

The fact is that women have no special capacities for love, and when a culture reaches a level where its women have nothing to do but "love" (as occurred in the Victorian upper classes and as is occurring now in the American middle classes), they prove to be very bad at it. The modern American wife is not noted for her love of her husband or of her children; she is noted for her driving (or should I say driven?) domination of them. She displays an aberrant, aggressive ambition for her mate and for her offspring which can be explained only by the most vicious feelings toward the self. The reasons are obvious. The woman who must love for a living, the woman who has no self, no objective external reality to take her own measure by, no work to discipline her, no goal to provide the illusion of progress, no internal resources, no separate mental existence, is constitutionally incapable of the emotional distance that is one of the real requirements of love. She cannot separate herself from her husband and children because all the passionate and multiple needs of her being are centered on them. That's why women "take everything personally." It's all they've got to take. "Loving" must substitute for an entire range of feeling and interest. The man, who is not raised to be a husband and father specifically, and who simply loves as a single function of his existence, cannot understand her abnormal "emotionality" and concludes that this is the female nature. (Why shouldn't he? She does too.) But this is not so. It is a result of a psychology achieved by cultural attitudes that run so deep and have gone on for so long that they are mistaken for "nature" or "instinct."

A good example of what I mean are the multiple legends of our culture regarding motherhood. Let's use our heads for a moment. What on earth is holy about motherhood? I mean, why motherhood rather than fatherhood? If anything is holy, it is the consecration of sexual union. A man plants a seed in a woman; the seed matures and eventually is expelled by the woman; a child is born to both of them; each contributed the necessary parts to bring about procreation; each is responsible to and necessary to the child; to claim that the woman is more so than the man is simply not true; certainly it cannot be proved biologically or psychologically (please, no comparisons with baboons and penguins just now—I am sure I can supply fifty examples from nature to counter any assertion made on the subject); all that can be proved is that some *one* is necessary to the newborn baby; to have instilled in women the belief that their childbearing and housewifely obligations supersede all other needs, that indeed what they fundamentally *want* and need is to be wives and mothers as distinguished from being anything else, is to have accomplished an act of trickery, an act which has deprived women of the proper forms of expression alive in every talking creature, an act which has indeed mutilated their natural selves and deprived them of their womanhood, *whatever* that may be, deprived them of the right to say "I" and have it mean something. This understanding, grasped whole, is what underlies the current wave of feminism. It is felt by thousands of women today; it will be felt by millions tomorrow. You have only to examine briefly a fraction of the women's rights organizations already in existence to realize instantly that they form the nucleus of a genuine movement, complete with theoreticians, tacticians, agitators, manifestoes, journals, and thesis papers, running the entire political spectrum from conservative reform to visionary radicalism, and powered by an emotional conviction rooted in undeniable experience, and fed by a determination that is irreversible.

REDSTOCKINGS

Manifesto and Principles

The New York City radical feminist group Redstockings was founded by Ellen Willis (1941–2006) and Shulamith Firestone (1945–2012) in 1969 (see pages 433 and 117 in this volume), expanding the movement's reach by refining the technique of consciousness raising and deploying the "speakout" as a feminist organizing tool. After disrupting a New York state legislative hearing on abortion, where fourteen men and a nun testified as "experts," Redstockings held an abortion speakout on March 21, 1969, where women, "the true experts," broke a long taboo by publicly discussing their unwanted pregnancies and illegal abortions. The original group stopped meeting in 1970, but members revived it more than once in later years, most recently as a feminist archive and think tank. The Redstockings 1969 "Manifesto" and "Principles" are reprinted here in full.

Manifesto

I   After centuries of individual and preliminary political struggle, women are uniting to achieve their final liberation from male supremacy. Redstockings is dedicated to building this unity and winning our freedom.

II   Women are an oppressed class. Our oppression is total, affecting every facet of our lives. We are exploited as sex objects, breeders, domestic servants, and cheap labor. We are considered inferior beings, whose only purpose is to enhance men's lives. Our humanity is denied. Our prescribed behavior is enforced by the threat of physical violence.

Because we have lived so intimately with our oppressors, in isolation from each other, we have been kept from seeing our personal suffering as a political condition. This creates the illusion that a woman's relationship with her man is a matter of interplay between two unique personalities, and can be worked out individually. In reality, every such relationship is a *class* relationship, and the conflicts between individual men and women are *political* conflicts that can only be solved collectively.

III   We identify the agents of our oppression as men. Male supremacy is the oldest, most basic form of domination. All other forms of exploitation and oppression (racism, capitalism, imperialism, etc.) are extensions of male supremacy: men dominate women, a few men dominate the rest. All power structures throughout history have been male-dominated and male-oriented. Men have controlled all political, economic and cultural institutions and backed up this control with physical force. They have used their power to keep women in an inferior position. *All men* receive economic, sexual, and psychological benefits from male supremacy. *All men* have oppressed women.

IV   Attempts have been made to shift the burden of responsibility from men to institutions or to women themselves. We condemn these arguments as evasions. Institutions alone do not oppress; they are merely tools of the oppressor. To blame institutions implies that men and women are equally victimized, obscures the fact that men benefit from the subordination of women, and gives men the excuse that they are forced to be oppressors. On the contrary, any man is free to renounce his superior position provided that he is willing to be treated like a woman by other men.

We also reject the idea that women consent to or are to blame for their own oppression. Women's submission is not the result of brainwashing, stupidity, or mental illness but of continual, daily pressure from men. We do not need to change ourselves, but to change men.

The most slanderous evasion of all is that women can oppress men. The basis for this illusion is the isolation of individual relationships from their political context and the tendency of men to see any legitimate challenge to their privileges as persecution.

V   We regard our personal experience, and our feelings about that experience, as the basis for an analysis of our common situation. We cannot rely on existing ideologies as they are all products of male supremacist culture. We question every generalization and accept none that are not confirmed by our experience.

Our chief task at present is to develop female class consciousness through sharing experience and publicly exposing the sexist foundation of all our institutions. Consciousness-raising is not "therapy," which implies the existence of individual solutions and falsely assumes that the male-female relationship is purely personal, but the only method by which we can ensure that our program for liberation is based on the concrete realities of our lives.

The first requirement for raising class consciousness is honesty, in private and in public, with ourselves and other women.

VI   We identify with all women. We define our best interest as that of the poorest, most brutally exploited woman.

We repudiate all economic, racial, educational or status privileges that divide us from other women. We are determined to recognize and eliminate any prejudices we may hold against other women.

We are committed to achieving internal democracy. We will do whatever is necessary to ensure that every woman in our movement has an equal chance to participate, assume responsibility, and develop her political potential.

VII   We call on all our sisters to unite with us in struggle.

We call on all men to give up their male privileges and support women's liberation in the interest of our humanity and their own.

In fighting for our liberation we will always take the side of women against their oppressors. We will not ask what is "revolutionary" or "reformist," only what is good for women.

The time for individual skirmishes has passed. This time we are going all the way.

PRINCIPLES

We take the woman's side in everything.

We ask not if something is "reformist," "radical," "revolutionary," or "moral." We ask: is it good for women or bad for women?

We ask not if something is "political." We ask: is it effective? Does it get us closest to what we really want in the fastest way?

We define the best interests of women as the best interests of the poorest, most insulted, most despised, most abused woman on earth. Her lot, her suffering and abuse is the threat that men use against all of us to keep us in line. She is what all women fear being called, fear being treated as and yet what we all really are in the eyes of men. She is Everywoman: ugly, dumb (dumb broad, dumb cunt), bitch, nag, hag, whore, fucking and breeding machine, mother of us all. Until Everywoman is free, no woman will be free. When her beauty and knowledge is revealed and seen, the new day will be at hand.

We are critical of all past ideology, literature and philosophy, products as they are of male supremacist culture. We are re-examining even our words, language itself.

We take as our source the hitherto unrecognized culture of women, a culture which from long experience of oppression developed an intense appreciation for life, a sensitivity to unspoken thoughts and the complexity of simple things, a powerful knowledge of human needs and feelings.

We regard our feelings as our most important source of political understanding.

We see the key to our liberation in our collective wisdom and our collective strength.

▲

1970–1979

▼

SHULAMITH FIRESTONE

(from) *The Dialectic of Sex*
The Culture of Romance

Visual artist Shulamith Firestone (1945–2012) was a founding member of Chicago's West Side Group in 1967, considered the country's first women's liberation group. Later that year she moved to New York City, where she successively cofounded New York Radical Women, Redstockings, and New York Radical Feminists, and edited the important 1968 mimeographed collection *Notes from the First Year*. In 1970, at age twenty-five, she published her first book, *The Dialectic of Sex: The Case for Feminist Revolution*. In separate chapters, this visionary manifesto critiques, among other topics, racism, love, male culture, and, in this excerpt, romance; a final chapter presents a sweeping "utopian speculation" on organizing a truly feminist society.

So FAR we have not distinguished "romance" from love. For there are no two kinds of love, one healthy (dull) and one not (painful) ("My dear, what you need is a mature love relationship. Get over this romantic nonsense."), but only less-than-love or daily agony. When love takes place in a power context, everyone's "love life" must be affected. Because power and love don't make it together.

So when we talk about romantic love we mean love corrupted by its power context—the sex class system—into a diseased form of love that then in turn reinforces this sex class system. We have seen that the psychological dependence of women upon men is created by continuing real economic and social oppression. However, in the modern world the economic and social bases of the oppression are no longer *alone* enough to maintain it. So the apparatus of romanticism is hauled in. (Looks like we'll have to help her out, Boys!)

Romanticism develops in proportion to the liberation of women from their biology. As civilization advances and the biological bases of sex class crumble, male supremacy must shore itself up with artificial institutions, or exaggerations of previous institutions, e.g., where previously the family had a loose, permeable form, it now tightens and rigidifies into the patriarchal nuclear family. Or, where formerly women had been held openly in contempt, now they are elevated to states of mock worship.* Romanticism is a cultural tool of male power to keep women from knowing their condition. It is especially needed—and therefore strongest—in Western countries with the highest rate of industrialization. Today, with technology enabling women to break out of their roles for good—it was a near miss in the early twentieth century—romanticism is at an all-time high.

How does romanticism work as a cultural tool to reinforce sex class? Let us examine its components, refined over centuries, and the modern methods of its diffusion—cultural techniques so sophisticated and penetrating that even men are damaged by them.

1) *Eroticism.* A prime component of romanticism is eroticism. All animal needs (the affection of a kitten that has never seen heat) for love and warmth are channeled into genital sex: people must never touch others of the same sex, and may touch those of the opposite sex only when preparing for a genital sexual encounter ("a pass"). Isolation from others makes people starved for physical affection; and if the only kind they can get is genital sex, that's soon all they crave. In this state of hypersensitivity the least sensual stimulus produces an exaggerated effect, enough to inspire everything from schools of master painting to rock and roll. Thus *eroticism is the concentration of sexuality—often into highly-charged objects ("Chantilly Lace")—signifying the displacement of other social/affection needs onto sex*. To be plain old needy-for-affection makes one a "drip," to need a kiss is embarrassing, unless it is an erotic kiss; only "sex" is O.K., in fact it proves one's mettle. Virility and sexual performance become confused with social worth.†

Constant erotic stimulation of male sexuality coupled with its forbidden release through most normal channels are designed to encourage men to look at women as only things whose resistance to entrance must be overcome. For notice that this eroticism operates in only one direction. Women are the only "love" objects in our society, so much so that women regard *themselves*

---

* Gallantry has been commonly defined as "excessive attention to women without serious purpose," but the purpose is very serious: through a false flattery, to keep women from awareness of their lower-class condition.

† But as every woman has discovered, a man who seems to be pressuring for sex is often greatly relieved to be excused from the literal performance: His ego has been made dependent on his continuously proving himself through sexual conquest; but all he may have really wanted was the excuse to indulge in affection without the loss of manly self-respect. That men are more restrained than are women about exhibiting emotion is because, in addition to the results of the Oedipus Complex, to express tenderness to a woman is to acknowledge her equality. Unless, of course, one tempers one's tenderness—takes it back—with some evidence of domination.

as erotic.* This functions to preserve direct sex pleasure for the male, rein-forcing female dependence: women can be fulfilled sexually only by vicarious identification with the man who enjoys them. Thus eroticism preserves the sex class system.

The only exception to this concentration of all emotional needs into erotic relationships is the (sometimes) affection within the family. But here, too, unless they are *his* children, a man can no more express affection for children than he can for women. Thus his affection for the young is also a trap to saddle him into the marriage structure, reinforcing the patriarchal system.

2) *The Sex Privatization of Women.* Eroticism is only the topmost layer of the romanticism that reinforces female inferiority. As with any lower class, group awareness must be deadened to keep them from rebelling. In this case, because the distinguishing characteristic of women's exploitation as a class is sexual, a special means must be found to make them unaware that they are consid-ered all alike sexually ("cunts"). Perhaps when a man marries he chooses from this undistinguishable lot with care, for as we have seen, he holds a special high place in his mental reserve for "The One," by virtue of her close associ-ation with himself; but in general he can't tell the difference between chicks (Blondes, Brunettes, Redheads).† And he likes it that way. ("A wiggle in your walk, a giggle in your talk, THAT'S WHAT I LIKE!") When a man believes all women are alike, but wants to keep women from guessing, what does he do? He keeps his beliefs to himself, and pretends, to allay her suspicions, that what she has in common with other women is precisely what makes her different. Thus her sexuality eventually becomes synonymous with her individuality. *The sex privatization of women is the process whereby women are blinded to their generality as a class which renders them invisible as individuals to the male eye.* Is not that strange Mrs. Lady next to the President in his entourage reminiscent of the discreet black servant at White House functions?

The process is insidious: When a man exclaims, "I love Blondes!" all the secretaries in the vicinity sit up; they take it personally because they have been sex-privatized. The blonde one feels personally complimented because she has come to measure her worth through the physical attributes that differentiate her from other women. She no longer recalls that any physical attribute you could name is shared by many others, that these are accidental attributes not of her own creation, that her sexuality is shared by half of humanity. But in an

---

* Homosexuals are so ridiculed because in viewing the male as sex object they go doubly against the norm: even women don't read Pretty Boy magazines.

† "As for his other sports," says a recent blurb about football hero Joe Namath, "he prefers Blondes."

authentic recognition of her individuality, her blondeness would be loved, but in a different way: She would be loved first as an irreplaceable totality, and then her blondeness would be loved as one of the characteristics of that totality.

The apparatus of sex privatization is so sophisticated that it may take years to detect—if detectable at all. It explains many puzzling traits of female psychology that take such form as:

> Women who are personally complimented by compliments to their sex, i.e., "Hats off to the Little Woman!"

> Women who are not insulted when addressed regularly and impersonally as Dear, Honey, Sweetie, Sugar, Kitten, Darling, Angel, Queen, Princess, Doll, Woman.

> Women who are secretly flattered to have their asses pinched in Rome. (Much wiser to count the number of times other girls' asses are pinched!)

> The joys of "prickteasing" (generalized male horniness taken as a sign of personal value and desirability).

> The "clotheshorse" phenomenon. (Women, denied legitimate outlets for expression of their individuality, "express" themselves physically, as in "I want to see something 'different'.")

These are only some of the reactions to the sex privatization process, the confusion of one's sexuality with one's individuality. The process is so effective that most women have come to believe seriously that the world needs their particular sexual contributions to go on. ("She thinks her pussy is made of gold.") But the love songs would still be written without them.

Women may be duped, but men are quite conscious of this as a valuable manipulative technique. That is why they go to great pains to avoid talking about women in front of them ("not in front of a lady")—it would give their game away. To overhear a bull session is traumatic to a woman: So all this time she has been considered only "ass," "meat," "twat," or "stuff," to be gotten a "piece of," "that bitch," or "this broad" to be tricked out of money or sex or love! To understand finally that she is no better than other women but completely indistinguishable comes not just as a blow but as a total annihilation. But perhaps the time that women more often have to confront their own sex privatization is in a lover's quarrel, when the truth spills out: then a man might get careless and admit that the only thing he ever *really* liked her for was her bust ("Built like a brick shithouse") or legs anyway ("Hey, Legs!"), and he can find that somewhere else if he has to.

Thus sex privatization stereotypes women: it encourages men to see women as "dolls" differentiated only by superficial attributes—not of the same species as themselves—and it blinds women to their sexploitation as a class, keeping them from uniting against it, thus effectively segregating the two classes. A side-effect is the converse: if women are differentiated only by superficial physical attributes, men appear more individual and irreplaceable than they really are.

Women, because social recognition is granted only for a *false* individuality, are kept from developing the tough individuality that would enable breaking through such a ruse. If one's existence in its generality is the only thing acknowledged, why go to the trouble to develop real character? It is much less hassle to "light up the room with a smile"—until that day when the "chick" graduates to "old bag," to find that her smile is no longer "inimitable."

3) *The Beauty Ideal.* Every society has promoted a certain ideal of beauty over all others. What that ideal is is unimportant, for any ideal leaves the majority out; ideals, by definition, are modeled on *rare* qualities. For example, in America, the present fashion vogue of French models, or the erotic ideal Voluptuous Blonde is modeled on qualities rare indeed: few Americans are of French birth, most don't look French and never will (and besides they eat too much); voluptuous brunettes can bleach their hair (as did Marilyn Monroe, the sex queen herself), but blondes can't develop curves at will—and most of them, being Anglo-Saxon, simply aren't built like that. If and when, by artificial methods, the majority can squeeze into the ideal, the ideal changes. If it were attainable, what good would it be?

For the exclusivity of the beauty ideal serves a clear political function. Someone—most women—will be left out. And left scrambling, because as we have seen, women have been allowed to achieve individuality only through their appearance—looks being defined as "good" not out of love for the bearer, but because of her more or less successful approximation to an external standard. This image, defined by men (and currently by homosexual men, often misogynists of the worst order), becomes the ideal. What happens? Women everywhere rush to squeeze into the glass slipper, forcing and mutilating their bodies with diets and beauty programs, clothes and makeup, anything to become the punk prince's dream girl. But they have no choice. If they don't the penalties are enormous: their social legitimacy is at stake.

Thus women become more and more look-alike. But at the same time they are expected to express their individuality through their physical appearance.

Thus they are kept coming and going, at one and the same time trying to express their similarity and their uniqueness. The demands of Sex Privatization contradict the demands of the Beauty Ideal, causing the severe feminine neurosis about personal appearance.

But this conflict itself has an important political function. When women begin to look more and more alike, distinguished only by the degree to which they differ from a paper ideal, they can be more easily stereotyped as a class: They look alike, they think alike, and even worse, they are so stupid they believe they are not alike.

———— ▲▼ ————

These are some of the major components of the cultural apparatus, romanticism, which, with the weakening of "natural" limitations on women, keep sex oppression going strong. The political uses of romanticism over the centuries became increasingly complex. Operating subtly or blatantly, on every cultural level, romanticism is now—in this time of greatest threat to the male power role—amplified by new techniques of communication so all-pervasive that men get entangled in their own line. How does this amplification work?

With the cultural portrayal of the smallest details of existence (e.g., deodorizing one's underarms), the distance between one's experience and one's perceptions of it becomes enlarged by a vast interpretive network; If our direct experience contradicts its interpretation by this ubiquitous cultural network, the experience must be denied. This process, of course, does not apply only to women. The pervasion of image has so deeply altered our very relationships to ourselves that even men have become objects—if never *erotic* objects. Images become extensions of oneself; it gets hard to distinguish the real person from his latest image, if indeed, the Person Underneath hasn't evaporated altogether. Arnie, the kid who sat in back of you in the sixth grade, picking his nose and cracking jokes, the one who had a crook in his left shoulder, is lost under successive layers of adopted images: the High School Comedian, the Campus Rebel, James Bond, the Salem Springtime Lover, and so on, each image hitting new highs of sophistication until the person himself doesn't know who he is. Moreover, he deals with others through this image-extension (Boy-Image meets Girl-Image and consummates Image-Romance). Even if a woman could get beneath this intricate image facade—and it would take months, even years, of a painful, almost therapeutic relationship—she would be met not with gratitude that she had (painfully) loved the man for his real self, but with shocked repulsion and terror that she had found him out. What he wants instead is The Pepsi-Cola Girl, to smile pleasantly to his Johnny Walker Red in front of a ski-lodge fire.

But, while this reification affects both men and women alike, in the case of women it is profoundly complicated by the forms of sexploitation I have described. Woman is not only an Image, she is the Image of Sex Appeal. The stereotyping of women expands: now there is no longer the excuse of ignorance. Every woman is constantly and explicitly informed on how to "improve" what nature gave her, where to buy the products to do it with, and how to count the calories she should never have eaten—indeed, the "ugly" woman is now so nearly extinct even she is fast becoming "exotic." The competition becomes frantic, because everyone is now plugged into the same circuit. The current beauty ideal becomes all-pervasive ("Blondes have more fun . . .").

And eroticism becomes erotomania. Stimulated to the limit, it has reached an epidemic level unequalled in history. From every magazine cover, film screen, TV tube, subway sign, jump breasts, legs, shoulders, thighs. Men walk about in a state of constant sexual excitement. Even with the best of intentions, it is difficult to focus on anything else. This bombardment of the senses, in turn, escalates sexual provocation still further: ordinary means of arousal have lost all effect. Clothing becomes more provocative: hemlines climb, bras are shed. See-through materials become ordinary. But in all this barrage of erotic stimuli, men themselves are seldom portrayed as erotic objects. Women's eroticism, as well as men's, becomes increasingly directed toward women.

One of the internal contradictions of this highly effective propaganda system is to expose to men as well as women the stereotyping process women undergo. Though the idea was to better acquaint women with their feminine role, men who turn on the TV are also treated to the latest in tummy-control, false eyelashes, and floor waxes (Does she . . . or doesn't she?). Such a cross-current of sexual tease and exposé would be enough to make any man hate women, if he didn't already.

Thus the extension of romanticism through modern media enormously magnified its effects. If before culture maintained male supremacy through Eroticism, Sex Privatization, and the Beauty Ideal, these cultural processes are now almost too effectively carried out: the media are guilty of "overkill." The regeneration of the women's movement at this moment in history may be due to a backfiring, an internal contradiction of our modern cultural indoctrination system. For in its amplification of sex indoctrination, the media have unconsciously exposed the degradation of "femininity."

In conclusion, I want to add a note about the special difficulties of attacking the sex class system through its means of cultural indoctrination. Sex objects *are* beautiful. An attack on them can be confused with an attack on beauty itself. Feminists need not get so pious in their efforts that they feel they must flatly deny the beauty of the face on the cover of *Vogue*. For this is not the point. The real question is: is the face beautiful in a *human* way—does it allow for growth and flux and decay, does it express negative as well as positive emotions, does it fall apart without artificial props—or does it falsely imitate the very different beauty of an *inanimate* object, like wood trying to be metal?

To attack eroticism creates similar problems. Eroticism is *exciting*. No one wants to get rid of it. Life would be a drab and routine affair without at least that spark. That's just the point. Why has all joy and excitement been concentrated, driven into one narrow, difficult-to-find alley of human experience, and all the rest laid waste? When we demand the elimination of eroticism, we mean not the elimination of sexual joy and excitement but its rediffusion over—there's plenty to go around, it increases with use—the spectrum of our lives.

KATE MILLETT

(from) *Sexual Politics*

When Kate Millett's *Sexual Politics* was published in 1970, it created such a sensation that *Time* magazine made it a cover story. A book-length argument for women's liberation adapted from Millett's Columbia University doctoral thesis, it employs feminist literary criticism and theory to expose patriarchal ideology as a socially constructed belief system so pervasive that it passes for nature. Even as it was embraced by feminists, bringing throngs of new adherents to the movement and international fame to its author, *Sexual Politics* was vilified by the male literary establishment. In her 1974 memoir *Flying*, Millett (1934–2017) described the psychological damage she suffered from her sudden notoriety and the controversies surrounding her. Afterward, she nevertheless persisted in her activism, enjoying a long career as an artist, prolific writer, and filmmaker. Here are two excerpts from "Theory of Sexual Politics," Chapter Two of her groundbreaking book.

THE WORD "politics" is enlisted here when speaking of the sexes primarily because such a word is eminently useful in outlining the real nature of their relative status, historically and at the present. It is opportune, perhaps today even mandatory, that we develop a more relevant psychology and philosophy of power relationships beyond the simple conceptual framework provided by our traditional formal politics. Indeed, it may be imperative that we give some attention to defining a theory of politics which treats of power relationships on grounds less conventional than those to which we are accustomed.[1] I have therefore found it pertinent to define them on grounds of personal contact and interaction between members of well-defined and coherent groups: races, castes, classes, and sexes. For it is precisely because certain groups have no representation in a number of recognized political structures that their position tends to be so stable, their oppression so continuous.

1. I am indebted here to Ronald V. Samson's *The Psychology of Power* (New York: Random House, 1968) for his intelligent investigation of the connection between formal power structures and the family and for his analysis of how power corrupts basic human relationships.

In America, recent events have forced us to acknowledge at last that the relationship between the races is indeed a political one which involves the general control of one collectivity, defined by birth, over another collectivity, also defined by birth. Groups who rule by birthright are fast disappearing, yet there remains one ancient and universal scheme for the domination of one birth group by another—the scheme that prevails in the area of sex. The study of racism has convinced us that a truly political state of affairs operates between the races to perpetuate a series of oppressive circumstances. The subordinated group has inadequate redress through existing political institutions, and is deterred thereby from organizing into conventional political struggle and opposition.

Quite in the same manner, a disinterested examination of our system of sexual relationship must point out that the situation between the sexes now, and throughout history, is a case of that phenomenon Max Weber defined as *herrschaft*, a relationship of dominance and subordinance.[2] What goes largely unexamined, often even unacknowledged (yet is institutionalized nonetheless) in our social order, is the birthright priority whereby males rule females. Through this system a most ingenious form of "interior colonization" has been achieved. It is one which tends moreover to be sturdier than any form of segregation, and more rigorous than class stratification, more uniform, certainly more enduring. However muted its present appearance may be, sexual dominion obtains nevertheless as perhaps the most pervasive ideology of our culture and provides its most fundamental concept of power.

This is so because our society, like all other historical civilizations, is a patriarchy.[3] The fact is evident at once if one recalls that the military, industry, technology, universities, science, political office, and finance—in short, every avenue of power within the society, including the coercive force of the police, is entirely in male hands. As the essence of politics is power, such realization

2. "Domination in the quite general sense of power, i.e. the possibility of imposing one's will upon the behavior of other persons, can emerge in the most diverse forms." In this central passage of *Wirtschaft und Gesellschaft* Weber is particularly interested in two such forms: control through social authority ("patriarchal, magisterial, or princely") and control through economic force. In patriarchy as in other forms of domination "that control over economic goods, i.e. economic power, is a frequent, often purposively willed, consequence of domination as well as one of its most important instruments." Quoted from Max Rheinstein's and Edward Shil's translation of portions of *Wirtschaft und Gesellschaft* entitled *Max Weber on Law in Economy and Society* (New York: Simon and Schuster, 1967), pp. 323–24.

3. No matriarchal societies are known to exist at present. Matrilineality, which may be, as some anthropologists have held, a residue or a transitional stage of matriarchy, does not constitute an exception to patriarchal rule, it simply channels the power held by males through female descent—, e.g. the Avunculate.

cannot fail to carry impact. What lingers of supernatural authority, the Deity, "His" ministry, together with the ethics and values, the philosophy and art of our culture—its very civilization—as T. S. Eliot once observed, is of male manufacture.

If one takes patriarchal government to be the institution whereby that half of the populace which is female is controlled by that half which is male, the principles of patriarchy appear to be two fold: male shall dominate female, elder male shall dominate younger. However, just as with any human institution, there is frequently a distance between the real and the ideal; contradictions and exceptions do exist within the system. While patriarchy as an institution is a social constant so deeply entrenched as to run through all other political, social, or economic forms, whether of caste or class, feudality or bureaucracy, just as it pervades all major religions, it also exhibits great variety in history and locale. In democracies,[4] for example, females have often held no office or do so (as now) in such minuscule numbers as to be below even token representation. Aristocracy, on the other hand, with its emphasis upon the magic and dynastic properties of blood, may at times permit women to hold power. The principle of rule by elder males is violated even more frequently. Bearing in mind the variation and degree in patriarchy—as say between Saudi Arabia and Sweden, Indonesia and Red China—we also recognize our own form in the U.S. and Europe to be much altered and attenuated by the reforms described in the next chapter.

I IDEOLOGICAL

Hannah Arendt[5] has observed that government is upheld by power supported either through consent or imposed through violence. Conditioning to an ideology amounts to the former. Sexual politics obtains consent through the "socialization" of both sexes to basic patriarchal polities with regard to temperament, role, and status. As to status, a pervasive assent to the prejudice of male superiority guarantees superior status in the male, inferior in the female. The first item, temperament, involves the formation of human personality along stereotyped lines of sex category ("masculine" and "feminine"), based on the needs and values of the dominant group and dictated by what its members

4. Radical democracy would, of course, preclude patriarchy. One might find evidence of a general satisfaction with a less than perfect democracy in the fact that women have so rarely held power within modern "democracies."

5. Hannah Arendt, "Speculations on Violence," *The New York Review of Books*, Vol. XII No. 4, February 27, 1969, p. 24.

cherish in themselves and find convenient in subordinates: aggression, intelligence, force, and efficacy in the male; passivity, ignorance, docility, "virtue," and ineffectuality in the female. This is complemented by a second factor, sex role, which decrees a consonant and highly elaborate code of conduct, gesture and attitude for each sex. In terms of activity, sex role assigns domestic service and attendance upon infants to the female, the rest of human achievement, interest, and ambition to the male. The limited role allotted the female tends to arrest her at the level of biological experience. Therefore, nearly all that can be described as distinctly human rather than animal activity (in their own way animals also give birth and care for their young) is largely reserved for the male. Of course, status again follows from such an assignment. Were one to analyze the three categories one might designate status as the political component, role as the sociological, and temperament as the psychological—yet their interdependence is unquestionable and they form a chain. Those awarded higher status tend to adopt roles of mastery, largely because they are first encouraged to develop temperaments of dominance. That this is true of caste and class as well is self-evident.

VIII PSYCHOLOGICAL

The aspects of patriarchy already described have each an effect upon the psychology of both sexes. Their principal result is the interiorization of patriarchal ideology. Status, temperament, and role are all value systems with endless psychological ramifications for each sex. Patriarchal marriage and the family with its ranks and division of labor play a large part in enforcing them. The male's superior economic position, the female's inferior one have also grave implications. The large quantity of guilt attached to sexuality in patriarchy is overwhelmingly placed upon the female, who is, culturally speaking, held to be the culpable or the more culpable party in nearly any sexual liaison, whatever the extenuating circumstances. A tendency toward the reification of the female makes her more often a sexual object than a person. This is particularly so when she is denied human rights through chattel status. Even where this has been partly amended the cumulative effect of religion and custom is still very powerful and has enormous psychological consequences. Woman is still denied sexual freedom and the biological control over her body through the cult of virginity, the double standard, the proscription against abortion, and in many places because contraception is physically or psychically unavailable to her.

The continual surveillance in which she is held tends to perpetuate the infantilization of women even in situations such as those of higher education. The female is continually obliged to seek survival or advancement through the approval of males as those who hold power. She may do this either through appeasement or through the exchange of her sexuality for support and status. As the history of patriarchal culture and the representations of herself within all levels of its cultural media, past and present, have a devastating effect upon her self image, she is customarily deprived of any but the most trivial sources of dignity or self-respect. In many patriarchies, language, as well as cultural tradition, reserve the human condition for the male. With the Indo-European languages this is a nearly inescapable habit of mind, for despite all the customary pretense that "man" and "humanity" are terms which apply equally to both sexes, the fact is hardly obscured that in practice, general application favors the male far more often than the female as referent, or even sole referent, for such designations.[6]

When in any group of persons, the ego is subjected to such invidious versions of itself through social beliefs, ideology, and tradition, the effect is bound to be pernicious. This coupled with the persistent though frequently subtle denigration women encounter daily through personal contacts, the impressions gathered from the images and media about them, and the discrimination in matters of behavior, employment, and education which they endure, should make it no very special cause for surprise that women develop group characteristics common to those who suffer minority status and a marginal existence. A witty experiment by Philip Goldberg proves what everyone knows, that having internalized the disesteem in which they are held, women despise both themselves and each other.[7] This simple test consisted of asking women undergraduates to respond to the scholarship in an essay signed alternately by one John McKay and one Joan McKay. In making their assessments the students generally agreed that John was a remarkable thinker, Joan an unimpressive mind. Yet the articles were identical: the reaction was dependent on the sex of the supposed author.

As women in patriarchy are for the most part marginal citizens when they are citizens at all, their situation is like that of other minorities, here defined not as dependent upon numerical size of the group, but on its status. "A minority group is any group of people who because of their physical or cultural characteristics, are singled out from others in the society in which they live

---

6. Languages outside the Indo-European group are instructive. Japanese, for example, has one word for man (*otōko*), another for woman (*ōnna*) and a third for human being (*ningen*). It would be as unthinkable to use the first to cover the third as it would be to use the second.
7. Philip Goldberg, "Are Women Prejudiced Against Women?" *Transaction*, April 1968.

for differential and unequal treatment"[8] Only a handful of sociologists have ever addressed themselves in any meaningful way to the minority status of women.[9] And psychology has yet to produce relevant studies on the subject of ego damage to the female which might bear comparison to the excellent work done on the effects of racism on the minds of blacks and colonials. The remarkably small amount of modern research devoted to the psychological and social effects of masculine supremacy on the female and on the culture in general attests to the widespread ignorance or unconcern of a conservative social science which takes patriarchy to be both the status quo and the state of nature.

8. Louis Wirth, "Problems of Minority Groups," in *The Science of Man in the World Crisis*, ed. by Ralph Linton (New York, Appleton, 1945), p. 347. Wirth also stipulates that the group see itself as discriminated against. It is interesting that many women do not recognize themselves as discriminated against; no better proof could be found of the totality of their conditioning.

9. The productive handful in question include the following:

Helen Mayer Hacker, "Women as a Minority Group," *Social Forces*, Vol. XXX, October 1951.

Gunnar Myrdal, *An American Dilemma*, Appendix 5 is a parallel of black minority status with women's minority status.

Everett C. Hughes, "Social Change and Status Protest: An Essay on the Marginal Man," *Phylon*, Vol. X, First Quarter, 1949.

Joseph K. Folsom, *The Family and Democratic Society*, 1943.

Godwin Watson, "Psychological Aspects of Sex Roles," *Social Psychology, Issues and Insights* (Philadelphia, Lippincott, 1966).

SHIRLEY CHISHOLM

(from) The 51% Minority

With the slogan "unbought and unbossed," Democrat Shirley Chisholm (1924–2005) was the first African American congresswoman, representing New York's 12th District from 1969 to 1983, and in 1972 became the first African American to run for the presidential nomination of either major party. Once elected to Congress, she hired an all-female staff, saying she faced more gender than racial discrimination in politics. She was a founding member of NOW, the National Women's Political Caucus, and both the Congressional Black Caucus and the Congressional Women's Caucus, and was the first co-president of the National Association for the Repeal of Abortion Laws (NARAL). Chisholm was also a champion of the Equal Rights Amendment (ERA), first introduced to Congress in 1923. Focusing on women, people of color, veterans, and the poor, her often radical legislative agenda stressed childcare funding, expanded public education, reproductive rights, minimum wage for domestic workers, guaranteed annual family income, and ending the Vietnam War. In this speech to a 1970 NOW-sponsored Conference on Women's Employment, Chisholm urges women to "become revolutionaries" while at the same time cautioning that "we must prepare ourselves educationally, economically, and psychologically" for the inevitable backlash.

M Y SISTERS all, I am very glad to be here this afternoon because I think that we are beginning to recognize that indeed, women have to become very active in the social struggle that is occurring in the United States of America today, and that we too no longer must indulge in jargon and lots of words. We must now begin to suit the action to the words in order to acquire *our* unequivocal place in the American society just as black people are acting for their unequivocal share in American society.

Do women dare to take an active part in society? And particularly, do they dare to take a part in the present social revolution? I find the questions are as much of an insult as I would the question, "Are you, as a black person, willing to fight for your rights?" America has been sufficiently sensitized to the answer, whether or not black people are willing to both die and fight for their rights, to make the question asinine and superfluous. America is not yet sufficiently aware that such a question, applied to women, is equally asinine and superfluous.

I am, as it is obvious, both black and a woman. And that is a good vantage point from which to view at least two elements of what is becoming a social revolution: the American black revolution and the women's liberation movement. But it is also a horrible disadvantage. It is a disadvantage because America as a nation is both racist and anti-feminist. Racism and anti-feminism are two of the prime traditions of this country. For any individual, breaking with social tradition is a giant step—a giant step because there are no social traditions which do not have corresponding social sanctions—the sole purpose of which are to protect the sanctity of those traditions.

That's when we ask the question, "Do women dare?" We're not asking whether women are capable of a break with tradition so much as we're asking whether they are capable of bearing the sanctions that will be placed upon them. Coupled with the hypothesis presented by some social thinkers and philosophers that in any given society, the most active group are those who are nearest to the particular freedom that they desire, it does not surprise me that those women both active and vocal on the issue of freedom for women are those who are white and middle class. Nor is it too surprising that there are not more from that group involved in the women's liberation movement. There certainly are reasons why more women are not involved.

This country, as I have said, is both racist and anti-feminist. Few, if any, Americans are free of the psychological wounds imposed by racism and anti-feminism. A few months ago, while testifying before the Office of Federal Contract Compliance, I noted that anti-feminism, like every form of discrimination, is destructive both to those who perpetrate it and to their victims—that males with their anti-feminism, hurt both themselves and their women.

In *Soul on Ice*, Eldridge Cleaver pointed out how America's racial and sexual stereotypes were supposed to work. Whether his insight is correct or not, it bears close examination. Cleaver, in the chapter, "The Primeval Mitosis", describes in detail the four major roles. There is the white female, who he considers to be ultra-feminine, because she is required to present and project an image that is in sharp contrast to the white male's image as omnipotent administrator—all brains and no body.

He goes on to identify the black female as subfeminine, or amazon, by virtue of her assignment to the lowly household chores and those corresponding jobs of a tedious nature. He sums up the role of the black male as a supermasculine menial—all body and no brains—because he was expected to supply society with its store of brute power. What the roles and the interplay between them have led to in America Cleaver goes on to point out quite well.

But what he does not say, and what I think must be said is that because of the bizarre aspect of the roles and the influence that non-habitual contact between them has on this general society, black and white, male and female, must operate almost independently of each other in order to escape from the quicksand of psychological slavery.

Each—black male and black female, white male and white female—must escape first from their own intolerable trap before they can be fully effective in helping others to free themselves. Therein lies one of the major reasons that there are not more involved in the women's liberation movement. Women cannot, for the most part, operate independently of men because they often do not have sufficient economic freedom.

In 1966, the median earnings of women who worked full time for the whole year was less than the median income for males who worked full time for the whole year. In fact, white women workers made less than black male workers, and of course, black women workers made the least of all. Whether it is intentional or not, women are paid less than men for the same work, no matter what their chosen field of work. Whether it is intentional or not, employment for women is regulated more in terms of the jobs that are available to them. This is almost as true for white women as it is for black women. Whether it is intentional or not, when it becomes time for a high school girl to think about preparing for her career, her counselors, whether they be male or female, will think first of her so-called natural career—housewife and mother—and begin to program her for a field with which children and marriage will not unduly interfere.

That's exactly the same as the situation of the young black students who the racist counselor advises to prepare for service-oriented occupations, because he does not even think of them entering the professions. And the response of the average young female is precisely the same as the response of the average young black or Puerto Rican—tacit agreement—because the odds seem to be stacked against them.

This is not happening as much as it once did to young minority group people. It is not happening because they have been radicalized, and the country is becoming sensitized to its racist attitudes. Women must learn a lesson from that experience. They must rebel.

They must react to the traditional stereotyped education mapped out for them by society. Their education and training is programmed and planned for them from the moment the doctor says, "Mrs. Jones, it's a beautiful baby girl." And Mrs. Jones begins deleting mentally the things that she might have been, and adds the things that society says that she must be. That young woman—for society begins to see her as a stereotype the moment that her sex is determined—will be wrapped in a pink blanket—pink, because that's the color of her caste—and the unequal segregation of the sexes will have begun. Small wonder then, that the young girl sitting across the desk from her counselor will not be able to say "No!" to educational, economic and social slavery. Small wonder—because she has been a psychological slave and programmed as such from the moment of her birth.

On May 20th of last year, I introduced legislation concerning the equal employment opportunity for women. And at that time I pointed out that there were three-and-one-half million more women than men in America. But women held only two per cent of the managerial positions; no women sat on the AFL-CIO council or the Supreme Court; only two women had ever held cabinet rank; and there were at that time only two women of ambassadorial rank in the diplomatic corps. I stated then as I do now: this situation is outrageous. In my speech on the floor that day, I said, "It is true that part of the problem has been that women have not been aggressive in demanding their rights. This was also true of the black population for many years. They submitted to oppression, and they even cooperated with it. Women have done exactly the same thing. But now there is an awareness of this situation, particularly among the younger segment of the population. As in the field of equal rights for blacks, Spanish Americans, the Indians, and other groups, laws will not change such deep-seated problems overnight, but they can be used to provide protection for those who are most abused, and begin the process of evolutionary change by compelling the insensitive majority to reexamine its unconscious attitudes."

The law cannot do it for us. *We must do it for ourselves.* Women in this country must become revolutionaries. We must refuse to accept the old, the traditional roles and stereotypes. We must reject the Greek philosopher's thought, "It is thy place, woman, to hold thy peace, and keep within doors." We must reject the thought of St. Paul, who said, "Let the woman learn in silence." And we must reject the great German philosopher, Nietzsche, who said, "When a woman inclines to learning, there must be something wrong with her sexual apparatus." We must replace those thoughts and the concept that they symbolize with *positive values* based upon female experience.

A few short years ago, if you called most Negroes "blacks", it was tantamount to calling us niggers. But now black is beautiful, and black is proud. There are relatively few people, white or black, who do not recognize what has happened. Black people have freed themselves from the dead weight of albatross blackness that once hung around their necks. They have done it by picking it up in their arms and holding it out with pride for all the world to see. They have done it by embracing it, not in the dark of the moon, but in the searing light of the white sun. They have said "Yes!" to it, and they have found that the skin that was once seen as symbolizing their chains is in reality their badge of honor.

Now women must come to realize that the superficial symbolism that surrounds us, too, is negative only when we ourselves perceive and accept it as negative. We must replace the old, negative thoughts about our femininity with positive thoughts and positive action affirming it, and more. But we must also remember that we will be breaking with tradition, and so we must prepare ourselves educationally, economically, and psychologically in order that we will be able to accept and bear with the sanctions that society will immediately impose upon us.

LUCINDA CISLER

Abortion Law Repeal (Sort of): A Warning to Women

In the late 1960s, New York Radical Feminists distributed pages as a "model abortion law," graphically demonstrating their bedrock demand for repeal—not "reform"—of all abortion and contraception laws. Lucinda Cisler (born 1938) was repeal's foremost feminist organizer. Active in New York Radical Women and NOW, Cisler helped found both local and national associations for repeal of abortion laws in 1969. A consistent voice against the legislative compromise of women's reproductive rights, she presciently warned, in the April 1970 article presented here in full, that anything less than complete repeal would endanger full reproductive freedom—as happened that very year with the 1970 New York State abortion law as well as with the 1973 Supreme Court decision *Roe v. Wade*, and which continues to this day with many restrictive state laws. Cisler also compiled and annotated *Women: A Bibliography* (1968–70), a widely circulated bibliography of and by women that became an indispensable resource for early Women's Studies courses.

ONE OF the few things everyone in the women's movement seems to agree on is that we have to get rid of the abortion laws and make sure that any woman who wants an abortion can get one. We all recognize how basic this demand is; it sounds like a pretty clear and simple demand, too—hard to achieve, of course, but obviously a fundamental right just like any other method of birth control.

But just because it *sounds* so simple and so obvious and is such a great point of unity, a lot of us haven't really looked below the surface of the abortion fight and seen how complicated it may be to get what we want. The most important thing feminists have done and have to keep doing is to insist that the basic reason for repealing the laws and making abortions available is JUSTICE: women's right to abortion.

Everyone recognizes the cruder forms of opposition to abortion traditionally used by the forces of sexism and religious reaction. But a feminist philosophy must be able to deal with *all* the stumbling blocks that keep us from reaching our goal, and must develop a consciousness about the far more subtle dangers we face from many who honestly believe they are our friends.

In our disgust with the extreme oppression women experience under the present abortion laws, many of us are understandably tempted to accept insulting token changes that we would angrily shout down if they were offered to us in any other field of the struggle for women's liberation. We've waited so long for anything to happen that when we see our demands having any effect at all we're sorely tempted to convince ourselves that everything that sounds good in the short run will turn out to be good for women in the long run. And a lot of us are so fed up with "the system" that we don't even bother to find out what it's doing so we can fight it and demand what *we* want. This is the measure of our present oppression; a chain of aluminum *does* feel lighter around our necks than one made of iron, but it's still a chain, and our task is still to burst entirely free.

The abortion issue is one of the very few issues vital to the women's movement that well-meaning people outside the movement were dealing with on an organized basis even before the new feminism began to explode a couple of years ago. Whatever we may like to think, there *is* quite definitely an abortion movement that is distinct from the feminist movement, and the good intentions of most of the people in it can turn out to be either a tremendous source of support for our goals or the most tragic barrier to our ever achieving them. The choice is up to us: we must subject every proposal for change and every tactic to the clearest feminist scrutiny, demand only what is good for *all* women, and not let some of us be bought off at the expense of the rest.

Until just a couple of years ago the abortion movement was a tiny handful of good people who were still having to concentrate just on getting the taboo lifted from public discussions of the topic. They dared not even think about any proposals for legal change *beyond* "reform" (in which abortion is grudgingly parceled out by hospital committee fiat to the few women who can "prove" they've been raped, or who are crazy, or are in danger of bearing a defective baby). They spent a lot of time debating with priests about When Life Begins, and Which Abortions Are Justified. They were mostly doctors, lawyers, social workers, clergymen, professors, writers, and a few were just plain women—usually not particularly feminist.

Part of the reason the reform movement was very small was that it appealed mostly to altruism and very little to people's self-interest: the circumstances covered by "reform" *are* tragic but they affect very few women's lives, whereas repeal is compelling because most women know the fear of unwanted pregnancy and in fact get abortions for that reason.

Some people were involved with "reform"—and are in the abortion movement today—for very good reasons: they are concerned with important issues like the public health problem presented by illegal abortions, the doctor's right to provide patients with good medical care, the suffering of unwanted children and unhappy families, and the burgeoning of our population at a rate too high for *any* economic system to handle.

But the basis for all these good reasons to be concerned with abortion is, in the final analysis, simple expediency. Such reasons are peripheral to the central rationale for making abortion available: justice for women. And unless a well-thought-out feminism underlies the dedication of these people, they will accept all kinds of token gains from legislators and judges and the medical establishment in the name of "getting something done NOW"—never mind what that is, or how much it cuts the chances for real changes later by lulling the public into a false sense of accomplishment.

These people do deserve a lot of credit for their lonely and dogged insistence on raising the issue when everybody else wanted to pretend it didn't exist. But because they invested so much energy earlier in working for "reform" (and got it in ten states), they have an important stake in believing that their approach is the "realistic" one—that one must accept the small, so-called "steps in the right direction" that can be wrested from reluctant politicians, that it isn't quite dignified to demonstrate or shout what you want, that raising the women's rights issue will "alienate" politicians, and so on.

Others, however (especially in centers of stylish liberalism like New York City), are interested in abortion because they are essentially political fashion-mongers: Some of them aspire to public office and some just like to play around the pool. For them, it's "groovy" to be for something racy like abortion. You can make a name for yourself faster in a small movement, such as this one still is, than in something huge like the peace movement, and it's sexier than supporting the grape strikers in their struggle.

Unfortunately, the "good people" share with these pseudo-militants an over-awed attitude toward politicians, doctors, lawyers, and traditional "experts" of all kinds; they tend to view the women's movement as rather eccentric troops they can call upon to help them with colorful things like unavoidable demonstrations, rather than as the grassroots force whose feminist philosophy should be leading *them* in the right direction. Even those who have begun to say that the woman's right to abortion *is* the central issue show a good deal of half-concealed condescension toward the very movement that has brought this issue to the fore and inspired the fantastic change in public opinion witnessed in the last year or so.

Because of course, it *is* the women's movement whose demand for *repeal*—rather than "reform"—of the abortion laws has spurred the general acceleration in the abortion movement and its influence. Unfortunately, and ironically, the very rapidity of the change for which we are responsible is threatening to bring us to the point where we are offered something so close to what we want that our demands for true radical change may never be achieved.

Most of us recognize that "reforms" of the old rape–incest–fetal deformity variety are not in women's interest and in fact, in their very specificity, are almost more of an insult to our dignity as active, self-determining humans than are the old laws that simply forbid us to have abortions unless we are about to die. But the *new* reform legislation now being proposed all over the country is not in our interest either: it looks pretty good, and the improvements it seems to promise (at least for middle-class women) are almost irresistible to those who haven't informed themselves about the complexities of the abortion situation or developed a feminist critique of abortion that goes beyond "it's our right." And the courts are now handing down decisions that look good at a glance but that contain the same restrictions as the legislation.

All of the restrictions are of the kind that would be extremely difficult to get judges and legislators to throw out later (unlike the obvious grotesqueries in the old "reform" laws, which are already being challenged successfully in some courts and legislatures). A lot of people are being seriously misled because the legislation and the court decisions that incorporate these insidious limitations are being called abortion law "repeal" by the media. It's true that the media are not particularly interested in accuracy when they report news of interest to women, but the chief reason for this dangerous misuse of language is that media people are getting their information from the established abortion movement, which wants very badly to think that these laws and decisions *are* somehow repeal. (It seems pretty clear that when you repeal an abortion law you just get rid of it; you do not put things back into the statutes or make special rules that apply to abortion but not to other medical procedures.)

The following are the four major restrictions that have been cropping up lately in "repeal" bills, and some highly condensed reasons why feminists (and indeed anyone) must oppose them. No one can say for sure whether sexist ill-will, political horse-trading, or simple ignorance played the largest part in the lawmakers' decisions to include them, but all of them codify outmoded notions about medical technology, religion, or women's "role":

1. Abortions may only be performed in licensed hospitals. Abortion is almost always a simple procedure that can be carried out in a clinic or a doctor's office. Most women do need a place to lie down and rest for a while after a D&C or even a vacuum aspiration abortion, but they hardly need to occupy scarce hospital beds and go through all the hospital rigamarole that ties up the woman's money and the time of overworked staff people.

Hospital boards are extremely conservative and have always wanted to minimize the number of abortions performed within their walls: the "abortion committees" we now have were not invented by lawmakers but by hospital administrators. New laws that insure a hospital monopoly will hardly change this attitude. (The same committees regulate which women will be able to get the sterilizations they seek—even though voluntary sterilization is perfectly legal in all but one or two states.) The hospitals and accreditation agencies set up their own controls on who will get medical care, and doctors who want to retain their attending status are quite careful not to do "too many" abortions or sterilizations.

Hawaii's new law has this kind of restriction, and hospitals there are already busy setting up a new catechism of "guidelines," none of which insures that women will get more abortions and all of which insure that they will have to ask a lot of strangers for "permission" before they are allowed to spend the considerable amount of money hospitalizations inevitably cost. Maryland's new bill and the legislation proposed in several other states contain the same provisions that essentially shift the locus of control over women's decisions from the state to the hospital bureaucracies and their quasi-legal "regulations."

2. *Abortions may only be performed by licensed physicians.* This restriction sounds almost reasonable to most women who have always been fairly healthy and fairly prosperous, who are caught up in the medical mystique so many doctors have cultivated, and who accept the myth that abortion is incredibly risky and thus should cost a lot. But it is one of the most insidious restrictions of all, and is most oppressive to poor women.

Most doctors are not at all interested in performing abortions: even the ones who don't think it's dirty and who favor increasing the availability of abortion generally consider it a pretty boring procedure that they don't especially want to do. One reason they do find it tedious is that it is basically quite a simple operation, especially when the new vacuum aspiration technique is used, rather than the old dilation and curettage. The physicians who would like to see paramedical specialists trained to perform abortions with the aspirator (or who would like to perfect other promising new methods, such as hormone injections) would be completely thwarted by this restriction in their desire to provide efficient, inexpensive care on a mass basis. The general crisis in the medical delivery system in fact demands that paramedical people be trained to do a great many things that physicians do now.

If physicians themselves were to try to perform all the abortions that are needed, they would be swamped with requests and would have to charge a great deal for their specialized training. Childbirth is statistically eight or ten times more dangerous than abortion, and yet nurses are now being trained as midwives in many medical centers. Why can't they and other medical personnel also be specially trained to use the aspirator so that five or six of them can perform clinic abortions under the general supervision of one physician? Only if paramedicals are allowed to do abortions can we expect to have truly inexpensive (and eventually free) abortions available to all women.

In the fall of 1969 a Washington, D.C. court threw out the District's limitations on a doctor's right to perform abortions—but upheld the conviction of the doctor's paramedical aide who said she had wanted to help poor women. Anyone who knows what the present situation in D.C. is will know that abortion is *not* readily available when its performance is limited to doctors only. The public hospital where poor women go has clamped down on abortions almost completely; private hospitals that serve middle-class women still operate restrictively and charge a lot; a few doctors willing to brave the stigma of being "abortionists" are performing abortions in their offices for $300 or so. Although they work long hours, they are inundated with patients (one has a backlog of five weeks). Another is so swamped, partly because he continues to muddle through with D&C, that he does not even take the time to give the women an anesthetic (although they are assured before they arrive that they will get one).

Several attempts have been made to get D.C. doctors to devote a few volunteer hours each week to a free clinic for the poor; doctors have refused, expressing either indifference or fear of professional censure.

Some women insist that because *they* would prefer to go to a doctor, *all* women must be compelled by law to go to one. It is each woman's right to choose to spend $300 for an abortion from a doctor, but she is obviously oppressing other women when she insists that all must do as she does. An abortion performed by a paramedical person with special training in a given modern procedure could easily, in fact, be safer than a D&C performed by a physician who hasn't done many abortions before.

In any case, it is only when doctors have the right to train the people they need to help them meet the demand, and women have the right to get medical care at a price they can afford, that butchers and quacks will be put out of business. Existing medical practice codes provide for the punishment of quacks, but as long as poor women cannot find good abortions at a price they can pay, so long will butchers elude the law and women continue to die from their ministrations.

Looking not so far into the future, this restriction would also deny women themselves the right to use self-abortifacients when they are developed—and who is to say they will not be developed soon? The laws regulating contraception that still exist in thirty-one states were made before contraceptive foam was invented, at a time when all effective female contraception involved a visit to the doctor. That visit was frozen into a legal requirement in some states, and we still have the sad and ludicrous example of Massachusetts, where non-prescriptive foam cannot legally be bought without a prescription.

The "doctors only" clause is a favorite in legislation that masquerades as repeal. Hawaii, Maryland, Washington State, and New York are among the important states where this restriction was (rather quietly) included.

3. *Abortions may not be performed beyond a certain time in pregnancy, unless the woman's life is at stake.* Significantly enough, the magic time limit varies from bill to bill, from court decision to court decision, but this kind of restriction essentially says two things to women: (a) at a certain stage, your body suddenly belongs to the state and it can force you to have a child, whatever your own reasons for wanting an abortion late in pregnancy; (b) because late abortion entails more risk to you than early abortion, the state must "protect" you even if your considered decision is that you want to run that risk and your doctor is willing to help you. This restriction insults women in the same way the present "preservation-of life" laws do: it assumes that we must be in a state of tutelage and cannot assume responsibility for our own acts. Even many women's liberation writers are guilty of repeating the paternalistic explanation given to excuse the original passage of U.S. laws against abortion: in the nineteenth century abortion was more dangerous than childbirth, and women had to be protected against it. Was it somehow less dangerous in the eighteenth century? Were other kinds of surgery safe then? And, most important, weren't women wanting and getting abortions, even though they knew how much they were risking? "Protection" has often turned out to be but another means of control over the protected; labor law offers many examples. When childbirth becomes as safe as it should be, perhaps it will be safer than abortion: will we put back our abortion laws, to "protect women"?

And basically, of course, no one can ever know exactly when *any* stage of pregnancy is reached until birth itself. Conception can take place at any time within about three days of intercourse, so that any legal time limit reckoned from "conception" is meaningless because it cannot be determined precisely. All the talk about "quickening," "viability," and so on, is based on old religious myths (if the woman believes in them, of course, she won't look for an abortion) or tied to ever-shifting technology (who knows how soon a three-day-old fertilized egg may be considered "viable" because heroic mechanical devices allow it to survive and grow outside the woman's uterus?). To listen to judges and legislators play with the ghostly arithmetic of months and weeks is to hear the music by which angels used to dance on the head of a pin.

There are many reasons why a woman might seek a late abortion, and she should be able to find one legally if she wants it. She may suddenly discover that she had German measles in early pregnancy and that her fetus is deformed; she may have had a sudden mental breakdown; or some calamity may have changed the circumstances of her life: whatever her reasons, *she belongs to herself and not to the state.*

This limitation speaks to the hangups many people have, and it would be almost impossible to erase from a law once it were enacted—despite its possible constitutional vulnerability on the grounds of vagueness. It is incorporated in New York State's abortion bill, among many others, and in a recent Federal court decision in Wisconsin that has been gravely misrepresented as judicial "repeal." The Washington, D.C. decision discussed the "issue," and concluded that Congress should probably enact new laws for different stages of pregnancy. This is not repeal, it is a last-ditch attempt at retaining a little of the state ownership of pregnant women provided for under the worst laws we have now.

4. Abortions may only be performed when the married woman's husband or the young single woman's parents give their consent. The feminist objection to vesting a veto power in anyone other than the pregnant woman is too obvious to need any elaboration. It is utterly fantastic, then, to hear that some women's liberation groups in Washington State have actually been *supporting* an abortion bill with a consent provision. Although such a debasing restriction is written into law in most of the states that have "reform," some legal writers consider it of such little consequence that they fail to mention it in otherwise accurate summaries of U.S. abortion laws. The women's collective now putting out *Rat* in New York recently printed a very good map of the U.S., showing in ironic symbols the various restrictions on abortion in each state. For their source these radical women had used a legal checklist that did not include a mention of husband's consent—so their map didn't show this sexist restriction existing anywhere.

This may be the easiest of these restrictions to challenge constitutionally, but why should we have to? Instead we could prevent its enactment and fight to eradicate the hospital regulations that frequently impose it even where the law does not.

——— ▲▼ ———

All women are oppressed by the present abortion laws, by old-style "reforms," and by seductive new fake-repeal bills and court decisions. But the possibility of fake repeal—if it becomes reality—is the most dangerous: it will divide women from each other. It can buy off most middle-class women and make them believe things have really changed, while it leaves poor women to suffer and keeps us all saddled with abortion laws for many more years to come. There are many nice people who would like to see abortion made more or less legal, but their reasons are fuzzy and their tactics acquiescent. Because no one else except the women's movement is going to cry out against these restrictions, it is up to feminists to make the strongest and most precise demands upon the lawmakers—who ostensibly exist to serve *us*. We will not accept insults and call them "steps in the right direction."

Only if we know what we *don't* want, and why, and say so over and over again, will we be able to recognize and reject all the clever plastic imitations of our goal.

RADICALESBIANS

The Woman Identified Woman

On May 1, 1970, at the meeting of the Second Congress to Unite Women in New York City, organized by NOW to try to unite moderate and radical feminist branches of the movement, the lights of the crowded auditorium suddenly went out, to come up on seventeen women standing on the stage in lavender T-shirts silkscreened with the words "LAVENDER MENACE." The phrase quoted Betty Friedan who, at a 1969 NOW meeting, had insisted on deleting lesbian rights from the agenda of the First Congress to Unite Women. Now, at the audience's insistence, each lavender-clad woman on the stage told her story. This essay, written by Rita Mae Brown, Cynthia Funk, Lois Hart, Artemis March, Ellen Shumsky, and Barbara XX and distributed that night, articulated a theoretical basis not only for erotic and spousal relationships between women, but also for friendship and loyalty between and among feminists, bonds that could cross the divisions of sexual preference, race, class, religion, and politics. Friedan's apology and NOW's lesbian rights plank came the following year.

WHAT IS a lesbian? A lesbian is the rage of all women condensed to the point of explosion. She is the woman who, often beginning at an extremely early age, acts in accordance with her inner compulsion to be a more complete and freer human being than her society—perhaps then, but certainly later—cares to allow her. These needs and actions, over a period of years, bring her into painful conflict with people, situations, the accepted ways of thinking, feeling and behaving, until she is in a state of continual war with everything around her, and usually with her self. She may not be fully conscious of the political implications of what for her began as personal necessity, but on some level she has not been able to accept the limitations and oppression laid on her by the most basic role of her society—the female role. The turmoil she experiences tends to induce guilt proportional to the degree to which she feels she is not meeting social expectations, and/or eventually drives her to question and analyze what the rest of her society more or less accepts. She is forced to evolve her own life pattern, often living much of her life alone, learning usually much earlier than her "straight" (heterosexual) sisters about the essential aloneness of life (which the myth of marriage obscures) and about the reality of illusions. To the extent that she cannot expel the heavy socialization that goes with being female, she can never truly find peace with herself. For she is caught somewhere between accepting society's view of her—in which case she cannot accept herself—and coming to understand what this sexist society has done to her and why it is functional and necessary for it to do so. Those of us who work that through find ourselves on the other side of a tortuous journey through a night that may have been decades long. The perspective gained from that journey, the liberation of self, the inner peace, the real love of self and of all women, is something to be shared with all women—because we are all women.

It should first be understood that lesbianism, like male homosexuality, is a category of behavior possible only in a sexist society characterized by rigid sex roles and dominated by male supremacy. Those sex roles dehumanize women by defining us as a supportive/serving caste *in relation to* the master caste of men, and emotionally cripple men by demanding that they be alienated from their own bodies and emotions in order to perform their economic/political/military functions effectively. Homosexuality is a by-product of a particular way of setting up roles (or approved patterns of behavior) on the basis of sex; as such it is an inauthentic (not consonant with "reality") category. In a society in which men do not oppress women, and sexual expression is allowed to follow feelings, the categories of homosexuality and heterosexuality would disappear.

But lesbianism is also different from male homosexuality, and serves a different function in the society. "Dyke" is a different kind of put-down from "faggot," although both imply you are not playing your socially assigned sex role . . . are not therefore a "real woman" or a "real man." The grudging admiration felt for the tomboy, and the queasiness felt around a sissy boy point to the same thing: the contempt in which women—or those who play a female role—are held. And the investment in keeping women in that contemptuous role is very great. Lesbian is the word, the label, the condition that holds women in line. When a woman hears this word tossed her way, she knows she is stepping out of line. She knows that she has crossed the terrible boundary of her sex role. She recoils, she protests, she reshapes her actions to gain approval. Lesbian is a label invented by the Man to throw at any woman who dares to be his equal, who dares to challenge his prerogatives (including that of all women as part of the exchange medium among men), who dares to assert the primacy of her own needs. To have the label applied to people active in women's liberation is just the most recent instance of a long history; older women will recall that not so long ago, any woman who was successful, independent, not orienting her whole life about a man, would hear this word. For in this sexist society, for a woman to be independent means she *can't be* a woman—she must be a dyke. That in itself should tell us where women are at. It says as clearly as can be said: women and person are contradictory terms. For a lesbian is not considered a "real woman." And yet, in popular thinking, there is really only one essential difference between a lesbian and other women: that of sexual orientation—which is to say, when you strip off all the packaging, you must finally realize that the essence of being a "woman" is to get fucked by men.

"Lesbian" is one of the sexual categories by which men have divided up humanity. While all women are dehumanized as sex objects, as the objects of men they are given certain compensations: identification with his power, his ego, his status, his protection (from other males), feeling like a "real woman," finding social acceptance by adhering to her role, etc. Should a woman confront herself by confronting another woman, there are fewer rationalizations, fewer buffers by which to avoid the stark horror of her dehumanized condition. Herein we find the overriding fear of many women toward being used as a sexual object by a woman, which not only will bring her no male-connected compensations, but also will reveal the void which is woman's real situation. This dehumanization is expressed when a straight woman learns that a sister is a lesbian; she begins to relate to her lesbian sister as her potential sex object, laying a surrogate male role on the lesbian. This reveals her heterosexual conditioning to make herself into an object when sex is potentially involved in a relationship, and it denies the lesbian her full humanity. For women, especially those in the movement, to perceive their lesbian sisters through this male grid of role definitions is to accept this male cultural conditioning and to oppress their sisters much as they themselves have been oppressed by men. Are we going to continue the male classification system of defining all females in sexual relation to some other category of people? Affixing the label lesbian not only to a woman who aspires to be a person, but also to any situation of real love, real solidarity, real primacy among women, is a primary form of divisiveness among women: it is the condition which keeps women within the confines of the feminine role, and it is the debunking/scare term that keeps women from forming any primary attachments, groups, or associations among ourselves.

Women in the movement have in most cases gone to great lengths to avoid discussion and confrontation with the issue of lesbianism. It puts people uptight. They are hostile, evasive, or try to incorporate it into some "broader issue." They would rather not talk about it. If they have to, they try to dismiss it as a "lavender herring." But it is no side issue. It is absolutely essential to the success and fulfillment of the women's liberation movement that this issue be dealt with. As long as the label "dyke" can be used to frighten women into a less militant stand, keep her separate from her sisters, keep her from giving primacy to anything other than men and family—then to that extent she is controlled by the male culture. Until women see in each other the possibility of a primal commitment which includes sexual love, they will be denying themselves the love and value they readily accord to men, thus affirming their second-class status. As long as male acceptability is primary—both to individual women and to the movement as a whole—the term lesbian will be used effectively against women. Insofar as women want only more privileges within the system, they do not want to antagonize male power. They instead seek acceptability for women's liberation, and the most crucial aspect of the acceptability is to deny lesbianism—i.e., to deny any fundamental challenge to the basis of the female. It should also be said that some younger, more radical women have honestly begun to discuss lesbianism, but so far it has been primarily as a sexual "alternative" to men. This, however, is still giving primacy to men, both because the idea of relating more completely to women occurs as a negative reaction to men, and because the lesbian relationship is being characterized simply by sex, which is divisive and sexist. On one level, which is both personal and political, women may withdraw emotional and sexual energies from men, and work out various alternatives for those energies in their own lives. On a different political/psychological level, it must be understood that what is crucial is that women begin disengaging from male-defined response patterns. In the privacy of our own psyches, we must cut those cords to the core. For irrespective of where our love and sexual energies flow, if we are male-identified in our heads, we cannot realize our autonomy as human beings.

But why is it that women have related to and through men? By virtue of having been brought up in a male society, we have internalized the male culture's definition of ourselves. That definition consigns us to sexual and family functions, and excludes us from defining and shaping the terms of our lives. In exchange for our psychic servicing and for performing society's non-profit-making functions, the man confers on us just one thing: the slave status which makes us legitimate in the eyes of the society in which we live. This is called "femininity" or "being a real woman" in our cultural lingo. We are authentic, legitimate, real to the extent that we are the property of some man whose name we bear. To be a woman who belongs to no man is to be invisible, pathetic, inauthentic, unreal. He confirms his image of us—of what we have to be in order to be acceptable by him—but not our real selves; he confirms our womanhood—as he defines it, in relation to him—but cannot confirm our personhood, our own selves as absolutes. As long as we are dependent on the male culture for this definition, for this approval, we cannot be free.

The consequence of internalizing this role is an enormous reservoir of self-hate. This is not to say the self-hate is recognized or accepted as such; indeed most women would deny it. It may be experienced as discomfort with her role, as feeling empty, as numbness, as restlessness, as a paralyzing anxiety at the center. Alternatively, it may be expressed in shrill defensiveness of the glory and destiny of her role. But it does exist, often beneath the edge of her consciousness, poisoning her existence, keeping her alienated from herself, her own needs, and rendering her a stranger to other women. They try to escape by identifying with the oppressor, living through him, gaining status and identity from his ego, his power, his accomplishments. And by not identifying with other "empty vessels" like themselves. Women resist relating on all levels to other women who will reflect their own oppression, their own secondary status, their own self-hate. For to confront another woman is finally to confront one's self—the self we have gone to such lengths to avoid. And in that mirror we know we cannot really respect and love that which we have been made to be.

As the source of self-hate and the lack of real self are rooted in our male-given identity, we must create a new sense of self. As long as we cling to the idea of "being a woman," we will sense some conflict with that incipient self, that sense of I, that sense of a whole person. It is very difficult to realize and accept that being "feminine" and being a whole person are irreconcilable. Only women can give to each other a new sense of self. That identity we have to develop with reference to ourselves, and not in relation to men. This consciousness is the revolutionary force from which all else will follow, for ours is an organic revolution. For this we must be available and supportive to one another, give our commitment and our love, give the emotional support necessary to sustain this movement. Our energies must flow toward our sisters, not backward toward our oppressors. As long as woman's liberation tries to free women without facing the basic heterosexual structure that binds us in one-to-one relationship with our oppressors, tremendous energies will continue to flow into trying to straighten up each particular relationship with a man, into finding how to get better sex, how to turn his head around—into trying to make the "new man" out of him, in the delusion that this will allow us to be the "new woman." This obviously splits our energies and commitments, leaving us unable to be committed to the construction of the new patterns which will liberate us.

It is the primacy of women relating to women, of women creating a new consciousness of and with each other, which is at the heart of women's liberation, and the basis for the cultural revolution. Together we must find, reinforce, and validate our authentic selves. As we do this, we confirm in each other that struggling, incipient sense of pride and strength, the divisive barriers begin to melt, we feel this growing solidarity with our sisters. We see ourselves as prime, find our centers inside of ourselves. We find receding the sense of alienation, of being cut off, of being behind a locked window, of being unable to get out what we know is inside. We feel a real-ness, feel at last we are coinciding with ourselves. With that real self, with that consciousness, we begin a revolution to end the imposition of all coercive identifications, and to achieve maximum autonomy in human expression.

GENE BOYER

(from) Are Women Equal Under the Law?

Wisconsin businesswoman Gene Boyer (1925–2003) was attending the June 1966 Third National Conference of Commissions on the Status of Women in Washington, D.C., when she was called to Betty Friedan's hotel room for a meeting to discuss mobilizing women for action. There, twenty-eight frustrated conference attendees founded what would become NOW. Boyer served as NOW's first treasurer and helped organize and run the organization's Legal Defense and Education Fund (later renamed Legal Momentum). Passionate about economic inequality, she mentored women entrepreneurs, served on the Wisconsin Governor's Committee on Minority and Women-Owned Businesses, and pursued marital property reform. At the May 1970 hearings of the House Committee on Education and Labor, Boyer identified thirty-one areas of legal discrimination against women, in testimony excerpted here.

In Basic Civil and Political Rights

1. Are men and women treated equally under the law?

In several states, the punishments for some crimes are not only different, but of greater or lesser degree, depending on the sex of the criminal. Until as recently as 1968, two states (Pennsylvania and Connecticut) had laws which decreed that any woman convicted of a crime must be given the maximum penalty.

A prostitute is treated as a far worse criminal than the man caught consorting with her. He is, in fact, charged with a lesser crime and receives a lighter punishment for participating equally in the same illegal act.

2. Do men and women have the same freedoms to use public places?

Among other inequities sanctioned by the law, women are discriminated against in places of public accommodation. Many restaurants, clubs and cocktail lounges refuse to serve women, or restrict them to certain rooms and times, or require their being escorted by a male.

Golf courses have "men only" days and hours. Airlines encourage wives to accompany husbands on business trips by offering a bargain rate of one-half the regular fare for the wife . . . but a husband is not allowed to travel half-fare on his wife's business-trip ticket.

3. Do men and women have the same obligations as citizens?

One state (Mississippi) still prohibits women from serving on juries. Almost half the states permit women to be excused from serving on juries solely by reason of being a woman. In Louisiana, a woman must pre-register in order to be considered eligible for *jury service.*

Many women consider non-conscription during periods of compulsory *military service* an abrogation of their rights as citizens.

Women are still held to "handmaidenry" in our political system, rarely achieve appointments to policy-making bodies in *public life.* In Wisconsin, for example, the governor-appointed Council on Home and Family is composed of 16 men to 1 woman; the Council on Highway Safety has a ratio of 9 men to 1 woman; the Higher Educational Aids Board has 14 men, 1 woman. No woman serves on the parole board that decides the fate of women offenders in the prisons.

4. Does the United States subscribe to the principles expressed in the United Nations Declaration on the Political Rights of Women?

The United States has so far failed to ratify any of the 20 Human Rights Conventions of the United Nations, including the Declaration on the Elimination of Discrimination Against Women, but with the exception of the one against slavery.

5. Are both men and women guaranteed equal protection of the law under the United States Constitution?

The Supreme Court has never decreed that women are persons under the law and entitled to its equal protections under the 14th amendment to the Constitution.

6. Do men and women have the same rights to legal residence?

The domicile of a married woman automatically follows that of her husband. If he has moved to a separate domicile, or deserted her, this can seriously affect her rights to vote, to run for public office, serve on juries, have her estate properly administered, etc.

In 5 states (Alaska, Arkansas, Delaware, Hawaii and Wisconsin), a wife may take legal steps to establish separate domicile for all purposes.

In 13 additional states (California, Connecticut, Florida, Illinois, Indiana, Iowa, Maine, Massachusetts, Michigan, New Jersey, New York, North Dakota and Wyoming), she may do so for voting purposes. In 3 of these (Maine, New York and New Jersey) she may do so for the purpose of holding public office also.

In every case, the burden of special effort is upon the woman, while the man's legal residence follows him automatically.

7. Are men and women equally free to change their name?

In those cases where women have petitioned to legally retain their maiden names after marriage, the courts have uniformly rejected the effort.

Many states have statutes expressly denying to married women the right to change their surname to one other than their husband's. No comparable restriction is imposed on married men.

When a married man changes his surname, his wife's surname is automatically changed regardless of her wishes.

8. Do married women have equal rights to married men—or to single women—under the law?

Based in common law, many states have laws which cause a woman to forfeit rights when she marries, such as restricting married women from executing contracts, managing their own property, engaging in business without the consent of their husbands, etc.

Under common law, a man and wife become a single legal entity and the husband is the symbol and representative person for that entity. (The word "woman" means "wife-of-man.")

In Matters of Family Law and Policy

9. Do divorce laws favor women in the division of property?

Except in the 9 community property states (Arizona, California, Hawaii, Idaho, Louisiana, New Mexico, Nevada, Texas and Washington), the wife is financially at the husband's mercy upon divorce.

In the 41 common law states, all monies earned by a husband during marriage belong exclusively to him and no monetary value is attached to the wife's domestic services in helping to produce the family income or acquire property.

10. Do divorce laws favor women in the awarding of alimony and custody of children?

More than one-third of the states permit alimony to be awarded to either spouse at the discretion of the court.

Often child support payments are camouflaged as alimony because taxes on alimony payments to an ex-wife are payable by her, not the ex-husband, while the total amount of alimony is subtracted from the ex-husband's income (child support is deductible only up to the $600 exemption allowed). As a result of lumping child support payments together with alimony, the husband enjoys a tax advantage.

In only a very few states is the mother given automatic preference in custody of children, and then only if they are very young. The general rule today is to award custody in accordance with the child's best interests.

11. Do divorce laws favor women in establishing grounds for divorce?

The only grounds for divorce common to all 50 states and the District of Columbia is adultery. Cruelty is recognized as grounds for divorce in 45 states, but the definitions of cruelty differ widely. Incompatibility is recognized as a ground for divorce in only 4 states.

A woman who has been deserted by her husband must wait from 1 to 5 years before she can begin to sue him for divorce. The only state where a woman can begin suit after 6 months is Hawaii.

At present it is necessary to establish fault with the husband in order for the wife to receive alimony, a legal manipulation which adversely affects any possibilities for reconciliation between the parties or future amiable relationship.

It would not be necessary to establish fault in a divorce if alimony were viewed as recognition of the contribution made by a spouse to the family which is otherwise uncompensated; to reimburse for loss of earning capacity suffered by either spouse because of the marriage; and to continue the responsibility of a self-supporting spouse toward a financially dependent one until such time as the need is no longer acute (a form of "workmen's compensation" upon loss of job).

12. Do married men and women have the same rights to their earnings?

In the community property states (except Texas), all of an employed woman's earnings belong to a common fund which is legally under the control of the husband, the wife having no "say" as to how her income is spent.

A man need not pay wages to his wife who works in his business. This exemption, which is permitted in most states, does NOT apply to a husband employed by his wife, or children employed by their parents.

In no state does the law give the woman the right to tell her husband how to spend his earnings or to claim his labors without recompense.

13. Do married men and women have the same rights to property purchased by them from their individual earnings?

Unless there is a title or a record establishing otherwise, property purchased by the wife—such as a car or television set—is generally considered to be the property of the husband, even if the purchase was made entirely from her individual earnings.

A wife owns none of the property accumulated during marriage in her husband's name in the common law states. In some states, like Wisconsin, she has a "dower right" to only one-third of his estate when he dies.

14. Are married men and women equally responsible for each other?

In all states, a husband is liable for support of his wife regardless of her ability to support herself. This is based in the legal concept of "the perpetual tutelage of women."

A wife is not obliged to support a husband who is unable to support himself in 19 states, a denial of the mature woman's abilities to care for dependents. (Alabama, Colorado, Florida, Georgia, Hawaii, Indiana, Iowa, Kentucky, Maryland, Massachusetts, Mississippi, Missouri, Rhode Island, South Carolina, Tennessee, Texas, Virginia, Washington and Wyoming.)

15. Are parents equally responsible for their children?

In 4 states (Colorado, Montana, Ohio and Rhode Island), the father alone is required to support legitimate children. In 6 states (Alaska, Colorado, Minnesota, Mississippi, Ohio and Rhode Island) the father alone is required to support illegimate children.

Differential responsibility shows up in laws governing matters other than support. In Wisconsin, only the father's signature is acceptable on the driver's license application of a minor.

In Matters of Employment

16. Do the same labor standards apply to men and women? Are they equally protected in such matters as minimum wages, overtime pay, maximum hours, safety and health?

In 11 states there are no minimum wage laws at all. (Alabama, Florida, Georgia, Iowa, Mississippi, Missouri, Montana, South Carolina, Tennessee, Texas and Virginia.)

In 39 states, the District of Columbia and Puerto Rico there are minimum wage laws, but in 7 of these the laws apply to women and minors only. (Arizona, California, Colorado, Minnesota, Ohio, Utah and Wisconsin.)

When coupled with other restrictions—such as maximum hours, weight-lifting or night-work prohibitions—these so-called "protective" labor laws serve to bar women from equal opportunities in employment, in promotion and training for advancement.

Weight-lifting restrictions for women exist in 10 states (Alaska, California, Maryland, Massachusetts, New York, Oregon, Ohio, Utah, Washington, and in Puerto Rico). In California, for example, a woman who regularly carries growing children off to bed is prohibited from carrying as little as 10 pounds on the job!

Recently, decisions on test cases in state courts have declared these restrictive laws in conflict with, and overridden by, the federal laws providing equality of opportunity in employment.

17. Are women entitled to the same pay as men for the same work?

Only 31 states have equal pay laws guaranteeing women the same wage for the same work done by men on the same or similar job.

Only 15 states, including Wisconsin, have Fair Employment Practices laws which include prohibitions against discrimination in employment on the basis of sex. Equal pay is not always specified as a requirement in these laws.

Many employment contracts are written—including those for professionals, such as teachers—which pay premiums for head-of-household or additional dependents, and which serve to defeat the principle of equal pay for equal work.

18. Are women entitled to equal opportunities in hiring, training and promotion under Title VII of the Civil Rights Act of 1964?

This major piece of legislation, perhaps second only to women's suffrage in 1920 in securing equal rights for women, has shortcomings: women employed in government service or in the field of education are not covered; the Equal Employment Opportunity Commission, the enforcing agency, lacks effective powers.

While the law specifically prohibits the advertisement of jobs under sex-designated column headings, only a few major newspapers (such as the *New York Times*) are voluntarily complying.

Current practices in the professions, education, labor unions, among employers in business and industry, operate to prevent women from achieving promotions to supervisory and executive positions. Among these practices are: excluding women from conferences, from training courses, from membership in professional organizations, from quasi-social meetings, groups or facilities which are, in reality, arenas of business negotiations.

Women are often prevented from acquiring franchises, dealerships, distributorships and other opportunities for going into business as entrepreneurs by such "subtle" practices as requiring excessive financial resources or extra guarantors on loans from the female investor.

19. Are women in control of most of the wealth of our country?

Women own approximately 51% of the stock and securities issued in this country, which is not surprising in view of the fact that they constitute 53% of the adult population.

Less than 3% of women with income from any source earn over $10,000 per year, as compared to 24% of men.

Women are conspicuous by their absence from the ranks of stockbrokers, financiers, corporation and bank presidents, boards of directors of major corporations, insurance companies, high government officials and other elements of control over the economics and wealth of our country.

In Matters of Health, Education, and Welfare

20. Do boys and girls have the same rights to parental support?

In 7 states, boys have a right to parental support up to age 21 while girls have that right only to age 18. (Arkansas, Idaho, Nevada, North Dakota, Oklahoma, South Dakota, Utah.)

21. Are boys and girls equally entitled to a high school education?

High schools are permitted to refuse attendance to girls who are married or pregnant: married boys and unwed fathers are usually allowed to attend.

22. Do boys and girls have the same opportunity to enter college, if they qualify academically?

Quotas limiting registration of girls in certain classes and colleges are common; such quotas are invoked even at coeducational, tax-supported state institutions of higher learning.

Many more scholarships and other financial aids are available to male students.

Prejudice and discouraging counseling practices are responsible in large part for the continuing low enrollments of women in schools of medicine, law, engineering, business administration, and other "traditional" male fields.

23. Are men and women equally entitled to control their own reproductive processes?

The men who make the laws which control contraception and abortion have, in effect, control over the reproductive processes of women.

While the idea of legally required prevention of conception to mitigate the population explosion is regarded as an intolerable intervention in individual liberties, the woman who is victim of an accidental conception is forced by law to go through a pregnancy against her will and, in many cases, bear an unwanted child.

Since it is comparatively easier for the affluent woman to obtain an illegal abortion, it is the low-income woman whose liberty and freedom of choice is most often abrogated, and who frequently becomes the hapless victim of fatal quackery.

24. Are men and women living in poverty given equal opportunities toward a better life?

The latest available data shows that, among the poor, women outnumber men 8 to 5. Women and children together constitute over ⅔ of all persons living in poverty.

Many Federal programs designed to relieve poverty conditions fail to include women proportionately. Manpower Development and Training, Job

Corps, etc., concentrate on skills for males, while the unemployment rate among females is higher.

Adequate housing is also extremely difficult to find for the woman who is head-of-household, has dependents to support, is seasonally employed, unemployed, marginally or under-employed. Of the better than 5 million women heading a family, 35% are counted among the poor.

25. Are women, as well as men, on Aid to Families with Dependent Children (AFDC) entitled to retain some human dignity and pride?

In Wisconsin, and other states, the law requires a woman applicant for AFDC to declare her willingness to file criminal non-support charges against the father in order to be eligible for benefits.

In many cases, rather than jeopardize the possibility of a reconciliation with her deserting husband, a woman will refuse to file charges and will, instead, risk starvation for herself and children. The state does not need her charges to pursue a deserting father.

DORIS WRIGHT

(from) Angry Notes from a Black Feminist

"The Man to Sam may be Whitey, but the Man to women is any man," wrote Doris Wright, a militant feminist activist, in the 1970 essay excerpted here. Though she insists that feminism does not detract from the Black freedom struggle, her unflinching critique of male dominance, particularly by Black men, provoked accusations of disloyalty from some Black male leaders. After she convened a meeting of Black women to discuss "their relationship to the women's movement," Wright, an advisory board member of NOW, cofounded the National Black Feminist Organization (NBFO) in 1973.

THE MAN

As a Black woman, maybe you still believe that what the black man's putting down is somehow different from what Whitey has been propagating and diseasing the world with all these years. Up to now, you've thought that your situation in this society was very different from that of your white sister. In fact, you've never even considered her your "sister" at all. She was some alien enemy who belonged to the Arch-Oppressor, and who lived in enemy territory. Well, two minutes in the Movement will prove to you that when it comes to being a member of the female sex, we're all in the same bag. All you have to do is look around to see the evidence of what Whitey really thinks of our white sister, and how he's used and abused her for his purposes.

A pervasive myth in our society was the one which proclaimed the white man's reverential esteem for his white sister. Myth had it that he would risk life and limb to defend his woman's virtue, and that her welfare was the primary concern of the civilized world. In many parts of the country, he laid down strict laws governing the behavior of black men as regards white women, and the black man was severely punished for violating these laws. We now, of course, recognize the real factors behind these extreme and excessive measures. Whitey's treatment of our white sister as a prized possession never had anything to do with his regard for her human dignity. She was just another pawn in his war with the black man. Woman has always been used in this way. Men do battle with one another, and she is caught in the middle. The top dog gets to take advantage of, and even mutilate, the underdog's property, while a symbol of the slave breaking free of the master's domination is his ability finally to defile that which belongs to the master. One evidence of the subtle change in Whitey's attitudes toward white women is reflected in his present crop of movies, which depict our white sister as a kind of appeasement gift. Sam can have her now. Her usefulness is at an end in the white man's war with his brother, so she too can be offered to the wolves. And especially now that she has sullied herself in contact with other women, and is militantly proclaiming her right to control her own destiny, it's of no consequence *who* takes her to bed.

The Man is the Man and the color of his skin hasn't mattered for any woman up to this point in history, and never will matter so long as our destiny remains in his hands.

What the Black Man Wants

Only in a society where male-approved perversions of the kind that lead to violence and power struggles are discouraged—and where continual competitive combat with other human beings is not rewarded—will man stop viewing woman as just part of the "spoils" of his world. And, Black sister, that's all we are to the black man—part of the spoils that he now feels he deserves after all those years of "masculine" privation at the hands of Whitey. To someone whose identity is all caught up with his striving for middle class status, we represent yet another symbol of his success, of his having "made it." He now wants to be able to enjoy us in style. Although the white man has long since placed our white sister on a pedestal and thereby gotten rid of her, that is, removed her from all possible competition with him on an equal basis, the black man has to work harder to convince the Black woman of her innate inferiority to him. He thinks, however, that he can coerce us by messing up our minds. He thinks he can ply us with bon bons and doodads and we'll restrain any personal desires to have things our way, forgetting the noble history of our female ancestors, while he takes center stage and leads the race on the same ruinous and destructive course that has characterized Whitey's reign as master.

The Age of the Pedestal is about to dawn for us, Black sisters. Old Sam now wants us to keep out of his way and play with the family's toys in order that he can prove to Mr. Charlie what a successful provider and, therefore, Man he is. Although Eleanor Holmes Norton claims that black men do not want "wives like the white suburban chocolate eaters of Larchmont," there certainly has been no evidence to attest to the truth of her statement. On the contrary, there is evidence to indicate that just as many black men as white are eager to suburbanize lifetime servants. Black men may be, as she claims, ". . . the one group accustomed to women who are able and assertive, because their mothers and sisters were that way," but is she implying that they therefore hold these women in special regard? Are we to assume that black men encourage this assertiveness in the women in their lives? Or are they woefully forced to accept it out of sheer necessity? In terms of Black women ending up as "chocolate eaters," if the current rash of products being directed toward the Black female market (literature, cosmetics, et al.) is evidence of the society's forming image of the Black woman, we can assume that our sole aim is to emulate every bad trait adopted in self-defence by our white sister. One wonders at what stage in our development we are if the "culture" purveyors think us a target to barrage with their trifling, frothy junk. It's a sign of the times, sisters. We are about to be done in by the brothers for keeps, to be made their frivolous appendages through whom they can prove how well they've made it in Whitey's world.

Whitey's "success" is judged not only by what job he holds and in which section of town he resides, but also by whether or not he can afford to own a sexual object, namely, a woman. Men are proud they can "afford" families and boast of them in the same manner that they boast of their T-Birds. Now what Sam wants is easier access to owning all the things Whitey just takes for granted. He wants to be able to afford his chicks and cars with less hassle. The fact that the attainment of his inane, shallow goals has nothing to do with our self-fulfillment is of no consequence. He's been working to convince us that we really want to be made into mindless, over-pampered dolls—each of us an emotional dependent who is kept virtually powerless to explore life on her own. In spite of the fact that Sam fearfully acknowledges us as the descendants of those proud, independent Black women who for centuries spiritually carried this race and its woes on their backs, he is hopeful that we will submit to a way of life that would prove a negation of everything for which they suffered.

THE "STAND BEHIND YOUR MAN" CRUSADE

Although Sam did momentarily get angry over the conclusions arrived at in studies such as Moynihan's which explored the Black family in depth, he did so only because he felt they "exposed" him as a deficient father and, thereby, challenged his manhood. He nonetheless quickly closed ranks with the white establishment in virtually indicting Black women as "dominating bitches" who must abdicate their positions of authority in the family. Whoever defined the patriarchal family system as being the most wholesome and preferred one? The Man himself, of course, because he's top cat and one of the ways to stay on top is to cultivate a climate which equates male supremacy to godliness. They've sent many a white sister into guilt-ridden qualms over this patriarchy rubbish. They have also succeeded in intimidating some Black women into anxious remorse over the fact that when Sam ran out and left them with the brood they had the courage and the moral strength to become the family's breadwinner. Black women have proven over and over again that they are capable leaders, not only as necessary heads of families but out in the world as well. We should never allow Whitey or Sam to shame us on that score. Of course, we can always ask Sam where his gang was when our grandmother and her mother before her was out scrubbing floors and getting laid by Whitey to keep their children alive. Yeah, we all know the story. They were busy being castrated by society, or something.

Black women are cautioned to stay out of the women's movement on the grounds that their presence in it will tend to "drain" off energies from the bigger, more important struggle for Black civil rights. The black man never makes it clear, however, just how the efforts of a woman fighting for her right to have an abortion when she wants it, round-the-clock child care centers, and an end to discrimination against her sex, in any way interferes with a co-existent struggle, the main purpose of which is, initially, equal opportunity on all fronts, and, ultimately, self-determination. Although the black man claims the right of self-determination for the race as such, what he really has in mind is self-determination for the black man. He, like all men, is dismayed at the prospect of female self-determination. That women should demand the right to be their own masters, and to be shackled to no one, is a mind-blowing idea which he's too small to handle. What the Black woman must ask herself is, "When I'm free from the necessity of catering to the Great White Father, who's to free me from the necessity of catering to the Great Black Father?"

(from) Position Paper on Women

In 1969, a group of young, mostly Puerto Rican activists in Chicago founded the Young Lords Organization (later the Young Lords Party) to fight for self-determination and liberation for all Latino and "Third World" people. Inspired by the Black Panthers, the activists transformed a street gang named the Young Lords into a community organization providing childcare, free breakfasts, and clean streets. Young Lords women, like women in the Black Panthers and other radical groups of color, chose to struggle against sexism and machismo from within the organization rather than by breaking away. The following excerpt from a statement by women in the organization's New York City affiliate published in the Young Lords newspaper, *Palante*, in 1970, concludes, "We are fighting every day within our PARTY against male chauvinism because we want to make a revolution of brothers and sisters—together—in love and respect for each other."

PUERTO RICAN, Black, and other Third World (colonized) women are becoming more aware of their oppression in the past and today. They are suffering three different types of oppression under capitalism. First, they are oppressed as Puerto Ricans or Blacks. Second, they are oppressed as women. Third, they are oppressed by their own men. The Third World woman becomes the most oppressed person in the world today.

Economically, Third World women have always been used as a cheap source of labor and as sexual objects. Puerto Rican and Black women are used to fill working class positions in factories, mass assembly lines, hospitals and all other institutions. Puerto Rican and Black women are paid lower wages than whites and kept in the lowest positions within the society. At the same time, giving Puerto Rican and Black women jobs means the Puerto Rican and Black man is kept from gaining economic independence, and the family unit is broken down. Capitalism defines manhood according to money and status; the Puerto Rican and Black man's manhood is taken away by making the Puerto Rican and Black woman the breadwinner. This situation keeps the Third World man divided from his woman. The Puerto Rican and Black man either leaves the household or he stays and becomes economically dependent on the woman, undergoing psychological damage. He takes out all of his frustrations on his woman, beating her, repressing and limiting her freedom. Because this society produces these conditions, our major enemy is capitalism rather than our own oppressed men.

Third World Women have an integral role to play in the liberation of all oppressed people as well as in the struggle for the liberation of women. Puerto Rican and Black women make up over half of the revolutionary army, and in the struggle for national liberation they must press for the equality of women; the woman's struggle is the revolution within the revolution. Puerto Rican women will be neither behind nor in front of their brothers but always alongside them in mutual respect and love.

The Double Standard, Machismo, and Sexual Fascism

Capitalism sets up standards that are applied differently to Puerto Rican and Black men from the way they are applied to Puerto Rican and Black women. These standards are also applied differently to Third World peoples than they are applied to whites. These standards must be understood since they are created to divide oppressed people in order to maintain an economic system that is racist and oppressive.

Puerto Rican and Black men are looked upon as rough, athletic and sexual, but not as intellectuals. Puerto Rican women are not expected to know anything except about the home, kitchen and bedroom. All that they are expected to do is look pretty and add a little humor. The Puerto Rican man sees himself as superior to his woman, and his superiority, he feels, gives him license to do many things—curse, drink, use drugs, beat women, and run around with many women. As a matter of fact these things are considered natural for a man to do, and he must do them to be considered a man. A woman who curses, drinks, and runs around with a lot of men is considered dirty scum, crazy, and a whore.

Today Puerto Rican men are involved in a political movement. Yet the majority of their women are home taking care of the children. The Puerto Rican sister that involves herself is considered aggressive, castrating, hard and unwomanly. She is viewed by the brothers as sexually accessible because what else is she doing outside of the home. The Puerto Rican man tries to limit the woman's role because they feel the double standard is threatened; they feel insecure without it as a crutch.

Machismo has always been a very basic part of Latin American and Puerto Rican culture. Machismo is male chauvinism and more. Machismo means "mucho macho" or a man who puts himself selfishly at the head of everything without considering the woman. He can do whatever he wants because his woman is an object with certain already defined roles—wife, mother, and good woman.

Machismo means physical abuse, punishment and torture. A Puerto Rican man will beat his woman to keep her in place and show her who's boss. Most Puerto Rican men do not beat women publicly because in the eyes of other men that is a weak thing to do. So they usually wait until they're home. All the anger and violence of centuries of oppression which should be directed against the oppressor is directed at the Puerto Rican woman. The aggression is also directed at daughters. The daughters hear their fathers saying "the only way a woman is going to do anything or listen is by hitting her." The father applies this to the daughter, beating her so that she can learn "respeto." The daughters grow up with messed up attitudes about their role as women and about manhood. They grow to expect that men will always beat them.

Sexual fascists are very sick people. Their illness is caused in part by this system which mouths puritanical attitudes and laws and yet exploits the human body for profit.

Sexual Fascism is tied closely to the double standard and machismo. It means that a man or woman thinks of the opposite sex solely as sexual objects to be used for sexual gratification and then discarded. A sexual fascist does not consider people's feelings; all they see everywhere is a pussy or a dick. They will use any rap, especially political, to get sex.

PROSTITUTION

Under capitalism, Third World women are forced to compromise themselves because of their economic situation. The facts that her man cannot get a job and that the family is dependent on her for support mean she hustles money by any means necessary. Black and Puerto Rican sisters are put into a situation where jobs are scarce or nonexistent and are forced to compromise body, mind, and soul; they are then called whores or prostitutes.

Puerto Rican and Black sisters are made to prostitute themselves in many other ways. The majority of these sisters on the street are also hard-core drug addicts, taking drugs as an escape from oppression. These sisters are subjected to sexual abuse from dirty old men who are mainly white racists who view them as the ultimate sexual objects. Also he has the attitude that he cannot really prove his manhood until he has slept with a Black or Puerto Rican woman. The sisters also suffer abuse from the pimps, really small-time capitalists, who see the women as private property that must produce the largest possible profit.

Because this society controls and determines the economic situation of Puerto Rican and Black women, sisters are forced to take jobs at the lowest wages; at the same time take insults and other indignities in order to keep the job. In factories, our men are worked like animals and cannot complain because they will lose their jobs—their labor is considered abundant and cheap. In hospitals, our women comprise the majority of the nurse's aides, kitchen workers, and clerks. These jobs are unskilled, the pay is low, and there is no chance for advancement. In offices, our positions are usually as clerks, typists, and no-promotion jobs. In all of these jobs, our sisters are subjected to racial slurs, jokes, and other indignities such as being leered at, manhandled, propositioned, and assaulted. Our sisters are expected to prostitute themselves and take abuse of any kind or lose these subsistence jobs.

Everywhere our sisters are turned into prostitutes. The most obvious example is the sisters hustling their bodies on the streets, but the other forms of prostitution are also types of further exploitation of the Third World woman. The only way to eliminate prostitution is to eliminate this society which creates the need. Then we can establish a socialist society that meets the economic needs of all the people.

BIRTH CONTROL, ABORTION, STERILIZATION = GENOCIDE

We have no control over our bodies, because capitalism finds it necessary to control the woman's body to control population size. The choice of motherhood is being taken out of the mother's hands. She is sterilized to prevent her from having children, or she has to have a child because she cannot get an abortion.

Third World sisters are caught up in a complex situation. On one hand, we feel that genocide is being committed against our people. We know that Puerto Ricans will not be around on the face of the earth very long if Puerto Rican women are sterilized at the rate they are being sterilized now. The practice of sterilization in Puerto Rico goes back to the 1930's when doctors pushed it as the only means of contraception. In 1947–48, 7% of the women were sterilized; between 1953–54, 4 out of every 25; and by 1965, the number had increased to about 1 out of every 3 women. In many cases our sisters are told that their tubes are going to be "tied," but are never told that the "tying" is really "cutting" and that the tubes can never be "untied."

Part of this genocide is also the use of birth control pills which were tested for 15 years on Puerto Rican sisters (guinea pigs) before being sold on the market in the U.S. Even now many doctors feel that these pills cause cancer and death from blood clotting.

Abortions in hospitals that are butcher shops are little better than the illegal abortions our women used to get. The first abortion death in NYC under the new abortion law was Carmen Rodriguez, a Puerto Rican sister who died in Lincoln Hospital. Her abortion was legal, but the conditions in the hospital were deadly.

On the other hand, we believe that abortions should be legal if they are community controlled, if they are safe, if our people are educated about the risks and if doctors do not sterilize our sisters while performing abortions. We realize that under capitalism our sisters and brothers cannot support large families and the more children we have the harder it is to support them. We say, change the system so that women can freely be allowed to have as many children as they want without suffering any consequences.

JUDY SYFERS

Why I Want A Wife

During the strike for Black Studies at San Francisco State University (1968–69), Judy Brady Syfers, a thirty-one-year-old mother of two, plunged into the fight led by her husband, turning their home into "the strike annex," a five-month-long effort for which her husband, not she, was thanked. She soon joined the women's liberation movement, and, at the San Francisco celebration of the fiftieth anniversary of women's suffrage (August 26, 1970), read aloud "Why I Want A Wife," eliciting cheers from women in the audience and heckles from the men. First published in the Bay Area women's liberation newspaper *Mother Lode*, the piece was widely reprinted, including in the December 1971 preview issue of *Ms.*, where Syfers (1937–2017) appended a note stressing that under capitalism, all but a few privileged women "must necessarily be exploited as workers and as wives."

I BELONG TO that classification of people known as wives. I am A Wife. And, not altogether incidentally, I am a mother.

Not too long ago a male friend of mine appeared on the scene from the Midwest fresh from a recent divorce. He had one child, who is, of course, with his ex-wife. He is obviously looking for another wife. As I thought about him while I was ironing one evening, it suddenly occurred to me that I, too, would like to have a wife. Why do I want a wife?

I would like to go back to school so that I can become economically independent, support myself, and, if need be, support those dependent upon me. I want a wife who will work and send me to school. And while I am going to school I want a wife to take care of my children. I want a wife to keep track of the children's doctor and dentist appointments. And to keep track of mine, too. I want a wife to make sure my children eat properly and are kept clean. I want a wife who will wash the children's clothes and keep them mended. I want a wife who is a good nurturant attendant to my children, arranges for their schooling, makes sure that they have an adequate social life with their peers, takes them to the park, the zoo, etc. I want a wife who takes care of the children when they are sick, a wife who arranges to be around when the children need special care, because, of course, I cannot miss classes at school. My wife must arrange to lose time at work and not lose the job. It may mean a small cut in my wife's income from time to time, but I guess I can tolerate that. Needless to say, my wife will arrange and pay for the care of the children while my wife is working.

I want a wife who will take care of *my* physical needs. I want a wife who will keep my house clean. A wife who will pick up after my children, a wife who will pick up after me. I want a wife who will keep my clothes clean, ironed, mended, replaced when need be, and who will see to it that my personal things are kept in their proper place so that I can find what I need the minute I need it. I want a wife who cooks the meals, a wife who is a *good* cook. I want a wife who will plan the menus, do the necessary grocery shopping, prepare the meals, serve them pleasantly, and then do the cleaning up while I do my studying. I want a wife who will care for me when I am sick and sympathize with my pain and loss of time from school. I want a wife to go along when our family takes a vacation so that someone can continue to care for me and my children when I need a rest and a change of scene.

I want a wife who will not bother me with rambling complaints about a wife's duties. But I want a wife who will listen to me when I feel the need to explain a rather difficult point I have come across in my course of studies. And I want a wife who will type my papers for me when I have written them.

I want a wife who will take care of the details of my social life. When my wife and I are invited out by my friends, I want a wife who will take care of the babysitting arrangements. When I meet people at school that I like and want to entertain, I want a wife who will have the house clean, will prepare a special meal, serve it to me and my friends, and not interrupt when I talk about the things that interest me and my friends. I want a wife who will have arranged that the children are fed and ready for bed before my guests arrive so that the children do not bother us. I want a wife who takes care of the needs of my guests so that they feel comfortable, who makes sure that they have an ashtray, that they are passed the hor d'oeuvres, that they are offered a second helping of the food, that their wine glasses are replenished when necessary, that their coffee is served to them as they like it. And I want a wife who knows that sometimes I need a night out by myself.

I want a wife who is sensitive to my sexual needs, a wife who makes love passionately and eagerly when I feel like it, a wife who makes sure that I am satisfied. And, of course, I want a wife who will not demand sexual attention when I am not in the mood for it. I want a wife who assumes the complete responsibility for birth control, because I do not want more children. I want a wife who will remain sexually faithful to me so that I do not have to clutter up my intellectual life with jealousies. And I want a wife who understands that *my* sexual needs may entail more than strict adherence to monogamy. I must, after all, be able to relate to people as fully as possible.

If, by chance, I find another person more suitable as a wife than the wife I already have, I want the liberty to replace my present wife with another one. Naturally, I will expect a fresh, new life; my wife will take the children and be solely responsible for them so that I am left free.

When I am through with school and have acquired a job, I want my wife to quit working and remain at home so that my wife can more fully and completely take care of a wife's duties.

My God, who *wouldn't* want a wife?

ROBIN MORGAN

A Brief Elegy for Four Women

After a September 1970 mass shooting of four women in Albany, New York, Robin Morgan (born 1941)—polemicist, poet, cofounder of WITCH (see pages 73–74 in this volume)—issued this feminist call-to-arms in the countercultural New Left newspaper *Rat*. Earlier that year, outraged that the editorial collective behind *Rat* had published a sex-and-porn special issue, Morgan had stopped working on her feminist anthology *Sisterhood Is Powerful* to help launch a feminist takeover of *Rat*. The resulting all-women issue (February 1970) included "Goodbye to All That," Morgan's impassioned denunciation of sexism in the male Left—which may explain why the collective's male members were initially resistant to publishing this angry "Elegy" in the October 1970 issue.

PATRICIA CHROMICK, *22 years old*
SANDRA L. PETERS, *24 years old*
MARY ANN REINSCHE, *27 years old*
LINDA D. WILLIS, *21 years old*

L AST WEEK, Joseph White, a twenty-five-year-old administrative analyst in the State Employment Insurance Offices in Albany, New York, killed four women with a pump-action shotgun.

He had taken a sick leave from his job and had come in to pick up his first paycheck, which was not ready for him. Becoming enraged at the bureaucratic foul-up, he went on a rampage against the women in the office, and finally shot himself.

It was not a case of indiscriminate murder. White was in fact discriminating enough to pass up all the men he saw in between his killings of women. When one male bureaucrat tried to question him, White ran past him—until he found another woman to kill.

White had been screwed by his employer. So his natural response was to take out his rage on the people he had power over—women, all of whom were themselves powerless to live a decent life or even die a meaningful death. They were all four workers in the secretarial pool.

No matter where they are on the status ladder, men can always feel better as long as they can oppress women. White was a man who himself was oppressed, as a worker and a victim of bureaucracy, but his hatred detoured the real enemy—the System and his employer-job-whole-life-misery—and exploded instead against the convenient lightning rods: women.

Every day newspapers carry stories of atrocities committed against women: murder, rape, beatings, mutilations. Such news is presented as being either titillating or irrelevant. To us it is intensely political.

Sexual crimes are political assassinations, and at the rising rate and ferocity with which they are being committed, they approach attempted genocide of a people on the basis of sex and gender.

Only one thing can protect us. Women must defend our lives and bodies and minds against male violence, by any means necessary. We must learn and practice self- and sister-defense on all levels: physical, mental, emotional. We must learn to understand weapons. We are doing this already, but not fast enough, hard enough, seriously enough. *Too many sisters who would be willing to die defending a radical brother would on the other hand find it difficult, if not impossible, even to relate to the daily suffering of any woman in a secretarial pool.*

Such a shameful attitude must stop. We can afford no more arrogant dismissals of secretaries, housewives, file clerks, nurses, etc. No more snobbish, vicious statements like "But she's so *straight*. But that's so *bourgeois*. But they're not *hip*. But that one reminds me of my *mother*."

One of the four sisters who was murdered in Albany lay dying in a room where she had lived a daily death, in the midst of gray typewriters and gray metal file cabinets and gray chrome desks. Littered around her were squares of white paper to be typed and then filed—some "unfortunately" ruined now, because they were stained with her blood. She kept whimpering, "Please, please somebody help me. Somebody help."

Remember The Albany Four, sisters. Never forget. . . .

(from) The Children's House

Feminist organizations from the reformist NOW to the radical Bread and Roses demanded safe, non-sexist childcare as basic to women's freedom. Experimental feminist childcare projects included free workplace daycare centers and parent-run cooperatives with, ideally, women and men participating equally. One such effort was The Children's House, in Washington, D.C., described in this 1970 article by Marcia Sprinkle (born 1942) and Norma Allen Lesser (born 1946) and published in the feminist newspaper *off our backs*. In 1971 Congress passed a comprehensive childcare bill, introduced by representatives Shirley Chisholm and Bella Abzug, but President Richard Nixon vetoed it as undermining the family. The Children's House was forced to shut down and move several times by licensing and zoning authorities; eventually the parents managed to become fully licensed and to find a legal location. The Children's House existed for almost ten years.

——————— ▲▼ ———————

THE OUTSIDE badly needs paint and the porch tilts and sags but the front door is shocking pink. Inside is a furious amount of activity, most going on at three feet and under: The walls are covered with posters, notices and pictures of the children. The Children's House is a fully co-operative, parent-run day-care center. For most of the adults it is far more than just an adequate place to leave their children—it is a new way to care for and relate to children and each other. Two of us wrote this article to share the experience of what we are doing.

WHAT'S HAPPENING NOW

We have been operating full-time for eight months now and the mechanics of running a children's center have been fairly well worked out. Our group now Includes 25 children from the ages of 10 months to 3 years (most are around 2) and approximately 50 adults (19 to 35). The house is open Monday through Friday from 9 am to 5 pm.

Children are signed up for any combination of hours but in order to simplify planning the adults must come the morning shift (9–1) or the afternoon shift (1–5). We usually maintain a 1–3 ratio of adults to children or as close to that as possible. There also must be at least two adults at the house at all times.

Every couple comes 1/3 of the time their children are there, man and woman working equal time. Couples with two children spend the same amount of time as those with one child and single parents come only 1/6 of the time. We don't penalize people for having more than one child or for being a single parent. In addition there are many non-parents who also come. We can sign up ourselves and our children for different hours each week so the center is flexible enough to meet our fluctuating needs.

How We Do It

The administrative jobs are rotated weekly through the list of adults in the group. There are four jobs that have to be done:

1. *Scheduling.* The purpose of the scheduler is to make sure there are enough adults per children. The scheduler calls anyone who has not signed up. This helps wives who feel they must substitute when their husbands are unavailable. This mechanism makes it a group responsibility to deal with paternal reluctance to accept responsibility for child care. People find their own substitutes when they can't come. When there are extra people on the schedule, they are available for helping out if there are sick children or for going on special trips. The scheduler also writes the agenda for the bi-weekly meetings and notifies people about their jobs for the coming week.

2. *Buying supplies.* The supply person buys the food and pampers for the week, makes the menus so the morning people know what to prepare for lunch, including snacks for the kids and coffee for the adults. We have a continuing unresolved debate over whether to fix organic health food or supermarket variety. At this point the food person does what he or she wants each week.

3. *Laundry.* One person washes the sheets and extra clothes.

4. *Clean-up.* A thorough clean-up is done every weekend.

On a daily basis, the morning shift serves lunch, the afternoon shift cleans and we all do small jobs.

Every family unit contributes $5 to $30 a month depending on what they feel they can afford. People can change their pledges up or down depending on their finances. We have a standing finance committee which signs the checks, pays the bills, and keeps the records straight. So far we have had enough money to pay for rent, utilities, food, supplies and toys.

Our House

To get started everyone donated new or used toys, furniture and equipment. A standing equipment committee has bought some things and made others. The house is well supplied with riding vehicles, dolls, crayons, paper, pull toys, plastic crud, puzzles, balls, books, and other kid stuff. Toy shelves and doll beds were made out of fruit crates. Play houses were made by putting curtains across the front of a huge open cabinet. A really wonderful 4 foot wide group slide was made out of old boards and doors.

The first floor of the house has a kitchen and two rooms where most of the toys are kept. Upstairs are three bedrooms with cribs, cots, extra clothes and linens. The basement has larger toys such as a bouncing horse, a see-saw and the slide. At first we thought we'd have separate activities but the kids all travel in a pack from one room to another, so everything happens everywhere. The backyard contains a wading pool in the summer, another group slide and playhouse but is too confining for all day use.

Our Day

On a typical morning 13–16 children come. Weather permitting many of us take trips to museums, parks and go on walks. Lunch which is usually served around 11:30 is always a nice part of the day. Paper plates of easy finger food like cheese, apple slices and pieces of meatloaf are put out on an old coffee table. The children just take whatever they want. They sit down or stand or walk around, coming back to get more for themselves or more for someone else. The amazing thing is how quiet it gets and how rarely they fight over the food. They all eat without being pushed and there is relatively little mess. Afternoons are generally quieter because most of the children nap.

Licensing

At this writing we are unlicensed. We aren't willing to comply with some of the objectionable laws e.g., no children under six months and boys and girls must sleep in separate rooms. Even if we were willing to be licensed it's not likely we could find a house in the prescribed non-residential area that would meet the extensive safety code regulations. We would also be periodically investigated. Strangely, this city is very casual, even lax about the condition of houses rented to people to live in but very stringent with people who try to start a daycare center. Some of the health rules are meaningless and totally prohibitive. For example, we're illegal because we have only two toilets instead of five which the law requires. If we are caught and harassed we will make a big stink about the lack of good facilities for pre-school children. We don't want a place where brainwashing starts earlier, we want complete parent control and some degree of parent participation.

OUR COMMON IDEAS

Most of the people involved in our daycare center are similar: white, college educated and politically left of center, so some theories have evolved as important to the group as a whole.

We think it is very important for our children to have the freedom to grow, explore, learn and be. That means providing a secure, interesting environment. It also means respecting their ideas, emotions and business. There is little structure imposed on the children: all the toys are always available, all the space is open and free, and the children are free to do whatever they please. We try not to interfere in the relationships they have with each other. Fighting is infrequent and even the infants have the capacity to develop unique relationships. It also means ending the possessive/dependent relationship between parents and children so typical in isolated nuclear families.

It means, despite conventional wisdom, that parents should not always be the only important people to a child, even an infant. It means we must let our children be free to develop very special relationships with other adults and that we have the time and openness to develop the same loving concern for other children that we have for our own.

At first, some of us felt some guilt about involving young children in a daycare center since the prevailing myth is that children in that age group are insecure in large groups. But our experience is that it isn't true. Providing a secure environment means that for certain children we made sure there were always some familiar faces until the child got to know more people in the group. It seems that the younger the children join the group, the easier it is for them. However, parents have a problem no matter what their age. For instance, almost every parent is shocked the first few times their leavetaking goes unnoticed. The parent says three or four "good-bys" and "I'm going now" until the kid finally cries a little so the parent can leave reassured.

SUCCESS AND FAILURE

Control over our own lives and particularly the institutions and communities we are a part of is important to us. To this end we all participate fully in the responsibility of keeping the center going, rather than employing a staff or allowing (by default) a few of the more active, vocal parents to control the group. This means everybody doing their share of the work and participating at meetings in a process we like to think of as struggle. In place of taking votes or establishing rules, the group has tried thorough on-going discussion to reach a consensus that is satisfactory to everyone. Issues are always considered open for more discussion and new consensus. We have always hoped to relate to each other in an open, honest way that is supportive. This involves the very difficult tasks of really listening to each other, trying to understand each other, being tolerant of where others are at, and still expressing and working for what you think is correct. All of us have been concerned about solving our problems without making the meetings painful to attend. Sometimes issues have been settled but it hasn't always worked; the group is too large, we tend to polarize at meetings, meetings are repetitive and we often avoid dealing with issues. We don't yet know or trust each other and there hasn't been much true struggle or true support for each other. We find it very difficult to talk about child rearing without getting defensive about our own children and practices. Because we haven't been successful as a group, a woman whose husband wasn't doing his share would have to leave the group or fight him alone rather than having the group deal with him as an irresponsible member.

Some people feel the house provides just a decent and convenient place to leave their kids. They are resistant to allowing the group to change their lives in important ways and hold the whole group back from becoming more than just a daycare center.

SOCIALIZATION

We feel a special urgency about ending the usual socialization and sex-role programming of children and about helping each other break out of our own stereotyped sex roles. We want children to know men as well as they have traditionally known women, to see that all people have their good and bad, strong and weak times, to see that all jobs, all emotions, all ways of being are as appropriate for one sex as the other. We don't want our children to see women primarily dealing with children and that men go off to "work"—that mysterious place. We don't want our male children to oppress our female children. We don't want our children to grow up thinking that little boys become whatever they want while little girls grow up to be mothers. But it's hard for people to change and we have not really dealt with much of our own destructive socialization.

Parent Non-Parents

Non-parents' participation is varied. Some are as active as the parents; others are not. We have repeatedly discussed whether non-parents should be expected to carry the same responsibilities as parents at the Children's House. At first we felt so grateful to non-parents for helping at the center that we asked very little of them. Then we realized that if we wanted society to be responsible for all children, we must treat all adults as parents. This meant we didn't have to be grateful or expect less of the non-parents but it also meant we couldn't continue the old possessive/dictatorial role of parents.

Time Off

Another obviously important function of the center is to give people with children time away from them to dig other people and activities. This need is especially acute for women in the nuclear family. We are searching for new ways to be relieved part time of our child care responsibilities without exploiting spouses or hired help.

The center and the discussions we have there have pushed us to change our own life styles e.g., challenging work situations—Larry asking and fighting for a 2/3 time contract at his teaching job in order to work at the center. Marcia and Lorraine asking for release time when interviewed for jobs. Men cooking, washing dishes, and spending lots more time caring for their children.

Many of us want to go beyond just maintaining child care for our personal use and take more kinds of positive action including publicizing what we have been able to do so other people will have some knowledge and feeling about our children's house and perhaps be inspired to set up their own.

SUSAN GRIFFIN

(from) Rape: The All-American Crime

Illustrated in the September 1971 issue of the New Left magazine *Ramparts* by
painter Artemisia Gentileschi's depiction of Judith beheading her rapist Holofernes
(1610), this essay by poet and activist Susan Griffin (born 1943) demolished myths
that blamed women and protected men from responsibility for the "all-American
crime" of rape. Her pioneering analysis, excerpted here, shocked with its battery
of rebukes to existing assumptions about sexual assault. Griffin established terrain
now central to rape law—"no" does not mean "yes," a woman never asks for it—
and discredited the cultural undergirding that legitimized sexual assault, reframing
chivalry as "an age-old protection racket which depends for its existence on rape."
Griffin expanded this piece into her first nonfiction book, *Rape: The Politics of
Consciousness* (1979).

IN THE spectrum of male behavior, rape, the perfect combination of sex
and violence, is the penultimate act. Erotic pleasure cannot be separated
from culture, and in our culture male eroticism is wedded to power. Not only
should a man be taller and stronger than a female in the perfect love-match,
but he must also demonstrate his superior strength in gestures of dominance
which are perceived as amorous. Though the law attempts to make a clear
division between rape and sexual intercourse, in fact the courts find it difficult
to distinguish between a case where the decision to copulate was mutual and
one where a man forced himself upon his partner.

The scenario is even further complicated by the expectation that, not only
does a woman mean "yes" when she says "no," but that a really decent woman
ought to begin by saying "no," and then be led down the primrose path to
acquiescence. Ovid, the author of Western Civilization's most celebrated sex-
manual, makes this expectation perfectly clear:

> . . . and when I beg you to say "yes," say "no." Then let me lie out-
> side your bolted door. . . . So Love grows strong. . . .

That the basic elements of rape are involved in all heterosexual relationships may explain why men often identify with the offender in this crime. But to regard the rapist as the victim, a man driven by his inherent sexual needs to take what will not be given him, reveals a basic ignorance of sexual politics. For in our culture heterosexual love finds an erotic expression through male dominance and female submission. A man who derives pleasure from raping a woman clearly must enjoy force and dominance as much or more than the simple pleasures of the flesh. Coitus cannot be experienced in isolation. The weather, the state of the nation, the level of sugar in the blood—all will affect a man's ability to achieve orgasm. If a man can achieve sexual pleasure after terrorizing and humiliating the object of his passion, and in fact while inflicting pain upon her, one must assume he derives pleasure directly from terrorizing, humiliating and harming a woman. According to Amir's study of forcible rape, on a statistical average the man who has been convicted of rape was found to have a normal sexual personality, tending to be different from the normal, well-adjusted male only in having a greater tendency to express violence and rage.

And if the professional rapist is to be separated from the average dominant heterosexual, it may be mainly a quantitative difference. For the existence of rape as an index to masculinity is not entirely metaphorical. Though this measure of masculinity seems to be more publicly exhibited among "bad boys" or aging bikers who practice sexual initiation through group rape, in fact, "good boys" engage in the same rites to prove their manhood. In Stockton, a small town in California which epitomizes silent-majority America, a bachelor party was given last summer for a young man about to be married. A woman was hired to dance "topless" for the amusement of the guests. At the high point of the evening the bridegroom-to-be dragged the woman into a bedroom. No move was made by any of his companions to stop what was clearly going to be an attempted rape. Far from it. As the woman described, "I tried to keep him away—told him of my Herpes Genitalis, et cetera, but he couldn't face the guys if he didn't screw me." After the bridegroom had finished raping the woman and returned with her to the party, far from chastizing him, his friends heckled the woman and covered her with wine.

It was fortunate for the dancer that the bridegroom's friends did not follow him into the bedroom for, though one might suppose that in group rape, since the victim is outnumbered, less force would be inflicted on her, in fact, Amir's studies indicate, "the most excessive degrees of violence occurred in group rape." Far from discouraging violence, the presence of other men may in fact encourage sadism, and even cause the behavior. In an unpublished study of group rape by Gilbert Geis and Duncan Chappell, the authors refer to a study by W. H. Blanchard which relates, "The leader of the male group . . . apparently precipitated and maintained the activity, despite misgivings, because of a need to fulfill the role that the other two men had assigned to him. 'I was scared when it began to happen,' he says. 'I wanted to leave but I didn't want to say it to the other guys—you know—that I was scared.'"

Thus it becomes clear that not only does our culture teach men the rudiments of rape, but society, or more specifically other men, encourage the practice of it.

II

Every man I meet wants to protect me. Can't figure out what from.
                                                              —Mae West

If a male society rewards aggressive, domineering sexual behavior, it contains within itself a sexual schizophrenia. For the masculine man is also expected to prove his mettle as a protector of women. To the naive eye, this dichotomy implies that men fall into one of two categories: those who rape and those who protect. In fact, life does not prove so simple. In a study euphemistically entitled "Sex Aggression by College Men," it was discovered that men who believe in a double standard of morality for men and women, who in fact believe most fervently in the ultimate value of virginity, are more liable to commit "this aggressive variety of sexual exploitation."

(At this point in our narrative it should come as no surprise that Sir Thomas Malory, creator of that classic tale of chivalry, *The Knights of the Round Table*, was himself arrested and found guilty for repeated incidents of rape.)

In the system of chivalry, men protect women against men. This is not unlike the protection relationship which the mafia established with small businesses in the early part of this century. Indeed, chivalry is an age-old protection racket which depends for its existence on rape.

According to the male mythology which defines and perpetuates rape, it is an animal instinct inherent in the male. The story goes that sometime in our pre-historical past, the male, more hirsute and burly than today's counterparts, roamed about an uncivilized landscape until he found a desirable female. (Oddly enough, this female is *not* pictured as more muscular than the modern woman.) Her mate does not bother with courtship. He simply grabs her by the hair and drags her to the closest cave. Presumably, one of the major advantages of modern civilization for the female has been the civilizing of the male. We call it chivalry.

But women do not get chivalry for free. According to the logic of sexual politics, we too have to civilize our behavior. (Enter chastity. Enter virginity. Enter monogamy.) For the female, civilized behavior means chastity before marriage and faithfulness within it. Chivalrous behavior in the male is supposed to protect that chastity from involuntary defilement. The fly in the ointment of this otherwise peaceful system is the fallen woman. She does not behave. And therefore she does not deserve protection. Or, to use another argument, a major tenet of the same value system: what has once been defiled cannot again be violated. One begins to suspect that it is the behavior of the fallen woman, and not that of the male, that civilization aims to control.

The assumption that a woman who does not respect the double standard deserves whatever she gets (or at the very least "asks for it") operates in the courts today. While in some states a man's previous rape convictions are not considered admissible evidence, the sexual reputation of the rape victim is considered a crucial element of the facts upon which the court must decide innocence or guilt.

The court's respect for the double standard manifested itself particularly clearly in the case of the People v. Jerry Plotkin. Mr. Plotkin, a 36-year-old jeweler, was tried for rape last spring in a San Francisco Superior Court. According to the woman who brought the charges, Plotkin, along with three other men, forced her at gunpoint to enter a car one night in October 1970. She was taken to Mr. Plotkin's fashionable apartment where he and the three other men first raped her and then, in the delicate language of the *S.F. Chronicle*, "subjected her to perverted sex acts." She was, she said, set free in the morning with the warning that she would be killed if she spoke to anyone about the event. She did report the incident to the police who then searched Plotkin's apartment and discovered a long list of names of women. Her name was on the list and had been crossed out.

In addition to the woman's account of her abduction and rape, the prosecution submitted four of Plotkin's address books containing the names of hundreds of women. Plotkin claimed he did not know all of the women since some of the names had been given to him by friends and he had not yet called on them. Several women, however, did testify in court that Plotkin had, to cite the *Chronicle*, "lured them up to his apartment under one pretext or another, and forced his sexual attentions on them."

Plotkin's defense rested on two premises. First, through his own testimony Plotkin established a reputation for himself as a sexual libertine who frequently picked up girls in bars and took them to his house where sexual relations often took place. He was the Playboy. He claimed that the accusation of rape, therefore, was false—this incident had simply been one of many casual sexual relationships, the victim one of many playmates. The second premise of the defense was that his accuser was also a sexual libertine. However, the picture created of the young woman (fully 13 years younger than Plotkin) was not akin to the light-hearted, gay-bachelor image projected by the defendant. On the contrary, the day after the defense cross-examined the woman, the *Chronicle* printed a story headlined, "Grueling Day For Rape Case Victim." (A leaflet passed out by women in front of the courtroom was more succinct, "rape was committed by four men in a private apartment in October; on Thursday, it was done by a judge and a lawyer in a public courtroom.")

Through skillful questioning fraught with innuendo, Plotkin's defense attorney James Martin MacInnis portrayed the young woman as a licentious opportunist and unfit mother. MacInnis began by asking the young woman (then employed as a secretary) whether or not it was true that she was "familiar with liquor" and had worked as a "cocktail waitress." The young woman replied (the *Chronicle* wrote "admitted") that she had worked once or twice as a cocktail waitress. The attorney then asked if she had worked as a secretary in the financial district but had "left that employment after it was discovered that you had sexual intercourse on a couch in the office." The woman replied, "That is a lie. I left because I didn't like working in a one-girl office. It was too lonely." Then the defense asked if, while working as an attendant at a health club, "you were accused of having a sexual affair with a man?" Again the woman denied the story, "I was never accused of that."

Plotkin's attorney then sought to establish that his client's accuser was living with a married man. She responded that the man was separated from his wife. Finally he told the court that she had "spent the night" with another man who lived in the same building.

At this point in the testimony the woman asked Plotkin's defense attorney, "Am I on trial? . . . It is embarrassing and personal to admit these things to all these people. . . . I did not commit a crime. I am a human being." The lawyer, true to the chivalry of his class, apologized and immediately resumed questioning her, turning his attention to her children. (She is divorced, and the children at the time of the trial were in a foster home.) "Isn't it true that your two children have a sex game in which one gets on top of another and they—" "That is a lie!" the young woman interrupted him. She ended her testimony by explaining "They are wonderful children. They are not perverted."

The jury, divided in favor of acquittal ten to two, asked the court stenographer to read the woman's testimony back to them. After this reading, the Superior Court acquitted the defendant of both the charges of rape and kidnapping.

According to the double standard a woman who has had sexual intercourse out of wedlock cannot be raped. Rape is not only a crime of aggression against the body; it is a transgression against chastity as defined by men. When a woman is forced into a sexual relationship, she has, according to the male ethos, been violated. But she is also defiled if she does not behave according to the double standard, by maintaining her chastity, or confining her sexual activities to a monogamous relationship.

One should not assume, however, that a woman can avoid the possibility of rape simply by behaving. Though myth would have it that mainly "bad girls" are raped, this theory has no basis in fact. Available statistics would lead one to believe that a safer course is promiscuity. In a study of rape done in the District of Columbia, it was found that 82 percent of the rape victims had a "good reputation." Even the Police Inspector's advice to stay off the streets is rather useless, for almost half of reported rapes occur in the home of the victim and are committed by a man she has never before seen. Like indiscriminate terrorism, rape can happen to any woman, and few women are ever without this knowledge.

But the courts and the police, both dominated by white males, continue to suspect the rape victim, *sui generis*, of provoking or asking for her own assault. According to Amir's study, the police tend to believe that a woman without a good reputation cannot be raped. The rape victim is usually submitted to countless questions about her own sexual mores and behavior by the police investigator. This preoccupation is partially justified by the legal requirements for prosecution in a rape case. The rape victim must have been penetrated, and she must have made it clear to her assailant that she did not want penetration (unless of course she is unconscious). A refusal to accompany a man to some isolated place to allow him to touch her does not in the eyes of the court, constitute rape. She must have said "no" at the crucial genital moment. And the rape victim, to qualify as such, must also have put up a physical strug-gle—unless she can prove that to do so would have been to endanger her life.

But the zealous interest the police frequently exhibit in the physical details of a rape case is only partially explained by the requirements of the court. A woman who was raped in Berkeley was asked to tell the story of her rape four different times "right out in the street," while her assailant was escaping. She was then required to submit to a pelvic examination to prove that penetration had taken place. Later, she was taken to the police station where she was asked the same questions again: "Were you forced?" "Did he penetrate?" "Are you sure your life was in danger and you had no other choice?" This woman had been pulled off the street by a man who held a 10-inch knife at her throat and forcibly raped her. She was raped at midnight and was not able to return to her home until five in the morning. Police contacted her twice again in the next week, once by telephone at two in the morning and once at four in the morning. In her words, "The rape was probably the least traumatic incident of the whole evening. If I'm ever raped again, . . . I wouldn't report it to the police because of all the degradation. . . ."

If white women are subjected to unnecessary and often hostile questioning after having been raped, third world women are often not believed at all. According to the white male ethos (which is not only sexist but racist), third world women are defined from birth as "impure." Thus the white male is provided with a pool of women who are fair game for sexual imperialism. Third world women frequently do not report rape and for good reason. When blues singer Billie Holliday was 10 years old, she was taken off to a local house by a neighbor and raped. Her mother brought the police to rescue her, and she was taken to the local police station crying and bleeding:

> When we got there, instead of treating me and Mom like somebody who called the cops for help, they treated me like I'd killed somebody. . . . I guess they had me figured for having enticed this old goat into the whorehouse. . . . All I know for sure is they threw me into a cell . . . a fat white matron . . . saw I was still bleeding, she felt sorry for me and gave me a couple glasses of milk. But nobody else did anything for me except give me filthy looks and snicker to themselves.
>
> After a couple of days in a cell they dragged me into a court. Mr. Dick got sentenced to five years. They sentenced me to a Catholic institution.

Clearly the white man's chivalry is aimed only to protect the chastity of "his" women.

As a final irony, that same system of sexual values from which chivalry is derived has also provided womankind with an unwritten code of behavior, called femininity, which makes a feminine woman the perfect victim of sexual aggression. If being chaste does not ward off the possibility of assault, being feminine certainly increases the chances that it will succeed. To be submissive is to defer to masculine strength; is to lack muscular development or any interest in defending oneself; is to let doors be opened, to have one's arm held when crossing the street. To be feminine is to wear shoes which make it difficult to run; skirts which inhibit one's stride; underclothes which inhibit the circulation. Is it not an intriguing observation that those very clothes which are thought to be flattering to the female and attractive to the male are those which make it impossible for a woman to defend herself against aggression?

Each girl as she grows into womanhood is taught fear. Fear is the form in which the female internalizes both chivalry and the double standard. Since, biologically speaking, women in fact have the same if not greater potential for sexual expression as do men, the woman who is taught that she must behave differently from a man must also learn to distrust her own carnality. She must deny her own feelings and learn not to act from them. She fears herself. This is the essence of passivity, and of course, a woman's passivity is not simply sexual but functions to cripple her from self-expression in every area of her life.

Passivity itself prevents a woman from ever considering her own potential for self-defense and forces her to look to men for protection. The woman is taught fear, but this time fear of the other; and yet her only relief from this fear is to seek out the other. Moreover, the passive woman is taught to regard herself as impotent, unable to act, unable even to perceive, in no way self-sufficient, and, finally, as the object and not the subject of human behavior. It is in this sense that a woman is deprived of the status of a human being. She is not free to be.

MIRTA VIDAL

(from) New Voice of La Raza: Chicanas Speak Out

Frustrated by the reluctance of the male-dominated Chicano movement to take up women's issues, six hundred Chicana women traveled to Houston in May 1971 for the Conferencia de Mujeres. In workshops on birth control, abortion, childcare, and machismo, participants spoke with "our own voices for the first time." Argentinian American Mirta Vidal (1949–2004), a reporter for the international socialist weekly *The Militant*, was a participant. Her resulting essay, excerpted here, is considered a founding document of Chicana feminism. To join the struggle for women's liberation "would expand rather than divide Il Movimiento," she declared, adding furthermore that "on the basis of the subordination of women, there can be no real unity."

IN PHARR, Texas, women have organized pickets and demonstrations to protest police brutality and to demand the ousting of the city's mayor. And even in Crystal City, Texas, where La Raza Unida Party has won major victories, women have had to organize on their own for the right to be heard. While the men constituted the decision-making body of Ciudadanos Unidos (United Citizens)—the organization of the Chicano community of Crystal City—the women were organized into a women's auxiliary—Ciudadanas Unidas. Not satisfied with this role, the women got together, stormed into one of the meetings and demanded to be recognized as members on an equal basis. Although the vote was close, the women won.

The numerous articles and publications that have appeared recently on La Chicana are another important sign of the rising consciousness of Chicanas. Among the most outstanding of these are a special section in *El Grito del Norte*, an entire issue dedicated to and written by Chicanas published by *Regeneración* and a regular Chicana feminist newspaper put out by Las Hijas de Cuahtemoc in Long Beach, California. This last group and their newspaper are named after the feminist organization of Mexican women who fought for emancipation during the suffragist period in the early part of this century.

These facts, which are by no means exhaustive of what Chicanas have done in this last period, are plainly contradictory to the statement made by women participating in the 1969 Denver Youth Conference. At that time a workshop held to discuss the role of women in the movement came back to report to the conference: "It was the consensus of the group that the Chicana woman does not want to be liberated." Although there are still those who maintain that Chicanas not only do not want to be liberated, but do not *need* to be liberated, Chicanas themselves have decisively rejected that attitude through their actions.

"MACHISMO"

In part, this awakening of Chicana consciousness has been prompted by the "machismo" she encounters in the movement. It is adequately described by one Chicana, in an article entitled "Macho Attitudes," in which she says:

> When a freshman male comes to MECHA [Movimiento Estudian-til Chicano de Aztlan—a Chicano student organization in California], he is approached and welcomed. He is taught by observation that the Chicanas are only useful in areas of clerical and sexual activities. When something must be done there is always a Chicana there to do the work. "It is her place and duty to stand behind and back up her Macho!" . . . Another aspect of the MACHO attitude is their lack of respect for Chicanas. They play their games, plotting girl against girl for their own benefit . . . They use the movement and Chicanismo to take her to bed. And when she refuses, she is a *vendida* [sell-out] because she is not looking after the welfare of her men.[1]

This behavior, typical of Chicano men, is a serious obstacle to women anxious to play a role in the struggle for Chicano liberation.

The oppression suffered by Chicanas is different from that suffered by most women in this country. Because Chicanas are part of an oppressed nationality, they are subjected to the racism practiced against La Raza. Since the overwhelming majority of Chicanos are workers, Chicanas are also victims of the exploitation of the working class. But in addition, Chicanas, along with the rest of women, are relegated to an inferior position because of their sex. Thus, Raza women suffer a triple form of oppression: as members of an oppressed nationality, as workers, *and* as women. Chicanas have no trouble understanding this. At the Houston conference 84 percent of the women surveyed felt that "there is a distinction between the problems of the Chicana and those of other women."

On the other hand, they also understand that the struggle now unfolding against the oppression of women is not only relevant to them, but *is* their struggle.

Because sexism and male chauvinism are so deeply rooted in this society, there is a strong tendency, even within the Chicano movement, to deny the basic right of Chicanas to organize around their own concrete issues. Instead they are told to stay away from the women's liberation movement because it is an "Anglo thing."

One needs only to analyze the origins of male supremacy to expose that position for what it is—a distortion of reality and false. The inferior role of women in society does not date back to the beginning of time. In fact, before the Europeans came to this part of the world women enjoyed a high position of equality with men. The submission of women, along with institutions such as the church and the patriarchy, was imported by the European colonizers, and remains to this day part of Anglo society. Machismo—which, as it is commonly used, translates in English into male chauvinism—is the one thing, if any, which should be labeled an "Anglo thing."

When Chicano men oppose the efforts of women to move against their oppression, they are actually opposing the struggle of every woman in this country aimed at changing a society in which Chicanos themselves are oppressed. They are saying to 51 percent of this country's population that we have no right to fight for our liberation.

Moreover, they are denying one half of La Raza this basic right. They are denying Raza women, who are triply oppressed, the right to struggle around their specific, real, and immediate needs.

In essence, they are doing just what the white, male rulers of this country have done. The white male rulers would want Chicanas to accept their oppression precisely because they understand that when Chicanas begin a movement demanding legal abortions, child care, and equal pay for equal work, this movement will pose a real threat to their ability to rule.

Opposition to the struggles of women to break the chains of their oppression is not in the interests of the oppressed but only in the interest of the oppressor. And that is the logic of the arguments of those who say that Chicanas do not want to or need to be liberated.

The same problem arose when the masses of people in this country began to move in opposition to the war in Vietnam. Because Black people did not until recently participate in massive numbers in antiwar demonstrations, the bourgeois media went on a campaign to convince us that the reason Blacks were not a visible component of these demonstrations was because the antiwar movement was a "white thing." Although, for a while, this tactic was successful in slowing down the progress of the Black nationalist movement, for which the question of the war is of vital importance, Black antiwar activity is now clearly rising.

But once again the white males who run this country are up to their old tricks. Only this time around it is the women's liberation movement which is a "white thing," and again the bourgeois media is a key tool for perpetrating this myth. As one Chicana explains, in an article entitled "Chicanas Speak Out" in *Salsipuedes*, published in Santa Barbara, California: "The real issue of the women's liberation movement is fighting the established female role in society which has kept women enslaved as human beings. But the news media portrays women's liberation people as karate-chopping, man-hating hippies."[2]

Among the many distortions about the feminist movement is the argument that women are simply fighting against men. One such statement which exemplifies this point of view appeared in an article by Enriqueta Vasquez some months ago in *El Grito del Norte*. Vasquez wrote:

> In looking at women's lib [sic] we see issues that are relevant to that materialistic, competitive society of the Gringo. This society is only able to function through the sharpening of wits and development of the human instinct of rivalry. For this same dominant society and mentality to arrive at a point where there is now a white women's liberation movement is *dangerous* and *cruel* in that that social structure has reached the point of fracture and competition of the male and female.

Thus, since the feminist movement is "antimale," when Chicanas attempt to organize against their own oppression they are accused of trying to divide the Chicano movement.

The appeal for "unity" based on the continued submission of women is a false one. While it is true that the unity of La Raza is the basic foundation of the Chicano movement, when Chicano men talk about maintaining La Familia and the "cultural heritage" of La Raza, they are in fact talking about maintaining the age-old concept of keeping the woman barefoot, pregnant, and in the kitchen. On the basis of the subordination of women there can be no real unity.

---

1. *Las Hijas de Cuahtemoc*, unnumbered edition, p. 9.

2. *Salsipuedes*, Vol. I, No. 5, p. 4.

MARGARET SLOAN

Black & Blacklesbian

A journalist, organizer, and poet, Margaret Sloan-Hunter (1947–2004) began her activism at age fourteen in Chicago rent strikes alongside Jesse Jackson. In 1971, she moved to New York to become an editor at the new *Ms.* magazine and was later a cofounder and first chair of the National Black Feminist Organization. Committed to unity between Black and white women, she pioneered workshops for white women in "unlearning racism" and traveled the country lecturing with Gloria Steinem: "I'm not Black Monday, Tuesday and Wednesday and a woman Thursday, Friday and Saturday," Steinem remembered her saying. In this brief cri de coeur, first published in November 1971 in the Chicago lesbian periodical *The Lavender Woman*, Sloan renders her experience as a Black lesbian in the women's movement.

WHAT HAVE you got to offer us? You wonder where we are and we say right in front of you. You offer us psychological rhetoric and we give you feelings and emotions which you charge are loud and violent. You cry dry tears while we bleed. You like to watch us dance for you but you never ask us to dance with you. You imagine/think/fantasize we fuck better which either keeps you on our backs or miles away. You assume we are mostly all dykes and the fem in us you try to butch. You use our blackness as an excuse more than we do and you never try to see the pain behind all our laughter. When you are around us you talk black and we find ourselves talking white and you even come to our parties bringing a 1969 Aretha Franklin record and when we confront you, you say we're too powerful to deal with and you don't come to our neighborhood after dark except in groups when *your* men have raped us (you too) for over 300 years. I can't call you my sister until you stop participating in my oppression. You can't have a struggle without all oppressed people—and black women, particularly black lesbians, have struggled harder than anyone. You need us and we can work and will work with you if only you accept us where we've been, where we are, where we come from.

GLORIA STEINEM

Sisterhood

Journalist Gloria Steinem (born 1934) came to national attention with a gritty muck-raking account of working undercover as a bunny at the New York Playboy Club (*Show Magazine*, May 1963). After attending Redstockings' 1969 taboo-breaking abortion speakout, she began promoting feminism full-time, most prominently as a founding and contributing editor of *Ms.*, and on frequent national speaking tours where, whenever possible, she co-lectured with a woman of color. Her rapid elevation by the media to movement spokesperson drew harsh criticism from feminists whose more radical positions received little media attention and whom Steinem did not represent. This article, describing her journey from what she calls "dissembling" to "sisterhood," appeared in *Ms.*'s preview issue in December 1971.

A VERY, VERY long time ago (about three or four years), I took a certain secure and righteous pleasure in saying the things that women are supposed to say.

I remember with pain—

"My work won't interfere with marriage. After all, I can always keep my typewriter at home." Or:

"I don't want to write about women's stuff. I want to write about foreign policy." Or:

"Black families were forced into matriarchy, so I see why Black women have to step back and let their men get ahead." Or:

"I know we're helping Chicano groups that are tough on women, but *that's their culture.*" Or:

"Who would want to join a women's group? I've never been a joiner, have you?" Or (when bragging):

"He says I write about abstract ideas like a man."

I suppose it's obvious from the kinds of statements I chose that I was secretly nonconforming. (I wasn't married, I was earning a living at a profession I cared about, and I had basically—if quietly—opted out of the "feminine" role.) But that made it all the more necessary to repeat some Conventional Wisdom, even to look as conventional as I could manage, if I was to avoid the punishments reserved by society for women who don't do as society says. I therefore learned to Uncle Tom with subtlety, logic, and humor. Sometimes I even believed it myself.

If it weren't for the Women's Movement, I might still be dissembling away. But the ideas of this great sea-change in women's view of ourselves are contagious and irresistible. They hit women like a revelation, as if we had left a small dark room and walked into the sun.

At first my discoveries seemed complex and personal. In fact, they were the same ones so many millions of women have made and are making. Greatly simplified, they went like this: Women are human beings first, with minor differences from men that apply largely to the act of reproduction. We share the dreams, capabilities, and weaknesses of all human beings, but our occasional pregnancies and other visible differences have been used—even more pervasively, if less brutally, than racial differences have been used—to mark us for an elaborate division of labor that may once have been practical but has since become cruel and false. The division is continued for clear reason, consciously or not: the economic and social profit of men as a group.

Once this feminist realization dawned, I reacted in what turned out to be predictable ways. First, I was amazed at the simplicity and obviousness of a realization that made sense, at last, of my life experience: I couldn't figure out why I hadn't seen it before. Second, I realized, painfully, how far that new vision of life was from the system around us, and how tough it would be to explain the feminist realization at all, much less to get people (especially, though not only, men) to accept so drastic a change.

But I tried to explain. God knows (*she* knows) that women try. We make analogies with other groups that have been marked for subservient roles in order to assist blocked imaginations. We supply endless facts and statistics of injustice, reeling them off until we feel like human information-retrieval machines. We lean heavily on the device of reversal. (If there is a male reader to whom all my pre-realization statements seem perfectly logical, for instance, let him substitute "men" for "women" or himself for me in each sentence, and see how he feels. "My work won't interfere with marriage. . . ." ". . . Chicana groups that are tough on men. . . ." You get the idea.)

We even use logic. If a woman spends a year bearing and nursing a child, for instance, she is supposed to have the primary responsibility for raising that child to adulthood. That's logic by the male definition, but it often makes women feel children are their only function or discourages them from being mothers at all. Wouldn't it be just as logical to say that the child has two parents, both equally responsible for child-rearing, and that therefore the father should compensate for that extra year by spending *more* than his half of the time with the child? Now *that's* logic.

Occasionally, these efforts at explaining succeed. More often, I get the feeling that we are speaking Urdu and the men are speaking Pali. As for logic, it's in the eye of the logician.

Painful or not, both stages of reaction to our discovery have a great reward. They give birth to sisterhood.

First, we share with each other the exhilaration of growth and self-discovery, the sensation of having the scales fall from our eyes. Whether we are giving other women this new knowledge or receiving it from them, the pleasure for all concerned is enormous. And very moving.

In the second stage, when we're exhausted from dredging up facts and arguments for the men whom we had previously thought advanced and intelligent, we make another simple discovery. Women understand. We may share experiences, make jokes, paint pictures, and describe humiliations that mean nothing to men, but *women understand.*

The odd thing about these deep and personal connections of women is that they often ignore barriers of age, economics, worldly experience, race, culture—all the barriers that, in male or mixed society, had seemed so difficult to cross.

I remember meeting with a group of women in Missouri who, because they had come in equal numbers from the small town and from its nearby campus, seemed to be split between wives with white gloves welded to their wrists and students with boots who talked about "imperialism" and "oppression." Planning for a child care center had brought them together, but the meeting seemed hopeless until three of the booted young women began to argue among themselves about a young male professor, the leader of the radicals on campus, who accused all women unwilling to run mimeograph machines of not being sufficiently devoted to the cause. As for child care centers, he felt their effect of allowing women to compete with men for jobs was part of the "feminization" of the American male and American culture.

"He sounds just like my husband," said one of the white-gloved women, "only he wants me to have bake-sales and collect door-to-door for his Republican Party."

The young women had sense enough to take it from there. What did boots or white gloves matter if they were all getting treated like servants and children? Before they broke up, they were discussing the myth of the vaginal orgasm and planning to meet every week. "Men think we're whatever it is we do for men," explained one of the housewives. "It's only by getting together with other women that we'll ever find out who we are."

Even racial differences become a little less hopeless once we discover this mutuality of our life experience as women. At a meeting run by black women domestics who had formed a job cooperative in Alabama, a white housewife asked me about the consciousness-raising sessions or "rap groups" that are the basic unit of the Women's Movement. I explained that while men, even minority men, usually had someplace where they could get together every day and be themselves, women were isolated in their houses; isolated from each other. We had no street corners, no bars, no offices, no territory that was recognized as ours. Rap groups were an effort to create that free place: an occasional chance for total honesty and support from our sisters.

As I talked about isolation, the feeling that there must be something wrong with us if we weren't content to be housekeepers and mothers, tears began to stream down the cheeks of this dignified woman—clearly as much of a surprise to her as to us. For the black women, some barrier was broken down by seeing her cry.

"He does it to us both, honey," said the black woman next to her, putting an arm around her shoulders. "If it's your own kitchen or somebody else's, you still don't get treated like people. Women's work just doesn't count."

The meeting ended with the housewife organizing a support group of white women who would extract from their husbands a living wage for domestic workers and help them fight the local hierarchy: a support group without which the domestic workers felt their small and brave cooperative could not survive.

As for the "matriarchal" argument that I swallowed in pre-feminist days, I now understand why many black women resent it and feel that it's the white sociologist's way of encouraging the black community to imitate a white suburban life style. ("If I end up cooking grits for revolutionaries," explained a black woman poet from Chicago, "it isn't my revolution. Black men and women need to work together for partnership, not patriarchy. You can't have liberation for half a race.") In fact, some black women wonder if criticism of the strength they were forced to develop isn't a way to keep half the black community working at lowered capacity and lowered pay, as well as to attribute some of black men's sufferings to black women, instead of to their real source—white racism. I wonder with them.

Looking back at all those male-approved things I used to say, the basic hang-up seems clear: a lack of esteem for women—black women, Chicana women, white women—and for myself.

This is the most tragic punishment that society inflicts on any second-class group. Ultimately, the brainwashing works, and we ourselves come to believe our group is inferior. Even if we achieve a little success in the world and think of ourselves as "different," we don't want to associate with our group. We want to identify up, not down (clearly my problem in not wanting to write about women, and not wanting to join women's groups). We want to be the only woman in the office, or the only black family on the block, or the only Jew in the club.

The pain of looking back at wasted, imitative years is enormous. Trying to write like men. Valuing myself and other women according to the degree of our acceptance by men—socially, in politics, and in our professions. It's as painful as it is now to hear two grown-up female human beings competing with each other on the basis of their husbands' status, like servants whose identity rests on the wealth or accomplishments of their employers.

And this lack of esteem that makes us put each other down is still the major enemy of sisterhood. Women who are conforming to society's expectations view the non-conformists with justifiable alarm. "Those noisy, unfeminine women," they say to themselves. "They will only make trouble for us all." Women who are quietly non-conforming, hoping nobody will notice, are even more alarmed because they have more to lose. And that makes sense, too.

Because the status quo protects itself by punishing all challengers, especially women whose rebellion strikes at the most fundamental social organization: the sex roles that convince half the population its identity depends on being first in work or in war, and the other half that it must serve as docile ("feminine") unpaid or underpaid labor. There seems to be no punishment inside the white male club that quite equals the ridicule and personal viciousness reserved for women who rebel. Attractive or young women who act forcefully are assumed to be male-controlled. If they succeed, it could only have been sexually, through men. Old women or women considered unattractive by male standards are accused of acting only out of bitterness, because they could not get a man. Any woman who chooses to behave like a full human being should be warned that the armies of the status quo will treat her as something of a dirty joke; that's their natural and first weapon. She will *need* sisterhood.

All of that is meant to be a warning but not a discouragement. There are so many more rewards than punishments.

For myself, I can now admit anger, and use it constructively, where once I would have submerged it and let it fester into guilt or collect for some destructive explosion.

I have met brave women who are exploring the outer edge of human possibility, with no history to guide them, and with a courage to make themselves vulnerable that I find moving beyond the words to express it.

I no longer think that I do not exist, which was my version of that lack of self-esteem afflicting many women. (If male standards weren't natural to me, and they were the only standards, how could I exist?) This means that I am less likely to need male values to identify myself with and am less vulnerable to classic arguments ("If you don't like me, you're not a Real Woman"—said by a man who is Coming On. "If you don't like me, you are not a Real Person, and you can't relate to other people"— said by anyone who understands blackmail as an art).

I can sometimes deal with men as equals and therefore can afford to like them for the first time.

I have discovered politics that are not intellectual or superimposed. They are organic, because I finally understand why I for years inexplicably identified with "out" groups. I belong to one, too. It will take a coalition of such groups to achieve a society in which, at a minimum, no one is born into a second-class role because of visible difference, because of race or of sex.

I no longer feel strange by myself, or with a group of women in public. I feel just fine.

I am continually moved to discover I have sisters.

I am beginning, just beginning, to find out who I am.

(from) The Housewife's Moment of Truth

Jane O'Reilly (born 1936) was introduced to feminism by Gloria Steinem, her friend and collleague at *New York* magazine. Later, with Steinem and others, she became a founding contributor to *Ms.*, writing the new magazine's first cover story, which is excerpted here. Written as a personal essay, a form that women writers deployed with wit and skill to advance awareness, O'Reilly's piece named the kind of epiphany that was turning women, housewives or not, into feminists as quickly as you could say "Click!"

L AST SUMMER I got a letter, from a man who wrote: "I do not agree with your last article, and I am cancelling my wife's subscription." The next day I got a letter from his wife saying, "*I* am not cancelling *my* subscription." Click!

On Fire Island my weekend hostess and I had just finished cooking breakfast, lunch, and washing dishes for both. A male guest came wandering into the kitchen just as the last dish was being put away and said, "How about something to eat?" He sat down, expectantly, and started to read the paper. Click! "You work all week," said the hostess, "and *I* work all week, and if you want something to eat, you can get it, and wash up after it yourself."

In New York last fall, my neighbors—named Jones—had a couple named Smith over for dinner. Mr. Smith kept telling his wife to get up and help Mrs. Jones. Click! Click! Two women radicalized at once.

A woman I know in St. Louis, who had begun to enjoy a little success writing a grain company's newsletter, came home to tell her husband about lunch in the executive dining room. She had planned a funny little anecdote about the deeply humorous pomposity of executives, when she noticed her husband rocking with laughter. "Ho ho, my little wife in an executive dining room." Click!

Last August, I was on a boat leaving an island in Maine. Two families were with me, and the mothers were discussing the troubles of cleaning up after a rental summer. "Bob cleaned up the bathroom for me, didn't you honey?"

she confided, gratefully patting her husband's knee. "Well, what the hell, it's vacation," he said, fondly. The two women looked at each other, and the queerest change came over their faces. "I got up at six this morning to make the sandwiches for the trip home from this 'vacation,'" the first one said. "So I wonder why I've thanked him at least six times for cleaning the bathroom?" Click! Click!

Attitudes are expressed in semantic equations that simply turn out to be two languages; one for men and another for women. One morning a friend of mine told her husband she would like to hire a baby sitter so she could get back to her painting. "Maybe when you start to make money from your pictures, then we could think about it," said her husband. My friend didn't stop to argue the inherent fallacy in his point—how could she make money if no one was willing to free her for work? She suggested that, instead of hiring someone, he could help with the housework a little more. "Well, I don't know, honey," he said, "I guess sharing the housework is all right if the wife is really contributing something, brings in a salary. . . ." For a terrible minute my friend thought she would kill her husband, right there at breakfast, in front of the children. For ten years, she had been covering furniture, hanging wallpaper, making curtains and refinishing floors so that they could afford the mortgage on their apartment. She had planned the money-saving menus so they could afford the little dinners for prospective clients. She had crossed town to save money on clothes so the family could have a new hi-fi. All the little advances in station—the vacations, the theater tickets, the new car—had been made possible by her crafty, endless, worried manipulation of the household expenses. "I was under the impression," she said, "that I *was* contributing something. Evidently my life's blood is simply a non-deductible expense."

In suburban Chicago, the party consisted of three couples. The women were a writer, a doctor and a teacher. The men were all lawyers. As the last couple arrived, the host said, jovially, "With a roomful of lawyers, we ought to have a good evening." Silence. Click! "What are we?" asked the teacher. "Invisible?"

In an office, a political columnist, male, was waiting to see the editor-in-chief. Leaning against a doorway, the columnist turned to the first woman he saw and said, "Listen, call Barry Brown and tell him I'll be late." Click! It wasn't because she happened to be an editor herself that she refused to make the call.

In the end, we are all housewives, the natural people to turn to when there is something unpleasant, inconvenient or inconclusive to be done. It will not do for women who have jobs to pretend that society's ills will be cured if all women are gainfully employed. In Russia, 70 per cent of the doctors and 20 per cent of the construction workers are women, but women still do *all* the housework. Some revolution. As the Russian women's saying goes, it simply freed us to do twice the work.

It will not do for women who are mostly housewives to say that Women's Liberation is fine for women who work, but has no relevance for them. Equal pay for equal work is only part of the argument—usually described as "the part I'll go along with."

We are all housewives. We would prefer to be persons. That is the part they *don't* go along with.

TILLIE OLSEN

(from) Women Who Are Writers in Our Century: One Out of Twelve

Labor activist and pioneering feminist Tillie Olsen (1912–2007) began her first novel when she was just nineteen. Publication of an excerpt in *The Partisan Review* (Spring 1934) led, three years later, to a contract from Random House. Olsen never fulfilled that contract, abandoning her writing in the press of domestic life. In 1962, on the strength of the story collection *Tell Me a Riddle* (1961), she was named a fellow at the newly formed Radcliffe Institute, which supported women artists and scholars. There, she worked on an essay exploring the silences in the lives of writers, women in particular. She first presented this essay at the 1971 meeting of the Modern Language Association; and the abandoned novel *Yonnondio: From the Thirties*, was finally published in 1974. Her own interrupted promise lends painful context to this account of the toll that poverty, marriage, and motherhood have exacted on the female literary tradition.

COMPARED TO the countless centuries of the silence of women, compared to the century preceding ours—the first in which women wrote in any noticeable numbers—ours has been a favorable one.

The road was cut many years ago, as Virginia Woolf reminds us:

> by Fanny Burney, by Aphra Behn, by Harriet Martineau, by Jane Austen, by George Eliot, many famous women and many more unknown and forgotten. . . . Thus, when I came to write . . . writing was a reputable and harmless occupation.

Predecessors, ancestors, a body of literature, an acceptance of the right to write: each in themselves an advantage.

In this second century we have access to areas of work and of life experience previously denied; higher education; longer lives; for the first time in human history, freedom from compulsory childbearing; freer bodies and attitudes toward sexuality; and—of the greatest importance to those like myself who come from generations of illiterate women—increasing literacy, and higher degrees of it. Each one of these a vast gain.

And the results?

Productivity: books of all manner and kind. My own crude sampling, having to be made without benefit of research assistants, secretary, studies (nobody's made them), or computer (to feed *Books in Print* into, for instance) indicates that four books are written by men, to every one by a woman.

Comparative earnings: ("equal pay for equal work"): no figures available.

Achievement: as gauged by what supposedly designates it: appearance in 20th Century literature courses, required reading lists, textbooks; in quality anthologies; the year's best, the decade's best, the fifty years' best; consideration by critics or in current reviews: *one woman writer for every twelve men.* For a week or two, make your own survey whenever you pick up an anthology, course bibliography, quality magazine or quarterly, book review section, book of criticism.

One woman writer of achievement for every twelve men writers so ranked. Is this proof again—and in this so much more favorable century—of women's innately inferior capacity for creative achievement?

Only a few months ago, during a Harvard-Radcliffe panel on "Women's Liberation, Myth or Reality," Diana Trilling asking why it is that women

> have not made even a fraction of the intellectual, scientific or artistic-cultural contributions which men have made

could come only to the traditional conclusion that

> it is not enough to blame women's place in culture or culture itself, because that leaves certain fundamental questions unanswered . . . necessarily raises the question of the biological aspects of the problem.

Biology: that difference. Evidently unconsidered, unknown (?) to her and the others who share her conclusion, are the centuries of prehistory during which biology did not deny equal contribution; and the other determining difference—not biology—between male and female in the centuries after; the past of women that should be part of every human consciousness, certainly every woman's consciousness (in the same way that the 400 years of bondage, colonialism, the slave passage are to black humans).

Work first:

Within our bodies we bore the race. Through us it was shaped, fed
and clothed. . . . Labour more toilsome and unending than that of
man was ours. . . . No work was too hard, no labor too strenuous
to exclude us.[1]

True for most women in most of the world still.

Unclean; taboo. The Devil's Gateway. The three steps behind; the girl babies
drowned in the river; the baby strapped to the back. Buried alive with the
lord, burned alive on the funeral pyre, burned as witch at the stake. Stoned to
death for adultery. Beaten, raped. Bartered. Bought and sold. Concubinage,
prostitution, white slavery. The hunt, the sexual prey, "I am a lost creature, o
the poor Clarissa." Purdah, the veil of Islam, domestic confinement. Illiterate.
Excluded, excluded, excluded from council, ritual, activity, language, when
there was neither biological nor economic reason to be excluded.

Religion, when all believed. In sorrow shalt thou bring forth children. May
thy wife's womb never cease from bearing. Neither was the man created for
the woman but the woman for the man. Let the woman learn in silence and
in all subjection. (Contrary to biological birth fact) Adam's rib. The Jewish
male morning prayer: thank God I was not born a woman. Silence in holy
places, seated apart, or not permitted entrance at all; castration of boys because
women too profane to sing in church.

And for the comparative handful of women born into the privileged classes:
being, not doing; man does, woman is; to you the world says work, to us it
says seem. "God is thy law, thou mine." Isolated. Cabin'd, cribb'd, confin'd;
the private sphere. Bound feet: corseted, cosseted, bedecked; denied one's
body. Powerlessness. Fear of rape, male strength. Fear of aging. Subject to.
Fear of expressing capacities. Soft attractive graces; the mirror to magnify
man. Marriage as property arrangement. The vices of slaves:[2] dissembling, flattering, manipulating, appeasing. Bolstering. Vicarious living, infantilization,
trivialization. Parasitism, individualism, madness. Shut up, you're only a girl.
O Elizabeth, why couldn't you have been born a boy? Roles, discontinuities,
part self, part time: (20th century woman).

How is it that women have not made a fraction of the intellectual,
scientific, or artistic-cultural contributions that men have made?

1. Olive Schreiner, *Women and Labour.*
2. Elizabeth Barrett Browning's phrase.

Only in the context of this punitive difference in circumstance, in history, between the sexes; this past, hidden or evident, that though objectively obsolete, (yes, even the toil and the compulsory childbearing obsolete) continues so terribly, so determiningly to live on,—can the question be answered or my subject here today—the woman writer in our century: one out of twelve—be understood.

How much it takes to become a writer. Bent (far more common than we assume), circumstances, time, development of craft—but beyond that: how much conviction as to the importance of what one has to say, one's right to say it. And the will, the measureless store of belief in oneself to be able to come to, cleave to, find the form for one's own life comprehensions. Difficult for any male not born into a class that breeds such confidence. Almost impossible for a girl, a woman.

The leeching of belief, of will; the damaging of capacity; begin so early. Sparse indeed is the literature on the pain, the way of denial, to small girl children of the development of their endowment as born human: active, vigorous bodies; exercise of the power to do, to make, to investigate, to invent, to conquer obstacles; to resist violations of the self; to think, create, choose; to attain community, confidence in self. Little has been written on the harm of instilling constant concern with appearance; the need to please, to support; the training in acceptance, deferring. Little has been written in our century to add even to George Eliot's *Mill on the Floss* on the effect of the differing treatment—"climate of expectation"—for boys and for girls.

But it is there if one knows how to read for it, and indelibly there in the damage. One—out of twelve.

In the vulnerable girl years, unlike their sisters in the previous century, women writers go to college.[3] The kind of experience it may be for them is stunningly documented in Elaine Showalter's "Women and the Literary Curriculum."[4] Freshman texts in which women have little place, if at all; language itself, all achievement, anything to do with the human in male terms: *Man in Crises; The Individual and His World.* Three hundred thirteen male writers taught; seventeen women writers. That classic of adolescent rebellion: *Portrait of the Artist as a Young Man,* and sagas (male) of the quest for identity (but then Erikson, the father of the concept, propounds that identity concerns girls only insofar as making themselves into attractive beings for the right kind of man). Most, not all, of the predominantly male literature studied, written by

3. True almost without exception among the writers who are women in *20th Century Authors* and *Contemporary Authors.*
4. *College English,* May, 1971.

men whose understandings are not universal, but restrictively male; and in our time, as Mary Ellmann, Kate Millett, and Dolores Schmidt have pointed out, more and more surface, hostile, and stereotypic in portraying women.

In a writer's young years, susceptibility to the vision and style of the great is extreme. Add the aspiration-denying implication, consciously felt or not, that (as Woolf noted years ago) women writers, women's experience, and literature written by women, are by definition minor. (Mailer will not grant even the minor: "the one thing a writer has to have is balls.") No wonder that Showalter observes:

> Women (students) are estranged from their own experience and unable to perceive its shape and authenticity, in part because they do not see it mirrored and given resonance in literature. . . . They have no faith in the validity of their own perceptions and experiences, rarely seeing them confirmed in literature, or accepted in criticism . . . (They) notoriously lack the happy confidence, the exuberant sense of value of their individual observations which enables young men to risk making fools of themselves, for the sake of an idea.

Harms difficult to work through. Nevertheless, some young women (others are already lost) maintain their ardent intention to write—fed indeed by the very glories of some of this literature that puts them down.

But other invisible worms are finding out the bed of crimson joy. Self doubt; seriousness questioned by the hours agonizing over appearance; concentration shredded into attracting, being attractive; the absorbing, real need and love for working with words felt as hypocritical self delusion, for what seems (and is) esteemed is whether or not the phone rings for you, and how often. High aim, and accomplishment towards it, discounted by the prevalent attitude that, as girls will probably marry (attitudes not applied to boys who will probably marry) writing is no more than an attainment of a dowry to be spent later according to the needs and circumstances within the true vocation: husband and family. The growing conviction that going on will threaten other needs; that "a woman has to sacrifice all claims to femininity and family to be a writer."[5]

And the agony—peculiarly mid-century, escaped by their sisters of pre-Freudian, pre-Jungian times—that "creation and femininity are incompatible." Anaïs Nin's words:

5. Plath: a letter when a graduate student.

> The aggressive act of creation; the guilt for creating. I did not want to rival man; to steal man's creation, his thunder. I must protect them, not outshine them.

The acceptance—against one's experienced reality—of the sexist notion that the act of creation is not as inherently natural to a woman as to a man, but rooted instead in unnatural competition, or envy, or imitation, or thwarted sexuality.

And in all the usual college teaching—the English, history, psychology, sociology courses—little to help that young woman understand the source or nature of this inexplicable draining unsureness, self doubt, loss of aspiration, of confidence.

It is all there in the extreme in Plath's *Bell Jar*—that portrait of the artist as a young woman (significantly, one of the few that we have)—from the precarious sense of vocation to the paralyzing conviction that (in a sense different than she wrote years later)

> Perfection is terrible. It cannot have children.
> It tamps the womb.

And indeed, in our century as in the last, until very recently almost all distinguished achievement has come from childless women: Willa Cather, Ellen Glasgow, Gertrude Stein, Edith Wharton, Virginia Woolf, Elizabeth Bowen, Katherine Mansfield, Isak Dinesen, Katherine Anne Porter, Dorothy Richardson, Henry Handel Richardson, Susan Glaspell, Dorothy Parker, Lillian Hellman, Eudora Welty, Djuna Barnes, Anaïs Nin, Ivy Compton-Burnett, Elizabeth Madox Roberts, Christina Stead, Carson McCullers, Flannery O'Connor, Jean Stafford, May Sarton, Josephine Herbst, Janet Frame, Lillian Smith, Iris Murdoch, Joyce Carol Oates, Lorraine Hansberry.

Most never questioned, or at least accepted, this different condition for achievement, not required of men writers. Few asked the fundamental human equality question regarding it that Elizabeth Mann Borghese, Thomas Mann's daughter, asked when she was 18 and sent to a psychiatrist for help in getting over an unhappy love affair (revealing also an unrealistic working ambition to become a great musician although "women cannot be great musicians"). "You must choose between your art and fulfillment as a woman," the analyst told her, "between music and family life." "Why?" she asked, "Why must I choose? No one said to Toscanini or to Bach or my father, that they must choose between their art and fulfillment as a man, family life. . . . Injustice everywhere." Not where it is free choice. But where it is forced because of the circumstances for the sex into which one is born—a choice men do not have to make in order to do their work—that is not choice, that is a working of injustice. How much of the one to twelve ratio is accounted for by those lost here?

What possible difference, you may ask, does it make to literature whether or not a woman writer remains childless—free choice or not—especially in view of the marvels these childless women have created.

Might there not have been other marvels as well, or other dimensions to these marvels? Might there not have been present profound aspects and understandings of human life as yet largely absent in literature?

More and more women writers in our century, primarily in the last two decades, are assuming as their right fullness of work *and* family life, previously the prerogative of men. I hope and I fear for what will result. I hope for complex new richness that will come into literature. I fear, because unlike men writers who made the same choice, they do not have wives; nor a mother (except themselves) for their children.[6] So little has the fundamental situation changed that even those who can afford help, good schools, summer camps, may suffer what 70 years ago W.E.B. Du Bois called The Damnation of Women: "that only at the sacrifice of the chance to do their best work can women bear and rear children."

> Substantial creative achievement demands time . . . and with rare exceptions only full time workers have created it.[7]

I am quoting myself from "Silences,"[8] a talk nine years ago. In motherhood, as it is structured,

> circumstances for sustained creation are almost impossible. Not because the capacities to create no longer exist, or the need (though for a while as in any fullness of life the need may be obscured),

6. Among those with children: Harriet Arnow, Mary Lavin, Mary McCarthy, Elizabeth Janeway, Tess Slesinger, Storm Jameson, Janet Lewis, Jean Rhys, Kay Boyle, Dorothy Canfield Fisher, Pearl Buck, Josephine Johnson, Hortense Calisher, Grace Paley, Caroline Gordon, Shirley Jackson; and a sampling in the unparalleled last two decades: Doris Lessing, Edna O'Brien, Margaret Drabble, Cynthia Ozick, Pauli Murray, Joanne Greenberg (Hannah Green), Joan Didion, Penelope Mortimer, Alison Lurie, Doris Betts, Muriel Spark, Lael Wertenbraker, Maxine Kumin, Lore Segal, Alice Walker, Margaret Walker, Mary Gray Hughes, Sallie Bingham, Norma Rosen. Some wrote before children, some only in the middle or late years afterward.

7. This does not mean these full time writers were hermetic or denied themselves social or personal life (think of James, Turgenev, Tolstoy, Balzac, Joyce, etc.).

8. Reprinted in *Harper's*, October, 1965.

but . . . the need cannot be first. It can have at best only part self, part time. . . . Motherhood means being instantly interruptible, responsive, responsible. Children need one *now* (and remember, in our society, the family must often try to be the center for love and health the outside world is not). The very fact that these are needs of love, not duty, that one feels them as one's self; that there is no one else to be responsible for these needs, gives them primacy. It is distraction, not meditation, that becomes habitual; interruption, not continuity; spasmodic, not constant, toil. Work interrupted, deferred, postponed makes blockage—at best, lesser accomplishment. Unused capacities atrophy, cease to be.

There are other vulnerabilities to loss, diminishment. Rare is the woman writer who has not had bred into her what Virginia Woolf called "The Angel in the House," who "must charm, sympathize, conciliate . . . be extremely sensitive to the needs and moods and wishes of others before her own . . . excel in the difficult arts of family life."

It was she who used to come between me and my paper . . . who bothered me and wasted my time and so tormented me that at last I killed her . . . or she would have plucked out my heart as a writer.[9]

There is another angel, so lowly as to be invisible, although without her no art, or any human endeavor could be carried on for even one day—the essential angel, with whom Virginia Woolf (and most women writers, still in the privileged class) did not have to contend—the angel who must assume the physical responsibilities for daily living, for the maintenance of life.

Almost always in one form or another (usually in the wife, two-angel form) she has dwelt in the house of men. She it was who made it possible for Joseph Conrad to "wrestle with the Lord for his creation":

Mind and will and conscience engaged to the full, hour after hour, day after day . . . never aware of the even flow of daily life made easy and noiseless for me by a silent, watchful, tireless affection.

The angel who was "essential" to Rilke's "great task":

9. "Professions for Women"—Virginia Woolf, *Collected Essays.*

like a sister who would run the house like a friendly climate, there or not there as one wished . . . and would ask for nothing except just to be there working and warding at the frontiers of the invisible.

Men (even part time writers who must carry on work other than writing[10]) have had and have this inestimable advantage towards productivity. I cannot help but notice how curiously absent both of these angels, these watchers and warders at the frontiers of the invisible, are from the actual contents of most men's books, except perhaps on the dedication page:

To my wife, without whom. . . .

Mailer made clear that as a writer he was not so much a prisoner of sex as of service—supportive, secretarial, household.

I digress, and yet I do not; the disregard for the essential angel, the large absence of any sense of her in literature or elsewhere, has not only cost literature great contributions from those so occupied or partially occupied, but by failing to help create an arousing awareness (as literature has done in other realms) has contributed to the agonizingly slow elimination of this technologically and socially obsolete, human-wasting drudgery: Virginia Woolf's dream of a long since possible

economical, powerful and efficient future when houses will be cleaned by a puff of hot wind.

10. As do many women writers.

CHARLOTTE BUNCH

Lesbians in Revolt

After cofounding the Women's Liberation Center (1968–71) in Washington, D.C., and organizing one of the first national women's liberation conferences (held near Chicago, November 1968), Charlotte Bunch (born 1944) cofounded, in 1971, the D.C. lesbian-separatist collective The Furies. (The house where The Furies lived communally is listed on the National Register of Historic Places.) This essay for lesbian separatism and against male supremacy, homophobia, and heterosexism was described by Bunch as a "theoretical manifesto" for the collective and was published in the January 1972 inaugural issue of the group's eponymous national newspaper. In later writings Bunch questioned whether separatism is an effective long-term strategy and increasingly focused on international social justice.

THE DEVELOPMENT of Lesbian-feminist politics as the basis for the liberation of women is our top priority; this article outlines our present ideas. In our society which defines all people and institutions for the benefit of the rich, white male, the Lesbian is in revolt. In revolt because she defines herself in terms of women and rejects the male definitions of how she should feel, act, look, and live. To be a Lesbian is to love oneself, woman, in a culture that denigrates and despises women. The Lesbian rejects male sexual/political domination; she defies his world, his social organization, his ideology, and his definition of her as inferior. Lesbianism puts women first while the society declares the male supreme. Lesbianism threatens male supremacy at its core. When politically conscious and organized, it is central to destroying our sexist, racist, capitalist, imperialist system.

LESBIANISM IS A POLITICAL CHOICE

Male society defines Lesbianism as a sexual act, which reflects men's limited view of women: they think of us only in terms of sex. They also say Lesbians are not real women, so a real woman is one who gets fucked by men. We say that a Lesbian is a woman whose sense of self and energies, including sexual energies, center around women—she is woman identified. The woman-identified-woman commits herself to other women for political, emotional, physical, and economic support. Women are important to her. She is important to herself. Our society demands that commitment from women be reserved for men.

The Lesbian, woman-identified-woman, commits herself to women not only as an alternative to oppressive male/female relationships but primarily because she *loves* women. Whether consciously or not, by her actions, the Lesbian has recognized that giving support and love to men over women perpetuates the system that oppresses her. If women do not make a commitment to each other, which includes sexual love, we deny ourselves the love and value traditionally given to men. We accept our second class status. When women do give primary energies to other women, then it is possible to concentrate fully on building a movement for our liberation.

Woman-identified Lesbianism is, then, more than a sexual preference, it is a political choice. It is political because relationships between men and women are essentially political, they involve power and dominance. Since the Lesbian actively rejects that relationship and chooses women, she defies the established political system.

Lesbianism, by Itself, Is Not Enough

Of course, not all Lesbians are consciously woman-identified, nor are all committed to finding common solutions to the oppression they suffer as women and Lesbians. Being a Lesbian is part of challenging male supremacy, but not the end. For the Lesbian or heterosexual woman, there is no individual solution to oppression.

The Lesbian may think that she is free since she escapes the personal oppression of the individual male/female relationship. But to the society she is still a woman, or worse, a visible Lesbian. On the street, at the job, in the schools, she is treated as an inferior and is at the mercy of men's power and whims. (I've never heard of a rapist who stopped because his victim was a Lesbian.) This society hates women who love women, and so, the Lesbian, who escapes male dominance in her private home, receives it doubly at the hands of male society; she is harrassed, outcast, and shuttled to the bottom. Lesbians must become feminists and fight against woman oppression, just as feminists must become Lesbians if they hope to end male supremacy.

U.S. society encourages individual solutions, apolitical attitudes, and reformism to keep us from political revolt and out of power. Men who rule, and male leftists who seek to rule, try to depoliticize sex and the relations between men and women in order to prevent us from acting to end our oppression and challenging their power. As the question of homosexuality has become public, reformists define it as a private question of who you sleep with in order to sidetrack our understanding of the politics of sex. For the Lesbian-feminist, it is not private; it is a political matter of oppression, domination, and power. Reformists offer solutions which make no basic changes in the system that oppresses us, solutions which keep power in the hands of the oppressor. The only way oppressed people end their oppression is by seizing power: People whose rule depends on the subordination of others do not voluntarily stop oppressing others. Our subordination is the basis of male power.

SEXISM IS THE ROOT OF ALL OPPRESSION

The first division of labor, in pre-history, was based on sex: men hunted, women built the villages, took care of children, and farmed. Women collectively controlled the land, language, culture, and the communities. Men were able to conquer women with the weapons that they developed for hunting when it became clear that women were leading a more stable, peaceful, and desirable existence. We do not know exactly how this conquest took place, but it is clear that the original imperialism was male over female: the male claiming the female body and her service as his territory (or property).

Having secured the domination of women, men continued this pattern of suppressing people, now on the basis of tribe, race, and class. Although there have been numerous battles over class, race, and nation during the past 3000 years, none has brought the liberation of women. While these other forms of oppression must be ended, there is no reason to believe that our liberation will come with the smashing of capitalism, racism, or imperialism today. Women will be free only when we concentrate on fighting male supremacy.

Our war against male supremacy does, however, involve attacking the latter day dominations based on class, race, and nation. As Lesbians who are outcasts from every group, it would be suicidal to perpetuate these man-made divisions among ourselves. We have no heterosexual privileges, and when we publically assert our Lesbianism, those of us who had them lose many of our class and race privileges. Most of our privileges as women are granted to us by our relationships to men (fathers, husbands, boyfriends) whom we now reject. This does not mean that there is no racism or class chauvinism within us, but we must destroy these divisive remnants of privileged behavior among ourselves as the first step toward their destruction in the society. Race, class, and national oppressions come from men, serve ruling class white men's interests, and have no place in a woman-identified revolution.

Lesbianism Is the Basic Threat to Male Supremacy

Lesbianism is a threat to the ideological, political, personal, and economic basis of male supremacy. The Lesbian threatens the ideology of male supremacy by destroying the lie about female inferiority, weakness, passivity, and by denying women's "innate" need for men. Lesbians literally do not need men (even for procreation if the science of cloning is developed).

The Lesbian's independence and refusal to support one man undermines the personal power that men exercise over women. Our rejection of heterosexual sex challenges male domination in its most individual and common form. We offer all women something better than submission to personal oppression. We offer the beginning of the end of collective and individual male supremacy. Since men of all races and classes depend on female support and submission for practical tasks and feeling superior, our refusal to submit will force some to examine their sexist behavior, to break down their own destructive privileges over other humans, and to fight against those privileges in other men. They will have to build new selves that do not depend on oppressing women and learn to live in social structures that do not give them power over anyone.

Heterosexuality separates women from each other; it makes women define themselves through men; it forces women to compete against each other for men and the privilege which comes through men and their social standing. Heterosexual society offers women a few privileges as compensations if they give up their freedom: for example, mothers are respected and "honored," wives or lovers are socially accepted and given some economic and emotional security, a woman gets physical protection on the street when she stays with her man, etc. The privileges give heterosexual women a personal and political stake in maintaining the status quo.

The Lesbian receives none of these heterosexual privileges or compensations since she does not accept the male demands on her. She has little vested interest in maintaining the present political system since all of its institutions—church, state, media, health, schools—work to keep her down. If she understands her oppression, she has nothing to gain by supporting white rich male America and much to gain from fighting to change it. She is less prone to accept reformist solutions to women's oppression.

Economics is a crucial part of woman oppression, but our analysis of the relationship between capitalism and sexism is not complete. We know that Marxist economic theory does not sufficiently consider the role of women or Lesbians, and we are presently working on this area.

However, as a beginning, some of the ways that Lesbians threaten the economic system are clear: In this country, women work for men in order to survive, on the job and in the home. The Lesbian rejects this division of labor at its roots; she refuses to be a man's property, to submit to the unpaid labor system of housework and childcare. She rejects the nuclear family as the basic unit of production and consumption in capitalist society.

The Lesbian is also a threat on the job because she is not the passive/part-time woman worker that capitalism counts on to do boring work and be part of a surplus labor pool. Her identity and economic support do not come through men, so her job is crucial and she cares about job conditions, wages, promotion, and status. Capitalism cannot absorb large numbers of women demanding stable employment, decent salaries, and refusing to accept their traditional job exploitation. We do not understand yet the total effect that this increased job dissatisfaction will have. It is, however, clear that as women become more intent upon taking control of their lives, they will seek more control over their jobs, thus increasing the strains on capitalism and enhancing the power of women to change the economic system.

Lesbians Must Form Our Own Movement to Fight Male Supremacy

Feminist-lesbianism, as the most basic threat to male supremacy, picks up part of the Women's Liberation analysis of sexism and gives it force and direction. Women's Liberation lacks direction now because it has failed to understand the importance of heterosexuality in maintaining male supremacy and because it has failed to face class and race as real differences in women's behavior and political needs. As long as straight women see Lesbianism as a bedroom issue, they hold back the development of politics and strategies which would put an end to male supremacy and they give men an excuse for not dealing with their sexism.

Being a Lesbian means ending your identification with, allegiance to, dependence on, and support of heterosexuality. It means ending your personal stake in the male world so that you join women, individually and collectively, in the struggle to end your oppression. Lesbianism is the key to liberation and only women who cut their ties to male privilege can be trusted to remain serious in the struggle against male dominance. Those who remain tied to men, individually or in political theory, cannot always put women first. It is not that heterosexual women are evil or do not care about their sisters. It is because the very essence, definition, and nature of heterosexuality is men first. Every woman has experienced that desolation when her sister puts her man first in the final crunch: heterosexuality demands that she do so. As long as women still benefit from heterosexuality, receive its privileges and security, they will at some point have to betray their sisters, especially Lesbian sisters who do not receive those benefits.

Women in women's liberation have understood the importance of having meetings and other events for women only. It has been clear that dealing with men divides us and saps our energies and that it is not the job of the oppressed to explain our oppression to the oppressor. Women also have seen that collectively, men will not deal with their sexism until they are forced to do so. Yet, many of these same women continue to have primary relationships with men individually and do not understand why Lesbians find this oppressive. Lesbians cannot grow politically or personally in a situation which denies the basis of our politics: that Lesbianism is political, that heterosexuality is crucial to maintaining male supremacy.

Lesbians must form our own political movement in order to grow. Changes which will have more than token effects on our lives will be led by woman-identified Lesbians who understand the nature of our oppression and are therefore in a position to end it.

JOHNNIE TILLMON

Welfare Is a Women's Issue

Johnnie Tillmon (1926–1995), a leader of the welfare rights movement, published this celebrated call-to-arms in the premier issue of *Ms.* (Spring 1972). As a single mother of six and a new welfare recipient, Tillmon began organizing welfare mothers in her housing project in 1963; by 1972 she was executive director of the National Welfare Rights Organization (1966–75). Here Tillmon details the connections between sexism, racism, and class oppression in the government's brutal, paternalistic treatment of the poor, especially women on welfare.

I'M A WOMAN. I'm a black woman. I'm a poor woman. I'm a fat woman. I'm a middle-aged woman. And I'm on welfare.

In this country, if you're any one of those things—poor, black, fat, female, middle-aged, on welfare—you count less as a human being. If you're *all* those things, you don't count at all. Except as a statistic.

I am a statistic.

I am 45 years old. I have raised six children.

I grew up in Arkansas, and I worked there for fifteen years in a laundry, making about $20 or $30 a week, picking cotton on the side for carfare. I moved to California in 1959 and worked in a laundry there for nearly four years. In 1963, I got too sick to work anymore. My husband and I had split up. Friends helped me to go on welfare.

They didn't call it welfare. They called it A.F.D.C.—Aid to Families with Dependent Children. Each month I get $363 for my kids and me. I pay $128 a month rent; $30 for utilities, which include gas, electricity, and water; $120 for food and non-edible household essentials; $50 for school lunches for the three children in junior and senior high school who are not eligible for reduced-cost meal programs. This leaves exactly $5 per person per month for everything else—clothing, shoes, recreation, incidental personal expenses and transportation. This check allows $1 a month for transportation for me but none for my children. That's how we live.

There are millions of statistics like me. Some on welfare. Some not. And some, really poor, who don't even know they're entitled to welfare. Not all of them are black. Not at all. In fact, the majority—about two-thirds—of all the poor families in the country are white.

Welfare's like a traffic accident. It can happen to anybody, but especially it happens to women.

And that's why welfare is a women's issue. For a lot of middle-class women in this country, Women's Liberation is a matter of concern. For women on welfare it's a matter of survival.

Survival. That's why we had to go on welfare. And that's why we can't get off welfare now. Not us women. Not until we do something about liberating poor women in this country.

Because up until now we've been raised to expect to work, all our lives, for nothing. Because we are the worst-educated, the least-skilled, and the lowest-paid people there are. Because we have to be almost totally responsible for our children. Because we are regarded by everybody as dependents. That's why we are on welfare. And that's why we stay on it.

Welfare is all about dependency.

Welfare is the most prejudiced institution in this country, even more than marriage, which it tries to imitate. Let me explain that a little.

Forty-four per cent of all poor families are headed by women. That's bad enough. But the *families* on A.F.D.C. aren't really families. Because 99 per cent of them are headed by women. That means there is no man around. In half the states there really can't be men around because A.F.D.C. says if there is an "able-bodied" man around, then you can't be on welfare. If the kids are going to eat, and the man can't get a job, then he's got to go. So his kids can eat.

The truth is that A.F.D.C. is like a super-sexist marriage. You trade in *a* man for *the* man. But you can't divorce him if he treats you bad. He can divorce you, of course, cut you off anytime he wants. But in that case, *he* keeps the kids, not you.

The man runs everything. In ordinary marriage, sex is supposed to be for your husband. On A.F.D.C., you're not supposed to have any sex at all. You give up control of your own body. It's a condition of aid. You may even have to agree to get your tubes tied so you can never have more children just to avoid being cut off welfare.

The man, the welfare system, controls your money. He tells you what to buy, what not to buy, where to buy it, and how much things cost. If things—rent, for instance—really cost more than he says they do, it's just too bad for you. He's always right. Everything is budgeted down to the last penny; and you've got to make your money stretch.

The man can break into your house any time he wants to and poke into your things. You've got no right to protest. You've got no right to privacy when you go on welfare.

Like I said, welfare's a super-sexist marriage.

In fact, welfare was invented mostly for women. It grew out of something called the Mother's Pension Laws. To be eligible, you had to be female, you had to be a mother, you had to be "worthy." "Worthy" meant were your kids "legitimate," was your home "suitable," were you "proper"?

In 1935, the Mother's Pension Laws became part of the Social Security system. And they changed the name of the program to Aid to Families with Dependent Children.

Of course now there are other welfare programs, other kinds of people on welfare—the blind, the disabled, the aged. (Many of them are women, too, especially the aged.) Those others make up just over a third of all the welfare caseloads. We A.F.D.C.s are two-thirds. But when the politicians talk about the "welfare cancer eating at our vitals," they're not talking about the aged, blind and disabled. Nobody minds them. They're the "deserving poor." Politicians are talking about A.F.D.C. Politicians are talking about us—the women who head up 99 per cent of the A.F.D.C. families—and our kids. We're the "cancer," the "undeserving poor." Mothers and children.

In fact, welfare isn't even for mothers. It's for the children. It's like a bonus for reproducing the race. Some bonus—all of $720 a year or $60 a month for a family of four if you live in Mississippi. It's more in other places—up to $346 a month for a family of four in New Jersey. But nowhere, nohow, is it enough to live on.

In this country, we believe in something called the "work ethic." That means that your work is what gives you human worth. But the work ethic itself is a double standard. It applies to men, and to women on welfare. It doesn't apply to all women. If you're a society lady from Scarsdale and you spend all your time sitting on your prosperity paring your nails, well, that's okay. Women aren't supposed to work. They're supposed to be married.

But if you don't have a man to pay for everything, particularly if you have kids, then everything changes. You've "failed" as a woman, because you've failed to attract and keep a man. There's something wrong with you. It can't possibly be the man's fault, his lack of responsibility. It must be yours. That's why Governor Reagan can get away with slandering A.F.D.C. recipients, calling them "lazy parasites," "pigs at the trough," and such. We've been trained to believe that the only reason people are on welfare is because there's something wrong with their character. If people have "motivation," if people only *want* to work, they can, and they will be able to support themselves and their kids in decency.

If this were true, we wouldn't have the working poor. Right now, 66 per cent of the "employable" mothers are already employed—many full time—but at such pitifully low wages that we still need, and are entitled to, public assistance to survive.

The truth is a job doesn't necessarily mean an adequate income. A woman with three kids—not twelve kids, mind you, just three kids—that woman, earning the full Federal minimum wage of $1.60 an hour, is still stuck in poverty. She is below the Government's own official poverty line. There are some ten million jobs that now pay less than the minimum wage, and if you're a woman, you've got the best chance of getting one. Why would a 45-year-old woman work all day in a laundry ironing shirts at 90-some cents an hour? Because she knows there's some place lower she could be. She could be on welfare. Society needs women on welfare as "examples" to let every woman, factory workers and housewife workers alike, know what will happen if she lets up, if she's laid off, if she tries to go it alone without a man. So these ladies stay on their feet or on their knees all their lives instead of asking *why* they're only getting 90-some cents an hour, instead of daring to fight and complain.

And still, 33 per cent of the employable mothers are looking for work.

We are this country's source of cheap labor. But we can't, some of us, get any jobs.

The President keeps repeating the "dignity of work" idea. What dignity? Wages are the measure of dignity that society puts on a job. Wages and nothing else. There is no dignity in starvation. Nobody denies, least of all poor women, that there is dignity and satisfaction in being able to support your kids through honest labor.

We wish we could do it.

The problem is that our country's economic policies deny the dignity and satisfaction of self-sufficiency to millions of people—the millions who suffer every day in underpaid dirty jobs—and still don't have enough to survive.

People still believe that old lie that A.F.D.C. mothers keep on having kids just to get a bigger welfare check. On the average, another baby means another $35 a month—barely enough for food and clothing. Having babies for profit is a lie that only men could make up, and only men could believe. Men, who never have to bear the babies or have to raise them and maybe send them to war.

There are a lot of other lies that male society tells about welfare mothers: That A.F.D.C. mothers are immoral. That A.F.D.C. mothers are lazy, misuse their welfare checks, spend it all on booze and are stupid and incompetent.

If people are willing to believe these lies, it's partly because they're just special versions of the lies that society tells about *all* women.

For instance, the notion that all A.F.D.C. mothers are lazy: that's just a negative version of the idea that women don't work and don't want to. It's a way of rationalizing the male policy of keeping women as domestic slaves.

The notion that A.F.D.C. mothers are immoral is another way of saying that all women are likely to become whores unless they're kept under control by men and marriage.

A.F.D.C. mothers misuse their welfare checks? That's simply a justification for harassment. It comes from the male theory that women have no head for money, that they're naturally frivolous. In fact, an A.F.D.C. mother's probably got a better head for money than Rockefeller. She has to. She has so little to begin with that she's got to make every penny count, if she and her kids are even going to survive.

A.F.D.C. mothers are stupid, incompetent? That allows welfare officials to feel good about being paternalistic and justifies their policy of preventing A.F.D.C. mothers from making decisions about their own lives. It even explains why people are on welfare in the first place: because they're dumb, because there's something wrong with them.

A.F.D.C. mothers are the cause of slums and high taxes? Well, what's that but a special version of the notion that Eve, and Eve only, brought sin into the world? Welfare isn't the cause of high taxes. War is. Plus a lot of other things that poor women would like to see changed.

Society can continue to believe these lies only so long as women themselves believe them, as long as women sit still for them.

Even many of my own sisters on welfare believe these things about themselves.

Many ladies on welfare never get over their shame. But those of us who get beyond it are some of the strongest, most liberated women in this country.

To understand how this can be, you've got to remember that women on welfare are subject to all the same phony "female" ideals as all other women. But at the same time they're denied any opportunity to live up to those ideals.

On TV, a woman learns that human worth means beauty and that beauty means being thin, white, young and rich.

She learns that her body is really disgusting the way it is, and that she needs all kinds of expensive cosmetics to cover it up.

She learns that a "real woman" spends her time worrying about how her bathroom bowl smells; that being important means being middle class, having two cars, a house in the suburbs, and a minidress under your maxicoat. In other words, an A.F.D.C. mother learns that being a "real woman" means being all the things she isn't and having all the things she can't have.

Either it breaks you, and you start hating yourself, or you break it.

There's one good thing about welfare. It kills your illusions about yourself, and about where this society is really at. It's laid out for you straight. You have to learn to fight, to be aggressive, or you just don't make it. If you can survive being on welfare, you can survive anything. It gives you a kind of freedom, a sense of your own power and togetherness with other women.

Maybe it is we poor welfare women who will really liberate women in this country. We've already started on our own welfare plan. *

Along with other welfare recipients, we have organized together so we can have some voice. Our group is called the National Welfare Rights Organization (N.W.R.O.). We put together our own welfare plan, called Guaranteed Adequate Income (G.A.I.), which would eliminate sexism from welfare. There would be no "categories"—men, women, children, single, married, kids, no kids—just poor people who need aid. You'd get paid according to need and family size only—$6,500 for a family of four (which is the Department of Labor's estimate of what's adequate), and that would be upped as the cost of living goes up.

Of course, nobody in power—and that means rich, white men—wants anything to do with G.A.I. It's too "radical." The President has his own plan, the Family Assistance Plan (F.A.P.), before Congress now.

The President says we've got a "welfare crisis" in this country and that F.A.P.'s going to solve it. What he really means is that he's got a political problem, and that F.A.P.'s going to solve *it*. Because that's what F.A.P. is, really, politics.

The President calls F.A.P. a reform. It's not. It's a nice intellectual-sounding principle of an "income floor," but it won't help poor people a bit. Under F.A.P., a family of four would get $2,400 a year. Right now, 45 states and the District of Columbia are paying A.F.D.C. recipients over $2,400 a year in benefits and food stamps, and food stamps would be eliminated under F.A.P. That means that nine out of ten of all A.F.D.C. recipients—women and their children—would be even worse off under F.A.P. than they are now.

And that's not all.

First. There's a built-in "family maximum." If you've got seven kids you get $3,600 a year. If you've got ten kids, you still get $3,600 a year. If you have that eighth kid, by choice or by chance—maybe because you couldn't get birth control devices from the public clinic or because there was no clinic—then it's just too bad. That kid's invisible, as far as the Government is concerned.

Second. That $2,400 applies only to A.F.D.C.—to women and children. They've got a whole *different* schedule for the "deserving poor"—the aged, blind and disabled. A better schedule. For instance, an aged couple—just two people—will get almost exactly the same as an A.F.D.C. family of *four*.

Third. A single woman—not aged, not disabled, not a mother—gets nothing at all from F.A.P., no matter how hard up and desperate and unable to get work she is. If you don't have kids, you're not a person.

Fourth. If a mother refuses a job or job-training recommended for her by the welfare officials, she can be cut off and payments due her children are made to a "third party," someone outside her own family, someone she doesn't even choose. This brings up the most important point about F.A.P.: forced work.

Under F.A.P., a woman has to take any job offered her. She doesn't decide whether the job is suitable and pays a living wage. In fact, the job can pay as little as $1.20 an hour, or less, if "prevailing wages" are less. She doesn't decide whether child care facilities are good enough. The welfare people make these decisions for her. If she doesn't go along, her check is cut off.

"We can only put people in jobs that exist," the F.A.P. people say. We all know what kinds of jobs those are—maids get as low as $20 a week in Mississippi, living in five or six days, and only seeing their kids on weekends. And even these kinds of jobs, low as they are, are few and far between.

Child care provisions in F.A.P. don't make any sense either. They're just decorations to make it seem okay to force women with little children to work. In fact, the way it looks now, A.F.D.C. mothers may have to pay for all or part of their child care out of their own earnings, even though they only need child care because of the forced-work law.

There is an important point for women to remember when they fight for quality universal child care. Be careful that your enthusiasm doesn't get used to create a reservoir of cheap female labor. Because that's who's going to be working in those child care centers—poor women. If we don't watch it, an A.F.D.C. mother can end up paying a child-care center, which in turn will pay her less than the minimum wage to watch her children—and your children, too. Institutionalized, partially self-employed Mammies—that's what can happen to us.

A woman should be able to *choose* whether to work outside her home or in it, to choose whether she wants to care for her own children all the time or part-time. And the people who work in child care centers have to be paid decent wages or our kids won't get decent care.

The same thing goes for the birth control and abortion movements. Nobody realizes more than poor women that all women should have the right to control their own reproduction. But we also know how easily the lobby for birth control can be perverted into a weapon against poor women. The word is choice. Birth control as a right, not an obligation. A personal decision, not the condition of a welfare check.

As far as I'm concerned, the ladies of N.W.R.O. are the front-line troops of women's freedom. Both because we have so few illusions and because our issues are so important to all women—the right to a living wage for women's work, the right to life itself.

If I were President, I would solve this so-called welfare crisis in a minute and go a long way toward liberating every woman. I'd just issue a proclamation that women's work is *real* work. In other words, I'd start paying women a living wage for doing the work we are already doing—child-raising and housekeeping. And the welfare crisis would be over, just like that. Housewives would be getting wages, too—a legally-determined percentage of their husband's salary—instead of having to ask for and account for money they've already earned.

For me, Women's Liberation is simple. No woman in this country can feel dignified, no woman can be liberated, until all women get off their knees. That's what N.W.R.O. is all about—women standing together, on their feet.

If you agree, there are a lot of things you can do to help.

First, be honest about where your own head is at. Do you put down other women for being on welfare? Is it always "those people"? Well it could be you, and soon.

Stop for a minute and think what would happen to you and your kids if you suddenly had no husband and no savings.

Do you believe the "welfare Cadillac" myth? Inform yourself. Who's on welfare, why—and why can't they get off? N.W.R.O.'s got plenty of information out on the subject, and so do other groups. Write and get it.

Do you understand what F.A.P.'s about? Read the bill, or N.W.R.O.'s analysis of it.

Do you know how your Senator's going to vote on F.A.P.?

How does your own women's group stand on welfare? Push them a little. If we don't see that we're all women, all suffering from sexism, we'll never get anywhere. We have to work together.

Does your own community have people on welfare? Is there a local N.W.R.O. group? Help it.

Do you know your own rights to welfare? Find out.

Could you make it on a welfare budget (say, nineteen cents a meal)? Try it for a while. Just one week. Many women have done this—even wives of Congressmen—and they're shocked to see what even seven days is like. Do it in your community. Challenge people to a seven-day experiment to wake them up.

Inform yourself on welfare. You may have to live on it sooner or later.

Because you're a woman.

BARBARA SEAMAN

(from) Birth Control

A women's health activist and journalist, Barbara Seaman (1935–2008) was a pioneer in exposing sexism in healthcare and championing informed consent, and a vocal critic of the pharmaceutical industry. Her 1969 book *The Doctors' Case Against the Pill* challenged the safety of high-dose estrogen oral contraceptives and spurred the 1970 Senate hearings on the safety of the birth control pill. Feminists repeatedly disrupted the hearings, protesting the complete absence of women's testimony. As a result of the hearings, a warning about the Pill's side effects became the country's first informational insert for any prescription drug. At a time when barely 3 percent of OB-GYNs were female, Seaman pressed medical schools to admit more women. This excerpt from her 1972 book *Free and Female* wittily summarizes the contraceptive debate.

THE BIBLE tells us that God said to "Go forth and multiply." Apparently, She meant it. For a healthy young couple, fertility is a good deal more troublesome to curb than most modern birth control propaganda would lead you to believe.

On the other hand, the effective curbing of fertility is far from being an exclusive miracle of modern technology, and our current birth control technologists do not deserve quite the measure of undiluted gratitude that they ask and usually receive.

Historians tell us that Cleopatra had *some* effective method of birth control, probably crocodile dung which is highly spermicidal, if equally unappetizing. They also tell us that during the Middle Ages in Europe, the upper classes were so successful in curbing their fertility that population growth and the encouragement of babies became serious matters of royal concern. It may be that educated men became highly skilled at the practice of withdrawal. No historian or demographer has offered a better explanation, but all agree that few unwanted babies were conceived.

The point about birth control, ancient and modern, is that you don't get something for nothing. There are always certain drawbacks, either inconveniences or medical risks.

The older methods tend to be inconvenient; the newer ones risky. The perfect birth control method is safe, simple, totally reliable, very convenient and completely without risk. It hasn't been invented yet, and what's more, there is little reason to believe that it is about to come down the pike.

A lot of people with good intentions have been feeding you upbeat propaganda about birth control. They are concerned about the population explosion. They are concerned about teen-aged pregnancies and unsavory abortions and unwanted babies. They believe that it's in your interest to "have faith" in birth control, and they believe that you are too stupid or too selfish to use it consistently if you know that there are problems attached. So they lie to you.

They tell you that every method is marvelous, and you have merely to choose. They could better put it—"Every method has drawbacks: which troubles you the least? Which can *you* live with if you want to control your fertility?"

Every experienced woman knows that no birth control method is as safe and simple as proponents make it sound. Diaphragms are a nuisance to put in and take out. IUD's can hurt a lot when they are inserted and make your period heavier. Sterilization, even in men, is often a lot more painful than the propaganda says, and it may leave you feeling depressed and mutilated. Rhythm requires enormous self-discipline. The pill, that great sexual liberator, has more than fifty different side effects, some of them fatal, and the majority of users stop within a few years because of side effects. Condoms diminish sexual pleasure for many people. Foam diminishes sexual pleasure for some and may not be a sufficiently reliable method. Abortion, as an occasional backup, has much to recommend it, but at best it is not a pleasant experience, nor is it entirely safe, even when legal. You surely wouldn't want to have one every month.

The entire birth control situation is not unlike Dorothy Parker's famous discussion of suicide.[1] You almost feel like saying, "To hell with it all," and that is what many people do, to their regret, usually.

On the other hand, people are always hoping for something better, some

---

1. From *Enough Rope*, by Dorothy Parker (New York, Boni & Liveright, 1926).

> *Resume*
> Razors pain you;
> Rivers are damp;
> Acids stain you;
> And drugs cause cramp.
> Guns aren't lawful;
> Nooses give;
> Gas smells awful;
> You might as well live.

new miracle. If you have been keeping up with the birth control stories in magazines and newspapers, you know that we have long since been promised:

—A pill for men.

—Reversible sterilization.

—A permanent diaphragm.

—A safe morning-after pill.

—A safe once-a-month pill.

A Jane Brody story in a recent New York *Times* described a reversible vasectomy for men, involving a "tiny valve placed in the sperm duct that can be turned on and off like a faucet."[2] The urologists behind it estimate that the device will be ready for large-scale clinical trials within a few years.

Other stories of just-around-the-corner reversible vasectomies go back a decade or more. It's possible, of course, that sooner or later one of these new birth control wonders actually will prove out. But I'll believe it when I see it. The only thing new and available in mid-twentieth century is the pill.[3]

The pill has been widely promoted as a sexual liberator, almost, indeed, an aphrodisiac. For some women, it is. To *Time*'s Latin-American edition, a woman wrote, "To the pill I can credit harmony, communication, fulfillment, satisfaction, happiness, stability, understanding, acceptance, relaxation, achievement, compatibility, courage, love, peace, and Christ."

Nonetheless, sooner or later most of the women who take the pill do develop adverse symptoms, and most stop because of them. The latest study—reported at the 1971 annual meeting of the American Fertility Society—revealed that out of 2,000 women who had started on the pill in 1962, only 34 percent were still using it, at the end of six years.[4]

In 1960, the pill was approved for contraceptive use after having been tested for a full year or longer, continuously, on only 132 women.[5] And even among these women, the main thing being monitored was *effectiveness*. Several women died and were not even autopsied. At the time, their deaths were attributed to "heart attacks," but in retrospect it appears that pulmonary embolism was a more likely cause.[6]

It is not surprising that the undesirable side effects of the pill began to emerge only after it was in general use. The synthetic hormones in these pow-

2. New York *Times*, October 2, 1971.

3. The IUD is *not* a new method, as we shall see later. Vasectomy has been used on men since the nineteenth century to prevent those with hereditary defects from fathering children.

4. *Medical Tribune*, July 21, 1971.

5. Revealed in a 1963 investigation of the FDA by the Senate Committee on Government Operations.

6. Herbert Ratner, MD, *Child and Family* (Oak Park, Illinois, December, 1969)

erful drugs act through the pituitary, which has been called the "master gland" and even "the conductor of the endocrine symphony." There is no organ or tissue which is not affected by the pill to some degree, and the longer a woman stays on the pill, the more her organs and all her metabolic functions are apt to be subtly altered.[7] The 20,000,000 women who take the pill—and the doctors who prescribe it—are engaged in a massive and unprecedented human experiment. We delude ourselves if we believe that a similar experiment on *males* would have been allowed. One of the cornerstones of medical ethics is "First, do no harm." Until the pill—and except for the pill—it would be unthinkable to prescribe, for continuous long-term use by healthy persons, a powerful drug of which the side effects, and even the mechanisms of action, are imperfectly known.

If you doubt that there has been sex discrimination in the development of the pill, try to answer this question: Why *isn't* there a pill for men? Studies of the male reproductive system are well advanced, and a man's organs, being handily placed outside the body, are easier to work with than a woman's.

There are only a handful of researchers in male contraception, and they have a difficult time getting money, but most of them are inclined to believe that it could be easier and safer to interrupt the sperm production of men chemically than the egg production of women. It might be possible, for example, to interfere at the stage where the sperm are mixed with the seminal fluid instead of at the more dangerous level of the pituitary.

The British government has specifically rejected a proposal to channel research funds toward a pill for men. When the matter came up in the House of Lords, a Labour peer—to the accompaniment of much laughter—urged the government not to take too much notice of "those do-gooders who take all the fun out of life."

But women have always had to bear most of the risks associated with sex and reproduction. Therefore, governments and scientists reasoned, it would be all right to substitute one risk for another. One still hears this argument from certain doctors, such as Planned Parenthood's Malcolm Potts, who like to point out that the risks connected with the pill are less than the risks of pregnancy.

The trouble is, there are at least three reasons why it's not true.

One: You can't compare a known risk with an unknown risk, and the long-range dangers connected with the pill are still totally unknown. For example, close to 80 percent of the women who take the pill experience diabetic-like

7. Hilton Salhanick, ed., *Effects of Gonadal Hormones and Contraceptive Steroids* (New York, Plenum Press, 1969).

changes in their sugar metabolism. Some 15 percent actually test out as chemical diabetics. Will these women eventually come down with overt, clinical diabetes? Nobody can say yet, but the handful of diabetes specialists around the world who are studying the pill are extremely worried.[8]

The prospect of cancer is even more alarming. Estrogens can cause cancer in laboratory animals and can speed up the course of an existing cancer in humans. But cancer in humans takes many years to develop, so we will not know for some time whether the pill can actually *cause* it.

A new research report out of Harvard is not reassuring.[9] A synthetic estrogen given women during their pregnancy has caused a rare vaginal cancer in their daughters fifteen to twenty-two years later. The drug was administered between 1945 and 1951 to prevent miscarriages. A grown woman may not be as susceptible as a fetus, of course, but, as it happens, through the pill we are now giving these artificial estrogens to nursing babies. When their mothers take the pill, estrogens go right into the milk.

Two: The argument that the risks of pregnancy "outweigh" the risks of the pill rests on the absurd supposition that if you don't take the pill, you are going to be pregnant every year. A diaphragm—properly fitted and conscientiously used—is a 99 percent effective birth control method.[10] The newer IUD's are in the same range.[11] In fact, the leading biostatisticians of birth control, such as Dr. Christopher Tietze of the Population Council, have demonstrated repeatedly that the pill is *not* the best guardian of maternal health. The safest choice for women—in terms of mortality and morbidity statistics—is a local harmless method of contraception, backed up by readily available medical abortion.[12]

---

8. See testimony of Drs. Victor Wynn and William Spellacy at hearings before the Subcommittee on Monopoly of the Select Committee on Small Business ("Nelson" Hearings). (May be ordered from the Government Printing Office.)

See also Paul Vaughan, *The Pill on Trial* (New York, Coward-McCann, 1970), or Barbara Seaman, *The Doctors' Case Against the Pill* (New York, Wyden, 1969; Avon, 1970).

9. *New England Journal of Medicine*, 284:878 (1971).

10. See various papers of Charles Westoff (Princeton University).

11. Hugh Davis, *Intrauterine Devices for Contraception* (Baltimore, Williams and Wilkins Co., 1971).

12. Suppose 100,000 women are at risk of pregnancy for one year:

—Under condition one, these women use no contraception and have no abortions. 40,000 to 60,000 will become pregnant, and there will be 8 to 12 maternal deaths.

—Under condition two, the women use no contraception and all who become pregnant have illegal abortions. There will be an average of 1 pregnancy per woman, with 100 deaths.

—Under condition three, the women use no contraception, but all who become pregnant have legal abortions. There will be 3 deaths.

—Under condition four, the women use oral contraceptives. There will be 3 deaths from the contraceptives, as well as 50 hospitalizations for nonfatal blood clots.

And haven't men grown a little spoiled? When I was in high school, even the virginal (*especially* the virginal) boys used to carry condoms in their wallets. Now, I understand, high school boys have become so delicate that even *they* complain that condoms are "too much like raincoats." We know, of course, that if unmarried persons were still using condoms, VD would not have enjoyed its current renaissance.[13] We also know that a good brand of fresh condom is a reliable method, and we know that in Japan, where condoms come in many colors and some even glow in the dark, couples use them as part of their sex play, and the men rarely complain that their potency or pleasure is affected.

Do you know what the safest and simplest immediate solution to the population explosion might be? Vasectomize all boys at sixteen or eighteen, after having taken a sample of their sperm and frozen it. When they are ready for children, their wives could be artificially inseminated. It sounds repulsive, doesn't it? But it may be equally outrageous to encourage 20,000,000 women to play biological roulette with their own bodies and those of their unborn babies.

—Under condition five, the women use local contraception, such as the diaphragm or condom and have no abortions. There will be 2.5 deaths.

—Under condition six, the women use local contraception and have illegal abortions when the contraception fails. There will be 14.3 deaths.

—Under condition seven, the women use local contraception, backed up by legal abortions. There will be only 0.4 deaths, which, in Tietze's words, is "a whole different ball park."

13. Condoms were originally designed to prevent VD, and they remain an almost 100 percent safeguard against it. Furthermore, many investigators believe that the pill actually changes the chemical milieu of the vagina, from acidic, which tends to kill germs, to alkaline, which does not. If a woman who is not taking the pill is exposed to VD, her chances of getting it are estimated to be 20 to 30 percent. If she is taking the pill, her chances of getting VD approach 100 percent.

PHYLLIS CHESLER

(from) *Women and Madness*

To explain waves of protest as well as accounts by women writers—Sylvia Plath, Anne Sexton, and others—of the abuse of women by psychiatry, Phyllis Chesler (born 1940), a psychologist, published the 1972 best seller *Women and Madness*, which is excerpted here. Her wide-ranging analysis was both controversial and enormously influential, and her core perception that "depression, anxiety neuroses, suicide attempts and psychosomatic illness in women" were exacerbated rather than relieved by psychotherapy toppled paradigms about the psychology of women. In response to evolving feminist ideas about marriage, family, and female sexuality, a generation of women practitioners would revolutionize psychotherapy with modes of treatment that encouraged each woman to seek, in Chesler's words, "her own survival as a strong individual."

FOR MOST women (the middle-class-oriented) psychotherapeutic encounter is just one more instance of an unequal relationship, just one more opportunity to be rewarded for expressing distress and to be "helped" by being (expertly) dominated. Both psychotherapy and white or middle-class marriage isolate women from each other; both emphasize individual rather than collective solutions to woman's unhappiness; both are based on a woman's helplessness and dependence on a stronger male authority figure; both may, in fact, be viewed as re-enactments of a little girl's relation to her father in a patriarchal society; both control and oppress women similarly—yet, at the same time, are the two safest (most approved and familiar) havens for middle-class women in a society that offers them few—if any—alternatives.

Both psychotherapy and marriage enable women to express and defuse their anger by experiencing it as a form of emotional illness, by translating it into hysterical symptoms: frigidity, chronic depression, phobias, and the like. Each woman, as patient, thinks these symptoms are unique and are her own fault: she is "neurotic." She wants from a psychotherapist what she wants—and often cannot get—from a husband: attention, understanding, merciful relief, a *personal solution*—in the arms of the right husband, on the couch of the right therapist. The institutions of therapy and marriage not only mirror each other, they support each other. This is probably not a coincidence but is rather an expression of the American economic system's need for geographic and psychological mobility, i.e., for young, upwardly mobile "couples" to "survive," and to remain more or less intact in a succession of alien and anonymous urban locations, while they carry out the functions of socializing children and making money. Most therapists have a vested interest, financially and psychologically, in the supremacy of the nuclear family. Most husbands want their wives to "shape up" or at least not to interfere with male burdens, male pleasures, or male conscience.

The institution of psychotherapy may be used by many women as a way of keeping a bad marriage together or as a way of terminating it in order to form a good marriage. Some women, especially young and single women, may use psychotherapy as a way of learning how to catch a husband by practicing with a male therapist. Women probably spend more time during a therapy session talking about their husbands or boy friends—or lack of them—than they do talking about their lack of an independent identity or their relations to other women.

The institutions of middle-class psychotherapy and marriage both encourage women to talk—often endlessly—rather than to act (except in their socially prearranged roles as passive women or patients). In marriage, the talking is usually of an indirect and rather inarticulate nature. Open expressions of rage are too dangerous and too ineffective for the isolated and economically dependent women. Most often, such "kitchen" declarations end in tears, self-blame, and in the husband graciously agreeing with his wife that she was "not herself." Even control of a simple—but serious—conversation is usually impossible for most wives when several men, including their husbands, are present. The wife-women talk to each other, or they listen silently, while the men talk. Very rarely, if ever, do men listen silently to a group of women talking; even if there are a number of women talking and only one man present, the man will question the women, perhaps patiently, perhaps not, but always in order to ultimately control the conversation from a superior position.

In psychotherapy the patient-woman is encouraged—in fact directed—to talk, by a therapist who is at least expected to be, or is perceived as, superior or objective. The traditional therapist may be viewed as ultimately controlling what the patient says through a subtle system of rewards (attention, interpretations, and so forth) or rewards withheld—but, ultimately, controlling, in the sense that he is attempting to bring his patient to terms with the female role, i.e., he wants her to admit, accept, and "solve" her need for love. However, such acceptance of the human need for other people, or for "love," means something very different when women are already our culture's "acceptors" and men our culture's "rejectors." Such acceptance is further confused by the economic nature of the female need for "love."

Traditionally, the psychotherapist has ignored the objective facts of female oppression. Thus, in every sense, the female patient is still not having a "real" conversation—either with her husband or with her therapist. But how is it possible to have a "real" conversation with those who directly profit from her oppression? She would be laughed at, viewed as silly or crazy and, if she persisted, removed from her job—as secretary or wife, perhaps even as private patient.

Psychotherapeutic talking is indirect in the sense that it does not immediately or even ultimately involve the woman in any reality-based confrontations with the self. It is also indirect in that words—any words—are permitted, so long as certain actions of consequence are totally avoided—such as not paying one's bills.

Private psychoanalysis or psychotherapy is still a commodity available to those women who can buy it, that is, to women whose fathers, husbands, or boy friends can help them pay for it. Like the Calvinist elect, those women who can *afford* treatment are already "saved." Even if they are never happy, never free, they will be slow to rebel against their psychological and economic dependence on men. One look at their less privileged (poor, black, older and/or unmarried) sisters' position is enough to keep them silent and more or less gratefully in line. The less privileged women have no real or psychological silks to smooth down over, to disguise their unhappiness; they have no class to be "better than." As they sit facing the walls, in factories, offices, whorehouses, ghetto apartments, and mental asylums, at least one thing they must conclude is that "happiness" is on sale in America—but not at a price they can afford. They are poor.

FLORYNCE R. KENNEDY

(from) The Verbal Karate of Florynce R. Kennedy, Esq.

Legendary African American lawyer, activist, speaker, and hell-raiser Florynce R. Kennedy (1916–2000) was known throughout the civil rights and feminist movements as simply "Flo." As a lawyer, she represented Valerie Solanas and the Black Panthers and campaigned to decriminalize abortion and prostitution. Flamboyant and media savvy, Kennedy helped organize the 1966 antidiscrimination Media Workshop; the 1968 Miss America Pageant protest ("the best fun I can imagine anyone wanting to have on any single day of her life," see pages 45–47); the 1973 pee-in at Harvard, protesting the paucity of women's bathrooms; and several important antisexist, antiracist organizations. After founding the Feminist Party in 1971, she nominated Shirley Chisholm for U.S. president and led her campaign. She hosted *The Flo Kennedy Show* on Manhattan Cable TV (1978–95) and was known for her provocative pronouncements, such as these, excerpted from a collection compiled and introduced by her friend Gloria Steinem and published in *Ms.* in March 1973.

MOTHERHOOD

"BEING A mother is a noble status, right? Right. So why does it change when you put 'unwed' or 'welfare' in front of it?"

OPPRESSION

"Oppression has at least four dimensions: The personal or psychological—like when you yourself believe that you're a big zero because society keeps telling you so. The private—like when some employer tries to make out with you when you ask for a job. The public—like when the government takes the money you need for child-care centers, and uses it to kill people in Indochina. And the cultural—like when the history books attribute everything we did and invented to some guy we worked for."

"Niggerization is the result of oppression—and it doesn't just apply to black people. Old people, poor people, and students can also get niggerized. Sure, there are differences in degree, but we've got to stop comparing wounds and go out after the system that does the wounding."

"If you've been hit a lot, you tend to stay sore for a while. Trying to help an oppressed person is like trying to put your arm around somebody with a sunburn."

"As the struggle intensifies, the oppressor tends to pick more attractive agents—frequently from among the oppressed."

EMPLOYMENT

"There are very few jobs that actually require a penis or vagina. All other jobs should be open to everybody."

"People always ask if a woman can be a wife and mother and have a career at the same time. Why don't they ask if she can be a hostess, chauffeur, cook, gardener, nurse, seamstress, social secretary, purchasing agent, baby machine, and courtesan—and a wife and mother too?"

REVOLUTION

"Some people say they won't work 'inside the system'—they're 'waiting for the revolution.' Well, when the ramparts are open, honey, I'll be there. But until then, I'm going to go right on zapping the business and government delinquents, the jockocrats, the fetus fetishists, and all the other niggerizers any way I can. The biggest sin is sitting on your ass."

"You can't dump one cup of sugar into the ocean and expect to get syrup. If everybody sweetened her own cup of water, then things would begin to change."

TACTICS

"Unity in a Movement situation can be overrated. If you were the Establishment, which would you rather see coming in the door: one lion or five hundred mice?"

"Loserism is when oppressed people sit around and think up reasons why they can't do something. Well, just *do* it. Thinking up reasons why you can't is the Establishment's job."

"You don't cure malaria by getting in bed with the malaria patient, and you don't cure poverty by going to live in the ghetto. You go to Wall Street and Washington and put pressure on the people who've got the cure."

"If the ass is protecting the system, ass-kicking should be undertaken regardless of the sex, ethnicity, or charm of the ass involved."

"If you've had a broken leg, you don't get up and win the Olympics. The first step is to get out of bed."

"The innocence of good people is inexcusable. Naïveté is a luxury only the pigocrats can afford."

"When you spit on someone at a cocktail party, you don't want to drown him. You just want to let him know you don't like him."

"We've got to stop sucking and begin to bite."

"Don't agonize. Organize."

MARRIAGE

"Going in and out of a closet, your mind is on what you really want in there. But the minute the door locks, all you want is out."

POWER

"Women have at least three kinds of power: Dollar Power, to boycott with; Vote Power, to take over structures with, and maybe even get somebody elected; and Body Power, to get out and support our friends and make a damned nuisance of ourselves with everybody else."

"We don't say a word when Madison Avenue makes millions off us, but we get all resentful and suspicious when somebody in the Movement gets attention or makes a dime. That's Nigger Nobility. If you have to lose to prove you're a good person, we'll never get anywhere."

"Powerlessness is a dirty word."

REPRODUCTIVE FREEDOM

"If men could get pregnant, abortion would be a sacrament."

ON BEING A LAWYER

"Most lawyers are like whores. They serve the client who puts the highest fee on the table. The biggest law firms serve the richest johns."

"I don't practice law much any more. Even if you're honest, the law is still a one-ass-at-a-time proposition—and what we have to do is stop the wringer."

WOMEN WHO LIKE THINGS THE WAY THEY ARE

"Women who say they're contented just having a nice husband and two beautiful children—fine; I'm glad. Of course, I always wonder what happens if one of the children *isn't* beautiful . . . and if housework is so rewarding, why don't men do it, too? But this Movement isn't about getting some woman to leave her husband. It's about social justice."

"Just because you're not feeling sick doesn't mean you should close the hospitals."

SISTERHOOD

"Divide and conquer—that's what they try to do to any group trying to make social change. I call it D&C. Black people are supposed to turn against Puerto Ricans. Women are supposed to turn against their mothers and mothers-in-law. We're all supposed to compete with each other for the favors of the ruling class."

"We criticize each other instead of the oppressor because it's less dangerous. The oppressor fights back."

"In the name of elitism, we do a crabs-in-a-barrel number, and pull down any of our number who get public attention or a small success. As long as we're into piranha-ism and horizontal hostility, honey, we ain't going to get nowhere."

Sex

"Okay, roses are beautiful, fragrant, and desirable. But how much shit should you have to walk over to get one rose?"

The Press

"In a jockocratic society, you can turn on the TV and find out the score of some basketball game in Alaska—but you can't find out how many states have ratified the Equal Rights Amendment. You can turn on the radio, and hear every score in the country repeated all day long—but you don't hear how many women died from illegal abortions."

"Take a look at your local Weird Herald. On the Woman's Page, are they telling you how to make aprons out of artichokes and artichokes out of aprons? Well, protest! Picket! And if that doesn't work, try boycotting their biggest advertiser. That should turn the trick."

On Herself

"My parents gave us a fantastic sense of security and worth. By the time the bigots got around to telling us we were nobody, we already *knew* we were somebody."

"When we first moved to Kansas City, some Ku Klux Klansmen gave us ten minutes to get out of the neighborhood. My father went out with a shotgun and said, 'I'll shoot the first man who steps on this porch. After that, you can get me.' And you know, those Klansmen never came back?"

"At my age and in my condition, I'm going to do what I want—I haven't got time for anything else."

"I may seem radical, but I'm not. I'm just a worm, turning."

"I know we're termites. But if all the termites got together, the house would fall down."

"You've got to rattle your cage door. You've got to let them know that you're in there, and that you want out. Make noise. Cause trouble. You may not win right away, but you'll sure have a lot more fun."

KATHIE SARACHILD

(from) Consciousness-Raising: A Radical Weapon

Consciousness raising, practiced in many thousands of small, autonomous feminist groups nationwide, was the major information-gathering and galvanizing technique for spreading the women's liberation movement. From 1968 on, radical feminist organizer and theorist Kathie Sarachild, née Amatniek (born 1943), helped popularize consciousness raising through her speeches and writings. She was prominent in both New York Radical Women and Redstockings (see pages 45–47 and 110–113), early groups committed to consciousness raising. In 1968 Sarachild authored the popular slogan "Sisterhood is powerful" and took the matrilineal surname "Sarachild" to protest the long-established patriarchal tradition of patrilineal surnames. The speech excerpted here was delivered to the First Conference of Stewardesses for Women's Rights on March 12, 1973.

THE IDEA

To be able to understand what feminist consciousness-raising is all about, it is important to remember that it began as a program among women who all considered themselves radicals.

Before we go any further, let's examine the word "radical." It is a word that is often used to suggest extremist, but actually it doesn't mean that. The dictionary says radical means root, coming from the Latin word for root. And that is what we meant by calling ourselves radicals. We were interested in getting to the roots of problems in society. You might say we wanted to pull up weeds in the garden by their roots, not just pick off the leaves at the top to make things look good momentarily. Women's Liberation was started by women who considered themselves radicals in this sense.

Our aim in forming a women's liberation group was to start a *mass movement of women* to put an end to the barriers of segregation and discrimination based on sex. We knew radical thinking and radical action would be necessary to do this. We also believed it necessary to form Women's Liberation groups which excluded men from their meetings.

In order to have a radical approach, to get to the root, it seemed logical that we had to study the situation of women, not just take random action. How best to do this came up in the women's liberation group I was in—New York Radical Women, one of the first in the country—shortly after the group had formed. We were planning our first public action and wandered into a discussion about what to do next. One woman in the group, Anne Forer, spoke up: "I think we have a lot more to do just in the area of raising our consciousness," she said. "Raising consciousness?" I wondered what she meant by that. I'd never heard it applied to women before.

"I've only begun thinking about women as an oppressed group," she continued, "and each day, I'm still learning more about it—my consciousness gets higher."

Now I didn't consider that I had just started thinking about the oppression of women. In fact, I thought of myself as having done lots of thinking about it for quite a while, and lots of reading, too. But then Anne went on to give an example of something she'd noticed that turned out to be a deeper way of seeing it for me, too.

"I think a lot about being attractive," Anne said. "People don't find the real self of a woman attractive." And then she went on to give some examples. And I just sat there listening to her describe all the false ways women have to act: playing dumb, always being agreeable, always being nice, not to mention what we had to do to our bodies with the clothes and shoes we wore, the diets we had to go through, going blind not wearing glasses, all because men didn't find our real selves, our human freedom, our basic humanity "attractive." And I realized I still could learn a lot about how to understand and describe the particular oppression of women in ways that could reach other women in the way this had just reached me. The whole group was moved as I was, and we decided on the spot that what we needed—in the words Anne used—was to "raise our consciousness some more."

At the next meeting there was an argument in the group about how to do this. One woman—Peggy Dobbins—said that what she wanted to do was make a very intensive study of all the literature on the question of whether there really were any biological differences between men and women. I found myself angered by that idea.

"I think it would be a waste of time," I said. "For every scientific study we quote, the opposition can find their scientific studies to quote. Besides, the question is what *we* want to be, what we think we are, not what some authorities in the name of science are arguing over what we are. It is scientifically impossible to tell what the biological differences are between men and women—if there are any besides the obvious physical ones—until all the social and political factors applying to men and women are equal. Everything we have to know, have to prove, we can get from the realities of our own lives. For instance, on the subject of women's intelligence. We know from our own experience that women play dumb for men because, if we're too smart, men won't like us. I know, because I've done it. We've all done it. Therefore, we can simply deduce that women are smarter than men are aware of, and smarter than all those people who make studies are aware of, and that there are a lot of women around who are a lot smarter than they look and smarter than anybody but themselves and maybe a few of their friends know."

In the end the group decided to raise its consciousness by studying women's lives by topics like childhood, jobs, motherhood, etc. We'd do any outside reading we wanted to and thought was important. But our starting point for discussion, as well as our test of the accuracy of what any of the books said, would be the actual experience we had in these areas. One of the questions, suggested by Anne Forer, we would bring at all times to our studies would be—who and what has an *interest* in maintaining the oppression in our lives. The kind of actions the group should engage in, at this point, we decided— acting on an idea of Carol Hanisch, another woman in the group—would be consciousness-raising actions . . . actions brought to the public for the specific purpose of challenging old ideas and raising new ones, the very same issues of feminism we were studying ourselves. Our role was not to be a "service organization," we decided, nor a large "membership organization." What we were talking about being was, in effect, Carol explained, a "zap" action, political agitation and education group something like what the Student Non-Violent Coordinating Committee (S.N.C.C.) had been. We would be the first to dare to say and do the undareable, what women really felt and wanted. The first job now was to raise awareness and understanding, our own and others'— awareness that would prompt people to organize and to act on a mass scale.

The decision to emphasize our own feelings and experiences as women and to test all generalizations and reading we did by our own experience was actually the scientific method of research. We were in effect repeating the 17th century challenge of science to scholasticism: "study nature, not books," and put all theories to the test of living practice and action. It was also a method of radical organizing tested by other revolutions. We were applying to women and to ourselves as women's liberation organizers the practice a number of us had learned as organizers in the civil rights movement in the South in the early 1960's.

Consciousness-raising—studying the whole gamut of women's lives, starting with the full reality of one's own—would also be a way of keeping the movement radical by preventing it from getting sidetracked into single issue reforms and single issue organizing. It would be a way of carrying theory about women further than it had ever been carried before, as the groundwork for achieving a radical solution for women as yet attained nowhere.

It seemed clear that knowing how our own lives related to the general condition of women would make us better fighters on behalf of women as a whole. We felt that all women would have to see the fight of women as their own, not as something just to help "other women," that they would have to see this truth about their own lives before they would fight in a radical way for anyone. "Go fight your own oppressors," Stokely Carmichael had said to the white civil rights workers when the black power movement began. "You don't get radicalized fighting other people's battles," as Beverly Jones put it in the pioneering essay "Toward a Female Liberation Movement."

BOSTON WOMEN'S HEALTH COLLECTIVE

Preface to *Our Bodies, Ourselves*

In 1969, when twelve women formed a collective after a Boston women's liberation conference, American healthcare treated pregnancy, birth, menstruation, lesbianism, menopause, battering, sexual assault, and sexual abuse as illnesses to be passively endured by women. The Boston collective's determination to change the system evolved from researching health issues and teaching workshops to publishing *Our Bodies, Ourselves,* a book whose title became the central principle of a worldwide women's health movement. First a 193-page stapled newsprint coursebook (1970), then a paperback edition (1971), both from New England Free Press, the book's popularity soon outstripped the capacity of its small publisher, and the collective turned in 1973 to Simon and Schuster, a trade publisher, which agreed by contract to provide a 70 percent discount to nonprofit women's clinics. Taking no royalties individually, the collective gathered and refined the text in six editions, concluding in 2015, by which time the book had appeared in thirty languages. This preface is to the 1973 edition.

A GOOD STORY

THE HISTORY of this book, *Our Bodies, Ourselves*, is lengthy and satisfying. It began at a small discussion group on "women and their bodies" which was part of a women's conference held in Boston in the spring of 1969. These were the early days of the women's movement, one of the first gatherings of women meeting specifically to talk with other women. For many of us it was the very first time we got together with other women to talk and think about our lives and what we could do about them. Before the conference was over some of us decided to keep on meeting as a group to continue the discussion, and so we did.

In the beginning we called the group "the doctor's group." We had all experienced similar feelings of frustration and anger toward specific doctors and the medical maze in general, and initially we wanted to do something about those doctors who were condescending, paternalistic, judgmental and noninformative. As we talked and shared our experiences with one another, we realized just how much we had to learn about our bodies. So we decided on a summer project—to research those topics which we felt were particularly pertinent to learning about our bodies, to discuss in the group what we had learned, then to write papers individually or in small groups of two or three, and finally to present the results in the fall as a course for women on women and their bodies.

As we developed the course we realized more and more that we were really capable of collecting, understanding, and evaluating medical information. Together we evaluated our reading of books and journals, our talks with doctors and friends who were medical students. We found we could discuss, question and argue with each other in a new spirit of cooperation rather than competition. We were equally struck by how important it was for us to be able to open up with one another and share our feelings about our bodies. The process of talking was as crucial as the facts themselves. Over time the facts and feelings melted together in ways that touched us very deeply, and that is reflected in the changing titles of the course and then the book—from *Women and Their Bodies* to *Women and Our Bodies* to, finally, *Our Bodies, Ourselves.*

When we gave the course we met in any available free space we could get— in day schools, in nursery schools, in churches, in our homes. We expected the course to stimulate the same kind of talking and sharing that we who had prepared the course had experienced. We had something to say, but we had a lot to learn as well; we did not want a traditional teacher-student relationship. At the end of ten to twelve sessions—which roughly covered the material in the current book—we found that many women felt both eager and competent to get together in small groups and share what they had learned with other women. We saw it as a never-ending process always involving more and more women.

After the first teaching of the course, we decided to revise our initial papers and mimeograph them so that other women could have copies as the course expanded. Eventually we got them printed and bound together in an inexpensive edition published by the New England Free Press. It was fascinating and very exciting for us to see what a constant demand there was for our book. It came out in several editions, a larger number being printed each time, and the time from one printing to the next becoming shorter. The growing volume of requests began to strain the staff of the New England Free Press. Since our book was clearly speaking to many people, we wanted to reach beyond the audience who lived in the area or who were acquainted with the New England Free Press. For wider distribution it made sense to publish our book commercially.

You may want to know who we are. We are white, our ages range from 24 to 40, most of us are from middle-class backgrounds and have had at least some college education, and some of us have professional degrees. Some of us are married, some of us are separated, and some of us are single. Some of us have children of our own, some of us like spending time with children, and others of us are not sure we want to be with children. In short, we are both a very ordinary and a very special group, as women are everywhere. We are white middle-class women, and as such can describe only what life has been for us. But we do realize that poor women and non-white women have suffered far more from the kinds of misinformation and mistreatment that we are describing in this book. In some ways, learning about our womanhood from the inside out has allowed us to cross over the socially created barriers of race, color, income and class, and to feel a sense of identity with all women in the experience of being female.

We are twelve individuals and we are a group. (The group has been ongoing for three years and some of us have been together since the beginning. Others came in at later points. Our current collective has been together for one year.) We know each other well—our weaknesses as well as our strengths. We have learned through good times and bad how to work together (and how not to as well). We recognize our similarities and differences and are learning to respect each person for her uniqueness. We love each other.

Many, many other women have worked with us on the book. A group of gay women got together specifically to do the chapter on lesbianism. Other papers were done still differently. For instance, along with some friends the mother of one woman in the group volunteered to work on menopause with some of us who have not gone through that experience ourselves. Other women contributed thoughts, feelings and comments as they passed through town or passed through our kitchens or workrooms. There are still other voices from letters, phone conversations, a variety of discussions, etc., that are included in the chapters as excerpts of personal experiences. Many women have spoken for themselves in this book, though we in the collective do not agree with all that has been written. Some of us are even uncomfortable with part of the material. We have included it anyway, because we give more weight to accepting that we differ than to our uneasiness. We have been asked why this is exclusively a book about women, why we have restricted our course to women. Our answer is that we are women and, as women, do not consider ourselves experts on men (as men through the centuries have presumed to be experts on us). We are not implying that we think most twentieth-century men are much less alienated from their bodies than women are. But we know it is up to men to explore that for themselves, to come together and share their sense of themselves as we have done. We would like to read a book about men and their bodies.

We are offering a book that can be used in many different ways—individually, in a group, for a course. Our book contains real material about our bodies and ourselves that isn't available elsewhere, and we have tried to present it in a new way—an honest, humane, and powerful way of thinking about ourselves and our lives. We want to share the knowledge and power that comes with this way of thinking and we want to share the feelings we have for each other—supportive and loving feelings that show we can indeed help one another grow.

From the very beginning of working together, first on the course that led to this book and then on the book itself, we have felt exhilarated and energized by our new knowledge. Finding out about our bodies and our bodies' needs, starting to take control over that area of our life, has released for us an energy that has overflowed into our work, our friendships, our relationships with men and women, for some of us our marriages and our parenthood. In trying to figure out why this has had such a life-changing effect on us, we have come up with several important ways in which this kind of body education has been liberating for us and may be a starting point for the liberation of many other women.

First, we learned what we learned equally from professional sources—textbooks, medical journals, doctors, nurses—and from our own experiences. The facts were important, and we did careful research to get the information we had not had in the past. As we brought the facts to one another we learned a good deal, but in sharing our personal experiences relating to those facts we learned still more. Once we had learned what the "experts" had to tell us, we found that we still had a lot to teach and to learn from one another. For instance, many of us had "learned" about the menstrual cycle in science or biology classes—we had perhaps even memorized the names of the menstrual hormones and what they did. But most of us did not remember much of what we had learned. This time when we read in a text that the onset of menstruation is a normal and universal occurrence in young girls from ages ten to eighteen, we started to talk about our first menstrual periods. We found that, for many of us, beginning to menstruate had not felt normal at all, but scary, embarrassing, mysterious. We realized that what we had been told about menstruation and what we had not been told, even the tone of voice it had been told in—all had had an effect on our feelings about being female. Similarly, the information from enlightened texts describing masturbation as a normal, common sexual activity did not really become our own until we began to pull up from inside ourselves and share what we had never before expressed—the confusion and shame we had been made to feel, and often still felt, about touching our bodies in a sexual way.

Learning about our bodies in this way really turned us on. This is an exciting kind of learning, where information and feelings are allowed to interact. It has made the difference between rote memorization and relevant learning, between fragmented pieces of a puzzle and the integrated picture, between abstractions and real knowledge. We discovered that you don't learn very much when you are just a passive recipient of information. We found that each individual's response to information is valid and useful, and that by sharing our responses we can develop a base on which to be critical of what the experts tell us. Whatever we need to learn now, in whatever area of our life, we know more how to go about it.

A second important result of this kind of learning has been that we are better prepared to evaluate the institutions that are supposed to meet our health needs—the hospitals, clinics, doctors, medical schools, nursing schools, public health departments, Medicaid bureaucracies, and so on. For some of us it was the first time we had looked critically, and with strength, at the existing institutions serving us. The experience of learning just how little control we had over our lives and bodies, the coming together out of isolation to learn from each other in order to define what we needed, and the experience of supporting one another in demanding the changes that grew out of our developing critique—all were crucial and formative political experiences for us. We have felt our potential power as a force for political and social change.

The learning we have done while working on *Our Bodies, Ourselves* has been such a good basis for growth in other areas of life for still another reason. For women throughout the centuries, ignorance about our bodies has had one major consequence—pregnancy. Until very recently pregnancies were all but inevitable, biology *was* our destiny—that is, because our bodies are designed to get pregnant and give birth and lactate, that is what all or most of us did. The courageous and dedicated work of people like Margaret Sanger started in the early twentieth century to spread and make available birth control methods that women could use, thereby freeing us from the traditional lifetime of pregnancies. But the societal expectation that a woman above all else will have babies does not die easily. When we first started talking to each other about this we found that that old expectation had nudged most of us into a fairly rigid role of wife-and-motherhood from the moment we were born female. Even in 1969 when we first started the work that led to this book, we found that many of us were still getting pregnant when we didn't want to. It was not until we researched carefully and learned more about our reproductive systems, about birth-control methods and abortion, about laws governing birth control and abortion, not until we put all this information together with what it meant to us to be female, did we begin to feel that we could truly set out to control whether and when we would have babies.

This knowledge has freed us to a certain extent from the constant, energy-draining anxiety about becoming pregnant. It has made our pregnancies better, because they no longer happen to us; we actively choose them and enthusiastically participate in them. It has made our parenthood better, because it is our choice rather than our destiny. This knowledge has freed us from playing the role of mother if it is not a role that fits us. It has given us a sense of a larger life space to work in, an invigorating and challenging sense of time and room to discover the energies and talents that are in us, to do the work we want to do. And one of the things we most want to do is to help make this freedom of choice, this life space, available to every woman. That is why people in the women's movement have been so active in fighting against the inhumane legal restrictions, the imperfections of available contraceptives, the poor sex education, the highly priced and poorly administered health care that keeps too many women from having this crucial control over their bodies.

There is a fourth reason why knowledge about our bodies has generated so much new energy. For us, body education is core education. Our bodies are the physical bases from which we move out into the world; ignorance, uncertainty—even, at worst, shame—about our physical selves create in us an alienation from ourselves that keeps us from being the whole people that we could be. Picture a woman trying to do work and to enter into equal and satisfying relationships with other people—when she feels physically weak because she has never tried to be strong; when she drains her energy trying to change her face, her figure, her hair, her smells, to match some ideal norm set by magazines, movies, and TV; when she feels confused and ashamed of the menstrual blood that every month appears from some dark place in her body; when her internal body processes are a mystery to her and surface only to cause her trouble (an unplanned pregnancy, or cervical cancer); when she does not understand nor enjoy sex and concentrates her sexual drives into aimless romantic fantasies, perverting and misusing a potential energy because she has been brought up to deny it. Learning to understand, accept, and be responsible for our physical selves, we are freed of some of these preoccupations and can start to use our untapped energies. Our image of ourselves is on a firmer base, we can be better friends and better lovers, better *people*, more self-confident, more autonomous, stronger, and more whole.

CATHARINE R. STIMPSON

(from) The New Feminism and Women's Studies

An educator and academic activist, Catharine R. Stimpson (born 1936) was an early advocate of the Women's Studies movement. In the early 1970s, she helped launch both the Barnard College Women's Studies program and the Barnard Women's Center. In 1976 she chaired the emergent Women's Studies division of the Modern Language Association, becoming that organization's president in 1990. Stimpson was the founding editor-in-chief of the interdisciplinary *Signs: Journal of Women and Culture in Society,* which she edited from 1975 to 1980, and later served as a dean at New York University. In her 1973 article published in *Change,* Stimpson describes the late 1960s beginnings and phenomenal early growth of college Women's Studies courses and programs; in this excerpt, she explores the heterogeneous, contested movement's relation to feminism and the academy.

IT WOULD be, at best, grotesque to work to get a women's studies program without working to change the psychological, educational, social and political context in which such a program were to exist. It would be absurd for a student to talk about Mary Ellmann's notions of phallic criticism in the morning and then, in the afternoon, to have a historian tell her that the nineteenth-century feminists were crazed spinsters who ought to have been pouring tea or to have a man in the school health service lecture her about the wickedness of abortions. Consequently, women's studies and affirmative action are inseparable goals. Many people in women's studies would agree with Ann Scott, a vice-president of the National Organization for Women, when she writes: "I believe that a university must equip women to survive in our world of the overpowering institutions which have historically excluded them (including the university itself). It can do this through adopting a variety of intervention techniques designed for enabling women to intervene for themselves, through using its own resources to intervene for them, and through using its own structure as an arena for training in intervention."

This set of shared beliefs clearly embraces a mixture of hopes. Some are intellectual: women's studies will help us to think better and to know more accurately. Some are psychological: women's studies will help us to behave more humanely—women more freely, men less pompously. Some are political: women's studies will alter power relationships within institutions and between the sexes. A class itself may not engage in political activity—my literature class reads books—but students and faculty often share a sense of political engagement. Such an amalgam of intellectual, psychological and political ends helps to make women's studies less a monolithic movement than a multiplicity of groups.

The people in women's studies differ in temperament, values and in their approach to and ambition for women's studies. Some were pioneers, who took women as a serious academic subject before the new feminism made them a serious public issue; they may still take women as a serious academic subject, but they may not actively participate in the new feminism. Some are ideologues, who were feminists first and who now try to balance their politics and their profession. Some are radicals, who place both their feminism and their notion of women's studies within a large context of demands for revolutionary educational, political and social change. There are the late-comers, who recently discovered that women were an interesting academic subject and whose feminism is often enhanced when their new interest provokes resistance. Finally, there are bandwagoners of both sexes, whose attraction to women's studies is faddish and exploitative, and for whom women's studies may mean little more than writing a paper about the Wife of Bath instead of King Lear. I am an ideologue, who wondered how the insights that drove me on to a picket line might be applied to literature, and who wavers toward radicalism. Character, as well as a stubborn belief in the possibility of institutional change, softens my radicalism.

And I have found teaching women's studies courses exhilarating. For example, my first classes on Virginia Woolf's novel, *To the Lighthouse*, provoked paradigmatic quarrels among the students. At once moral and literary, the discussion whirled around the character of Mrs. Ramsey. The radicals loathed Mrs. Ramsey, to them a sheltered creature of the *bourgeoisie* who submitted to an oppressive husband's intolerable demands. The feminists were ambivalent. Ms. Ramsey, though she did take on a traditional role, had agreeable virtues: the desire to draw the alienated out of their psychological exile; the desire to unify the fragments of experience. The curious said the novel was a novel, not a tract, and that was that. As the quarrel, which I have oversimplified, went on, I felt the class exert a silent pressure upon me to exercise professorial authority and get it over with. Trying to dispel the notion that a teacher was *ipso facto* a greater authority than a class, I wanted the class to go on until its members had themselves articulated the terms of their disagreement. Finally, we had to compromise.

The men who had taken my course have been at once cheerful, smart, pleasant, modest and curious. Some of them have had encouraging girl friends. My sample is, however, highly selective. Talking about women's issues in general outside of the women's studies classroom but inside of the university community, I have found some male students marvelously receptive, but others either hostile, indifferent or nervous about women in authority. A favorite technique is to lecture uppity women and especially me, as their "representative," about feminism's flaws and failings. And to have a sophomore, who admits that he has never read Marx and Engels about women, announce that "a women's movement" has nothing to do with "the dialectic" strains both patience and credulity.

The questions that provoke internal quarrels, most intense between ideologues and radicals, haunt women's studies program after program. Some questions concern structure. Should a program be a separate department? If so, it may have more autonomy and self-control. On the other hand, a separate department may turn women's studies into a ghetto: older, more established departments may feel free blithely to ignore the scholarly discoveries and teaching methods of the women's studies group.

Other questions are conceptual. Is there such a thing as a woman's *gestalt*, and if so, should a program institutionalize that way of thinking, feeling, perceiving and responding? Still other questions are moral. What kind of person do I picture as the ideal product of a women's studies program? Would I, for example, celebrate if one of my students wanted to become the first woman president of a munitions factory? She would be exercising the freedom of choice that is a principle of the women's movement, but she would be choosing to make guns, which I find antithetical to other deep principles of the women's movement. Am I being either prissy or totalitarian even to ask what kind of a person a women's studies program ideally might produce?

The most perplexing questions are simultaneously structural, conceptual, political and moral. What, for example, is the relationship between a women's studies program and women in the larger community? What might that community be? Any woman in the surrounding neighborhood, or simply women of congenial intellectual concerns? If a women's liberation group in town helps to set up a women's studies program at a local university, should it have a say in that program? Should it have a veto over faculty hiring? Such a problem, for example, created tension between the Tampa Women's Center and the women's studies program at the University of South Florida. The women at the university, if for practical reasons alone, could not grant the women in the community the authority they sought.

What is the tie between a women's studies program and the women's movement? Does the former think of the latter simply as a fascinating phenomenon that history has obligingly cast up, or does someone in women's studies remain, as Marilyn Salzman-Webb says, "more closely tuned to an ongoing feminist movement than to the university proper"? Should a program take foundation money? Such money is useful, even necessary, but such money is also historically tainted. Even the laundering of philanthropy cannot wash out the ways in which great American fortunes were amassed.

The darkening quarrel about theory and practice is a psychological stain: an atavistic distrust that women often appear to feel toward other women who are either successful or have authority. That distrust may express itself in private gossip, public accusations or both. The code words in which the feeling is expressed—star, élitist, establishment sell-out, ripping off the movement—are easily deciphered. Clever administrators who wish to deflect pressure for women's studies as an academic program and for women's equity as an institutional policy—and who wish to do so without openly offending either women or HEW—increasingly manipulate such psychological guerilla wars for their own gain.

Clearly, some tensions are beyond immediate healing, some disagreements beyond reconciliation. Either a community woman has the power to vote on a university faculty member, or she does not. Either a program takes foundation money, or it does not. Either a senior male professor speaks to a 20-year-old traditionalist about chauvinism, or he does not. Yet some disagreements are more inflamed than necessary. It is clearly folly to say that working on a paper about Aphra Behn, that professional woman writer of the seventeenth century, renders me constitutionally incapable of demonstrating for day care during the same day. What may emerge from the women's studies movement is a temporary consensus that each program must work out its destiny; that no single program may claim an exclusive right to sanctity and perfection; that women's studies should be seen as a multiplicity of intersecting activities, not as a limited number of rigid models.

The internal turmoils also shrink in significance when they are compared to the larger quarrel between women's studies as a whole and its external opposition, which is far more ferocious than a casual observer might suspect. The habit of challenging women's studies either through scoffing ridicule or quiet gossip disguises its virulence. Doubts tend to surface rhetorically as a mixture of pejorative comment and question, and the verbal clusters, if dismembered, reveal some distressing attitudes. One such cluster, "Women's studies is female chauvinism. Aren't they going to study men?," arises from the false assumption that the practitioners of women's studies will simply invert the habits of the past, that women will now exclude the sex that once excluded them. Another cluster, "Women's studies is absurd. What's next? A Department of Male Studies?," reflects a refusal to take women seriously enough to make them a focus for the study of the world in general. A third cluster, "Women's studies is empty. Do they do anything besides scratch each other's consciousness?," ignores the solid accomplishments of women's studies and dismisses the respectable possibility that a liberal arts education might expand consciousness, personal and public.

Some of the sources of resistance are too powerful to be ignored, others too sympathetic on other grounds to be disdained. Institutional conservatives of both sexes dislike any disruption of current curriculum and intellectual practices. Women themselves often distrust any challenge to the notions of sexuality and sex roles that society has offered and they have accepted. Many, but not all, blacks resist women's studies, which seems to them the latest plaything of pampered, middle-class, white women, and a competitor for funds and administrative attention to black studies. The competition among black men, black women and white women for campus jobs affirmative action programs have opened up tends to stir the sour soup of suspicion. Young male faculty members, neurotically convinced that losing to a woman is more emasculating than losing to a man, are legitimately anxious about the academic job market and often too shrewd or too insecure to begin a career with a reputation as a boat-rocker. They may fear women's studies as the opening wedge of a social force that will threaten their personal security, intellectual values and ingrained ambitions.

Behind the resistance, of course, is a deep cultural bias against brainy women. The bias, which implies that women and studies are mutually contradictory, asserts that men are rational, women irrational; men use their heads, women their hearts; men inhabit and manage our great institutions, women the home. The belief is so obviously silly that people often refuse to admit it has influenced them. Certainly, intelligent people of both sexes have long protested against it. In 1792, for example, Mary Wollstonecraft, in the *Vindication of the Rights of Woman*, was attacking Rousseau, who declared in *Emile* that women were more or less incapable of reason. The necessity of protest remains.

ALICE WALKER

In Search of Our Mothers' Gardens

"Did you have a genius of a great-great-grandmother who died under some igno-rant and depraved white overseer's lash?" asks poet and novelist Alice Walker (born 1944). In this 1974 blend of memoir and polemic, Walker identifies the cre-ative achievements of African American women who fought the silence and invis-ibility of enslavement and poverty with the harmonies and power of the blues, the patterns of unsigned quilts, and gardens like that of her own mother. In her story "Coming Apart" (1979), Walker coined the term "Womanism" to describe the feminism of Black women whose activism is expressed in everyday life, a theme to which she would return in her Pulitzer Prize–winning 1982 novel *The Color Purple*.

> *I described her own nature and temperament. Told how they needed a larger life for their expression. . . . I pointed out that in lieu of proper channels, her emotions had overflowed into paths that dissipated them. I talked, beautifully I thought, about an art that would be born, an art that would open the way for women the likes of her. I asked her to hope, and build up an inner life against the coming of that day. . . . I sang, with a strange quiver in my voice, a promise song.*
>
> "Avey," Jean Toomer, *Cane*
> The poet speaking to a prostitute who falls asleep while he's talking—

WHEN THE poet Jean Toomer walked throuth the South in the early twenties, he discovered a curious thing: Black women whose spirituality was so intense, so deep, so *unconscious*, that they were themselves unaware of the richness they held. They stumbled blindly through their lives: creatures so abused and mutilated in body, so dimmed and confused by pain, that they considered themselves unworthy even of hope. In the selfless abstractions their bodies became to the men who used them, they became more than "sexual objects," more even than mere women: they became Saints. Instead of being perceived as whole persons, their bodies became shrines: what was thought to be their minds became temples suitable for worship. These crazy "Saints" stared out at the world, wildly, like lunatics—or quietly, like suicides; and the "God" that was in their gaze was as mute as a great stone.

Who were these "Saints"? These crazy, loony, pitiful women?

Some of them, without a doubt, were our mothers and grandmothers.

In the still heat of the Post-Reconstruction South, this is how they seemed to Jean Toomer: exquisite butterflies trapped in an evil honey, toiling away their lives in an era, a century, that did not acknowledge them, except as "the *mule* of the world." They dreamed dreams that no one knew—not even themselves, in any coherent fashion—and saw visions no one could understand. They wandered or sat about the countryside crooning lullabies to ghosts, and drawing the mother of Christ in charcoal on courthouse walls.

They forced their minds to desert their bodies and their striving spirits sought to rise, like frail whirlwinds from the hard red clay. And when those frail whirlwinds fell, in scattered particles, upon the ground, no one mourned. Instead, men lit candles to celebrate the emptiness that remained, as people do who enter a beautiful but vacant space to resurrect a God.

Our mothers and grandmothers, some of them: moving to music not yet written. And they waited.

They waited for a day when the unknown thing that was in them would be made known; but guessed, somehow in their darkness, that on the day of their revelation they would be long dead. Therefore to Toomer they walked, and even ran, in slow motion. For they were going nowhere immediate, and the future was not yet within their grasp. And men took our mothers and grandmothers, "but got no pleasure from it." So complex was their passion and their calm.

To Toomer, they lay vacant and fallow as autumn fields, with harvest time never in sight: and he saw them enter loveless marriages, without joy; and become prostitutes, without resistance; and become mothers of children, without fulfillment.

For these grandmothers and mothers of ours were not "Saints," but Artists; driven to a numb and bleeding madness by the springs of creativity in them for which there was no release. They were Creators, who lived lives of spiritual waste, because they were so rich in spirituality—which is the basis of Art—that the strain of enduring their unused and unwanted talent drove them insane. Throwing away this spirituality was their pathetic attempt to lighten the soul to a weight their work-worn, sexually abused bodies could bear.

What did it mean for a Black woman to be an artist in our grandmothers' time? In our great-grandmothers' day? It is a question with an answer cruel enough to stop the blood.

Did you have a genius of a great-great-grandmother who died under some ignorant and deprived white overseer's lash? Or was she required to bake biscuits for a lazy backwater tramp, when she cried out in her soul to paint watercolors of sunsets, or the rain falling on the green and peaceful pasturelands? Or was her body broken and forced to bear children (who were more often than not sold away from her)—eight, ten, fifteen, twenty children—when her one joy was the thought of modeling heroic figures of Rebellion, in stone or clay?

How was the creativity of the Black woman kept alive, year after year and century after century, when for most of the years Black people have been in America, it was a punishable crime for a Black person to read or write? And the freedom to paint, to sculpt, to expand the mind with action, did not exist. Consider, if you can bear to imagine it, what might have been the result if singing, too, had been forbidden by law. Listen to the voices of Bessie Smith, Billie Holiday, Nina Simone, Roberta Flack, and Aretha Franklin, among others, and imagine those voices muzzled for life. Then you may begin to comprehend the lives of our "crazy," "Sainted" mothers and grandmothers. The agony of the lives of women who might have been Poets, Novelists, Essayists, and Short Story Writers (over a period of centuries), who died with their real gifts stifled within them.

And, if this were the end of the story, we would have cause to cry out in my paraphrase of Okot p'Bitek's great poem:

> *O, my clanswomen*
> *Let us all cry together!*
> *Come,*
> *Let us mourn the death of our mother,*
> *The death of a Queen*
> *The ash that was produced*
> *By a great fire!*
> *O this homestead is utterly dead*
> *Close the gates*
> *With* lacari *thorns,*
> *For our mother*
> *The creator of the Stool is lost!*
> *And all the young women*
> *Have perished in the wilderness!*

But this is not the end of the story, for all the young women—our mothers and grandmothers, *ourselves*—have not perished in the wilderness. And if we ask ourselves why, and search for and find the answer, we will know beyond all efforts to erase it from our minds, just exactly who, and of what, we Black American women are.

One example, perhaps the most pathetic, most misunderstood one, can provide a backdrop for our mother's work: Phillis Wheatley, a slave in the 1700s.

Virginia Woolf, in her book, *A Room of One's Own*, wrote that in order for a woman to write fiction she must have two things, certainly: a room of her own (with key and lock) and enough money to support herself.

What then are we to make of Phillis Wheatley, a slave, who owned not even herself? This sickly, frail, Black girl who required a servant of her own at times—her health was so precarious—and who, had she been white, would have been easily considered the intellectual superior of all the women and most of the men in the society of her day.

Virginia Woolf wrote further, speaking of course not of our Phillis, that "any woman born with a great gift in the sixteenth century [insert *eighteenth century*, insert *Black woman*, insert *born or made a slave*] would certainly have gone crazed, shot herself, or ended her days in some lonely cottage outside the village, half witch, half wizard [insert *Saint*], feared and mocked at. For it needs little skill and psychology to be sure that a highly gifted girl who had tried to use her gift for poetry would have been so thwarted and hindered by contrary instincts [add *chains, guns, the lash, the ownership of one's body by someone else, submission to an alien religion*], that she must have lost her health and sanity to a certainty."

The key words, as they relate to Phillis, are "contrary instincts." For when we read the poetry of Phillis Wheatley—as when we read the novels of Nella Larsen or the oddly false-sounding autobiography of that freest of all Black women writers, Zora Hurston—evidence of "contrary instincts" is everywhere. Her loyalties were completely divided, as was, without question, her mind.

But how could this be otherwise? Captured at seven, a slave of wealthy, doting whites who instilled in her the "savagery" of the Africa they "rescued" her from . . . one wonders if she was even able to remember her homeland as she had known it, or as it really was.

Yet, because she did try to use her gift for poetry in a world that made her a slave, she was "so thwarted and hindered by . . . contrary instincts, that she . . . lost her health. . . ." In the last years of her brief life, burdened not only with the need to express her gift but also with a penniless, friendless "freedom" and several small children for whom she was forced to do strenuous work to feed, she lost her health, certainly. Suffering from malnutrition and neglect and who knows what mental agonies, Phillis Wheatley died.

So torn by "contrary instincts" was Black, kidnapped, enslaved Phillis that her description of "the Goddess"—as she poetically called the Liberty she did not have—is ironically, cruelly humorous. And, in fact, has held Phillis up to ridicule for more than a century. It is usually read prior to hanging Phillis's memory as that of a fool. She wrote:

> *The Goddess comes, she moves divinely fair,*
> *Olive and laurel binds her golden hair:*
> *Wherever shines this native of the skies,*
> *Unnumber'd charms and recent graces rise.*
> (Emphasis mine)

It is obvious that Phillis, the slave, combed the "Goddess's" hair every morning; prior, perhaps, to bringing in the milk, or fixing her mistress's lunch. She took her imagery from the one thing she saw elevated above all others.

With the benefit of hindsight we ask, "How could she?"

But at last, Phillis, we understand. No more snickering when your stiff, struggling, ambivalent lines are forced on us. We know now that you were not an idiot nor a traitor; only a sickly little Black girl, snatched from your home and country and made a slave; a woman who still struggled to sing the song that was your gift, although in a land of barbarians who praised you for your bewildered tongue. It is not so much what you sang, as that you kept alive, in so many of our ancestors, *the notion of song.*

II

Black women are called, in the folklore that so aptly identifies one's status in society, "the *mule* of the world," because we have been handed the burdens that everyone else—*everyone* else—refused to carry. We have also been called "Matriarchs," "Superwomen," and "Mean and Evil Bitches." Not to mention "Castraters" and "Sapphire's Mama." When we have pleaded for understanding, our character has been distorted; when we have asked for simple caring, we have been handed empty inspirational appellations, then stuck in the farthest corner. When we have asked for love, we have been given children. In short, even our plainer gifts, our labors of fidelity and love, have been knocked down our throats. To be an artist and a Black woman, even today, lowers our status in many respects, rather than raises it: and yet, artists we will be.

Therefore we must fearlessly pull out of ourselves and look at and identify with our lives the living creativity some of our great-grandmothers were not allowed to know. I stress *some* of them because it is well known that the majority of our great-grandmothers knew, even without "knowing" it, the reality of their spirituality, even if they didn't recognize it beyond what happened in the singing at church—and they never had any intention of giving it up.

How they did it: those millions of Black women who were not Phillis Wheatley, or Lucy Terry or Frances Harper or Zora Hurston or Nella Larsen or Bessie Smith—nor Elizabeth Catlett, nor Katherine Dunham, either—bring me to the title of this essay, "In Search of Our Mothers' Gardens," which is a personal account that is yet shared, in its theme and its meaning, by all of us. I found, while thinking about the far-reaching world of the creative Black woman, that often the truest answer to a question that really matters can be found very close. So I was not surprised when my own mother popped into my mind.

In the late 1920s my mother ran away from home to marry my father. Marriage, if not running away, was expected of 17-year-old girls. By the time she was 20, she had two children and was pregnant with a third. Five children later, I was born. And this is how I came to know my mother: she seemed a large, soft, loving-eyed woman who was rarely impatient in our home. Her quick, violent temper was on view only a few times a year, when she battled with the white landlord who had the misfortune to suggest to her that her children did not need to go to school.

She made all the clothes we wore, even my brothers' overalls. She made all the towels and sheets we used. She spent the summers canning vegetables and fruits. She spent the winter evenings making quilts enough to cover all our beds.

During the "working" day, she labored beside—not behind—my father in the fields. Her day began before sunup, and did not end until late at night. There was never a moment for her to sit down, undisturbed, to unravel her own private thoughts; never a time free from interruption—by work or the noisy inquiries of her many children. And yet, it is to my mother—and all our mothers who were not famous—that I went in search of the secret of what has fed that muzzled and often mutilated, but vibrant, creative spirit that the Black woman has inherited, and that pops out in wild and unlikely places to this day.

But when, you will ask, did my overworked mother have time to know or care about feeding the creative spirit?

The answer is so simple that many of us have spent years discovering it. We have constantly looked high, when we should have looked high—and low.

For example: in the Smithsonian Institution in Washington, D.C., there hangs a quilt unlike any other in the world. In fanciful, inspired, and yet simple and identifiable figures, it portrays the story of the Crucifixion. It is considered rare, beyond price. Though it follows no known pattern of quiltmaking, and though it is made of bits and pieces of worthless rags, it is obviously the work of a person of powerful imagination and deep spiritual feeling. Below this quilt I saw a note that says it was made by "an anonymous Black Woman in Alabama, a hundred years ago."

If we could locate this "anonymous" Black woman from Alabama, she would turn out to be one of our grandmothers—an artist who left her mark in the only materials she could afford, and in the only medium her position in society allowed her to use.

As Virginia Woolf wrote further, in *A Room of One's Own*:

"Yet genius of a sort must have existed among women as it must have existed among the working class. [Change this to *slaves* and *the wives and daughters of sharecroppers*.] Now and again an Emily Brontë or a Robert Burns [change this to *a Zora Hurston or a Richard Wright*] blazes out and proves its presence. But certainly it never got itself on to paper. When, however, one reads of a witch being ducked, of a woman possessed by devils [or *Sainthood*], of a wise woman selling herbs [our rootworkers], or even a very remarkable man who had a mother, then I think we are on the track of a lost novelist, a suppressed poet, of some mute and inglorious Jane Austen. . . . Indeed, I would venture to guess that Anon, who wrote so many poems without signing them, was often a woman. . . ."

And so our mothers and grandmothers have, more often than not anonymously, handed on the creative spark, the seed of the flower they themselves never hoped to see: or like a sealed letter they could not plainly read.

And so it is, certainly, with my own mother. Unlike "Ma" Rainey's songs, which retained their creator's name even while blasting forth from Bessie Smith's mouth, no song or poem will bear my mother's name. Yet so many of the stories that I write, that we all write, are my mother's stories. Only recently did I fully realize this: that through years of listening to my mother's stories of her life, I have absorbed not only the stories themselves, but something of the manner in which she spoke, something of the urgency that involves the knowledge that her stories—like her life—must be recorded. It is probably for this reason that so much of what I have written is about characters whose counterparts in real life are so much older than I am.

But the telling of these stories, which came from my mother's lips as naturally as breathing, was not the only way my mother showed herself as an artist. For stories, too, were subject to being distracted, to dying without conclusion. Dinners must be started, and cotton must be gathered before the big rains. The artist that was and is my mother showed itself to me only after many years. This is what I finally noticed:

Like Mem, a character in *The Third Life of Grange Copeland*, my mother adorned with flowers whatever shabby house we were forced to live in. And not just your typical straggly country stand of zinnias, either. She planted ambitious gardens—and still does—with over 50 different varieties of plants that bloom profusely from early March until late November. Before she left home for the fields, she watered her flowers, chopped up the grass, and laid out new beds. When she returned from the fields she might divide clumps of bulbs, dig a cold pit, uproot and replant roses, or prune branches from her taller bushes or trees—until night came and it was too dark to see.

Whatever she planted grew as if by magic, and her fame as a grower of flowers spread over three counties. Because of her creativity with her flowers, even my memories of poverty are seen through a screen of blooms—sunflowers, petunias, roses, dahlias, forsythia, spirea, delphiniums, verbena . . . and on and on.

And I remember people coming to my mother's yard to be given cuttings from her flowers; I hear again the praise showered on her because whatever rocky soil she landed on, she turned into a garden. A garden so brilliant with colors, so original in its design, so magnificent with life and creativity, that to this day people drive by our house in Georgia—perfect strangers and imperfect strangers—and ask to stand or walk among my mother's art.

I notice that it is only when my mother is working in her flowers that she is radiant, almost to the point of being invisible—except as Creator: hand and eye. She is involved in work her soul must have. Ordering the universe in the image of her personal conception of Beauty.

Her face, as she prepares the Art that is her gift, is a legacy of respect she leaves to me, for all that illuminates and cherishes life. She had handed down respect for the possibilities—and the will to grasp them.

For her, so hindered and intruded upon in so many ways, being an artist has still been a daily part of her life. This ability to hold on, even in very simple ways, is work Black women have done for a very long time.

This poem is not enough, but it is something, for the woman who literally covered the holes in our walls with sunflowers:

> *They were women then*
> *My mama's generation*
> *Husky of voice—Stout of*
> *Step*
> *With fists as well as*
> *Hands*
> *How they battered down*

Doors
And ironed
Starched white
Shirts
How they led
Armies
Headragged Generals
Across mined
Fields
Booby-trapped
Ditches
To discover books
Desks
A place for us
How they knew what we
Must *know*
Without knowing a page
Of it
Themselves.

Guided by my heritage of a love of beauty and a respect for strength—in search of my mother's garden, I found my own.

And perhaps in Africa over 200 years ago, there was just such a mother; perhaps she painted vivid and daring decorations in oranges and yellows and greens on the walls of her hut; perhaps she sang—in a voice like Roberta Flack's—*sweetly* over the compounds of her village; perhaps she wove the most stunning mats or told the most ingenious stories of all the village storytellers. Perhaps she was herself a poet—though only her daughter's name is signed to the poems that we know.

Perhaps Phillis Wheatley's mother was also an artist.

Perhaps in more than Phillis Wheatley's biological life is her mother's signature made clear.

SILVIA FEDERICI

Wages against Housework

A Marxist-feminist scholar and activist, Italian-born Silvia Federici (born 1942) was instrumental in raising consciousness in the U.S. about the true value of women's unpaid labor. In 1973, in New York, she cofounded the first Wages for House-work Committee, which soon spawned branches in half a dozen U.S. cities, as well as the autonomous group Black Women for Wages for Housework. With her 1974 book *Wages against Housework,* Federici emerged as a major theoreti-cian of the wages-for-housework movement, which held that unpaid "reproduc-tive" work (including housework, child and elder care, and emotional and sexual labor) shores up capitalism and enforces social and economic gender inequality, strengthening men's control over women's lives. Some opponents within the fem-inist movement argued, however, that payment for housework would reinforce the gendered division of labor that excuses men from assuming their fair share of domestic work.

> They say it is love. We say it is unwaged work.
> They call it frigidity. We call it absenteeism.
> Every miscarriage is a work accident.
> Homosexuality and heterosexuality are both working conditions
> . . . but homosexuality is workers' control of production, not
> the end of work.
> More smiles? More money. Nothing will be so powerful in
> destroying the healing virtues of a smile.
> Neuroses, suicides, desexualisation: occupational diseases of the
> housewife.

MANY TIMES the difficulties and ambiguities which women express in discussing wages for housework stem from the reduction of wages for housework to a thing, a lump of money, instead of viewing it as a political perspective. The difference between these two standpoints is enormous. To view wages for housework as a thing rather than a perspective is to detach the end result of our struggle from the struggle itself and to miss its significance in demystifying and subverting the role to which women have been confined in capitalist society.

When we view wages for housework in this reductive way we start asking ourselves: what difference could some more money make to our lives? We might even agree that for a lot of women who do not have any choice except for housework and marriage, it would indeed make a lot of difference. But for those of us who seem to have other choices—professional work, enlightened husband, communal way of life, gay relations or a combination of these—it would not make much of a difference at all. For us there are supposedly other ways of achieving economic independence, and the last thing we want is to get it by identifying ourselves as housewives, a fate which we all agree is, so to speak, worse than death. The problem with this position is that in our imagination we usually add a bit of money to the shitty lives we have now and then ask, so what? on the false premise that we could ever get that money without at the same time revolutionising—in the process of struggling for it—all our family and social relations. But if we take wages for housework as a political perspective, we can see that struggling for it is going to produce a revolution in our lives and in our social power as women. It is also clear that if we think we do not "need" that money, it is because we have accepted the particular forms of prostitution of body and mind by which we get the money to hide that need. As I will try to show, not only is wages for housework a revolutionary perspective, but *it is the only revolutionary perspective from a feminist viewpoint and ultimately for the entire working class.*

"A LABOUR OF LOVE"

It is important to recognise that when we speak of housework we are not speaking of a job as other jobs, but we are speaking of the most pervasive manipulation, the most subtle and mystified violence that capitalism has ever perpetrated against any section of the working class. True, under capitalism every worker is manipulated and exploited and his/her relation to capital is totally mystified. The wage gives the impression of a fair deal: you work and you get paid, hence you and your boss are equal; while in reality the wage, rather than paying for the work you do, hides all the unpaid work that goes into profit. But the wage at least recognises that you are a worker, and you can bargain and struggle around and against the terms and the quantity of that wage, the terms and the quantity of that work. To have a wage means to be part of a social contract, and there is no doubt concerning its meaning: you work, not because you like it, or because it comes naturally to you, but because it is the only condition under which you are allowed to live. But exploited as you might be, *you are not that work*. Today you are a postman, tomorrow a cabdriver. All that matters is how much of that work you have to do and how much of that money you can get.

But in the case of housework the situation is qualitatively different. The difference lies in the fact that not only has housework been imposed on women, but it has been transformed into a natural attribute of our female physique and personality, an internal need, an aspiration, supposedly coming from the depth of our female character. Housework had to be transformed into a natural attribute rather than be recognised as a social contract because from the beginning of capital's scheme for women this work was destined to be unwaged. Capital had to convince us that it is a natural, unavoidable and even fulfilling activity to make us accept our unwaged work. In its turn, the unwaged condition of housework has been the most powerful weapon in reinforcing the common assumption that *housework is not work*, thus preventing women from struggling against it, except in the privatised kitchen-bedroom quarrel that all society agrees to ridicule, thereby further reducing the protagonist of a struggle. We are seen as nagging bitches, not workers in struggle.

Yet just how natural it it to be a housewife is shown by the fact that it takes at least twenty years of socialisation—day-to-day training, performed by an unwaged mother—to prepare a woman for this role, to convince her that children and husband are the best she can expect from life. Even so, it hardly succeeds. No matter how well trained we are, few are the women who do not feel cheated when the bride's day is over and they find themselves in front of a dirty sink. Many of us still have the illusion that we marry for love. A lot of us recognise that we marry for money and security; but it is time to make it clear that while the love or money involved is very little, the work which awaits us is enormous. This is why older women always tell us "Enjoy your freedom while you can, buy whatever you want now . . ." But unfortunately it is almost impossible to enjoy any freedom if from the earliest days of life you are trained to be docile, subservient, dependent and most important to *sacrifice yourself* and even to get pleasure from it. If you don't like it, it is your problem, your failure, your guilt, your abnormality.

We must admit that capital has been very successful in hiding our work. It has created a true masterpiece at the expense of women. By denying housework a wage and transforming it into an act of love, capital has killed many birds with one stone. First of all, it has got a hell of a lot of work almost for free, and it has made sure that women, far from struggling against it, would seek that work as the best thing in life (the magic words: "Yes, darling, you are a real woman"). At the same time, it has disciplined the male worker also, by making *his* woman dependent on *his* work and *his* wage, and trapped him in this discipline by giving him a servant after he himself has done so much serving at the factory or the office. In fact, our role as women is to be the unwaged but happy, and most of all loving, servants of the "working class," i.e. those strata of the proletariat to which capital was forced to grant more social power. In the same way as god created Eve to give pleasure to Adam, so did capital create the housewife to service the male worker physically, emotionally and sexually—to raise *his* children, mend his socks, patch up his ego when it is crushed by the work and the social relations (which are relations of loneliness) that capital has reserved for him. It is precisely this peculiar combination of physical, emotional and sexual services that are involved in the role women must perform for capital that creates the specific character of that servant which is the housewife, that makes her work so burdensome and at the same time invisible. It is not an accident that most men start thinking of getting married as soon as they get their first job. This is not only because now they can afford it, but because having somebody at home who takes care of you is the only condition not to go crazy after a day spent on an assembly line or at a desk. Every woman knows that this is what she should be doing to be a true woman and have a "successful" marriage. And in this case too, the poorer the family the higher the enslavement of the woman, and not simply because of the monetary situation. In fact capital has a dual policy, one for the middle class and one for the proletarian family. It is no accident that we find the most unsophisticated machismo in the working class family: the more blows the man gets at work the more his wife must be trained to absorb them, the more he is allowed to recover his ego at her expense. You beat your wife and vent your rage against her when you are frustrated or overtired by your work or when you are defeated in a struggle (to go into a factory is itself a defeat). The more the man serves and is bossed around, the more he bosses around. A man's home is his castle . . . and his wife has to learn to wait in silence when he is moody, to put him back together when he is broken down and swears at the world, to turn around in bed when he says "I'm too tired tonight," or when he goes so fast at love-making that, as one woman put it, he might as well make it with a mayonnaise jar. (Women have always found ways of fighting back, or getting back at them, but always in an isolated and privatised way. The problem, then, becomes how to bring this struggle out of the kitchen and bedroom and into the streets.)

This fraud that goes under the name of love and marriage affects all of us, even if we are not married, because *once housework was totally naturalised and sexualised*, once it became a feminine attribute, all of us as females are characterised by it. If it is natural to do certain things, then all women are expected to do them and even like doing them—even those women who, due to their social position, could escape some of that work or most of it (their husbands can afford maids and shrinks and other forms of relaxation and amusement). We might not serve one man, but we are all in a servant relation with respect to the whole male world. This is why to be called a female is such a putdown, such a degrading thing. ("Smile, honey, what's the matter with you?" is something every man feels entitled to ask you, whether he is your husband, or the man who takes your ticket, or your boss at work.)

The Revolutionary Perspective

If we start from this analysis we can see the revolutionary implications of the demand for wages for housework. *It is the demand by which our nature ends and our struggle begins because just to want wages for housework means to refuse that work as the expression of our nature*, and therefore to refuse precisely the female role that capital has invented for us.

To ask for wages for housework will by itself undermine the expectations society has of us, since these expectations—the essence of our socialisation— are all functional to our wageless condition in the home. In this sense, it is absurd to compare the struggle of women for wages to the struggle of male workers in the factory for more wages. The waged worker in struggling for more wages challenges his social role but remains within it. When we struggle for wages *we struggle unambiguously and directly against our social role*. In the same way there is a qualitative difference between the struggles of the waged worker and the struggles of the slave *for a wage against that slavery*. It should be clear, however, that when we struggle for a wage we do not struggle to enter capitalist relations, because we have never been out of them. We struggle to break capital's plan for women, which is an essential moment of that planned division of labour and social power within the working class, through which capital has been able to maintain its power. Wages for housework, then, is a revolutionary demand not because by itself it destroys capital, but because it attacks capital and forces it to restructure social relations in terms more favourable to us and consequently *more favourable to the unity of the class*. In fact, to demand wages for housework does not mean to say that if we are paid we will continue to do it. It means precisely the opposite. To say that we want money for housework is the first step towards refusing to do it, because the demand for a wage makes our work visible, which is the most indispensable condition to begin to struggle against it, both in its immediate aspect as housework and its more insidious character as femininity.

Against any accusation of "economism" we should remember that *money is capital,* i.e. *it is the power to command labour.* Therefore to reappropriate that money which is the fruit of our labour—of our mothers' and grandmothers' labour—means at the same time to undermine capital's power to command forced labour from us. And we should not distrust the power of the wage in demystifying our femaleness and making visible our work—our femaleness as work—since the lack of a wage has been so powerful in shaping this role and hiding our work. To demand wages for housework is to make it visible that our minds, bodies and emotions have all been distorted for a specific function, in a specific function, and then have been thrown back at us as a model to which we should all conform if we want to be accepted as women in this society.

To say that we want wages for housework is to expose the fact that housework is already money for capital, that capital has made and makes money out of our cooking, smiling, fucking. At the same time, it shows that we have cooked, smiled, fucked throughout the years not because it was easier for us than for anybody else, but because we did not have any other choice. Our faces have become distorted from so much smiling, our feelings have got lost from so much loving, our oversexualisation has left us completely desexualised.

Wages for housework is only the beginning, but its message is clear: *from now on they have to pay us because as females we do not guarantee anything any longer.* We want to call work what is work so that eventually we might rediscover what is love and create what will be our sexuality which we have never known. And from the viewpoint of work we can ask not one wage but many wages, because we have been forced into many jobs at once. We are housemaids, prostitutes, nurses, shrinks; this is the essence of the "heroic" spouse who is celebrated on "Mother's Day." We say: stop celebrating our exploitation, our supposed heroism. From now on we want money for each moment of it, so that we can refuse some of it and eventually all of it. In this respect nothing can be more effective than to show that our female virtues have a calculable money value, until today only for capital, increased in the measure that we were defeated; from now on against capital *for us* in the measure we organise our power.

THE STRUGGLE FOR SOCIAL SERVICES

This is the most radical perspective we can adopt because although we can ask for everything, day care, equal pay, free laundromats, we will never achieve any real change unless we attack our female role at its roots. Our struggle for social services, i.e. for better working conditions, will always be frustrated if we do not first establish that our work is work. Unless we struggle against the totality of it we will never achieve victories with respect to any of its moments. We will fail in the struggle for the free laundromats unless we first struggle against the fact that we cannot love except at the price of endless work, which day after day cripples our bodies, our sexuality, our social relations, unless we first escape the blackmail whereby our need to give and receive affection is turned against us as a work duty for which we constantly feel resentful against our husbands, children and friends, and guilty for that resentment. Getting a second job does not change that role, as years and years of female work outside the house still witness. The second job not only increases our exploitation, but simply reproduces our role in different forms. Wherever we turn we can see that the jobs women perform are mere extensions of the housewife condition in all its implications. That is, not only do we become nurses, maids, teachers, secretaries—all functions for which we are well trained in the home—but we are in the same bind that hinders our struggles in the home: isolation, the fact that other people's lives depend on us, or the impossibility to see where our work begins and ends, where our work ends and our desires begin. Is bringing coffee to your boss and chatting with him about his marital problems secretarial work or is it a personal favour? Is the fact that we have to worry about our looks on the job a condition of work or is it the result of female vanity? (Until recently airline stewardesses in the United States were periodically weighed and had to be constantly on a diet—a torture that all women know—for fear of being laid off.) As is often said—when the needs of the waged labour market require her presence there—"A woman can do any job without losing her femininity," which simply means that no matter what you do you are still a cunt.

As for the proposal of socialisation and collectivisation of housework, a couple of examples will be sufficient to draw a line between these alternatives and our perspective. It is one thing to set up a day care centre the way we want it, and demand that the State pay for it. It is quite another thing to deliver our children to the State and ask the State to control them, discipline them, teach them to honour the American flag not for five hours, but for fifteen or twenty-four hours. It is one thing to organise communally the way we want to eat (by ourselves, in groups, etc.) and then ask the State to pay for it, and it is the opposite thing to ask the State to organise our meals. In one case we regain some control over our lives, in the other we extend the State's control over us.

THE STRUGGLE AGAINST HOUSEWORK

Some women say: how is wages for housework going to change the attitudes of our husbands towards us? Won't our husbands still expect the same duties as before and even more than before once we are paid for them? But these women do not see that they can expect so much from us precisely because we are not paid for our work, because they assume that it is "a woman's thing" which does not cost us much effort. Men are able to accept our services and take pleasure in them because they presume that housework is easy for us, that we enjoy it because we do it for their love. They actually expect us to be grateful because by marrying us or living with us they have given us the opportunity to express ourselves as women (i.e. to serve them), "You are lucky you have found a man like me." Only when men see our work as work—our love as work—and most important *our determination to refuse both*, will they change their attitude towards us. When hundreds and thousands of women are in the streets saying that endless cleaning, being always emotionally available, fucking at command for fear of losing our jobs is hard, hated work which wastes our lives, then they will be scared and feel undermined as men. But this is the best thing that can happen from their own point of view, because by exposing the way capital has kept us divided (capital has disciplined them through us and us through them—each other, against each other), we—their crutches, their slaves, their chains—open the process of their liberation. In this sense wages for housework will be much more educational than trying to prove that we can work as well as them, that we can do the same jobs. We leave this worthwhile effort to the "career woman," the woman who escapes from her oppression not through the power of unity and struggle, but through the power of the master, the power to oppress—usually other women. And we don't have to prove that we can "break the blue collar barrier." A lot of us broke that barrier a long time ago and have discovered that the overalls did not give us more power than the apron; if possible even less, because now we had to wear both and had less time and energy to struggle against them. *The things we have to prove are our capacity to expose what we are already doing, what capital is doing to us and our power in the struggle against it.*

Unfortunately, many women—particularly single women—are afraid of the perspective of wages for housework because they are afraid of identifying even for a second with the housewife. They know that this is the most power-less position in society and so they do not want to realise that they are house-wives too. This is precisely their weakness, a weakness which is maintained and perpetuated through the lack of self-identification. We want and have to say that we are all housewives, we are all prostitutes and we are all gay, because until we recognise our slavery we cannot recognise our struggle against it, because as long as we think we are something better, something different than a housewife, we accept the logic of the master, which is a logic of division, and for us the logic of slavery. We are all housewives because no matter where we are they can always count on more work from us, more fear on our side to put forward our demands, and less pressure on them for money, since hopefully our minds are directed elsewhere, to that man in our present or our future who will "take care of us."

And we also delude ourselves that we can escape housework. But how many of us, in spite of working outside the house, have escaped it? And can we really so easily disregard the idea of living with a man? What if we lose our jobs? What about ageing and losing even the minimal amount of power that youth (productivity) and attractiveness (female productivity) afford us today? And what about children? Will we ever regret having chosen not to have them, not even having been able to realistically ask that question? And can we afford gay relations? Are we willing to pay the possible price of isolation and exclusion? But can we really afford relations with men?

The question is: why are these our only alternatives and what kind of struggle will move us beyond them?

LOLLY HIRSCH

Practicing Health Without a License

A civil rights and peace activist, Lolly Hirsch (1922–1987) joined the women's health movement, calling on women to take back control of their bodies from male doctors. While the Boston Women's Health Collective produced *Our Bodies, Ourselves* (see also pp. 242–47 in this volume), California activists, as Hirsch reports in this 1975 article, developed and taught techniques of gynecological self-examination and early-stage self-abortion (menstrual extraction) to women throughout the country. (See photo insert.) In 1972, Los Angeles police raided California's first Feminist Women's Health Center, arresting cofounders Carol Downer and Coleen Wilson for "practicing medicine without a license." Wilson pleaded guilty to fitting a diaphragm, while Downer was acquitted by a jury on all counts, including inserting yogurt vaginally to relieve a yeast infection. Known as The Yogurt Case, it became a feminist cause célèbre. With her daughters, Hirsch founded New Moon Communications, which published several books and the newsletter *The Monthly Extract: An Irregular Periodical*, which they printed in Hirsch's basement until 1978.

O N APRIL 7, 1971 Carol Downer inserted a plastic speculum into her vaginal area and invited friends at a N.O.W. meeting to view her vagina and cervix.

A REVOLUTION WAS BORN!

Carol Downer's cervical canal that had expanded to deliver her six children was now the birth place of a revolution in women's health that would sweep around the world in several short years effecting drastic, basic changes in the field of obstetrics and gynecology.

Just as Carol had been transfixed by her first view of her vagina in a Seattle, Washington abortion clinic, the other women present that night were fascinated by the view that previously had been reserved for men only—men in medicine.

Today thousands and thousands of women throughout the world have observed the cervix of a real woman. Time and time again, after gynecological self help slide presentations, when women look at the female vagina for the first time, they say, "Is *that* all they've been looking at?"

The purity and simplicity of a woman's inner sanctum have been transformed by the medical profession into a mysterious, complicated territory forbidden-to-women that involves expensive, humiliating and often sadistic medical treatment, drugs, and surgical procedures. The normal functions of the human female—menstruation, ovulation, child birth, termination of pregnancy and menopause—have been designated by medicine through medical textbooks as the manifestations of disorder, dysfunction, and disease.

With political astuteness, men staked out the birthing canal as their property, first by liquidating millions of women health healers and midwives in the witch hunts and Inquisition of the 14th to 17th centuries; next, by bringing women's health under the control of professional (male) medicine; and, finally, by excluding women from medicine through the enforcement of stiff quotas at medical schools.

Medical men have become the army of occupation guarding the birthing canal for the patriarchy.

In 1920 Margaret Sanger asked this question of a German gynecologist: "Why is it such an act of enmity to advocate contraceptives rather than abortions? Abortions, as you know yourself, may be quite dangerous, whereas reliable contraceptives are harmless. Why do you oppose them?"

In her autobiography Margaret Sanger relates that, to her horror, he answered, "We will never give over the control of our numbers to the women themselves. What, let them control the future of the human race? With abortions it is in our hands; *we* must make the decisions, and they must come to us."

The control of the birth canal through which the human race passes, gives to men control of *all* humanity. All the nations of the world are patriarchal. East and West. North and South. Developed and developing. Capitalist and socialist.

In 1920 Russia liberalized the abortion laws. In 1936 the laws were rescinded.

In 1956 Romania liberalized contraception and abortion. In 1966 women were legally placed back into forced breeding.

In 1956 Hungary liberalized contraception. Then, rather than rescind the laws, breeding inducements were offered, in the style of the 1930's Fuhrers and Duces.

In China today the preferred method of birth control is sterilization. *Female* parents of more than two children are "persuaded" to give up their reproductive capacities—even though the operation is simpler and safer for men.

Carol Downer, Lorraine Rothman, and the Feminist Women's Health Center women of Los Angeles, for the most part non-professional laywomen, released women from thousands of years of subjugation with the simple but radical ideas of gynecological self help which encompass vaginal self-examination and menstrual extraction.

It has been reported that women in nursing and medical schools have looked at themselves with specula. It is known that some women after modern child delivery have had the temerity to view their gaping episiotomies with a mirror. But for the most part, women in Western society have been thoroughly socialized not to look at ourselves, not to touch ourselves, and never to experience the joyousness of our own sexuality.

Carol and Lorraine carried the idea of self help to women across the country. They did not beg professionals to treat women humanely. They did not set up teaching units. They *shared* their ideas and the physical view of their bodies with *women*, in groups of *women only*.

This is the cornerstone of the modern feminist women's health movement in the world. This is what differentiates the late Twentieth Century women's health movement from all other health movements of the past. This is the key to womanpower. Real womanpower.

A Gynecological Self-Help Presentation shows a set of slides that illustrate the changes in color and texture that take place in the vagina and cervix during the reproductive cycle—ovulation, menstruation, pregnancy—and in the presence of infection such as cervicitis or when an imbalance of yeast develops. A woman who keeps a file card on the appearance of *her* cervix as compared to the cervixes of other women in her group, can detect color and texture changes which indicate pregnancy within three to five days after conception. This releases the woman to choose whether to terminate the pregnancy early and non-traumatically or to plan for a baby with care and concern.

The slide presentation is accompanied by an explanation in lay terms, and as much interaction between participants as numbers and time allow. It is, however, essential that the slides *be followed by a volunteer who demonstrates the use of the plastic speculum to view her vagina.* That moment of shared observation between women is the magic breakthrough of consciousness. *It is the touch of genius.* Women look with awe at the actual cervix of a living woman wherever the presentation takes place—in university classrooms on tilted desks, in church basements on altars, women's living room couches, in bedrooms, on kitchen tables or nursery school play-tables. Anyplace where women are alone with women, the observation, information and experience exchange is normal and natural. A slide presentation can end there or can include the technology of menstrual extraction as invented by Lorraine Rothman.

The Gynecological Self-Help Clinic is not a place. It can be any group of women using consciousness-raising methods to discuss each woman's unique personal experiences in obstetrics and gynecology in the supportive environment and privacy of a woman's home with only women present. Here women listen and sympathize with each other.

After experience and information sharing, women proceed to vaginal self-examination. With the mirror, flashlight, and plastic speculum, each woman views her vagina and cervix while someone records the observations on a file card. This file card charts a woman's vaginal history.

Locally, groups of women are also keeping file cards of their experiences with doctors which serve as a consumer-guide for women needing medical consultation. Furthermore, a woman can ask medical questions on behalf of her entire group when she seeks professional services, in order to receive a full return on her medical dollar.

After achieving ease in the use of the plastic speculum, women learn to do pelvic examinations. This is a procedure by which an index finger is inserted into the vagina, locating the cervix, then palpating the cervix up and down while the other hand feels the abdominal area for the uterus. It actually takes many "pelvics" to develop a sensitivity to the size, shape, and texture of the hidden organ in order to distinguish its position, the development of a pregnancy, and/or unusual growths.

Breast examination follows the guidelines of the cancer societies but with the healthy interaction of women in a group situation rather than in isolation or in contact with a male authority figure. Since most unnecessary surgery is in the field of obstetrics and gynecology, women have learned that we must protect ourselves in every way possible against the mutilation and disfigurement of modern "cures."

Pap smears are simple procedures but represent another area where law and medicine have made it illegal for analyses to be given to anyone other than an M.D. On college and university campuses, women are doing their research, term papers, and theses in this area, thereby legitimatizing the availability of this information.

Patriarchal institutions program women to be helpless. Gynecological self help provides a woman with the tools to overcome that helplessness. Her emerging self-confidence is based on the fact that *she* has complete control of her reproductive cycle and of her physical self.

The most exciting outgrowth of this newly found power and control is that women who have a sustained interest in the physical, mental, and emotional health and well-being of the human female and her progeny are establishing: *women-controlled women's health centers, abortion clinics, birth centers, and hospitals.*

Women moving into health and medicine from gynecological self help are a totally new breed of women, separate and distinct from those women who have reached this field via the inhumane training and institutions of men.

Through self help, women have reclaimed our uterii, within our territorial possession. We are reidentifying with our Mother Earth, who, like each of us, has been raped, traumatized, brutalized, mutilated and disfigured by man's technology and his loss of the human touch.

This revolution in women's health is basic to a new era. If we move fast enough, if men don't decide in one last fit of rage to murder us off as they did in the Middle Ages, there is a chance that women can literally save our fragile planet Earth and future generations of *our* children.

ANNE FORER

Sex and Women's Liberation

Anne Forer (1945–2018), a kindergarten teacher, fiction writer, and early activist in New York Radical Women, helped create the feminist technique of consciousness raising. (See also pages 238–241 in this volume.) In this personal reflection, written pseudonymously for the 1975 Redstockings book *Feminist Revolution*, Forer recalls the liberating effect of consciousness raising on her sex life. She also argues strenuously against dropping the word "liberation" from "women's liberation movement," as was becoming common.

So you go to a meeting entitled women rap about sex 1975 and you imagine you will learn things that will enrich your own personal life. However you get to the meeting and you rediscover the women's liberation movement as some whole that is greater than your life. The movement is bigger than your own personal life. But after the experience you return to your life, perhaps equipped with the perceptions you thought you would gain—maybe not— but you return to your life more liberated on a deeper more pervasive level because of your participation and experience of the women's liberation movement. I would like to stress here a minor point or an apparent minor point, which is that many women, myself included, out of laziness but really out of something deeper than laziness, have fallen into the habit of calling it the women's movement, rather than the women's liberation movement. I think the dropping of the word liberation from every reference to the women's liberation movement is a serious loss. All three words are key: WOMEN'S LIBERA-TION MOVEMENT. Without a movement nothing can be accomplished, nothing strong and revolutionary can be accomplished without a movement. Women is where you fit in. It is you and your life. But LIBERATION. Liberation is the clue. Liberation is the meaning. Liberation is the common goal. Liberation is a word we should not get into the habit of avoiding just because it is so powerful and maybe intimidating in its implications. Liberation is what it is all about. And every inclusion of the word LIBERATION is a step forward in consciousness: just to have said the word in your brain and sent it out through speech. And every avoidance of the word liberation is a step backward or a step away from liberation. I have been saying women's movement for years and it wasn't until I was copying over my notes that I realized Kathie had said the women's liberation movement and I had subconsciously translated it to women's movement and when I realized the serious implications of that I wanted it to be part of this article. BUT IT CAME DIRECTLY FROM THE MEETING. THE MEETING OF THE WOMEN'S LIBERATION MOVEMENT.

The women at the meeting were involved in the women's liberation movement during its earliest, freshest, most creative and strongest days. If we were young and unconscious and ignorant, we were also strong. The women's liberation movement made it possible for each woman to participate from her STRONGEST SELF. The movement made that possible but the liberation went directly into the lives of the women participants. Liberation began immediately. There was a spirit of strength, honesty and unity and never to be forgotten, never to be slighted over, never to go unmentioned and unrecognized, tremendous INTELLIGENCE. I remember the first meeting I attended in 1967 and my vivid impression and amazement that everyone was so INTELLIGENT. And that never before, in no other radical or revolutionary meeting (and therefore the words do not apply) had I ever experienced the continuous use and display of intelligence. And so, women, I want to share this lesson I have learned: if ever you want to distinguish the authenticity of something or someone in the women's liberation movement—if it is to be deserving of that name—ask yourself: is it really INTELLIGENT and is it LIBERATING? And you will always know the truth. It is important in this era of *Ms.* magazine and other false spokeswomen purporting to be an organ of the women's liberation movement.

I will say that the immediate effect of being in that room with the women from the early women's liberation movement was profoundly liberating to me. The intervening years of being cut off from the women's liberation movement and struggling alone as a woman in this society had a regressive, anti-liberating effect on me. When Alix talked about her experiences she specifically mentioned backsliding and said "I think none of this would have happened (operating out of her weakest and most self-defeating self) if I had been in the movement." Being out of the movement has taken a serious toll on my courage, honesty and strength. I have given up fighting for things. My soul has become caked in mud and it began to crack open at that meeting. Just being at that meeting had an immediate and liberating effect. OF COMING BACK TO MYSELF.

Perhaps it would be useful to communicate my history of sex and the women's liberation movement. When I first began coming around the women's liberation movement I was 23 years old and had been sleeping with boys since I was 19. Even though I was mad about my first lover and was crazy to have sex with him I never had an orgasm. In fact I had never had any kind of orgasm ever and had never masturbated. Somehow I realized I had to simulate orgasm for him to feel the act was complete or successful or maybe just to get him off me. After that when I would sleep around boys would always say to me afterwards "did you come, did you come?" and I would always simulate orgasm and tell them yes. I thought two things. One that all other women must be having orgasms, or why would they assume like that that I "came"? And two that something was deeply wrong with me as a woman. I was inferior sexually. I was missing. To be a true sexual woman was vital to my self image. Along with looks it ranked at the top of my needs for my self image—with things like intelligence, et cetera, much lower on the scale.

In other words I would have gladly exchanged any intelligence I had or any other abilities for beauty and to be truly sexual. I guess truly sexual was defined at that time of my life as vaginal orgasm in the Freudian sense which was pervasive in the era of my young womanhood. I know there are many women who rank intelligence much higher. Although when I was 20 I used to ask men what their secret wish was and they would always say something like to write in the prose style of Nietzsche and I would always dream of looking like Anna Karina the French actress I admired. At that time I generalized to say that women care most deeply for beauty, and men for intelligence. Although I know this is not true. Because many women have told me they care more about their intelligence. So if they were honest then it is not true what I thought. I will say here, however, what I always said at my early meetings, that I think women are more intelligent than men and I have always taken women's high and extraordinary intelligence for granted, although now I have met intelligent men. So I will leave the question open as to whether or not men are as intelligent as women. I don't know the answer.

Anyway I had been faking orgasm for four years when I encountered the women's liberation movement and I had not mentioned it to A SINGLE OTHER WOMAN. I carried my sexual inferiority as a dark secret. When the subject of sex initially came up in women's liberation—or should I say when the subject of sex got liberated—everyone admitted to faking orgasms. And also based on those initial conversations—everyone faking vaginal orgasm— Anne Koedt developed her theory about The Myth of the Vaginal Orgasm. I don't know what to say about that. Old myths die hard. And I never committed myself to Anne Koedt's theory. What I did do however was stop faking orgasms after that. I was now permitted or was it liberated to have a genuine sexual response—whatever it was—although I think I held on to the vaginal myth. Maybe because other women said they had them. What they said was that they had a total body response and not a local response. I didn't know what to say. I would say maybe it was the myth of my sexual inferiority that I could not let go of. There wasn't enough true evidence.

Out of these discussions came Shulamith Firestone's article "Women Rap about Sex" where the issue of faking orgasms was made public as well as other truths about sexual relations between the sexes. A major and important article. The following year there was a nationwide conference on women's liberation held in Chicago. One of the workshops was a sex workshop organized by a woman and her friend. Luckily I went to this workshop. The two women had organized it specifically to get women to give up sex with men. Images like going to the brink but afraid to go over. The thesis was that the truly liberated thing for a liberated woman to do was to give up sex. Anything else comprised a cop out on liberation. I was dismayed by this—dismayed is a small word—I didn't believe it and I thought her image about going over the brink was apt and she wanted to take the whole women's liberation movement with her. I never for a second considered giving up men—and really at that time the only contacts I had with men were sexual—but I hoped I would find love eventually. Actually that was all I cared about then.

This rap was very rational and well-thought out, very pseudo-intelligent and pseudo-convincing and everything else. Who would dare to say anything after that? Joyce dared. She was sitting on the floor. And after this impressive delivery she said "I don't know. After I had my baby my whole vagina opened up and became much more feeling. Before that I was a clitoris girl all the way. I would just as soon have skipped intercourse completely but after my baby my vagina became much more feeling and now I really like intercourse." Brave and courageous and honest Joyce. Sitting on the floor. Next to this tall impassioned woman. Like a tigress she was. She terrified me. After Joyce talked everyone opened up about sex. It was really incredible. One woman said she and her husband would sing while they climaxed. Fantasies were discussed. "I can only get sexually excited if I have a rape fantasy." There was practically complete union on the subject of "masochistic" fantasies except one woman said she didn't have them.

And I must interject at this point that there were thirty or forty women in that room. So never be fooled by the false argument that meetings are too big. I will always say the bigger the better. It is a divisive argument, that argument about groups being too big for things to happen. I think too that masturbation was opened up at that meeting. And the woman who organized the workshop, I will give her the credit, after being silent for a long time while this discussion was going on, said: "I had heard about these conversations going on in Women's Liberation but I never thought I would be in one. . . ." and then opened up about her sexual fantasies also. The excitement from this meeting carried over and the women who hadn't been at the meeting of course wanted to talk about their experiences with sex and masturbation and the truth about sex for them. The subject of sex was opened up and women could tell the truth about themselves sexually for the first time. Many women who had never "dared" to masturbate began to when they heard other women were. I will not go into the ramifications of any of this—it is just a few pieces of history.

ANGELA DAVIS

(from) Joan Little: The Dialectics of Rape

The celebrated activist Angela Davis (born 1944) was a young academic who had been fired from UCLA because of her membership in the U.S. Communist Party when she first came to national attention in 1970. After guns registered in her name were used in a deadly protest in a Marin County courtroom, Davis was arrested and imprisoned for sixteen months before being acquitted of conspiracy, kidnapping, and murder. In 1974, Joan Little, a twenty-two-year-old Black prisoner in a North Carolina jail, was indicted for the first-degree murder of her white prison guard, whom she accused of rape. Davis, who had benefitted from a worldwide support campaign during her own incarceration, was a leader in Little's defense. This essay, published in *Ms.* in June 1975 and excerpted here, was enormously influential in building support for Little; her trial by a jury of six whites and six African Americans, nine of them women, ended in acquittal, making Little the first woman in U.S. history to be acquitted of murder committed in self-defense against sexual assault.

RAPE, LYNCH NEGRO MOTHER

Columbus, Miss., Dec. 17—Thursday a week ago Cordella Stevenson was found early in the morning hanging to the limb of a tree, without any clothing, dead. . . . The body was found about fifty yards north of the Mobile & Ohio R.R., and the thousands and thousands of passengers that came in and out of this city last Thursday morning were horrified at the sight. She was hung there from the night before by a bloodthirsty mob who had gone to her home, snatched her from slumber, and dragged her through the streets without any resistance. They carried her to a far-off spot, did their dirt and then strung her up. —Chicago *Defender* December 18, 1915

NO ONE—not even the men in the mob—had bothered to accuse Cordella Stevenson of committing a crime. She was black and that was reason enough. She was black and a woman, trapped in a society pervaded with myths of white superiority and male supremacy. She could be raped and murdered with absolute impunity. The white mob simply claimed that, a few months earlier, Cordella Stevenson's son had burned down a white man's barn.

It was 60 years ago when this black woman was raped and strung up on a tree. There are many who believe that incidents such as these belong to an era of racist terror now forever buried under the historical progress of the intervening years. But history itself allows only the naive to honestly claim these last 60 years as a time of unequivocal progress—especially when the elimination of racism and male supremacy is used as the yardstick.

Today, black women continue to be sexually attacked—and, in some cases, even murdered—by white men who know that, in all likelihood, they will never have to face the consequences of their crimes.

Twenty-year-old Joan Little, one of the most recent victims in this racist and sexist tradition, is the cultural grandchild of Cordella Stevenson. She says that she resisted when she was sexually assaulted, but as a result she is currently being tried on charges of first-degree murder. In the event of a conviction, she will automatically get a death sentence and will be placed on North Carolina's death row—the result of a "legal" process, but still too close to the lynch law of the past.

The story begins last August 27, when a guard at the jail in Beaufort County, North Carolina, was found dead in the cell of a missing prisoner. He had been stabbed 11 times with an ice pick, the same ice pick that he had kept in his own desk drawer. The jailer, Clarence Alligood, was white. The missing prisoner was black, and the only woman in the entire jail. Because of a conviction on charges of breaking and entering, larceny, and receiving stolen property, Joan Little was serving a sentence of seven to ten years and had already been kept in the Beaufort County jail for three months at the time of her disappearance.

When the autopsy report was released, it contained this evidence of recent sexual activity on the part of Alligood: "His shoes were in the corridor, his socks on his feet. He was otherwise naked from the waist down. . . . The left arm was under the body and clutching his pants. . . . His right hand contained an ice pick. There was blood on the sheet, cell floor, corridor. . . . Beneath his buttocks was a decorated, partially torn woman's kerchief. On the floor was a night gown and on the cell door was a brassiere and night jacket. . . . Extending from his penis to his thigh skin was a stream of what appeared to be seminal fluid. . . . The urethral fluid was loaded with spermatozoa."

After a week of evading police—who conducted their search with riot weapons and helicopters—Joan Little turned herself in, stating nothing publicly about the case except that she did what she had to do in self-defense. At her own insistence, Jerry Paul, the lawyer she contacted, received assurances that she would be incarcerated in the women's prison in Raleigh—not in the jail where the incident took place, and where she feared that she would be subjected to further sexual assault and perhaps even that her life would be in danger.

Shortly thereafter, Joan Little was charged with murder in the first degree.

The circumstances surrounding this case deserve careful attention, for they raise fundamental questions about the bringing of murder charges against her. Moreover, they expose conditions and situations many women prisoners must confront, especially in the small-town jails of this country.

1. Joan Little was being detained in a jail in which she was the only woman— among prisoners and guards alike. Since the Beaufort County Jail had served as a detention center for other women prisoners in the past, why were all the jailers assigned to it men? (Three months later—according to Karen Galloway, one of Joan's lawyers—the prison authorities began to claim that there had been a matron on duty during the daytime.)

2. Like any other prisoner, Sister Joan was being held under lock and key. Only her jailer, Clarence Alligood, had access to the key to her cell that night. Therefore, how could he have been present there against his will? A part of an escape attempt on the part of Joan Little, as the authorities then charged?

3. Alligood was apparently killed by stab wounds inflicted by the same ice pick which he was known to keep in his desk. What was a jail guard doing with an ice pick in the first place? And for what legitimate purpose could he have taken it into a prisoner's cell?

4. Alligood was discovered naked from the waist down. According to Karen Galloway and Jerry Paul, Joan Little's attorneys, the authorities maintained for a full three weeks that Alligood's pants were nowhere to be found. Were they afraid that the public would discover that, although he had been stabbed in the legs, there were no such holes in his pants? Were they afraid people would therefore realize that Alligood had removed his pants before the struggle began? In any case, how could such crucial evidence be allowed to disappear?

In fact, the reality of Joan Little's life as a prisoner, even before the rape, may have been one of sexual exploitation: a fate she consistently resisted. Jerry Paul has said, "One possibility is that she was being kept in Beaufort County Jail for openly sexual purposes." She should have been moved to the women's prison in Raleigh shortly after her original conviction, for instance, but she was never transferred. According to Paul, a TV camera was focused on her cell at all times, leaving her no privacy whatever even when she changed clothes or took a shower. When she used her sheets to block the view, they were taken from her. Joan Little's lawyers have said that on one occasion a highway patrolman visiting the jail on business unrelated to Joan, came into her cell and urinated on the floor.

If one wonders why Joan Little fled even though circumstances on their face tended to be greatly exculpatory, consider that, when she left, Alligood was still alive. From the appearance of the jail cell, a tremendous struggle must have taken place. She then fled, distraught, out of fear for her life. Alligood, according to the autopsy report, was found still clutching the ice pick. Sister Joan may well have felt that, if she hadn't left the jail when she did, she would have become just another number in the statistics surrounding prison deaths.

Essential to a clear perspective on the Joan Little case is an analysis of what might have happened if the situation had been reversed. What if Alligood had overpowered her? What if *he* had stabbed *her* with the ice pick—as he may have intended to do if she could not otherwise be raped? What if the sexually violated body of Joan Little had been discovered in that cell on the night of August 27?

There has never, to my knowledge, been a conviction—perhaps not even an indictment—of a white jailer for the murder of a black or any other minority prisoner. We can look to the 1970 case of W. L. Nolen, Alvin Miller, and Cleveland Edwards, for instance, who were shot down, unarmed and in cold blood, in the Soledad recreation yard by a guard perched in a gun tower; killings which the Grand Jury ruled justifiable homicides. There are also the 31 prisoners killed during the Attica Rebellion. No one denies that they were victims of gunfire, yet not a single one of the guards or policemen has been charged with a crime. Or consider Tito Perez, a prisoner recently discovered in a New York jail cell, hanged with a belt that did not belong to him. People who knew him insisted it had to be murder, yet police called it suicide. As one of the policemen then added, "It happens all the time."

There can be little speculation about the turn events would have taken had Joan Little been killed by Alligood. A verdict of "justifiable homicide" would have probably closed the books on such a case.

But she had the courage to fend off her assailant. The price of her resistance was a new threat of death, this time issuing from the government of North Carolina.

And so she is being tried—by the same state whose Supreme Court decided, in the 19th century, that no white man could be convicted of fornication with a slave woman. By the same state whose judicial apparatus in 1972 permitted Marie Hill to be sentenced to death at the age of 21; convicted by an all-white jury of murder of a white man on the basis of a confession which she insisted had been made under threat of death.

Joan Little stands accused by a court system which, proportionate to its population, has sentenced more political activists to prison than any other state in the country. (Reverend Ben Chavis and the others of the Wilmington Ten, for instance; as well as the Charlotte Three, the Ayden Eleven, and many Tuscarora Indians.) The number of state prison units in North Carolina is staggering; more than five times greater than in California, the most populous state in the country. In fact, North Carolina, along with Georgia, can claim more prisoners per capita than any other state—and they include, of course, an enormously disproportionate number of black men and women.

As this article is being written, there are 71 prisoners on death row in North Carolina, making that state Number One in the nation in condemning people to legal death. In the event of a conviction, the state's present sentencing policy could make Sister Joan Little the third woman in the country to be sentenced to death since the Supreme Court ruled in 1972 that the death penalty imposed at the discretion of judges and juries was cruel and unusual punishment. North Carolina subsequently mandated that a conviction on a first-degree murder charge automatically carried the death penalty. This procedure was appealed to the Supreme Court in late April. The other two women presently on death row are also in North Carolina; a black and a Native American respectively.

Even during the short time Joan Little hid from the police, the Sheriff was planning to ask that the courts initiate the procedure of declaring her an outlaw. The result of this declaration would have been, in effect, a call to all state citizens to arrest her on sight and to shoot if she resisted. North Carolina is the only state in the country where this law is still on the books.

Joan Little's attorneys relate numerous possibilities of judicial bias against her. In Beaufort County, for instance, where families are generations old, virtually everyone knows everyone else. Living in the area are numerous Alligoods. One of these Alligoods sat on the Grand Jury which returned the indictment against Joan Little.

Without exception, every pretrial motion filed, as of this writing, has been flatly denied. Despite inflammatory publicity about Joan Little—including unfounded and malicious charges that she was a prostitute—and in spite of the unconcealed public sympathy for Alligood, the courts have refused to grant a change of venue for the trial.

Although Joan Little is indigent, her motion to have the court assume the costs of expert witnesses has been denied. It was denied even though the court does not have to pay her attorneys' fees, since the lawyers are donating their services.

Efforts to gain access to the evidence, in the form of discovery motions, have also been thwarted. The sheriff at first refused to release a list of female prisoners previously incarcerated in the jail, leading to a belief that the authorities feared the exposure of other sexual assaults by Alligood and his colleagues. Later, after the State Bureau of Investigation had questioned 65 former prisoners, their names were released to Joan Little's lawyers—but even this SBI report stated that some of these inmates claimed Alligood and other jailers made sexual advances toward them.

After the difficulty in locating Alligood's pants, the defense attempted to have all the evidence assembled and placed in protective custody. This was denied.

Although Sister Joan seemed clearly eligible to be released on bail, District Attorney William Griffin employed every trick of his trade to prevent her release. When the defense attorneys attempted to post bail, for instance, Griffin, relying on a technicality, ordered the clerk not to accept the bond. Finally, as a result of a nationwide outcry, she was released in February on bail of $115,000; an amount that is itself clearly exorbitant.

Through the case of Joan Little, the courts of North Carolina seem to have decided to extend their long record of racist injustices and betrayal of the rights of poor people. How can these same courts be trusted to fairly determine the fate of the defendant herself?

If justice is to prevail, there must be a struggle. And the only force powerful enough to reverse the normal, repressive course of events is the organized might of great numbers of people.

Protests have already erupted. Mass actions have been organized in North Carolina—both by black community groups and women's organizations. The North Carolina Alliance Against Racist and Political Repression has taken on the case as one of its major concentrations, and the Southern Poverty Law Center, directed by Julian Bond, is vigorously supporting Sister Joan.

These beginnings must be utilized as the foundation of a movement which can ignite massive and militant protests on a national—and even international—scale. Only a movement of this magnitude can rescue Joan Little from the gas chamber.

Over the last few years, widespread concern about the increasing incidence of sexual assaults on women has crystallized into a militant campaign against rape. In the Joan Little case, as well as in all other instances of sexual assault, it is essential to place the specific incident in its sociohistorical context. For rape is not one-dimensional and homogeneous—but one feature that does remain constant is the overt and flagrant treatment of women, through rape, as property.

SUSAN BROWNMILLER

(from) *Against Our Will: Men, Women and Rape*

Rape early emerged as a central feminist issue. In 1975, journalist and activist
Susan Brownmiller (born 1935) published *Against Our Will: Men, Women and Rape*,
the first comprehensive feminist study of rape in law, war, and history. For her
thesis that rape is a political crime—"a conscious process of intimidation by which
all men keep *all women* in a state of fear"—Brownmiller was both extolled and
excoriated. In 1995 the New York Public Library named *Against Our Will* one of
the hundred most important books of the twentieth century. Two excerpts from
chapter three, "War," are presented here: the opening section and the section
on rape in Bangladesh during the 1971 Bangladesh war for independence from
Pakistan, which shocked the world with its brutality at the time Brownmiller was
writing her book.

WAR

> *This is my weapon, this is my gun*
> *This is for business, this is for fun*
> > —DRILL SERGEANT'S DITTY

> I then told him that, in spite of my most diligent efforts, there
> would unquestionably be some raping, and that I should like to
> have the details as early as possible so that the offenders could be
> properly hanged.
> > —GENERAL GEORGE S. PATTON, JR.
> > *War As I Knew It*

IT'S FUNNY about man's attitude toward rape in war. *Unquestionably* there
shall be some raping. Unconscionable, but nevertheless inevitable. When
men are men, slugging it out among themselves, conquering new land, sub-
jugating new people, driving on toward victory, *unquestionably* there shall be
some raping.

And so it has been. Rape has accompanied wars of religion: knights and pilgrims took time off for sexual assault as they marched toward Constantinople in the First Crusade. Rape has accompanied wars of revolution: George Washington's papers for July 22, 1780, record that one Thomas Brown of the Seventh Pennsylvania Regiment was sentenced to death for rape at Paramus, and it was Brown's second conviction at that. Rape in warfare is not bound by definitions of which wars are "just" or "unjust." Rape was a weapon of terror as the German Hun marched through Belgium in World War I. Rape was a weapon of revenge as the Russian Army marched to Berlin in World War II. Rape flourishes in warfare irrespective of nationality or geographic location. Rape got out of hand—"regrettably," as the foreign minister was later to say— when the Pakistani Army battled Bangladesh. Rape reared its head as a way to relieve boredom as American GI's searched and destroyed in the highlands of Vietnam.

In modern times, rape is outlawed as a criminal act under the international rules of war. Rape is punishable by death or imprisonment under Article 120 of the American Uniform Code of Military Justice. Yet rape persists as a common act of war.

It has been argued that when killing is viewed as not only permissible but heroic behavior sanctioned by one's government or cause, the distinction between taking a human life and other forms of impermissible violence gets lost, and rape becomes an unfortunate but inevitable by-product of the necessary game called war. Women, by this reasoning, are simply regrettable victims—incidental, unavoidable casualties—like civilian victims of bombing, lumped together with children, homes, personal belongings, a church, a dike, a water buffalo or next year's crop. But rape in war is qualitatively different from a bomb that misses its military target, different from impersonal looting and burning, different from deliberate ambush, mass murder or torture during interrogation, although it contains elements of all of the above. Rape is more than a symptom of war or evidence of its violent excess. Rape in war is a familiar act with a familiar excuse.

War provides men with the perfect psychologic backdrop to give vent to their contempt for women. The very maleness of the military—the brute power of weaponry exclusive to their hands, the spiritual bonding of men at arms, the manly discipline of orders given and orders obeyed, the simple logic of the hierarchical command—confirms for men what they long suspect, that women are peripheral, irrelevant to the world that counts, passive spectators to the action in the center ring.

Men who rape in war are ordinary Joes, made unordinary by entry into the most exclusive male-only club in the world. Victory in arms brings group power undreamed of in civilian life. Power for men alone. The unreal situation of a world without women becomes the prime reality. To take a life looms more significant than to make a life, and the gun in the hand is power. The sickness of warfare feeds on itself. A certain number of soldiers must prove their newly won superiority—prove it to a woman, to themselves, to other men. In the name of victory and the power of the gun, war provides men with a tacit license to rape. In the act and in the excuse, rape in war reveals the male psyche in its boldest form, without the veneer of "chivalry" or civilization.

Bangladesh

Indira Gandhi's Indian Army had successfully routed the West Pakistanis and had abruptly concluded the war in Bangladesh when small stories hinting at the mass rape of Bengali women began to appear in American newspapers. The first account I read, from the Los Angeles *Times* syndicated service, appeared in the New York *Post* a few days before Christmas, 1971. It reported that the Bangladesh government of Sheik Mujibur Rahman, in recognition of the particular suffering of Bengali women at the hands of Pakistani soldiers, had proclaimed all raped women "heroines" of the war for independence. Farther on in the story came this ominous sentence: "In traditional Bengali village society, where women lead cloistered lives, rape victims often are ostracized."

Two days after Christmas a more explicit story, by war correspondent Joseph Fried, appeared in the New York *Daily News*, datelined Jessore. Fried described the reappearance of young Bengali women on the city streets after an absence of nine months. Some had been packed off to live with relatives in the countryside and others had gone into hiding. "The precautions," he wrote, "proved wise, if not always effective."

> A stream of victims and eyewitnesses tell how truckloads of Pakistani soldiers and their hireling *razakars* swooped down on villages in the night, rounding up women by force. Some were raped on the spot. Others were carried off to military compounds. Some women were still there when Indian troops battled their way into Pakistani strongholds. Weeping survivors of villages razed because they were suspected of siding with the Mukti Bahini freedom fighters told of how wives were raped before the eyes of their bound husbands,

who were then put to death. Just how much of it was the work of Pakistani "regulars" is not clear. Pakistani officers maintain that their men were too disciplined "for that sort of thing."

Fearing I had missed the story in other papers, I put in a call to a friend on the foreign desk of *The New York Times*. "Rape of Bengali women?" He laughed. "I don't think so. It doesn't sound like a *Times* story." A friend at *Newsweek* was similarly skeptical. Both said they'd keep a lookout for whatever copy passed their way. I got the distinct impression that both men, good journalists, thought I was barking up an odd tree.*

In the middle of January the story gained sudden credence. An Asian relief secretary for the World Council of Churches called a press conference in Geneva to discuss his two-week mission to Bangladesh. The Reverend Kentaro Buma reported that more than 200,000 Bengali women had been raped by Pakistani soldiers during the nine-month conflict, a figure that had been supplied to him by Bangladesh authorities in Dacca. Thousands of the raped women had become pregnant, he said. And by tradition, no Moslem husband would take back a wife who had been touched by another man, even if she had been subdued by force. "The new authorities of Bangladesh are trying their best to break that tradition," Buma informed the newsmen. "They tell the husbands the women were victims and must be considered national heroines. Some men have taken their spouses back home, but these are very, very few."

A story that most reporters couldn't find in Bangladesh was carried by AP and UPI under a Geneva dateline. Boiled down to four paragraphs, it even made *The New York Times*.

Organized response from humanitarian and feminist groups was immediate in London, New York, Los Angeles, Stockholm and elsewhere. "It is unthinkable that innocent wives whose lives were virtually destroyed by war are now being totally destroyed by their own husbands," a group of eleven women wrote to *The New York Times* that January. "This . . . vividly demonstrates the blindness of men to injustices they practice against their own women even while struggling for liberation." Galvanized for the first time in history over the issue of rape in war, international aid for Bengali victims was coordinated by alert officials in the London office of the International Planned Parenthood Federation. The Bangladesh government, at first, was most cooperative. In the months to come, the extent of the aggravated plight of the women of Bangladesh during the war for independence would be slowly revealed.

---

*NBC's Liz Trotta was one of the few American reporters to investigate the Bangladesh rape story at this time. She filed a TV report for the weekend news.

Bengal was a state of 75 million people, officially East Pakistan, when the Bangladesh government declared its independence in March of 1971 with the support of India. Troops from West Pakistan were flown to the East to put down the rebellion. During the nine-month terror, terminated by the two-week armed intervention of India, a possible three million persons lost their lives, ten million fled across the border to India, and 200,000, 300,000 or possibly 400,000 women (three sets of statistics have been variously quoted) were raped. Eighty percent of the raped women were Moslems, reflecting the population of Bangladesh, but Hindu and Christian women were not exempt. As Moslems, most Bengali women were used to living in purdah, strict, veiled isolation that includes separate, secluded shelter arrangements apart from men, even in their own homes. The Pakistanis were also Moslem, but there the similarity stopped. Despite a shared religious heritage, Punjabi Pakistanis are taller, lighter-skinned and "rawboned" compared to dark, small-boned Bengalis. This racial difference would provide added anguish to those Bengali women who found themselves pregnant after their physical ordeal.

Hit-and-run rape of large numbers of Bengali women was brutally simple in terms of logistics as the Pakistani regulars swept through and occupied the tiny, populous land, an area little larger than the state of New York. (Bangladesh is the most overcrowded country in the world.) The Mukti Bahini "freedom fighters" were hardly an effective counterforce. According to victims, Moslem Biharis who collaborated with the Pakistani Army—the hireling *razakars*—were most enthusiastic rapists. In the general breakdown of law and order, Mukti Bahini themselves committed rape, a situation reminiscent of World War II when Greek and Italian peasant women became victims of whatever soldiers happened to pass through their village.

MICHELE WALLACE

(from) A Black Feminist's Search for Sisterhood

In this 1975 personal essay, first published in the *Village Voice*, Michele Wallace (born 1952) traces her childhood and college experiences—at Howard University and at City College in New York City—as an African American woman in search of the beginnings of her feminism. In the excerpt presented here, she discusses the sexism of Black men and the often contradictory behavior of white women in relation to Black men. Wishing to share and develop these ideas, Wallace longs for an independent Black feminist movement. In 1979, she would publish her important book *Black Macho and the Myth of the Superwoman*, which, like Ntozake Shange's 1975 play *for colored girls who have considered suicide when the rainbow is enuf* and Alice Walker's *The Color Purple*, would draw fire from critics (almost always men) for its portrayal of Black men.

WHEN I chose to go to Howard University in 1969, it was because it was all black. I envisioned a super-black utopia where for the first time in life I would be completely surrounded by people who totally understood me. The problem in New York had been that there were too many white people.

Thirty pounds overweight, my hair in the ultimate Afro—washed and left to dry without combing—my skin blue-black from a summer in the sun. Howard's students, the future polite society of NAACP cocktail parties, did not exactly greet me with open arms. I sought out a new clique each day and found a home in none. Finally I found a place of revelation, if not of happiness, with other misfits in the girls' dorm on Friday and Saturday nights.

These misfits, all dark without exception, all with Afros that were too nappy, chose to stay in and watch television or listen to records rather than take advantage of the score of one-night stands they could probably achieve before being taunted into running home to their parents as "fallen women." They came to Howard to get husbands; if you slept around, or if it got out that you had slept with someone you weren't practically engaged to, then there would be very little possibility of a husband for you at Howard.

Such restrictions are not unique in this world, but at Howard, the scene of student takeovers just the previous year, of riots and much revolutionary talk about casting aside Western values, archaic, Victorian morals seemed curiously "unblack." Baffled by my new environment, I did something I've never done before—I spent most of my time with women, often turning down the inevitable humiliation or, worse, boredom of a date (a growing possibility as I shed the extra pounds) even when it was offered to me. Most of the women were from small southern and midwestern communities. They thought me definitely strait-jacket material with my well-polished set of "sophisticated" New York views on premarital sex and atheism. I learned to listen more than I spoke.

But no one talked about why we stayed in on Friday and Saturday nights on a campus that was well-known for its parties and nightlife. No one talked about why we drank so much or why our hunger for Big Macs was insatiable. We talked about men—all kinds, black and white, Joe Namath, Richard Roundtree, the class president who earned quite a reputation for driving coeds out on the highway and offering them a quick screw or a long walk home. "But girl, ain't he fine?" We talked about movie stars and singing groups into the wee hours of the morning. Guzzling gin, cheating at poker, choking on cigarettes that dangled precariously from the corners of our mouths, we'd signify. "If we could only be woman (white) enough" was the general feeling of most of us as we trotted off to bed.

Meanwhile the males on the campus had successfully buried the old standards of light, curly haired young men with straight noses. They sported large, unruly Afros, dashikis, and flaring nostrils. Their coal-black eyes seemed to say "The nights *and* the days belong to me," as we'd pass one another on the campus green, a fashionable, thin, colorless little creature always on their arm.

Enough was enough. I left Howard for City College after one term, and the significance of all I'd seen there had not entirely escaped me, because I remember becoming a feminist about then. No one had been doing very well when I had left New York but now it seemed even worse—the "new blackness" was fast becoming the new slavery for sisters.

I discovered my voice and when brothers talked to me, I talked back. This had its hazards. Almost got my eye blackened several times. My social life was like guerilla warfare. Here was the logic behind our grandmothers' old saying, "A nigga man ain't shit." It was shorthand for "The black man has learned to hate himself and to hate you even more. Be careful. He will hurt you."

I am reminded of a conversation I had with a brother up at City College one mild spring day. We were standing on a corner in front of the South Campus gates and he was telling me what the role of the black woman was. When a pause came in his monologue, I asked him what the role of the black man was. He mumbled something about, "Simply to be a man." When I suggested that might not be enough, he went completely ape. He turned purple. He started screaming, "The black man doesn't have to do anything. He's a man he's a man he's a man!"

Whenever I raised the question of a black woman's humanity in conversation with a black man, I got a similar reaction. Black men, at least the ones I knew, seemed totally confounded when it came to treating black women like people. Trying to be what we were told to be by the brothers of the "nation"—sweet and smiling—a young black woman I knew had warmly greeted a brother in passing on Riverside Drive. He responded by raping her. When she asked the brothers what she should do, they told her not to go to the police and to have the baby though she was only seventeen.

Young black female friends of mine were dropping out of school because their boyfriends had convinced them that it was "not correct" and "counterrevolutionary" to strive to do anything but have babies and clean house. "Help the brother get his thing together," they were told. Other black women submitted to polygamous situations where sometimes they were called upon to sleep with the friends of their "husband." This latter duty was explained to me once by a "priest" of the New York Yoruban Temple. "If your brother has to go to the bathroom and there is no toilet in his house then wouldn't you let him use your toilet?" For toilet read black woman.

The sisters got along by keeping their mouths shut, by refusing to see what was daily growing more difficult to ignore—a lot of brothers were doing double time, uptown with the sisters and downtown with the white women whom they always vigorously claimed to hate. Some of the bolder brothers were quite frank about it. "The white woman lets me be a man."

The most popular justification black women had for not becoming feminists was their hatred of white women. They often repeated this for approving black male ears. (Obviously the brother had an interest in keeping black and white women apart—"Women will chatter.") But what I figured out was that the same black man who trembled with hatred for white men found the white woman irresistible because she was not a human being but a possession in his eyes—the higher-priced spread of women he saw on television. "I know that the white man made the white woman the symbol of freedom and the black woman the symbol of slavery." ("Soul on Ice," Eldridge Cleaver.)

When I first became a feminist, my black friends used to cast pitying eyes upon me and say, "That's whitey's thing." I used to laugh it off, thinking, yes there are some slight problems, a few things white women don't completely understand but we can work them out. In Ebony, Jet, and Encore, and even in the New York Times, various black writers cautioned black women to be wary of smiling white feminists. The Women's Movement enlists the support of black women only to lend credibility to an essentially middle-class, irrelevant movement, they asserted. Time has shown that there was more truth to these claims than their shrillness indicated. Today when many white feminists think of black women, they too often think of faceless masses of welfare mothers and rape victims to flesh out their statistical studies of woman's plight.

One unusually awkward moment for me as a black feminist was when I found out that white feminists often don't view black men as men but as fellow victims. I've got no pressing quarrel with the notion that white men have been the worst offenders but that isn't very helpful for a black woman from day to day. White women don't check out a white man's bank account or stockholdings before they accuse him of being sexist—they confront white men with and without jobs, with and without membership in a male consciousness-raising group. Yet when it comes to the black man, it's hands off.

A black friend of mine was fired by a black news service because she was pregnant. When she proposed doing an article on this for Ms., an editor there turned down the proposal with these words: "We've got a special policy for the black man." For a while I thought that was just the conservative feminist position until I overheard a certified radical feminist explaining why she dated only black men and other nonwhite men. "They're less of a threat to women; they're less oppressive."

Being a black woman means frequent spells of impotent, self-consuming rage. Such a spell came upon me when I recently attended a panel discussion at a women artists' conference. One of the panel members, a museum director and a white feminist, had come with a young black man in sweat shirt, Pro-Keds, and rag tied around the kind of gigantic afro you don't see much anymore. When asked about her commitment to black women artists, she responded with, "Well, what about Puerto Rican women artists, and Mexican women artists, and Indian women artists?" But she doesn't exhibit Hispanic women any more than she does black women (do I have to say anything about Indian women?), which is seldom indeed, though her museum is located in an area that is predominantly black and Puerto Rican. Yet she was confident in the position she took because the living proof of her liberalism and good intentions sat in the front row, black and unsmiling, six foot something and militant-*looking*.

In the spring of 1973, Doris Wright, a black feminist writer, called a meeting to discuss "Black Women and Their Relationship to the Women's Movement." The result was the National Black Feminist Organization, and I was fully delighted until, true to Women's Movement form, we got bogged down in an array of ideological disputes, the primary one being lesbianism versus heterosexuality. Dominated by the myths and facts of what white feminists had done and not done before us, it was nearly impossible to come to any agreement about our position on anything; and action was unthinkable.

Many of the prime movers in the organization seemed to be representing other interest groups and whatever commitment they might have had to black women's issues appeared to take a backseat to that. Women who had initiative and spirit usually attended one meeting, were turned off by the hopelessness of ever getting anything accomplished, and never returned again. Each meeting brought almost all new faces. Overhearing an aspiring political candidate say only half-jokingly at NBFO's first conference, "I'm gonna get me some votes out of these niggas," convinced me that black feminists were not ready to form a movement in which I could, with clear conscience, participate.

It is very possible that NBFO was not meant to happen when it did, that the time was not yet ripe for such an organization.

I started a black women's consciousness-raising group around the same time. When I heard one of my friends, whom I considered the closest thing to a feminist in the room, saying at one of our sessions, "I feel sorry for any woman who tries to take my husband away from me because she's just going to have a man who has to pay alimony and child support," even though she was not married to the man in question, I felt a great sinking somewhere in the chest area. Here was a woman, who had insisted (at least to me) upon her right to bear a child outside of marriage, trying to convince a few black women that she was really married, unlike they, who were mostly single and very worried about it. In fact, one of the first women to leave the group was a recent graduate of Sarah Lawrence, her excuse being, "I want to place myself in situations where I will meet more men." The group eventually disintegrated. We had no strength to give to one another. Is that possible? At any rate, that's the way it seemed, and perhaps it was the same on a larger scale with NBFO.

Despite a sizable number of black feminists who have contributed much to the leadership of the Women's Movement, there is still no Black Women's Movement, and it appears there won't be for some time to come. It is conceivable that the level of consciousness feminism would demand in black women wouldn't lead to any sort of separatist movement anyway—despite our very separate problems. Perhaps a multicultural women's movement is somewhere in the future.

But for now, black feminists, of necessity it seems, exist as individuals—some well-known, like Eleanor Holmes Norton, Florynce Kennedy, Faith

Ringgold, Shirley Chisholm, Alice Walker, and some unknown like me. We exist as women who are black who are feminists, each stranded for the moment, working independently because there is not yet an environment in this society remotely congenial to our struggle—because, being on the bottom, we would have to do what no else has done: we would have to fight the world.

MAXINE HONG KINGSTON

(from) *The Woman Warrior*
No Name Woman

As the literature of women's liberation began to expand to new areas, many women turned to writing about "lost" women, and exploring the heretofore hidden lives of their "foremothers," mining their family, cultural, and social histories, often without written records, to expose the patriarchal construction of inheritance. Maxine Hong Kingston's *The Woman Warrior: Memoirs of a Girlhood Among Ghosts* (1976) was one of the first in the wave of late twentieth-century American memoirs by women to expand the reach of the genre, and it remains among the most influential. In imagistic prose, drawing on her mother's rendering of myth, dream, and memory, Kingston (born 1940) indelibly renders the contradictory experience of growing up female in Chinese and Chinese American culture. *The Woman Warrior* won the National Book Critics Circle Award in 1977.

A T THE mirror my aunt combed individuality into her bob. A bun could have been contrived to escape into black streamers blowing in the wind or in quiet wisps about her face, but only the older women in our picture album wear buns. She brushed her hair back from her forehead, tucking the flaps behind her ears. She looped a piece of thread, knotted into a circle between her index fingers and thumbs, and ran the double strand across her forehead. When she closed her fingers as if she were making a pair of shadow geese bite, the string twisted together catching the little hairs. Then she pulled the thread away from her skin, ripping the hairs out neatly, her eyes watering from the needles of pain. Opening her fingers, she cleaned the thread, then rolled it along her hairline and the tops of her eyebrows. My mother did the same to me and my sisters and herself. I used to believe that the expression "caught by the short hairs" meant a captive held with a depilatory string. It especially hurt at the temples, but my mother said we were lucky we didn't have to have our feet bound when we were seven. Sisters used to sit on their beds and cry together, she said, as their mothers or their slaves removed the bandages for a few minutes each night and let the blood gush back into their veins. I hope that the man my aunt loved appreciated a smooth brow, that he wasn't just a tits-and-ass man.

Once my aunt found a freckle on her chin, at a spot that the almanac said predestined her for unhappiness. She dug it out with a hot needle and washed the wound with peroxide.

More attention to her looks than these pullings of hairs and pickings at spots would have caused gossip among the villagers. They owned work clothes and good clothes, and they wore good clothes for feasting the new seasons. But since a woman combing her hair hexes beginnings, my aunt rarely found an occasion to look her best. Women looked like great sea snails—the corded wood, babies, and laundry they carried were the whorls on their backs. The Chinese did not admire a bent back; goddesses and warriors stood straight. Still there must have been a marvelous freeing of beauty when a worker laid down her burden and stretched and arched.

Such commonplace loveliness, however, was not enough for my aunt. She dreamed of a lover for the fifteen days of New Year's, the time for families to exchange visits, money, and food. She plied her secret comb. And sure enough she cursed the year, the family, the village, and herself.

Even as her hair lured her imminent lover, many other men looked at her. Uncles, cousins, nephews, brothers would have looked, too, had they been home between journeys. Perhaps they had already been restraining their curiosity, and they left, fearful that their glances, like a field of nesting birds, might be startled and caught. Poverty hurt, and that was their first reason for leaving. But another, final reason for leaving the crowded house was the never-said.

She may have been unusually beloved, the precious only daughter, spoiled and mirror gazing because of the affection the family lavished on her. When her husband left, they welcomed the chance to take her back from the in-laws; she could live like the little daughter for just a while longer. There are stories that my grandfather was different from other people, "crazy ever since the little Jap bayoneted him in the head." He used to put his naked penis on the dinner table, laughing. And one day he brought home a baby girl, wrapped up inside his brown western-style greatcoat. He had traded one of his sons, probably my father, the youngest, for her. My grandmother made him trade back. When he finally got a daughter of his own, he doted on her. They must have all loved her, except perhaps my father, the only brother who never went back to China, having once been traded for a girl.

Brothers and sisters, newly men and women, had to efface their sexual color and present plain miens. Disturbing hair and eyes, a smile like no other threatened the ideal of five generations living under one roof. To focus blurs, people shouted face to face and yelled from room to room. The immigrants I know have loud voices, unmodulated to American tones even after years away from the village where they called their friendships out across the fields. I have not been able to stop my mother's screams in public libraries or over telephones. Walking erect (knees straight, toes pointed forward, not pigeon-toed, which is Chinese-feminine) and speaking in an inaudible voice, I have tried to turn myself American-feminine. Chinese communication was loud, public. Only sick people had to whisper. But at the dinner table, where the family members came nearest one another, no one could talk, not the outcasts nor any eaters. Every word that falls from the mouth is a coin lost. Silently they gave and accepted food with both hands. A preoccupied child who took his bowl with one hand got a sideways glare. A complete moment of total attention is due everyone alike. Children and lovers have no singularity here, but my aunt used a secret voice, a separate attentiveness.

She kept the man's name to herself throughout her labor and dying; she did not accuse him that he be punished with her. To save her inseminator's name she gave silent birth.

He may have been somebody in her own household, but intercourse with a man outside the family would have been no less abhorrent. All the village were kinsmen, and the titles shouted in loud country voices never let kinship be forgotten. Any man within visiting distance would have been neutralized as a lover—"brother," "younger brother," "older brother"—one hundred and fifteen relationship titles. Parents researched birth charts probably not so much to assure good fortune as to circumvent incest in a population that has but one hundred surnames. Everybody has eight million relatives. How useless then sexual mannerisms, how dangerous.

As if it came from an atavism deeper than fear, I used to add "brother" silently to boys' names. It hexed the boys, who would or would not ask me to dance, and made them less scary and as familiar and deserving of benevolence as girls.

But, of course, I hexed myself also—no dates. I should have stood up, both arms waving, and shouted out across libraries, "Hey, you! Love me back." I had no idea, though, how to make attraction selective, how to control its direction and magnitude. If I made myself American-pretty so that the five or six Chinese boys in the class fell in love with me, everyone else—the Caucasian, Negro, and Japanese boys—would too. Sisterliness, dignified and honorable, made much more sense.

Attraction eludes control so stubbornly that whole societies designed to organize relationships among people cannot keep order, not even when they bind people to one another from childhood and raise them together. Among the very poor and the wealthy, brothers married their adopted sisters, like doves. Our family allowed some romance, paying adult brides' prices and providing dowries so that their sons and daughters could marry strangers. Marriage promises to turn strangers into friendly relatives—a nation of siblings.

In the village structure, spirits shimmered among the live creatures, balanced and held in equilibrium by time and land. But one human being flaring up into violence could open up a black hole, a maelstrom that pulled in the sky. The frightened villagers, who depended on one another to maintain the real, went to my aunt to show her a personal, physical representation of the break she had made in the "roundness." Misallying couples snapped off the future, which was to be embodied in true offspring. The villagers punished her for acting as if she could have a private life, secret and apart from them.

If my aunt had betrayed the family at a time of large grain yields and peace, when many boys were born, and wings were being built on many houses, perhaps she might have escaped such severe punishment. But the men—hungry, greedy, tired of planting in dry soil, cuckolded—had had to leave the village in order to send food-money home. There were ghost plagues, bandit plagues, wars with the Japanese, floods. My Chinese brother and sister had died of an unknown sickness. Adultery, perhaps only a mistake during good times, became a crime when the village needed food.

The round moon cakes and round doorways, the round tables of graduated size that fit one roundness inside another, round windows and rice bowls—these talismen had lost their power to warn this family of the law: a family must be whole, faithfully keeping the descent line by having sons to feed the old and the dead, who in turn look after the family. The villagers came to show my aunt and her lover-in-hiding a broken house. The villagers were speeding up the circling of events because she was too shortsighted to see that her infidelity had already harmed the village, that waves of consequences would return unpredictably, sometimes in disguise, as now, to hurt her. This roundness had to be made coin-sized so that she would see its circumference: punish her at the birth of her baby. Awaken her to the inexorable. People who refused fatalism because they could invent small resources insisted on culpability. Deny accidents and wrest fault from the stars.

After the villagers left, their lanterns now scattering in various directions toward home, the family broke their silence and cursed her. "Aiaa, we're going to die. Death is coming. Death is coming. Look what you've done. You've killed us. Ghost! Dead ghost! Ghost! You've never been born." She ran out into the fields, far enough from the house so that she could no longer hear their voices, and pressed herself against the earth, her own land no more. When she felt the birth coming, she thought that she had been hurt. Her body seized together. "They've hurt me too much," she thought. "This is gall, and it will kill me." Her forehead and knees against the earth, her body convulsed and then released her onto her back. The black well of sky and stars went out and out and out forever; her body and her complexity seemed to disappear. She was one of the stars, a bright dot in blackness, without home, without a companion, in eternal cold and silence. An agoraphobia rose in her, speeding higher and higher, bigger and bigger; she would not be able to contain it; there would be no end to fear.

Flayed, unprotected against space, she felt pain return, focusing her body. This pain chilled her—a cold, steady kind of surface pain. Inside, spasmodically, the other pain, the pain of the child, heated her. For hours she lay on the ground, alternately body and space. Sometimes a vision of normal comfort obliterated reality: she saw the family in the evening gambling at the dinner table, the young people massaging their elders' backs. She saw them congratulating one another, high joy on the mornings the rice shoots came up. When these pictures burst, the stars drew yet further apart. Black space opened.

She got to her feet to fight better and remembered that old-fashioned women gave birth in their pigsties to fool the jealous, pain-dealing gods, who do not snatch piglets. Before the next spasms could stop her, she ran to the pigsty, each step a rushing out into emptiness. She climbed over the fence and knelt in the dirt. It was good to have a fence enclosing her, a tribal person alone.

Laboring, this woman who had carried her child as a foreign growth that sickened her every day, expelled it at last. She reached down to touch the hot, wet, moving mass, surely smaller than anything human, and could feel that it was human after all—fingers, toes, nails, nose. She pulled it up on to her belly, and it lay curled there, butt in the air, feet precisely tucked one under the other. She opened her loose shirt and buttoned the child inside. After resting, it squirmed and thrashed and she pushed it up to her breast. It turned its head this way and that until it found her nipple. There, it made little snuffling noises. She clenched her teeth at its preciousness, lovely as a young calf, a piglet, a little dog.

She may have gone to the pigsty as a last act of responsibility: she would protect this child as she had protected its father. It would look after her soul, leaving supplies on her grave. But how would this tiny child without family find her grave when there would be no marker for her anywhere, neither in the earth nor the family hall? No one would give her a family hall name. She had taken the child with her into the wastes. At its birth the two of them had felt the same raw pain of separation, a wound that only the family pressing tight could close. A child with no descent line would not soften her life but only trail after her, ghost-like, begging her to give it purpose. At dawn the villagers on their way to the fields would stand around the fence and look.

Full of milk, the little ghost slept. When it awoke, she hardened her breasts against the milk that crying loosens. Toward morning she picked up the baby and walked to the well.

Carrying the baby to the well shows loving. Otherwise abandon it. Turn its face into the mud. Mothers who love their children take them along. It was probably a girl; there is some hope of forgiveness for boys.

"Don't tell anyone you had an aunt. Your father does not want to hear her name. She has never been born." I have believed that sex was unspeakable and words so strong and fathers so frail that "aunt" would do my father mysterious harm. I have thought that my family, having settled among immigrants who had also been their neighbors in the ancestral land, needed to clean their name, and a wrong word would incite the kinspeople even here. But there is more to this silence: they want me to participate in her punishment. And I have.

In the twenty years since I heard this story I have not asked for details nor said my aunt's name; I do not know it. People who can comfort the dead can also chase after them to hurt them further—a reverse ancestor worship. The real punishment was not the raid swiftly inflicted by the villagers, but the family's deliberately forgetting her. Her betrayal so maddened them, they saw to it that she would suffer forever, even after death. Always hungry, always needing, she would have to beg food from other ghosts, snatch and steal it from those whose living descendants give them gifts. She would have to fight the ghosts massed at crossroads for the buns a few thoughtful citizens leave to decoy her away from village and home so that the ancestral spirits could feast unharassed. At peace, they could act like gods, not ghosts, their descent lines providing them with paper suits and dresses, spirit money, paper houses, paper automobiles, chicken, meat, and rice into eternity—essences delivered up in smoke and flames, steam and incense rising from each rice bowl. In an attempt to make the Chinese care for people outside the family, Chairman Mao encourages us now to give our paper replicas to the spirits of outstanding soldiers and workers, no matter whose ancestors they may be. My aunt remains forever hungry. Goods are not distributed evenly among the dead.

My aunt haunts me—her ghost drawn to me because now, after fifty years of neglect, I alone devote pages of paper to her, though not origamied into houses and clothes. I do not think she always means me well. I am telling on her, and she was a spite suicide, drowning herself in the drinking water. The Chinese are always very frightened of the drowned one, whose weeping ghost, wet hair hanging and skin bloated, waits silently by the water to pull down a substitute.

JUDY CHICAGO

(from) *Through the Flower: My Struggle as a Woman Artist*

In this excerpt from her 1975 memoir, Judy Chicago, née Cohen (born 1939), recounts her struggle within the male-dominated art establishment, the impact of reading feminist literature, and her quest for an art language in which to make visible her life as a woman. With the artist Miriam Schapiro, Chicago created the first feminist art programs, in 1970 at California State University at Fresno and the following year at the California Institute for the Arts, and, in 1973, with art historian Arlene Raven and graphic designer Sheila Levrant de Bretteville, the Feminist Studio Workshop at the Woman's Building in Los Angeles, a vibrant center for feminist art in all disciplines until it closed in 1991. Her room-size installation *The Dinner Party* opened in San Francisco in 1979, toured six countries on three continents, and is now permanently installed at the Brooklyn Museum.

I TRIED TO pursue my work the best I could. Then, the first material from the slowly developing women's movement reached the West Coast. When I read it, I couldn't believe it. Here were women saying the things I had been feeling, saying them out loud. I trembled when I read them, remembering the put-downs I encountered whenever I had tried to express the facts of my life as a woman artist. I had so internalized the taboo about mentioning it that I shuddered with terror reading Valerie Solanas' book and some of the early journals of the women's movement. Even though I thought Solanas extreme, I recognized the truth of many of her observations, and I identified with all the material in those early tracts as I had never identified with anything in my whole life.

As I read, I slowly allowed the information to seep into my pores, realizing that at last there was an alternative to the isolation, the silence, the repressed anger, the rejection, the depreciation, and the denial I had been facing. If these women could say how they felt, so could I. Coincidentally, I had been invited by several colleges in the area to speak about my work. I decided to use the opportunities to express my real feelings, to reveal what I had been going through as a woman and an artist. I was so scared. My voice shook, I could hardly talk. I spoke about the isolation and the rejection, the put-downs and the distortions. I spoke about my anger toward men because they had used me sexually. Everyone was shocked; there were angry reactions from the men. I drove home and trembled in terror at the fantasies that told me that something terrible was going to happen because I was saying the unsayable. I was telling the truth about my experiences as a woman, and I felt sure that I would be punished for it, that someone would break into my studio and destroy all my paintings or would shoot me or beat me up.

For one entire year, I lived in terror. I recognized that my fear reflected how deeply I had internalized society's taboos about revealing my real feelings. I had been told that if I told men the truth, I would "castrate" them, and I was afraid that they would retaliate. But I felt that I *had* to reach out and take this opportunity to be myself, offered implicitly by the women's movement. I accepted the fear as part of my day-to-day experience and just felt it every day, every time I attempted to reveal my own point of view. Even now, five years later, each time I make another step in exposing my real feelings, the fears engulf me again. The difference is that I have tangible support from women now; then I was alone and had only a few books to tell me that there were other women who were also speaking out.

Throughout this period, the only person I had to depend on was Lloyd. Even though he himself was trapped in the role of "nice guy" and was often unable to express his real feelings, he identified with my struggle and supported me every step of the way, even when my growth made him feel threatened. By the beginning of 1969, we had worked through many of the problems that had prevented us from realizing the relationship that we both wanted—one that allowed us to be ourselves, to realize our personal ambitions and to be able to relate easily and directly. After the big scene in San Diego, things had calmed down considerably between us. Lloyd's therapy was beginning to pay off, and he was establishing new and healthier behavior patterns. I was becoming more independent and self-sufficient. In the spring of 1969, we decided to get married, probably as a way of affirming the relationship we were making, which was so untypical in so many ways that we both felt the need to give it *some* shape that related to social mores. Also, after having experienced the destruction of my first marriage, I needed to feel the security of being married and having someone in the world to count on. Lloyd had been married briefly when he was twenty-five, only to have the marriage end badly, leaving him with a sense of failure that a successful marriage with me helped erase.

We married while I was still painting "Pasadena Livesavers." Lloyd was beginning a series of works that were to lead him to a personal, sculptural format that allowed him to speak of his own emotional states, though often even more indirectly than I. The link that existed in our work when I borrowed his symmetrical structure in 1963 had continued over the years, with mutual borrowing, influencing, and sharing of ideas. But even when we got married, we continued to live separately, feeling that it helped both of us maintain our separate identities. We had discovered that, although we had many things in common, our natural life styles were very different. I liked to get up in the morning and go directly about my business, going into my studio without talking to anyone. Then I liked to work all day and go out at night. Lloyd, on the other hand, preferred to work at night, sleep later than I, and he loved to talk in the morning. We also didn't like the same kinds of food: I preferred a broccoli and lamb chop diet (not exclusively, of course), while Lloyd liked one-dish dinners with very little meat. In 1971, when we finally began to live together again, we worked out a system of cooking our respective meals side by side and then eating together. But by that time we had both learned how to live according to our own needs and to help each other have the psychic privacy so essential to our work.

By the end of 1969, I felt that I was in a new place in my life and work. Painting "Pasadena Lifesavers," resolving and stabilizing my relationship with Lloyd, expressing my real experiences as a woman in lectures all conjoined to make me feel that I had more permission to be myself. I had not shown my work in Los Angeles for some time, and I decided that it was important to try to establish my range as an artist. I felt that I was not seen in the art world in a way that was commensurate with my achievements, and I still hoped that I could change that. I had been creating coherent bodies of work for some time, had worked across various media, including painting, sculpture, and process art, was dealing with the subject matter of my own identity as a woman, and had developed technical procedures in spraying and in fireworks that no one had done before. I wanted to share what I had done with my community, and arranged to have a show of the domes, the atmospheres in photo and film form, and the entire "Pasadena Lifesavers" series. I also wanted my being a woman to be visible in the work and had thus decided to change my name from Judy Gerowitz to Judy Chicago as an act of identifying myself as an independent woman.

The show, held at California State College at Fullerton, directed by Dextra Frankel, was beautiful, and Dextra's installation was fantastic. My name change was on the wall directly across from the entrance. It said:

Judy Gerowitz hereby divests herself of all names imposed upon her through male social dominance and freely chooses her own name *Judy Chicago*.

But, even though my position was so visibly stated, male reviewers refused to accept that my work was intimately connected to my femaleness. Rather, they denied that my statement had anything at all to do with my art. Many people interpreted the work in the same way they interpreted my earlier, more neutralized work, as if I were working only with formal issues. Admittedly the content of the work was not clear, but it seems that people could have made an effort to see the work in relation to the statement I had chosen to include. Moreover, no one even dealt with the range of ideas expressed or with the discrepancy between my status as an artist in the world and the obvious level of my development. Instead, there was only denial. At that time, there was no acknowledgment in the art community that a woman might have a different point of view than a man, or if difference was acknowledged, that difference meant inferiority.

As I look back on this, I realize that many issues were involved in the situation. I had come out of a formalist background and had learned how to neutralize my subject matter. In order to be considered a "serious" artist, I had *had* to suppress my femaleness. In fact, making a place as an artist had depended upon my ability to move away from the direct expression of my womanliness. Although I was trying to make my images clearer, I was still working in a frame of reference that people had learned to perceive in a particular, non-content-oriented way. But what other frame of reference existed then for abstract art? I was expecting the art community to actually "see" my work differently, to look at it in new terms, to respond to it on an emotional level. I realize that most people didn't know how to "read form" as I did. When Miriam Schapiro, the well-known painter from the East Coast who had recently moved to L.A., brought her class to the show, it was obvious that she could "read" my work, identify with it, and affirm it. On the other hand, a male artist friend of mine had told me: "Judy, I could look at these paintings for twenty years and it would never occur to me that they were cunts." The idea that my forms were cunts was an oversimplification, obviously, but at that time, even a greatly simplified perception seemed better than no perception at all of the relationship between my femaleness and my art.

When the achievement and meaning of my show went unrecognized, I was very upset. Not only had the exhibition not resulted in an increased understanding of my stature and intent as an artist, but it had produced a level of denial of my integrity that appalled me. I was accused of "mixing up" politics and art, "taking advantage" of the women's movement, of being "rigid" because I used a structure in my paintings, and of copying a male artist in my domes. I wanted my show to speak to people, to tell them that women possessed all aspects of human personality, that society's conception of the female was distorted and that other values in the culture that grew out of that distortion were also questionable. Fundamental to my work was an attempt to challenge the values of the society, but either my work was not speaking, society didn't know how to hear it, or both.

The full impact of my alienation struck me. I had tried to challenge society's conception of what it is to be a woman. At the same time, I had, in trying to make myself into an artist who was taken seriously in a male-dominated art community, submerged the very aspects of myself that could make my work intelligible. How could I make my voice heard, have access to the channels of the society that allow one's work to be visible, and be myself as a woman? I had tried to deal with the issues that were crucial to me "within" the structure of male art language and a male-oriented art community, a group whose values reflected the patriarchal culture in which we live. My accommodation had been self-defeating, however, for I could see by the results of my show and the evidence of my life as an artist that the male-dominated value structure, by its very nature, could not give me what I wanted and deserved. To honor a woman *in her own terms* would require a fundamental change in the culture and in the cultural values as they are expressed in art.

Men had constructed their community on the basis of their interests and needs as men. I realized that men (and women invested in that male community) *could not* respond to my work the way I wanted them to. There was no frame of reference in 1970 to understand a woman's struggle, to value it, or to read and respond to imagery that grew out of it. What did men know or care about what a struggle it was for a woman to overcome her conditioning as a woman, to feel comfortable about being assertive, to struggle to use tools that she had never been educated to use? And even if the male world could acknowledge that struggle, could it ever allow it to be considered "important" art, as important as the art that grew out of men's lives? I could not be content with having my work seen as trivial, limited, or "unimportant" if it dealt openly with my experiences as a woman, something I had seen happen to women who had not neutralized their subject matter. I also could no longer accept denying my experiences as a woman in order to be considered a "serious" artist, especially if my stature was going to be diminished anyway by the male-dominated community.

I realized that if the art community as it existed could not provide me with what I needed in order to realize myself, then I would have to commit myself to developing an alternative and that the meaning of the women's movement was that there was, probably for the first time in history, a chance to do just that. If my needs, values, and interests differed from male artists' who were invested in the values of the culture, then it was up to me to help develop a community that was relevant to me and other women artists. In fact, I was beginning to suspect that the reason there were so few visible women artists signified that the art community, as it existed, could not really serve the needs of women artists, unless they were willing to do what I had done and make art that did not deal directly with their experiences as women.

Perhaps I and other women would have to develop all aspects of an art community ourselves—making art, showing art, selling and distributing it, teaching other women artmaking skills, writing about art, and establishing our own art history, one that allowed us to discover the contributions of women artists past and present. I had been reading women's novels for several years, having given up male literature because I couldn't respond to the female characters. I had found a wealth of work by women I never knew existed, work with which I identified, and I was sure that there must likewise be unknown visual art by women. If making art according to male standards had resulted in making my subject matter unintelligible, perhaps looking at the work of women artists would give me clues about how to communicate my point of view more directly. But first, I would have to go back to the point where I had begun to hide my content and learn how to expose rather than cover that content.

I didn't know how to do that in Los Angeles, where the values of the male art community pervaded the environment—values that asserted form over content, protection over exposure, toughness over vulnerability. I decided to go away from the city for a year, to look for a job at a college, something that I had never done before, having supported myself by teaching occasional extension classes. When I graduated from college I had vowed not to become involved with day school teaching, as I didn't want to be like my teachers who had become more invested with their teaching than their art-making. Now I wanted to teach—but I wanted to teach women. I wanted to try to communicate to female students, to tell them what I had gone through in making myself into an artist. I felt that by externalizing the process I had gone through, I could examine it, which would be the first step in turning it around, and the women's class might also be the first step in making an alternative female art community.

ADRIENNE RICH

(from) *Of Woman Born*
Anger and Tenderness

"A thinking woman sleeps with monsters," wrote Adrienne Rich (1929–2012) in "Snapshots of a Daughter-in-Law" (1958–60), the first of her major poems in which a consciousness she later identified as feminist began to reveal itself. Winning the National Book Award in poetry in 1974 for *Diving into the Wreck*, she refused individual recognition, instead joining cofinalists Audre Lorde and Alice Walker to accept the prize on behalf of women writers "whose voices have gone and still go unheard in a patriarchal world." Rich soon became an important and influential feminist essayist and theorist. Here is an excerpt from her only book-length prose work, *Of Woman Born: Motherhood as Experience and Institution*, published in 1976, in which she extends her radical rethinking of women's lives under patriarchy, using an approach that fuses memoir with historical and anthropological analysis.

BEFORE MY third child was born I decided to have no more children, to be sterilized. (Nothing is removed from a woman's body during this operation; ovulation and menstruation continue. Yet the language suggests a cutting- or burning-away of her essential womanhood, just as the old word "barren" suggests a woman eternally empty and lacking.) My husband, although he supported my decision, asked whether I was sure it would not leave me feeling "less feminine." In order to have the operation at all, I had to present a letter, counter-signed by my husband, assuring the committee of physicians who approved such operations that I had already produced three children, and stating my reasons for having no more. Since I had had rheumatoid arthritis for some years, I could give a reason acceptable to the male panel who sat on my case; my own judgment would not have been acceptable. When I awoke from the operation, twenty-four hours after my child's birth, a young nurse looked at my chart and remarked coldly: "Had yourself spayed, did you?"

The first great birth-control crusader, Margaret Sanger, remarks that of the hundreds of women who wrote to her pleading for contraceptive information in the early part of the twentieth century, all spoke of wanting the health and strength to be better mothers to the children they already had; or of wanting to be physically affectionate to their husbands without dread of conceiving. None was refusing motherhood altogether, or asking for an easy life. These women—mostly poor, many still in their teens, all with several children—simply felt they could no longer do "right" by their families, whom they expected to go on serving and rearing. Yet there always has been, and there remains, intense fear of the suggestion that women shall have the final say as to how our bodies are to be used. It is as if the suffering of the mother, the primary identification of woman *as* the mother—were so necessary to the emotional grounding of human society that the mitigation, or removal, of that suffering, that identification, must be fought at every level, including the level of refusing to question it at all.

3

"Vous travaillez pour l'armée, madame?" (You are working for the army?), a Frenchwoman said to me early in the Vietnam war, on hearing I had three sons.

> *April 1965*
> Anger, weariness, demoralization. Sudden bouts of weeping. A sense of insufficiency to the moment and to eternity . . .

> Paralyzed by the sense that there exists a mesh of relations, between e.g. my rejection and anger at [my eldest child], my sensual life, pacifism, sex (I mean in its broadest significance, not merely physical desire)—an interconnectedness which, if I could see it, make it valid, would give me back myself, make it possible to function lucidly and passionately—Yet I grope in and out among these dark webs—

> I weep, and weep, and the sense of powerlessness spreads like a cancer through my being.

> *August 1965, 3:30 A.M.*
> Necessity for a more unyielding discipline of my life.
> Recognize the uselessness of blind anger.
> Limit society.

Use children's school hours better, for work & solitude.
Refuse to be distracted from own style of life.
    Less waste.
Be harder & harder on poems.

Once in a while someone used to ask me, "Don't you ever write poems about your children?" The male poets of my generation did write poems about their children—especially their daughters. For me, poetry was where I lived as no-one's mother, where I existed as myself.

The bad and the good moments are inseparable for me. I recall the times when, suckling each of my children, I saw his eyes open full to mine, and realized each of us was fastened to the other, not only by mouth and breast, but through our mutual gaze: the depth, calm, passion, of that dark blue, maturely focused look. I recall the physical pleasure of having my full breast suckled at a time when I had no other physical pleasure in the world except the guilt-ridden pleasure of addictive eating. I remember early the sense of conflict, of a battleground none of us had chosen, of being an observer who, like it or not, was also an actor in an endless contest of wills. This was what it meant to me to have three children under the age of seven. But I recall too each child's individual body, his slenderness, wiriness, softness, grace, the beauty of little boys who have not been taught that the male body must be rigid. I remember moments of peace when for some reason it was possible to go to the bathroom alone. I remember being uprooted from already meager sleep to answer a childish nightmare, pull up a blanket, warm a consoling bottle, lead a half-asleep child to the toilet. I remember going back to bed starkly awake, brittle with anger, knowing that my broken sleep would make next day a hell, that there would be more nightmares, more need for consolation, because out of my weariness I would rage at those children for no reason they could understand. I remember thinking I would never dream again (the unconscious of the young mother—where does it entrust its messages, when dream-sleep is denied her for years?).

For many years I shrank from looking back on the first decade of my children's lives. In snapshots of the period I see a smiling young woman, in maternity clothes or bent over a half-naked baby; gradually she stops smiling, wears a distant, half-melancholy look, as if she were listening for something. In time my sons grew older, I began changing my own life, we began to talk to each other as equals. Together we lived through my leaving the marriage, and through their father's suicide. We became survivors, four distinct people with strong bonds connecting us. Because I always tried to tell them the truth, because their every new independence meant new freedom for me, because we trusted each other even when we wanted different things, they became, at a fairly young age, self-reliant and open to the unfamiliar. Something told me that if they had survived my angers, my self-reproaches, and still trusted my love and each others,' they were strong. Their lives have not been, will not be, easy; but their very existences seem a gift to me, their vitality, humor, intelligence, gentleness, love of life, their separate life-currents which here and there stream into my own. I don't know how we made it from their embattled childhood and my embattled motherhood into a mutual recognition of ourselves and each other. Probably that mutual recognition, overlaid by social and traditional circumstance, was always there, from the first gaze between the mother and the infant at the breast. But I do know that for years I believed I should never have been anyone's mother, that because I felt my own needs acutely and often expressed them violently, I was Kali, Medea, the sow that devours her farrow, the unwomanly woman in flight from womanhood, a Nietzschean monster. Even today, rereading old journals, remembering, I feel grief and anger; but their objects are no longer myself and my children. I feel grief at the waste of myself in those years, anger at the mutilation and manipulation of the relationship between mother and child, which is the great original source and experience of love.

On an early spring day in the 1970s, I meet a young woman friend on the street. She has a tiny infant against her breast, in a bright cotton sling; its face is pressed against her blouse, its tiny hand clutches a piece of the cloth. "How old is she?" I ask. "Just two weeks old," the mother tells me. I am amazed to feel in myself a passionate longing to have, once again, such a small, new being clasped against my body. The baby belongs there, curled, suspended asleep between her mother's breasts, as she belonged curled in the womb. The young mother—who already has a three-year-old—speaks of how quickly one forgets the pure pleasure of having this new creature, immaculate, perfect. And I walk away from her drenched with memory, with envy. Yet I know other things: that her life is far from simple; she is a mathematician who now has two children under the age of four; she is living even now in the rhythms of other lives—not only the regular cry of the infant but her three-year-old's needs, her husband's problems. In the building where I live, women are still raising children alone, living day in and day out within their individual family units, doing the laundry, herding the tricycles to the park, waiting for the husbands to come home. There is a baby-sitting pool and a children's playroom, young fathers push prams on weekends, but child-care is still the individual responsibility of the individual woman. I envy the sensuality of having an infant of two weeks curled against one's breast; I do not envy the turmoil of the elevator full of small children, babies howling in the laundromat, the apartment in winter where pent-up seven- and eight-year-olds have one adult to look to for their frustrations, reassurances, the grounding of their lives.

4

But, it will be said, this is the human condition, this interpenetration of pain and pleasure, frustration and fulfillment. I might have told myself the same thing, fifteen or eighteen years ago. But the patriarchal institution of motherhood is not the "human condition" any more than rape, prostitution, and slavery are. (Those who speak largely of the human condition are usually those most exempt from its oppressions—whether of sex, race, or servitude.)

Motherhood—unmentioned in the histories of conquest and serfdom, wars and treaties, exploration and imperialism—has a history, it has an ideology, it is more fundamental than tribalism or nationalism. My individual, seemingly private pains as a mother, the individual, seemingly private pains of the mothers around me and before me, whatever our class or color, the regulation of women's reproductive power by men in every totalitarian system and every socialist revolution, the legal and technical control by men of contraception, fertility, abortion, obstetrics, gynecology, and extrauterine reproductive experiments—all are essential to the patriarchal system, as is the negative or suspect status of women who are not mothers.

Throughout patriarchal mythology, dream-symbolism, theology, language, two ideas flow side by side: one, that the female body is impure, corrupt, the site of discharges, bleedings, dangerous to masculinity, a source of moral and physical contamination, "the devil's gateway." On the other hand, as mother the woman is beneficent, sacred, pure, asexual, nourishing; and the physical potential for motherhood—that same body with its bleedings and mysteries—is her single destiny and justification in life. These two ideas have become deeply internalized in women, even in the most independent of us, those who seem to lead the freest lives.

In order to maintain two such notions, each in its contradictory purity, the masculine imagination has had to divide women, to see us, and force us to see ourselves, as polarized into good or evil, fertile or barren, pure or impure. The asexual Victorian angel-wife and the Victorian prostitute were institutions created by this double thinking, which had nothing to do with women's actual sensuality and everything to do with the male's subjective experience of women. The political and economic expediency of this kind of thinking is most unashamedly and dramatically to be found where sexism and racism become one. The social historian A. W. Calhoun describes the encouragement of the rape of black women by the sons of white planters, in a deliberate effort to produce more mulatto slaves, mulattos being considered more valuable. He quotes two mid–nineteenth-century southern writers on the subject of women:

> "The heaviest part of the white racial burden in slavery was the African woman of strong sex instincts and devoid of a sexual conscience, at the white man's door, in the white man's dwelling." . . .
> "Under the institution of slavery, the attack against the integrity of white civilization was made by the insidious influence of the lascivious hybrid woman at the point of weakest resistance. In the uncompromising purity of the white mother and wife of the upper classes lay the one assurance of the future purity of the race."[1]

The motherhood created by rape is not only degraded; the raped woman is turned into the criminal, the *attacker*. But who brought the black woman to the white man's door, whose absence of a sexual conscience produced the financially profitable mulatto children? Is it asked whether the "pure" white mother and wife was not also raped by the white planter, since she was assumed to be devoid of "strong sexual instinct"? In the American South, as elsewhere, it was economically necessary that children be produced; the mothers, black and white, were a means to this end.

Neither the "pure" nor the "lascivious" woman, neither the so-called mistress nor the slave woman, neither the woman praised for reducing herself to a brood animal nor the woman scorned and penalized as an "old maid" or a "dyke," has had any real autonomy or selfhood to gain from this subversion of the female body (and hence of the female mind). Yet, because short-term advantages are often the only ones visible to the powerless, we, too, have played our parts in continuing this subversion.

5

Most of the literature of infant care and psychology has assumed that the process toward individuation is essentially the *child's* drama, played out against and with a parent or parents who are, for better or worse, givens. Nothing could have prepared me for the realization that I *was* a mother, one of those givens, when I knew I was still in a state of uncreation myself. That calm, sure, unambivalent woman who moved through the pages of the manuals I read seemed as unlike me as an astronaut. Nothing, to be sure, had prepared me for the intensity of relationship already existing between me and a creature I had carried in my body and now held in my arms and fed from my breasts. Throughout pregnancy and nursing, women are urged to relax, to mime the serenity of madonnas. No one mentions the psychic crisis of bearing a first child, the excitation of long-buried feelings about one's own mother, the sense of confused power and powerlessness, of being taken over on the one hand and of touching new physical and psychic potentialities on the other, a heightened sensibility which can be exhilarating, bewildering, and exhausting. No one mentions the strangeness of attraction—which can be as single-minded and overwhelming as the early days of a love affair—to a being so tiny, so dependent, so folded-in to itself—who is, and yet is not, part of oneself.

From the beginning the mother caring for her child is involved in a continually changing dialogue, crystallized in such moments as when, hearing her child's cry, she feels milk rush into her breasts; when, as the child first suckles, the uterus begins contracting and returning to its normal size, and when later, the child's mouth, caressing the nipple, creates waves of sensuality in the womb where it once lay; or when, smelling the breast even in sleep, the child starts to root and grope for the nipple.

The child gains her first sense of her own existence from the mother's responsive gestures and expressions. It's as if, in the mother's eyes, her smile, her stroking touch, the child first reads the message: *You are there!* And the mother, too, is discovering her own existence newly. She is connected with this other being, by the most mundane and the most invisible strands, in a way she can be connected with no one else except in the deep past of her infant connection with her own mother. And she, too, needs to struggle from that one-to-one intensity into new realization, or reaffirmation, of her being-unto-herself.

The act of suckling a child, like a sexual act, may be tense, physically painful, charged with cultural feelings of inadequacy and guilt; or, like a sexual act, it can be a physically delicious, elementally soothing experience, filled with a tender sensuality. But just as lovers have to break apart after sex and become separate individuals again, so the mother has to wean herself from the infant and the infant from herself. In psychologies of child-rearing the emphasis is placed on "letting the child go" for the child's sake. But the mother needs to let it go as much or more for her own.

Motherhood, in the sense of an intense, reciprocal relationship with a particular child, or children, is *one part* of female process; it is not an identity for all time. The housewife in her mid-forties may jokingly say, "I feel like someone out of a job." But in the eyes of society, once having been mothers, what are we, if not always mothers? The process of "letting-go"—though we are charged with blame if we do not—is an act of revolt against the grain of patriarchal culture. But it is not enough to let our children go; we need selves of our own to return to.

To have borne and reared a child is to have done that thing which patriarchy joins with physiology to render into the definition of femaleness. But also, it can mean the experiencing of one's own body and emotions in a powerful way. We experience not only physical, fleshly changes but the feeling of a change in character. We learn, often through painful self-discipline and self-cauterization, those qualities which are supposed to be "innate" in us: patience, self-sacrifice, the willingness to repeat endlessly the small, routine chores of socializing a human being. We are also, often to our amazement, flooded with feelings both of love and violence intenser and fiercer than any we had ever known. (A well-known pacifist, also a mother, said recently on a platform: "If anyone laid a hand on *my* child, I'd murder him.")

These and similar experiences are not easily put aside. Small wonder that women gritting their teeth at the incessant demands of child-care still find it hard to acknowledge their children's growing independence of them; still feel they must be at home, on the *qui vive*, be that ear always tuned for the sound of emergency, of being needed. Children grow up, not in a smooth ascending curve, but jaggedly, their needs inconstant as weather. Cultural "norms" are marvelously powerless to decide, in a child of eight or ten, what gender s/he will assume on a given day, or how s/he will meet emergency, loneliness, pain, hunger. One is constantly made aware that a human existence is anything but linear, long before the labyrinth of puberty; because a human being of six is still a human being.

In a tribal or even a feudal culture a child of six would have serious obligations; ours have none. But also, the woman at home with children is not believed to be doing serious work; she is just supposed to be acting out of maternal instinct, doing chores a man would never take on, largely uncritical of the meaning of what she does. So child and mother alike are depreciated, because only grown men and women in the paid labor force are supposed to be "productive."

The power-relations between mother and child are often simply a reflection of power-relations in patriarchal society: "You will do this because I know what is good for you" is difficult to distinguish from "You will do this because I can *make* you." Powerless women have always used mothering as a channel—narrow but deep—for their own human will to power, their need to return upon the world what it has visited on them. The child dragged by the arm across the room to be washed, the child cajoled, bullied, and bribed into taking "one more bite" of a detested food, is more than just a child which must be reared according to cultural traditions of "good mothering." S/he is a piece of reality, of the world, which can be acted on, even modified, by a woman restricted from acting on anything else except inert materials like dust and food.

6

When I try to return to the body of the young woman of twenty-six, pregnant for the first time, who fled from the physical knowledge of her pregnancy and at the same time from her intellect and vocation, I realize that I was effectively alienated from my real body and my real spirit by the institution—not the fact—of motherhood. This institution—the foundation of human society as we know it—allowed me only certain views, certain expectations, whether embodied in the booklet in my obstetrician's waiting room, the novels I had read, my mother-in-law's approval, my memories of my own mother, the Sistine Madonna or she of the Michelangelo *Pietà*, the floating notion that a woman pregnant is a woman calm in her fulfillment or, simply, a woman waiting. Women have always been seen as waiting: waiting to be asked, waiting for our menses, in fear lest they do or do not come, waiting for men to come home from wars, or from work, waiting for children to grow up, or for the birth of a new child, or for menopause.

In my own pregnancy I dealt with this waiting, this female fate, by denying every active, powerful aspect of myself. I became dissociated both from my immediate, present, bodily experience and from my reading, thinking, writing life. Like a traveler in an airport where her plane is several hours delayed, who leafs through magazines she would never ordinarily read, surveys shops whose contents do not interest her, I committed myself to an outward serenity and a profound inner boredom. If boredom is simply a mask for anxiety, then I had learned, as a woman, to be supremely bored rather than to examine the anxiety underlying my Sistine tranquility. My body, finally truthful, paid me back in the end: I was allergic to pregnancy.

I have come to believe, as will be clear throughout this book, that female biology—the diffuse, intense sensuality radiating out from clitoris, breasts, uterus, vagina; the lunar cycles of menstruation; the gestation and fruition of life which can take place in the female body—has far more radical implications than we have yet come to appreciate. Patriarchal thought has limited female biology to its own narrow specifications. The feminist vision has recoiled from female biology for these reasons; it will, I believe, come to view our physicality as a resource, rather than a destiny. In order to live a fully human life we require not only *control* of our bodies (though control is a prerequisite); we must touch the unity and resonance of our physicality, our bond with the natural order, the corporeal ground of our intelligence.

The ancient, continuing envy, awe, and dread of the male for the female capacity to create life has repeatedly taken the form of hatred for every other female aspect of creativity. Not only have women been told to stick to motherhood, but we have been told that our intellectual or aesthetic creations were inappropriate, inconsequential, or scandalous, an attempt to become "like men," or to escape from the "real" tasks of adult womanhood: marriage and childbearing. To "think like a man" has been both praise and prison for women trying to escape the body-trap. No wonder that many intellectual and creative women have insisted that they were "human beings" first and women only incidentally, have minimized their physicality and their bonds with other women. The body has been made so problematic for women that it has often seemed easier to shrug it off and travel as a disembodied spirit.

But this reaction against the body is now coming into synthesis with new inquiries into the actual—as opposed to the culturally warped—power inherent in female biology, however we choose to use it, and by no means limited to the maternal function.

My own story, which is woven throughout this book, is only one story. What I carried away in the end was a determination to heal—insofar as an individual woman can, and as much as possible with other women—the separation between mind and body; never again to lose myself both psychically and physically in that way. Slowly I came to understand the paradox contained in "my" experience of motherhood; that, although different from many other women's experiences it was not unique; and that only in shedding the illusion of my uniqueness could I hope, as a woman, to have any authentic life at all.

---

1. Arthur W. Calhoun, *A Social History of the American Family from Colonial Times to the Present* (Cleveland: 1917). See also Gerda Lerner, *Black Women in White America: A Documentary History* (New York: Vintage, 1973), pp. 149–50 ff.

JO FREEMAN

(from) Trashing: The Dark Side of Sisterhood

Years of civil rights activism led Jo Freeman (born 1945) to a deep understanding of the need for feminism, and she became one of the pioneers of the women's liberation movement. She cofounded Chicago's West Side Group, considered the country's first women's liberation group, in 1967, and founded and edited the first movement newsletter, *Voice of the Women's Liberation Movement,* giving the new movement its name. Distressed by radical feminism's widespread rejection of formal structure and, in the name of equality, its extreme suspicion of leaders, including herself, Freeman published, under her movement pen name Joreen, two widely read articles: "The Tyranny of Structurelessness" (1970) and "Trashing: The Dark Side of Sisterhood," published in *Ms.* in April 1976 and excerpted here. Freeman has played major roles in the traditionally structured NOW for the past five decades.

IT'S BEEN a long time since I was trashed. I was one of the first in the country, perhaps the first in Chicago, to have my character, my commitment, and my very self attacked in such a way by Movement women that it left me torn in little pieces and unable to function. It took me years to recover, and even today the wounds have not entirely healed. Thus I hang around the fringes of the Movement, feeding off it because I need it, but too fearful to plunge once more into its midst. I don't even know what I am afraid of. I keep telling myself there's no reason why it should happen again—if I am cautious—yet in the back of my head there is a pervasive, irrational certainty that says if I stick my neck out, it will once again be a lightning rod for hostility.

For years I have written this spiel in my head, usually as a speech for a variety of imaginary Movement audiences. But I have never thought to express myself on it publicly because I have been a firm believer in not washing the Movement's dirty linen in public. I am beginning to change my mind.

First of all, so much dirty linen is being publicly exposed that I doubt that what I have to reveal will add much to the pile. To those women who have been active in the Movement, it is not even a revelation. Second, I have been watching for years with increasing dismay as the Movement consciously destroys anyone within it who stands out in any way. I had long hoped that this self-destructive tendency would wither away with time and experience. Thus I sympathized with, supported, but did not speak out about, the many women whose talents have been lost to the Movement because their attempts to use them had been met with hostility. Conversations with friends in Boston, Los Angeles, and Berkeley who have been trashed as recently as 1975 have convinced me that the Movement has not learned from its unexamined experience. Instead, trashing has reached epidemic proportions. Perhaps taking it out of the closet will clear the air.

What is "trashing," this colloquial term that expresses so much, yet explains so little? It is not disagreement; it is not conflict; it is not opposition. These are perfectly ordinary phenomena which, when engaged in mutually, honestly, and not excessively, are necessary to keep an organism or organization healthy and active. Trashing is a particularly vicious form of character assassination which amounts to psychological rape. It is manipulative, dishonest, and excessive. It is occasionally disguised by the rhetoric of honest conflict, or covered up by denying that any disapproval exists at all. But it is not done to expose disagreements or resolve differences. It is done to disparage and destroy.

The means vary. Trashing can be done privately or in a group situation; to one's face or behind one's back; through ostracism or open denunciation. The trasher may give you false reports of what (horrible things) others think of you; tell your friends false stories of what you think of them; interpret whatever you say or do in the most negative light; project unrealistic expectations on you so that when you fail to meet them, you become a "legitimate" target for anger; deny your perceptions of reality; or pretend you don't exist at all. Trashing may even be thinly veiled by the newest group techniques of criticism/self-criticism, mediation, and therapy. Whatever methods are used, trashing involves a violation of one's integrity, a declaration of one's worthlessness, and an impugning of one's motives. In effect, what is attacked is not one's actions, or one's ideas, but one's self.

This attack is accomplished by making you feel that your very existence is inimical to the Movement and that nothing can change this short of ceasing to exist. These feelings are reinforced when you are isolated from your friends as they become convinced that their association with you is similarly inimical to the Movement and to themselves. Any support of you will taint them. Eventually all your colleagues join in a chorus of condemnation which cannot be silenced, and you are reduced to a mere parody of your previous self.

It took three trashings to convince me to drop out. Finally, at the end of 1969, I felt psychologically mangled to the point where I knew I couldn't go on. Until then I interpreted my experiences as due to personality conflicts or political disagreements which I could rectify with time and effort. But the harder I tried, the worse things got, until I was finally forced to face the incomprehensible reality that the problem was not what I did, but what I was.

This was communicated so subtly that I never could get anyone to talk about it. There were no big confrontations, just many little slights. Each by itself was insignificant; but added one to another they were like a thousand cuts with a whip. Step by step I was ostracized: if a collective article was written, my attempts to contribute were ignored; if I wrote an article, no one would read it; when I spoke in meetings, everyone would listen politely, and then take up the discussion as though I hadn't said anything; meeting dates were changed without my being told; when it was my turn to coordinate a work project, no one would help; when I didn't receive mailings, and discovered that my name was not on the mailing list, I was told I had just looked in the wrong place. My group once decided on joint fund-raising efforts to send people to a conference until I said I wanted to go, and then it was decided that everyone was on her own (in fairness, one member did call me afterward to contribute $5 to my fare, provided that I not tell anyone. She was trashed a few years later).

My response to this was bewilderment. I felt as though I were wandering blindfolded in a field full of sharp objects and deep holes while being reassured that I could see perfectly and was in a smooth, grassy pasture. It was as if I had unwittingly entered a new society, one operating by rules of which I wasn't aware, and couldn't know. When I tried to get my group(s) to discuss what I thought was happening to me, they either denied my perception of reality by saying nothing was out of the ordinary, or dismissed the incidents as trivial (which individually they were). One woman, in private phone conversations, did admit that I was being poorly treated. But she never supported me publicly, and admitted quite frankly that it was because she feared to lose the group's approval. She too was trashed in another group.

Month after month the message was pounded in: get out, the Movement was saying: Get Out, *Get Out!* One day I found myself confessing to my roommate that I didn't think I existed; that I was a figment of my own imagination. That's when I knew it was time to leave. My departure was very quiet. I told two people, and stopped going to the Women's Center. The response convinced me that I had read the message correctly. No one called, no one sent me any mailings, no reaction came back through the grapevine. Half my life had been voided, and no one was aware of it but me. Three months later word drifted back that I had been denounced by the Chicago Women's Liberation Union, founded after I dropped out of the Movement, for allowing myself to be quoted in a recent news article without their permission. That was all.

The worst of it was that I really didn't know why I was so deeply affected. I had survived growing up in a very conservative, conformist, sexist suburb where my right to my own identity was constantly under assault. The need to defend my right to be myself made me tougher, not tattered. My thickening skin was further annealed by my experiences in other political organizations and movements, where I learned the use of rhetoric and argument as weapons in political struggle, and how to spot personality conflicts masquerading as political ones. Such conflicts were usually articulated impersonally, as attacks on one's ideas, and while they may not have been productive, they were not as destructive as those that I later saw in the feminist movement. One can rethink one's ideas as a result of their being attacked. It's much harder to rethink one's personality. Character assassination was occasionally used, but it was not considered legitimate, and thus was limited in both extent and effectiveness. As people's actions counted more than their personalities, such attacks would not so readily result in isolation. When they were employed, they only rarely got under one's skin.

But the feminist movement got under mine. For the first time in my life, I found myself believing all the horrible things people said about me. When I was treated like shit, I interpreted it to mean that I was shit. My reaction unnerved me as much as my experience. Having survived so much unscathed, why should I now succumb? The answer took me years to arrive at. It is a personally painful one because it admits of vulnerability I thought I had escaped. I had survived my youth because I had never given anyone or any group the right to judge me. That right I had reserved to myself. But the Movement seduced me by its sweet promise of sisterhood. It claimed to provide a haven from the ravages of a sexist society; a place where one would be understood. It was my very need for feminism and feminists that made me vulnerable. I gave the movement the right to judge me because I trusted it. And when it judged me worthless, I accepted that judgment.

For at least six months I lived in a kind of numb despair, completely internalizing my failure as a personal one. In June, 1970, I found myself in New York coincidentally with several feminists from four different cities. We gathered one night for a general discussion on the state of the Movement, and instead found ourselves discussing what had happened to us. We had two things in common; all of us had Movement-wide reputations, and all had been trashed. Anselma Dell'Olio read us a speech on "Divisiveness and Self-

Destruction in the Women's Movement" she had recently given at the Congress To Unite Women (sic) as a result of her own trashing.

"I learned . . . years ago that women had always been divided against one another, self-destructive and filled with impotent rage. I thought the Movement would change all that. I never dreamed that I would see the day when this rage, masquerading as a pseudo-egalitarian radicalism [would be] used within the Movement to strike down sisters singled out for punishment. . . .

"I am referring . . . to the personal attacks, both overt and insidious, to which women in the Movement who had painfully managed any degree of achievement have been subjected. These attacks take different forms. The most common and pervasive is character assassination: the attempt to undermine and destroy belief in the integrity of the individual under attack. . . . Another form is the 'purge.' . . . The ultimate tactic is to isolate her. . . .

"And who do they attack? Generally two categories. . . . Achievement or accomplishment of any kind would seem to be the worst crime: . . . do anything . . . that every other woman secretly or otherwise feels she could do just as well—and . . . you're in for it. If then . . . you are assertive, have what is generally described as a 'forceful personality,' if . . . you do not fit the conventional stereotype of a 'feminine' woman, . . . it's all over. . . .

"If you are in the first category (an achiever), you are immediately labeled a thrill-seeking opportunist, a ruthless mercenary, out to make her fame and fortune over the dead bodies of selfless sisters who have buried their abilities and sacrificed their ambitions for the greater glory of Feminism. Productivity seems to be the major crime—but if you have the misfortune of being outspoken and articulate, you are also accused of being power-mad, elitist, fascist, and finally the worst epithet of all: *a male-identifier. Aaaarrrrggg!*"

As I listened to her, a great feeling of relief washed over me. It was my experience she was describing. If I was crazy, I wasn't the only one. Our talk continued late into the evening. When we left, we sardonically dubbed ourselves the "feminist refugees" and agreed to meet sometime again. We never did. Instead we each slipped back into our own isolation, and dealt with the problem only on a personal level. The result was that most of the women at that meeting dropped out as I had done. Two ended up in the hospital with nervous breakdowns. Although all remained dedicated feminists, none have really contributed their talents to the Movement as they might have. Though we never met again, our numbers grew as the disease of self-destructiveness slowly engulfed the Movement.

Over the years I have talked with many women who have been trashed. Like a cancer, the attacks spread from those who had reputations to those who were merely strong; from those who were active to those who merely had ideas;

from those who stood out as individuals to those who failed to conform rapidly enough to the twists and turns of the changing line. With each new story, my conviction grew that trashing was not an individual problem brought on by individual actions nor was it a result of political conflicts between those of differing ideas. It was a social disease.

The disease has been ignored so long because it is frequently masked under the rhetoric of sisterhood. In my own case, the ethic of sisterhood prevented a recognition of my ostracism. The new values of the Movement said that every woman was a sister, every woman was acceptable. I clearly was not. Yet no one could admit that I was not acceptable without admitting that they were not being sisters. It was easier to deny the reality of my unacceptability. With other trashings, sisterhood has been used as the knife rather than the cover-up. A vague standard of sisterly behavior is set up by anonymous judges who then condemn those who do not meet their standards. As long as the standard is vague and utopian, it can never be met. But it can be shifted with circumstances to exclude those not desired as sisters. Thus Ti-Grace Atkinson's memorable adage that "sisterhood is powerful: it kills sisters" is reaffirmed again and again.

DEL MARTIN

A Letter from a Battered Wife

Viewing domestic violence as misogyny in action, feminist groups founded battered women's shelters; by 1979 there were over 250 in the U.S. This letter from an
anonymous woman, published in Del Martin's trailblazing book *Battered Women*
(1976), describes the complex dynamics of what came to be called "battered wife
syndrome." Martin (1921–2008) was the first openly lesbian board member of NOW
and, with her partner and later wife Phyllis Lyon, a founder of the lesbian social
and rights organization Daughters of Bilitis (1955) and the Council on Religion and
the Homosexual (1964). She shifted her activist focus from lesbian rights to the
situation of battered women when, answering phones at a gay counseling center,
Martin began to receive calls from women beaten by their husbands: "I didn't want
to be a single issue feminist," she later wrote.

A FRIEND OF mine received the following letter after discussing wife-
beating at a public meeting.

I am in my thirties and so is my husband. I have a high school diploma
and am presently attending a local college, trying to obtain the additional
education I need. My husband is a college graduate and a professional in his
field. We are both attractive and, for the most part, respected and well-liked.
We have four children and live in a middle-class home with all the comforts
we could possibly want.

I have everything, except life without fear.

For most of my married life I have been periodically beaten by my husband.
What do I mean by "beaten"? I mean that parts of my body have been hit
violently and repeatedly, and that painful bruises, swelling, bleeding wounds,
unconciousness, and combinations of these things have resulted.

Beating should be distinguished from all other kinds of physical abuse—
including being hit and shoved around. When I say my husband threatens me
with abuse I do not mean he warns me that he may lose control. I mean that he

shakes a fist against my face or nose, makes punching-bag jabs at my shoulder, or makes similar gestures which may quickly turn into a full-fledged beating.

I have had glasses thrown at me. I have been kicked in the abdomen when I was visibly pregnant. I have been kicked off the bed and hit while lying on the floor—again, while I was pregnant. I have been whipped, kicked and thrown, picked up again and thrown down again. I have been punched and kicked in the head, chest, face, and abdomen more times than I can count.

I have been slapped for saying something about politics, for having a different view about religion, for swearing, for crying, for wanting to have intercourse.

I have been threatened when I wouldn't do something he told me to do. I have been threatened when he's had a bad day and when he's had a good day.

I have been threatened, slapped, and beaten after stating bitterly that I didn't like what he was doing with another woman.

After each beating my husband has left the house and remained away for days.

Few people have ever seen my black and blue face or swollen lips because I have always stayed indoors afterwards, feeling ashamed. I was never able to drive following one of these beatings, so I could not get myself to a hospital for care. I could never have left my young children alone, even if I could have driven a car.

Hysteria inevitably sets in after a beating. This hysteria—the shaking and crying and mumbling—is not accepted by anyone, so there has never been anyone to call.

My husband on a few occasions did phone a day or so later so we could agree on the excuse I would use for returning to work, the grocery store, the dentist appointment, and so on. I used the excuses—a car accident, oral surgery, things like that.

Now, the first response to this story, which I myself think of, will be "Why didn't you seek help?"

I did. Early in our marriage I went to a clergyman who, after a few visits, told me that my husband meant no real harm, that he was just confused and felt insecure. I was encouraged to be more tolerant and understanding. Most important, I was told to forgive him the beatings just as Christ had forgiven me from the cross. I did that, too.

Things continued. Next time I turned to a doctor. I was given little pills to relax me and told to take things a little easier. I was just too nervous.

I turned to a friend, and when her husband found out, he accused me of either making things up or exaggerating the situation. She was told to stay away from me. She didn't, but she could no longer really help me. Just by believing me she was made to feel disloyal.

I turned to a professional family guidance agency. I was told there that my husband needed help and that I should find a way to control the incidents. I couldn't control the beatings—that was the whole point of my seeking help. At the agency I found I had to defend myself against the suspicion that I wanted to be hit, that I invited the beatings. Good God! Did the Jews invite themselves to be slaughtered in Germany?

I did go to two more doctors. One asked me what I had done to provoke my husband. The other asked if we had made up yet.

I called the police one time. They not only did not respond to the call, they called several hours later to ask if things had "settled down." I could have been dead by then!

I have nowhere to go if it happens again. No one wants to take in a woman with four children. Even if there were someone kind enough to care, no one wants to become involved in what is commonly referred to as a "domestic situation."

Everyone I have gone to for help has somehow wanted to blame me and vindicate my husband. I can see it lying there between their words and at the end of their sentences. The clergyman, the doctor, the counselor, my friend's husband, the police—all of them have found a way to vindicate my husband.

No one has to "provoke" a wife-beater. He will strike out when he's ready and for whatever reason he has at the moment.

I may be his excuse, but I have never been the reason.

I know that I do not want to be hit. I know, too, that I will be beaten again unless I can find a way out for myself and my children. I am terrified for them also.

As a married woman I have no recourse but to remain in the situation which is causing me to be painfully abused. I have suffered physical and emotional battering and spiritual rape because the social structure of my world says I cannot do anything about a man who wants to beat me. . . . But staying with my husband means that my children must be subjected to the emotional battering caused when they see their mother's beaten face or hear her screams in the middle of the night.

I know that I have to get out. But when you have nowhere to go, you know that you must go on your own and expect no support. I have to be ready for that. I have to be ready to support myself and the children completely, and still provide a decent environment for them. I pray that I can do that before I am murdered in my own home.

I have learned that no one believes me and that I cannot depend upon any outside help. All I have left is the hope that I can get away before it is too late.

I have learned also that the doctors, the police, the clergy, and my friends will excuse my husband for distorting my face, but won't forgive me for looking bruised and broken. The greatest tragedy is that I am still praying, and there is not a human person to listen.

Being beaten is a terrible thing; it is most terrible of all if you are not equipped to fight back. I recall an occasion when I tried to defend myself and actually tore my husband's shirt. Later, he showed it to a relative as proof that I had done something terribly wrong. The fact that at that moment I had several raised spots on my head hidden by my hair, a swollen lip that was bleeding, and a severely damaged cheek with a blood clot that caused a permanent dimple didn't matter to him. What mattered was that I tore his shirt! That I tore it in self-defense didn't mean anything to him.

My situation is so untenable I would guess that anyone who has not experienced one like it would find it incomprehensible. I find it difficult to believe myself.

It must be pointed out that while a husband can beat, slap, or threaten his wife, there are "good days." These days tend to wear away the effects of the beating. They tend to cause the wife to put aside the traumas and look to the good—first, because there is nothing else to do; second, because there is nowhere and no one to turn to; and third, because the defeat is the beating and the hope is that it will not happen again. A loving woman like myself always hopes that it will not happen again. When it does, she simply hopes again, until it becomes obvious after a third beating that there is no hope. That is when she turns outward for help to find an answer. When that help is denied, she either resigns herself to the situation she is in or pulls herself together and starts making plans for a future life that includes only herself and her children.

For many the third beating may be too late. Several of the times I have been abused I have been amazed that I have remained alive. Imagine that I have been thrown to a very hard slate floor several times, kicked in the abdomen, the head, and the chest, and still remained alive!

What determines who is lucky and who isn't? I could have been dead a long time ago had I been hit the wrong way. My baby could have been killed or deformed had I been kicked the wrong way. What saved me?

I don't know. I only know that it has happened and that each night I dread the final blow that will kill me and leave my children motherless. I hope I can hang on until I complete my education, get a good job, and become self-sufficient enough to care for my children on my own.

BARBARA EHRENREICH

What Is Socialist Feminism?

Starting in the 1960s, socialist- and Marxist-feminist ideas, championed by feminists from the New Left, spread through the radical women's movement in America. By the mid-1970s, in the Northeast alone, there were three active Marxist-feminist women's groups, each convening semiannually for weekend-long retreats to examine the interconnections between class and gender oppression. Some members, called "politicos," believed that women's oppression would end when capitalism ended; others, while embracing socialism, believed that women's oppression had preceded capitalism and could survive its demise. The writer and activist Barbara Ehrenreich (born 1941) came to the movement in the early 1970s, initially through a focus on women's health, authoring a cover article in *Ms.* debunking the myth that feminism caused heart disease. Her speech to a National Socialist/Feminist Conference in Yellow Springs, Ohio, in 1975 was revised for the 1976 *WIN Magazine* essay presented here. Introducing a 2018 reprint, Ehrenreich wrote that she winces over the original essay's "casual postponement of issues like race and homophobia."

A T SOME level, perhaps not too well articulated, socialist feminism has been around for a long time. You are a woman in a capitalist society. You get pissed off: about the job, about the bills, about your husband (or ex), about the kids' school, the housework, being pretty, not being pretty, being looked at, not being looked at (and either way, not listened to), etc. If you think about all these things and how they fit together and what has to be changed, and then you look around for some words to hold all these thoughts together in abbreviated form, you'd almost have to come up with "socialist feminism."

A lot of us came to socialist feminism in just that kind of way. We were reaching for a word/term/phrase which would begin to express *all* of our concerns, all of our principles, in a way that neither "socialist" nor "feminist" seemed to. I have to admit that most socialist feminists I know are not too happy with the term "socialist feminist" either. On the one hand it is too long (I have no hopes for a hyphenated mass movement); on the other hand it is much too short for what is, after all, really socialist internationalist anti-racist anti-heterosexist feminism.

The trouble with taking a new label of any kind is that it creates an instant aura of sectarianism. "Socialist feminism" becomes a challenge, a mystery, an issue in and of itself. We have speakers, conferences, articles on "socialist feminism"—though we know perfectly well that both "socialism" and "feminism" are too huge and too inclusive to be subjects for any sensible speech, conference, article, etc. People, including avowed socialist feminists, ask themselves anxiously, "What *is* socialist feminism?" There is a kind of expectation that it is (or is about to be at any moment, maybe in the next speech, conference, or article) a brilliant synthesis of world historical proportions—an evolutionary leap beyond Marx, Freud and Wollstonecraft. Or that it will turn out to be a nothing, a fad seized on by a few disgruntled feminists and female socialists, a temporary distraction.

I want to try to cut through some of the mystery which has grown up around socialist feminism. A logical way to start is to look at socialism and feminism separately. How does a socialist, more precisely, a Marxist, look at the world? How does a feminist? To begin with, Marxism and feminism have an important thing in common: they are *critical* ways of looking at the world. Both rip away popular mythology and "common sense" wisdom and force us to look at experience in a new way. Both seek to understand the world—not in terms of static balances, symmetries etc. (as in conventional social science)—but in terms of *antagonisms*. They lead to conclusions which are jarring and disturbing at the same time that they are liberating. There is no way to have a Marxist or a feminist outlook and remain a spectator. To understand the reality laid bare by these analyses is to move into action to change it.

Marxism addresses itself to the class dynamics of capitalist society. Every social scientist knows that capitalist societies are characterized by more or less severe, systemic inequality. Marxism understands this inequality to arise from processes which are *intrinsic* to capitalism as an economic system. A minority of people (the capitalist class) own all the factories/energy sources/resources etc. which everyone else depends on in order to live. The great majority (the working class) must work, out of sheer necessity, under conditions set by the capitalists, for the wages the capitalists pay. Since the capitalists make their profits by paying less in wages than the value of what the workers actually produce, the relationship between these two classes is necessarily one of irreconcilable antagonism. The capitalist class owes its very existence to the continued exploitation of the working class. What maintains this system of class rule is, in the last analysis, force. The capitalist class controls (directly or indirectly) the means of organized violence represented by the state—police, jails, etc. Only by waging a revolutionary struggle aimed at the seizure of state power can the working class free itself, and, ultimately, all people.

Feminism addresses itself to another familiar inequality. All human societies are marked by some degree of inequality between the sexes. If we survey human societies at a glance, sweeping through history and across continents, we see that they have commonly been characterized by: the subjugation of women to male authority, both within the family and in the community in general; the objectification of women as a form of property; a sexual division of labor in which women are confined to such activities as childraising, performing personal services for adult males, and specified (usually low prestige) forms of productive labor.

Feminists, struck by the near-universality of these things, have looked for explanations in the biological "givens" which underlie all human social existence. Men are physically stronger than women on the average, especially compared to pregnant women or women who are nursing babies. Furthermore, men have the power to make women pregnant. Thus, the forms that sexual inequality takes—however various they may be from culture to culture—rest, in the last analysis, on what is clearly a physical advantage males hold over females. That is to say, they rest ultimately on violence, or the threat of violence.

The ancient, biological root of male supremacy—the fact of male violence—is commonly obscured by the laws and conventions which regulate the relations between the sexes in any particular culture. But it is there, according to a feminist analysis. The possibility of male assault stands as a constant warning to "bad" (rebellious, aggressive) women, and drives "good" women into complicity with male supremacy. The reward for being "good" ("pretty," submissive) is protection from random male violence and, in some cases, economic security.

Marxism rips away the myths about "democracy" and "pluralism" to reveal a system of class rule that rests on *forcible* exploitation. Feminism cuts through myths about "instinct" and romantic love to expose male rule as a rule of *force*. Both analyses compel us to look at a fundamental injustice. The choice is to reach for the comfort of the myths or, as Marx put it, to work for a social order which does not require myths to sustain it.

It is possible to add up Marxism and feminism and call the sum "socialist feminism." In fact, this is probably how most socialist feminists operate most of the time—as a kind of hybrid, pushing our feminism in socialist circles, our socialism in feminist circles. One trouble with leaving things like that, though, is that it keeps people wondering "Well, what is she *really*?" or demanding of us "What is the principal contradiction?" These kinds of questions, which sound so compelling and authoritative, often stop us in our tracks: "Make a choice!" "Be one or another!" But we know that there is a political consistency to socialist feminism. We are not hybrids or fence-sitters.

To get to that political consistency we have to differentiate ourselves, as feminists, from other kinds of feminists, and, as Marxists, from other kinds of Marxists. We have to stake out a (pardon the terminology here) socialist feminist kind of feminism and a socialist feminist kind of socialism. Only then is there a possibility that things will "add up" to something more than an uneasy juxtaposition.

I think most radical feminists and socialist feminists would agree with my capsule characterization of feminism *as far as it goes*. The trouble with radical feminism, from a socialist feminist point of view, is that it doesn't go any farther. It remains transfixed with the universality of male supremacy—things have never really changed; all social systems are "patriarchies"; imperialism, militarism and capitalism are all simply expressions of innate male aggressiveness. And so on.

The problem with this, from a socialist feminist point of view, is not only that it leaves out men (and the possibility of reconciliation with them on a truly human and egalitarian basis) but that it leaves out an awful lot about women. For example, to discount a socialist country such as China as a "patriarchy"—as I have heard radical feminists do—is to ignore the real struggles and achievements of millions of women. Socialist feminists, while agreeing that there is something timeless and universal about women's oppression, have insisted that it takes different forms in different settings, and that the *differences* are of vital importance. There is a difference between a society in which sexism is expressed in the form of female infanticide and a society in which sexism takes the form of unequal representation on the Central Committee. And the difference is worth dying for.

One of the historical variations on the theme of sexism which ought to concern all feminists is the set of changes that came with the transition from an agrarian society to industrial capitalism. This is no academic issue. The social system which industrial capitalism replaced was in fact a *patriarchal* one, and I am using that term now in its original sense, to mean a system in which production is centered in the household and is presided over by the oldest male. The fact is that industrial capitalism came along and tore the rug out from under patriarchy. Production went into the factories and individuals broke off from the family to become "free" wage earners. To say that capitalism disrupted the patriarchal organization of production and family life is not, of course, to say that capitalism abolished male supremacy! But it is to say that the particular forms of sex oppression we experience today are, to a significant degree, *recent* developments. A huge historical discontinuity lies between us and true patriarchy. If we are to understand our experience as women today, we must move to a consideration of *capitalism* as a system.

There are obviously other ways I could have gotten to the same point. I could have simply said that, as feminists, we are most interested in the most oppressed women—poor and working class women, third world women, etc., and for *that* reason we are led to a need to comprehend and confront capitalism. I could have said that we need to address ourselves to the class system simply because women are members of classes. But I am trying to bring out something else about our perspective as feminists: there is no way to understand sexism as it acts on our lives without putting it in the historical context of capitalism.

I think most socialist feminists would also agree with the capsule summary of Marxist theory *as far as it goes*. And the trouble again is that there are a lot of people (I'll call them "mechanical Marxists") who do not go any further. To these people, the only "real" and important things that go on in capitalist society are those things that relate to the productive process or the conventional political sphere. From such a point of view, every other part of experience and social existence—things having to do with education, sexuality, recreation, the family, art, music, housework (you name it)—is peripheral to the central dynamics of social change; it is part of the "superstructure" or "culture."

Socialist feminists are in a very different camp from what I am calling "mechanical Marxists." We (along with many, many Marxists who are not feminists) see capitalism as a social and cultural *totality*. We understand that, in its search for markets, capitalism is driven to penetrate every nook and cranny of social existence. Especially in the phase of monopoly capitalism, the realm of consumption is every bit as important, just from an economic point of view, as the realm of production. So we cannot understand class struggle as something confined to issues of wages and hours, or confined only to workplace issues. Class struggle occurs in every arena where the interests of classes conflict, and that includes education, health, art, music, etc. We aim to transform not only the ownership of the means of production, but the totality of social existence.

As Marxists, we come to feminism from a completely different place than the mechanical Marxists. Because we see monopoly capitalism as a political/ economic/cultural totality, we have room within our Marxist framework for feminist issues which have nothing ostensibly to do with production or "politics," issues that have to do with the family, health care, "private" life.

Furthermore, in our brand of Marxism, there is no "woman question" because we never compartmentalized women off to the "superstructure" or somewhere in the first place. Marxists of a mechanical bent continually ponder the issue of the unwaged woman (the housewife): Is she really a member of the working class? That is, does she really produce surplus value? We say, of course housewives are members of the working class—*not* because we have some elaborate proof that they really do produce surplus value—but because we understand a class as being composed of *people*, and as having a *social* existence quite apart from the capitalist-dominated realm of production. When we think of class in this way, then we see that in fact the women who seemed most peripheral, the housewives, are at the very heart of their class—raising children, holding together families, maintaining the cultural and social networks of the community.

We are coming out of a kind of feminism and a kind of Marxism whose interests quite naturally flow together. I think we are in a position now to see why it is that socialist feminism has been so mystified. The idea of socialist feminism is a great mystery, or a paradox, so long as what you mean by socialism is really what I have called "mechanical Marxism" and what you mean by feminism is an ahistorical kind of radical feminism. These things just don't add up; they have nothing in common.

But if you put together another kind of socialism and another kind of feminism, as I have tried to define them, you do get some common ground and that is one of the most important things about socialist feminism today. It is a space—free from the constrictions of a truncated kind of feminism and a truncated version of Marxism—in which we can develop the kind of politics that addresses the political/economic/cultural *totality* of monopoly capitalist society. We could go only so far with the available kinds of feminism, the conventional kind of Marxism, and then we had to break out to something that is not so restrictive and incomplete in its view of the world. We had to take a new name, "socialist feminism," in order to assert our determination to comprehend the *whole* of our experience and to forge a politics that reflects the totality of that comprehension.

However, I don't want to leave socialist feminist theory as a "space" or a common ground. Things are beginning to grow in that "ground." We are closer to a synthesis in our understanding of sex and class, capitalism and male domination, than we were a few years ago. Here I will indicate only very sketchily one such line of thinking:

1. The Marxist/feminist understanding that class and sex domination rest ultimately on force is correct, and this remains the most devastating critique of sexist/capitalist society. But there is a lot to that "ultimately." In a day to

day sense, most people acquiesce to sex and class domination without being held in line by the threat of violence, and often without even the threat of material deprivation.

2. It is very important, then, to figure out what it is, if not the direct application of force, that keeps things going. In the case of class, a great deal has been written already about why the US working class lacks militant class consciousness. Certainly ethnic divisions, especially the black/white division, are a key part of the answer. But, I would argue, in addition to being divided, the working class has been socially *atomized*. Working class neighborhoods have been destroyed and are allowed to decay; life has become increasingly privatized and inward-looking; skills once possessed by the working class have been expropriated by the capitalist class; and capitalist controlled "mass culture" has edged out almost all indigenous working class culture and institutions. Instead of collectivity and self-reliance as a class, there is mutual isolation and collective *dependency* on the capitalist class.

3. The subjugation of women, in the ways which are characteristic of late capitalist society, has been key to this process of class atomization. To put it another way, the forces which have atomized working class life and promoted cultural/material dependence on the capitalist class are the same forces which have served to perpetuate the subjugation of women. It is women who are most isolated in what has become an increasingly privatized family existence (even when they work outside the home too). It is, in many key instances, women's skills (productive skills, healing, midwifery, etc.) which have been discredited or banned to make way for commodities. It is, above all, women who are encouraged to be utterly passive/uncritical/dependent (i.e., "feminine") in the face of the pervasive capitalist penetration of private life. Historically, late capitalist penetration of working class life has singled out women as prime targets of pacification/"feminization"—because *women are the culture-bearers of their class*.

4. It follows that there is a fundamental interconnection between women's struggle and what is traditionally conceived as class struggle. Not all women's struggles have an inherently anti-capitalist thrust (particularly not those which seek only to advance the power and wealth of special groups of women), but all those which build *collectivity* and *collective confidence* among women are vitally important to the building of class consciousness. Conversely, not all class struggles have an inherently anti-sexist thrust (especially not those which cling to pre-industrial patriarchal values) but all those which seek to build the social and cultural autonomy of the working class are necessarily linked to the struggle for women's liberation.

This, in very rough outline, is one direction which socialist feminist analysis is taking. No one is expecting a synthesis to emerge which will collapse socialist and feminist struggle into the same thing. The capsule summaries I gave earlier retain their "ultimate" truth: there are crucial aspects of capitalist domination (such as racial oppression) which a purely feminist perspective simply cannot account for or deal with—without bizarre distortions, that is. There are crucial aspects of sex oppression (such as male violence within the family) which socialist thought has little insight into—again, not without a lot of stretching and distortion. Hence the need to continue to be socialists *and* feminists. But there *is* enough of a synthesis, both in what we think and what we do, for us to begin to have a self-confident identity as *socialist feminists*.

GERDA LERNER

The Majority Finds Its Past

It was Gerda Lerner's leadership—"Arguing, cajoling, even twisting arms," wrote her colleague Amy Swerdlow—that won funding in 1972 from the Rockefeller Foundation to launch at Sarah Lawrence College the first master's degree program in women's history. A poet and feminist active in the anti-Nazi resistance, Lerner (1920–2013) fled Vienna at age nineteen, settling first in New York and eventually in Los Angeles, where she worked as a screenwriter. When her film director husband was blacklisted in 1951 from the film industry for his communist activism, the couple returned to New York. There, while still an undergraduate at the New School, Lerner began her life's work, teaching what is considered the first course in women's history in 1963. Presented here is her 1976 essay "The Majority Finds Its Past," a roadmap for the future study of women's history collected in her 1979 book of the same title. In 1992, the Organization of American Historians, which Lerner had led as president in the early 1980s, established the annual Lerner-Scott Prize, named for her and historian Anne Firor Scott and awarded annually to the writer of the best doctoral dissertation in U.S. women's history.

WOMEN'S EXPERIENCE encompasses all that is human; they share—and always have shared—the world equally with men. Equally in the sense that half, at least, of all the world's experience has been theirs, half of the world's work and many of its products. In one sense, then, to write the history of women means documenting all of history: women have always been making history, living it and shaping it. But the history of women has a special character, a built-in distortion: it comes to us refracted through the lens of men's observations; refracted again through values which consider man the measure. What we know of the past experience of women has been transmitted to us largely through the reflections of men: how we see and interpret what we know about women has been shaped for us through a value system defined by men. And so, to construct a new history that will with true equality reflect the dual nature of humankind—its male and female aspect—we must first pause to reconstruct the missing half—the female experience: women's history.

Women's history must contain not only the activities and events in which women participated, but the record of changes and shifts in their perception of themselves and their roles. Historically, women began their public activities by extending their concerns from home and family to the larger community. With this broadening of female concerns came the questioning of tradition, often followed by tentative steps in new directions: Anne Hutchinson holding weekly meetings for men and women in which she, not the male clergy, commented on the Bible; Frances Wright daring to assert women's freedom of sexual choice; Margaret Sanger discovering in one moment of insight and empathy that societally enforced motherhood was a wrong no longer to be tolerated.

Then came the reaching out toward other women: sewing circles and female clubs; women workers organizing themselves; women's rights conventions; the building of mass movements of women. By such steps women became "woman-oriented." Out of such activities grew a new self-consciousness, based on the recognition of the separate interests of women as a group. Out of communality and collectivity emerged feminist consciousness—a system of ideas that not only challenged patriarchal values and assumptions, but attempted to substitute for them a feminist system of values and ideas.

The most advanced conceptual level by which women's history can now be defined must include an account of the female experience as it changes over time and should include the development of feminist consciousness as an essential aspect of women's historical past. This past includes the quest for rights, equality, and justice which can be subsumed under "women's rights," i.e., the civil rights of women. But the quest for female emancipation from patriarchally determined subordination encompasses more than the striving for equality and rights. It can be defined best as the quest for autonomy. Autonomy means women defining themselves and the values by which they will live, and beginning to think of institutional arrangements that will order their environment in line with their needs. It means to some the evolution of practical programs, to others the reforming of existing social arrangements, to still others the building of new institutions. Autonomy for women means moving out from a world in which one is born to marginality, bound to a past without meaning, and prepared for a future determined by others. It means moving into a world in which one acts and chooses, aware of a meaningful past and free to shape one's future.

The central question raised by women's history is: what would history be like if it were seen through the eyes of women and ordered by values they define?

Is one justified in speaking of a female historical experience different from that of men?[1] To find an answer to this basic question, it is useful to examine the life cycles and the turning points in individual lives of men and women of the past. Are there significant differences in childhood, education, maturity? Are social expectations different for boys and girls? Taking full cognizance of the wide range of variations, are there any universals by which we can define the female past? Material for answering such questions as far as they pertain to women can be found in many primary sources, some virtually untapped, others familiar. Autobiographical letters and diaries, even those frequently used, yield new information if approached with these questions and rearranged from the female point of view.[2]

There are basic differences in the way boys and girls now and in the past experienced the world and, more important, the social roles they were trained to fulfill. From childhood on, the talents and drives of girls were channeled into different directions from those of boys. For boys, the family was the place from which one sprang and to which one returned for comfort and support, but the field of action was the larger world of wilderness, adventure, industry, labor, and politics. For girls, the family was to be the world, their field of action was the domestic circle. He was to express himself in his work, and through it and social action help to transform his environment; her individual growth and choices were restricted to lead her to express herself through love, wifehood, and motherhood—through the support and nurturance of others who would act for her. The ways in which these gender-differentiated patterns would find expression would change in the course of historical development; the differences in the function assigned to the sexes might widen or narrow, but the fact of different sex role indoctrination remained.

Throughout most of America's past, life was experienced at a different rhythm by men and women. For a boy, education was directed toward a vocational or professional goal, his life ideally moved upward and outward in a straight line until it reached a plateau of fulfillment; the girl's education was sporadic and often interrupted: it did not lead to the fulfillment of her life role, but rather competed with it. Her development was dependent on her relationship to others and was often determined by them; it moved in wavelike, circuitous motion. In the boy's case, life crises were connected to vocational goals: separation from the family for purposes of greater educational opportunity; success or failures in achievement and career; economic decisions or setbacks. For the girl, such crises were more closely connected to stages in her biological life: the transition from childhood to adolescence, and then to marriage, which usually meant, in the past, greater restraint rather than the broadening out which it meant for the boy. Love and marriage for her implied a shifting of domesticity from one household to another, and the onset of her serious responsibilities: childbirth, child-rearing, and the nurture of the family. Finally came the crisis of widowhood and bereavement which could, depending on her economic circumstances, mean increasing freedom and autonomy or a difficult struggle for economic survival.

All people, in every society, are assigned specific roles and indoctrinated to perform to the expectations and values of that society. But for women this has always meant social indoctrination to a value system that imposed upon them greater restrictions of the range of choices than those of men. During much of the historic past, some of these restrictions were based on women's function as childbearers and the necessity of their bearing many children in order to guarantee the survival of some. With a declining infant mortality rate and advances in medical knowledge that made widely accessible birth-control methods possible, the gender-based role indoctrination of women was no longer functional but anachronistic. Women's indoctrination to motherhood as their primary and life-long function became oppressive, a patriarchal cultural myth. Additionally, even after educational restrictions were removed, women have been trained to fit into institutions shaped, determined, and ruled by men. As a result, their definitions of selfhood and self-fulfillment have remained subordinated to those of others.

American women have always shared in the economic life of the nation: in agriculture as equal partners performing separate, but essential work; in industry usually as low-paid unskilled workers; and in the professions overcoming barriers formed by educational discrimination and traditional male dominance. Although the majority of women have always worked for the same reasons as men—self-support and the support of dependents—their work has been characterized by marginality, temporariness, and low status. Typically, they have moved into the male-defined work world as outsiders, often treated as intruders. Thus, after each of the major wars in which the nation engaged, women who during wartime did all essential work and services, were at war's end shunted back to their traditional jobs. As workers, women have been handicapped by direct discrimination in hiring, training, and advancement, and, more profoundly, by their sex-role indoctrination that made them consider any work they did as subsidiary to their main job: wife and motherhood.

Thus, women often participated in their own subordination by internalizing the ideology and values that oppressed them and by passing these on to their children. Yet they were not *passive* victims; they always involved themselves actively in the world in their own way. Starting on a stage defined by their life cycle, they often rebelled against and defied societal indoctrination, developed their own definitions of community, and built their own female culture.

In addition to their participation in the economic life of society, women have shaped history through community-building and participation in politics. American women built community life as members of families, as carriers of cultural and religious values, as founders and supporters of organizations and institutions.[3] So far, historians have taken notice mostly of the first of these functions and of the organizational work of women only insofar as they "contributed" to social reforms. Women's political work has been recognized only as it pertains to women's rights and woman suffrage.

Historical interpretation of the community-building work of women is urgently needed. The voluminous national and local records that document the network of community institutions founded and maintained by women are available. They should be studied against the traditional record of institution-building, which focuses on the activities of men. The research and the monographic work that form the essential groundwork for such interpretations have yet to be done.

The history of women's struggles for the ballot has received a good deal of attention by historians, but this narrow focus has led to the impression that the main political activity in which women engaged in the past was working for woman suffrage.[4] While the importance of that issue is undeniable, it is impossible to understand the involvement of American women in every aspect of the nation's life, if their political activity is so narrowly defined. Women were involved in most of the political struggles of the 19th century, but the form of their participation and their activities were different from those of men. It is one of the urgent and as yet unfulfilled tasks of women's history to study the ways in which women influenced and participated in political events, directly or through the mass organizations they built.

The involvement of American women in the important events of American history—the political and electoral crises, the wars, expansion, diplomacy—is overshadowed by the fact of the exclusion of women from political power throughout 300 years of the nation's life. Thus women, half of the nation, are cast in the marginal role of a powerless minority—acted upon, but not acting. That this impression of the female past is a distortion is by now obvious. It is premature to attempt a critical evaluation or synthesis of the role women played in the building of American society. It is not premature to suggest that the fact of the exclusion of women from all those institutions that make essential decisions for the nation is itself an important aspect of the nation's past. In short, what needs to be explained is not why women were so little evident in American history as currently recorded, but why and how patriarchal values affected that history.

The steps by which women moved toward self-respect, self-definition, a recognition of their true position and from there toward a sense of sisterhood are tentative and varied and have occurred throughout our history. Exceptional women often defied traditional roles, at times explicitly, at other times simply by expressing their individuality to its fullest. The creation of new role models for women included the development of the professional woman, the political leader, the executive, as well as the anonymous working woman, the club woman, the trade unionist.[5] These types were created in the process of changing social activities, but they also were the elements that helped to create a new feminist consciousness. The emergence of feminist consciousness as a historical phenomenon is an essential part of the history of women.

The process of creating a theory of female emancipation is still under way. The challenges of modern American women are grounded in past experience, in the buried and neglected female past. Women have always made history as much as men have, not "contributed" to it, only they did not know what they had made and had no tools to interpret their own experience. What is new at this time, is that women are fully claiming their past and shaping the tools by means of which they can interpret it.

Women are not a marginal "minority," and women's history is not a collection of "missing facts and views" to be incorporated into traditional categories. Women are at least half and often a majority of all Americans and are distributed through all classes and categories of American society. Their history inevitably reflects variations in economic class, race, religion, and ethnicity. But the overriding fact is that women's history is the history of the *majority* of humankind.

---

1. See Carroll Smith-Rosenberg, "The New Woman and the New History," *Feminist Studies*, Vol. III, No. 1/2 (Fall 1975), 185–98, for a methodological discussion.

    For historical work which has accepted the concept of a female culture or highlighted aspects of it, see Nancy Cott, "Young Women in the Second Great Awakening in New England," *Feminist Studies*, Vol. III, No. 1/2 (Fall 1975), 15–29; C. Smith-Rosenberg, "Beauty, the Beast and the Militant Woman," *American Quarterly*, Vol. 23, No. 3 (Oct. 1971), 562–84; C. Smith-Rosenberg, "Female World . . . ," *Signs* (Fall 1975); Anne Firor Scott, *The Southern Lady: From Pedestal to Politics, 1830–1930* (Chicago, 1970); Kathryn Kish Sklar, *Catharine Beecher: A Study in American Domesticity* (New Haven, 1973); Barbara Welter, "Feminization of American Religion: 1800–1860," in William O'Neill (ed.), *Problems and Issues in American Social History* (Minneapolis, 1974); Ann Douglas Wood, "The Scribbling Women and Fanny Fern: Why Women Wrote," *American Quarterly*, Vol. 23, No. 3 (Oct. 1971), 3–24.

2. G. Lerner, *Female Experience: An American Documentary* (New York and Indianapolis, 1977), Part I.

3. The first historian to call attention to this aspect of Women's History was Mary Beard. Her *Woman's Work in Municipalities* (New York, 1915; reprint 1972) merely indicates the

availability of sources without organizing or interpreting them. This weakness is shared by other early collections of women's club activities, such as Jane Cunningham Croly, *The History of the Women's Club Movement in America* (New York, 1898); Elizabeth Lindsay Davis, *Lifting as They Climb* (n.p., 1933); Maud Nathan, *The Story of an Epoch-Making Movement* (New York, 1926).

Also see: Clarke A. Chambers, *A Seedtime of Reform* (Ann Arbor, 1967), chaps. 2, 5, 6; Jill Conway, "Women Reformers and American Culture, 1870–1930," *Journal of Social History*, Vol. V, No. 2 (Winter 1971–72), 164–77; Richard Jensen, "Family, Career and Reform: Women Leaders of the Progressive Era," in Michael Gordon (ed.), *The American Family in Social-Historical Perspective* (New York, 1973); Keith Melder, "Ladies Bountiful: Organized Women's Benevolence in Early 19th Century America," *New York History* (July 1967), 231–54; Gerda Lerner, *Black Women in White America* (New York, 1972), chap. 8; Frances Willard, *Glimpses of Fifty Years* (Chicago, 1899); Mildred White Wells, *Unity in Diversity: The History of the General Federation of Women's Clubs* (Washington, D.C., 1953).

An indication of the range of available untapped sources on the community and institution-building work of women can be gleaned from perusing the biographies in James (ed.), *Notable American Women* (Cambridge, Mass., 1972) of women listed under one or all of the following headings: "Kindergartners," "Religious Founders and Leaders," "School Founders and Administrators," "Social and Civic Reformers," "Temperance Advocates," "Welfare Work Leaders," "Women's Club Leaders."

4. For monographs on woman suffrage see: Carrie Chapman Catt and Nattie R. Schuler, *Women Suffrage and Politics* (New York, 1926); William Chafe, *Women and Equality* (New York, 1977); Alan P. Grimes, *The Puritan Ethic and Woman Suffrage* (New York, 1967); Ida Husted Harper, *Story of the National Amendment for Woman Suffrage* (New York, 1919); Mrs. Inez Haynes Irwin, *The Story of the Woman's Party* (New York, 1921), and *Up Hill with Banners Flying* (Penobscot, Me., 1964); Aileen S. Kraditor, *Ideas . . .* (New York, 1965); David Morgan, *Suffragists and Democrats in America* (East Lansing, 1972); Anne F. Scott and Andrew Scott, *One Half the People: The Fight for Woman's Suffrage* (Philadelphia, 1975); Doris Stevens, *Jailed for Freedom* (New York, 1920; reprint, 1976).

For a broader-based treatment of the subject see: Barbara Berg, *The Remembered Gate: Origins of American Feminism: The Woman and the City, 1800–1860* (New York, 1978); Ellen Dubois, *Feminism and Suffrage: The Emergence of an Independent Women's Movement in America, 1848–1869* (Ithaca, 1978); Eleanor Flexner, *Century of Struggle* (Cambridge, Mass., 1959); Keith Melder, *Beginnings of Sisterhood* (New York, 1977); William O'Neill, *Everyone Was Brave* (Chicago, 1969); Ross Evans Paulson, *Woman's Suffrage and Prohibition* (Glenview, Ill., 1973).

5. Lerner, *Female Experience*, Part III.

A Black Feminist Statement

In 1974, a group of Black activists in Boston left the National Black Feminist Organization to forge a more radical Black feminism. Frustrated by hierarchy, they became a collective, naming themselves for the river in South Carolina where Harriet Tubman led Black Union soldiers in a raid that freed 750 enslaved people in 1863. All had come to feminism from groups—Students for a Democratic Society (SDS), the Congress of Racial Equality (CORE), the Black Panther Party—where the particularity of their lives as Black women went unexamined or, in the case of lesbians, unmentioned. As organizers, they looked anew for sources of Black female oppression in the origins of capitalism and patriarchy, and, through their activism and study, emerged with a fresh analysis that enlarged the scope of feminism. Included here in full is "A Black Feminist Statement," drafted in April 1977 by Demita Frazier, Barbara Smith (see also pp. 373–376 in this volume), and Beverly Smith after group discussions.

WE ARE a collective of black feminists who have been meeting together since 1974.[1] During that time we have been involved in the process of defining and clarifying our politics, while at the same time doing political work within our own group and in coalition with other progressive organizations and movements. The most general statement of our politics at the present time would be that we are actively committed to struggling against racial, sexual, heterosexual, and class oppression and see as our particular task the development of integrated analysis and practice based upon the fact that the major systems of oppression are interlocking. The synthesis of these oppressions creates the conditions of our lives. As black women we see black feminism as the logical political movement to combat the manifold and simultaneous oppressions that all women of color face.

We will discuss four major topics in the paper that follows: (1) The genesis of contemporary black feminism; (2) what we believe, i.e., the specific province of our politics; (3) the problems in organizing black feminists, including a brief herstory of our collective; and (4) black feminist issues and practice.

1. THE GENESIS OF CONTEMPORARY BLACK FEMINISM

Before looking at the recent development of black feminism, we would like to affirm that we find our origins in the historical reality of Afro-American women's continuous life-and-death struggle for survival and liberation. Black women's extremely negative relationship to the American political system (a system of white male rule) has always been determined by our membership in two oppressed racial and sexual castes. As Angela Davis points out in "Reflections on the Black Woman's Role in the Community of Slaves," black women have always embodied, if only in their physical manifestation, an adversary stance to white male rule and have actively resisted its inroads upon them and their communities in both dramatic and subtle ways. There have always been black women activists—some known, like Sojourner Truth, Harriet Tubman, Frances E. W. Harper, Ida B. Wells Barnett, and Mary Church Terrell, and thousands upon thousands unknown—who had a shared awareness of how their sexual identity combined with their racial identity to make their whole life situation and the focus of their political struggles unique. Contemporary black feminism is the outgrowth of countless generations of personal sacrifice, militancy, and work by our mothers and sisters.

A black feminist presence has evolved most obviously in connection with the second wave of the American women's movement beginning in the late 1960s. Black, other Third World, and working women have been involved in the feminist movement from its start, but both outside reactionary forces and racism and elitism within the movement itself have served to obscure our participation. In 1973 black feminists, primarily located in New York, felt the necessity of forming a separate black feminist group. This became the National Black Feminist Organization (NBFO).

Black feminist politics also have an obvious connection to movements for black liberation, particularly those of the 1960s and 1970s. Many of us were active in those movements (civil rights, black nationalism, the Black Panthers), and all of our lives were greatly affected and changed by their ideology, their goals, and the tactics used to achieve their goals. It was our experience and disillusionment within these liberation movements, as well as experience on the periphery of the white male left, that led to the need to develop a politics that was antiracist, unlike those of white women, and antisexist, unlike those of black and white men.

There is also undeniably a personal genesis for black feminism, that is, the political realization that comes from the seemingly personal experiences of individual black women's lives. Black feminists and many more black women who do not define themselves as feminists have all experienced sexual oppression as a constant factor in our day-to-day existence.

Black feminists often talk about their feelings of craziness before becoming conscious of the concepts of sexual politics, patriarchal rule, and, most importantly, feminism, the political analysis and practice that we women use to struggle against our oppression. The fact that racial politics and indeed racism are pervasive factors in our lives did not allow us, and still does not allow most black women, to look more deeply into our own experiences and define those things that make our lives what they are and our oppression specific to us. In the process of consciousness-raising, actually life-sharing, we began to recognize the commonality of our experiences and, from that sharing and growing consciousness, to build a politics that will change our lives and inevitably end our oppression.

Our development also must be tied to the contemporary economic and political position of black people. The post–World War II generation of black youth was the first to be able to minimally partake of certain educational and employment options, previously closed completely to black people. Although our economic position is still at the very bottom of the American capitalist economy, a handful of us have been able to gain certain tools as a result of tokenism in education and employment which potentially enable us to more effectively fight our oppression.

A combined antiracist and antisexist position drew us together initially, and as we developed politically we addressed ourselves to heterosexism and economic oppression under capitalism.

2. What We Believe

Above all else, our politics initially sprang from the shared belief that black women are inherently valuable, that our liberation is a necessity not as an adjunct to somebody else's but because of our need as human persons for autonomy. This may seem so obvious as to sound simplistic, but it is apparent that no other ostensibly progressive movement has ever considered our specific oppression a priority or worked seriously for the ending of that oppression. Merely naming the pejorative stereotypes attributed to black women (e.g., mammy, matriarch, Sapphire, whore, bulldagger), let alone cataloguing the cruel, often murderous, treatment we receive, indicates how little value has been placed upon our lives during four centuries of bondage in the Western hemisphere. We realize that the only people who care enough about us to work consistently for our liberation is us. Our politics evolve from a healthy love for ourselves, our sisters, and our community which allows us to continue our struggle and work.

This focusing upon our own oppression is embodied in the concept of identity politics. We believe that the most profound and potentially the most radical politics come directly out of our own identity, as opposed to working to end somebody else's oppression. In the case of black women this is a particularly repugnant, dangerous, threatening, and therefore revolutionary concept because it is obvious from looking at all the political movements that have preceded us that anyone is more worthy of liberation than ourselves. We reject pedestals, queenhood, and walking ten paces behind. To be recognized as human, levelly human, is enough.

We believe that sexual politics under patriarchy is as pervasive in black women's lives as are the politics of class and race. We also often find it difficult to separate race from class from sex oppression because in our lives they are most often experienced simultaneously. We know that there is such a thing as racial-sexual oppression which is neither solely racial nor solely sexual, e.g., the history of rape of black women by white men as a weapon of political repression.

Although we are feminists and lesbians, we feel solidarity with progressive black men and do not advocate the fractionalization that white women who are separatists demand. Our situation as black people necessitates that we have solidarity around the fact of race, which white women of course do not need to have with white men, unless it is their negative solidarity as racial oppressors. We struggle together with black men against racism, while we also struggle with black men about sexism.

We realize that the liberation of all oppressed peoples necessitates the destruction of the political-economic systems of capitalism and imperialism as well as patriarchy. We are socialists because we believe the work must be organized for the collective benefit of those who do the work and create the products and not for the profit of the bosses. Material resources must be equally distributed among those who create these resources. We are not convinced, however, that a socialist revolution that is not also a feminist and antiracist revolution will guarantee our liberation. We have arrived at the necessity for developing an understanding of class relationships that takes into account the specific class position of black women who are generally marginal in the labor force, while at this particular time some of us are temporarily viewed as doubly desirable tokens at white-collar and professional levels. We need to articulate the real class situation of persons who are not merely raceless, sexless workers, but for whom racial and sexual oppression are significant determinants in their working/economic lives. Although we are in essential agreement with Marx's theory as it applied to the very specific economic relationships he analyzed, we know that this analysis must be extended further in order for us to understand our specific economic situation as black women.

A political contribution which we feel we have already made is the expansion of the feminist principle that the personal is political. In our consciousness-raising sessions, for example, we have in many ways gone beyond white women's revelations because we are dealing with the implications of race and class as well as sex. Even our black women's style of talking/testifying in black language about what we have experienced has a resonance that is both cultural and political. We have spent a great deal of energy delving into the cultural and experiential nature of our oppression out of necessity because none of these matters have ever been looked at before. No one before has ever examined the multilayered texture of black women's lives.

As we have already stated, we reject the stance of lesbian separatism because it is not a viable political analysis or strategy for us. It leaves out far too much and far too many people, particularly black men, women, and children. We have a great deal of criticism and loathing for what men have been socialized to be in this society: what they support, how they act, and how they oppress. But we do not have the misguided notion that it is their maleness, per se—i.e., their biological maleness—that makes them what they are. As black women we find any type of biological determinism a particularly dangerous and reactionary basis upon which to build a politic. We must also question whether lesbian separatism is an adequate and progressive political analysis and strategy, even for those who practice it, since it so completely denies any but the sexual sources of women's oppression, negating the facts of class and race.

3. PROBLEMS IN ORGANIZING BLACK FEMINISTS

During our years together as a black feminist collective we have experienced success and defeat, joy and pain, victory and failure. We have found that it is very difficult to organize around black feminist issues, difficult even to announce in certain contexts that we *are* black feminists. We have tried to think about the reasons for our difficulties, particularly since the white women's movement continues to be strong and to grow in many directions. In this section we will discuss some of the general reasons for the organizing problems we face and also talk specifically about the stages in organizing our own collective.

The major source of difficulty in our political work is that we are not just trying to fight oppression on one front or even two, but instead to address a whole range of oppressions. We do not have racial, sexual, heterosexual, or class privilege to rely upon, nor do we have even the minimal access to resources and power that groups who possess any one of these types of privilege have.

The psychological toll of being a black woman and the difficulties this presents in reaching political consciousness and doing political work can never be underestimated. There is a very low value placed upon black women's psyches in this society, which is both racist and sexist. As an early group member once said, "We are all damaged people merely by virtue of being black women." We are dispossessed psychologically and on every other level, and yet we feel the necessity to struggle to change our condition and the condition of all black women. In "A Black Feminist's Search for Sisterhood," Michele Wallace arrives at this conclusion:

> We exist as women who are black who are feminists, each stranded for the moment, working independently because there is not yet an environment in this society remotely congenial to our struggle—because, being on the bottom, we would have to do what no one else has done: we would have to fight the world.[2]

Wallace is not pessimistic but realistic in her assessment of black feminists' position, particularly in her allusion to the nearly classic isolation most of us face. We might use our position at the bottom, however, to make a clear leap into revolutionary action. If black women were free, it would mean that everyone else would have to be free since our freedom would necessitate the destruction of all the systems of oppression.

Feminism is, nevertheless, very threatening to the majority of black people because it calls into question some of the most basic assumptions about our existence, i.e., that gender should be a determinant of power relationships. Here is the way male and female roles were defined in a black nationalist pamphlet from the early 1970s.

> We understand that it is and has been traditional that the man is the head of the house. He is the leader of the house/nation because his knowledge of the world is broader, his awareness is greater, his understanding is fuller and his application of this information is wiser. . . . After all, it is only reasonable that the man be the head of the house because he is able to defend and protect the development of his home. . . . Women cannot do the same things as men—they are made by nature to function differently. Equality of men and women is something that cannot happen even in the abstract

world. Men are not equal to other men, i.e., ability, experience, or even understanding. The value of men and women can be seen as in the value of gold and silver—they are not equal but both have great value. We must realize that men and women are a complement to each other because there is no house/family without a man and his wife. Both are essential to the development of any life.[3]

The material conditions of most black women would hardly lead them to upset both economic and sexual arrangements that seem to represent some stability in their lives. Many black women have a good understanding of both sexism and racism, but because of the everyday constrictions of their lives cannot risk struggling against them both.

The reaction of black men to feminism has been notoriously negative. They are, of course, even more threatened than black women by the possibility that black feminists might organize around our own needs. They realize that they might not only lose valuable and hard-working allies in their struggles but that they might also be forced to change their habitually sexist ways of interacting with and oppressing black women. Accusations that black feminism divides the black struggle are powerful deterrents to the growth of an autonomous black women's movement.

Still, hundreds of women have been active at different times during the three-year existence of our group. And every black woman who came, came out of a strongly felt need for some level of possibility that did not previously exist in her life.

When we first started meeting early in 1974 after the NBFO first eastern regional conference, we did not have a strategy for organizing, or even a focus. We just wanted to see what we had. After a period of months of not meeting, we began to meet again late in the year and started doing an intense variety of consciousness-raising. The overwhelming feeling that we had is that after years and years we had finally found each other. Although we were not doing political work as a group, individuals continued their involvement in lesbian politics, sterilization abuse and abortion rights work, Third World Women's International Women's Day activities, and support activity for the trials of Dr. Kenneth Edelin, Joan Little, and Inez Garcia. During our first summer, when membership had dropped off considerably, those of us remaining devoted serious discussion to the possibility of opening a refuge for battered women in a black community. (There was no refuge in Boston at that time.) We also decided around that time to become an independent collective since we had serious disagreements with NBFOs bourgeois-feminist stance and their lack of a clear political focus.

We also were contacted at that time by socialist feminists, with whom we had worked on abortion rights activities, who wanted to encourage us to attend the National Socialist Feminist Conference in Yellow Springs. One of our members did attend and despite the narrowness of the ideology that was promoted at that particular conference, we became more aware of the need for us to understand our own economic situation and to make our own economic analysis.

In the fall, when some members returned, we experienced several months of comparative inactivity and internal disagreements which were first conceptualized as a lesbian-straight split but which were also the result of class and political differences. During the summer those of us who were still meeting had determined the need to do political work and to move beyond consciousness-raising and serving exclusively as an emotional support group. At the beginning of 1976, when some of the women who had not wanted to do political work and who also had voiced disagreements stopped attending of their own accord, we again looked for a focus. We decided at that time, with the addition of new members, to become a study group. We had always shared our reading with each other, and some of us had written papers on black feminism for group discussion a few months before this decision was made. We began functioning as a study group and also began discussing the possibility of starting a black feminist publication. We had a retreat in the late spring which provided a time for both political discussion and working out interpersonal issues. Currently we are planning to gather together a collection of black feminist writing. We feel that it is absolutely essential to demonstrate the reality of our politics to other black women and believe that we can do this through writing and distributing our work. The fact that individual black feminists are living in isolation all over the country, that our own numbers are small, and that we have some skills in writing, printing, and publishing makes us want to carry out these kinds of projects as a means of organizing black feminists as we continue to do political work in coalition with other groups.

4. Black Feminist Issues and Practice

During our time together we have identified and worked on many issues of particular relevance to black women. The inclusiveness of our politics makes us concerned with any situation that impinges upon the lives of women, Third World, and working people. We are of course particularly committed to working on those struggles in which race, sex, and class are simultaneous factors in oppression. We might, for example, become involved in workplace organizing at a factory that employs Third World women or picket a hospital that is cutting back on already inadequate health care to a Third World community, or set up a rape crisis center in a black neighborhood. Organizing around welfare or daycare concerns might also be a focus. The work to be done and the countless issues that this work represents merely reflect the pervasiveness of our oppression.

Issues and projects that collective members have actually worked on are sterilization abuse, abortion rights, battered women, rape, and health care. We have also done many workshops and educationals on black feminism on college campuses, at women's conferences, and most recently for high school women.

One issue that is of major concern to us and that we have begun to publicly address is racism in the white women's movement. As black feminists we are made constantly and painfully aware of how little effort white women have made to understand and combat their racism, which requires among other things that they have a more than superficial comprehension of race, color, and black history and culture. Eliminating racism in the white women's movement is by definition work for white women to do, but we will continue to speak to and demand accountability on this issue.

In the practice of our politics we do not believe that the end always justifies the means. Many reactionary and destructive acts have been done in the name of achieving "correct" political goals. As feminists we do not want to mess over people in the name of politics. We believe in collective process and a nonhierarchical distribution of power within our own group and in our vision of a revolutionary society. We are committed to a continual examination of our politics as they develop through criticism and self-criticism as an essential aspect of our practice. As black feminists and lesbians we know that we have a very definite revolutionary task to perform and we are ready for the lifetime of work and struggle before us.

---

1. This statement is dated April 1977.

2. Michele Wallace, "A Black Feminist's Search for Sisterhood"; see pages 292–297 in this volume.

3. Mumininas of Committee for Unified Newark, *Mwanamke Mwananchi (The Nationalist Woman)*, Newark, N.J., c. 1971, pp. 4–5.

(from) In Mourning and In Rage . . .

In 1969, Suzanne Lacy (with artist Faith Wilding) started a consciousness raising group at California State University at Fresno, which led to their joining the new feminist art program there. During the 1970s in Los Angeles, Lacy (born 1945) collaborated with artist Leslie Labowitz (born 1946), who was then working at the Woman's Building, on performances pivotal in the development of a public performance art that merged feminist art with social activism. In December 1977, "In Mourning and in Rage . . ." called out the graphic media coverage of the rape murders by the Hillside Strangler (actually two men, cousins), which the artists believed terrorized women. Framed as a public act of mourning, the event led to a pledge from the city rape hotline to publicize self-defense classes to train women to combat, not merely endure, violence. Later that year, Lacy and Labowitz founded ARIADNE, a network to formalize and support the coalition of artists, activists, media reporters, and politicians built during their performances protesting violence against women. (See the insert to this volume for a photograph of the performance.)

"IN MOURNING and In Rage . . ." was conceived as a response to Leslie and Suzanne's very personal grief and rage over the incidents of rape-murder in Los Angeles which are labeled the "Hillside Strangler Case." After reading about the tenth victim, they decided to design a media event which would include the collaborative participation of women's organizations, city government, and members of the women's community.

Seventy women dressed in black gathered at the Woman's Building in Los Angeles. The women received instructions for the event which began when ten actresses dressed in black mourning emerged from the Building and entered a hearse. The hearse and two motorcycle escorts departed from the Building, followed by twenty-two cars filled with women in black. Each car had its lights on and displayed two stickers: "Funeral" and "Stop Violence Against Women." The motorcade circled City Hall twice and stopped in front of the assembled members of the news media.

One at a time, nine seven-foot-tall veiled women mourners emerged from the hearse and stood in a line on the sidewalk. The final figure emerged, an active woman clothed in scarlet. The ten women faced the street as the hearse departed while women from the motorcade procession drove slowly past in silent homage to the mourners. Forming a procession three abreast, the mourners walked toward the steps in front of City Hall.

Women from the motorcade positioned themselves on either side of the steps forming a black-clothed chorus from a modern tragedy. They unfurled a banner which read "In Memory of Our Sisters, Women Fight Back."

As soon as the media had positioned itself to record this second part of the event, the first mourner walked toward the microphone and in a loud, clear voice said "I am here for the ten women who have been raped and strangled between October 18 and November 29!" The chorus echoed her with "In memory of our sisters, we fight back!" as she was wrapped with a brilliant red scarf by the woman clothed in red. She took her place on the steps, followed by the second mourner. Each of the nine women made her statement which connected this seemingly random incident of violence in Los Angeles with the greater picture of nationwide violence toward women; each received her red cloak; and each was greeted by the chorus, "We fight back." Finally the woman in red approached the microphone. Unveiled, speaking directly and powerfully, she declared "I am here for the *rage* of all women. I am here for women fighting back!"

The ten women on the steps, the chorus and their banner, served as a background of unified woman-strength against which the remainder of the piece unfolded. A short statement, directed at the press, was read explaining the artists' rationale for the piece. A member of the Los Angeles Commission on Assaults Against Women read a prepared list of three demands for women's self-defense. These were presented to three members of City Council: Pat Russell, Joy Picus, and Dave Cunningham, and the Deputy Mayor, Grace Davis. The final image consisted of a song, written especially for the event, sung by Holly Near. The audience joined in this and a spontaneous circle dance as the artists and political organizers met with and answered questions from the press.

Script

Actress 1: I am here for the ten women who have been raped and strangled between October 18 and November 29.

> *Chorus*: In memory of our sisters, we fight back!

Actress 2: I am here for the 388 women who were raped between October 18 and November 29.

  Chorus: In memory of our sisters, we fight back!

Actress 3: I am here for the 4,033 women who were raped last year in Los Angeles.

  Chorus: In memory of our sisters, we fight back!

Actress 4: I am here for the half-million women who are being beaten in their own homes.

  Chorus: In memory of our sisters, we fight back!

Actress 5: I am here for the one out of four of us who is sexually abused before the age of eighteen.

  Chorus: In memory of our sisters, we fight back!

Actress 6: I am here for the hundreds of women who are portrayed as victims of assault in films, television, and magazines.

  Chorus: In memory of our sisters, we fight back!

Actress 7: I am here to speak for the thousands of women who are raped and beaten and have not yet found their voices.

  Chorus: In memory of our sisters, we fight back!

Actress 8: I am here for the women whose lives are limited daily by the threat of violence.

  Chorus: In memory of our sisters, we fight back!

Actress 9: I am here to mourn the reality of violence against women.

  Chorus: In memory of our sisters, we fight back!

Actress 10: I am here for the rage of all women. I am here for women fighting back.

Chorus: In memory of our sisters, we fight back!

STATEMENT READ DURING THE PERFORMANCE

For all of the women here now, for all the women who will see this: we are here today in memory of the ten women who were recently slain in Los Angeles, *and* we are here in memory of all women who have been, and are being, battered, raped, and killed throughout this country, a result of the pervasive and ongoing attitude of violence toward women.

We are here because we want you to know that we know that these ten women are not isolated cases of random, unexplainable violence. That this violence wreaked upon them is not different, except perhaps in degree and detail, from all of the daily real-life reports which reach the news media, from those fictionalized mutilations shown by our entertainment industries, and from the countless unreported cases of brutalization of our relatives, friends, and loved ones who are women.

Today we are here to share our grief and our understanding and our rage in a public manner. That concern, which before was only expressed as isolated fear by each individual woman, we now express together, through our combined voices, and we are mourning each other loudly, mourning in rage, as we recognize our own collective strength through action. We are fighting back.

MARY DALY

(from) *Gyn/Ecology*
The Metapatriarchal Journey of Exorcism and Ecstasy

A professor of theology and philosophy at Boston College, a Jesuit university, and a self-described radical lesbian, Mary Daly (1928–2010) pushed at the boundaries of her Catholic faith, becoming a leading feminist theorist. Drawing upon deep knowledge acquired in three doctorates—religion, theology, and philosophy—she launched a radical feminist critique of Christian theory and practice in *The Church and the Second Sex* (1968) and *Beyond God the Father* (1973). After she was told her teaching contract would not be renewed in a not-so-veiled censure of her first book, public outcry and support from the then all-male student body resulted in Daly's being granted tenure. With *Gyn/Ecology: The Meta-Ethic of Radical Feminism* (1978), whose introduction is excerpted here, Daly began "wrenching back wordpower" in a quest to reveal how Christian theology buttresses patriarchal structures through language itself.

THE RADICAL be-ing of women is very much an Otherworld Journey. It is both discovery and creation of a world other than patriarchy. Patriarchy appears to be "everywhere." Even outer space and the future have been colonized. As a rule, even the more imaginative science-fiction writers (allegedly the most foretelling futurists) cannot/will not create a space and time in which women get far beyond the role of space stewardess. Nor does this colonization exist simply "outside" women's minds, securely fastened into institutions we can physically leave behind. Rather, it is also internalized, festering inside women's heads, even feminist heads.

The Journey, then, involves exorcism of the internalized Godfather in his various manifestations (his name is legion). It involves dangerous encounters with these demons. Within the christian tradition, particularly in medieval times, evil spirits have sometimes been associated with the "Seven Deadly Sins," both as personifications and as causes.[1] A standard listing of the Sins is the following: pride, avarice, anger, lust, gluttony, envy, and sloth.[2] The feminist voyage discloses that these have all been radically misnamed, that is, inadequately and perversely "understood." They are particularized expressions of the overall use of "evil" to victimize women. Our journey involves confrontations with the demonic manifestations of evil.

Why has it seemed "appropriate" in this culture that the plot of a popular book and film (*The Exorcist*) centers around a Jesuit who "exorcises" a girl who is "possessed"? Why is there no book or film about a woman who exorcises a Jesuit?[3] From a radical feminist perspective it is clear that "Father" is precisely the one who cannot exorcise, for he is allied with and identified with The Possessor. The fact that he is himself possessed should not be women's essential concern. It is a mistake to see men as pitiable victims or vessels to be "saved" through female self-sacrifice. However possessed males may be within patriarchy, it is *their* order; it is they who feed on women's stolen energy. It is a trap to imagine that women should "save" men from the dynamics of demonic possession; and to attempt this is to fall deeper into the pit of patriarchal possession. It is women ourselves who will have to expel the Father from ourselves, becoming our own exorcists.

Within a culture possessed by the myth of feminine evil, the naming, describing, and theorizing about good and evil has constituted a maze/haze of deception. The journey of women becoming is breaking through this maze—springing into free space, which is an a-mazing process.

Breaking through the Male Maze is both exorcism and ecstasy. It is spinning through and beyond the fathers' foreground which is the arena of games. This spinning involves encountering the demons who block the various thresholds as we move through gateway after gateway into the deepest chambers of our homeland, which is the Background of our Selves. As Denise Connors has pointed out, the Background is the realm of the wild reality of women's Selves. Objectification and alienation take place when we are locked into the male-centered, monodimensional foreground.[4] Thus the monitors of the foreground, the male myth-masters, fashion prominent and eminently forgettable images of women in their art, literature, and mass media—images intended to mold women for male purposes.

The Background into which feminist journeying spins is the wild realm of Hags and Crones. It is Hag-ocracy. The demons who attempt to block the gateways to the deep spaces of this realm often take ghostly/ghastly forms, comparable to noxious gases not noticeable by ordinary sense perception.[5] Each time we move into deeper space, these numbing ghostly gases work to paralyze us, to trap us, so that we will be unable to move further. Each time we succeed in overcoming their numbing effect, more dormant senses come alive.

Our inner eyes open, our inner ears become unblocked. We are strengthened to move through the next gateway and the next. This movement inward/ outward is be-ing. It is spinning cosmic tapestries. It is spinning and whirling into the Background.

The spinning process requires seeking out the sources of the ghostly gases that have seeped into the deep chambers of our minds. "The way back to reality is to destroy our perceptions of it," said Bergson. Yes, but these deceptive perceptions were/are implanted through language—the all-pervasive language of myth, conveyed overtly and subliminally through religion, "great art," literature, the dogmas of professionalism, the media, grammar. Indeed, deception is embedded in the very texture of the words we use, and here is where our exorcism can begin. Thus, for example, the word *spinster* is commonly used as a deprecating term, but it can only function this way when apprehended exclusively on a superficial (foreground) level. Its deep meaning, which has receded into the Background so far that we have to spin deeply in order to retrieve it, is clear and strong: "a woman whose occupation is to spin." There is no reason to limit the meaning of this rich and cosmic verb. A woman whose occupation is to spin participates in the whirling movement of creation. She who has chosen her Self, who defines her Self, by choice, neither in relation to children nor to men, who is Self-identified, is a Spinster, a whirling dervish, spinning in a new time/space. Another example is the term *glamour*, whose first definition as given in Merriam-Webster is "a magic spell." Originally it was believed that witches possessed the power of glamour, and according to the authors of the *Malleus Maleficarum*, witches by their glamour could cause the male "member" to disappear. In modern usage, this meaning has almost disappeared into the Background, and the power of the term is masked and suffocated by such foreground images as those associated with *Glamour* magazine.

Journeying is multidimensional. The various meanings and images conjured up by the word are not sharply distinguishable. We can think of mystical journeys, quests, adventurous travel, advancement in skills, in physical and intellectual prowess. So also the barriers are multiple and intertwined. These barriers are not mere immobile blocks, but are more like deceptive tongues that prevent us from hearing our Selves, as they babble incessantly in the Tower of Babel which is the erection of phallocracy.[6] The voices and the silences of Babel pierce all of our senses. They are the invasive extensions of the enemy of women's hearing, dreaming, creating. *Babel* is said to be derived from an Assyrian-Babylonian word meaning "gate of god." When women break through this multiple barrier composed of deceptions ejaculated by "god" we can begin to glimpse the true gateways to our depths, which are the Gates of the Goddess.

Spinsters can find our way back to reality by destroying the false perceptions of it inflicted upon us by the language and myths of Babel. We must learn to dis-spell the language of phallocracy, which keeps us under the spell of brokenness. This spell splits our perceptions of our Selves and of the cosmos, overtly and subliminally. Journeying into our Background will mean recognizing that both the "spirit" and the "matter" presented to us in the fathers' foreground are reifications, condensations. They are not really "opposites," for they have much in common: both are dead, inert. This is unmasked when we begin to see through patriarchal language. Thus, the Latin term *texere*, meaning to weave, is the origin and root both for *textile* and for *text*. It is important for women to note the irony in this split of meanings. For our process of cosmic weaving has been stunted and minimized to the level of the manufacture and maintenance of textiles. While there is nothing demeaning about this occupation in itself, the limitation of women to the realm of "distaff" has mutilated and condensed our Divine Right of creative weaving to the darning of socks. If we look at the term *text* in contrast to *textile*, we see that this represents the other side of the schizoid condensations of weaving/spinning. "Texts" are the kingdom of males; they are the realm of the reified word, of condensed spirit. In patriarchal tradition, sewing and spinning are for girls; books are for boys.

Small wonder that many women feel repugnance for the realm of the distaff, which has literally been the sweatshop and prison of female bodies and spirits. Small wonder that many women have seen the male kingdom of texts as an appealing escape from the tomb-town of textiles which has symbolized the confinement/reduction of female energy.* The kingdom of male-authored texts has appeared to be the ideal realm to be reached/entered, for we have been educated to forget that professional "knowledge" is our stolen process. As Andrée Collard remarked, in the society of cops and robbers, we learn to forget that the cops are the robbers, that they rob us of everything: our myths, our energy, our divinity, our Selves.[7]

Women's minds have been mutilated and muted to such a state that "Free Spirit" has been branded into them as a brand name for girdles and bras rather than as the name of our verb-ing, be-ing Selves. Such brand names brand women "Morons." Moronized, women believe that male-written texts (biblical, literary, medical, legal, scientific) are "true." Thus manipulated, women become eager for acceptance as docile tokens mouthing male texts, employing technology for male ends, accepting male fabrications as the true texture of

---

*We should not forget that countless women's lives have been consumed in the sweatshops of textile manufacturers and garment makers as well as in the everyday tedium of sewing, mending, laundering, and ironing.

reality. Patriarchy has stolen our cosmos and returned it in the form of *Cosmopolitan* magazine and cosmetics. They have made up our cosmos, our Selves. Spinning deeper into the Background is courageous sinning against the Sins of the Fathers. As our senses become more alive we can see/hear/feel how we have been tricked by their texts. We begin unweaving our winding sheets. The process of exorcism, of peeling off the layers of mindbindings and cosmetics, is movement past the patriarchally imposed sense of reality and identity. This demystification process, a-mazing The Lies, *is* ecstasy.

Journeying centerward is Self-centering movement in all directions. It erases implanted pseudodichotomies between the Self and "other" reality, while it unmasks the unreality of both "self" and "world" as these are portrayed, betrayed, in the language of the fathers' foreground. Adrienne Rich has written:

> In bringing the light of critical thinking to bear on her subject, in the very act of *becoming more conscious* of her situation in the world, a woman may feel herself coming deeper than ever into touch with her unconscious and with her body.[8]

Moving into the Background/Center is not navel-gazing. It is be-ing in the world. The foreground fathers offer dual decoys labeled "thought" and "action," which distract from the reality both of deep knowing and of external action. There is no authentic separation possible.

The Journey is itself participation in Paradise. This word, which is said to be from the Iranian *pairi* (meaning around) and *daēza* (meaning wall), is commonly used to conjure an image of a walled-in pleasure garden. Patriarchal Paradise, as projected in Western and Eastern religious mythology, is imaged as a place or a state in which the souls of the righteous after death enjoy eternal bliss, that is, heaven. Despite theological attempts to make this seem lively, the image is one of stagnation (in a stag-nation) as suggested in the expression, "the Afterlife." In contrast to this, the Paradise which is cosmic spinning is not containment within walls. Rather, it is movement that is not containable, weaving around and past walls, leaving them in the past. It moves into the Background which is the moving center of the Self, enabling the Self to act "outwardly" in the cosmos as she comes alive. This metapatriarchal movement is not Afterlife, but Living now, dis-covering Life.

A primary definition of *paradise* is "pleasure park." The walls of the Patriarchal Pleasure Park represent the condition of being perpetually parked, locked into the parking lot of the past. A basic meaning of *park* is a "game preserve."

The fathers' foreground is precisely this: an arena where the wildness of nature and of women's Selves is domesticated, preserved. It is the place for the preservation of females who are the "fair game" of the fathers, that they may be served to these predatory Park Owners, and service them at their pleasure. Patriarchal Paradise is the arena of games, the place where the pleas of women are silenced, where the law is: Please the Patrons. Women who break through the imprisoning walls of the Playboys' Playground are entering the process which is our happening/happiness. This is Paradise beyond the boundaries of "paradise." Since our passage into this process requires making breaks in the walls, it means setting free the fair game, breaking the rules of the games, breaking the names of the games. Breaking through the foreground which is the Playboys' Playground means letting out the bunnies, the bitches, the beavers, the squirrels, the chicks, the pussycats, the cows, the nags, the foxy ladies, the old bats and biddies, so that they can at last begin naming themselves.

I have coined the term *metapatriarchal* to describe the journey, because the prefix *meta* has multiple meanings. It incorporates the idea of "post-patriarchal," for it means occurring later. It puts patriarchy in the past without denying that its walls/ruins and demons are still around. Since *meta* also means "situated behind," it suggests that the direction of the journey is into the Background. Another meaning of this prefix is "change in, transformation of." This, of course, suggests the transforming power of the journey. By this I do not mean that women's movement "reforms" patriarchy, but that it transforms our Selves. Since *meta* means "beyond, transcending," it contains a built-in corrective to reductive notions of mere reformism.

This metapatriarchal process of encountering the unknown involves also a continual conversion of the previously unknown into the familiar.[9] Since the "unknown" is stolen/hidden know-ing, frozen and stored by the Abominable Snowmen of Androcratic Academia, Spinsters must melt these masses of "knowledge" with the fire of Female Fury.

Amazon expeditions into the male-controlled "fields" are necessary in order to leave the fathers' caves and live in the sun. A crucial problem for us has been to learn how to re-possess righteously while avoiding being caught too long in the caves. In universities, and in all of the professions, the omnipresent poisonous gases gradually stifle women's minds and spirits. Those who carry out the necessary expeditions run the risk of shrinking into the mold of the mystified Athena, the twice-born, who forgets and denies her Mother and Sisters, because she has forgotten her original Self. "Re-born" from Zeus, she becomes Daddy's Girl, the mutant who serves the master's purposes. The token woman, who in reality is enchained, possessed, "knows" that she is free.

She is a useful tool of the patriarchs, particularly against her sister Artemis, who knows better, respects her Self, bonds with her Sisters, and refuses to sell her freedom, her original birthright, for a mess of respectability.

A-mazing Amazons must be aware of the male methods of mystification. Elsewhere I have discussed four methods which are essential to the games of the fathers.[10] First, there is *erasure* of women. (The massacre of millions of women as witches is erased in patriarchal scholarship.) Second, there is *reversal*. (Adam gives birth to Eve, Zeus to Athena, in patriarchal myth.) Third, there is *false polarization*. (Male-defined "feminism" is set up against male-defined "sexism" in the patriarchal media.) Fourth, there is *divide and conquer*. (Token women are trained to kill off feminists in patriarchal professions.) As we move further on the metapatriarchal journey, we find deeper and deeper layers of these demonic patterns embedded in the culture, implanted in our souls. These constitute mindbindings comparable to the footbindings which mutilated millions of Chinese women for a thousand years. Stripping away layer after layer of these mindbinding societal/mental embeds is the a-mazing essential to the journey.

Spinsters are not only A-mazing Amazons cutting away layers of deceptions. Spinsters are also Survivors. We must survive, not merely in the sense of "living on," but in the sense of living beyond. Surviving (from the Latin *super* plus *vivere*) I take to mean living above, through, around the obstacles thrown in our paths. This is hardly the dead "living on" of possessed tokens. The process of Survivors is meta-living, be-ing.

---

1. See Morton W. Bloomfield, *The Seven Deadly Sins: An Introduction to the History of a Religious Concept, with Special Reference to Medieval English Literature* (Michigan State University Press, 1967), especially pp. 7–27. Bloomfield discusses the tradition of the Otherworld Journey in connection with the Deadly Sins. On p. 12 he writes: "The Sins are a by-product of an eschatological belief which has been called the Soul Drama or Soul Journey. . . . The seven cardinal sins are the remnant of some Gnostic Soul Journey which existed probably in Egypt or Syria in the early Christian centuries. But the Soul Journey is itself part of a much vaster eschatological conception, the Otherworld Journey. . . ."

2. This listing became common in catholic doctrine. The number seven came to be favored for the cardinal sins, although there have been many different lists of the sins. See Bloomfield, *The Seven Deadly Sins*.

3. See Dolores Bargowski, "Moving Media: The Exorcist," *Quest: A Feminist Quarterly*, Vol. 1, No. 1 (summer 1974), pp. 53–57.

4. Conversation, Boston, October 1976.

5. See Mary Daly, "The Qualitative Leap Beyond Patriarchal Religion," *Quest: A Feminist Quarterly*, Vol. 1, No. 4 (spring 1975), pp. 20–40.

6. Françoise d'Eaubonne uses the term *phallocratisme* in her book, *Le Féminisme ou la mort* (Paris: Pierre Horay, 1974), especially pp. 113–24.

7. Conversation, Boston, September 1976.

8. Adrienne Rich, *Of Woman Born: Motherhood as Experience and Institution* (New York: W. W. Norton, 1976), p. 95.

9. See Daly, "The Qualitative Leap."

10. See Mary Daly, *Beyond God the Father: Toward a Philosophy of Women's Liberation* (Boston: Beacon Press, 1973), passim.

SUSAN JACOBY

Notes from a Free-Speech Junkie

In what became known as the feminist "sex wars" of the late 1970s and 1980s, feminists publicly battled over pornography and other issues concerning sexuality. With antipornography feminists allied in practice with right-wing conservatives, they were named "conservative feminists" by their movement opponents, who were sometimes called "sex-positive" feminists. Both sides, however, adamantly laid claim to the "radical feminist" label. One prominent argument in the debate centered on the issue of free speech and censorship—here addressed by journalist Susan Jacoby (born 1945) in a January 1978 *New York Times* "Hers" column, a series that ran from 1977 to 1996 as an occasional forum for women writers, on a rotating basis. No comparable "His" column was needed.

IT IS no news that many women are defecting from the ranks of civil libertarians on the issue of obscenity. The conviction of Larry Flynt, publisher of *Hustler* magazine—before his metamorphosis into a born-again Christian— was greeted with unabashed feminist approval. Harry Reems, the unknown actor who was convicted by a Memphis jury for conspiring to distribute the movie *Deep Throat*, has carried on his legal battles with almost no help from women who ordinarily regard themselves as supporters of the First Amendment. Feminist writers and scholars have even discussed the possibility of making common cause against pornography with adversaries of the women's movement—including opponents of the Equal Rights Amendment and "right to life" forces.

All of this is deeply disturbing to a woman who believes, as I always have and still do, in an absolute interpretation of the First Amendment. Nothing in Larry Flynt's garbage convinces me that the late Justice Hugo L. Black was wrong in his opinion that "the Federal government is without any power whatsoever under the Constitution to put any type of burden on free speech and expression of ideas of any kind (as distinguished from conduct)." Many women I like and respect tell me I am wrong; I cannot remember having become involved in so many heated discussions of a public issue since the end of the Vietnam war. A feminist writer described my views as those of a "First Amendment junkie."

Many feminist arguments for controls on pornography carry the implicit conviction that porn books, magazines, and movies pose a greater threat to women than similarly repulsive exercises of free speech pose to other offended groups. This conviction has, of course, been shared by everyone—regardless of race, creed, or sex—who has ever argued in favor of abridging the First Amendment. It is the argument used by some Jews who have withdrawn their support from the American Civil Liberties Union because it has defended the right of American Nazis to march through a community inhabited by survivors of Hitler's concentration camps.

If feminists want to argue that the protection of the Constitution should not be extended to *any* particularly odious or threatening form of speech, they have a reasonable argument (although I don't agree with it). But it is ridiculous to suggest that the porn shops in Times Square are more disgusting to women than a march of neo-Nazis is to survivors of the extermination camps.

The arguments over pornography also blur the vital distinction between expression of ideas and conduct. When I say I believe unreservedly in the First Amendment, someone always comes back at me with the issue of "kiddie porn." But kiddie porn is not a First Amendment issue. It is an issue of the abuse of power—the power adults have over children—and not of obscenity. Parents and promoters have no more right to use their children to make porn movies than they do to send them to work in coal mines. The responsible adults should be prosecuted, just as adults who use children for backbreaking farm labor should be prosecuted.

Susan Brownmiller, in *Against Our Will: Men, Women and Rape*, has described pornography as "the undiluted essence of anti-female propaganda." I think this is a fair description of some types of pornography, especially of the brutish subspecies that equates sex with death and portrays women primarily as objects of violence.

The equation of sex and violence, personified by some glossy rock record album covers as well as by *Hustler*, has fed the illusion that censorship of pornography can be conducted on a more rational basis than other types of censorship. Are all pictures of naked women obscene? Clearly not, says a friend. A Renoir nude is art, she says, and *Hustler* is trash. "Any reasonable person" knows that.

But what about something between art and trash—something, say, along the lines of *Playboy* or *Penthouse* magazines? I asked five women for their reactions to one picture in *Penthouse* and got responses that ranged from "lovely" and "sensuous" to "revolting" and "demeaning." Feminists, like everyone else, seldom have rational reasons for their preferences in erotica. Like members of juries, they tend to disagree when confronted with something that falls short of 100 per cent vulgarity.

In any case, feminists will not be the arbiters of good taste if it becomes easier to harass, prosecute, and convict people on obscenity charges. Most of the people who want to censor girlie magazines are equally opposed to open discussion of issues that are of vital concern to women: rape, abortion, menstruation, contraception, lesbianism—in fact, the entire range of sexual experience from a woman's viewpoint.

Feminist writers and editors and filmmakers have limited financial resources: Confronted by a determined prosecutor, Hugh Hefner will fare better than Susan Brownmiller. Would the Memphis jurors who convicted Harry Reems for his role in *Deep Throat* be inclined to take a more positive view of paintings of the female genitalia done by sensitive feminist artists? *Ms.* magazine has printed color reproductions of some of those art works; *Ms.* is already banned from a number of high school libraries because someone considers it threatening and/or obscene.

Feminists who want to censor what they regard as harmful pornography have essentially the same motivation as other would-be censors: They want to use the power of the state to accomplish what they have been unable to achieve in the marketplace of ideas and images. The impulse to censor places no faith in the possibilities of democratic persuasion.

It isn't easy to persuade certain men that they have better uses for $1.95 each month than to spend it on a copy of *Hustler*? Well, then, give the men no choice in the matter.

I believe there is also a connection between the impulse toward censorship on the part of people who used to consider themselves civil libertarians and a more general desire to shift responsibility from individuals to institutions. When I saw the movie *Looking for Mr. Goodbar*, I was stunned by its series of visual images equating sex and violence, coupled with what seems to me the mindless message (a distortion of the fine Judith Rossner novel) that casual sex equals death. When I came out of the movie, I was even more shocked to see parents standing in line with children between the ages of ten and fourteen.

I simply don't know why a parent would take a child to see such a movie, any more than I understand why people feel they can't turn off a television set their child is watching. Whenever I say that, my friends tell me I don't know how it is because I don't have children. True, but I do have parents. When I was a child, they did turn off the TV. They didn't expect the Federal Communications Commission to do their job for them.

I am a First Amendment junkie. You can't OD on the First Amendment, because free speech is its own best antidote.

LIN FARLEY

Eleven Ways to Fight Sexual Harassment

When Lin Farley (born 1942) was hired in 1974 to direct the Women's Section of Human Affairs at Cornell University, the term "sexual harassment," describing a range of discriminatory behaviors against women from verbal harassment to sexual assault, had not yet been coined. Only after Farley and other activists organized a speakout supporting a Cornell coworker who had been repeatedly sexually abused by the professor she worked for, did their brainstorming produce the term. That first-ever "sexual harassment" speakout, attended by several hundred women on May 4, 1975, in Ithaca, New York, sparked national media coverage, raising awareness about sexual harassment in the workplace. In 1978, Farley published her trailblazing book *Sexual Shakedown: The Sexual Harassment of Women on the Job,* of which this selection is the final chapter.

1. Sexual harassment is Criminal Activity. Rape because it occurs in an office or factory is no less a crime than elsewhere in our society. The same holds true for sexual assault, abuse, misuse and physical violation. No less importantly, when a manager, boss, supervisor or foreman tells a woman she can't get a job or keep one without "putting out" sexually, he is soliciting for prostitution. All of these forms of sexual harassment are *already* outlawed by criminal statutes. Take your complaint to your local police department. Don't be timid. Demand your protection under the law. Prosecute your assailant.

2. Sexual Harassment on-the-job is Sex Discrimination. Because this abuse deprives women of the right to equal employment opportunity, you can seek justice and/or compensation under a variety of government enforcement agencies:

> ▶ The Equal Employment Opportunity Commission (EEOC) is the federal remedy. Within 180 days of filing a complaint with the EEOC you can obtain a lawyer (often on a contingency basis which means you pay nothing until the successful conclusion of your suit)

and you can, if fired, sue for re-instatement to your job plus up to three years' back-pay dating from the time of termination.

▶ Closer to home, your local city or state human rights agency is empowered to intervene in your behalf at any point you experience sexual harassment. This can be before or after you are either forced to quit your job and/or are fired. All it takes is a phone call to determine if you have a complaint. Don't wait! Act immediately. You have nothing to lose and it could save your job.

▶ Private suits are a third legal option. You can sue for damages as a result of the trauma of being coerced sexually on your job. Consult a lawyer.

3. You deserve Unemployment Compensation. A bill now pending in the New York State Legislature will make sexual harassment good cause for leaving a job; Wisconsin has already passed a similar statute. File your claim immediately. Fair and just economic compensation for sexual harassment that results in loss of employment is your right.

4. File a Grievance/Go to your Union. Internal grievance procedures and unions are your on-the-job remedies. Use them. Even if you feel they will not take your claim seriously or are prejudiced against your complaint, these channels must be pursued if you are serious about stopping sexual harassment. No court, for example, can rule in favor of a female complainant if she has not first exhausted all internal remedies.

5. Document Your Case. Your job is in jeopardy from the second the sexual harassment begins. Prepare yourself accordingly. Keep memos that detail the attacks. For example, "On such and such day and time, so and so came into my office, met me in the hall, cornered me in the elevator and he either/and-or said or did thus." You don't have to post these memos on the company bulletin board, but you should send them privately to someone else at work, preferably a superior. Now you have a record of the harassment. Combined with your good employment record this documentation can eventually save your job.

6. Take Direct Action. This is particularly successful with co-workers. State your discomfort, say "NO" immediately. If necessary, pinch back. Many men will stop when faced by a determined woman who forcefully communicates that this behavior is intolerable.

7. Get Help from Women's Groups. The experience of sexual harassment at work is a serious trauma. Women's organizations including N.O.W. and a variety of local working women's organizations such as the Alliance Against Sexual Coercion in Boston, the Interfaith Project on Working Women in

Philadelphia and Work Options for Women in Wichita, Kansas are on your side. You need their emotional/legal resources. Don't hesitate. If your town doesn't have a women's organization to deal with women's job problems—start one.

8. Use the Power of the Press. Never underestimate the value of adverse publicity. Go public. Expose the situation. Sexual harassment can only succeed in secrecy and public exposure is a great asset.

9. Female Solidarity on-the-job is a Powerful Weapon. Ask for help from your female co-workers. Give help without being asked. Become friends of the women with whom you work. The company and the harasser can always pick us off one-by-one. When we stand up together we have power—the power of unity in numbers. Just think, he can fire you, but he can't fire all ten of you in the office at the same time.

10. Organize. This is the *whole* solution. When women have organized to protect their rights on-the-job as vigorously as men have organized to protect theirs, the world of work for women will be transformed. This is the future. It won't be long before a national women's union or federation of unions of women will negotiate decent working conditions for all women who work for pay, but you can begin now. Form a women's committee, a women's caucus, a female rap group. You have nothing to lose and your job may depend on it.

11. In school. While it is not strictly on-the-job, female students in University and College graduate schools frequently are blocked by sexual harassment from obtaining the degrees necessary to get skilled jobs. Because the abuse in this setting deprives women of the right to an equal education, students should file grievances against the offending professor as well as sue the institution under all the government statutes and agencies which prohibit sex discrimination in education.

AUDRE LORDE

(from) Uses of the Erotic: The Erotic as Power

Poet, activist, essayist, and feminist Audre Lorde (1934–1992) began her career in Harlem, publishing her first poem at age seventeen and becoming a major poet first in the Black Arts movement of the 1960s and later in the feminist movement where she identified as Black and lesbian. "I am defined as other in every group I'm part of," she once wrote, "lesbian, mother, warrior, poet." In her essays and speeches, she elaborated on that idea. "Difference," she wrote, is "that raw and powerful connection from which our personal power is forged," and "survival is learning how to take our differences and make them strengths." Her purpose in publicly revealing her breast cancer in *The Cancer Journals* (1980) was not mere confession but the transformation of "silence into language and action." This excerpt from "Uses of the Erotic: The Erotic as Power" was delivered as a speech at the Fourth Berkshire Conference on the History of Women in August 1978 and collected in *Sister Outsider: Essays and Speeches* (1984).

THERE ARE MANY kinds of power, used and unused, acknowledged or otherwise. The erotic is a resource within each of us that lies in a deeply female and spiritual plane, firmly rooted in the power of our unexpressed or unrecognized feeling. In order to perpetuate itself, every oppression must corrupt or distort those various sources of power within the culture of the oppressed that can provide energy for change. For women, this has meant a suppression of the erotic as a considered source of power and information within our lives.

We have been taught to suspect this resource, vilified, abused, and devalued within western society. On the one hand, the superficially erotic has been encouraged as a sign of female inferiority; on the other hand, women have been made to suffer and to feel both contemptible and suspect by virtue of its existence.

It is a short step from there to the false belief that only by the suppression of the erotic within our lives and consciousness can women be truly strong.

But that strength is illusory, for it is fashioned within the context of male models of power.

As women, we have come to distrust that power which rises from our deepest and nonrational knowledge. We have been warned against it all our lives by the male world, which values this depth of feeling enough to keep women around in order to exercise it in the service of men, but which fears this same depth too much to examine the possibilities of it within themselves. So women are maintained at a distant/inferior position to be psychically milked, much the same way ants maintain colonies of aphids to provide a life-giving substance for their masters.

But the erotic offers a well of replenishing and provocative force to the woman who does not fear its revelation, nor succumbs to the belief that sensation is enough.

The erotic has often been misnamed by men and used against women. It has been made into the confused, the trivial, the psychotic, the plasticized sensation. For this reason, we have often turned away from the exploration and consideration of the erotic as a source of power and information, confusing it with its opposite, the pornographic. But pornography is a direct denial of the power of the erotic, for it represents the suppression of true feeling. Pornography emphasizes sensation without feeling.

The erotic is a measure between the beginnings of our sense of self and the chaos of our strongest feelings. It is an internal sense of satisfaction to which, once we have experienced it, we know we can aspire. For having experienced the fullness of this depth of feeling and recognizing its power, in honor and self-respect we can require no less of ourselves.

It is never easy to demand the most from ourselves, from our lives, from our work. To encourage excellence is to go beyond the encouraged mediocrity of our society. But giving in to the fear of feeling and working to capacity is a luxury only the unintentional can afford, and the unintentional are those who do not wish to guide their own destinies.

This internal requirement toward excellence which we learn from the erotic must not be misconstrued as demanding the impossible from ourselves nor from others. Such a demand incapacitates everyone in the process. For the erotic is not a question only of what we do; it is a question of how acutely and fully we can feel in the doing. Once we know the extent to which we are capable of feeling that sense of satisfaction and completion, we can then observe which of our various life endeavors bring us closest to that fullness.

The aim of each thing which we do is to make our lives and the lives of our children richer and more possible. Within the celebration of the erotic in all our endeavors, my work becomes a conscious decision—a longed-for bed which I enter gratefully and from which I rise up empowered.

Of course, women so empowered are dangerous. So we are taught to separate the erotic demand from most vital areas of our lives other than sex. And the lack of concern for the erotic root and satisfactions of our work is felt in our disaffection from so much of what we do. For instance, how often do we truly love our work even at its most difficult?

The principal horror of any system which defines the good in terms of profit rather than in terms of human need, or which defines human need to the exclusion of the psychic and emotional components of that need—the principal horror of such a system is that it robs our work of its erotic value, its erotic power and life appeal and fulfillment. Such a system reduces work to a travesty of necessities, a duty by which we earn bread or oblivion for ourselves and those we love. But this is tantamount to blinding a painter and then telling her to improve her work, and to enjoy the act of painting. It is not only next to impossible, it is also profoundly cruel.

As women, we need to examine the ways in which our world can be truly different. I am speaking here of the necessity for reassessing the quality of all the aspects of our lives and of our work, and of how we move toward and through them.

The very word *erotic* comes from the Greek word *eros*, the personification of love in all its aspects—born of Chaos, and personifying creative power and harmony. When I speak of the erotic, then, I speak of it as an assertion of the lifeforce of women; of that creative energy empowered, the knowledge and use of which we are now reclaiming in our language, our history, our dancing, our loving, our work, our lives.

There are frequent attempts to equate pornography and eroticism, two diametrically opposed uses of the sexual. Because of these attempts, it has become fashionable to separate the spiritual (psychic and emotional) from the political, to see them as contradictory or antithetical. "What do you mean, a poetic revolutionary, a meditating gunrunner?" In the same way, we have attempted to separate the spiritual and the erotic, thereby reducing the spiritual to a world of flattened affect, a world of the ascetic who aspires to feel nothing. But nothing is farther from the truth. For the ascetic position is one of the highest fear, the gravest immobility. The severe abstinence of the ascetic becomes the ruling obsession. And it is one not of self-discipline but of self-abnegation.

The dichotomy between the spiritual and the political is also false, resulting from an incomplete attention to our erotic knowledge. For the bridge which connects them is formed by the erotic—the sensual—those physical, emotional, and psychic expressions of what is deepest and strongest and richest within each of us, being shared: the passions of love, in its deepest meanings.

Beyond the superficial, the considered phrase, "It feels right to me," acknowledges the strength of the erotic into a true knowledge, for what that means is the first and most powerful guiding light toward any understanding. And understanding is a handmaiden which can only wait upon, or clarify, that knowledge, deeply born. The erotic is the nurturer or nursemaid of all our deepest knowledge.

The erotic functions for me in several ways, and the first is in providing the power which comes from sharing deeply any pursuit with another person. The sharing of joy, whether physical, emotional, psychic, or intellectual, forms a bridge between the sharers which can be the basis for understanding much of what is not shared between them, and lessens the threat of their difference.

BARBARA SMITH

Racism and Women's Studies

In June 1979, activist, educator, and writer Barbara Smith (born 1946) was invited to speak on Black women's studies at the first National Women's Studies Association Conference. She took the opportunity to address instead racial divisions among feminists. In her speech, presented in full here, Smith, who had spent the previous four months organizing in response to the murders of twelve Black women in Boston, criticized white feminists for not prioritizing "eradicating racism," insisting that unity, however difficult to realize, is "crucial to the survival of both Third World and white women." A founder with other women of color of such important Black feminist institutions as the Combahee River Collective (see pages 345–353 in this volume) and Kitchen Table: Women of Color Press, Smith has long been a coalition builder, working to bridge differences in race, class, and sexual identity among activists with shared political and social goals.

ALTHOUGH MY proposed topic is Black women's studies, I've decided to focus my remarks in a different way. Given that this is a gathering of predominantly white women, and given what has occurred during this conference, it makes much more sense to discuss the issue of racism: racism in women's studies and racism in the women's movement generally.

"Oh no," I can hear some of you groaning inwardly. "Not that again. That's all we've talked about since we got here." This, of course, is not true. If it had been all we had all talked about since we got here, we might be at a point of radical transformation on the last day of this conference that we clearly are not. For those of you who are tired of hearing about racism, imagine how much more tired *we* are of constantly experiencing it, second by literal second, how much more exhausted we are to see it constantly in your eyes. The degree to which it is hard or uncomfortable for you to have the issue raised is the degree to which you know inside of yourself that you aren't dealing with the issue, the degree to which you are hiding from the oppression that undermines Third World women's lives. I want to say right here that this is not a "guilt trip." It's a fact trip. The assessment of what's actually going on.

Why is racism being viewed and taken up as a pressing feminist issue at this time, and why is it being talked about in the context of women's studies? As usual, the impetus comes from the grassroots, activist women's movement. In my six years of being an avowed Black feminist, I have seen much change in how white women take responsibility for their racism, particularly within the last year. The formation of consciousness-raising groups to deal solely with this issue, study groups, and community meetings and workshops; the appearance of articles in our publications and letters in newspapers; and the beginning of real and equal coalitions between Third World and white women are all phenomena that have really begun to happen, and I feel confident that there will be no turning back.

The reason racism is a feminist issue is easily explained by the inherent definition of feminism. Feminism is the political theory and practice that struggles to free *all* women: women of color, working-class women, poor women, disabled women, Jewish women, lesbians, old women—as well as white, economically privileged, heterosexual women. Anything less than this vision of total freedom is not feminism, but merely female self-aggrandizement.

Let me make quite clear, before going any further, something you must understand. White women don't work on racism to do a favor for someone else, solely to benefit Third World women. You have to comprehend how racism distorts and lessens your own lives as white women—that racism affects your chances for survival, too, and that it is very definitely your issue. Until you understand this, no fundamental change will come about.

Racism is being talked about in the context of women's studies because of its being raised in the women's movement generally, but also because women's studies is a context in which white and Third World women actually come together, a context that should be about studying and learning about all of our lives. I feel at this point that it is not only about getting Third World women's materials into the curriculum, although this must be done. This has been happening, and it is clear that racism still thrives, just as the inclusion of women's materials in a college curriculum does not prevent sexism from thriving. The stage we are at now is having to decide to change fundamental attitudes and behavior—the way people treat each other. In other words, we are at a stage of having to take some frightening risks.

I am sure that many women here are telling themselves they aren't racists because they are capable of being civil to Black women, having been raised by their parents to be anything but. It's not about merely being polite: "I'm not racist because I do not snarl and snap at Black people." It's much more subtle than that. It's not white women's fault that they have been raised, for the most part, not knowing how to talk to Black women, not knowing how to look us in the eye and laugh *with* us. Racism and racist behavior are our white patriarchal legacy. What is your fault is making no serious effort to change old patterns of contempt—to look at how you still believe yourselves to be superior to Third World women and how you communicate these attitudes in blatant and subtle ways.

A major roadblock for women involved in women's studies to changing their individual racism and challenging it institutionally is the pernicious ideology of professionalism. That word *professionalism* covers such a multitude of sins. I always cringe when I hear *anyone* describe herself as "professional," because what usually follows is an excuse for inaction, an excuse for ethical irresponsibility. It's a word and concept we don't need, because it is ultimately a way of dividing ourselves from others and escaping from reality. I think the way to be "successful" is to do work with integrity and work that is good. Not to play cutthroat tricks and insist on being called "Doctor." When I got involved in women's studies six years ago, and particularly during my three and a half years as the first Third World woman on the Modern Language Association Commission on the Status of Women, I began to recognize what I call women's studies or academic feminists: women who teach, research, and publish about women, but who are not involved in any way in making radical social and political change; women who are not involved in making the lives of living, breathing women more viable. The grassroots/community women's movement has given women's studies its life. How do we relate to it? How do we bring our gifts and our educational privilege back to it? Do we realize also how very much there is to learn in doing this essential work? Ask yourself what the women's movement is working on in your town or city. Are you a part of it? Ask yourself which women are living in the worst conditions in your town and how your work positively affects and directly touches their lives? If it doesn't, why not?

The question has been raised here whether this should be an activist association or an academic one. In many ways, this is an immoral question, an immoral and false dichotomy. The answer lies in the emphasis and the kinds of work that will lift oppression off of not only women, but all oppressed people: poor and working-class people, people of color in this country and in the colonized Third World. If lifting this oppression is not a priority to you, then it's problematic whether you are a part of the actual feminist movement.

There are two other roadblocks to our making feminism real which I'll mention briefly. First, there is Third World women's antifeminism, which I sometimes sense gets mixed up with opposition to white women's racism and is fueled by a history of justified distrust. To me, racist white women cannot be said to be actually feminist, at least not in the way I think and feel about the word. Feminism in and of itself would be fine. The problems arise with the mortals who practice it. As Third World women we must define a responsible and radical feminism for ourselves and not assume that bourgeois female self-aggrandizement is all that feminism is and therefore attack feminism wholesale.

The other roadblock is homophobia, that is, antilesbianism, an issue that both white and Third World women still have to deal with. Need I explicate in 1979 how enforced heterosexuality is the extreme manifestation of male domination and patriarchal rule and that women must not collude in the oppression of women who have chosen each other, that is, lesbians? I wish I had time here to speak also about the connections between the lesbian-feminist movement, being woman-identified, and the effective antiracist work that is being done by many, though not all, lesbians.

In conclusion, I'll say that I don't consider my talk today to be in any way conclusive or exhaustive. It has merely scratched the surface. I don't know exactly what's going on in your schools or in your lives. I can only talk about those qualities and skills that will help you to bring about change: integrity, awareness, courage, and redefining your own success.

I also feel that the women's movement will deal with racism in a way that it has not been dealt with before in any other movement: fundamentally, organically, and nonrhetorically. White women have a materially different relationship to the system of racism than white men. They get less out of it and often function as its pawns, whether they recognize this or not. It is something that living under white-male rule has imposed on us; and overthrowing racism is the inherent work of feminism and by extension feminist studies.

1980–1991

ROSARIO MORALES

We're All in the Same Boat

Born in Puerto Rico and raised in Spanish Harlem, Rosario Morales (1930–2011) became politically active after moving back to Puerto Rico with her American Jewish husband and, inspired by its nationalism, joining the Communist Party there. Returning to New York in the early 1960s, she first encountered feminism when she found in Communist Party literature a critique of the machismo she encountered in Puerto Rican men. Moving to Chicago, she became active in the Chicago Women's Liberation Union, founded in 1969. From the beginning, Morales, a poet whose life bridged cultures, fully embraced the complex intersections of identity. This essay, completed in April 1980 and included here in full, first appeared in *This Bridge Called My Back* (1981).

November 1979

I AM not white. I am not middle class.
I am white skinned and puertorican. I was born into the working class and married into the middle class. I object to the label white & middle class both because they don't include my working class life and my puertoricanness, but also because "white & middle class" stands for a kind of politics. *Color and class don't define people or politics.* I get angry with those in the women's movement and out of it who deal with class & color as if they defined politics and people.

My experience in the Puerto Rican communist & independence movements has made me suspicious of and angry at Puerto Rican (& other Latin American) activist women. They have been sexist and supported the macho line that we *needed to fight against imperialism first—only later could we think about women as women.* I desperately want Latina women in the feminist movement while I fear the entry of hispanic & often black women because I fear they will play an anti-feminist role.

Racism is an ideology. Everyone is capable of being racist whatever their color and condition. Only some of us are liable to racist attack. Understanding the racist ideology—where and how it penetrates—is what is important for the feminist movement, not "including" women of color or talking about "including" men. *Guilt* is a fact for us all, white & colored: an identification with the oppressor and oppressive ideology. Let us, instead, identify, understand, and feel with the oppressed as a way out of the morass of racism and guilt.

I want to be whole. I want to claim my self to be puertorican, and U.S. american, working class & middle class, housewife and intellectual, feminist, marxist, and anti-imperialist. I want to claim my racism, especially that directed at myself, so I can struggle with it, so I can use my energy to be a woman, creative and revolutionary.

April 1980

This society this incredible way of living divides us by class   by color   It says   we are individual and alone and don't you forget it   It says the only way out of our doom   of our sex our class our race is some individual gift and character and hard work and then all we get   all we ever get is to change class or color or sex   to rise   to bleach   to masculinize   an enormous game of musical chairs and that's only at its fairy tale Horatio Alger best   that's only at its best

From all directions we get all the beliefs to go with these divisions   we believe all kinds of things about: what real men really are   what women must want   what black people feel and smell like   what white people do and deserve   how rich people earn their comforts and cadillacs   how poor people get what's coming to them

O we are all racist   we are all sexist   some of us only some of us are the targets of racism of sexism of homophobia of class denigration   but we all   all breathe in racism with the dust in the streets   with the words we read and we struggle those of us who struggle   we struggle endlessly endlessly to think and be and act differently from all that

Listen you and listen hard   I carry within me a vicious anti-semite voice that says   jew him down   that says dirty jew   that says things that stop me dead in the street and make the blood leave my face   I have fought that voice for 45 years   all the years that I lived with and among jews who are almost me   whose rhythms of speech and ways of laughing are close beside me   are dear to me   whose sorrows reach deep inside me   that voice that has tried to tell me that that love and identification are unreal   fake   cannot be   and I refuse it I refuse its message

I carry a shell   a white and crisp voiced shell to hide my brown golden soft spanish voiced inner self   to pass   to hide my puertoricanness

I carry a pole 18 inches long to hold me at the correct distance from black-skinned people

I carry hard metal armor with spikes   with shooting weapons in every joint   with fire breathing from every hole   to protect me   to prepare me to assault any man from 13 to 89

I am a whole circus by myself   a whole dance company with stance and posture for being in middle class homes   in upper class buildings   for talking to men   for speaking with blacks   for carefully angling and directing   for choreographing my way thru the maze of classes of people and places thru the little boxes of sex   race   class   nationality   sexual orientation   intellectual standing   political preference   the automatic contortions   the exhausting camouflage with which I go thru this social space called

CAPITALIST PATRIARCHY

a daunting but oh so nicely covering name   this is no way to live

Listen   listen with care   class and color and sex do not define people do not define politics   a class society defines people by class   a racist society defines people by color   We   feminists   socialists   radicals   define people by their struggles against the racism   sexism   classism   that they harbor   that surrounds them

So stop saying that she acts that way because she's middle class   that that's all you can expect from that group because it's white   that they're just men, quit it!

We know different things   some very much more unpleasant things if we've been women poor black or lesbian or all of those   we know different things depending on what sex   what color   what lives we live   where we grew up   What schooling   what beatings   with or without shoes   steak or beans   but what politics each of us is going to be and do is anybody's guess

Being female doesn't stop us from being sexist   we've had to choose early or late at 7 14 27 56 to think different   dress different   act different   to struggle   to organize   to picket   to argue   to change other women's minds   to change our own minds   to change our feelings   ours   yours   and mine constantly   to change and change and change   to fight the onslaught   on our minds and bodies and feelings

I'm saying that the basis of our unity is that in the most important way we are all in the same boat   all subjected to the violent pernicious ideas we have learned to hate   that we must all struggle against them and exchange ways and means   hints and how tos   that only some of us are victims of sexism   only some of us are victims of racism   of the directed arrows of oppression   but all of us are   sexist   racist   all of us.

GLORIA ANZALDÚA

(from) Speaking In Tongues:
A Letter to 3rd World Women Writers

A self-described "chicana dyke-feminist, tejana patlache poet, writer, and cultural theorist," Gloria Anzaldúa (1942–2004) was descended from Spanish colonists who settled in Texas in the sixteenth and seventeenth centuries as well as from indigenous ancestors and grew up in a sharecropping family. Claiming the psychic divisions of her borderland heritage as the source of her thinking and writing, Anzaldúa coedited the anthology *This Bridge Called My Back* to address all women writers of color who sought authentic voices in a culture that rendered them "inaudible." Excerpted here, from that book, is her iconic 1980 essay, "Speaking In Tongues."

21 mayo 80

Dear mujeres de color, companions in writing—

I sit here naked in the sun, typewriter against my knee trying to visualize you. Black woman huddles over a desk in the fifth floor of some New York tenement. Sitting on a porch in south Texas, a Chicana fanning away mosquitos and the hot air, trying to arouse the smouldering embers of writing. Indian woman walking to school or work lamenting the lack of time to weave writing into your life. Asian American, lesbian, single mother, tugged in all directions by children, lover or ex-husband, and the writing.

It is not easy writing this letter. It began as a poem, a long poem. I tried to turn it into an essay but the result was wooden, cold. I have not yet unlearned the esoteric bullshit and pseudo-intellectualizing that school brainwashed into my writing.

How to begin again. How to approximate the intimacy and immediacy I want. What form? A letter, of course.

My dear *hermanas*, the dangers we face as women writers of color are not the same as those of white women though we have many in common. We don't have as much to lose—we never had any privileges. I wanted to call the dangers "obstacles" but that would be a kind of lying. We can't *transcend* the dangers, can't rise above them. We must go through them and hope we won't have to repeat the performance.

Unlikely to be friends of people in high literary places, the beginning woman of color is invisible both in the white male mainstream world and in the white women's feminist world, though in the latter this is gradually changing. The *lesbian* of color is not only invisible, she doesn't even exist. Our speech, too, is inaudible. We speak in tongues like the outcast and the insane.

Because white eyes do not want to know us, they do not bother to learn our language, the language which reflects us, our culture, our spirit. The schools we attended or didn't attend did not give us the skills for writing nor the confidence that we were correct in using our class and ethnic languages. I, for one, became adept at, and majored in English to spite, to show up, the arrogant racist teachers who thought all Chicano children were dumb and dirty. And Spanish was not taught in grade school. And Spanish was not required in High School. And though now I write my poems in Spanish as well as English I feel the rip-off of my native tongue.

> I *lack imagination* you say
>
> *No.* I lack language.
> The language to clarify
> my resistance to the literate.
> Words are a war to me.
> They threaten my family.
>
> To gain the word
> to describe the loss
> I risk losing everything.
> I may create a monster
> the word's length and body
> swelling up colorful and thrilling
> looming over my *mother*, characterized.
> Her voice in the distance
> *unintelligible illiterate.*
> These are the monster's words.[1]
>
> Cherríe Moraga

Who gave us permission to perform the act of writing? Why does writing seem so unnatural for me? I'll do anything to postpone it—empty the trash, answer the telephone. The voice recurs in me: *Who am I, a poor Chicanita from the sticks, to think I could write?* How dare I even considered becoming a writer as I stooped over the tomato fields bending, bending under the hot sun, hands broadened and calloused, not fit to hold the quill, numbed into an animal stupor by the heat.

How hard it is for us to *think* we can choose to become writers, much less *feel* and *believe* that we can. What have we to contribute, to give? Our own expectations condition us. Does not our class, our culture as well as the white man tell us writing is not for women such as us?

The white man speaks: *Perhaps if you scrape the dark off of your face. Maybe if you bleach your bones. Stop speaking in tongues, stop writing left-handed. Don't cultivate your colored skins nor tongues of fire if you want to make it in a right-handed world.*

> "Man, like all the other animals, fears and is repelled by that which he does not understand, and mere difference is apt to connote something malign."[2]

I think, yes, perhaps if we go to the university. Perhaps if we become male-women or as middleclass as we can. Perhaps if we give up loving women, we will be worthy of having something to say worth saying. They convince us that we must cultivate art for art's sake. Bow down to the sacred bull, form. Put frames and metaframes around the writing. Achieve distance in order to win the coveted title "literary writer" or "professional writer." Above all do not be simple, direct, nor immediate.

Why do they fight us? Because they think we are dangerous beasts? Why *are* we dangerous beasts? Because we shake and often break the white's comfortable stereotypic images they have of us: the Black domestic, the lumbering nanny with twelve babies sucking her tits, the slant-eyed Chinese with her expert hand—"They know how to treat a man in bed," the flat-faced Chicana or Indian, passively lying on her back, being fucked by the Man *a la* La Chingada.

The Third World woman revolts: *We revoke, we erase your white male imprint. When you come knocking on our doors with your rubber stamps to brand our faces with DUMB, HYSTERICAL, PASSIVE PUTA, PERVERT, when you come with your branding irons to burn MY PROPERTY on our buttocks, we will vomit the guilt, self-denial and race-hatred you have force-fed into us right back into your mouth. We are done being cushions for your projected fears. We are tired of being your sacrificial lambs and scapegoats.*

I can write this and yet I realize that many of us women of color who have strung degrees, credentials and published books around our necks like pearls that we hang onto for dear life are in danger of contributing to the invisibility of our sister-writers. "La Vendida," the sell-out.

The danger of selling out one's own ideologies. For the Third World woman, who has, at best, one foot in the feminist literary world, the temptation is great to adopt the current feeling-fads and theory fads, the latest half truths in political thought, the half-digested new age psychological axioms that are preached by the white feminist establishment. Its followers are notorious for "adopting" women of color as their "cause" while still expecting us to adapt to *their* expectations and *their* language.

How dare we get out of our colored faces. How dare we reveal the human flesh underneath and bleed red blood like the white folks. It takes tremendous energy and courage not to acquiesce, not to capitulate to a definition of feminism that still renders most of us invisible. Even as I write this I am disturbed that I am the only Third World woman writer in this handbook. Over and over I have found myself to be the only Third World woman at readings, workshops, and meetings.

We cannot allow ourselves to be tokenized. We must make our own writing and that of Third World women the first priority. We cannot educate white women and take them by the hand. Most of us are willing to help but we can't do the white woman's homework for her. That's an energy drain. More times than she cares to remember, Nellie Wong, Asian American feminist writer, has been called by white women wanting a list of Asian American women who can give readings or workshops. We are in danger of being reduced to purveyors of resource lists.

Coming face to face with one's limitations. There are only so many things I can do in one day. Luisah Teish addressing a group of predominantly white feminist writers had this to say of Third World women's experience:

> "If you are not caught in the maze that (we) are in, it's very difficult to explain to you the hours in the day we do not have. And the hours that we do not have are hours that are translated into survival skills and money. And when one of those hours is taken away it means an hour not that we don't have to lie back and stare at the ceiling or an hour that we don't have to talk to a friend. For me it's a loaf of bread."

> Understand.
> My family is poor.
> Poor. I can't afford

a new ribbon. The risk
of this one is enough
to keep me moving
through it, accountable.
The repetition like my mother's
stories retold, *each* time
reveals more particulars
gains more familiarity.

You can't get me in your car so fast.[3]

Cherríe Moraga

"Complacency is a far more dangerous attitude than outrage."[4]

Naomi Littlebear

Why am I compelled to write? Because the writing saves me from this complacency I fear. Because I have no choice. Because I must keep the spirit of my revolt and myself alive. Because the world I create in the writing compensates for what the real world does not give me. By writing I put order in the world, give it a handle so I can grasp it. I write because life does not appease my appetites and hunger. I write to record what others erase when I speak, to rewrite the stories others have miswritten about me, about you. To become more intimate with myself and you. To discover myself, to preserve myself, to make myself, to achieve self-autonomy. To dispel the myths that I am a mad prophet or a poor suffering soul. To convince myself that I am worthy and that what I have to say is not a pile of shit. To show that I *can* and that I *will* write, never mind their admonitions to the contrary. And I will write about the unmentionables, never mind the outraged gasp of the censor and the audience. Finally I write because I'm scared of writing but I'm more scared of not writing.

---

[1] Cherríe Moraga's poem, "It's the Poverty" from *Loving in the War Years*, an unpublished book of poems.

[2] Alice Walker, editor, "What White Publishers Won't Print," *I Love Myself When I Am Laughing—A Zora Neale Hurston Reader* (New York: The Feminist Press, 1979), p. 169.

[3] Moraga, *Ibid.*

[4] Naomi Littlebear, *The Dark of the Moon* (Portland: Olive Press, 1977), p. 36.

CATHARINE MACKINNON

To Change the World for Women

Among the first to position sexual harassment as sex discrimination under Title IX of the Civil Rights Act of 1964, lawyer and legal scholar Catharine MacKinnon (born 1946) later offered arguments that rape and pornography also violated a woman's civil rights, articulating "a feminist theory of the state that looks at law from women's point of view." While rape law developed along these lines, pornography continued to be considered legally as free speech. This philosophical difference exploded in the feminist "sex wars" that divided the movement in the early 1980s. Invited by the city of Minneapolis, MacKinnon and Andrea Dworkin drafted an Antipornography Civil Rights Ordinance, which was vetoed twice by the mayor there, but passed in Indianapolis in 1984, only to be struck down by the Seventh Circuit Court of Appeals as a violation of the First Amendment. This 1980 speech to the Midwest Regional Women and the Law Conference in Minneapolis was first published in 2017 by MacKinnon, who added the endnotes.

I WENT TO law school because I wanted to change the world for women. One of the first things I learned there—something that pervaded my legal education whether my teachers, with exceptions, meant it to or not—was that in order to be a lawyer, it was necessary to strip oneself of passion, commitment, identification, feelings, community loyalties. Become objective, disinterested, fair, dispassionate. In a word: legal. The law is or should be neutral, was the idea, so a proper lawyer is a neutral instrument.

Together with this was a view that the law is everything. To change society—or what is responsible for society being the way it is—change law. John Stuart Mill's work illustrated the place of this idea in liberalism.[1] In this view, women were subjected in society because they were subjected in the law of the family. Implicit is a notion that law is all-powerful. Lawyers have a particular investment in this idea; it makes us the primary social activists.

Law school also taught the opposite idea: that the law is nothing. All law does is reflect the way society is. To produce social changes, work at a social level, abdicate the legal arena, because it is only a passive tool in the hands of society's manipulators. It merely reflects the way things are, the interests of those with power. Nothing can be done with it for the powerless.

Neither of these views seems adequate to the social system of women and law's relation to it. As legal advocates for women, we do not, I think, have a theory of what we are doing in the specific political context of sex inequality. Yes, the law is powerful in constructing social options. Yes, the law reflects forms of power that exist. But we need to devise what I would call a feminist theory of the state that looks at law from women's point of view, to see what can be done with it from there.

This may sound simple, but it is profoundly difficult and complex. Systematically, it has never been tried. Looking at the law from women's point of view has, of course, to embrace all women including all our sisters who are not with us today, each of us in our complexity, ambiguity, and divisions in our identifications, along with our attempts to reject the stereotypes we have been saddled with. "All women" includes not only those who do not identify as feminist but also those who deny that women and men are socially unequal. It includes women who embrace subordination to men. To have a feminist theory of law, hence a theory of our role as lawyers, we need to examine the law from the standpoint of this "all women." Quite obviously, this must encompass Black women, Latinas, all third-world women, including those, for example, who believe that if they still have a clitoris, they are ugly and unclean, and those who bound their own and each other's feet because they thought that it was (and it was) essential to their attractiveness and future. If they are not here, our equivalent to them is; participation and complicity in our own oppression is hard to avoid.

I pursue this task here through three issues: rape, sexual harassment, and pornography. These issues were chosen because I believe that women's sexuality is at the core of the way we are socially defined and therefore denigrated as women and because sexuality has been largely ignored as a factor in women's inequality to men. This means that the way the law treats issues of women's sexuality is a crucial indicator and determinant of women's status as a sex.

Over the past ten years, many women have attempted to pursue changes in the rape law and its administration. Rape is legally defined as sexual intercourse with force and without consent. The idea is to know it through its distinction from ordinary sexual intercourse, which is not forced and is consensual. Presumably, what makes it criminal distinguishes it from what most men do and from what most women experience.

Intercourse without consent—the one-sidedness is striking. Consent means somebody else initiates; you agree or not. But sexuality is supposed to be mutual. If rape means lack of consent, sex is apparently not envisioned to be mutual, but only consented to, acceded to. Equal initiation is not fundamental to the model. This is consistent with what has been found about much heterosexual intercourse. Women know from our own lives about the everyday construction of sexual intercourse. We are told that sex is something men do to women—men initiate it. Women at most approve that initiation or don't. At least, that is the dominant model, and it is built into the rape law.

Rape is also distinguished from sex by virtue of force. A fundamental question is whether the presence of force can be distinguished with a hard line from what ordinarily goes on between women and men under conditions of social inequality. As convicted rapists see themselves and are seen by other prison inmates, all they did wrong was get caught. They think that they are in prison for doing something that is little different from what most men do most of the time. Life taught them this. Add this to the fact that most rapes, it appears from studies, are not reported.[2] This indicates that women do not think the legal system will recognize their violation and vindicate their interests.

Many women who have gone through rape trials see the trial as an extension of the rape.[3] The burdens of proof, the legal assumptions, the disbelief they encounter, mean that their sexuality can be violated without consequences to the violator. The perspective they encounter is that what they said happened to them is not so different from what happens to most women much of the time. If this man is to be put away, the woman will have to show what happened to her is an extraordinary, exceptional occurrence. Often she cannot. If it is hard for a trier of fact to distinguish a rape clearly, perhaps that should indict the ordinary experience of heterosexual intercourse. Instead, it exonerates the rapist. Indicting intercourse does not directly help a woman who is trying, through the legal process, to establish that she has been raped, as the law defines it, either.

Discussing this analysis is sensitive in part because it can feed the implicit views of some judges and juries who converge rape with sex to let rapists off the hook. Men accused of rape often plead, in effect, that they did not use any more force than is usual during the preliminaries.[4] Studies show that most rapists are not psychologically abnormal men.[5]

Once a woman is married, unless she lives in a state with a still-exceptional marital rape statute, or with an interpretation of the rape law that extends to rape in marriage, any legal right to mutuality in a sexual relationship with her husband is given up, in the sense that the law does not stand behind her if she is not interested tonight. Under the pervasive assumptions about women's sexual availability, any woman who charges rape risks being undercut as a "whore," as someone who has had sex before, so cannot be violated. This assumption is used particularly invidiously against Black women, who are assumed, on a racist basis, to be hypersexual, labeled with one side of the madonna/whore distinction. When a Black woman who complains of sexual mistreatment is disbelieved, it is often because it is seen to be her nature to wish to be sexually used—she must have consented, so it was not a rape.

Women vote with our feet. We do not report rape because we do not believe we will get justice. The accuracy of this perception can be found in the animating requirements of the legal system on the issue of rape, which reflect rather than stand against the values of the unequal social system.[6] Those are male values, meaning values from the male point of view, unequal on the basis of sex.

Viewpoints don't have genitals. This refers to a social perspective in the interest and from the standpoint of a particular group of people. It doesn't matter whether members of dominant groups enjoy their position or not, although often they do. What does matter is that this system gives dominant groups social power to actualize themselves, to assert themselves at the expense of, over and against, other groups with impunity. To be white in a white supremacist society is to be a member of a socially dominant group. The phrase "from the experience and to the advantage of white people" describes a social standpoint—a dominant one that anyone can adopt if permitted to. Women, if permitted, can have male dominant attitudes. Men, with much struggle and perhaps decades of commitment, can learn women's standpoint. To speak of male attitudes is not to speak of the physical or the natural. That it does, is what *they* think.

With this state, as these fragments of evidence, logic, and experiences suggest, we are caught between letting rapists off the hook and demanding that they be energetically prosecuted. Successful prosecution means rapists go to jail, where they will likely be raped. They will be brutalized, at constant risk, much like what women experience every day walking down the street. Jail keeps them away from most women but changes nothing in the ultimate risk they pose to women. Men who go to jail and are raped do not usually come to identify with their victims. They cannot wait to get out, to be no longer the victim. Then they often rape again.[7] Women have no place to get out to. If we insist that the state protect us, we may get more rapes reported, but we do not seem to produce many more convictions. At the same time, Black men are often disproportionately convicted of rape, including those they did not commit, which is not in women's interest either. These initiatives do not change the predominately male behavior or attitudes of the society or the legal system. But what are our alternatives?

We are presented the choice of attempting to get the state to protect us, with dubious benefits, or abdicating the state as recourse and forum altogether. Back to the law as everything or nothing, no rights except those that power will accede or those that can be extracted or enforced socially. Abdicating the state altogether encourages rape. There would be even less risk in forcing a woman than there is now, men could rape with absolute, not just nearly total, impunity. That strategy leaves women, including Black women, to the rapists. There has to be a better way to use the state—maybe civil rights.

With sexual harassment, which has been pursued in this way, there has been more progress. Some of the same problems of credibility, and a similar set of social forces of gender and sexuality, animate this issue as they do the issue of rape. But this time, with sexual harassment women have so far defined the injury. The crime of rape was never defined by women but by male legislators and judges, who seem to have difficulty understanding that women are injured by sexual abuse. The rape law shows it; the damage to the victim of rape is nowhere central to it. What women lose when raped eludes it. The law of sexual harassment, by contrast, recognizes that this fairly standard set of social sexual behaviors is injurious. I am often asked what the difference is between sexual harassment and what goes on between men and women all the time. The answer is often very little. Their implication is, How can it be illegal to do something that goes on all the time? How can you be against it? The answer is, if it goes on all the time, maybe that is a reason to be *more* against it. That it is common supports the view that it is discrimination—implicit in discrimination is the notion that the behavior is pervasive, unlike the view taken by criminal law that the prohibited behavior is exceptional. Of course, particular acts of discrimination are often thought exceptional rather than systemic, but the concept makes it possible to argue that it is part of a larger phenomenon or pattern, shared by a group of victims who also share a lesser status.

Sexual harassment is the unwanted imposition of sexual attention on someone who is not in a position to refuse it. Now ask: In what circumstances do women tend to be in a position to refuse men's sexual attentions? In the workplace? Not usually. Women are systematically the structural subordinates of men in the workplace; therefore men can require pretty much anything, and hold women's jobs as hostage. Educational institutions? Some women are teachers, some women are in positions of power, but on the whole it is men who are at the upper reaches of that hierarchy too. Women students are not usually in a position to refuse men teachers' sexual attentions. Employment and education have been litigated because there are laws against discrimination there. But what about areas in which there is no equality law—say, the home? Women in the home are not necessarily in a position to refuse the sexual attention of their husbands either. The need to survive economically may make women who are beaten in their homes unable to leave or refuse the men who batter them. If women cannot avoid being beaten, then they are not in a position to resist sexual harassment—pinching, leering, unwelcome sexual acts—in the home either.

As a legal idea, it has been a struggle, but possible, to get legal actions for sexual harassment accepted. It has been a great deal more difficult to win individual women's sexual harassment cases. This dynamic is shared with rape cases. As an idea in the mind, everyone is against rape. Most men think of it as something they do not do. But most real-life situations in which women are raped, including many in which they charge rape, do not fit the male mental construct. When a woman presents herself in flesh and blood, in a real-life sexual situation involving a particular man, few realities look like the ideal outrages that those (mostly men) who make these determinations have imagined, what they are looking for and have distinguished themselves from. Many men can identify with the idea that sexual preconditions could prevent a woman from getting a job she should have. But real charges by women of propositions, pressure for dates, jokes, and cartoons at work engender disbelief and incredulity that this is an injury, similar to the disbelief women encounter that acts they call rape are injuries. Men who are accused of sexual harassment, like many imprisoned for rape, often also cannot see that they did anything very wrong, nor can their supporters. In their view, it was no different from what they, and other men, do all the time. They were just unlucky enough to get caught.

The point being, there is a difference between the ideal image of injury to the abstract woman and real injury to a real woman. Consider, for example, a faculty man saying to a woman student: "Sleep with me and I'll give you an A." This is what was alleged was said in *Alexander v. Yale.* The magistrate judge agreed with our theory that if these facts were proven, Title IX's prohibition on sex discrimination in education was violated.[8] But when the real woman actually walked into court and told what a man did, and he walked in and said I did not do this, the case lost at trial. The testimony of the real woman, who in this case is Black, against this white man was approximately as follows. I went to turn in my late paper, I sat down at his desk, he engaged me in discussion about my grade, mentioning that I might get a C. He asked me if I wanted an A in his course. I said I would like an A. He asked me how much do I want an A in the course. I said, I guess I could use one. Do I want an A in the course very, very much? Well, no, it really is not an insane desire, but I thought the final paper was a good paper. Then he said, God, you have a turn-on body. Stunned, she just looks back at him. And then she said he said (she was not believed at trial, so it is not a legal fact that any of this occurred, but I believe her), would she sleep with him? No, she said, no, no, no. (You should see this woman shake her head when she says no.) Then she ran out of his office.

He said that she did come there; she did turn in her paper. He was there. He made a phone call to his wife; it was on the phone bill. But what she said happened in that room did not happen and was not said. She complained orally and in writing shortly thereafter and tried to pursue her complaint persistently. Yale did little, having no procedure to follow in such instances. The trial judge believed the man.[9] No explicit judgment about credibility or assessment of evidence was made. These facts were found so as to insulate them from appeal. The legal cause of action for sexual harassment under Title IX was recognized in this case for the first time, so anyone can now use it, but this plaintiff's appeal on her specific facts was lost a few days ago.[10]

The idea that sexual harassment violates women is easier to accept against a man's denials than the real violation of a real woman is. It seemingly does not matter how much women seek control over the reproductive consequences of sex or over the depiction of our bodies, itself a form of sexual access. No matter how much we argue that the real issue is altering our powerlessness, what is encountered is the use, meaning the withholding of the use for us, of male power. Will the courts protect us, vindicate us, or not? Protection is always on their terms. Being protected is not the same as having rights. Women who men think are worthy of protection, precious few who can be presented as having no sexuality, are most likely to be protected. But who is that? The minute a woman walks in and has a body, she is a walking provocation to rape and sexual harassment and a form of pornography. We are available to be taken as sexual beings, meaning as sexual objects who can properly be acted upon. As is clear from the *Alexander v. Yale* example, a woman can take this approach to women too. Take seriously that the woman judge in *Alexander* is white.

Sexual harassment is a new issue. In women's lives, it's been going on for-ever, but as a legal issue, it's emerged in the recent context of a women's move-ment. So there is still some potential to keep control over its definition. One way to do that is to be very careful and conscious about how we, as lawyers, use the law. The benefit of making sexual harassment illegal is not the progress of the law but the progress of women taking power over our own lives. Making sexual harassment illegal has legitimized women's discontent and dissent. It is changing women's feelings about what we have to put up with. It is redrawing dignity lines between and within people. As an example, in Minnesota's *Continental Can* case,[11] for the first time in a reported judicial opinion, persistent sexual harassment without indices of economic deprivation that most men understand was recognized as discrimination. The woman wasn't deprived of money or a promotion or a job. She was in a job situation, an environmental condition of work, that her tolerance of persistent sexual abuse was a precon-dition for keeping. She could have quit at any point—her option. To stay, she only had to put up with constant sexual byplay. This, exclusively a sexual injury, was found to be sex discrimination.

One concern is that, once law is used to legitimize women's discontent, the minute law cuts back, women's outrage will diminish to what the law says we can be outraged about. What will be found illegal will necessarily be narrower than what we want to protest politically and in our own lives. Women have not had, and still do not have, the resources, access, or authority to get our injuries, as we define them, recognized as abuses by courts. We need to keep control over our own outrage and the definition of our own injuries and never allow courts to tell us what constitutes our oppression.

Just as in law, rape is supposed to be distinguishable from intercourse, and sexual harassment is to be distinguished from ordinary sexual initiation, in obscenity law, pornography is supposed to be distinguishable from eroticism and art. As with the other issues, left out is, to whom? If pornographers were providing something found satisfying or gratifying or interesting or educational, women would not avoid it as most of us do. Men, mainly, buy it, make it, and sell it—or us—to one another at a phenomenal financial return. Over the last ten years, the success of the film *Deep Throat* showed that pornography could be conventionally lucrative; it legitimized it as a medium. Pornography, increasingly, is everywhere. Seen from the standpoint of the status of women, what is happening in pornography looks a lot like what is happening in many legitimate magazines, fashion, films, and advertising: the bondage, the violence, the bruises, being spread-eagled across car hoods like a bagged deer, the "I'm all black and blue from the Rolling Stones and I love it,"[12] the bloody-mouth and blackened-eye makeup, the "Hit me with a club" ad,[13] and so on. Women, like everyone else, are bombarded by these materials, but most women do not consume pornography itself if we can help it. If you do, you tend to know it means you. It targets women. It makes promises to men that women are expected to keep. Men we know consume it, not just other men. Whatever is available is what is allowed, is what in fact is not obscene, is what does not violate their community standards. It is what turns men on.

In the context of sex inequality, a hard line between obscenity and what is allowed as art and beauty is problematic. Hugh Hefner defends *Playboy* as just showing the natural woman's body and asks how looking at anything so beautiful can be exploitive.[14] Look at the pictures and ask whether you look like that or have ever found yourself in the normal pursuit of life, in such a circumstance or posture; or whether, if you had, you would feel about it the way the women in the pictures are said to feel. It is not that women do not have pornographic life experiences. It is not that these depictions of our bodies are pornography because they are always extraordinarily violent or exceptionally anything. It is that the material does not present what women experience under those conditions: the use, the abuse, the access, the humiliation, the violation. It is clear that men, not women, are its intended consumers. Is *that* what men want?

We are looking for a place and a way to confront this issue. When we consider the courts, we are effectively told it is not our place. What are women up against in using courts as forums? What social process are we a part of? What would it mean, for example, to expand the definition of obscenity through the courts? I do not trust this state to see obscenity from the point of view of women, and we do not have a definition of pornography from that vantage point. I am not against censorship of pornography as a First Amendment absolutist; the First Amendment, no matter how absolute, has not protected our right to speak. Women are silenced when we speak as and for women, as well as in pornography. To try to use obscenity law for these ends, though, would misunderstand the values and interest that this law has historically served.[15] A possible strategy lies in supporting pornography models who are coerced. Pornography means literally the graphic depiction of whores, historically the lowest class of women, whose sexuality is freely available to men. Consider those women who are forced to be there. We need to learn more from them and think about their civil rights and all of ours.

So, the legal system can be a means of legitimizing women's outrage and of promoting resistance to our status. If we are creative, it can be part of women's empowerment. But, as it stands, it also supports much of what we are attempting to change when we advocate for change for women. Men are allowed to get their sense of self out of women's selflessness, their sense of worth out of a projection of our worthlessness, their sense of power out of our powerlessness, their definition of beauty out of our degradation, their eroticism out of our denigration. Implicitly, we have been searching for a theory and practice of what this state is—the state that has supported and enforced these legal doctrines and social institutions—for those of us who want to change them.

We need to identify with the interests of women as a whole, so that each initiative we take as lawyers empowers women's resistance to this system. Only then will we recover our own passion, the passion many of us began this pursuit with, which we were taught in law school we had to abandon. We need to recover our identification as women, our commitment, our belief that we can and must be, as lawyers, committed to that in ourselves that is inseparable from that in the world that is all women. We need to develop an autonomous definition of our own direction, to search for forums and means and doctrines of struggle on behalf of women's equality that cannot be turned against us or taken away.

1. John Stuart Mill, *The Subjection of Women* 30 (Cambridge, MA: M.I.T. Press 1970) (1869) (arguing that women are subjected through society because they are unequal in the law of marriage).

2. Diana E. H. Russell, *Sexual Exploitation: Rape, Child Sexual Abuse, and Workplace Harassment* 31 (Thousand Oaks, CA: Sage Publications 1984) (documenting 9.5 percent of rapes reported); National Victim Center, Crime Victims Research and Treatment Center, *Rape in America: A Report to the Nation* 5 (1992) (finding 16 percent of rapes reported); Catharine A. MacKinnon, *Sex Equality* 854 (3d ed., New York: Foundation Press 2016) (compiling research to date).

3. This report was taken directly from women's experience as reported at the time. Subsequent research proved it to be widespread. See generally Lynda Lytle Holmstrom and Ann Wolbert Burgess, *The Victim of Rape: Institutional Reactions* (1991); Lee Madigan and Nancy C. Gamble, *The Second Rape* (New York: Lexington Books 1991); MacKinnon, *Sex Equality* 866 (compiling research to date).

4. At the time this talk was given, support for this observation was mainly anecdotal. For a reasonably contemporary instance, one case that was discussed in the press at the time held that acts of a defendant wrestling, kissing, and pressing himself against the victim without her consent "when such acts are merely the preliminaries to consensual sexual intercourse" are not enough to put a reasonable person in fear of bodily harm, hence are not a lesser included offense of assault. State v. Jeffries, 291 S.E.2d 859, 861 (N.C. App. 1982). Actually, the State's evidence here showed that the defendant grabbed the victim, pulled her onto his lap despite her telling him "No," whereupon she burned him with a cigarette and tried to break away; he held onto her and threw her on the bed and started kissing her and pressing his body down on her despite her crying and pleading that he stop, after which he forcefully wrestled with her, and despite her continued resistance and threats to prosecute, forcibly removed her clothing while she continued to try to push him off her; she hit him in the face with her fist, he struck her back, and he eventually had sexual intercourse with her. Id. at 860. (His testimony was that she hugged and kissed him and then he hit her while they were having sex. Id. at 861.) He was convicted of second degree rape; that conviction was upheld. Id. at 864. In other words, the jury did not believe his version. Regrettably, substantial case law support for this kind of judicial normalization of forcibly abusive sexual initiation being deemed even potentially consensual—the *Jeffries* court actually said that the acts mentioned above "may constitute assault," but when they initiate sex, they don't, id. at 861—has developed substantially since. See MacKinnon, "Rape Redefined," 459–462.

5. At the time of delivery, this fact was supported by Richard Rada, ed., *Clinical Aspects of the Rapist* (New York: Grune & Stratton 1978); Clifford Kirkpatrick and Eugene Kanin, "Males Sex Aggression on a University Campus," *American Sociological Review* 22, 52–58 (1957); Neil Malamuth, Scott Haber, and Seymour Feshbach, "Testing Hypotheses Regarding Rape: Exposure to Sexual Violence, Sex Differences, and the 'Normality' of Rapists," 14 *Journal of Research in Personality* 121 (1980). Soon after, it was further documented by James Check and Neil Malamuth, "An Empirical Assessment of Some Feminist Hypotheses About Rape," 8 *International Journal of Women's Studies* 414, 415 (1985), Diana Scully, *Understanding Sexual Violence: A Study of Convicted Rapists* (Boston: Unwin Hyman 1990), and others.

6. Much later, the process described here came to be termed "rape attrition" by researchers. For extensive documentation of it, see MacKinnon, *Sex Equality* 854–855.

7. These rates, known from experience at the time, have been variously documented since. See, e.g., Vernon L. Quinsey et al., "Actuarial Prediction of Sexual Recidivism," 10 *Journal of Interpersonal Violence* 85 (1995).

8. Alexander v. Yale University, 459 F. Supp. 1, 5 (D. Conn. 1977) (adopting the ruling of Magistrate Judge Arthur H. Latimer).

9. Id.

10. Alexander v. Yale University, 631 F.2d 178, 184 (2d Cir. 1980).

11. Continental Can Co. Inc. v. State of Minnesota, 291 N.W.2d 241, 250 (Minn. 1980).

12. "I'm Black and Blue from the Rolling Stones—and I Love It!," *Rolling Stone*, July 1, 1976.

13. "Hit Me with a Club," Heublein's Club Cocktail, 1975.

14. Hugh M. Hefner, "The Playboy Philosophy," 1 *Playboy* 41 (Jan. 1963).

15. This analysis was later pursued in detail in Catharine A. MacKinnon, "Not a Moral Issue," in Catharine A. MacKinnon, *Feminism Unmodified: Discourses on Life and Law* (Cambridge, MA: Harvard University Press 1987).

ANDREA DWORKIN

(from) *Pornography*

A spellbinding orator and polarizing writer, Andrea Dworkin (1946–2005) was perhaps the leading figure of the feminist antipornography movement in the late 1970s and 1980s. The 1983 Minneapolis ordinance she drafted with Catharine MacKinnon was supported by Women Against Pornography (WAP), which launched demonstrations, conferences, "educational tours" of sex-related businesses, and lobbying campaigns. WAP's feminist opponents, sometimes called "sex-positive" feminists, were outraged by the ordinance, which they considered to be repressive censorship harmful to women, and organized the Feminist Anti-Censorship Taskforce (FACT, 1982–86) to counter it in court and oppose WAP. Though eventually struck down by the courts, the ordinance exacerbated the "sex wars" that divided feminists, further inflaming conflicts that had erupted at the 1982 Barnard Conference on Sexuality and that continue to this day. Presented here is chapter 6 from Dworkin's 1981 book *Pornography/Men Possessing Women*.

THE WORD *pornography*, derived from the ancient Greek *pornē* and *graphos*, means "writing about whores." *Pornē* means "whore," specifically and exclusively the lowest class of whore, which in ancient Greece was the brothel slut available to all male citizens. The *pornē* was the cheapest (in the literal sense), least regarded, least protected of all women, including slaves. She was, simply and clearly and absolutely, a sexual slave. *Graphos* means "writing, etching, or drawing."

The word *pornography* does not mean "writing about sex" or "depictions of the erotic" or "depictions of sexual acts" or "depictions of nude bodies" or "sexual representations" or any other such euphemism. It means the graphic depiction of women as vile whores. In ancient Greece, not all prostitutes were considered vile: only the *porneia*.

Contemporary pornography strictly and literally conforms to the word's root meaning: the graphic depiction of vile whores, or, in our language, sluts, cows (as in: sexual cattle, sexual chattel), cunts. The word has not changed its meaning and the genre is not misnamed. The only change in the meaning of the word is with respect to its second part, *graphos*: now there are cameras—there is still photography, film, video. The methods of graphic depiction have increased in number and in kind: the content is the same; the meaning is the same; the purpose is the same; the status of the women depicted is the same; the sexuality of the women depicted is the same; the value of the women depicted is the same. With the technologically advanced methods of graphic depiction, real women are required for the depiction as such to exist.

The word *pornography* does not have any other meaning than the one cited here, the graphic depiction of the lowest whores. Whores exist to serve men sexually. Whores exist only within a framework of male sexual domination. Indeed, outside that framework the notion of whores would be absurd and the usage of women as whores would be impossible. The word *whore* is incomprehensible unless one is immersed in the lexicon of male domination. Men have created the group, the type, the concept, the epithet, the insult, the industry, the trade, the commodity, the reality of woman as whore. Woman as whore exists within the objective and real system of male sexual domination. The pornography itself is objective and real and central to the male sexual system. The valuation of women's sexuality in pornography is objective and real because women are so regarded and so valued. The force depicted in pornography is objective and real because force is so used against women. The debasing of women depicted in pornography and intrinsic to it is objective and real in that women are so debased. The uses of women depicted in pornography are objective and real because women are so used. The women used in pornography are used in pornography. The definition of women articulated systematically and consistently in pornography is objective and real in that real women exist within and must live with constant reference to the boundaries of this definition. The fact that pornography is widely believed to be "sexual representations" or "depictions of sex" emphasizes only that the valuation of women as low whores is widespread and that the sexuality of women is perceived as low and whorish in and of itself. The fact that pornography is widely believed to be "depictions of the erotic" means only that the debasing of women is held to be the real pleasure of sex. As Kate Millett wrote, women's sexuality is reduced to the one essential: "cunt . . . our essence, our offense."[1] The idea that pornography is "dirty" originates in the conviction that the sexuality of women is dirty and is actually portrayed in pornography; that women's bodies (especially women's genitals) are dirty and lewd in themselves. Pornography does not, as some claim, refute the idea that female sexuality is dirty: instead, pornography embodies and exploits this idea; pornography sells and promotes it.

In the United States, the pornography industry is larger than the record and film industries combined. In a time of widespread economic impoverishment, it is growing: more and more male consumers are eager to spend more and more money on pornography—on depictions of women as vile whores. Pornography is now carried by cable television; it is now being marketed for home use in video machines. The technology itself demands the creation of more and more *porneia* to meet the market opened up by the technology. Real women are tied up, stretched, hanged, fucked, gang-banged, whipped, beaten, and begging for more. In the photographs and films, real women are used as *porneia* and real women are depicted as *porneia*. To profit, the pimps must supply the *porneia* as the technology widens the market for the visual consumption of women being brutalized and loving it. One picture is worth a thousand words. The number of pictures required to meet the demands of the marketplace determines the number of *porneia* required to meet the demands of graphic depiction. The numbers grow as the technology and its accessibility grow. The technology by its very nature encourages more and more passive acquiescence to the graphic depictions. Passivity makes the already credulous consumer more credulous. He comes to the pornography a believer; he goes away from it a missionary. The technology itself legitimizes the uses of women conveyed by it.

In the male system, women are sex; sex is the whore. The whore is *pornē*, the lowest whore, the whore who belongs to *all* male citizens: the slut, the cunt. Buying her is buying pornography. Having her is having pornography. Seeing her is seeing pornography. Seeing her sex, especially her genitals, is seeing pornography. Seeing her in sex is seeing the whore in sex. Using her is using pornography. Wanting her means wanting pornography. Being her means being pornography.

---

1. Kate Millett, *The Prostitution Papers* (New York: Avon Books, 1973), p. 95.

PAULA WEBSTER

Pornography and Pleasure

"Pornography and Pleasure," by anthropologist Paula Webster (born 1943), was published in *Heresies: A Feminist Publication on Art and Politics,* edited and produced by the New York–based Heresies Collective (1977–93). Each *Heresies* issue was devoted to women's experiences of a specific theme: violence, education, environment, racism, art, and music, among others. Editors of the "Sex Issue" (1981) asked, "Where do our desires come from?" and called for "more pleasure, more variety, more analysis, more debate, more honesty." In this essay Webster analyzes her complicated response to a Women Against Pornography (WAP) presentation.

E VERY FEMINIST in the New York metropolitan area has heard of Women Against Pornography. Indeed, in the last few years, pornography has become the focus for a great deal of feminist activity. In one of the best-organized and best-funded campaigns in movement history, women have been encouraged to examine their gut reactions to sexually explicit material and to take a political stand that condemns pornography as a major cause of violence against women.

Women from every part of the movement, and women who would have no part of the movement, came together around this issue. Political differences, both in theory and practice, were set aside as pornography was assigned a privileged position in the discourse on women's oppression. At least publicly, the link was unquestioned. Pornography caused violence against women. Moreover, not only did pornography *cause* violence against women, it *was* violence against women. Pornography made women victims, for it depicted women as subject to men's sexual lusts. The very existence of 42nd Street was an assault on women. All those pictures, films, advertisements degraded and therefore violated women.

A vast sea of feminist solidarity swelled around the issue of pornography. To move against the wave felt truly threatening. Although a few voices addressed contradictions in the anti-porn analysis,[1] no dissenting movement developed. Criticism was kept to a minimum. It is one thing to disagree with a group you are fighting against, but serious discord within your own movement is problematic. We seem to fear that feminist solidarity, so precious to us all, will not survive any rigorous criticism.

Yet many women, under their breath, confided that something was missing from all this discussion of the production and consumption of sexually explicit material. Dogmatism, moralizing, and censorial mystifying tended to dominate the anti-porn campaign. What about encouraging an honest dialogue about *our* sexual imagination? The shifting of discourse might have opened the floodgates of many passions. So much remains unsaid about our eroticism, our fantasies, our sexual activities, our longings for satisfaction. Our pleasure, as it is constituted inside and out of heterosexuality and patriarchy, never got center stage. Because this was a movement to chastise men for their vices, women were not encouraged to talk about their relationship to sexuality.

But what did we really feel under the onslaught of sexual imagery provided by the campaign? I remember seeing a slide show with about 30 images of predominantly heterosexual couples engaged in intercourse (genital and anal), bondage, and sadomasochism. There were shots of individual women, bound and gagged, pictures of female dominatrixes, assorted album covers, posters, clothing advertisements, as well as a handful of very jarring images of self-mutilation and the now-infamous *Hustler* photos of women arranged as food on a platter or put through a meat grinder.

Despite the lecturer's claim that *all* reactions to the slides were encouraged, each slide was interpreted to reveal its implicit pernicious meaning. One viewer, for example, asked why the photo of a young girl about to have anal intercourse was described as "the violent rape of a child." The reply was that she was obviously under age, so at the least it was statutory rape. The lecturer added that anal intercourse was "very painful"; therefore it was unlikely that this "tiny young girl" could have been anything other than *brutally injured*. I thought this reply indicated certain biases about pain and pleasure and preferred positions. Yet the most important misunderstanding was that a mere representation was spoken of as a reality—as an actual event recorded by some Candid Camera. The multiplicity of issues around gender, power, and sexuality embedded in each slide was disregarded; only one way of seeing was acceptable. Our "visual guide" invariably revealed the real or implied violence of the slide. *All* images of women were suspect.

In one department store ad for girls' shirts the seductive looks of the child models were offered as proof positive that the evil influence of pornography had filtered down to the truly mass media and was spreading like a contagious plague through even the most mundane images. Such photos, not unlike ones we could all find in family scrapbooks of ourselves as preteens, were indicted as encouragement to incest. No one thought it strange that these ads, directed primarily at women consumers, did not incite these women's lust for their sons, daughters, and other women.

To discourage and deny the charge that the campaign was anti-sex, erotica was held up as the *only* sexually explicit material that did not represent violence or cause it. "Erotica" became the code word for stimulation appropriate to a feminist consciousness, while "pornography" was defined as exclusively male and therefore "naturally" devoid of distinctions between sex and violence. The implications of this neat dichotomization and sex-typing of desire reflect, unchanged, the Victorian ideology of innate differences in the nature of male and female libido and fantasy. Men, we are to presume, because of their "excessive" drive, prefer the hard edge of pornography. Women, less driven by the "beast," find erotica just their cup of tea.

Given this map of the sexual world, it was most distressing that during the slide show no erotica was ever presented, leaving the impression that erotica itself is very rare, or so mundane that we can trust our memories to recall its charge. This category of images, absent and therefore mute, was considered essentially unproblematic. It was good, healthy sexual imagery—the standard against which pornography and perhaps our own sexual lives were to be judged. The subjectivity involved in dividing explicitly sexual material into hard-core, soft-core, and erotic was never challenged by the audience.

What is defined as pornography and what is defined as erotica no doubt depends on personal taste, moral boundaries, sexual preferences, cultural and class biases. These definitions have contracted and expanded over time; advocates of one or the other form of imagery have switched camps or staunchly defended their own. Just as normative attitudes about sexual behavior, masculinity and femininity, and the social relations between the sexes have shifted, so have attitudes about sexually explicit material. There are no universal, unchanging criteria for drawing the line between acceptable and unacceptable sexual images. As feminists, we might question the very impulse to make such a rigid separation, to let a small group of women dictate the boundaries of our morality and our pleasure.

No discussion immediately followed the slide show. Divided into groups, we walked down 42nd Street, entering the shops and arcades where films, magazines, and live sex shows are offered to the male public. For the price of a subway ride, I could actually watch for a few minutes, in my own private booth, the act that for all my years in the nuclear family was considered dirty, disgusting, and therefore taboo. If pornography is propaganda, and I do believe that it is, it is not promoting the violation and degradation of women, but traditional heterosexual intercourse and gender relations. (Perhaps they overlap, but that is another story.) What is missing is romance, shared social status, worries about contraception and shame. The short film I saw was not about love, but it was undeniably about sex.

I was grateful for this opportunity to demystify a territory that had been off-limits to me as a woman. I felt relieved about the dangers of pornography, since I had viewed little violence and a lot of consensual sex. However, I was more curious than ever about the meaning and function of such a zone dedicated to solitary sexual stimulation and voyeuristic fantasies. The secrecy surrounding sexual activity had been, for me, the price all women paid for femininity. We were not to speak of our desires, only answer "yes" or "no." The tour evoked complex reactions, including envy, fear, and sexual arousal. The social and psychic repression of my female desire was giving way, ever so slightly, under the barrage of sexual imagery. I was a fascinated tourist in an exotic, erotic, and forbidden land.

The tour and slide show raised many questions for me. What is the underlying appeal of pornography? And what does the volume of business done on 42nd Street say about sexual relations? What can pornography tell us about the nature of desire and its relation to fantasy? Is pornography really any more dangerous to women than fashion magazines, television commercials, and cinema? Otherness in the guise of domestic purity and mindless submission seems more pernicious than Otherness in the guise of sexual activity. How, I wondered, can we begin to measure the effects of objectification in pornography when the Otherness ascribed to us at birth because we are not male already labels us as socially inferior? Such an ancient Otherness leaves little room for any avowal of our subjectivity. Moreover, reality and representation of reality are not the same. Objectification may be a function of representation. All the actors (male and female) in pornography are objectified. They do not speak. They are not individuals. They have no depth, no contours. They are the ritual performers of the culture's sexual paradigms. They are not the real, but a commentary on the real.

What I felt after the tour and slide show was the need for discussion of our many contradictory reactions to what we had seen. Yet the lines had already been drawn between bad and good sex, brainwashed fantasies and uncontaminated desire, danger and purity. The excitement of the unknown, the delight and terror at seeing so much active flesh (male and female), was never acknowledged. Like Mom and Dad, the tour leaders responded exclusively to our reactions of disgust. Our worst adolescent fantasies (or our best) were true. "They" will do anything to get *it*, to have *it*, to use *us*. To see pornography as a safety valve for the aggressive sexuality of men was mistaken. Pornography "really" acts to disinhibit male violence. If it is not done away with, we will see an increase in rape, battery, and child molestation. This final volley of dooms-day prediction was not easy to recover from. To disagree was to be aligned with the brainwashed or the naive.

I am convinced that the current anti-porn campaign holds significant dangers for feminists interested in developing an analysis of violence against women and extending an analysis of female sexuality. The provocative claims of the campaign create an enormous obstacle in the form of moral righteous-ness; they feed the old and voracious anxiety we experience when confronted with sexual imagery. Even more important, the campaign has chosen to orga-nize and theorize around our victimization, our Otherness, not our subjec-tivity and self-definition. In focusing on what male pornography has done to us, rather than on our own sexual desires, we tend to embrace our sexually deprived condition and begin to police the borders of the double standard that has been used effectively to silence us. It is not in the interests of feminism to circumvent the vast area of sexual repression. And pornography is primarily about sexuality. It is important to wrench this ground out from under the barrage of moralizing so that we can understand the social construction of all our ideas about our own and male sexuality. While it is equally important to understand the cultural determinants of violence against women, I would suggest that these tasks remain separate for the moment.

I have serious reservations about certain tendencies within the anti-porn movement. Are we seeking to protect the ideal of Womanhood by claiming some natural female superiority in the realm of morality and decency? And don't we ignore the sexual socialization of both men and women in asserting that men "by nature" prefer this and women that? What about the subver-sive elements in pornography, which might help feminists to understand the conditions under which all sexual behavior is negotiated in a sexist society? If women are humiliated by pornography and feel degraded watching women get pleasure, then we might pause to ask if women feel humiliated by real, everyday heterosexuality and its demands. Power relations play an important role in our actual sexual lives. Can we really expect the realm of fantasy to be free of the residues of that power struggle?

As women, we have been brought up in a society where to be sexual in an active or "promiscuous" fashion is to transgress the rules for femininity. Not just the rules set up by men but the rules set and enforced by other women. We learned that men were the princes/beasts and we were their expectant prin-cesses/martyrs, waiting to be aroused by a kiss, leading to love and marriage and the protection of our vulnerable sexuality. The pursuit of sex threatens to make good girls bad, so we usually accept the cultural standard of sexual minimalism . . . few partners, fewer positions, less pleasure, and no changing of preference. Nice girls don't talk about desiring sex. We talk about what *they* did to us. Women are allowed to be the objects of desire, to attract attention. But we have tended to refuse the role of sexual subject. Being forward, pushy, seeking sex are not acceptable. Being passive, teasing to please are still preferred to seizing our own pleasure. Pornography might be seen as challenging this protected and confining corner into which women's sexuality has been pushed, for it negates the sacramental character of our sexual desires.

Indeed, I am convinced that pornography, even in its present form, contains important messages for women. As Angela Carter suggests,[2] it does not tie women's sexuality to reproduction or to a domesticated couple or exclusively to men. It is true that this depiction is created by men, but perhaps it can encourage us to think of what our own images and imaginings might be like.

Television, film, and our mothers all reinforce the notion that only bad girls like sex. If we reject this good girl/bad girl distinction, the split between the mother and the whore, the tour guide and the topless dancer, we begin to understand that neither has a better deal under patriarchy. The comfortable separation between feminists, especially academic feminists, and prostitutes, office workers, and other "exploited women" crumbles when we realize the extent to which all our bodies become commodities, whether within or outside the nuclear family. In placing the gratification of men above our own, we pose absolutely no danger to male-dominated society. What I am suggesting here is not a withdrawal from sex, but an active pursuit of *our* gratification, with a sense of responsibility, entitlement, and enthusiasm. The good girl/bad girl distinction will fail to terrorize us and control our access to pleasure *only* if we set out to destroy the double standard.

Specifically, what we might take *from* male pornography is a vision of the mutability of sexual experience and a variety of directions for sexual experimentation. Whatever its limitations, pornography does demystify a number of sexual practices that have been taboo for women. As voyeurs, we can participate in homosexual activity, domination, group sex, and masochistic and sadistic orgies. With the clues we gather here about our own fantasies, we can begin to map out the zones of cerebral and fleshly arousal.

Pornography also offers women a multiplicity of vantage points for analyzing the sexual paradigms that frame all gender relations and constrain our sexual interactions. Pornography implies that we could find all races, genders, ages, and shapes sexually interesting, if only in our minds. Compare this to the pinched reality of a liberal ideology that snidely prods us to do our own thing against a background of political repression. While pornography itself is not a critique of society, its very existence in such a deeply anti-pleasure society speaks to an attempt to introduce a non-moralistic view of sexual practice. Of course, pornography is not a substitute for sexual practice, though it might be an addition to it. Even if women were to miraculously take over this industry, we would only be able to change the content so that *our* masturbatory pleasure was considered. It would not give us permission to act. That permission can only come when we accept that our desires will not make us victims, that our sensuality is not dangerous to our well-being. This will inspire us at the same time that we work to restructure society to be more hospitable to our desires.

My point is that a stance of moralizing about sexual imagery and, by implication, practice gets us no closer to defining how sexual activity and fantasy fit into our lives or our analysis of oppression. If we think that women can only be the victims of sex, what strategies do we propose for taking control and altering this situation? Each heterosexually involved woman must ask herself if she will continue to refuse sexual autonomy and subjectivity in the name of femininity.

Perhaps it is premature to call for a truly radical feminist pornography-erotica. But to speak of our own desires and to organize for our own and our collective sexual pleasure would be a beginning. We could open the debate about the nature of female sexual desire. It is precisely in the private, secret, and "shameful" realm of our own sexuality that we have feared to take responsibility for being subjects. We easily talk about denying men pornographic pleasure, but this does not bring us closer to gaining our own.

The training we received as girls encouraged us to renounce acting on our own behalf and for our own pleasure. Our own sexual desires threatened Mom and Dad, and they told us how dangerous sex was, especially curiosity or experimentation. They warned us about men. The good ones would protect us and the bad ones would exploit us. Now we are hearing these same echoes in a feminist campaign. Men are lustful and women are loving. They are violent and we are peaceful. They like rough sex . . . we don't.

Some feminists reject this classification of genders which stresses natural, immutable differences. The essence of male sexuality is not barely repressed violence or insatiable bestiality. Nor is female sexuality passive or characterized by efficiently sanitized longings. As we have come to understand that women are made and not born, we must conclude that men too undergo a similar social construction. Masculinity and femininity are social products that establish but do not reveal the true natures of these hierarchically opposed groups. Are we ready to give up the eternal enemy and challenge our feminization, which leaves us mute about our desires for pleasure, and so many other things? Once we take our eyes off *them* and renounce our obsessive concern with *their* thoughts, feelings, and actions, we can move from blaming to assessing our vision for change.

It is time to organize for our pleasure as well as our protection, to use pornographic images to raise consciousness about our desires and our fears. If we can switch our focus from men's pleasure to our own, then we have the potential of creating the discourse that will challenge the values of "good girls" (non-sexual women) and explore the bridge that connects and divides expression and repression. If we could imagine operating without all the internal and external constraints society has imposed on us, feminists might create a truly radical pornography that spoke of female desire as we are beginning to know it and as we would like to see it acted out.

---

[1] See Dierdre English, "The Politics of Porn," *Mother Jones*, Vol. 5, No. 3 (April 1980), p. 20; Ellen Willis, in *Village Voice* (Oct. 15, 1979).

[2] Angela Carter, *The Sadeian Woman and the Ideology of Pornography* (New York: Pantheon, 1978).

JOAN NESTLE

My Mother Liked to Fuck

Politicized in the fight for civil rights, women's rights, and gay rights, Joan Nestle (born 1940) became a feminist archivist, writer, teacher, and editor. In 1972 she helped found the Gay Academic Union and in 1974 she cofounded the Lesbian Herstory Archives. A participant in the butch-femme bar scene of the 1950s, Nestle began writing erotic lesbian fiction in the late 1970s. When her writings were attacked by members of the antipornography movement during the 1980s "sex wars," she became a prominent sex-positive activist, embracing "a feminism that does not run from the full complexity of women's lives, from the vital differences between us as well as the connections that bind us." The full text of her pro-sex essay "My Mother Liked to Fuck," first published in *Womanews* in 1981, is presented here.

(A response to the "Eros, Language and Pornography" panel at the American Writers Congress, Oct. 9, 1981. Dedicated to Amber who speaks to the best parts of ourselves.)

M Y MOTHER Regina was not a matriarchal goddess or a spiritual advisor. She worshipped at no altars and many times scorned the label mother. She was a Jewish working class widowed woman who from the age of 14 worked as a bookkeeper in New York's garment district. My father died before I was born when my mother was twenty-nine and left her with two children to raise. My mother liked sex and let me know throughout the years both the punishments and rewards she earned because she dared to be clear about enjoying fucking.

Regina was in my mind that October afternoon I sat in the front row of 1199's auditorium to tape the panel discussion on pornography and eros. When my mother died, she left no money, no possessions, no property, no insurance policies. She left me only a sheaf of writings, scrawled letters and poems written on the back of yellow ledger sheets. I have written a longer piece about her and I, incorporating these letters but for now I only want to talk about the courage of her sexual legacy and the sexual secrets I found in her writings and how she stood in my mind, the mind of her Lesbian daughter who has loved women for over twenty years, the afternoon of the panel.

Like many working class single parents, my mother used me as a confidante, a supporter, a witness. I had to grow up fast to learn how to duck the repossessors, the eviction notices, the subpoenas. I learned how to be quiet and good in the homes of others. We never had large apartments and my mother had many boyfriends so sex and her enjoyment of it were not secrets. I knew the phrase blowjob before I knew there was a right way to brush one's teeth. What I learned from her writings was how hard bought this sexual freedom was.

At age thirteen, my mother allowed herself to be picked up on a Coney Island beach and have sex with a good looking Jewish boy who was in his twenties; three weeks later he invited her to his apartment where she was gang raped by three of his friends. She became pregnant and had to have an abortion at age fourteen. The year was 1924. Her German father threatened to kill her and she left school in the ninth grade to go to work. When my mother writes of these experiences she tells of her sexual passions, of how she wanted sex.

> I remember as a little girl, the impatiency with my own youth. I recognized that I was someone, someone to be reckoned with. I SENSED THE SEXUAL ORDER OF LIFE. I felt its pull. I wanted to be quickly and passionately involved. God, so young and yet so old. I recognized my youth only in the physical sense as when I exposed my own body to my own vision, saw the beautiful breasts, the flat stomach, the sturdy limbs, the eyes that hid sadness, needed love, a hell of a lot of grit and already acknowledging this to be one hell of a life. I was going to find the key. I knew the hunger but I did not know how to appease it.

She goes on to speak of her shock, pain and hurt and later of her anger at the rape but she ends the narrative with a sexual credo, that she would not let this ugliness take away her right to sexual freedom, her enjoyment of "the penis and the vagina" as she puts it.

Respectable ladies did not speak to my mother for most of her widowed life. She picked up men at the race track, at OTB offices, slept with them, had affairs with her bosses and generally lived a sexualised life. Several times she was beaten by the men she brought home. In her fifties, she was beaten unconscious by a merchant seaman when she refused to hand over her paycheck. My mother, in short, was both a sexual victim and a sexual adventurer: her courage grew as the voices of condemnation and threats of violence increased against her. I watched it all and her belief in a woman's undeniable right to enjoy sex, to actively seek it, became a part of me but I chose women. I wanted to kill the men who beat her, who took her week's pay. I wanted her not to need them and to come into my world of Lesbian friendship and passion, but she chose not to. We faced each other as two women for whom sex was important and after initial skirmishes, she accepted my world of adventure as I did hers.

The week before she died, she was sexually challenging her doctor in the hospital, telling him he probably did it too quick for a woman like her. He, red faced and young, drew the curtain around her hurriedly. At sixty-seven my mother still wanted sex and made jokes about what she could do when she didn't have her teeth in. My mother was not a goddess, not a matriarchal figure who looms up over my life big bellied with womyn rituals. She was a working woman who liked to fuck, who believed she had a right to have a penis inside of her if she liked it and who sought deeply for love but knew that was much harder to find.

As Andrea Dworkin's litany against the penis rang out that afternoon, I saw my mother's small figure, with her ink stained calloused hands never without a cigarette held out towards me and I saw her face with a slight smile: "so nu, Joan is this the world you wanted for me, the world you wanted me to have, where I should feel shame and guilt for what I like. I did for all the years of my life. I fought the rapist and the batterer and I didn't give up my knowledge of what I liked. I looked at those dirty pictures and I saw lonely people. Sometimes I did those things they do in dirty pictures and wives would not speak to me. Their husbands fucked me first and then went home for shabbas. I made lots of mistakes but one thing I never did. I never allowed anyone to bully me out of my sexual needs. Just like you Joan when in the fifties I took you to doctors to see if you were a Lesbian and they said you had too much hair on your face, you were a freak and they never stopped you either. They called you freak and me whore and maybe they always will but we fight them the best when we keep on doing what they say we should not want or need for the joy we find in doing it. I fucked because I liked it and Joan the ugly ones, the ones who beat me or fucked me too hard, they didn't run me out of town and neither can the women who don't walk my streets of loneliness and of need. Don't scream penis at me but help to change the world so no woman feels shame or fear because she likes to fuck."

CHERRÍE MORAGA

(from) La Güera

Born in 1952 to a Chicana mother and a white father, Cherríe Moraga was raised and educated in Los Angeles, where, at the Woman's Building, she began to write lesbian poems, later turning also to memoir, essays, and plays. Moraga was still in her twenties when she edited, with Gloria Anzaldúa, the breakthrough 1981 anthology *This Bridge Called My Back: Writings by Radical Women of Color.* The contributors, Moraga declared in her preface, wrote from "the exhaustion we feel in our bones at the end of the day, the fire we feel in our hearts when we are insulted, the knife we feel in our backs when we are betrayed, the nausea we feel in our bellies when we are afraid, even the hunger we feel between our hips when we long to be touched." Excerpted here is her 1979 essay "La Güera," which appears in the anthology.

I WAS EDUCATED, and wore it with a keen sense of pride and satisfaction, my head propped up with the knowledge, from my mother, that my life would be easier than hers. I was educated; but more than this, I was "la güera": fair-skinned. Born with the features of my Chicana mother, but the skin of my Anglo father, I had it made.

No one ever quite told me this (that light was right), but I knew that being light was something valued in my family (who were all Chicano, with the exception of my father). In fact, everything about my upbringing (at least what occurred on a conscious level) attempted to bleach me of what color I did have. Although my mother was fluent in it, I was never taught much Spanish at home. I picked up what I did learn from school and from over-heard snatches of conversation among my relatives and mother. She often called other lower-income Mexicans "braceros", or "wet-backs", referring to herself and her family as "a different class of people." And yet, the real story was that my family, too, had been poor (some still are) and farmworkers. My mother can remember this in her blood as if it were yesterday. But this is something she would like to forget (and rightfully), for to her, on a basic economic level, being Chicana meant being "less." It was through my mother's desire to protect her children from poverty and illiteracy that we became "anglocized"; the more effectively we could pass in the white world, the better guaranteed our future.

From all of this, I experience, daily, a huge disparity between what I was born into and what I was to grow up to become. Because, (as Goldman suggests) these stories my mother told me crept under my "güera" skin. I had no choice but to enter into the life of my mother. *I had no choice.* I took her life into my heart, but managed to keep a lid on it as long as I feigned being the happy, upwardly mobile heterosexual.

When I finally lifted the lid to my lesbianism, a profound connection with my mother reawakened in me. It wasn't until I acknowledged and confronted my own lesbianism in the flesh, that my heartfelt identification with and empathy for my mother's oppression—due to being poor, uneducated, and Chicana—was realized. My lesbianism is the avenue through which I have learned the most about silence and oppression, and it continues to be the most tactile reminder to me that we are not free human beings.

You see, one follows the other. I had known for years that I was a lesbian, had felt it in my bones, had ached with the knowledge, gone crazed with the knowledge, wallowed in the silence of it. Silence *is* like starvation. Don't be fooled. It's nothing short of that, and felt most sharply when one has had a full belly most of her life. When we are not physically starving, we have the luxury to realize psychic and emotional starvation. It is from this starvation that other starvations can be recognized—if one is willing to take the risk of making the connection—if one is willing to be responsible to the result of the connection. For me, the connection is an inevitable one.

What I am saying is that the joys of looking like a white girl ain't so great since I realized I could be beaten on the street for being a dyke. If my sister's being beaten because she's Black, it's pretty much the same principle. We're both getting beaten any way you look at it. The connection is blatant; and in the case of my own family, the difference in the privileges attached to looking white instead of brown are merely a generation apart.

In this country, lesbianism is a poverty—as is being brown, as is being a woman, as is being just plain poor. The danger lies in ranking the oppressions. *The danger lies in failing to acknowledge the specificity of the oppression.* The danger lies in attempting to deal with oppression purely from a theoretical base. Without an emotional, heartfelt grappling with the source of our own oppression, without naming the enemy within ourselves and outside of us, no authentic, non-hierarchical connection among oppressed groups can take place.

When the going gets rough, will we abandon our so-called comrades in a flurry of racist/heterosexist/what-have-you panic? To whose camp, then, should the lesbian of color retreat? Her very presence violates the ranking and abstraction of oppression. Do we merely live hand to mouth? Do we merely struggle with the "ism" that's sitting on top of our own heads?

The answer is: yes, I think first we do; and we must do so thoroughly and deeply. But to fail to move out from there will only isolate us in our own oppression—will only insulate, rather than radicalize us.

To illustrate: a gay male friend of mine once confided to me that he continued to feel that, on some level, I didn't trust him because he was male; that he felt, really, if it ever came down to a "battle of the sexes", I might kill him. I admitted that I might very well. He wanted to understand the source of my distrust. I responded, "You're not a woman. Be a woman for a day. Imagine being a woman." He confessed that the thought terrified him because, to him, being a woman meant being raped by men. He *had* felt raped by men; he wanted to forget what that meant. What grew from that discussion was the realization that in order for him to create an authentic alliance with me, he must deal with the primary source of his own sense of oppression. He must, first, emotionally come to terms with what it feels like to be a victim. If he—or anyone—were to truly do this, it would be impossible to discount the oppression of others, except by again forgetting how we have been hurt.

And yet, oppressed groups are forgetting all the time. There are instances of this in the rising Black middle class, and certainly an obvious trend of such "unconsciousness" among white gay men. Because to remember may mean giving up whatever privileges we have managed to squeeze out of this society by virtue of our gender, race, class, or sexuality.

Within the women's movement, the connections among women of different backgrounds and sexual orientations have been fragile, at best. I think this phenomenon is indicative of our failure to seriously address ourselves to some very frightening questions: How have I internalized my own oppression? How have I oppressed? Instead, we have let rhetoric do the job of poetry. Even the word "oppression" has lost its power. We need a new language, better words that can more closely describe women's fear of and resistance to one another; words that will not always come out sounding like dogma.

1. The Women's Strike for Equality organized by the National Organization for Women (NOW) on New York's Fifth Avenue on August 26, 1970, the 50th anniversary of the Nineteenth Amendment. The movement's first mass demonstration drew 50,000 participants, plus thousands more in sister cities nationwide.

2. "The Myth of the Vaginal Orgasm" author Anne Koedt, left, and Carol Hanisch, right, originator of the slogan "the personal is political," carrying a banner at a 1968 rally to legalize abortion.

3. New York Radical Women at a consciousness-raising meeting in New York City, 1968. NYRW member Kathie Sarachild, who coined the slogan "Sisterhood is powerful," is at the far right.

4. Consciousness-raising group at the Women's Center, New York City, 1970.

5. Protesters tossing bras, brooms, and other "instruments of female torture" into a Freedom Trash Can, at the September 7, 1968, Miss America Pageant protest in Atlantic City. Contrary to legend, no bras were burned.

6. The National Welfare Rights Organization, marching in the Poor People's Campaign, Washington, D.C., in 1968, with NWRO's first chair and later executive director Johnnie Tillmon, front row, left.

7. Carol Downer, of the Los Angeles–based Feminist Women's Health Center, teaching the technique of vaginal self-examination to a group of women in Washington, D.C., in 1974, as part of a program to wrest control of women's bodies from male doctors.

8. A member of the University of Chicago WITCH hexing the Sociology Department for firing a popular woman professor, January 16, 1969.

9. Ti-Grace Atkinson being arrested at an anti-Nixon protest, October 23, 1972. A six-month sentence for resisting arrest was suspended. From left: Ruth Simpson, Atkinson, and Ellen Povill.

10. FBI 1970 Wanted poster for political activist and philosopher Angela Davis, charged with "kidnaping and murder." She was acquitted of all charges in 1972.

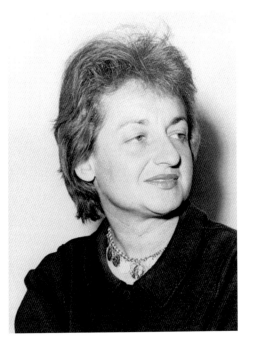

11–13. Clockwise from top left: Betty Friedan, author of *The Feminine Mystique* (1963)—which launched the modern feminist movement in the U.S.—and cofounder in 1966 of the National Organization for Women (NOW); Kate Millett, sculptor, filmmaker, and author of many books, including the groundbreaking *Sexual Politics* (1970); Shulamith Firestone, cofounder of the earliest U.S. radical feminist groups, in Chicago and New York City, and author of the feminist classic *The Dialectic of Sex: The Case for Feminist Revolution* (1970), written at age twenty-five.

14–15. Author Maxine Hong Kingston, above, and playwright and poet Ntozake Shange pictured on the poster for the 1976 Broadway production of her play.

16. Congresswoman Shirley Chisholm's campaign poster for the Democratic presidential
    nomination, 1972.

17. Florynce (Flo) Kennedy, left, who served as Chisholm's campaign manager, with Comanche
    LaDonna Harris, the Citizens Party's 1980 vice presidential candidate.

18. Alabama native Minnie Bruce Pratt, poet and former member of the North Carolina Feminary collective, at an anti-Klan march in Washington, D.C., November 27, 1982.

19. From left: Judy Reif, Fran Winant, and Martha Shelley, of the Lavender Menace, at the Second Congress to Unite Women (1970).

20. From left: Tennis champion Billie Jean King; Susan B. Anthony II; conference chair Bella Abzug; and Betty Friedan, far right, join torch runners Sylvia Ortiz, Peggy Kokernot, and Michele Cearcy for the final mile of the relay from Seneca Falls, NY, site of the first women's rights convention (1848), to the National Women's Conference in Houston, November 18, 1977.

21. Robin Morgan, Susan Brownmiller, and Gloria Steinem in New York City, 1979.

22. Beth Brant, also known as Degonwadonti, poet and essayist. A member of the Bay of Quinte Mohawk, she was editor of *A Gathering of Spirit* (1988), the first anthology of works by Indigenous women edited by an Indigenous woman.

23. Attendees at the Native American Women's Rights Conference, New York City, 1975.

24. Founders of Kitchen Table: Women of Color Press, launched in 1980 to circumvent bias against feminist and lesbian writers of color in publishing, Washington, D.C., 1981. From left: Barbara Smith, poets Audre Lorde, Cherríe Moraga, and Hattie Gossett.

25. Protest of a threatened day care closure in New York City, 1974. In 1972 President Richard Nixon vetoed a comprehensive federal childcare bill.

26. "The Liberation of Aunt Jemima," by Los Angeles artist Betye Saar: "I used the derogatory image to empower black women by making her a revolutionary."

27. Harlem-born artist Faith Ringgold in her studio, 1971, with her painting "Soul Sister." She and her daughter Michele Wallace organized for inclusion of women and people of color in the art world.

28. A 1989 poster by The Guerrilla Girls, an anonymous collective of women artists founded in 1985.

YOU'RE SEEING LESS THAN HALF THE PICTURE

WITHOUT THE VISION OF WOMEN ARTISTS AND ARTISTS OF COLOR.

Please send $ and comments to: Box 1056 Cooper Sta. NY, NY 10276 **GUERRILLA GIRLS** CONSCIENCE OF THE ART WORLD

29. "In Mourning and in Rage . . ." a 1977 performance by Suzanne Lacy, at the microphone, and Leslie Labowitz. The piece protested media coverage of the Los Angeles Hillside Strangler. See also pp. 354–57.

30. In the October 1970 issue of *Artforum*, artist Judy Chicago's ad for a one-woman show.

31. Democratic congresswomen marching up the Capitol steps to demand a delay of the Senate's vote to confirm Clarence Thomas to the Supreme Court, October 1991. The all-male Senate Judiciary Committee's failure to take seriously Anita Hill's and other women's accusations of sexual harassment against Thomas was a win for the anti-feminist backlash.

MITSUYE YAMADA

(from) Invisibility Is an Unnatural Disaster: Reflections of an Asian American Woman

Japanese American Mitsuye Yamada was nineteen in 1942 when she and her mother and brothers, U.S. citizens all, were interned for two years during World War II at the Mindoka War Relocation Center in Idaho. Two decades later, a feminist consciousness born of growing up in an Asian household that overtly privileged the needs of men drew her to Betty Friedan's *The Feminine Mystique* and later to the Bay Area community of women writers. There the feminist poet Alta introduced her to the stories of Tillie Olsen (see pages 201–209 in this volume); "I cried and cried," Yamada said. She soon met Olsen, who encouraged her to revisit poems she'd written while interned. *Camp Notes* appeared in 1977. Excerpted here is the pioneering essay Yamada wrote for *This Bridge Called My Back*.

MY EXPERIENCE leads me to believe that contrary to what I thought, I had actually been contributing to my own stereotyping. Like the hero in Ralph Ellison's novel *The Invisible Man*, I had become invisible to white Americans, and it clung to me like a bad habit. Like most bad habits, this one crept up on me because I took it in minute doses like Mithradates' poison and my mind and body adapted so well to it I hardly noticed it was there.

For the past eleven years I have busied myself with the usual chores of an English teacher, a wife of a research chemist, and a mother of four rapidly growing children. I hadn't even done much to shatter this particular stereotype: the middle class woman happy to be bringing home the extra income and quietly fitting into the man's world of work. When the Asian American woman is lulled into believing that people perceive her as being different from other Asian women (the submissive, subservient, ready-to-please, easy-to-get-along-with Asian woman), she is kept comfortably content with the state of things. She becomes ineffectual in the milieu in which she moves. The seemingly apolitical middle class woman and the apolitical Asian woman constituted a double invisibility.

I had created an underground culture of survival for myself and had become in the eyes of others the person I was trying not to be. Because I was permitted to go to college, permitted to take a stab at a career or two along the way, given "free choice" to marry and have a family, given a "choice" to eventually do both, I had assumed I was more or less free, not realizing that those who are free make and take choices; they do not choose from options proffered by "those out there."

I, personally, had not "emerged" until I was almost fifty years old. Apparently through a long conditioning process, I had learned how *not* to be seen for what I am. A long history of ineffectual activities had been, I realize now, initiation rites toward my eventual invisibility. The training begins in childhood; and for women and minorities, whatever is started in childhood is continued throughout their adult lives. I first recognized just how invisible I was in my first real confrontation with my parents a few years after the outbreak of World War II.

During the early years of the war, my older brother, Mike, and I left the concentration camp in Idaho to work and study at the University of Cincinnati. My parents came to Cincinnati soon after my father's release from Internment Camp (these were POW camps to which many of the Issei* men, leaders in their communities, were sent by the FBI), and worked as domestics in the suburbs. I did not see them too often because by this time I had met and was much influenced by a pacifist who was out on a "furlough" from a conscientious objectors' camp in Trenton, North Dakota. When my parents learned about my "boy friend" they were appalled and frightened. After all, this was the period when everyone in the country was expected to be one-hundred percent behind the war effort, and the Nisei† boys who had volunteered for the Armed Forces were out there fighting and dying to prove how American we really were. However, during interminable arguments with my father and overheard arguments between my parents, I was devastated to learn they were not so much concerned about my having become a pacifist, but they were more concerned about the possibility of my marrying one. They were understandably frightened (my father's prison years of course were still fresh on his mind) about repercussions on the rest of the family. In an attempt to make my father understand me, I argued that even if I didn't marry him, I'd still be a pacifist; but my father reassured me that it was "all right" for me to be a pacifist because as a Japanese national and a "girl" *it didn't make any difference to anyone*. In frustration I remember shouting, "But can't you see, *I'm* philosophically committed to the pacifist cause," but he dismissed this with

* Issei—Immigrant Japanese, living in the U.S.
† Nisei—Second generation Japanese, born in the U.S.

"In my college days we used to call philosophy, foolosophy," and that was the end of that. When they were finally convinced I was not going to marry "my pacifist," the subject was dropped and we never discussed it again.

As if to confirm my father's assessment of the harmlessness of my opinions, my brother Mike, an American citizen, was suddenly expelled from the University of Cincinnati while I, "an enemy alien", was permitted to stay. We assumed that his stand as a pacifist, although he was classified a 4-F because of his health, contributed to his expulsion. We were told the Air Force was conducting sensitive wartime research on campus and requested his removal, but they apparently felt my presence on campus was not as threatening.

I left Cincinnati in 1945, hoping to leave behind this and other unpleasant memories gathered there during the war years, and plunged right into the politically active atmosphere at New York University where students, many of them returning veterans, were continuously promoting one cause or other by making speeches in Washington Square, passing out petitions, or staging demonstrations. On one occasion, I tagged along with a group of students who took a train to Albany to demonstrate on the steps of the State Capitol. I think I was the only Asian in this group of predominantly Jewish students from NYU. People who passed us were amused and shouted "Go home and grow up." I suppose Governor Dewey, who refused to see us, assumed we were a group of adolescents without a cause as most college students were considered to be during those days. It appears they weren't expecting any results from our demonstration. There were no newspersons, no security persons, no police. No one tried to stop us from doing what we were doing. We simply did "our thing" and went back to our studies until next time, and my father's words were again confirmed: it made no difference to anyone, being a young student demonstrator in peacetime, 1947.

Not only the young, but those who feel powerless over their own lives know what it is like not to make a difference on anyone or anything. The poor know it only too well, and we women have known it since we were little girls. The most insidious part of this conditioning process, I realize now, was that we have been trained not to expect a response in ways that mattered. We may be listened to and responded to with placating words and gestures, but our psychological mind set has already told us time and again that we were born into a ready-made world into which we must fit ourselves, and that many of us do it very well.

This mind set is the result of not believing that the political and social forces affecting our lives are determined by some person, or a group of persons, probably sitting behind a desk or around a conference table.

Just recently I read an article about "the remarkable track record of success" of the Nisei in the United States. One Nisei was quoted as saying he attributed our stamina and endurance to our ancestors whose characters had been shaped, he said, by their living in a country which has been contantly besieged by all manner of natural disasters, such as earthquakes and hurricanes. He said the Nisei has inherited a steely will, a will to endure and hence, to survive.

This evolutionary explanation disturbs me, because it equates the "act of God" (i.e., natural disasters) to the "act of man" (i.e., the war, the evacuation). The former is not within our power to alter, but the latter, I should think, is. By putting the "acts of God" on par with the acts of man, we shrug off personal responsibilities.

I have, for too long a period of time accepted the opinion of others (even though they were directly affecting my life) as if they were objective events totally out of my control. Because I separated such opinions from the persons who were making them, I accepted them the way I accepted natural disasters; and I endured them as inevitable. I have tried to cope with people whose points of view alarmed me in the same way that I had adjusted to natural phenomena, such as hurricanes, which plowed into my life from time to time. I would readjust my dismantled feelings in the same way that we repaired the broken shutters after the storm. The Japanese have an all-purpose expression in their language for this attitude of resigned acceptance: "Shikataganai." "It can't be helped." "There's nothing I can do about it." It is said with the shrug of the shoulders and tone of finality, perhaps not unlike the "those-were-my-orders" tone that was used at the Nuremberg trials. With all the sociological studies that have been made about the causes of the evacuations of the Japanese Americans during World War II, we should know by now that "they" knew that the West Coast Japanese Americans would go without too much protest, and of course, "they" were right, for most of us (with the exception of those notable few), resigned to our fate, albeit bewildered and not willingly. We were not perceived by our government as responsive Americans; we were objects that happened to be standing in the path of the storm.

Perhaps this kind of acceptance is a way of coping with the "real" world. One stands against the wind for a time, and then succumbs eventually because there is no point to being stubborn against all odds. The wind will not respond to entreaties anyway, one reasons; one should have sense enough to know that. I'm not ready to accept this evolutionary reasoning. It is too rigid for me; I would like to think that my new awareness is going to make me more visible than ever, and to allow me to make some changes in the "man made disaster" I live in at the present time. Part of being visible is refusing to separate the actors from their actions, and demanding that they be responsible for them.

By now, riding along with the minorities' and women's movements, I think we are making a wedge into the main body of American life, but people are still looking right through and around us, assuming we are simply tagging along. Asian American women still remain in the background and we are heard but not really listened to. Like Musak, they think we are piped into the airwaves by someone else. We must remember that one of the most insidious ways of keeping women and minorities powerless is to let them only talk about harmless and inconsequential subjects, or let them speak freely and not listen to them with serious intent.

We need to raise our voices a little more, even as they say to us "This is so uncharacteristic of you." To finally recognize our own invisibility is to finally be on the path toward visibility. Invisibility is not a natural state for anyone.

SONIA JOHNSON

(from) *From Housewife to Heretic*

A devout member of the Church of Jesus Christ of Latter-day Saints, Sonia Johnson (born 1936) heard about feminism at an informal meeting of Mormon women
and began to read feminist texts with her initially supportive husband. Quickly
becoming active in the burgeoning Mormon feminist movement, she defied
church opposition to the Equal Rights Amendment (ERA) by testifying before a
U.S. Senate Judiciary Subcommittee in favor of extending the deadline for the
amendment's passage. Her activist support of the ERA—including a thirty-seven-
day hunger strike at the Illinois House of Representatives and chaining herself to
the White House gates—led to her excommunication from the Mormon church
and the end of her marriage. The excerpt presented here is from her 1981 memoir,
From Housewife to Heretic.

I WAS NOT yet in touch with the serious anger that had built up in me
over my lifetime. The full emotional realization of it, the full fury, lay
unplumbed for several more months. I still felt no need to act, no need to
change the world. Like most Mormon and other traditional women, I had not
yet learned to dare to feel angry at men and their institutions, preferring to
turn my anger inward and let it eat away at my well-being instead. It was less
frightening to be depressed than to be angry at men.

To be angry at men was to be angry at God.

I was beginning where many begin with feminism—grappling intellectually
with the fact of the systematic, millennia-old degradation of females. I turned
page after page in feminist books, nodding my head in violent agreement,
shouting aloud to whomever, "Hey, listen to this. It's so hideously true! This
is the way it *is*!" marveling, as I read about incidents in other women's lives,
how I'd experienced similar things myself and had not *seen*. How could I have
been so blind?

But I didn't really understand the revolutionary implications of what I was
reading and of what was beginning to happen to me. Ideas and insights were
crashing about in my head, but their yeasty meaning hadn't penetrated my

bones, weren't yet swimming in my blood, beating with my heart. I was intellectually engaged, but the business of re-creating myself had barely begun.

Ironically, but naturally enough, it was the church that catapulted me into the appropriate state of anger. And it took the church to force me to transmute that anger into the energy necessary to go forth and fight to right the ancient wrongs.

Over the coming months, as the church cooperated so fully in my transformation, I began to mine and unleash years of pent-up rage upon Rick. Knowing very well that he had not invented sexism, knowing that he was a product of his culture, knowing that he was trying to understand, to be patient, and best of all, to change his own attitudes and behavior—for which I loved him more than ever—still, to me he represented the destructiveness of male supremacy to females, and every new insight into the incredible maiming done to women would fill me with such pain and wrath that rays of my rage would pierce him many times a day.

He had, of course, not been guiltless of dozens of varieties of sexism on a personal level in his relationship with me. Over the years he had made me feel incompetent and not very bright hundreds of times. I had so little self-confidence, I always assumed that he knew what he was talking about and that therefore I did not. While seeming to be eminently just and fair, he condescended mightily and knew very well how to put me down hard. Though somewhere I believe I always knew he bluffed a lot, perhaps I refused to face the fact that in subtle but devastating ways he bullied and belittled me, because I needed to believe in his superiority, too. After all, I'd sacrificed a great deal to be allowed to become part of him. I could not let myself see that I had put all my eggs into one less-than-perfect basket.

In defense against my anger, he resisted feeling personally responsible for women's oppression, including mine. (We both knew that for the most part he had been an unwitting accomplice in the past. But that was *then*. *Now* I couldn't bear it anymore.) But if he expressed his anger at being made to bear what he felt was an unfair measure of the blame, he felt guiltier than ever, so in true Rick fashion, he kept his anger to himself most of the time—a defense that proved ultimately disastrous. Feminism, a simple ideology of equality, is not easy to live. We have no models.

By spring I had come to the end of my capacity to repress my anger and to continue to dodge the issue. One afternoon I sat on the basement stairs and wondered why I felt so depressed. We had a lovely house, I had a part-time editing job (which I didn't enjoy much, but I could do it at home and it left plenty of time for the children and church work); the house was clean, supper was ready to go into the oven, and I had several free hours before everyone came home. Ordinarily all this, plus the fact that we were all well and our lives were going smoothly, should have given me a feeling of contentment. But there I was, swamped with despair and praying aloud, "Why, Father, why do I feel so *awful*? What's wrong with me?"

Just a few days before, on May 3, I'd written a letter to my parents:

"I don't know whether I asked you to offer prayers that I would get the teaching job at the state university in the fall. The classes would be in the evening when Rick's home and would be the salvation of my soul, as I feel now. I am so enormously and thoroughly bored and so much needing to do what I love to do and do so well. I feel certain that can't be offensive to the Lord, and hope you'll join us in asking him for that boon if it would be right for me and the family. When we first moved here, I told Heavenly Father not to worry about me for a while but to get my husband and children established and happy first and I would help with that and not ask for more—for a while. It seems to me that those things have about been accomplished and that—this may sound selfish—it's my turn now. I am really unhappy when my mind is not stimulated and employed, and when I have to rely on church associations for all my fulfillment and stimulation. It makes me dissatisfied with the church. But I don't think the church should have to bear that burden, since the Lord has allowed me to prepare myself to find fulfillment in secular ways as well. Has not only allowed me, but seemed to encourage and bless me so that I could."

Sitting there on the stairs, I wondered briefly whether my malaise might really be what I'd thought when I wrote that letter: that I was bored. So I prayed about it. Was this it? But I knew without asking that lack of mental exercise alone could never cause the kind of despair I was struggling against. I prayed on and on, aloud, as is my wont when I'm alone, but the deadly, leaden feeling refused to budge. And then I remembered a talk I'd heard in church the Sunday before, which suggested that since we don't always understand ourselves well enough to know what we should pray for, we should ask God.

So I did. And no sooner had I done so than I surprised myself by saying, still in vocal prayer: "Father, I know there's something I've been trying to avoid knowing for a very long time—probably all my life—because I've been too afraid to face it, afraid of what it might do to my life and family, afraid I couldn't handle it, that it might overwhelm me and maybe even drive me insane. But I have become so unhappy by not dealing with it, that doing so could not make me any more miserable. So no matter what it is, I am ready to know it. I want to know it. I must know it!"

Immediately, I heard my own voice in my mind say clearly, "Patriarchy is a sham."

Z. BUDAPEST

(from) The Vows, Wows, & Joys of the High Priestess or What Do You People Do Anyway?

In the 1970s, religious women began to think and worship, in Mary Daly's words, "beyond God the father": Jewish women composed feminist Haggadahs, Catholic nuns threw off their habits, and eleven Episcopalian women, in defiance of church policy, became priests in a 1974 renegade ordination. In 1971, the feminist Z. (Zsuzsanna) Budapest (born 1940)—Hungarian immigrant daughter of a practicing witch—founded Dianic Wicca, which worshipped female deities only, serving as founding high priestess of Susan B. Anthony Coven Number One. In what she described in this 1981 essay as "the first witch trial in the US since Salem," Budapest was arrested in 1975 in an LAPD sting for reading the tarot in her Venice, California, candle store—fortune-telling was illegal at the time—then tried and convicted. After a decade of appeals arguing that reading the tarot was a practice of a legitimate religion, Dianic Wicca, she was acquitted under the California Freedom of Religion Act and the offending laws were struck from the books.

I HAVE BEEN a Dianic High Priestess for ten years now. My coven, The Susan B. Anthony Coven Number One, is one of the oldest spiritual groups of revolutionary women in this country, or maybe the world. It's wonderful to lay back, to sigh a sigh of relief—ten years! Not many women's groups have lasted that long in the patriarchy. How did we do it? What have we accomplished in a decade of the Goddess movement?

Such continuity certainly did not come about from assigning power to "higher" beings. In ten years we have had thousands of politically conscious women participate in our rituals. The results speak highly: I have three large flour-sacks of letters from women who changed their lives because of this Goddess exposure. This long tenure didn't come about by "hugging" information either; if there is continuity, there is teaching going on. "Oaths of secrecy," as in the old tradition of Wicca, have been discarded by me and many other feminist Witches. How can you spread information if you have to keep it secret? The "new" women's religion doesn't need extra baggage. As for hierarchy, Oh

Goddess! We carried over our normal revolutionary customs, namely, all are equal, somebody facilitated, and somebody was the High Priestess. Taking responsibility has been hard, but the ten years have testified that many were trained through practicing while "on the job."

I asked Starhawk, a very active High Priestess herself, about hierarchy and she responded:

> I don't know anyone in the Craft setting herself up as a guru-type, and I know even fewer Witches who would be impressed in the least with anyone who did. Leadership and hierarchy are strictly coven matters—and covens vary. Some are more authoritarian, some are quite collective. That's as it should be—because people need different situations in order to develop and grow. Diversity is a Craft value.

For myself, I prefer a coven of equals in which all are leaders. Praise Goddess, I've got one—but it didn't come about instantly or easily. Leadership skills are something women, in this culture, need to learn. We don't get them automatically or by accident; everything in the mainstream culture is set up to keep us from ever getting them, from ever coming into our own power. To discuss that question fully would take a volume. Let me just say that sometimes we need to be trained in order to eventually lead, and that training can take place within a coven. Sometimes we need role models, other women who are leaders. I feel we should encourage women to be strong, to take power-that-comes-from-within (not power-over).

HISTORY OF THE SUSAN B. ANTHONY COVEN NUMBER ONE

In 1971 we were a political group who wanted to accomplish the goals of women's liberation. We decided to combine our spiritual skills with our revolutionary activism in order to speed up the process of arriving at those goals. The traditional Pagan community had never seen such a blend of independent/politico women Witches before. They argued that we were "just using the Goddess for politics" and accused us of being "political, not real Pagans." To this we replied, "Witches have always been political." The legend of Aradia, the first avatar who taught the oppressed to use magical skills to defeat their oppressors, is evidence of such politics. If you define politics as a statement of power relationships among people, it can easily be seen that all religions are "political." In the Goddess religion, the natural, nurturing relationship between mothers and their children is promoted as a model of human relationships. It is not a religion which advocates hierarchical, power-over relationships. The Judeo-Christians, on the other hand, relate to a god who is angry, punitive, vindictive, and who constantly chastises "his" children. Worship of this god is the prototype for competitive, blaming, guilt-ridden relationships among people.

In the early Seventies, it was heretical to say, "The Goddess is using us to bring about social and spiritual change," or to say, as we also did, "We are the Goddess." In those days, High Priestesses were housewives during the six weeks between sabbaths. Only briefly, in circles, were they permitted to acknowledge themselves as Goddess. Priests talked about "their High Priestesses" the way they were accustomed to talking about "their wives." The emerging Dianic tradition shook up the crowns on many heads.

In the mid-Seventies, we faced different opposition: "How can you have balanced energy with no men?" In 1976, we invited priestesses in Ukiah to attend our Midsummer women's circle. As we headed for the woods, many women from traditions other than Dianic followed. As I looked back from halfway up the mountain, I suddenly understood what the men feared. There they were, a small group of men left to themselves with nobody to reflect their glory that evening. In the circle of sixty-eight women, it became clear to all why we didn't need men to raise energy or "balance" ourselves. As they danced naked on the mountaintop in complete freedom and leapt over Midsummer fires, they understood that nothing was wanting there. We all felt blessed. Since then, in many parts of the world, Dianic covens have been founded, bonds have formed, and we have learned about each other and rejoiced.

RELIGION = POLITICS = RELIGION

The police also discovered the Dianics, however. When we opened the Feminist Wicca, our occult supply store, we were constantly watched by the Los Angeles Police Department. One day they arrested me for reading the Tarot for an undercover policewoman. There was a silver lining to this crisis, however: Women's religion was suddenly seen as politically threatening to the patriarchy. Although it was a dubious way to become well known, Goddess religion was being responded to very seriously. There were mass demonstrations in my behalf. Losing the case made us more aware of how political religion really is. We fought the rap for three years before giving up. The Boston conference, later in 1976, seemed almost like a victory celebration. Thousands of women celebrated their personal connections with the Goddess. Morgan McFarland led a beautiful ritual, and some danced naked in the church where the conference was held. We birthed renewed energy for the longer-lasting struggles to follow.

There was opposition within the feminist movement toward the spiritual movement. Those who didn't share the experiences wondered why intelligent women would want to "worship the Goddess." They missed the crucial meaning: It is self-worship. If the Goddess is seen as being "out there" (or "up there"), it is because all living things are a part of Her: trees, stars, moon, honeybees, rocks, and us. Just as She has thousands of different names, She can be worshipped in thousands of different ways. It will take time for women to get rid of patriarchal ways of worshipping. If some see Her as sitting up on a cloud with Her magic wand blessing them, maybe this is a step toward seeing Her inside themselves. In the Susan B. Coven, we teach that women are the Goddess every time we make a choice.

Soon composers started making Goddess songs, and sculptors made Goddess images. The Woman's Building in Los Angeles had an exhibit of altars that women had built for themselves. Our Goddess teaching had inspired women artists, and they are now teaching through their own culture. Such things, however, cannot be learned in one introductory workshop; they may take years and must be taught in a very personal way.

As High Priestess, I wrote, gave lectures, and promoted Goddess-consciousness by ordaining priestesses, hiving new covens, and initiating new members yearly. (I also worked at holding the coven together and at making it possible for us to work and have fun at the same time.) I regularly mail 3,000 copies of our newsletter, *Themis*, sometimes with only the help of my roommate. One of my more frightening duties was finding a place of worship. The coven has been arrested twice for trespassing in Malibu. At our old covenstead, we worshipped undisturbed for three years until one night some rich neighbors noticed the light of about one hundred of our candles burning. My students got a taste of what it's like to belong to an unpopular religion when six police cars came after us with shotguns, looking for "female sacrifices." Two years later, the police knew our names and did not arrest us; they just made us leave. They had received a complaint from a house lower down on the mountain. I angrily stomped my foot, pointed to the house which had twice called the police on us and said, "The third time YOU GO!" (This place today is known as the Great Malibu Landslide.)

CAROL GILLIGAN

(from) *In a Different Voice: Psychological Theory and Women's Development*

Feminist psychologists were already questioning the deep, sometimes subconscious structures of patriarchy when, in the mid-1970s, Carol Gilligan (born 1936), a psychology professor at the Harvard School of Education, noticed that studies of morality left women out when theorizing about all of humanity. While interviewing women about "conceptions of self and morality," she began to hear "a different voice," more likely to consider morality in terms of relationship and community—"an ethic of care"—than the prevailing moral voice, which emphasized abstract principles of justice. Some feminists decried Gilligan's observation of gendered difference as a danger to the struggle for women's equality, while others welcomed her conclusion that "an ethic of care" be more evenly shared by the sexes. Here is an excerpt from her book *In a Different Voice* (1982).

"IT IS obvious," Virginia Woolf says, "that the values of women differ very often from the values which have been made by the other sex" (1929, p. 76). Yet, she adds, "it is the masculine values that prevail." As a result, women come to question the normality of their feelings and to alter their judgments in deference to the opinion of others. In the nineteenth century novels written by women, Woolf sees at work "a mind which was slightly pulled from the straight and made to alter its clear vision in deference to external authority." The same deference to the values and opinions of others can be seen in the judgments of twentieth century women. The difficulty women experience in finding or speaking publicly in their own voices emerges repeatedly in the form of qualification and self-doubt, but also in intimations of a divided judgment, a public assessment and private assessment which are fundamentally at odds.

Yet the deference and confusion that Woolf criticizes in women derive from the values she sees as their strength. Women's deference is rooted not only in their social subordination but also in the substance of their moral concern. Sensitivity to the needs of others and the assumption of responsibility for taking care lead women to attend to voices other than their own and to include in their judgment other points of view. Women's moral weakness, manifest in an apparent diffusion and confusion of judgment, is thus inseparable from women's moral strength, an overriding concern with relationships and responsibilities. The reluctance to judge may itself be indicative of the care and concern for others that infuse the psychology of women's development and are responsible for what is generally seen as problematic in its nature.

Thus women not only define themselves in a context of human relationship but also judge themselves in terms of their ability to care. Women's place in man's life cycle has been that of nurturer, caretaker, and helpmate, the weaver of those networks of relationships on which she in turn relies. But while women have thus taken care of men, men have, in their theories of psychological development, as in their economic arrangements, tended to assume or devalue that care. When the focus on individuation and individual achievement extends into adulthood and maturity is equated with personal autonomy, concern with relationships appears as a weakness of women rather than as a human strength (Miller, 1976).

The discrepancy between womanhood and adulthood is nowhere more evident than in the studies on sex-role stereotypes reported by Broverman, Vogel, Broverman, Clarkson, and Rosenkrantz (1972). The repeated finding of these studies is that the qualities deemed necessary for adulthood—the capacity for autonomous thinking, clear decision-making, and responsible action—are those associated with masculinity and considered undesirable as attributes of the feminine self. The stereotypes suggest a splitting of love and work that relegates expressive capacities to women while placing instrumental abilities in the masculine domain. Yet looked at from a different perspective, these stereotypes reflect a conception of adulthood that is itself out of balance, favoring the separateness of the individual self over connection to others, and leaning more toward an autonomous life of work than toward the interdependence of love and care.

The discovery now being celebrated by men in mid-life of the importance of intimacy, relationships, and care is something that women have known from the beginning. However, because that knowledge in women has been considered "intuitive" or "instinctive," a function of anatomy coupled with destiny, psychologists have neglected to describe its development. In my research, I have found that women's moral development centers on the elaboration of that knowledge and thus delineates a critical line of psychological development in the lives of both of the sexes. The subject of moral development not only provides the final illustration of the reiterative pattern in the observation and assessment of sex differences in the literature on human development, but also indicates more particularly why the nature and significance of women's development has been for so long obscured and shrouded in mystery.

ELLEN WILLIS

(from) Toward a Feminist Sexual Revolution

A journalist and cultural critic—she was *The New Yorker's* first pop music critic—
Ellen Willis (1941–2006) was a major radical feminist thinker and organizer (she
cofounded, in 1969, the radical feminist group Redstockings). A self-described
"left libertarian," she championed the 1960s counterculture. Her essays, published
in five collections (two of them posthumous), constitute a crucial body of radical
feminist theory. Over four decades, she took on right-wing religious radicalism and
left-wing social conservatism in her writing, analyzing such key feminist concerns
as sexuality, the family, abortion, pornography, popular culture, and divisions within
feminism. In this excerpt from her searching 1982 essay "Toward a Feminist Sexual
Revolution," originally published in *Social Text*, Willis considers women's sexual
oppression and argues for women's sexual freedom.

I

THE TRADITIONAL patriarchal family maintains sexual law and order on
two fronts. It regulates the relations between the sexes, enforcing male
dominance, female subordination, and the segregation of "masculine" and
"feminine" spheres. It also regulates sexuality per se, defining as illicit any
sexual activity unrelated to reproduction or outside the bounds of heterosexual, monogamous marriage. Accordingly, the new right's militant defense
of the traditional family and its values has a dual thrust: it is at once a male-
supremacist backlash against feminism and a reaction by cultural conservatives
of both sexes against the "sexual revolution" of the past twenty years.

There is, of course, an integral connection between sexism and sexual
repression. The suppression of women's sexual desire and pleasure, the denial
of our right to control reproduction, and the enforcement of female abstinence outside marriage have been—together with our exclusion from equal
participation in economic and political activity—primary underpinnings of
male supremacy. Conversely, a restrictive sexual morality inevitably constrains
women more than men, even in religious subcultures that profess a single

standard. Not only is unwanted pregnancy a built-in punishment for female participation in sex (assuming the prohibition of birth control and abortion on the one hand, and lesbianism on the other) and therefore a powerful inhibitor; it is visible evidence of sexual "delinquency," which subjects women who break the rules to social sanctions their male partners never have to face. Still, it is important to recognize that the right's opposition to sexual permissiveness— as expressed in its attacks on abortion, homosexuality, "pornography" (defined as any sexually explicit material), sex education, and adolescents' access to contraception and abortion without parental consent—has consequences for both sexes. Gays and teenagers are obvious targets. But the success of the "pro-family" agenda would also impinge on the lives of adult heterosexual men, who would have to contend with the unwanted pregnancies of their wives and lovers, women's increased sexual fears and inhibitions, restrictions on frank discussion and public legitimation of sex and sexual fantasy, and a general chilling of the sexual atmosphere. While some men are willing to accept such constraints on their own freedom in order to reassert certain traditional controls over women, many are not.

The dual focus of pro-family politics, on feminism and on sex itself, has serious implications for feminist theory and strategy. It means that feminists cannot define their opposition to the pro-family movement solely in terms of defending female autonomy against male power, nor can they ignore the fact that conflict over sexual morality cuts across gender lines. If the women's movement is to organize effectively against the right, it will have to develop a political theory of sexuality and in particular an analysis of the relation between feminism and sexual freedom. Such an analysis would help feminists to identify and avoid responses to sexual issues that unwittingly undercut feminist aims. It would clarify many disagreements among women who regard themselves as feminists. It would also enable feminists to seek alliances with male opponents of the right's sexual politics—alliances that are undoubtedly necessary if the battle is to be won—on the basis of a clear understanding of mutual interests, differences that need to be resolved to achieve a working coalition, and issues on which it is possible to agree to disagree. The intensity of current debate on sex among feminists and gay activists reflects a visceral comprehension—if not always an articulate understanding—of how much is at stake.

At present, the right has its feminist opponents at an enormous disadvantage. The pro-family movement has a coherent ideology and program whose anti-feminist and anti-sexual aspects reinforce each other. In contrast, feminists are ambivalent, confused, and divided in their views on sexual freedom. While there have been feminist sexual libertarians in both the 19th century and contemporary movements, for the most part women's liberation and sexual liberation have developed as separate, often antagonistic causes. The sexual libertarian movement that began in the 1950s was conspicuously male-dominated and male-supremacist. Though it advocated a single standard of freedom from sexual guilt and conventional moral restrictions, it displayed no insight into the social reasons for women's greater inhibition and conformity to moral norms. On the contrary, women were blamed—often in virulently misogynist terms—for adhering to the sexual prohibitions men and a patriarchal society had forced on them. At the same time male libertarians intensified women's sexual anxieties by equating repression with the desire for love and commitment, and exalting sex without emotion or attachment as the ideal. From this perspective liberation for men meant rebelling against the demands of women, while liberation for women meant the opportunity (read obligation) to shuck their "hangups" about casual sex.

The question that remained unasked was whether men had sexual hangups of their own. Was the rejection of any link between sexual desire and emotional involvement really an expression of freedom—or merely another form of repression? To what extent did men's demand for "pure" sex represent a predatory disregard of women as people—an attitude that could only reinforce the conventionally feminine sexual reluctance, passivity, and unresponsiveness that men found so frustrating? There was also the touchy issue of whether sex as conventionally initiated and orchestrated by men was pleasurable for women. In theory there was much concern with female orgasm and the need for men to satisfy women; in practice that concern often translated into a demand that women corroborate men's ideas about female sexuality and protect men's egos by acting satisfied whether they were or not. A conservative popular Freudianism neatly coopted the idea that women had a right to sexual fulfillment by preaching that such fulfillment could be achieved only through "mature" acceptance of the feminine role: in effect women were told that to actively assert their sexual needs would make satisfaction of those needs impossible; if they were submissive and yet unsatisfied it meant they weren't submissive enough. For women trapped in this logic, the theoretical right to orgasm became a new source of pain, inadequacy, and self-blame. Finally, the sexual revolution did not seriously challenge the taboo on lesbianism (or homosexuality in general).

At its inception, the contemporary women's liberation movement was dominated by young women who had grown up during or since the emergence of sexual libertarian ideology; many radical feminists came out of the left and the counterculture, where that ideology was particularly strong. Unsurprisingly, one of the first issues to surface in the movement was women's pent-up rage at men's one-sided, exploitative view of sexual freedom. From our consciousness-raising sessions we concluded that women couldn't win no matter how they behaved. We were still oppressed by a sexual double standard that while less rigid was by no means obsolete: women who took too literally their supposed right to sexual freedom and pleasure were regularly put down as "easy," "aggressive," or "promiscuous." Heterosexual women still lived in fear of unwanted pregnancy; in 1968 abortion was illegal—except in the most dire circumstances—in every state. Yet at the same time men were demanding that women have sex on their terms, unmindful of the possible consequences, and without reference to our own feelings and needs. In addition to suffering sexual frustration from the inhibitions instilled by repressive parents, fear of pregnancy, and men's sexual judgments and exploitative behavior, we had to swallow the same men's humiliating complaints about how neurotic, frigid, and unliberated we were. Unfortunately, the movement's efforts to make political sense of this double bind led to confusions in feminist thinking about sexuality that are still unresolved.

At least in theory, organized feminism from the 60s to the present has been united in endorsing sexual freedom for women, including the right to express our sexual needs freely, to engage in sexual activity for our own pleasure, to have sex and bear children outside marriage, to control our fertility, to refuse sex with any particular man or all men, to be lesbians. Almost as universally, feminists have regarded male sexuality with suspicion if not outright hostility. From the beginning radical feminists argued that freedom as men defined it was against women's interests; if anything men already had too much freedom, at women's expense. One faction in the movement strongly defended women's traditional demands for marriage and monogamy against the anti–nuclear family, sexual liberationist rhetoric of the counterculture. Proponents of this view held that the sexual revolution simply legitimized the age-old tendency of men in a male-supremacist society to coerce, cajole, or fool women into giving them sex without getting anything—love, respect, responsibility for the children, or even erotic pleasure—in return.[1] At the other extreme were feminists who argued that under present conditions, any kind of sexual contact

1. Some radical feminists argued that there was nothing wrong with marriage, per se, only with sex roles within marriage. (In a sense this position was an early version of Betty Friedan's "pro-family" feminism, minus the sentimental glossing over of male power.) Others maintained that while sexual freedom in the context of women's liberation was an ultimate goal, for now it was in our interest to resist the sexual revolution. See, for example, Shulamith Firestone, *The Dialectic of Sex* (Morrow, 1970), pp. 160–163. Another version of this argument was advanced by Kathie Sarachild, an influential theorist in the early movement, in "Hot and Cold Flashes," *The Newsletter*, Vol. I #3, May 1, 1969: "We women can use marriage as the

with men, in marriage or out, was oppressive, and that the issue for women was how to resist the relentless social pressure to be with a man.[2] Later, lesbian separatists elaborated this argument, claiming that only women were capable of understanding and satisfying women's sexual needs.

Although the idea that in order to achieve equality women's sexual freedom must be expanded and men's restricted has a surface common-sense logic, in practice it is full of contradictions. For one thing, the same social changes that allow greater freedom for women inevitably mean greater freedom for men. Historically, a woman's main protection from sexual exploitation has been to be a "good girl" and demand marriage as the price of sex—in other words, relinquish the freedom to spontaneously express her sexuality in order to pre-serve its bargaining power. Furthermore, this traditional strategy will not work for individual women if most women "scab" by abandoning it, which implies the need for some form of social or moral pressure to keep women in line. (If one assumes that women will voluntarily decline to take advantage of their increased freedom, then demanding it makes no sense in the first place.) In practice, relaxing social condemnation of female "unchastity" and permitting women access to birth control and abortion allays social concern about men's "ruining" or impregnating respectable women, and so invariably reduces the pressure on men—both from women and from other men—to restrain their demands for casual sex. Thus the feminist critique of male sexuality tends to bolster the familiar conservative argument that a morality restricting sex to marriage is in women's interest—indeed, that its purpose is to protect women from selfish male lust.

Another difficulty is that judgments of men's heterosexual behavior nec-essarily imply judgments about what women want. Dissenters within fem-inist groups immediately challenged the prevailing judgments, arguing with monogamists that they wanted to sleep with more than one man, or that they didn't want the state messing into their sex lives, and arguing with separatists that they enjoyed sex with men. As a result, assumptions about what women want were soon amended to authoritative pronouncements on what women *really* want/ought to want/would want if they were not intimidated/bought off/brainwashed by men. The ironic consequence has been the development of feminist sexual orthodoxies that curtail women's freedom by setting up the

---

'dictatorship of the proletariat' in the family revolution. When male supremacy is completely eliminated, marriage, like the state, will wither away."

2. Of the early radical feminist groups taking a female separatist position, the most influential were The Feminists in New York City and Cell 16 in Boston.

movement as yet another source of guilt-provoking rules about what women should do and feel.

That irony is compounded by another: the orthodoxies in question dovetail all too well with traditional patriarchal ideology. This is most obviously true of polemics in favor of heterosexual monogamy, but it is no less true of lesbian separatism, which in recent years has had far more impact on feminist thinking. There have been two overlapping but distinct tendencies in lesbian feminist politics: the first has emphasized lesbianism as a forbidden erotic choice and lesbians as an oppressed sexual minority; the other—aligning itself with the separatist faction that surfaced in the radical feminist movement before lesbianism as such became an issue—has defined lesbianism primarily as a political commitment to separate from men and bond with women.[3] The latter tendency has generated a sexual ideology best described as neo-Victorian. It regards heterosexual relations as more or less synonymous with rape, on the the grounds that male sexuality is by definition predatory and sadistic: men are exclusively "genitally-oriented" (a phrase that is always used pejoratively) and uninterested in loving relationships. Female sexuality, in contrast, is defined as tender, nonviolent, and not necessarily focused on the genitals; intimacy and physical warmth are more important to us than orgasm. The early pre-lesbian separatists argued that celibacy was a reasonable alternative to sleeping with men, and some suggested that the whole idea of a compelling sexual drive was a male invention designed to keep women in their place; women didn't need sex, and men's lust was less for pleasure than for power.[4] In short, to the neo-Victorians men are beasts who are only after one thing, while women are nice girls who would just as soon skip it. The inescapable implication is that women who profess to enjoy sex with men, especially penile-vaginal intercourse itself, are liars or masochists; in either case they have chosen (or been forced) to be victims and to uphold an oppressive system. Nor are lesbians automatically exempt from criticism; gay women whose sexual proclivities do not conform to the approved feminine stereotype are assumed to be corrupted by heterosexism.

Though neo-Victorianism has been most militantly promoted by lesbian separatists, in modified form—i.e., allowing that men (some men at least)

3. For a lucid exposition of this distinction I am indebted to Alice Echols' paper, "Cultural Feminism: Feminist Capitalism and the Anti-Pornography Movement." Versions of this paper will be published in a future issue of *Social Text* and in the forthcoming anthology on feminism and sexuality, *The Powers of Desire*, ed. Ann Snitow, Christine Stansell, and Sharon Thompson, to be published in 1983 by Monthly Review Press.

4. The best known exponents of these views were Ti-Grace Atkinson, of the Feminists, and Dana Densmore, of Cell 16.

can change their ways and be good lovers—it has also had wide appeal for heterosexual feminists. (Conversely, lesbians have been among its loudest critics; this is not a gay-straight split.) Its most popular current expression is the anti-pornography movement, which has seized on pornography as an all-purpose symbol of sex that is genitally-oriented, hence male, hence sadistic and violent, while invoking the concept of "erotica" as code for sex that is gentle, romantic, relationship-oriented—in a word, feminine. Clearly, this conventional view of female as opposed to male sexuality is consistent with many women's subjective experience. Indeed, there are probably few women who don't identify with it to some degree. But to take that experience at face value is to ignore its context: a patriarchal society that has systematically inhibited female sexuality and defined direct, active physical desire as a male prerogative. Feminist neo-Victorians have made the same mistake—only with the sexes reversed—as male libertarians who criticize female sexual behavior while adopting stereotypical male sexuality as the standard for judging sexual health and happiness. In the process they have actively reinforced the larger society's taboos on women's genital sexuality. From a conservative perspective, a woman who has aggressive genital desires and acts on them is "bad" and "unwomanly"; from the neo-Victorian perspective she is "brainwashed" and "male-identified."

Overtly or implicitly, many feminists have argued that sexual coercion is a more important problem for women than sexual repression. In the last few years, the women's movement has increasingly emphasized violence against women as a primary—if not *the* primary—concern. While sexual violence, coercion, and harassment have always been feminist issues, earlier feminist analyses tended to regard physical force as one of several ways that men insure women's compliance to a sexist system, and in particular to their subordinate wife-and-mother role. The main function of sexual coercion, in this view, is to curb women's freedom, including their sexual freedom. Rape and the tacit social tolerance of it convey the message that simply by being sexual, women are "provocative" and deserve punishment, especially if they step out of their place (the home) or transgress society's definition of the "good" (inhibited) woman. Similarly, sexual harassment on the street or on the job, and exploitative sexual demands by male "sexual revolutionaries," punish women for asserting themselves, sexually and otherwise, in the world.

The current feminist preoccupation with male violence has a very different focus. Rape and pornography, redefined as a form of rape, are regarded not as aspects of a larger sexist system but as the foundation and essence of sexism, while sexual victimization is seen as the central fact of women's oppression. Just as male violence against women is equated with male supremacy, freedom from violence is equated with women's liberation.[5] From this standpoint the positive aspect of freedom—freedom for women to *act*—is at best a secondary concern, and freedom for women to assert an active genital sexuality is, by the logic of neo-Victorianism, a contradiction in terms.

Whatever its intent, the objective effect of feminists' emphasis on controlling male sexuality—particularly when that emphasis is combined with a neo-Victorian view of women's nature and the conviction that securing women's safety from male aggression should be the chief priority of the women's movement—is to undercut feminist opposition to the pro-family backlash. It provides powerful reinforcement for the right's efforts to manipulate women's fear of untrammeled male sexuality, thus intimidating women into stifling their own impulses toward freedom in order to cling to what little protection the traditional roles still offer. The convergence of neo-Victorian and pro-family ideology is most striking in the recent attempts by so-called "feminists for life" to argue that abortion is "violence against women" and a way for men to escape responsibility for their sexual behavior. While this argument did not come from within the feminist movement but from anti-abortion pacifists seeking to justify their position to feminists, it is perfectly consistent with neo-Victorian logic. No tendency in organized feminism has yet advocated outlawing abortion, but one does occasionally hear the argument that feminists should spend less energy defending abortion and more on educating women to understand that the real solution to unwanted pregnancy is to stop sleeping with men.[6]

Neo-Victorians have also undermined feminist opposition to the right by equating feminism with their own sexual attitudes, in effect reading out of the

5. The following is a good example of this kind of thinking: ". . . if we are going to destroy the effects of pornography in our lives . . . We must each be able to visualize on a grand scale what it is that we want for ourselves and for our society . . . Would you try now to think of what it would be like to live in a society in which we are not, every minute, bombarded with sexual violence? Would you try to visualize what it would be like to go to the movies and not see it, to be able to walk home and not be afraid of it . . . If we set that as our goal and demand nothing less, we will not stop fighting until we've achieved it."—Kathleen Barry, "Beyond Pornography: From Defensive Politics to Creating a Vision," in *Take Back The Night: Women on Pornography*, ed. Laura Lederer (Morrow, 1980), p. 312.

6. The June, 1981, issue of the feminist newspaper *off our backs* published two letters to the editor on this theme. One of the writers, while affirming her unequivocal stand in favor of legal abortion, protests, "Why are we fighting so hard to make it 'safe' to fuck with men? . . . Why don't we focus on eliminating the need for abortion and birth control?" The other letter states, "Compulsory pregnancy results from compulsory penetration . . . So I'm getting impatient to know when we will really take control over our bodies and not let ourselves be penetrated?" and goes on to assert "the inescapable fact that since I did not allow men to have control over my body, I could not then turn around and claim control over my baby's body."

movement any woman who disagrees with them. Since their notion of proper feminist sexuality echoes conventional moral judgments and the anti-sexual propaganda presently coming from the right, their guilt-mongering has been quite effective. Many feminists who are aware that their sexual feelings contradict the neo-Victorian ideal have lapsed into confused and apologetic silence. No doubt there are also thousands of women who have quietly concluded that if this ideal is feminism, then feminism has nothing to do with them. The result is widespread apathy, dishonesty, and profound disunity in a movement faced with a determined enemy that is threatening its very existence.

II

The foregoing suggests that feminists are at a theoretical impasse. If a feminist politics that advocates restrictions on male sexuality leads inexorably to the sexual repression of women and the strengthening of anti-feminist forces, such a politics is obviously untenable. But how can women support sexual freedom for both sexes without legitimizing the most oppressive aspects of male sexual behavior? I believe our hope for resolving this dilemma lies in reexamining certain widely shared assumptions about sex, male versus female sexuality, and the meaning of sexual liberation.

The philosophy of the "sexual revolution" as we know it is an extension of liberalism: it defines sexual freedom as the simple absence of external restrictions—laws and overt social taboos—on sexual information and activity. Since most people accept this definition, there is widespread agreement that we are already a sexually emancipated society. The easy availability of casual sex, the virtual lack of restrictions (at least for adults) on sexual information and sexually explicit material, the accessibility (for adults again) of contraception, the legalization of abortion, the proliferation of massage parlors and sex clubs, the ubiquity of sexual images and references in the mass media, the relaxation of taboos against "deviant" sexual practices—all are regularly cited as evidence that this culture has largely overcome its anti-sexual history. At the same time, sexual liberalism has clearly not brought nirvana. Noting that "liberated" sexuality is often depressingly shallow, exploitative, and joyless, many men as well as women have concluded that sexual liberation has been tried and found wanting, that it is irrelevant or even inimical to a serious program for social change.

This is a superficial view. In the first place, this society is far from endorsing, even in principle, people's right to consensual sexual relations, of whatever sort they prefer, as a basic liberty. (Skeptics are invited to imagine public reaction to a proposed constitutional amendment guaranteeing freedom of sexual association.) There is strong and stubborn resistance to legalizing—let alone accepting as socially and morally legitimate—all sexual acts between consent- ing adults; children have no recognized sexual rights at all, and adolescents virtually none.[7] But the basic problem with this dismissal of sexual freedom as a valid political issue is that it focuses on the quantity and variety of sexual activity, rather than the quality of sexual experience. Political opposition to restrictive sexual mores is ultimately based on the premise that a gratifying sexual life is a human need whose denial causes unnecessary and unjustified suffering. Certainly, establishing people's right to pursue sexual happiness with a consenting partner is a precondition for ending that suffering. Yet as most of us have had occasion to discover, it is entirely possible to "freely" partici- pate in a sexual act and feel frustrated, indifferent, or even repelled. From a radical standpoint, then, sexual liberation involves not only the abolition of restrictions but the positive presence of social and psychological conditions that foster satisfying sexual relations. And from that standpoint, this culture is still deeply repressive. Most obviously, sexual inequality and the resulting antagonism between men and women constitute a devastating barrier to sex- ual happiness. I will argue in addition that sexual liberalism notwithstanding, most children's upbringing produces adults with profoundly negative attitudes toward sex. Under these conditions, the relaxation of sexual restrictions leads people to try desperately to overcome the obstacles to satisfaction through compulsive sexual activity and preoccupation with sex. The emphasis on sex that currently permeates our public life—especially the enormous demand for sexual advice and therapy—attests not to our sexual freedom but to our continuing sexual frustration.

It is in this context that we need to examine the male sexual pattern femi- nists have protested—the emphasis on conquest and dominance, the tendency to abstract sex from love and social responsibility. Sexual liberalism has allowed many men to assert these patterns in ways that were once socially taboo, and to impose them on reluctant women. But to conclude from this fact that male sexual freedom is inherently oppressive is to make the uncritical assumption that men find predatory, solipsistic sexual relations satisfying and inherently preferable to sex with affection and mutuality. As I have noted, some femi- nists argue that male sexuality is naturally sadistic. Others grant that men's

---

7. In the ongoing debate over "the epidemic of teenage pregnancy" and whether it is best dealt with by providing teenagers with contraceptives or giving them lectures on chastity, birth control advocates have argued that access to contraception does not increase teenage sexual activity. So far as I know, no "responsible" organization has dared to suggest that adolescents have sexual needs and should have the right to satisfy them.

predatory tendencies are a function of sexism, but assume that they are a simple, direct expression of men's (excessive) freedom and power, the implication being that anyone who has the opportunity to dominate and use other people sexually will of course want to take advantage of it.

This assumption is open to serious question. If one pays attention to what men consciously or unwittingly reveal about their sexual attitudes—in their fiction and confessional writing (see *Portnoy's Complaint* and its epigoni), in their political polemics (see George Gilder's *Sexual Suicide*), in sociological and psychological studies (see *The Hite Report on Male Sexuality* or Lillian Rubin's *Worlds of Pain*), in everyday interaction with women—the picture that emerges is far more complicated and ambiguous. Most men, in fact, profess to want and need mutual sexual love, and often behave accordingly, though they have plenty of opportunity to do otherwise. Many men experience both tender and predatory sexual feelings, toward the same or different women, and find the contradiction bewildering and disturbing; others express enormous pain over their inability to combine sex with love. Often men's impulses to coerce and degrade women seem to express not a confident assumption of dominance but a desire to retaliate for feelings of rejection, humiliation, and impotence: as many men see it, they need women sexually more than women need them, an intolerable imbalance of power.[8] Furthermore, much male sexual behavior clearly reflects men's irrational fears that loss of dominance means loss of maleness itself, that their choice is to "act like a man" or be castrated, to embrace the role of oppressor or be degraded to the status of victim.

None of this is to deny men's objective social power over women, their reluctance to give up that power, or their tendency to blame women for their unhappiness rather than recognize that their own oppressive behavior is largely responsible for women's sexual diffidence. My point is only that the behavior that causes women so much grief evidently brings men very little joy; on the contrary, men appear to be consumed with sexual frustration, rage, and anxiety. With their compulsive assertions of power they continually sabotage their efforts to love and be loved. Such self-defeating behavior cannot, in any meaningful sense, be described as free. Rather it suggests that for all the unquestionable advantages men derive from "acting like a man" in a male-supremacist society, the price is repression and deformation of spontaneous sexual feeling.

---

8. Shere Hite's *The Hite Report on Male Sexuality* (Knopf, 1981) includes many revealing comments from men on this particular theme: see her chapters on "Men's View of Women and Sex" and "Rape, Paying Women for Sex, and Pornography."

DEIRDRE ENGLISH

The Fear That Feminism Will Free Men First

Deirdre English (born 1948) was editor-in-chief of the progressive San Francisco–based magazine *Mother Jones* from 1980 to 1986, years during which she was the only woman to head a national opinion magazine other than *Ms.* English brought a feminist sensibility to *Mother Jones*, publishing many feminist authors, such as Barbara Ehrenreich, Maxine Hong Kingston, and Alice Walker (see their separate entries in this volume). She also led the way in featuring female investigative reporters, cartoonists, photographers, and artists. In the essay presented here, from the anthology *Powers of Desire* (1983), English uses a feminist analysis to present a sympathetic portrait of right-wing antifeminist women.

FOR FEMINISTS, the most difficult aspect of the 1980s' backlash against women's abortion rights, and other emancipatory new rights and attitudes related to sex, is the fact that a large part of the anti-choice ("pro-life") movement is made up of women. What we have for the past ten years grown accustomed to calling the "women's movement" claimed to represent the collective good of all women: the opposition was expected to be male. But now we are faced with an opposing women's movement, and one that also claims to stand for the best interests of all women. It is as confusing, as frustrating, as if, at the height of the civil rights movement, a large percentage of blacks had suddenly organized to say: "Wait a minute. We don't want equal rights. We like things just the way they are."

The very existence of such a movement represents a deep crisis in the community of women, and a profound challenge to the analytical and synthetical powers of feminist theory. Before proceeding, an old feminist touchstone is a good reminder: though we may be in conflict with them, other women rarely prove to be our real enemies. Even in opposing the politics of the anti-feminist woman, we must begin by recognizing and honoring her experiences, her prospects, her hopes and fears.

To do that, it is essential to separate the motivations of those men who organize against women's rights and the women who do so, even when they are found holding the same credo in the same organizations. For while men in the anti-abortion movement stand to increase the measure of male control over women, the women can gain nothing but greater sexual submission. Now that is a suspicious thing in itself, because any people asking only to give in to a more powerful group must be well convinced that their survival is at stake. After all, the anti-feminist woman is neither stupid nor incompetent, whatever she may wish her male leaders to believe. Legitimately enough, she has her own self-interest in mind, in a world in which she did not create the options.

THE OTHER WOMAN

Clearly, the anti-choice activist is not primarily concerned with refusing an abortion for herself; that she has the power to do no matter what the laws are. (By contrast, women in the pro-choice movement are almost invariably women who feel, at some level, a personal need for abortion rights.) But no one is taking away another person's right to bear children, no feminist is circumscribing individual ethical or religious beliefs that would prohibit abortion. What is solely at question to the anti-choice activist is the *other* woman's right to make this decision herself; her objective is to refuse social legitimation for abortion decisions that are not her own.

The anti-abortionists are, as they have been accused, seeking to impose their morality on society. But that is part of the very definition of moralism: a *moralist* is "one concerned with regulating the morals of others." The anti-abortion movement is a perfect example of a moralistic movement, and it demonstrates some interesting things about the functions of moral systems.

In opposing the Right-to-Lifers, pro-choice advocates most frequently argue that a woman has an absolute right to control her own body. The insistence on individual rights is at the foundation of the feminist position. A woman's right to control her own body encompasses endless new meanings in feminism: from the right to refuse sex (as in marital rape) to the right to a freely chosen sexuality; from the right to be protected from sexual violence to the right to plan one's own reproductivity. The complete realization of those rights alone would mark a new era for women. For now, the recognition of woman's body as the *terra firma* of female liberation must be counted as one of the great political accomplishments of our day. But it is far from enough.

After all, this is a society: we are interdependent; individual actions have repercussions. The struggle is not and can never be only over the actual act of abortion. The struggle is necessarily over a larger sexual morality—and moral systems do have a bearing on virtually everybody's behavior. The anti-abortion people have tried to insist on single-issue politics partly because it is much easier for them to attack the keystone of abortion than to defend the system of morality that is tied to compulsory motherhood. It falls to us to identify the moral system they are upholding and, at the same time, to define our own.

The anti-feminist woman is right about one crucial thing: the other woman's right to have an abortion does affect her. It does something very simple and, to many women, very upsetting: it takes away their ability *not* to choose. Where abortion is available, the birth of every baby becomes a willed choice, a purposeful act. And that new factor destroys the set of basic assumptions on which many traditional marriages have been based. It breaks the rules and wrecks the game.

The Sex Contract

Remember the rules of the old game? They began with this: men did not get to have sex with women (at least not women of their own class or higher) unless they married them. Then men were morally obligated to provide for the children they had helped to conceive. In other words, sex was supposed to incur a major responsibility for men—as it did for women. Only thirty years ago, the average marrying age in the United States was twenty for women and twenty-two for men, and hundreds of thousands of brides have been pregnant on their wedding day.

Men always complained about this sexual bargain. "Nature kidded us," said a young Irish Catholic father of two in a short story by Frank O'Connor. "We had our freedom and we didn't value it. Now our lives are run for us by women." But men's regrets, however deeply felt, were still the complaints of the relatively more powerful party. It was women who, for physical and financial reasons, really *needed* marriage.

In a society that effectively condoned widespread male sexual violence and severely restricted economic opportunities for women outside of marriage, the deck was heavily stacked. If men did not "value their freedom," women had little freedom to value. The one short-lived power women had was withholding sex; and even that was only good until marriage—possibly periodically thereafter, with the more tolerant husbands. But in general, women had to earn their keep not only with sex, but with submissiveness, and acceptance of the male not as an equal partner but as a superior. Seen in these terms, the marriage contract seems a little more like extortion under the threat of abandonment.

But to point this out is not the way to play the game. The essential thing about the system—like moral systems in general—is that everyone must play by the same rules. In the past, the community of women has often been hard on those who "give away" for free—or for money—what the rest trade for love and marriage. Then came birth control, the sexual revolution, and legalized abortion.

THE ESCAPE CLAUSE

It was the availability of relatively reliable contraception that provided the first escape clause to the old marital Russian roulette, both for men and women. The "99 percent effective" pill sparked the sexual revolution in the 1960s and 1970s and permitted women for the first time in history to decisively separate intercourse from reproduction. (Only after that historic schism could the modern woman's new fascination with discovering her own sexuality begin to emerge.)

For the most part, women of all classes and religions enthusiastically welcomed the advent of reliable contraception. True, it did have the effect of releasing men from some responsibility for their sexual acts, but the gains for women seemed much greater. Sexual liberation and birth control brought women new-found sexual pleasure, began to erode the double standard, allowed women to plan their pregnancies—and therefore participate in the work world on new terms—and in general seemed to tend to equalize the sexes. Other things, unfortunately, did not change so fast. Especially not the economy.

CATCH 22

Most women who want to have children still cannot make it, financially, without a man. In an era in which an increasingly larger number of people are spending significant parts of their lives outside of the marriage coupling, the socioeconomic differences between men and women become increasingly, painfully obvious. According to 1978 Bureau of Labor statistics, only some 7 percent of women make more than $15,000 per year, while more than 46 percent of men do. Marriage is still the major means of economic stability—even survival—for women.

In this sense, men have reaped more than their share of benefits from women's liberation. If women hold jobs, no matter how poorly paid, men may more easily renounce any responsibility for the economic support of women and children. Thus woman's meager new economic independence, and her greater sexual freedom outside the bounds of marriage, have allowed men to garner great new freedoms. Because there is no "trick of nature" to make the link between sex and fatherhood, and little social stigma on he who loves and leaves, a woman faces the abdication of any male responsibility for pregnancy—let alone for any ensuing children. If a woman gets pregnant, the man who twenty years ago might have married her may feel today that he is gallant if he splits the cost of an abortion. The man who might have remained in a dead-end marriage out of a sense of duty finds increasingly that he faces no great social disapproval if he walks out on his family, even while his kids are still in diapers.

Divorce leaves women putting a higher percentage of both their incomes and their time into child care. According to the U.S. Census, the number of one-parent families headed by divorced women jumped almost 200 percent in one decade—from 956,000 in 1970 to 2.7 million in 1981. During the same period, the number of single-parent families headed by men actually declined. (Nationally, there are more youthful products of divorce cared for by relatives other than a parent than by their fathers alone.)

It is also worth noting the difference in the economic impact of divorce on fathers versus mothers. Roughly 40 percent of absent fathers contribute *no* money for child support after divorce, and the other 60 percent average a contribution of less than $2,000 per year. A recent study of 3,000 divorces showed, shockingly, that men improved their standard of living an average of 42 percent in the first year following divorce, while women with children saw their living standard decline by 73 percent. Under these circumstances, the fear has risen that feminism will free men first—and might never get around to freeing women.

All this is not to imply that either men or women *should* stay in loveless, unhappy marriages out of some sense of duty. Rather, both sexes need the right to change their circumstances. So far, our progress, like all progress, has been ragged: men, more independent to begin with, have been able to profit from women's new independence sometimes more fully than women themselves.

It seems revealing that the anti-feminist backlash, as well as the anti-sexual-liberation backlash, took so long to develop the momentum that it has today. It is the period of unremitting economic decline that has brought it on, the nightfall of economic prospects for women. It is as though the country reserved judgment during ten or fifteen years of experimentation with sexual politics, as long as economic conditions permitted it. In a climate of affluence, women had more hope of successfully freeing themselves from male-dominant relationships. But today, a greater number of working women are perceiving that the feminist revolution may not rapidly succeed in actually equalizing the material opportunities of the sexes. When working-class men no longer hold their own against unemployment, union-management rollbacks or even inflation, what hope is there for women to close the economic gap between the male and female worker?

Giving up marriage and children for an interesting career may be one thing (although this is an either/or choice that men rarely face), but it may not be a decent trade for a dead-end job in the pink-collar ghetto. If men can no longer support families on a single paycheck, most women certainly cannot. The media presents us with the image of successful management-level women, but in fact even these women are almost always contained in middle-management positions, at under $20,000 a year. For the less-than-fervent feminist who is not prepared to pay any price at all for independence, the future looks bleak.

FEAR AND REACTION

It begins to seem clearer that the anti-feminist woman, like other women, is grappling with the terms of her survival. She is responding to social circumstances—a worsening economy, a lack of support and commitment from men—that feminists did not create and from which feminists also suffer the consequences. The conditions she faces face all women.

The differences lie in our strategies for dealing with all this. The anti-feminist woman's strategy is defensive: reactionary in the sense of reacting to change, with the desire to return to the supposedly simple solutions of the past. Like other patriotic or fundamentalist solutions, like going to war or being "born again," the longed-for return to the old feminine style seems to promise an end to complexity, compromise, and ambivalence. For many of the advocates of the anti-choice movement, the ideal is ready-made and well polished. It is the American family of the 1950s: dad in the den with his pipe, mom in her sunny kitchen with cafe curtains, the girls dressed in pink and the boys in blue. It could be called nostalgic utopianism—the glorification of a lost past rather than an undiscovered future. What has not been accepted is that the road to that ideal is as impossible to find—and to many people, as little desired—as the road back to childhood.

To feminists, the only response to the dilemma of the present lies in pressing onward. We must continue to show how a complete feminist sexual and reproductive politics could lead to the transformation of all society, without curtailing the freedom of any individual. True reproductive freedom, for example, would inevitably require fair opportunities for financial equality, so that women could bear children without facing either dependency or impoverishment. There would be practical child-care support for working parents of both sexes and an equal affirmation by men of their responsibility for parenthood. Yet, the individual's right to choose whether to bear a child would remain at the heart of the feminist position.

Today, the individual decision to have an abortion remains a sobering one; it puts a woman face-to-face with her dreams and her prospects and with the frequently startling fact that she is choosing not to be a passive victim, but rather an active shaper of her existence. The difficulties she will encounter as she continues to try to create her own destiny will repeatedly call for that same strength of will. In demonstrating it, she is already helping to bring about a new order of sexual equality, a world more worthy of the next generation. Few who have clearly seen the vision of that new world will want to turn back.

BETH BRANT

(from) A Gathering of Spirit

As feminist publishing grew, new anthologies reflected both the inclusion of marginalized women writers and the desire of those writers to create their own literary contexts. In late 1978, Bay of Quinte Mohawk poet and writer Beth Brant (1941–2015), also known by her tribal name, Degonwadonti, was invited by Michelle Cliff and Adrienne Rich, editors of the feminist journal *Sinister Wisdom*, to edit an issue devoted to American Indian women. A double issue was published in 1983, titled "A Gathering of Spirit," which included Brant's introduction, excerpted here. It became the basis of the 1988 anthology of the same title published by the lesbian feminist press Firebrand Books. Writers from forty tribes were represented in this first-ever published collection of writing by North American indigenous women to be edited by an indigenous woman.

THE PHYSICAL

I HAVE A two-page list of names, the Native American Directory, and my own list of correspondence. I buy a roll of stamps. I begin sending out the flyer that took me weeks to write. Did it say enough? Did it say too much? Always the questions.

I buy another roll of stamps. Send out the flyer to Indian newspapers, journals, associations, organizations, for I know that what I am looking for will not be gotten from feminist or lesbian/feminist sources. I write personal letters requesting support and help in this important project. I buy yet another roll of stamps, more envelopes, have to get more flyers printed. And the fact is, if *Sinister Wisdom* were not paying for these endless stamps, xeroxing, printing, etc., this would be impossible for me to do.

I wrote everywhere I thought there was a story to tell. I wanted to hear from the women yet unheard. I wanted the voices traditionally silenced to be a part of this collection. So I wrote to prison organizations in the U.S. and Canada. I made contact with the anti-psychiatry network, Native women's health projects. I sent to everyone I could possibly think of and then looked for more. Some women requested flyers of their own to distribute among their friends, their relatives, their workmates. To these women I am indebted. Because they took us seriously. Because they had faith.

After a while it became impossible to keep track of how many letters and flyers were going out. My life from June 1982 to February 1983 seems a flurry of typing, going to the post office, going to the printer, making phone calls, writing more letters. I felt I was heading off something. My own writing suffered. My life became measured by *The Issue*. It had taken over. It had become my work.

As the first letters and poems and stories and photographs came to me, I had to reassess, once again, who it is that we are. And why I was doing this. The answers seemed obvious, but were knotted together in a pattern not quite recognizable. I am doing this because I have to. I am doing this because no one else will do it. I am doing this because it is my work. But there was more. It would come when I was ready.

THE SPIRITUAL

"Dear Beth,

Please help me find out who I am. My mother was Indian, but we were taken from her and put in foster homes. They were white and didn't want to tell us about our mother. I have a name and maybe a place of birth. Do you think you can help me? I always wanted a sister."

"Dear Sister,

These poems might not be what you are looking for, but I send them anyway. I never wrote before, but wanted to share my memories of my grandma with you. My spelling is not so good, but maybe you could clean it up."

"Sehkon,

How good it is that you are doing this for Indian women. Please accept this story in the spirit I give it to you. I am glad a sister is doing this work."

"Dear Beth,

I am in prison. It is hard to be an Indian woman here. But I think about the res, and my father and mother. When I get the loneliest, my grandma comes to visit me. It is very strange to be away from the land. A part of me stays out there with the birds. Please write to me."

Sister. The word comes easily to most of us. Sisterhood. What holds us to that word is our commonness as Indians—as women. We come from different Nations. Our stories are not the same. Our dress is not the same. Our color is not the same. *Yet, we are the same.* Can I tell you how lonely I have been for you? That my search for the spirit had to begin with you?

The letters. The poetry. Telling the stories. Drawing the pictures. As each day begins, there is new language and image sitting in my mailbox. But it is old too. And as I sort through and sift over the words, it becomes clearer to me. *The power of spirit.* Spirit manifested in the land we walk on, the food that faithfully grows out of that dirt. The wool that comes from the sheep we have raised and sheared. The spinning of that wool into cloth for our families, for ourselves. The story that hasn't changed for hundreds, maybe thousands of years. The retelling. The continuity of spirit. We believe in that. We believe in community in its most basic form. We recognize each other. Visible spirit.

I light a candle that has a picture of the Lady of Guadalupe etched on the glass. I do not light the candle because I'm a christian, but because she is an Indian.

On my bulletin board is a holy card of Kateri Tekakwitha. "Bless me Kateri," not because I believe in the racist and misogynist vision of the Blackrobes, but because she is an Indian.

I want to talk about blessings, and endurance, and facing the machine. The everyday shit. The everyday joy. We make no excuses for the way we are, the way we live, the way we paint and write. We are not "stoic" and "noble," we are strong-willed and resisting.

We have a spirit of rage. We are angry women. Angry at white men and their perversions. Their excessive greed and abuse of the earth, sky, and water. Their techno-christian approach to anything that lives, including our children, our people. We are angry at Indian men for their refusals of us. For their limited vision of what constitutes a strong Nation. We are angry at a so-called "women's movement" that always seems to forget we exist. Except in romantic fantasies of earth mother, or equally romantic and dangerous fantasies about Indian-woman-as victim. Women lament our *lack* of participation in feminist events, yet we are either referred to as *et ceteras* in the naming of women of color, or simply not referred to at all. *We are not victims.* We are organizers, we are freedom fighters, we are feminists, we are healers. This is not anything new. For centuries it has been so.

There is not one of us who has not been touched by the life-destroying effects of alcohol. We have lost our mothers, an uncle, barely knew a father. We have lost our children. We have lost stories. Our spirit holds loss, held in the center, tightly. We never have to remind ourselves of what has come down. It is an instinct, like smelling autumn, or shaking pollen.

And the core, the pivot, is love. We love with passion and sensuality. We love—with humor—our lovers, our relations, our tricksters. We have a great fondness for laughter. And we do lots of it. Loud, gutsy noises that fill up empty spaces. We laugh at the strange behavior of *wasicu*, we laugh about being Indians. Our spirit is making a little bit of Indian country wherever we travel or live. In cities with the confusing limitations. In universities, where the customs and language are so removed from ours. On the res, where time is often measured by how long it will be safe to drink the water.

I light my candle again. I think of the Lady and her magic. Magic that was *almost* whitened and christianized beyond recognition. Her magic of being a woman, being Indio. Kateri's holy card depicts a white-looking girl, piously praying for the redemption of her people's souls. *But you are familiar to me.* You were dark seers of the future. You were scarred visitations. Beautiful and horrible. *You are us.* Ladies, you frightened them. Sisters, you give nurturance to me.

We made the fires. We are the fire-tenders. We are the ones who do not allow anyone to speak for us *but* us.

Spirit. Sisterhood. No longer can the two be separated.

PAULA GUNN ALLEN

(from) Who Is Your Mother? Red Roots of White Feminism

Born in New Mexico of Laguna, Sioux, Scottish, and Lebanese descent, Paula Gunn Allen (1939–2008) identified with her mother's people of the Laguna Pueblo, among whom she spent her childhood. In her poetry and fiction, she drew on American Indian oral traditions; she also edited four collections of American Indian traditional and contemporary writing. As an anthropologist, Allen brought her personal experience to her pathbreaking study *The Sacred Hoop* (1986), which restored women's central role in Pueblo cultural life and political power. Excerpted here is an essay first published in *Sinister Wisdom 25*.

RE/MEMBERING CONNECTIONS AND HISTORIES

THE BELIEF that rejection of tradition (as well as of history) is a useful response to life is reflected in America's amazing loss of memory concerning its origins in the matrix and context of Native America. America does not seem to remember that it derived its wealth, its values, its food, much of its medicine and a large part of its "dream" from Native America. It is ignorant of the genesis of its culture in this Native American land, and that ignorance helps to perpetuate the long standing European and Middle Eastern mono-theistic, hierarchical, patriarchal cultures' oppression of women, gays and les-bians, people of color, working class and unemployed people. Hardly anyone in America speculates that the constitutional system of government implaced here might be as much a product of American Indian ideas and practices as it is of colonial American and/or Anglo-European revolutionary fervor.

However Indians are officially and informally ignored as intellectual mov-ers and shapers in the United States, Britain and Europe, they are peoples with ancient tenure on this soil. During the ages when the tribal societies existed in the Americas largely untouched by patriarchal oppression, they developed elaborate systems of thought that included sciences, philosophy and governmental systems based on a belief in the central importance of female energies, systems that highly valued autonomy of individuals, cooperation, human dignity, human freedom, and egalitarian distribution of status, goods and services. Respect for others, reverence for life, and as a by-product of this value, pacifism as a way of life, importance of kinship ties and customary ordering of social transactions, a sense of the sacredness and mystery of existence, balance and harmony in relationships both sacred and secular were all features of life among the tribal confederacies and nations. And in those that lived by the largest number of these principles, gynarchy was the norm rather than the exception. Those systems are as yet unmatched in any contemporary industrial, agrarian, or post-industrial society on earth.

GRANDMOTHER, THE OLD WOMAN WHO THINKS CREATION

The name by which the tribes and nations refer to the greatest kind of woman-power is "Grandmother" or "elder woman power." As the Keres remember (celebrate) our origins, "In the beginning, Thought Woman thought all that is into being." By this, they don't mean there is a beginning in the sense that first there's nothing and then there's something, but that at the source of our particular life-system a creation/power/being who is female in the kind of energies she possesses and expresses gave life to all that we know by the expedient of thinking it/us. They mean that she did and does that, and that without her thought nothing would exist then or now.

The Iroquois trace their origins to the descent of Sky Woman, who gave birth to a spirit daughter. When that daughter died giving birth to her twin sons, Sky Woman flung her body into the sky where it became the moon and hung her body on a tree near her lodge where it became the sun. For so powerful was the spirit woman's being that even in "death" she continued to live. (And of course this myth expresses the Iroquoian idea that death is a change of state rather than an end, as well as their view of women as primary to life on earth.)

In ancient Meso-America, the Grandmother power was Gucumatz, the Feathered One, who thought and meditated and spoke with her cohorts. She was later to be called "Quetzal"—another word that designates the same bird and, by extension, the same ritual force. This being later became known as Quetzacoatl, the feathered or winged serpent among the Aztecs who were by all accounts a latter-day people descended of more ancient peoples. One of their major deities, Quetzacoatl, reflected the masculine shift that was beginning to take place in the western hemisphere about the time the Aztecs descended into the valley of Mexico and began building their masculine-oriented system.[1] It appears that Quetzacoatl combines in his person the earliest female deities, Gucumatz and Cihuacoatl, or "Bird Woman" and "Serpent Woman" (who might both be better understood if called "Eldest Female Spirit Who Circles Above" and "Eldest Female Spirit Who Meanders Within"). In essence, the title of this best known Aztec deity, Quetzacoatl, reflects a female nature, for the highest Aztec deity, whose original identity (all but lost in the patriarchal ages since her coming) was Grandmother.

Changing Woman, as the Grandmother power is known among the Navajo, does just that, she changes. Ancient crone, seductive maiden, mature woman, mother, creator, grandmother, mistress of the sun, she wields the powers of Creative Thinking to the ends that best meet the needs of the universe of people, spirits and other creatures. According to an account recorded by Gladys A. Reichard, Changing Woman and her sister, Sand Altar Woman, were the sole inhabitants of this fourth or fifth world and made it safe for the human beings who eventually came here from the previous world.[2]

Like Changing Woman, Hard Beings Woman has the ability to change from young woman to old crone. And, in the words of Hamilton A. Tyler, ". . . as every Hopi knows, the world was created by Huruing Wuhti, Hard Beings Woman."[3] This creation-goddess is referred to as Spider Woman among the Hopi, and as creator she possesses many of the attributes of the Keres Thinking Woman, who is also informally known as Spider Woman. She is most often seen as the agent of human welfare and the benefactor of those who have good hearts and think no evil in their hearts. Often she is the champion of those who are weak, helpless, oppressed or suffering.

Speaking of goddesses with creative potency, the Zuni tell of Shi'wano'kia who "expectorated into the palm of her left hand and slapped the saliva with the fingers of her right, and the spittle foamed like yucca suds, running over her hand and flowing everywhere; and thus she created A'wilelin Si'ta (Earth Mother)."[4]

On the Plains walks White Buffalo Woman. The director of wind powers, the significator of the quadrants, directions, seasons and solstices, she gave the sacred medicine pipe to the Lakota, and with it the rules for how they should be a people, and how they should live within their traditional tribal mind. She is the heart of the people, the psychically-charged center that gives their being as a people its structure, meaning and vitality. In that way she, like the Keresan Iyatiko (Corn Woman, the Mother of the katsina, the people and the animals and plants) or the Navajo Changing Woman, is the center of the people, the true source of their power to live and to prosper.

These are only a bare hint of the sorts of female gods that were recognized and honored by the tribes and nations, but even such a brief account indicates that femaleness was not devalued among them. Rather it was highly valued, both respected and feared, and social institutions of every sort reflected this attitude. Even modern sayings, such as the Cheyenne statement that a people is not conquered until the hearts of the women are on the ground, reflect their understanding that without the power of woman the people will not live, but with it, they will endure, and they will prosper.

Nor did they confine this belief in the central importance of female energy to matters of worship. Among many of the tribes (perhaps as many as 70% of them in North America alone), this belief was reflected in all of their social institutions. The Iroquois Constitution or White Roots of Peace, also called the Great Law of the Iroquois, codified the Matrons' decision-making and economic power. For example, Articles 19, 44 and 45 provide:

> The lineal descent of the people of the Five Fires [the Iroquois Nations] shall run in the female line. Women shall be considered the progenitors of the Nation. They shall own the land and the soil. Men and women shall follow the status of their mothers. (Article 44)
>
> The women heirs of the chieftainship titles of the League shall be called Oiner or Otinner [Noble] for all time to come. (Article 45)
>
> If a disobedient chief persists in his disobedience after three warnings [by his female relatives, by his male relatives and by one of his fellow council members, in that order], the matter shall go to the council of War Chiefs. The Chiefs shall then take away the title of the erring chief *by order of the women in whom the title is vested*. [My emphasis] When the chief is deposed, the women shall notify the chiefs of the League . . . and the chiefs of the League shall sanction the act. The women will then select another of their sons as a candidate and the chiefs shall elect him. (Article 19)

Beliefs, attitudes and laws such as these resulted in systems that featured all that is best in the vision of American feminists and in human liberation movements around the world. Yet feminists too often believe that no one has ever experienced the kind of society that empowered women and made that empowerment the basis of its rules of civilization. The price the feminist community must pay because it is not aware of the recent if not contemporary presence of gynarchical societies on this continent is unnecessary confusion, division, and much lost time. Wouldn't it be good for feminists to know that there have been recent social models from which its dream descends and to which its adherents can look for models?

1 At least, this seems to have been the case, though the apparent shift might be a result of Spanish Catholic destruction of all records and informal sources of information about a gynocratic system, for such would have given serious cause for alarm among European potentates, namely the officers of the Inquisition and the Pope himself. The Spaniards who were destroying documents all over Latin America during that period were largely interested in a peaceful conquest, and were unlikely to be willing to acknowledge gynocracy there if they were to find it. But it is interesting (and perhaps not a meaningless coincidence), that the Aztec ritual or ceremonial calendar was based on a year of 20 13-day months, and that that same 13 is, in Europe, the number of the wiccan covens and all allied cultures.

2 Gladys A. Reichard, *Spider Woman, A Story of Navajo Weavers and Chanters* (Glorieta, New Mexico: The Rio Grande Press, Inc., 1971), 169–79; cf. 236.

3 Hamilton A. Tyler, *Pueblo Gods and Myths* (Norman: University of Oklahoma, The Civilization of the American Indian Series, 1964), 37.

4 Tyler, p 94, citing Stevenson "The Zuni Indians," *BAE Twenty-Third Annual Report*, 1901–02, Washington, 1904, 23–24.

KATE SHANLEY

(from) Thoughts on Indian Feminism

Born and raised on the Fort Peck reservation and a member of the Assiniboine and Sioux tribes of Montana, Kate Shanley was a committed feminist and a University of Michigan Ph.D. student focusing on American Indian literature when she attended a 1983 conference on Indian women's leadership. Finding few feminists there, she began to ask herself why. Did becoming a feminist require abandoning identification with tribal sovereignty and tradition? Did being a feminist mean no longer engaging in the struggle to keep and care for ancestral land? Arguing that no such compromises should hinder indigenous women, Shanley sought to navigate a path to feminism not only for native women but also for other women of color. Her 1984 essay from *A Gathering of Spirit* is excerpted here.

TOWARD THE end of the 1983 Ohoyo Indian Women's Conference on Leadership, I began to notice that the participants were not referring to themselves as feminists, although the group of women present are as strong and committed as any group of women in America today who are working for change. Why, then, do Indian women avoid the designation "feminist"? The more I thought about it, the more that question began proliferating into many questions: how many other women (of all colors and creeds) have I encountered in my travels (plenty!) who do not choose to identify as feminists? What do they have in common with Indian women? What is a feminist, anyway?

My thoughts on the questions raised thus far by no means represent a consensus among Indian women; in fact, before I could begin to deal objectively with the subject of Indian feminism, I had to come to terms with my own defensiveness about representing other women, particularly other Indian women. On the one hand, I am a woman who refers to herself as a feminist. If most Indian women do not refer to themselves as feminists, does that fact make me somehow *less* representative, *less* Indian? On the other hand, does the theoretical feminism of the university constitute something different from (though, perhaps giving it the benefit of the doubt, correlated to) the "grass-roots" feminism Ohoyo represents? To some extent I know that I suffer the conflicts of an "academic squaw" (to borrow a term from poet and educator Wendy Rose), a certain distance from the "real world."

Attending the Ohoyo conference in Grand Forks, North Dakota was a returning home for me in a spiritual sense—taking my place beside other Indian women, and an actual sense—being with my relatives and loved ones after finally finishing my pre-doctoral requirements at the university. Although I have been a full-time student for the past six years, I brought to the academic experience many years in the workaday world as a mother, registered nurse, volunteer tutor, social worker aide, and high school outreach worker. What I am offering in this article are my thoughts as an Indian woman on feminism. Mine is a political perspective that seeks to re-view the real-life positions of women in relation to the theories that attempt to address the needs of those women.

Issues such as equal pay for equal work, child health and welfare, and a woman's right to make her own choices regarding contraceptive use, sterilization and abortion—key issues to the majority women's movement—affect Indian women as well; however, equality *per se*, may have a different meaning for Indian women and Indian people. That difference begins with personal and tribal sovereignty—the right to be legally recognized as peoples empowered to determine our own destinies. Thus, the Indian women's movement seeks equality in two ways that do not concern mainstream women: (1) on the individual level, the Indian woman struggles to promote the survival of a social structure whose organizational principles represent notions of family different from those of the mainstream; and (2) on the societal level, the People seek sovereignty as a people in order to maintain a vital legal and spiritual connection to the land, in order to *survive* as a people.

The nuclear family has little relevance to Indian women; in fact, in many ways, mainstream feminists now are striving to redefine family and community in a way that Indian women have long known. The American lifestyle from which white middle-class women are fighting to free themselves, has not taken hold in Indian communities. Tribal and communal values have survived after four hundred years of colonial oppression.

It may be that the desire on the part of mainstream feminists to include Indian women, however sincere, represents tokenism just now, because too often Indian people, by being thought of as spiritual "mascots" to the American endeavor, are seen more as artifacts than as real people able to speak for ourselves. Given the public's general ignorance about Indian people, in other words, it is possible that Indian people's real-life concerns are not relevant to the mainstream feminist movement in a way that constitutes anything more than a "representative" facade. Charges against the women's movement of heterosexism and racism abound these days; it is not my intention to add to them except to stress that we must all be vigilant in examining the underlying assumptions that motivate us. Internalization of negative (that is, sexist and racist) attitudes towards ourselves and others can and quite often does result from colonialist (white patriarchal) oppression. It is more useful to attack the systems that keep us ignorant of each other's histories.

The other way in which the Indian women's movement differs in emphasis from the majority women's movement, lies in the importance Indian people place on tribal sovereignty—it is the single most pressing political issue in Indian country today. For Indian people to survive culturally as well as materially, many battles must be fought and won in the courts of law, precisely because it is the legal recognition that enables Indian people to govern ourselves according to our own world view—a world view that is antithetical to the *wasicu* (the Lakota term for "takers of the fat") definition of progress. Equality for Indian women within tribal communities, therefore, holds more significance than equality in terms of the general rubric "American."

Up to now I have been referring to the women's movement as though it were a single, well-defined organization. It is not. Perhaps in many ways socialist feminists hold views similar to the views of many Indian people regarding private property and the nuclear family. Certainly, there are some Indian people who are capitalistic. The point I would like to stress, however, is that rather than seeing differences according to a hierarchy of oppressions (white over Indian, male over female), we must practice a politics that allows for diversity in cultural identity as well as in sexual identity.

The word "feminism" has special meanings to Indian women, including the idea of promoting the continuity of tradition, and consequently, pursuing the recognition of tribal sovereignty. Even so, Indian feminists are united with mainstream feminists in outrage against woman and child battering, sexist employment and educational practices, and in many other social concerns. Just as sovereignty cannot be granted but *must be recognized* as an inherent right to self-determination, so Indian feminism must also be recognized as powerful in its own terms, in its own right.

Feminism becomes an incredibly powerful term when it incorporates diversity—not as a superficial political position, but as a practice. The women's movement and the Indian movement for sovereignty suffer similar trivialization, because narrow factions turn ignorance to their own benefit so that they can exploit human beings and the lands they live on for corporate profit. The time has come for Indian women and Indian people to be known on our own terms. This nuclear age demands new terms of communication for all people. Our survival depends on it. Peace.

BELL HOOKS

Ending Female Sexual Oppression

Prolific author of more than thirty books, bell hooks—born Gloria Jean Watkins in Kentucky in 1952—took the name of her maternal great-grandmother, Bell Blair Hooks, "known for her snappy and bold tongue," removing capital letters to emphasize "the substance of the books rather than who I am." In this powerfully argued 1984 essay, hooks examines several positions of feminist activists that she believes may enhance or undermine ending female sexual oppression. Affirming political feminists' right to "freely choose sexual partners," or no partner, she warns against turning legitimate feminist critiques of heterosexism (compulsory heterosexuality) into attacks on heterosexual practices.

DURING THE early stages of contemporary feminist movement, women's liberation was often equated with sexual liberation. On the cover of Germaine Greer's *The Female Eunuch* (one of the most widely read feminist works in the '70s), the book is described as "the ultimate word on sexual freedom." On the back cover, Greer is described as "a woman with a sense of humor who is proud of her sexuality." (Germaine Greer's work *Sex and Destiny* is an interesting rethinking of the politics of fertility that challenges many notions of sexual freedom for women advocated by the author in her earlier work.) Feminist thinkers like Greer believed that assertion of the primacy of sexuality would be a liberatory gesture. They urged women to initiate sexual advances, to enjoy sex, to experiment with new relationships, to be sexually "free." Yet most women did not have the leisure, the mobility, the contacts, or even the desire to indulge in this so-called "sexual liberation." Young heterosexual women, single and childless; teenagers and college students; and political progressives were the groups most eager and able to pattern their sexual behavior after what was essentially an inversion of the male notion of sexual liberation. Advocating genuine sexual liberty was positive, and women learned from experience that the freedom to initiate sexual relationships; to be non-monogamous; to experiment with group sex, sexualized sado-masochism, etc. could sometimes be exciting and pleasurable; it did not, however, deconstruct the power relations between men and women in the sexual sphere. Many women felt disillusioned with the idea of sexual liberation. While some participants in feminist circles continued to emphasize the importance of sexual freedom, rejecting the idea that it should be patterned after a male model, a larger contingent, heterosexual and lesbian, began to denounce the idea of sexual freedom and even of sexual contact with men because they felt women were still exploited by the old sexual paradigms. Increasingly, these feminists came to see male sexuality as disgusting and necessarily exploitive of women.

Whether or not sexual freedom should be a feminist issue is currently a much-debated topic. (Since the writing of this chapter much new feminist writing discussing sexuality has emerged, including *Loving in the War Years*, by Cherríe Moraga; *Powers of Desire*, edited by Ann Snitow, Christine Stansell, and Sharon Thompson; *Female Desire*, by Rosalind Coward; and *Sex and Love*, edited by Sue Cartledge and Joanna Ryan; to name a few.) Concluding her essay "Sexuality as the Mainstay of Identity: Psychoanalytic Perspectives," Ethel Person writes:

> In sum, then, sexual liberation, while important and even crucial to some individuals, has significant limitations as social critique and political policy. At its worst, sexual liberation is part of the cult of individuality which only demands legitimation of the expression of the individual's need, what appears to be her raw "impulse" life, against the demands of society without considering a political reordering of the social order itself. The achievement of the conditions necessary to female autonomy is a precondition for authentic sexual liberation.

Person does not add that rethinking sexuality, changing the norms of sexuality, is a pre-condition for female sexual autonomy; therefore sexuality, and by implication "sexual freedom," is an important, relevant issue for feminist politics.

It has been a simple task for women to describe and criticize negative aspects of sexuality as it has been socially constructed in sexist society; to expose male objectification and dehumanization of women; to denounce rape, pornography, sexualized violence, incest, etc. It has been a far more difficult task for women to envision new sexual paradigms, to change the norms of sexuality. The inspiration for such work can only emerge in an environment where sexual well-being is valued. Ironically, some feminists have tended to dismiss issues of sexual pleasure, well-being, and contentedness as irrelevant. Contemporary emphasis on sexual revolution or anything-goes sexual expression has led many women and men to assume that sexual freedom already exists and is even overvalued in our society. However, this is *not* a culture that affirms real sexual freedom. Criticizing the assumption that this is a sexually liberated society because there is an absence of many restrictions, Ellen Willis asserts in her essay "Toward a Feminist Sexual Revolution":

> From a radical standpoint, then, sexual liberation involves not only the abolition of restrictions but the positive presence of social and psychological conditions that foster satisfying sexual relations. And from that standpoint, this culture is still deeply repressive. Most obviously, sexual inequality and the resulting antagonism between men and women constitute a devastating barrier to sexual happiness. I will argue in addition that, sexual liberalism notwithstanding, most children's upbringing produces adults with profoundly negative attitudes towards sex. Under these conditions, the relaxation of sexual restrictions leads people to try desperately to overcome the obstacles to satisfaction through compulsive sexual activity and preoccupation with sex. The emphasis on sex that currently permeates our public life—especially the enormous demands for sexual advice and therapy—attest not to our sexual freedom but to our continuing sexual frustration.

Feminist activists who see male sexuality as inherently despicable have been those most willing to de-emphasize issues of sexual freedom. Focusing solely on those aspects of male sexual expression that have to do with reinforcing male domination of women, they are reluctant and downright unwilling to acknowledge that sexuality as it is constructed in sexist society is no more "liberating" for men than it is for women (even though it is obviously oppressive to women in ways that are not oppressive to men). Willis argues that recognition of "sexual destructiveness can be seen as a perversion that both reflects and perpetuates a repressive system" so that it is possible "to envision a coherent feminist politics in which a commitment to sexual freedom plays an integral part." Sexual freedom can exist only when individuals are no longer oppressed by a socially constructed sexuality based on biologically determined definitions of sexuality: repression, guilt, shame, dominance, conquest, and exploitation. To set the stage for the development of that sexual freedom, feminist movement must continue to focus on ending female sexual oppression.

The focus on "sexual liberation" has always carried with it the assumption that the goal of such effort is to make it possible for individuals to engage in more and/or better sexual activity. Yet one aspect of sexual norms that many people find oppressive is the assumption that one "should" be engaged in sexual activity. This "should" is one expression of sexual coercion. Advocates of sexual liberation often imply that any individual who is not concerned about the quality of their experience or exercising greater sexual freedom is mentally disturbed or sexually repressed. When primary emphasis is placed on ending sexual oppression rather than on sexual liberation, it is possible to envision a society in which it is as much an expression of sexual freedom to choose not to participate in sexual activity as it is to choose to participate.

Sexual norms as they are currently socially constructed have always privileged active sexual expression over sexual desire. To act sexually is deemed natural, normal; to not act, unnatural, abnormal. Such thinking corresponds with sexist role patterning. Men are socialized to act sexually, women not to act (or to simply react to male sexual advances). Women's liberationists' insistence that women should be sexually active as a gesture of liberation helped free female sexuality from the restraints imposed upon it by repressive double standards, but it did not remove the stigma attached to sexual inactivity. Until that stigma is removed, women and men will not feel free to participate in sexual activity when they desire. They will continue to respond to coercion, either the sexist coercion that pushes young men to act sexually to prove their "masculinity" (i.e., their heterosexuality) or the sexual coercion that compels young women to respond to such advances to prove their "femininity" (i.e., their willingness to be heterosexual sex objects). The removal of the social stigma attached to sexual inactivity would amount to a change in sexual norms. It would have many positive implications for women and men, especially teenagers, who are at this historical moment most likely to be victimized by sexist sexual norms. Recent focus on sex between heterosexual teenagers indicates that coercion remains a central motivation for participation in sexual activity. Girls "do it for the boy," as one seventeen-year-old daughter told her mother (quoted in Ellen Goodman's essay "The Turmoil of Teenage Sexuality"), and boys do it to prove to other boys that they are heterosexual and that they can exert "masculine" power over girls.

Feminist movement to eradicate heterosexism—compulsory heterosexuality—is central to efforts to end sexual oppression. In the introduction to *No Turning Back: Lesbian and Gay Liberation of the '80s*, Gerre Goodman, George Lakey, Judy Lakey, and Erika Thorne define heterosexism as the:

> suppression and denial of homosexuality with the assumption that everyone is or should be heterosexual and, second, a belief in the inherent superiority of the dominant-male/passive-female role pattern. Heterosexism results in compulsory heterosexuality which

cripples the free expression and mutually supportive relationships of heterosexuals as well as of lesbians and gay men.

Within the feminist movement lesbian women have worked hardest to call attention to the struggle to end heterosexist oppression. Lesbians have been on both sides of the larger sexual-liberation debate. They have shown many heterosexual women that their prejudices against lesbians support and perpetuate compulsory heterosexuality. They have also shown women that we can find emotional and mutual sexual fulfillment in relationships with one another. Some lesbians have suggested that homosexuality may be the most direct expression of pro-sex politics, since it is unconnected to procreation. Feminist movement to end female sexual oppression is linked to lesbian liberation. The struggle to end prejudice, exploitation, and oppression of lesbians and gay men is a crucial feminist agenda. It is a necessary component of the movement to end female sexual oppression. Affirming lesbianism, women of varied sexual preferences resist the perpetuation of compulsory heterosexuality.

Throughout feminist movement, there has been a tendency to make the struggle to end sexual oppression a competition: heterosexuality versus lesbianism. Early in the movement, attempts to exclude and silence lesbians were justified through the specter of a "lavender menace." Later, lesbianism was presented as a choice that would eliminate the need to deal with issues of heterosexual conflict or as the most politically correct choice for a feminist woman. Even though many feminists acknowledge that fighting sexual oppression, particularly male domination of women, is not the same as man-hating, within feminist gatherings and organizations intense anti-male sentiments are sometimes expressed by heterosexual women and lesbians alike, and women who are not lesbians, who may or may not be in relationships with men, feel that they are not "real" feminists. This is especially true of women who may support feminism but who do not publicly support lesbian rights. It is often forgotten that we are all in the process of developing radical political consciousness, that it is a "process," and that it defeats efforts to build solidarity to condemn or judge women politically incorrect when they do not immediately support all the issues we deem relevant.

The suggestion that the truly feminist woman is lesbian (made by heterosexuals and lesbians alike) sets up another sexual standard by which women are to be judged and found wanting. Although it is not common for women in the feminist movement to state that women should be lesbian, the message is transmitted via discussions of heterosexuality that suggest all genital contact between women and men is rape, that the woman who is emotionally and sexually committed to an individual man is necessarily incapable of loyal, woman-identified political commitment. Just as the struggle to end sexual oppression aims to eliminate heterosexism, it should not endorse any one sexual choice: celibacy, bisexuality, homosexuality, or heterosexuality. Feminist activists need to remember that the political choices we make are not determined by whom we choose to have genital sexual contact with. In her introduction to *Home Girls: A Black Feminist Anthology*, Barbara Smith asserts: "Black feminism and Black Lesbianism are not interchangeable. Feminism is a political movement, and many Lesbians are not feminists." This is also true for many heterosexual women. It is important for women, especially those who are heterosexual, to know that they can make a radical political commitment to feminist struggle even though they are sexually involved with men (many of us know from experience that political choice will undoubtedly alter the nature of individual relationships). All women need to know that they can be politically committed to feminism regardless of their sexual preference. They need to know that the goal of feminist movement is not to establish codes for a "politically correct" sexuality. Politically, feminist activists committed to ending sexual oppression must work to eliminate the oppression of lesbians and gay men as part of an overall movement to enable all women (and men) to freely choose sexual partners.

Feminist activists must take care that our legitimate critiques of heterosexism are not attacks on heterosexual *practice*. As feminists, we must confront those women who do in fact believe that women with heterosexual preferences are either traitors or likely to be anti-lesbian. Condemnation of heterosexual practice has led women who desire sexual relationships with men to feel they cannot participate in feminist movement. They have gotten the message that to be "truly" feminist is not to be heterosexual. It is easy to confuse support for non-oppressive heterosexual practice with the belief in heterosexism. For example, responding to a statement in *Ain't I a Woman* that said, "Attacking heterosexuality does little to strengthen the self-concept of the masses of women who desire to be with men," lesbian feminist Cheryl Clarke writes in her essay "The Failure to Transform: Homophobia in the Black Community":

> Hooks delivers a backhanded slap at lesbian feminists, a considerable number of whom are black. Hooks would have done well to attack the institution of heterosexuality, as it is a prime cause of black women's oppression in America.

Clearly Clarke misunderstands and misinterprets my point. I made no reference to heterosexism, and it is the equation of heterosexual practice with heterosexism that makes it appear that Clarke is attacking the practice itself and not only heterosexism. My point is that feminism will never appeal to a mass-based group of women in our society who are heterosexual if they think that they will be looked down upon or seen as doing something wrong. My comment was not intended to reflect in any way on lesbians, because they are not the only group of feminists that criticizes and in some cases condemns all heterosexual practice.

Just as feminist movement to end sexual oppression should create a social climate in which lesbians and gay men are no longer oppressed, a climate in which their sexual choices are affirmed, it should also create a climate in which heterosexual practice is freed from the constraints of heterosexism and can also be affirmed. One of the practical reasons for doing this is the recognition that the advancement of feminism as a political movement depends on the involvement of masses of women, a vast majority of whom are heterosexual. As long as feminist women (be they celibate, lesbian, heterosexual, etc.) condemn male sexuality, and by extension women who are involved sexually with men, feminist movement is undermined. Useless and unnecessary divisions are created. Concurrently, as long as any pro-heterosexuality statement is read as a hidden attack upon homosexuality, we continue to perpetuate the idea that these are, and should be, competing sexualities. It is possible to delineate the positive or negative aspects of lesbianism without referring in any way to heterosexuality, and vice versa. Although Ellen Willis does not in her essay discuss the notion that lesbianism is a more politically correct sexual choice for feminist women, or that this represents yet another attempt to impose on women a sexual standard, her comments about neo-Victorian logic apply to attacks on female sexual contact with men:

> Neo-Victorians have also undermined feminist opposition to the right, by equating feminism with their own sexual attitudes, in effect reading out of the movement any woman who disagrees with them. Since their notion of proper feminist sexuality echoes conventional moral judgments and the anti-sexual propaganda presently coming from the right their guilt-mongering has been quite effective. Many feminists who are aware that their sexual feelings contradict the neo-Victorian ideal have lapsed into confused and apologetic silence. No doubt there are also thousands of women who have quietly concluded that if this ideal is feminism, then feminism has nothing to do with them. The result is widespread apathy, dishonesty, and profound disunity in a movement faced with a determined enemy that is threatening its very existence.

A feminist movement that aims to eliminate sexist oppression, and in that context sexual oppression, cannot ignore or dismiss the choice women make to be heterosexual. Despite heterosexism, many women have acknowledged and accepted that they do not have to be heterosexual (that there are other options) and have chosen to be exclusively or primarily heterosexual. Their choices should be respected. By choosing they exercise sexual freedom. Their choices may not, as those who oppose them suggest, be influenced by hetero-sexual privilege. Most heterosexual privilege is diminished when compared to the degree of exploitation and oppression a woman is likely to encounter in most heterosexual relationships. There are exceptions. Many women choose to be heterosexual because they enjoy genital contact with individual men. Feminist movement has enriched and added new dimensions to lesbian sexuality, and there is no reason it cannot do the same for heterosexuality. Women with heterosexual preferences need to know that feminism is a political movement that does not negate their choices even as it offers a framework to challenge and oppose male sexual exploitation of women.

There are some feminists (and I am one) who believe that feminist move-ment to end sexual oppression will not change destructive sexual norms if individuals are taught that they must choose between competing sexualities (the most obvious being heterosexuality and homosexuality) and conform to the expectations of the chosen norm. Sexual desire has varied and multiple dimensions and is rarely as "exclusive" as any norm would suggest. A liberatory sexuality would not teach women to see their bodies as accessible to all men, or to all women, for that matter. It would favor instead a sexuality that is open or closed based on the nature of individual interaction. Implicit in the idea of sexual preference is the assumption that anyone of the preferred sex can seek access to one's body. This is a concept that promotes objectification. In a heterosexual context it makes everyone, especially women, into sex objects. Given the power differential created by sexist politics, women are likely to be approached by any man since all men are taught to assume they should have access to the bodies of all women. Sexuality would be transformed if the codes and labels that strip sexual desire of its specificity and particularity were abandoned. As Stephen Heath summarized in *The Sexual Fix*:

> The end of oppression is a recasting of social relations that leaves men and women free, outside of any commodification of the sex-ual, removed from any of the violence and alienation of circulation and exchange as a sexual identity, the identity of a sex, being fixed to this or that image, this or that norm, to this thing "sexuality."

Though labeled "heterosexual," many women in this society feel little sexual desire for men because of the politics of sexual oppression; male domination destroys and perverts that desire. It is the enormity of acts of sexual oppression imposed on women by men that has made it difficult for women to speak of positive sexual interactions with men. Increasingly, feminist women who are heterosexual are making the point that they choose to have a relationship with an individual man and resist the heterosexist notion that they welcome or are open to the sexual advances of any male. This action attacks the compulsory heterosexuality that denies women the right to choose male sexual partners by evaluating whether such interactions support and affirm them. Asserting their right to choose, women challenge the assumption that female sexuality exists to serve the sexual needs of men. Their efforts enhance the struggle to end sexual oppression. The right to choose must characterize all sexual interactions between individuals.

A shift that will undoubtedly emerge as the struggle to end sexual oppression progresses will be decreased obsession with sexuality. This does not necessarily mean that there will be decreased sexual activity. It means that sexuality will no longer have the importance attributed to it in a society that uses sexuality for the express purposes of maintaining gender inequality, male domination, con-sumerism, and the sexual frustration and unhappiness that deflect attention away from the need to make social revolution. As Stephen Heath comments:

> The real problem and task is always one of social revolution. Priv-
> ileging the sexual has nothing necessarily liberating about it at all;
> indeed, it functions only too easily as an instance by development
> of and reference to which society guarantees its order outside of any
> effective process of transformation, produces precisely a containing
> area and ideology of "revolution" or "liberation."

Feminist efforts to develop a political theory of sexuality must continue if sex-ist oppression is to be eliminated. Yet we must keep in mind that the struggle to end sexual oppression is only one component of a larger struggle to trans-form society and establish a new social order.

URSULA K. LE GUIN

(from) The Mother Tongue, Bryn Mawr Commencement Address

The acclaimed writer Ursula K. Le Guin (1929–2018) was a self-identified feminist who viewed her fictions, "science" or otherwise, as "mind experiments" about bedrock political and social arrangements, including gender and sexuality. Her best-known antipatriarchal novels include *The Left Hand of Darkness* (1969) and *The Dispossessed* (1974). In her later years she criticized some of her own early work as insufficiently feminist, leading her to publish revised versions of several stories. In her 1986 Bryn Mawr Commencement Address, Le Guin examined our gendered ways of speaking and writing under patriarchy, identifying three languages we all speak: the father tongue, the mother tongue, and "our native tongue," the language of art. Excerpted here is her discussion of the first two.

THINKING ABOUT what I should say to you made me think about what we learn in college; and what we unlearn in college; and then how we learn to unlearn what we learned in college and relearn what we unlearned in college, and so on. And I thought how I have learned, more or less well, three languages, all of them English; and how one of these languages is the one I went to college to learn. I thought I was going to study French and Italian, and I did, but what I learned was the language of power—of social power; I shall call it the father tongue.

This is the public discourse, and one dialect of it is speechmaking—by politicians, commencement speakers, or the old man who used to get up early in a village in Central California a couple of hundred years ago and say things very loudly on the order of "People need to be getting up now, there are things we might be doing, the repairs on the sweathouse aren't finished and the tarweed is in seed over on Bald Hill; this is a good time of day for doing things, and there'll be plenty of time for lying around when it gets hot this afternoon." So everybody would get up grumbling slightly, and some of them would go pick tarweed—probably the women. This is the effect, ideally, of the public discourse. It makes something happen, makes somebody—usually somebody else—do something, or at least it gratifies the ego of the speaker. The difference between our politics and that of a native Californian people is clear in the style of the public discourse. The difference wasn't clear to the White invaders, who insisted on calling any Indian who made a speech a "chief," because they couldn't comprehend, they wouldn't admit, an authority without supremacy—a non-dominating authority. But it is such an authority that I possess for the brief—we all hope it is decently brief—time I speak to you. I have no right to speak to you. What I have is the responsibility you have given me to speak to you.

The political tongue speaks aloud—and look how radio and television have brought the language of politics right back where it belongs—but the dialect of the father tongue that you and I learned best in college is a written one. It doesn't speak itself. It only lectures. It began to develop when printing made written language common rather than rare, five hundred years ago or so, and with electronic processing and copying it continues to develop and proliferate so powerfully, so dominatingly, that many believe this dialect—the expository and particularly the scientific discourse—is the *highest* form of language, the true language, of which all other uses of words are primitive vestiges.

And it is indeed an excellent dialect. Newton's *Principia* was written in it in Latin, and Descartes wrote Latin and French in it, establishing some of its basic vocabulary, and Kant wrote German in it, and Marx, Darwin, Freud, Boas, Foucault—all the great scientists and social thinkers wrote it. It is the language of thought that seeks objectivity.

I do not say it is the language of rational thought. Reason is a faculty far larger than mere objective thought. When either the political or the scientific discourse announces itself as the voice of reason, it is playing God, and should be spanked and stood in the corner. The essential gesture of the father tongue is not reasoning but distancing—making a gap, a space, between the subject or self and the object or other. Enormous energy is generated by that rending, that forcing of a gap between Man and World. So the continuous growth of technology and science fuels itself; the Industrial Revolution began with splitting the world-atom, and still by breaking the continuum into unequal parts we keep the imbalance from which our society draws the power that enables it to dominate every other culture, so that everywhere now everybody speaks the same language in laboratories and government buildings and headquarters and offices of business, and those who don't know it or won't speak it are silent, or silenced, or unheard.

You came here to college to learn the language of power—to be empowered.

If you want to succeed in business, government, law, engineering, science, education, the media, if you want to succeed, you have to be fluent in the language in which "success" is a meaningful word.

White man speak with forked tongue; White man speak dichotomy. His language expresses the values of the split world, valuing the positive and devaluing the negative in each redivision: subject/object, self/other, mind/body, dominant/submissive, active/passive, Man/Nature, man/woman, and so on. The father tongue is spoken from above. It goes one way. No answer is expected, or heard.

In our Constitution and the works of law, philosophy, social thought, and science, in its everyday uses in the service of justice and clarity, what I call the father tongue is immensely noble and indispensably useful. When it claims a privileged relationship to reality, it becomes dangerous and potentially destructive. It describes with exquisite accuracy the continuing destruction of the planet's ecosystem by its speakers. This word from its vocabulary, "ecosystem," is a word unnecessary except in a discourse that excludes its speakers from the ecosystem in a subject/object dichotomy of terminal irresponsibility.

The language of the fathers, of Man Ascending, Man the Conqueror, Civilized Man, is not your native tongue. It isn't anybody's native tongue. You didn't even hear the father tongue your first few years, except on the radio or TV, and then you didn't listen, and neither did your little brother, because it was some old politician with hairs in his nose yammering. And you and your brother had better things to do. You had another kind of power to learn. You were learning your mother tongue.

Using the father tongue, I can speak of the mother tongue only, inevitably, to distance it—to exclude it. It is the other, inferior. It is primitive: inaccurate, unclear, coarse, limited, trivial, banal. It's repetitive, the same over and over, like the work called women's work; earthbound, housebound. It's vulgar, the vulgar tongue, common, common speech, colloquial, low, ordinary, plebeian, like the work ordinary people do, the lives common people live. The mother tongue, spoken or written, expects an answer. It is conversation, a word the root of which means "turning together." The mother tongue is language not as mere communication but as relation, relationship. It connects. It goes two ways, many ways, an exchange, a network. Its power is not in dividing but in binding, not in distancing but in uniting. It is written, but not by scribes and secretaries for posterity; it flies from the mouth on the breath that is our life and is gone, like the outbreath, utterly gone and yet returning, repeated, the breath the same again always, everywhere, and we all know it by heart. John have you got your umbrella I think it's going to rain. Can you come play with me? If I told you once I told you a hundred times. Things here just aren't the same without Mother, I will now sign your affectionate brother James. Oh what am I going to do? So I said to her I said if he thinks she's going to stand for that but then there's his arthritis poor thing and no work. I love you. I hate you. I hate liver. Joan dear did you feed the sheep, don't just stand around mooning. Tell me what they said, tell me what you did. Oh how my feet do hurt. My heart is breaking. Touch me here, touch me again. Once bit twice shy. You look like what the cat dragged in. What a beautiful night. Good morning, hello, goodbye, have a nice day, thanks. God damn you to hell you lying cheat. Pass the soy sauce please. Oh shit. Is it grandma's own sweet pretty dear? What am I going to tell her? There there don't cry. Go to sleep now, go to sleep. . . . Don't go to sleep!

It is a language always on the verge of silence and often on the verge of song. It is the language stories are told in. It is the language spoken by all children and most women, and so I call it the mother tongue, for we learn it from our mothers and speak it to our kids. I'm trying to use it here in public where it isn't appropriate, not suited to the occasion, but I want to speak it to you because we are women and I can't say what I want to say about women in the language of capital M Man. If I try to be objective I will say, "This is higher and that is lower," I'll make a commencement speech about being successful in the battle of life, I'll lie to you; and I don't want to.

Early this spring I met a musician, the composer Pauline Oliveros, a beautiful woman like a grey rock in a streambed; and to a group of us, women, who were beginning to quarrel over theories in abstract, objective language—and I with my splendid Eastern-women's-college training in the father tongue was in the thick of the fight and going for the kill—to us, Pauline, who is sparing with words, said after clearing her throat, "Offer your experience as your truth." There was a short silence. When we started talking again, we didn't talk objectively, and we didn't fight. We went back to feeling our way into ideas, using the whole intellect not half of it, talking with one another, which involves listening. We tried to offer our experience to one another. Not claiming something: offering something.

How, after all, can one experience deny, negate, disprove, another experience? Even if I've had a lot more of it, *your* experience is your truth. How can one being prove another being wrong? Even if you're a lot younger and smarter than me, *my* being is my truth. I can offer it; you don't have to take it. People can't contradict each other, only words can: words separated from experience for use as weapons, words that make the wound, the split between subject and object, exposing and exploiting the object but disguising and defending the subject.

People crave objectivity because to be subjective is to be embodied, to be a body, vulnerable, violable. Men especially aren't used to that; they're trained not to offer but to attack. It's often easier for women to trust one another, to try to speak our experience in our own language, the language we talk to each other in, the mother tongue; so we empower one another.

But you and I have learned to use the mother tongue only at home or safe among friends, and many men learn not to speak it at all. They're taught that there's no safe place for them. From adolescence on, they talk a kind of degraded version of the father tongue with each other—sports scores, job technicalities, sex technicalities, and TV politics. At home, to women and children talking mother tongue, they respond with a grunt and turn on the ball game. They have let themselves be silenced, and dimly they know it, and so resent speakers of the mother tongue; women babble, gabble all the time. . . . Can't listen to that stuff.

Our schools and colleges, institutions of the patriarchy, generally teach us to listen to people in power, men or women speaking the father tongue; and so they teach us not to listen to the mother tongue, to what the powerless say, poor men, women, children: not to hear that as valid discourse.

I am trying to unlearn these lessons, along with other lessons I was taught by my society, particularly lessons concerning the minds, work, works, and being of women. I am a slow unlearner. But I love my unteachers—the feminist thinkers and writers and talkers and poets and artists and singers and critics and friends, from Wollstonecraft and Woolf through the furies and glories of the seventies and eighties—I celebrate here and now the women who for two centuries have worked for our freedom, the unteachers, the unmasters, the unconquerors, the unwarriors, women who have at risk and at high cost offered their experience as truth. "Let us NOT praise famous women!" Virginia Woolf scribbled in a margin when she was writing *Three Guineas*, and she's right, but still I have to praise these women and thank them for setting me free in my old age to learn my own language.

SONIA SANCHEZ

style no. 1

Born in 1934, the poet and activist Sonia Sanchez has forged a celebrated body of work, writing "to offer a black woman's view of the world." In this brief piece, she claims her right to walk the terrain of the night despite the threatening possibility of a male predator, echoing the concerns of the Take Back the Night marches feminists organized across the U.S., and eventually around the world. The first such rally and march was held in Philadelphia in 1975 in response to the death of Susan Alexander Speeth, a young microbiologist who was stabbed and killed walking home, less than a block from her house.

i COME FROM a long line of rough mamas.

so here i was walking down market street. coming out of a city hall meeting. night wind at my back, dressed in my finest. black cashmere coat caressing the rim of my gray suede boots. hat sitting acey duecy. anointing the avenue with my black smell.

and this old dude. red as his car inching its way on the sidewalk. honked his horn. slid his body almost out of his skin. toward me. psst. psst. hey. let's you and me have some fun. psst. psst. c'mon babe. don't you want some of this?

and he pulled his penis out of his pants. held the temporal wonder of men in his hands.

i stopped. looked at him. a memory from deep in the eye. a memory of saturday afternoon moviehouses where knowledge comes with a tremulous cry. old white men. spiderlike. spinning their webs towards young girls legs and our budabbot and loucostello smiles melted. and we moved in the high noon walk of black girls. smelling the breath of an old undertow.

and i saw mama Dixon. dancing on his head. mama Dixon. big loud friend of the family. who stunned us with her curses and liquor. being herself. whose skin breathed hilarious breaths. and i greased my words on her tongue. and she gave them back to me like newly tasted wine.

motha fucka. you even offend the night i said. you look like an old mole coming out of its hole. take yo slimy sat ole ass home. fo you get what's coming to you. and yo generation. ask yo mama to skin you. that is if you have had one cuz anybody ugly as you couldna been born.

   and i turned my eyes eastward. toward the garage. waking up the incipient night with my steps. ready for the short days. the wind singing in my veins.

Don't You Talk About My Mama!

The release in 1965 of a government report entitled *The Negro Family: The Case for National Action*—better known today as the Moynihan Report for its author, the sociologist and future senator Daniel Patrick Moynihan—would have pernicious lasting effects on the way Black women, especially Black mothers, were perceived in American society. In this 1987 address to a Williams College conference on the Black family, the poet, essayist, and activist June Jordan (1936–2002) excoriates the idea that single Black motherhood was the source of Black poverty. With polemical intensity and cutting humor, Jordan denounces as racist and sexist a society that privileges father-led families while neglecting mothers and children: "Now I would agree that the Black family is not white. I do not agree that the problem is 'female-headedness.'" Despite hosts of obstacles, Black women, she declares, have been responsible for the survival of their families and "our continuation as a people in America." The speech, included here in full, was published both in the Black women's lifestyle magazine *Essence* and in *Ms*. It culminates with a thirteen-point program that still resonates, proposing such measures as a basic national income, free universal childcare, and equal pay for equal work.

I GOT UP that morning, with malice toward no one. Drank my coffee and scanned the front page of *The New York Times*. And there it was. I remember, even now, the effrontery of that headline four years ago: "Breakup of Black Family Imperils Gains of Decades." I could hardly believe it. Here were these clowns dumping on us yet again. That was 1983, three years into the shameless Real Deal of Ronald Reagan. He'd taken or he'd shaken everything we Black folks needed just to hang in here, breathing in and out. And yet the headline absolutely failed to give credit where it was due. Instead, "politicians and scholars—black and white" dared to identify the *victims*—the Black single mothers raising 55 percent of all of our Black children *with no help from anybody anywhere*—as the cause of Black poverty! These expense-account professionals presumed to identify "the family crisis" of Black folks as "a threat to the future of Black people without equal." And this was not somebody's weird idea about how to say "thank you." (I could relate to that: somebody finally saying thank you to Black women!) No: This was just another dumb, bold insult to my mother.

Now when I was growing up, the one sure trigger to a down-and-out fight was to say something—anything—about somebody's mother. As a matter of fact, we refined things eventually to the point where you didn't have to get specific. All you had to do was push into the face of another girl or boy, close as you could, almost nose to nose, and just spit out the two words: "Your mother!" This item of our code of honor was not negotiable, and clearly we took it pretty seriously: Even daring to refer to someone's mother put you off-limits. From the time you learned how to talk, everybody's mama remained the holiest of the holies. And we did not ever forget it, this fact, that the first, the last and the most, that the number-one persevering, resourceful, resilient and devoted person in our lives was, and would always be, your mother and my mother.

But sometimes, as you know, we grow up without growing wise. Sometimes we become so sophisticated we have to read *The New York Times* in order to figure out whether it's a hot or a rainy day. We read the fine print in order to find out the names of our so-called leaders. But what truly surprises me is Black folks listening to a whole lot of white blasphemy against Black feats of survival, Black folks paying attention to people who never even notice us except to describe us as "female-headed" or something equally weird. (I would like to know, for a fact, has anybody ever seen a female-headed anything at all? What did it look like? What did it do?)

Now I am not opposed to sophistication per se, but when you lose touch with your mama, when you take the word of an absolute, hostile stranger over and above the unarguable truth of your own miraculous, hard-won history, and when you don't remember to ask, again and again, "Compared to what?" I think you don't need to worry about enemies anymore. You'd better just worry about yourself.

Back in 1965, Daniel P. Moynihan (now a U.S. senator from New York) issued a broadside insult to the national Black community. With the full support of a Democratic administration that was tired of Negroes carrying on about citizenship rights and integration and white racist violence, Moynihan came through with the theory that we, Black folks, and that we, Black women in particular, constituted "the problem." And now there are Black voices joining the choruses of the absurd. There are national Black organizations and purported Black theoreticians who have become indistinguishable from the verified enemies of Black folks in this country.

These sophisticated Black voices jump to the forefront of delighted mass-media exposure because they are willing to lament and to defame the incredible triumph of Black women, the victory of Black mothers that is the victory of our continuation as a people in America.

Archly delivering jargon phrases about "the collapse of Black family structure" and "the destructive culture of poverty in the ghetto" and, of course, "the crisis of female-headedness," with an additional screaming reference to "the shame of teenage pregnancy," these Black voices come to us as the disembodied blatherings of peculiar offspring: Black men and women who wish to deny the Black mother of their origins and who wish to adopt white Daniel P. Moynihan as their father. I happen to lack the imagination necessary to forgive, or understand, this phenomenon. But the possible consequences of this oddball public outcry demand our calm examination.

According to these new Black voices fathered by Mr. Moynihan, it would seem that the Black family subsists in a terrible, deteriorating state. That's the problem. The source of the problem is The Black Family (that is, it is not white; it suffers from "female-headedness"). The solution to The Black Family Problem is—you guessed it—The Black Family. It must become more white—more patriarchal, less "female-headed," more employed more steadily at better and better-paying jobs.

Now I would agree that the Black family is not white. I do not agree that the problem is "female-headedness." I would rather suggest that the problem is that women in general and that Black women in particular cannot raise our children and secure adequately paying jobs because this is a society that hates women and that believes we are replaceable, that we are dispensable, ridiculous, irksome facts of life. American social and economic hatred of women means that any work primarily identified as women's work will be poorly paid, if at all. Any work open to women will be poorly paid, at best, in comparison to work open to men. Any work done by women will receive a maximum of 64 cents on the dollar compared with wages for the same work done by men. Prenatal, well-baby care, day care for children, children's allowances, housing allowances for parents, paid maternity leave—all of the elemental provisions for the equally entitled citizenship of women and children are ordinary attributes of industrialized nations, except for one: the United States.

The problem, clearly, does not originate with women in general or Black women specifically, who, whether it's hard or whether it's virtually impossible, nevertheless keep things together. Our hardships follow from the uncivilized political and economic status enjoined upon women and children in our country, which has the highest infant mortality rate among its industrial peers. And, evidently, feels fine, thank you, about that. (Not incidentally, Black infant-mortality rates hold at levels twice that for whites.)

The Black Family persists *despite* the terrible deteriorating state of affairs prevailing in the United States. This is a nation unwilling and progressively unable to provide for the well-being of most of its citizens: Our economic system increasingly concentrates our national wealth in the hands of fewer and fewer interest groups. Our economic system increasingly augments the wealth of the richest sector of the citizenry, while it diminishes the real wages and the available livelihood of the poor. Our economic system refuses responsibility for the equitable sharing of national services and monies among its various peoples. Our economic system remains insensitive to the political demands of a democracy, and therefore it does not yield to the requirements of equal entitlement of all women and all children and Black, Hispanic and Native American men, the elderly and the disabled. If you total the American people you have an obvious majority of Americans squeezed outside the putative benefits of "free enterprise."

Our economic system continues its trillion-dollar commitment *not* to the betterment of the lives of its citizens but, rather, to the development and lunatic replication of a military-industrial complex. In this context, then, the Black family persists, yes, in a terrible deteriorating state. But we did not create this state. Nor do we control it. And we are not suffering "collapse." Change does not signify collapse. The nuclear, patriarchal family structure of white America was never our own; it was not *African*. And when we arrived to slavery here, why or how should we have emulated the overseer and the master? We who were counted in the Constitution as three-fifths of a human being? We who could by law neither marry nor retain our children against the predations of the slave economy? Nonetheless, from under the whip through underpaid underemployment and worse, Black folks have formulated our own family, our own home base for nurture and for pride. We have done this through extended kinship methods. And even Black teenage parents are trying, in their own way, to perpetuate the Black family.

The bizarre analysis of the Black family that blames the Black family for being not white and not patriarchal, not endowed with steadily employed Black husbands and fathers who enjoy access to middle-income occupations is just that: a bizarre analysis, a heartless joke. If Black men and Black women *wanted* Black men to become patriarchs of their families, if Black men wanted to function as head of the house—shouldn't they probably have some kind of a job? Can anyone truly dare to suggest that the catastrophic 46-percent unemployment rate now crippling working-age Black men is something that either Black men or Black women view as positive or desirable? Forty-six percent! What is the meaning of a man in the house if he cannot hold out his hand to help his family make it through the month, and if he cannot hold up his head with the pride and authority that regular, satisfying work for good pay provides? How or whom shall he marry and on what basis? Is it honestly puzzling to anyone that the 46-percent, Depression-era rate of unemployment that imprisons Black men almost exactly mirrors the 50 percent of Black households now maintained by Black women? Our Black families persist despite a racist arrangement of rewards such as the fact that the median Black family has only about 56 cents to spend for every dollar that white families have to spend. And a Black college graduate still cannot realistically expect to earn more than a white high-school graduate.

We, children and parents of Black families, neither created nor do we control the terrible, deteriorating state of our unjust and meanly discriminating national affairs. In its structure, the traditional Black family has always reflected our particular jeopardy within these unwelcome circumstances. We have never been "standard" or predictable or stabilized in any normative sense, even as our Black lives have never been standard or predictable or stabilized in a benign national environment. We have been flexible, ingenious and innovative or we have perished. And we have not perished. We remain and we remain different, and we have become necessarily deft at distinguishing between the negative differences—those imposed upon us—and the positive differences—those that joyously attest to our distinctive, survivalist attributes as a people.

Today we must distinguish between responsibility and consequence. We are not responsible for the systematic underemployment and unemployment of Black men or women. We are not responsible for racist hatred of us, and we are not responsible for the American contempt for women per se. We are not responsible for a dominant value system that quibbles over welfare benefits for children and squanders deficit billions of dollars on American pie in the sky. But we must outlive the consequences of this inhumane, disposable-life ideology. We have no choice. And because this ideology underpins our economic system and the political system that supports our economy, we no longer constitute a minority inside America. We are joined in our precarious quandary here by all women and by children, Hispanic Americans and Native Americans and the quickly expanding population of the aged, as well as the temporarily or permanently disabled.

At issue now is the "universal entitlement" of American citizens (as author Ruth Sidel terms it in her important book *Women and Children Last: The Plight of Poor Women in Affluent America* [Viking Press, 1986]): What should American citizenship confer? What are the duties of the state in relation to the citizens it presumes to tax and to govern?

It is not the Black family in crisis but American democracy in crisis when the majority of our people oppose U.S. intervention in Central America and, nevertheless, the President proceeds to intervene. It is not the Black family in crisis but American democracy at stake when the majority of our people abhor South African apartheid and, nonetheless, the President proceeds to collaborate with the leadership of that evil. It is not the Black family in crisis but American democracy at risk when a majority of American citizens may no longer assume that social programs beneficial to them will be preserved and/or developed.

But if we, Black children and parents, have been joined by so many others in our precarious quandary here, may we not also now actively join with these other jeopardized Americans to redefine and to finally secure universal entitlement of citizenship that will at last conclude the shameful American history of our oppression? And what should these universal entitlements—our new American Bill of Rights—include?

1. Guaranteed jobs and/or guaranteed income to ensure each and every American in each and every one of the 50 states an existence *above* the poverty line.

2. Higher domestic minimum wages and, for the sake of both our narrowest and broadest self-interests, a coordinated, international minimum wage so that exhausted economic exploitation in Detroit can no longer be replaced by economic exploitation in Taiwan or Soweto or Manila.

3. Government guarantees of an adequate minimum allowance for every child regardless of the marital status of the parents.

4. Equal pay for equal work.

5. Affirmative action to ensure broadly democratic access to higher-paying occupations.

6. Compensation for "women's work" equal to compensation for "men's work."

7. Housing allowances and/or state commitments to build and/or to subsidize acceptable, safe and affordable housing for every citizen.

8. Comprehensive, national health insurance from prenatal through geriatric care.

9. Availability of state education and perpetual reeducation through graduate levels of study on the basis of student interest and aptitude rather than financial capacity.

10. A national budget that will invariably commit the main portion of our collective monies to our collective domestic needs for a good life.

11. Comprehensive provision for the well-being of all our children commensurate with the kind of future we are hoping to help construct. These provisions must include paid maternity and paternity leave and universal, state-controlled, public child-care programs for working parents.

12. Nationalization of vital industries to protect citizen consumers and citizen workers alike from the greed-driven vagaries of a "free market."

13. Aggressive nuclear-disarmament policies and, concurrently, aggressive state protection of what's left of the life-supportive elements of our global environment.

I do not believe that a just, a civilized nation can properly regard any one of these 13 entitlements as optional. And yet not one of them is legally in place in the United States. And why not? I think that, as a people, we have yet to learn how to say thank you in real ways to those who have loved us enough to keep us alive despite inhumane and unforgivable opposition to our well-being. For myself, I do not need any super-sophisticated charts and magical graphs to tell me my own mama done better than she could, and my mama's mama, *she* done better than I could. And *everybody's mama* done better than anybody had any right to expect she would. And that's the truth!

And I hope you've been able to follow my meaning. And a word to the wise, they say, should be sufficient. So, I'm telling you real nice: Don't you talk about my mama!

While universally condemning sex trafficking and all forms of nonconsensual, underage, and violent sex, feminists have long held differing positions on prostitution; the two major views are (1) to abolish prostitution as inherently oppressive and exploitive, or (2) to support sex workers' rights and decriminalize sex work. These and other views were presented in the feminist anthology *Sex Work*, published by the women-led Cleis Press in 1987. In the following pair of excerpts from the anthology, Sarah Wynter (aka Evelina Giobbe), a former prostitute and founder of the New York WHISPER (Women Hurt in Systems of Prostitution Engaged in Revolt) Program, speaks for the abolitionist view while Rachel West, founder of the San Francisco–based U.S. PROStitutes Collective (U.S. PROS), a multiracial sex workers' rights organization, offers the sex workers' rights view. U.S. PROS began in New York, where a group of Black women formed New York Prostitutes Collective, and went national in 1980.

WHISPER: Women Hurt in Systems of Prostitution Engaged in Revolt (Sarah Wynter)

THERE HAS been a deliberate attempt to validate men's perceived need, and self-proclaimed right, to buy and sell women's bodies for sexual use. This has been accomplished, in part, by euphemizing prostitution as an occupation. Men have promoted the cultural myth that women actively seek out prostitution as a pleasurable economic alternative to low-paying, low-skilled, monotonous labor, conveniently ignoring the conditions that insure women's inequality and the preconditions which make women vulnerable to prostitution. Men have been so successful in reinforcing this myth by controlling the culture that their central role in the commercial sexual exploitation of women has become invisible. The myth is so pervasive that when women come forward and expose the conditions they've endured, the injuries they've sustained through systems of prostitution, they are most often disbelieved or considered to be the exception rather than the rule.

Men's distortion about the realities of women's lives to serve their own self-interest is not new to feminists. Not long ago, we struggled to debunk the lie that women invited, and in fact enjoyed rape. That we "asked for it." Not that long ago, we struggled to expose the lie that battered wives provoked attacks, that they "must like it or they would leave." It was not that long ago that we unmasked the lie that children were complicit in incestuous abuse, that they "must have liked it or they would have told."

When rape victims failed to report their attacks, when battered wives remained in abusive relationships, when incest survivors kept childhood molestations a secret, we, as feminists, didn't interpret their silence as support for the culture's denial of their victimization. Instead, we joined together to condemn rape, battery, and sexual abuse and to demand legislation that would empower the victims.

These women, the raped, the battered, the incest survivors, along with their poor and disadvantaged sisters, are the selfsame women who are actively recruited and coerced into systems of prostitution. And the male hierarchy is spreading the same lies about the same women again: "They want it. They like it. If they didn't they would leave."

Another way that men attempt to validate prostitution as a career for women is by proposing that because of women's economic subordination (which men have insured), it is unfair to deprive women of the opportunity to earn a living wage by selling a service that they are compelled (by men) to offer for free. As feminists, we are bound to not only criticize and attempt to rectify economic subordination and compulsory sexual submission (which we have defined as rape), but the institution of prostitution which is the commerce of sexual abuse and inequality.

In parts of Europe and South America, drug kingpins hire poor women to transport heroin and cocaine into the United States. These women are called "mules," and they smuggle the drugs past customs by swallowing huge and potentially fatal doses in latex balloons. If there are no delays in the woman's voyage, when she arrives at her destination, the balloons are passed through her stool intact. This is not always the case. Sometimes one of the balloons is eaten away by the acids in the woman's stomach and she dies in transit from a massive overdose.

Some people claim that drug smuggling is a lucrative industry. And it is, for the dealer safe at home in France, or Italy, or Bogotà. But for the woman captured by customs officials, or lying on the coroner's table, it was an act of desperation. Shall we then say that because a woman coerced by poverty gambles with her life to secure an income that being a mule is a valid occupational alternative that she freely chooses? Every time a prostitute climbs into a car or walks into a hotel with a strange man, coerced by the circumstances of her existence, sexual abuse, rape, battery or just plain poverty, she risks her freedom and her very life. Can we then say that prostitution is a valid occupational alternative that she freely chooses?

Prostitution is taught in the home, socially validated by a sexual libertarian ideology, and enforced by both the church and the state. That is to say that both the conservative right and the liberal left male hierarchies collude to teach and keep women in prostitution. The right, by demanding that women be sexually and socially subordinate to one man in marriage, and the left, by demanding that women be sexually and socially subordinate to all men through prostitution and pornography. Their common goal is to exercise their prerogative to control and own women in both the private and public spheres.

Prostitution is taught to women in the home when the courts uphold the moral imperatives of the church (that women be unconditionally sexually available to their husbands), by maintaining the marital rape exemption in the penal code of most states. Prostitution is taught to girls in the home through paternal sexual abuse. The fact that social scientists have reported that upwards of seventy-five percent of women in the sex industry were sexually abused as children suggests that the ramifications of incest and sexual assault in childhood are causal factors in prostitution. Prostitution is taught through the social sanctioning of the commercial sexual exploitation of pornographers which maintains women's second class status and yet is touted by the liberal left as women's sexual liberation.

Prostitution isn't like anything else. Rather everything else is like prostitution, because it is the model for women's condition, for gender stratification and its logical extension, sex discrimination. Prostitution is founded on enforced sexual abuse under a system of male supremacy that is itself built along a continuum of coercion—fear, force, racism and poverty. For every real difference between women, prostitution exists to erase our diversity, distinction, and accomplishment while reducing all of us to meat to be bought, sold, traded, used, discarded, degraded, ridiculed, humiliated, maimed, tortured, and all too often, murdered for sex.

Prostitution is the foundation upon which pornography is built. Pornography is the vehicle by which men sexualize women's chattel status. Pornography cannot exist without prostitution. They are interdependent and create a sexual ghetto that insures women's inequality. It is impossible to separate pornography from prostitution. The acts are identical except that in pornography there is a permanent record of the woman's abuse.

The emerging profile of women used in prostitution clearly does not reflect the lies promoted in pornography and the mainstream media. As these social science ethnologies document, these are women with few resources; most are poor and have been subjected to sexual assault, rape, and battery. The average

age for women entering prostitution is sixteen, although the number of nine-, ten-, and eleven-year-old girls in the industry is on the rise. Over half of adult prostitutes were adolescent runaways; approximately seventy-five percent of these teenagers were victims of sexual abuse. Between half and seventy-five percent of prostitutes have pimps, and almost all of them have had pimps at one time in the past. Many are women of color. Many are substance abusers or drug addicts. Many have dependent children. Many were battered wives who have escaped from, or were abandoned by, abusive husbands and forced into prostitution in order to support themselves and their children.

We, the women of WHISPER, reject the lie that women freely choose prostitution from a whole array of economic alternatives that exist under civil equity. In the United States women have been unable to pass the Equal Rights Amendment. Eighty percent of the people in poverty in this country are women with dependent children. Women earn approximately sixty-seven cents for every dollar men earn. It is estimated that one out of every four girls will be sexually abused before the age of sixteen, that a woman is battered every eighteen seconds, raped every four minutes, that two thousand to four thousand women are beaten to death by their husbands annually, and most states still carry a marital exemption in their penal code. Clearly this does not reflect civil equality.

We reject the lie that turning tricks is sexual pleasure or agency for women. We reject the lie that women can and do become wealthy in systems of prostitution. We reject the lie that women control and are empowered in systems of prostitution. We reject the false divisions imposed by society which differentiate between pornography, peep shows, live sex shows, and prostitution as it is commonly defined. Each is a type of commercial sexual exploitation and abuse which reduces women to commodities for the pleasure and profit of men. Each is premised on inequality due to a condition of birth: gender. Because the only prerequisite necessary to be targeted for this abuse is to be born female, the commercial trafficking in women is by definition a form of sex discrimination.

We reject the false hierarchy imposed on women by men which claims that "call girls" are inherently better off than "street walkers," when the only real difference between the two is the private abuse of women juxtaposed to the public abuse of women. The equivalent of this would be stranger rape juxtaposed to marital rape.

We oppose current and proposed legislation (including *current* versions of criminalization, legalization, and decriminalization *with* zoning or regulatory provisions) which treat the institution of prostitution as an "urban blight" or an "eyesore" that needs to be hidden from view yet kept available to men.

These "solutions" insure men's unconditional sexual access to women without consideration for the physical and psychological consequences to individual women and the overall damage to the civil and social status of all women (by defining us as genitals that can be bought, sold, or traded). We want the state to stop defining prostitution as a "victimless" crime or as a crime committed by women, and acknowledge it for what it is—a crime committed against women by men. We want the state to stop arresting prostitutes and to start enforcing laws against men who traffic in women's bodies for their own pleasure and profit.

WHISPER has been founded by women who have escaped systems of prostitution to create a forum for us to speak out about the realities of our lives and to explore ideas for change. We have chosen the acronym WHISPER because women in systems of prostitution do whisper among ourselves about the coercion, degradation, sexual abuse and battery in our lives, while the myths about prostitution are shouted out in pornography, in mainstream media, and by self-appointed "experts" who have admittedly never experienced prostitution. We expect WHISPER to be a tool for change in our lives, and in our lifetime. Our purpose is to make the sexual enslavement of women history.

(from) U.S. PROStitutes Collective (Rachel West)

THE UNITED STATES Prostitutes Collective (U.S. PROS) is a national network of women who work in the sex industry as well as other women who support our goals. We are part of the International Prostitutes Collective (IPC) and a sister organization of the English Collective of Prostitutes (ECP). U.S. PROS is an independent network that is part of the International Wages for Housework Campaign. Women in our network are working or have worked in all levels of the sex industry: women who work the streets, massage parlors, escort services, hotels, clubs, houses, strippers, dancers, mistresses, models, etc., full-time and part-time, black, Latino and white women.

We are campaigning for the abolition of the laws against prostitute women—not legalization or decriminalization—so that women can work as independent business women, controlling our own working conditions. Legalization in Nevada, in the United States, and in the Eros Centers of West Germany are basically the new sex assembly lines. The women have no control over working conditions, hours worked, the number of clients they see, tips they receive, etc. Women, when working, have to register with the police and therefore are registered as "known prostitute women." They are also subject to health checks and are restricted in their movements outside the brothels. Decriminalization in some countries has come to mean the same as legalization. Therefore the IPC is very careful to make the distinction between legalization/decriminalization and abolition of the laws. It is a dangerous game to go along with the "program" of some state planners for legalization that in no way would end the vulnerability that prostitute women face. We are not building a movement to carry out our oppression under the guise of legalization or decriminalization.

We are also campaigning for economic independence for women, so that none of us will be forced into prostitution for economic reasons: safe houses for juvenile runaways, increases in all income transfer payments such as welfare (a study in San Francisco has shown that when welfare is cut, the number of AFDC mothers picked up for prostitution increases) and against immigration controls so that women and children can move freely from one country to another.

WHO ARE PROSTITUTE WOMEN?

In the United States women began to form support groups for the work of U.S. PROS in cities without active U.S. PROS chapters entitled No Bad Women, Just Bad Laws in Tulsa, Oklahoma; Boston, Massachusetts; New Haven, Connecticut and Portland, Oregon. They organized coalitions, pickets, press conferences, wrote letters, etc., on behalf of the rights of prostitute women. They stated clearly that the rights of prostitute women are the rights of all women. Both No Bad Women and the U.S. PROS networks are raising the public's awareness of who prostitutes are—in reality as diverse a group as any. We are mostly single mothers with children to support, women on welfare, women helping to support elderly relatives on fixed incomes, secretaries and other office workers supplementing low wages, students putting themselves through school, full-time housewives, nurses, teachers, juvenile runaways refusing to be raped and battered or emotionally abused at home, and other women refusing the low wages available to women in the straight job market. In other words, there is no real stereotype of who a prostitute woman is—she could be any of us. Prostitute women as drug addicts is one very common stereotype. Given how widespread the use of drugs in society is, we doubt there is much difference in the percentage of prostitute women on drugs and the percentage of others on drugs. AIDS is also misrepresented as being spread by prostitute women.

Another view we've had to challenge is that of feminists and anti-porn campaigners who like to blame sex industry workers for rape and violence against women. In Los Angeles we were instrumental, along with other women's groups, in overturning an anti-porn ordinance. We spoke out publicly about the devastating effects that greater censorship, and forcing sex industry workers underground, would have on working conditions and safety of women in the sex industry. The stereotype of prostitute women is promoted by the police, media and prostitute movement careerists whose funding and media access depends on putting forward the stereotype as the typical prostitute woman.

RACISM AND POLICE ILLEGALITY

Our day to day organizing includes fighting for the immediate civil rights of prostitute women and against the tremendous level of violence that prostitutes face because we are illegal. Our illegality makes us vulnerable to police brutality and racism, to extortion, kidnapping etc. by others who pimp off our vulnerability. The enforcement of the prostitution laws is both selective and racist. Although the majority of prostitute women are white, the majority of those in jail for prostitution are black. Prostitute women are constantly subject to illegal arrests in street sweeps; they are beaten up and forced to have sex with police officers. U.S. PROS often organizes pickets outside the courthouse to protest these abuses and to bring to the public's attention just how much taxpayer money is wasted on harassing, prosecuting and jailing prostitute women. Money could be better spent on programs to assist women with childcare, housing, health care, academic scholarships, waged job training programs, increased welfare payments etc., all of which would reduce the reasons women go into prostitution in the first place. Prostitution is about money, not about sex. If women's basic economic situation does not change, then women will continue to work as prostitutes.

Given the economic status of women, how many of us are forced to rent our bodies, stay in marriages we want to get out of, make deals with the landlord, shop keeper, put up with sexual harassment on the job, smile when we don't want to, put out or get fired etc.? How many wives put in a greater effort at being sexy when they need extra money from their husbands? How many women choose the man who has better career prospects over the man who is a heartthrob? How much do we all have to prostitute ourselves because women internationally have so little to show for the tremendous amount of work we do? Perhaps in thinking over these things, non-prostitute women can see that they are really not so very far apart from the rest of us.

LEGAL ACTION FOR WOMEN (LAW)

U.S. PROS has also organized Legal Action for Women (LAW) in San Francisco, based on LAW in London (see ECP), a grassroots legal service for all women to challenge police and court practices. We've helped women plead not guilty to illegal arrests and win their cases. Since its formulation in 1984, LAW has helped hundreds of women, not only prostitute women, but any women who can't afford legal services. We have also set up a Prostitutes Complaint Bureau where we document cases of police and customer harassment or brutality.

FIGHTING VIGILANTES

We have organized against vigilante harassment of prostitute women in Berkeley, Sacramento, Portland, Oregon and Tulsa, Oklahoma where vigilantes protected by the police patrolled the streets hunting down women they suspected of being prostitutes. We picketed City Hall protesting their support of the vigilantes, spoke at City Council meetings, met with local residents, spoke out to the public on television and radio. In a recent poll taken by a radio station in Berkeley in the neighborhood where the vigilantes patrolled, ninety-five percent of the residents interviewed were on our side.

ANN SNITOW

(from) Pages From a Gender Diary: Basic Divisions in Feminism

Ann Snitow (1943–2019) was a radical feminist organizer, writer, and teacher, cofounder of such groups as New York Radical Feminists (1969), the pro-choice street theater group No More Nice Girls (1977), the Feminist Anti-Censorship Task-force (FACT, 1982), and the Network of East-West Women (1990). In this essay, published in *Dissent* in 1989, Snitow analyzes what she sees as a basic, recurring "feminist divide" over how to conceive of the category *woman*. Among the aspects of the divide she discusses are "Radical and Cultural Feminists," "Essentialists and Social Constructionists," "Motherists and Feminists," and "Equality and Difference." This excerpt includes Snitow's introduction to the divide and her elucidation of "Equality and Difference."

In the early days of this wave of the women's movement, I sat in a weekly consciousness-raising group with my friend A. We compared notes recently: What did you think was happening? How did you think our own lives were going to change? A. said she had felt, "Now I can be a woman; it's no longer so humiliating. I can stop fantasizing that secretly I am a man, as I used to, before I had children. Now I can value what was once my shame." Her answer amazed me. Sitting in the same meetings during those years, my thoughts were roughly the reverse: "Now I don't have to be a woman anymore. I need never become a mother. Being a woman has always been humiliating, but I used to assume there was no exit. Now the very idea 'woman' is up for grabs. 'Woman' is my slave name; feminism will give me freedom to seek some other identity altogether."

ON ITS face this clash of theoretical and practical positions may seem absurd, but it is my goal to explore such contradictions, to show why they are not absurd at all. Feminism is inevitably a mixed form, requiring in its very nature such inconsistencies. In what follows I try to show first, that a common divide keeps forming in both feminist thought and action between the need to build the identity "woman" and give it solid political meaning and the need to tear down the very category "woman" and dismantle its all-too-solid history. Feminists often split along the lines of some version of this argument, and that splitting is my subject. Second, I argue that though a settled compromise between these positions is currently impossible, and though a constant choosing of sides is tactically unavoidable, feminists—and indeed most women—live in a complex relationship to this central feminist divide. From moment to moment we perform subtle psychological and social negotiations about just how gendered we choose to be.

This tension—between needing to act as women and needing an identity not overdetermined by our gender—is as old as Western feminism. It is at the core of what feminism is. The divide runs, twisting and turning, right through movement history. The problem of identity it poses was barely conceivable before the eighteenth century, when almost everyone saw women as a separate species. Since then absolute definitions of gender difference have fundamentally eroded, and the idea "woman" has become a question rather than a given.

In the current wave of the movement, the divide is more urgent and central a part of feminism than ever before. On the one hand, many women moved by feminism are engaged by its promise of solidarity, the poetry of a retrieved worth. It feels glorious to "reclaim an identity they taught [us] to despise." (The line is Michelle Cliff's.) Movement passion rescues women-only groups from contempt; female intimacy acquires new meanings and becomes more threatening to the male exclusiveness so long considered "the world."

On the other hand, other feminists, often equally stirred by solidarity, rebel against having to be "women" at all. They argue that whenever we uncritically accept the monolith "woman," we run the risk of merely relocating ourselves inside the old closed ring of an unchanging feminine nature. But is there any such reliable nature? These feminists question the eternal sisterhood. It may be a pleasure to be "we," and it may be strategically imperative to struggle as "we," but who, they ask, are "we"?[1]

EQUALITY AND DIFFERENCE

By now anyone who has spent time wrangling with feminist issues has recognized the divide and is no doubt waiting for me to produce the name for it that is probably the oldest, certainly the most all-encompassing: "equality" versus "difference." Most feminist thought grapples unavoidably with some aspect of the equality-difference problem at both the level of theory and of strategy. In theory, this version of the divide might be stated: Do women want to be equal to men (with the meaning of "equal" hotly contested),[2] or do women see biology as establishing a difference that will always require a strong recognition and that might ultimately define quite separate possibilities inside "the human"?

Some difference-feminists would argue that women have a special morality, or aesthetic, or capacity for community that it is feminism's responsibility to maximize. Others would put the theoretical case for difference more neutrally and would argue that woman, no matter *what* she is like, is unassimilable. Because she is biologically and therefore psychologically separable from man, she is enduring proof that there is no universally representative human being, no "human wholeness."[3] In contrast, the equality-feminists would argue that it is possible for the biological difference to wither away as a basis for social organization, either by moving men and women toward some shared center (androgyny) or toward some experience of human variety in which biology is but one small variable.

Difference theory tends to emphasize the body (and more recently the unconscious where the body's psychic meaning develops); equality theory tends to deemphasize the body and to place faith in each individual's capacity to develop a self not ultimately circumscribed by a collective law of gender. For difference theorists the body can be either the site of pain and oppression or the site of orgasmic ecstasy and maternal joy. For equality theorists neither extreme is as compelling as the overriding idea that the difference between male and female bodies is a problem in need of solution. In this view, therefore, sexual hierarchy and sexual oppression are bound to continue unless the body is transcended or displaced as the center of female identity.

At the level of practical strategy, the equality-difference divide is just as ubiquitous as it is in theory. Willingly or not, activist lawyers find themselves pitted against each other because they disagree about whether "equal treatment" before the law is better or worse for women than "special treatment," for example, in cases about pregnancy benefits or child custody. (Should pregnancy be defined as unique, requiring special legal provisions, or will pregnant women get more actual economic support if pregnancy, when incapacitating, is grouped with other temporary conditions that keep people from work? Should women who give birth and are almost always the ones who care for children therefore get an automatic preference in custody battles, or will women gain more ultimately if men are defined by law as equally responsible for children, hence equally eligible to be awarded custody?)[4] Sometimes activists find themselves pressured by events to pit the mainstreaming of information about women in the school curriculum against the need for separate programs for women's studies. Or they find themselves having to choose between working to get traditionally male jobs (for example in construction) and working to get fair pay in the women-only jobs they are already doing.

One rushes to respond that these strategic alternatives should not be mutually exclusive, but often, in the heat of local struggles, they temporarily become so. No matter what their theoretical position on the divide, activists find themselves having to make painfully unsatisfactory short-term decisions about the rival claims of equality and difference.[5]

Regrettably, these definitions, these examples flatten out the oscillations of the equality-difference debate; they obscure the class struggles that have shaped the development of the argument; they offer neat parallels where there should be asymmetries. Viewed historically, the oscillation between a feminism of equality and one of difference is a bitter disagreement about which path is more progressive, more able to change women's basic condition of subordination.

In this history each side has taken more than one turn at calling the other reactionary and each has had its genuine vanguard moments. "Difference" gained some working women protection at a time when any social legislation to regulate work was rare, while "equality" lay behind middle-class women's demand for the vote, a drive Ellen DuBois has called "the most radical program for women's emancipation possible in the nineteenth century."[6] At the same time, bourgeois women's demands that men should have to be as sexually pure as women finessed the divide between difference and equality and gave rise to interesting cross-class alliances of women seeking ways to make men conform to women's standard, rather than the usual way round—a notion of equality with a difference.[7] As DuBois points out, it is difficult to decide which of these varied political constructions gave nineteenth-century women the most real leverage to make change:

> My hypothesis is that the significance of the woman suffrage movement rested precisely on the fact that it bypassed women's oppression within the family, or private sphere, and demanded instead her admission to citizenship, and through it admission to the public arena.[8]

In other words, at a time when criticism of women's separate family role was still unthinkable, imagining a place outside the family where such a role would make no difference was—for a time—a most radical act.

Equality and difference are broad ideas and have included a range of definitions and political expressions. Equality, for example, can mean anything from the mildest liberal reform (this is piece-of-the-pie feminism, in which women are merely to be included in the world as it is) to the most radical reduction of gender to insignificance. Difference can mean anything from Mary Daly's belief in the natural superiority of women to psychoanalytic theories of how women are inevitably cast as "the Other" because they lack penises.[9]

---

1. The "we" problem has no more simple solution than does the divide itself, but in spite of its false promise of unity, the "we" remains politically important. In this piece, "we" includes anyone who calls herself a feminist, anyone who is actively engaged with the struggles described here.

2. Alison M. Jaggar gives an account of the contemporary feminist debate about the meaning and value of the demand for "equality" in Jaggar, "Sexual Difference and Sexual Equality." For some general accounts of the debate, also see Donovan, *Feminist Theory*; Eisenstein, *Contemporary Feminist Thought*; Eisenstein and Jardine, eds., *The Future of Difference*; Eisenstein, *Feminism and Sexual Equality*; Mitchell, *Women's Estate*; Mitchell and Oakley, eds., *What Is Feminism?* The debates about Carol Gilligan's *In a Different Voice* often turn on the equality-difference problem. See Broughton, ed., *New Ideas in Psychology* and his "Women's Rationality and Men's Virtues"; Kerber et al., "On *In a Different Voice*"; and Benhabib, "The Generalized and the Concrete Other." Similarly, the feminist response to Illich, *Gender*, has tended to raise these issues. See, for example, Benería, "Meditations on Ivan Illich's *Gender*."

3. The phrase "human wholeness" comes from Friedan, *The Second Stage*, and the concept receives a valuable and devastating critique in Jehlen, "Against Human Wholeness."

4. For the pregnancy issue, see Bertin, "Brief of the American Civil Liberties Union et al."; Chavkin, "Walking a Tightrope: Pregnancy, Parenting, and Work"; Vogel, "Debating Difference"; Bird and Holland, "Capitol Letter"; Williams, "Equality's Riddle"; Kay, "Equality and Difference." For the custody issue, see Bartlett and Stack, "Joint Custody, Feminism and the Dependency Dilemma"; Chesler, *Mothers on Trial*; Weitzman, *The Divorce Revolution*. The work of Nadine Taub, director of the Women's Rights Litigation Clinic, School of Law, Rutgers/Newark, has frequent bearing on both issues and on the larger questions in equality-difference debates. See Taub, "Defining and Combatting Sexual Harassment"; Taub, "Feminist Tensions"; Taub, "A Public Policy of Private Caring"; Taub and Williams, "Will Equality Require More Than Assimilation, Accommodation or Separation from the Existing Social Structure?" The burgeoning feminist work on the new reproductive technologies also reproduces the divide. For complete references to all aspects of these debates, see Taub and Cohen, *Reproductive Laws for the 1990s*.

5. If I had to come up with an example of a feminist strategy that faced the power of the divide squarely yet at the same time undermined the oppression the divide represents, I'd choose recent feminist comparable worth legislation. Humble and earthshaking, comparable worth asserts two things: First, because women and men do different work, the concept "equal pay" has little effect on raising women's low wages; and, second, if work were to be judged by standards of difficulty, educational preparation, experience, and so on (standards preferably developed by workers themselves), then antidiscrimination laws might enforce that men and women doing work of comparable worth be paid the same. (Perhaps nurses and auto mechanics? Or teachers and middle managers?) The

activists who have proposed comparable worth have singularly few pretensions. They are the first to point out that on its face, the proposal ignores the work women do in the family, ignores the noneconomic reasons why women and men have different kinds of jobs, ignores what's wrong with job hierarchies and with "worth" as the sole basis for determining pay. Yet this little brown mouse of a liberal reform, narrow in its present political potential and limited by its nature, has a touch of deconstructive genius. Without hoping to get women doing men's work tomorrow, the comparable worth model erodes the economic advantages to employers of consistently undervaluing women's work and channeling women into stigmatized work ghettoes where pay is always lower. With comparable worth, the stigma might well continue to haunt women's work, but women would be better paid. Men might start wanting a "woman's" job that paid well, while women might have new psychological incentives to cross gender work categories. Who knows, perhaps stigma might not catch up as categories of work got rethought and their gender markers moved around. And if the stigma clung to women's work, if men refused to be nurses even if nurses were paid as well as construction workers, a woman earning money is an independent woman. She can change the family; she can consider leaving it. Comparable worth asserts the divide, yet, slyly, it goes to work on the basic economic and psychological underpinnings of the divide; it undermines the idea that all work has a natural gender. See Evans and Nelson, *Wage Justice*. The mixtures of progressive and conservative impulses that have characterized both sides of the divide at different moments get a nuanced reading from Nancy F. Cott in her historical study of American feminism, *The Grounding of Modern Feminism*.

6. DuBois, "The Radicalism of the Woman Suffrage Movement," 128.

7. See, for example, Walkowitz, *Prostitution and Victorian Society*, 128.

8. DuBois, "The Radicalism of the Woman Suffrage Movement," 128.

9. See Daly, *Gyn/Ecology*. Maggie McFadden gives an account of this range in her useful taxonomy piece, "Anatomy of Difference." Adrienne Harris has pointed out to me that essentialism comes and goes in feminist psychoanalytic discussions of the penis: "The concept slips, moves in and breaks apart."

SUSAN FALUDI

(from) *Backlash*
Blame It on Feminism

Born in 1959, Susan Faludi came of age when the feminist movement was already under relentless attack. In her 1991 best seller *Backlash: The Undeclared War Against American Women*, Faludi, a Pulitzer Prize–winning journalist, employs precise statistics, personal interviews, and original research to debunk media myths disparaging women and feminism. From the 1980 article on sexual harassment she wrote for the *Harvard Crimson* as an undergraduate, which led to the dismissal of a guilty professor, to her 2013 *New Yorker* profile of women's liberation leader Shulamith Firestone, "Death of a Revolutionary," Faludi has been an outspoken champion of American feminism. Here, in full, is "Blame It on Feminism," the introduction to *Backlash*.

To be a woman in America at the close of the 20th century—what good fortune. That's what we keep hearing, anyway. The barricades have fallen, politicians assure us. Women have "made it," Madison Avenue cheers. Women's fight for equality has "largely been won," *Time* magazine announces. Enroll at any university, join any law firm, apply for credit at any bank. Women have so many opportunities now, corporate leaders say, that we don't really need equal opportunity policies. Women are so equal now, lawmakers say, that we no longer need an Equal Rights Amendment. Women have "so much," former President Ronald Reagan says, that the White House no longer needs to appoint them to higher office. Even American Express ads are saluting a woman's freedom to charge it. At last, women have received their full citizenship papers.

And yet . . .

Behind this celebration of the American woman's victory, behind the news, cheerfully and endlessly repeated, that the struggle for women's rights is won, another message flashes. You may be free and equal now, it says to women, but you have never been more miserable.

This bulletin of despair is posted everywhere—at the newsstand, on the

TV set, at the movies, in advertisements and doctors' offices and academic journals. Professional women are suffering "burnout" and succumbing to an "infertility epidemic." Single women are grieving from a "man shortage." The *New York Times* reports: Childless women are "depressed and confused" and their ranks are swelling. *Newsweek* says: Unwed women are "hysterical" and crumbling under a "profound crisis of confidence." The health advice manuals inform: High-powered career women are stricken with unprecedented outbreaks of "stress-induced disorders," hair loss, bad nerves, alcoholism, and even heart attacks. The psychology books advise: Independent women's loneliness represents "a major mental health problem today." Even founding feminist Betty Friedan has been spreading the word: she warns that women now suffer from a new identity crisis and "new 'problems that have no name.'"

How can American women be in so much trouble at the same time that they are supposed to be so blessed? If the status of women has never been higher, why is their emotional state so low? If women got what they asked for, what could possibly be the matter now?

The prevailing wisdom of the past decade has supported one, and only one, answer to this riddle: it must be all that equality that's causing all that pain. Women are unhappy precisely *because* they are free. Women are enslaved by their own liberation. They have grabbed at the gold ring of independence, only to miss the one ring that really matters. They have gained control of their fertility, only to destroy it. They have pursued their own professional dreams—and lost out on the greatest female adventure. The women's movement, as we are told time and again, has proved women's own worst enemy.

"In dispensing its spoils, women's liberation has given my generation high incomes, our own cigarette, the option of single parenthood, rape crisis centers, personal lines of credit, free love, and female gynecologists," Mona Charen, a young law student, writes in the *National Review*, in an article titled "The Feminist Mistake." "In return it has effectively robbed us of one thing upon which the happiness of most women rests—men." The *National Review* is a conservative publication, but such charges against the women's movement are not confined to its pages. "Our generation was the human sacrifice" to the women's movement, *Los Angeles Times* feature writer Elizabeth Mehren contends in a *Time* cover story. Baby-boom women like her, she says, have been duped by feminism: "We believed the rhetoric." In *Newsweek*, writer Kay Ebeling dubs feminism "the Great Experiment That Failed" and asserts "women in my generation, its perpetrators, are the casualties." Even the beauty magazines are saying it: *Harper's Bazaar* accuses the women's movement of having "lost us [women] ground instead of gaining it."

In the last decade, publications from the *New York Times* to *Vanity Fair* to the *Nation* have issued a steady stream of indictments against the women's movement, with such headlines as WHEN FEMINISM FAILED or THE AWFUL TRUTH ABOUT WOMEN'S LIB. They hold the campaign for women's equality responsible for nearly every woe besetting women, from mental depression to meager savings accounts, from teenage suicides to eating disorders to bad complexions. The "Today" show says women's liberation is to blame for bag ladies. A guest columnist in the *Baltimore Sun* even proposes that feminists produced the rise in slasher movies. By making the "violence" of abortion more acceptable, the author reasons, women's rights activists made it all right to show graphic murders on screen.

At the same time, other outlets of popular culture have been forging the same connection: in Hollywood films, of which *Fatal Attraction* is only the most famous, emancipated women with condominiums of their own slink wild-eyed between bare walls, paying for their liberty with an empty bed, a barren womb. "My biological clock is ticking so loud it keeps me awake at night," Sally Field cries in the film *Surrender*, as, in an all too common transformation in the cinema of the '80s, an actress who once played scrappy working heroines is now showcased groveling for a groom. In prime-time television shows, from "thirtysomething" to "Family Man," single, professional, and feminist women are humiliated, turned into harpies, or hit by nervous breakdowns; the wise ones recant their independent ways by the closing sequence. In popular novels, from Gail Parent's *A Sign of the Eighties* to Stephen King's *Misery*, unwed women shrink to sniveling spinsters or inflate to fire-breathing she-devils; renouncing all aspirations but marriage, they beg for wedding bands from strangers or swing sledgehammers at reluctant bachelors. We "blew it by waiting," a typically remorseful careerist sobs in Freda Bright's *Singular Women*; she and her sister professionals are "condemned to be childless forever." Even Erica Jong's high-flying independent heroine literally crashes by the end of the decade, as the author supplants *Fear of Flying*'s saucy Isadora Wing, a symbol of female sexual emancipation in the '70s, with an embittered careerist-turned-recovering-"co-dependent" in *Any Woman's Blues*—a book that is intended, as the narrator bluntly states, "to demonstrate what a deadend the so-called sexual revolution had become, and how desperate so-called free women were in the last few years of our decadent epoch."

Popular psychology manuals peddle the same diagnosis for contemporary female distress. "Feminism, having promised her a stronger sense of her own identity, has given her little more than an identity *crisis*," the best-selling advice manual *Being a Woman* asserts. The authors of the era's self-help classic *Smart Women/Foolish Choices* proclaim that women's distress was "an unfortunate consequence of feminism," because "it created a myth among women that the apex of self-realization could be achieved only through autonomy, independence, and career."

In the Reagan and Bush years, government officials have needed no prompting to endorse this thesis. Reagan spokeswoman Faith Whittlesey declared feminism a "straitjacket" for women, in the White House's only policy speech on the status of the American female population—entitled "Radical Feminism in Retreat." Law enforcement officers and judges, too, have pointed a damning finger at feminism, claiming that they can chart a path from rising female independence to rising female pathology. As a California sheriff explained it to the press, "Women are enjoying a lot more freedom now, and as a result, they are committing more crimes." The U.S. Attorney General's Commission on Pornography even proposed that women's professional advancement might be responsible for rising rape rates. With more women in college and at work now, the commission members reasoned in their report, women just have more opportunities to be raped.

Some academics have signed on to the consensus, too—and they are the "experts" who have enjoyed the highest profiles on the media circuit. On network news and talk shows, they have advised millions of women that feminism has condemned them to "a lesser life." Legal scholars have railed against "the equality trap." Sociologists have claimed that "feminist-inspired" legislative reforms have stripped women of special "protections." Economists have argued that well-paid working women have created "a less stable American family." And demographers, with greatest fanfare, have legitimated the prevailing wisdom with so-called neutral data on sex ratios and fertility trends; they say they actually have the numbers to prove that equality doesn't mix with marriage and motherhood.

Finally, some "liberated" women themselves have joined the lamentations. In confessional accounts, works that invariably receive a hearty greeting from the publishing industry, "recovering Superwomen" tell all. In *The Cost of Loving: Women and the New Fear of Intimacy*, Megan Marshall, a Harvard-pedigreed writer, asserts that the feminist "Myth of Independence" has turned her generation into unloved and unhappy fast-trackers, "dehumanized" by careers and "uncertain of their gender identity." Other diaries of mad Super-women charge that "the hard-core feminist viewpoint," as one of them puts it, has relegated educated executive achievers to solitary nights of frozen dinners and closet drinking. The triumph of equality, they report, has merely given women hives, stomach cramps, eye-twitching disorders, even comas.

But what "equality" are all these authorities talking about?

If American women are so equal, why do they represent two-thirds of all poor adults? Why are nearly 75 percent of full-time working women making less than $20,000 a year, nearly double the male rate? Why are they still far more likely than men to live in poor housing and receive no health insurance, and twice as likely to draw no pension? Why does the average working woman's salary still lag as far behind the average man's as it did twenty years ago? Why does the average female college graduate today earn less than a man with no more than a high school diploma (just as she did in the '50s)—and why does the average female high school graduate today earn less than a male high school dropout? Why do American women, in fact, face one of the worst gender-based pay gaps in the developed world?

If women have "made it," then why are nearly 80 percent of working women still stuck in traditional "female" jobs—as secretaries, administrative "support" workers and salesclerks? And, conversely, why are they less than 8 percent of all federal and state judges, less than 6 percent of all law partners, and less than one half of 1 percent of top corporate managers? Why are there only three female state governors, two female U.S. senators, and two Fortune 500 chief executives? Why are only nineteen of the four thousand corporate officers and directors women—and why do more than half the boards of Fortune companies still lack even one female member?

If women "have it all," then why don't they have the most basic requirements to achieve equality in the work force? Unlike virtually all other industrialized nations, the U.S. government still has no family-leave and child care programs—and more than 99 percent of American private employers don't offer child care either. Though business leaders say they are aware of and deplore sex discrimination, corporate America has yet to make an honest effort toward eradicating it. In a 1990 national poll of chief executives at Fortune 1000 companies, more than 80 percent acknowledged that discrimination impedes female employees' progress—yet, less than 1 percent of these same companies regarded *remedying* sex discrimination as a goal that their personnel departments should pursue. In fact, when the companies' human resource officers were asked to rate their department's priorities, women's advancement ranked last.

If women are so "free," why are their reproductive freedoms in greater jeopardy today than a decade earlier? Why do women who want to postpone childbearing now have fewer options than ten years ago? The availability of different forms of contraception has declined, research for new birth control has virtually halted, new laws restricting abortion—or even *information* about abortion—for young and poor women have been passed, and the U.S. Supreme Court has shown little ardor in defending the right it granted in 1973.

Nor is women's struggle for equal education over; as a 1989 study found, three-fourths of all high schools still violate the federal law banning sex discrimination in education. In colleges, undergraduate women receive only 70 percent of the aid undergraduate men get in grants and work-study jobs—and women's sports programs receive a pittance compared with men's. A review of state equal-education laws in the late '80s found that only thirteen states had adopted the minimum provisions required by the federal Title IX law—and only seven states had anti-discrimination regulations that covered all education levels.

Nor do women enjoy equality in their own homes, where they still shoulder 70 percent of the household duties—and the only major change in the last fifteen years is that now middle-class men *think* they do more around the house. (In fact, a national poll finds the ranks of women saying their husbands share equally in child care shrunk to 31 percent in 1987 from 40 percent three years earlier.) Furthermore, in thirty states, it is still generally legal for husbands to rape their wives; and only ten states have laws mandating arrest for domestic violence—even though battering was the leading cause of injury of women in the late '80s. Women who have no other option but to flee find that isn't much of an alternative either. Federal funding for battered women's shelters has been withheld and one third of the 1 million battered women who seek emergency shelter each year can find none. Blows from men contributed far more to the rising numbers of "bag ladies" than the ill effects of feminism. In the '80s, almost half of all homeless women (the fastest growing segment of the homeless) were refugees of domestic violence.

The word may be that women have been "liberated," but women themselves seem to feel otherwise. Repeatedly in national surveys, majorities of women say they are still far from equality. Nearly 70 percent of women polled by the *New York Times* in 1989 said the movement for women's rights had only just begun. Most women in the 1990 Virginia Slims opinion poll agreed with the statement that conditions for their sex in American society had improved "a little, not a lot." In poll after poll in the decade, overwhelming majorities of women said they needed equal pay and equal job opportunities, they needed an Equal Rights Amendment, they needed the right to an abortion without government interference, they needed a federal law guaranteeing maternity leave, they needed decent child care services. They have none of these. So how exactly have we "won" the war for women's rights?

Seen against this background, the much ballyhooed claim that feminism is responsible for making women miserable becomes absurd—and irrelevant. As we shall see in the chapters to follow, the afflictions ascribed to feminism are all myths. From "the man shortage" to "the infertility epidemic" to "female burnout" to "toxic day care," these so-called female crises have had their origins not in the actual conditions of women's lives but rather in a closed system that starts and ends in the media, popular culture, and advertising—an endless feedback loop that perpetuates and exaggerates its own false images of womanhood.

Women themselves don't single out the women's movement as the source of their misery. To the contrary, in national surveys 75 to 95 percent of women credit the feminist campaign with *improving* their lives, and a similar proportion say that the women's movement should keep pushing for change. Less than 8 percent think the women's movement might have actually made their lot worse.

What actually is troubling the American female population, then? If the many ponderers of the Woman Question really wanted to know, they might have asked their subjects. In public opinion surveys, women consistently rank their own *inequality*, at work and at home, among their most urgent concerns. Over and over, women complain to pollsters about a lack of economic, not marital, opportunities; they protest that working men, not working women, fail to spend time in the nursery and the kitchen. The Roper Organization's survey analysts find that men's opposition to equality is "a major cause of resentment and stress" and "a major irritant for most women today." It is justice for their gender, not wedding rings and bassinets, that women believe to be in desperately short supply. When the *New York Times* polled women in 1989 about "the most important problem facing women today," job discrimination was the overwhelming winner; none of the crises the media and popular culture had so assiduously promoted even made the charts. In the 1990 Virginia Slims poll, women were most upset by their lack of money, followed by the refusal of their men to shoulder child care and domestic duties. By contrast, when the women were asked where the quest for a husband or the desire to hold a "less pressured" job or to stay at home ranked on their list of concerns, they placed them at the bottom.

As the last decade ran its course, women's unhappiness with inequality only mounted. In national polls, the ranks of women protesting discriminatory treatment in business, political, and personal life climbed sharply. The proportion of women complaining of unequal employment opportunities jumped more than ten points from the '70s, and the number of women complaining of unequal barriers to job advancement climbed even higher. By the end of the decade, 80 percent to 95 percent of women said they suffered from job discrimination and unequal pay. Sex discrimination charges filed with the Equal Employment Opportunity Commission rose nearly 25 percent in the Reagan years, and charges of general harassment directed at working women more than doubled. In the decade, complaints of sexual harassment nearly doubled. At home, a much increased proportion of women complained to pollsters of male mistreatment, unequal relationships, and male efforts to, in the words of the Virginia Slims poll, "keep women down." The share of women in the Roper surveys who agreed that men were "basically kind, gentle, and thoughtful" fell from almost 70 percent in 1970 to 50 percent by 1990. And outside their homes, women felt more threatened, too: in the 1990 Virginia Slims poll, 72 percent of women said they felt "more afraid and uneasy on the streets today" than they did a few years ago. Lest this be attributed only to a general rise in criminal activity, by contrast only 49 percent of men felt this way.

While the women's movement has certainly made women more cognizant of their own inequality, the rising chorus of female protest shouldn't be written off as feminist-induced "oversensitivity." The monitors that serve to track slippage in women's status have been working overtime since the early '80s. Government and private surveys are showing that women's already vast representation in the lowliest occupations is rising, their tiny presence in higher-paying trade and craft jobs stalled or backsliding, their minuscule representation in upper management posts stagnant or falling, and their pay dropping in the very occupations where they have made the most "progress." The status of women lowest on the income ladder has plunged most perilously; government budget cuts in the first four years of the Reagan administration alone pushed nearly 2 million female-headed families and nearly 5 million women below the poverty line. And the prime target of government rollbacks has been one sex only: one-third of the Reagan budget cuts, for example, came out of programs that predominantly serve women—even more extraordinary when one considers that all these programs combined represent only 10 percent of the federal budget.

The alarms aren't just going off in the work force. In national politics, the already small numbers of women in both elective posts and political appointments fell during the '80s. In private life, the average amount that a divorced man paid in child support fell by about 25 percent from the late '70s to the mid-'80s (to a mere $140 a month). Domestic-violence shelters recorded a more than 100 percent increase in the numbers of women taking refuge in their quarters between 1983 and 1987. And government records chronicled a spectacular rise in sexual violence against women. Reported rapes more than doubled from the early '70s—at nearly twice the rate of all other violent crimes and four times the overall crime rate in the United States. While the homicide rate declined, sex-related murders rose 160 percent between 1976 and 1984. And these murders weren't simply the random, impersonal by-product of a violent society; at least one-third of the women were killed by their husbands or boyfriends, and the majority of that group were murdered just after declaring their independence in the most intimate manner—by filing for divorce and leaving home.

By the end of the decade, women were starting to tell pollsters that they feared their sex's social status was once again beginning to slip. They believed they were facing an "erosion of respect," as the 1990 Virginia Slims poll summed up the sentiment. After years in which an increasing percentage of women had said their status had improved from a decade earlier, the proportion suddenly shrunk by 5 percent in the last half of the '80s, the Roper Organization reported. And it fell most sharply among women in their thirties—the age group most targeted by the media and advertisers—dropping about ten percentage points between 1985 and 1990.

Some women began to piece the picture together. In the 1989 *New York Times* poll, more than half of black women and one-fourth of white women put it into words. They told pollsters they believed men were now trying to retract the gains women had made in the last twenty years. "I wanted more autonomy," was how one woman, a thirty-seven-year-old nurse, put it. And her estranged husband "wanted to take it away."

The truth is that the last decade has seen a powerful counterassault on women's rights, a backlash, an attempt to retract the handful of small and hard-won victories that the feminist movement did manage to win for women. This counterassault is largely insidious: in a kind of pop-culture version of the Big Lie, it stands the truth boldly on its head and proclaims that the very steps that have elevated women's position have actually led to their downfall.

The backlash is at once sophisticated and banal, deceptively "progressive" and proudly backward. It deploys both the "new" findings of "scientific research" and the dime-store moralism of yesteryear; it turns into media sound bites both the glib pronouncements of pop-psych trend-watchers and the frenzied rhetoric of New Right preachers. The backlash has succeeded in framing virtually the whole issue of women's rights in its own language. Just as Reaganism shifted political discourse far to the right and demonized liberalism, so the backlash convinced the public that women's "liberation" was the true contemporary American scourge—the source of an endless laundry list of personal, social, and economic problems.

But what has made women unhappy in the last decade is not their "equality"—which they don't yet have—but the rising pressure to halt, and even reverse, women's quest for that equality. The "man shortage" and the "infertility epidemic" are not the price of liberation; in fact, they do not even exist. But these chimeras are the chisels of a society-wide backlash. They are part of a relentless whittling-down process—much of it amounting to outright propaganda—that has served to stir women's private anxieties and break their political wills. Identifying feminism as women's enemy only furthers the ends of a backlash against women's equality, simultaneously deflecting attention from the backlash's central role and recruiting women to attack their own cause.

Some social observers may well ask whether the current pressures on women actually constitute a backlash—or just a continuation of American society's long-standing resistance to women's rights. Certainly hostility to female independence has always been with us. But if fear and loathing of feminism is a sort of perpetual viral condition in our culture, it is not always in an acute stage; its symptoms subside and resurface periodically. And it is these episodes of resurgence, such as the one we face now, that can accurately be termed "backlashes" to women's advancement. If we trace these occurrences in American history (as we will do in a later chapter), we find such flare-ups are hardly random; they have always been triggered by the perception—accurate or not—that women are making great strides. These outbreaks are backlashes because they have always arisen in reaction to women's "progress," caused not simply by a bedrock of misogyny but by the specific efforts of contemporary women to improve their status, efforts that have been interpreted time and again by men—especially men grappling with real threats to their economic and social well-being on other fronts—as spelling their own masculine doom.

The most recent round of backlash first surfaced in the late '70s on the fringes, among the evangelical right. By the early '80s, the fundamentalist ideology had shouldered its way into the White House. By the mid-'80s, as resistance to women's rights acquired political and social acceptability, it passed into the popular culture. And in every case, the timing coincided with signs that women were believed to be on the verge of breakthrough.

Just when women's quest for equal rights seemed closest to achieving its objectives, the backlash struck it down. Just when a "gender gap" at the voting booth surfaced in 1980, and women in politics began to talk of capitalizing on it, the Republican party elevated Ronald Reagan and both political parties began to shunt women's rights off their platforms. Just when support for feminism and the Equal Rights Amendment reached a record high in 1981, the amendment was defeated the following year. Just when women were starting to mobilize against battering and sexual assaults, the federal government stalled funding for battered-women's programs, defeated bills to fund shelters, and shut down its Office of Domestic Violence—only two years after opening it in 1979. Just when record numbers of younger women were supporting feminist goals in the mid-'80s (more of them, in fact, than older women) and a majority of all women were calling themselves feminists, the media declared the advent of a younger "postfeminist generation" that supposedly reviled the women's movement. Just when women racked up their largest percentage ever supporting the right to abortion, the U.S. Supreme Court moved toward reconsidering it.

In other words, the antifeminist backlash has been set off not by women's achievement of full equality but by the increased possibility that they might win it. It is a preemptive strike that stops women long before they reach the finish line. "A backlash may be an indication that women really have had an effect," feminist psychologist Dr. Jean Baker Miller has written, "but backlashes occur when advances have been small, before changes are sufficient to help many people. . . . It is almost as if the leaders of backlashes use the fear of change as a threat before major change has occurred." In the last decade, some women did make substantial advances before the backlash hit, but millions of others were left behind, stranded. Some women now enjoy the right to legal abortion—but not the 44 million women, from the indigent to the military work force, who depend on the federal government for their medical care. Some women can now walk into high-paying professional careers—but not the more than 19 million still in the typing pools or behind the department store sales counters. (Contrary to popular myth about the "have-it-all" baby-boom women, the largest percentage of women in this generation remain typists and clerks.)

As the backlash has gathered force, it has cut off the few from the many—and the few women who have advanced seek to prove, as a social survival tactic, that they aren't so interested in advancement after all. Some of them parade their defection from the women's movement, while their working-class peers founder and cling to the splintered remains of the feminist cause. While a very few affluent and celebrity women who are showcased in news articles boast about having "found my niche as Mrs. Andy Mill" and going home to "bake bread," the many working-class women appeal for their economic rights—flocking to unions in record numbers, striking on their own for pay equity and establishing their own fledgling groups for working women's rights. In 1986, while 41 percent of upper-income women were claiming in the Gallup poll that they were not feminists, only 26 percent of low-income women were making the same claim.

———— ▲▼ ————

Women's advances and retreats are generally described in military terms: battles won, battles lost, points and territory gained and surrendered. The metaphor of combat is not without its merits in this context and, clearly, the same sort of martial accounting and vocabulary is already surfacing here. But by imagining the conflict as two battalions neatly arrayed on either side of the line, we miss the entangled nature, the locked embrace, of a "war" between women and the male culture they inhabit. We miss the reactive nature of a backlash, which, by definition, can exist only in response to another force.

In times when feminism is at a low ebb, women assume the reactive role—privately and most often covertly struggling to assert themselves against the dominant cultural tide. But when feminism itself becomes the tide, the opposition doesn't simply go along with the reversal: it digs in its heels, brandishes its fists, builds walls and dams. And its resistance creates countercurrents and treacherous undertows.

The force and furor of the backlash churn beneath the surface, largely invisible to the public eye. On occasion in the last decade, they have burst into view. We have seen New Right politicians condemn women's independence, antiabortion protesters firebomb women's clinics, fundamentalist preachers damn feminists as "whores" and "witches." Other signs of the backlash's wrath, by their sheer brutality, can push their way into public consciousness for a time—the sharp increase in rape, for example, or the rise in pornography that depicts extreme violence against women.

More subtle indicators in popular culture may receive momentary, and often bemused, media notice, then quickly slip from social awareness: A report, for instance, that the image of women on prime-time TV shows has suddenly degenerated. A survey of mystery fiction finding the numbers of female characters tortured and mutilated mysteriously multiplying. The puzzling news that, as one commentator put it, "So many hit songs have the B-word [bitch] to refer to women that some rap music seems to be veering toward rape music." The ascendancy of virulently misogynist comics like Andrew Dice Clay—who called women "pigs" and "sluts" and strutted in films in which women were beaten, tortured, and blown up—or radio hosts like Rush Limbaugh, whose broadsides against "femi-Nazi" feminists made his syndicated program the most popular radio talk show in the nation. Or word that in 1987, the American Women in Radio & Television couldn't award its annual prize for ads that feature women positively: it could find no ad that qualified.

These phenomena are all related, but that doesn't mean they are somehow coordinated. The backlash is not a conspiracy, with a council dispatching agents from some central control room, nor are the people who serve its ends often aware of their role; some even consider themselves feminists. For the most part, its workings are encoded and internalized, diffuse and chameleonic. Not all of the manifestations of the backlash are of equal weight or significance either; some are mere ephemera, generated by a culture machine that is always scrounging for a "fresh" angle. Taken as a whole, however, these codes and cajolings, these whispers and threats and myths, move overwhelmingly in one direction: they try to push women back into their "acceptable" roles—whether as Daddy's girl or fluttery romantic, active nester or passive love object.

Although the backlash is not an organized movement, that doesn't make it any less destructive. In fact, the lack of orchestration, the absence of a single string-puller, only makes it harder to see—and perhaps more effective. A backlash against women's rights succeeds to the degree that it appears *not* to be political, that it appears not to be a struggle at all. It is most powerful when it goes private, when it lodges inside a woman's mind and turns her vision inward, until she imagines the pressure is all in her head, until she begins to enforce the backlash, too—on herself.

In the last decade, the backlash has moved through the culture's secret chambers, traveling through passageways of flattery and fear. Along the way, it has adopted disguises: a mask of mild derision or the painted face of deep "concern." Its lips profess pity for any woman who won't fit the mold, while it tries to clamp the mold around her ears. It pursues a divide-and-conquer strategy: single versus married women, working women versus homemakers, middle- versus working-class. It manipulates a system of rewards and punishments, elevating women who follow its rules, isolating those who don't. The backlash remarkets old myths about women as new facts and ignores all appeals to reason. Cornered, it denies its own existence, points an accusatory finger at feminism, and burrows deeper underground.

Backlash happens to be the title of a 1947 Hollywood movie in which a man frames his wife for a murder he's committed. The backlash against women's rights works in much the same way: its rhetoric charges feminists with all the crimes it perpetrates. The backlash line blames the women's movement for the "feminization of poverty"—while the backlash's own instigators in Washington pushed through the budget cuts that helped impoverish millions of women, fought pay equity proposals, and undermined equal opportunity laws. The backlash line claims the women's movement cares nothing for children's rights—while its own representatives in the capital and state legislatures have blocked one bill after another to improve child care, slashed billions of dollars in federal aid for children, and relaxed state licensing standards for day care centers. The backlash line accuses the women's movement of creating a generation of unhappy single and childless women—but its purveyors in the media are the ones guilty of making single and childless women feel like circus freaks.

To blame feminism for women's "lesser life" is to miss entirely the point of feminism, which is to win women a wider range of experience. Feminism remains a pretty simple concept, despite repeated—and enormously effective—efforts to dress it up in greasepaint and turn its proponents into gargoyles. As Rebecca West wrote sardonically in 1913, "I myself have never been able to find out precisely what feminism is: I only know that people call me a feminist whenever I express sentiments that differentiate me from a doormat."

The meaning of the word "feminist" has not really changed since it first appeared in a book review in the *Athenaeum* of April 27, 1895, describing a woman who "has in her the capacity of fighting her way back to independence." It is the basic proposition that, as Nora put it in Ibsen's *A Doll's House* a century ago, "Before everything else I'm a human being." It is the simply worded sign hoisted by a little girl in the 1970 Women's Strike for Equality: I AM NOT A BARBIE DOLL. Feminism asks the world to recognize at long last that women aren't decorative ornaments, worthy vessels, members of a "special-interest group." They are half (in fact, now more than half) of the national population, and just as deserving of rights and opportunities, just as capable of participating in the world's events, as the other half. Feminism's agenda is basic: It asks that women not be forced to "choose" between public justice and private happiness. It asks that women be free to define themselves—instead of having their identity defined for them, time and again, by their culture and their men.

The fact that these are still such incendiary notions should tell us that American women have a way to go before they enter the promised land of equality.

500 Women's fight for . . . : Nancy Gibbs, "The Dreams of Youth," *Time*, Special Issue: "Women: The Road Ahead," Fall 1990, p. 12.

500 Women have "so much" . . . : Eleanor Smeal, *Why and How Women Will Elect the Next President* (New York: Harper & Row, 1984) p. 56.

501 The *New York Times* reports . . . : Georgia Dullea, "Women Reconsider Childbearing Over 30," *New York Times*, Feb. 25, 1982, p. C1.

501 *Newsweek* says: Unwed women . . . : Eloise Salholz, "The Marriage Crunch," *Newsweek*, June 2, 1986, p. 55.

501 The health advice manuals . . . : See, for example, Dr. Herbert J. Freudenberger and Gail North, *Women's Burnout* (New York: Viking Penguin, 1985); Marjorie Hansen Shaevitz, *The Superwoman Syndrome* (New York: Warner Books, 1984); Harriet Braiker, *The Type E Woman* (New York: Dodd, Mead, 1986); Donald Morse and M. Lawrence Furst, *Women Under Stress* (New York: Van Nostrand Reinhold Co., 1982); Georgia Witkin-Lanoil, *The Female Stress Syndrome* (New York: Newmarket Press, 1984).

501 The psychology books . . . : Dr. Stephen and Susan Price, *No More Lonely Nights: Overcoming the Hidden Fears That Keep You from Getting Married* (New York: G.P. Putnam's Sons, 1988) p. 19.

501   Even founding feminist Betty Friedan . . . : Betty Friedan, *The Second Stage* (New York: Summit Books, 1981) p. 9.

501   "In dispensing its spoils . . .": Mona Charen, "The Feminist Mistake," *National Review*, March 23, 1984, p. 24.

501   "Our generation was the human sacrifice . . .": Claudia Wallis, "Women Face the '90s," *Time*, Dec. 4, 1989, p. 82.

501   In *Newsweek*, writer . . . : Kay Ebeling, "The Failure of Feminism," *Newsweek*, Nov. 19, 1990, p. 9.

501   Even the beauty magazines . . . : Marilyn Webb, "His Fault Divorce," *Harper's Bazaar*, Aug. 1988, p. 156.

501   In the last decade . . . : Mary Anne Dolan, "When Feminism Failed," *The New York Times Magazine*, June 26, 1988, p. 21; Erica Jong, "The Awful Truth About Women's Liberation," *Vanity Fair*, April 1986, p. 92.

502   The "Today" show . . . : Jane Birnbaum, "The Dark Side of Women's Liberation," *Los Angeles Herald Examiner*, May 24, 1986.

502   A guest columnist . . . : Robert J. Hooper, "Slasher Movies Owe Success to Abortion" (originally printed in the *Baltimore Sun*), *Minneapolis Star Tribune*, Feb. 1, 1990, p. 17A.

502   In popular novels . . . : Gail Parent, *A Sign of the Eighties* (New York: G.P. Putnam's Sons, 1987); Stephen King, *Misery* (New York: Viking, 1987).

502   We "blew it by . . .": Freda Bright, *Singular Women* (New York: Bantam Books, 1988) p. 12.

502   Even Erica Jong's . . . : Erica Jong, *Any Woman's Blues* (New York: Harper & Row, 1989) pp. 2–3. A new generation of young "post-feminist" female writers, such as Mary Gaitskill and Susan Minot, also produced a bumper crop of grim-faced unwed heroines. These passive and masochistic "girls" wandered the city, zombie-like; they came alive and took action only in seeking out male abuse. For a good analysis of this genre, see James Wolcott, "The Good-Bad Girls," *Vanity Fair*, Dec. 1988, p. 43.

502   "Feminism, having promised her . . .": Dr. Toni Grant, *Being a Woman: Fulfilling Your Femininity and Finding Love* (New York: Random House, 1988) p. 25.

502   The authors of . . . : Dr. Connell Cowan and Dr. Melvyn Kinder, *Smart Women/Foolish Choices* (New York: New American Library, 1985) p. 16.

503   Reagan spokeswoman Faith . . . : Faith Whittlesey, "Radical Feminism in Retreat," Dec. 8, 1984, speech at the Center for the Study of the Presidency, 15th Annual Leadership Conference, St. Louis, Mo., p. 7.

503   As a California sheriff . . . : Don Martinez, "More Women Ending Up in Prisons," *San Francisco Examiner*, Sept. 4, 1990, p. A1. Judges have blamed women's increasing economic independence for increasing *male* crime, too: "What do we do [about crowded prisons]?" Texas District Judge John McKellips asked, rhetorically. "Well, we can start in our homes. Mothers can stay home and raise their children during the formative years." See "For the Record," *Ms.*, May 1988, p. 69.

503   The U.S. Attorney General's . . . : Attorney General's Commission on Pornography, Final Report, July 1986, p. 144. The commissioner's report goes on to undermine its

own logic, conceding that since women raped by acquaintances are the least likely to report the crime, it might be difficult to attribute a rise in reported rape rates to them, after all.

503 On network news . . . : Sylvia Ann Hewlett, *A Lesser Life: The Myth of Women's Liberation in America* (New York: William Morrow, 1986).

503 Legal scholars have . . . : Mary Ann Mason, *The Equality Trap* (New York: Simon and Schuster, 1988).

503 Economists have argued . . . : James P. Smith and Michael Ward, "Women in the Labor Market and in the Family," *The Journal of Economic Perspectives*, Winter 1989, 3, no. 1: 9–23.

503 In *The Cost of Loving* . . . : Megan Marshall, *The Cost of Loving: Women and the New Fear of Intimacy* (New York: G.P. Putnam's Sons, 1984) p. 218.

503 Other diaries of . . . : Hilary Cosell, *Woman on a Seesaw: The Ups and Downs of Making It* (New York: G.P. Putnam's Sons, 1985); Deborah Fallows, *A Mother's Work* (Boston: Houghton Mifflin, 1985); Carol Orsborn, *Enough is Enough* (New York: Pocket Books, 1986); Susan Bakos, *This Wasn't Supposed to Happen* (New York: Continuum, 1985). Even when the women aren't really renouncing their liberation, their publishers promote the texts as if they were. Mary Kay Blakely's *Wake Me When It's Over* (New York: Random House, 1989), an account of the author's diabetes-induced coma, is billed on the dust jacket as "a chilling memoir in which a working supermom exceeds her limit and discovers the thin line between sanity and lunacy and between life and death."

503 If American women are so equal . . . : "Money, Income and Poverty Status in the U.S.," 1989, Current Population Reports, U.S. Bureau of the Census, Department of Commerce, Series P-60, # 168.

504 Why are nearly 75 percent . . . : Margaret W. Newton, "Women and Pension Coverage," *The American Woman 1988–89: A Status Report*, ed. by Sara E. Rix (New York: W.W. Norton & Co., 1989) p. 268.

504 Why are they still . . . : Cushing N. Dolbeare and Anne J. Stone, "Women and Affordable Housing," *The American Woman 1990–91: A Status Report*, ed. by Sara E. Rix (W.W. Norton & Co., 1990) p. 106; Newton, "Pension Coverage," p. 268; "1990 Profile," 9 to 5/National Association of Working Women; Salaried and Professional Women's Commission Report, 1989, p. 2.

504 Why does the average . . . : "Briefing Paper on the Wage Gap," National Committee on Pay Equity, p. 3; "Average Earnings of Year-Round, Full-Time Workers by Sex and Educational Attainment," 1987, U.S. Bureau of the Census, February 1989, cited in *The American Woman 1990–91*, p. 392.

504 If women have "made it," then . . . : Susanna Downie, "Decade of Achievement, 1977–1987," The National Women's Conference Center, May 1988, p. 35; statistics from 9 to 5/National Association of Working Women.

504 And, conversely, . . . : Statistics from Women's Research & Education Institute, U.S. Bureau of the Census, U.S. Bureau of Labor Statistics, Catalyst, Center for the American Woman and Politics. See also *The American Woman 1990–91*, p. 359; Deborah L. Rhode, "Perspectives on Professional Women," *Stanford Law Review*, 40, no. 5 (May 1988): 1178–79; Anne Jardim and Margaret Hennig, "The Last Barrier," *Working*

Woman, Nov. 1990, p. 130; Jaclyn Fierman, "Why Women Still Don't Hit the Top," *Fortune*, July 30, 1990, p. 40.

504   Unlike virtually . . . : "1990 Profile," 9 to 5/National Association of Working Women; Bureau of Labor Statistics, 1987 survey of nation's employers. See also "Who Gives and Who Gets," *American Demographics*, May 1988, p. 16; "Children and Families: Public Policies and Outcomes, A Fact Sheet of International Comparisons," U.S. House of Representatives, Select Committee on Children, Youth and Families.

504   In a 1990 national poll . . . : "Women in Corporate Management," national poll of Fortune 1000 companies by Catalyst, 1990.

504   Why do women who want . . . : Data from Alan Guttmacher Institute.

504   Nor is women's struggle for equal education . . . : *The American Woman 1990–91*, p. 63; "Feminization of Power Campaign Extends to the Campus," Eleanor Smeal Report, 6, no. 1, Aug. 31, 1988; Project on Equal Education Rights, National Organization for Women's Legal Defense and Education Fund, 1987.

505   Nor do women . . . : Rhode, "Professional Women," p. 1183; Mark Clements Research Inc.'s Annual Study of Women's Attitudes, 1987; Arlie Hochschild, *The Second Shift: Working Parents and the Revolution at Home* (New York: Viking, 1989), p. 227. In fact, Hochschild's twelve-year survey, from 1976 to 1988, found that the men who said they were helping tended to be the ones who did the least.

505   Furthermore, in thirty states . . . : Statistics from National Center on Women and Family Law, 1987; National Woman Abuse Prevention Project; Cynthia Diehm and Margo Ross, "Battered Women," *The American Woman 1988–89*, p. 292.

505   Federal funding . . . : "Unlocking the Door: An Action Program for Meeting the Housing Needs of Women," Women and Housing Task Force, 1988, National Low-Income Housing Coalition, pp. 6, 8.

505   In the '80s, almost half of all homeless . . . : Katha Pollitt, "Georgie Porgie Is a Bully," *Time*, Fall 1990, Special Issue, p. 24. A survey in New York City found as many as 40 percent of all homeless people are battered women: "Understanding Domestic Violence Fact Sheets," National Woman Abuse Prevention Project.

505   Nearly 70 percent . . . : E. J. Dionne, Jr., "Struggle for Work and Family Fueling Women's Movement," *New York Times*, Aug. 22, 1989, p. A1. The Yankelovich Clancy Shulman poll (Oct. 23–25, 1989, for *Time*/CNN) and the 1990 Virginia Slims Opinion Poll (The Roper Organization Inc., 1990) found similarly large majorities of women who said that they needed a strong women's movement to keep pushing for change.

505   Most women in the . . . : The 1990 Virginia Slims Opinion Poll, The Roper Organization Inc., pp. 8, 18.

505   In poll after . . . : The Louis Harris poll, 1984, found 64 percent of women wanted the Equal Rights Amendment and 65 percent favored affirmative action. Similar results emerged from the national *Woman's Day* poll (Feb. 17, 1984) by *Woman's Day* and Wellesley College Center for Research on Women, which emphasized middle-American conventional women (80 percent were mothers and 30 percent were full-time homemakers). The *Woman's Day* poll found a majority of women, from all economic classes, seeking a wide range of women's rights. For instance, 68 percent of the women said they wanted the ERA, 79 percent supported a woman's right to choose an abortion,

and 61 percent favored a federally subsidized national child-care program. Mark Clements Research Inc.'s Annual Study of Women's Attitudes found in 1987 that 87 percent of women wanted a federal law guaranteeing maternity leave and about 94 percent said that more child care should be available. (In addition, 86 percent wanted a federal law enforcing the payment of child support.) The Louis Harris Poll found 80 percent of women calling for the creation of more day-care centers. See *The Eleanor Smeal Report*, June 28, 1984, p. 3; Warren T. Brookes, "Day Care: Is It a Real Crisis or a War Over Political Turf?" *San Francisco Chronicle*, April 27, 1988, p. 6; Louis Harris, *Inside America* (New York: Vintage Books, 1987), p. 96.

506 To the contrary . . . : In the 1989 *Time*/CNN poll, 94 percent of women polled said the movement made them more independent; 82 percent said it is still improving women's lives. Only 8 percent said it may have made their lives worse. A 1986 *Newsweek* Gallup poll found that 56 percent of women identified themselves as "feminists," and only 4 percent described themselves as "anti-feminists."

506 In public opinion . . . : In the Annual Study of Women's Attitudes (1988, Mark Clements Research), when women were asked, "What makes you angry?" they picked three items as their top concerns: poverty, crime, and their own inequality. In the 1989 *New York Times* Poll, when women were asked what was the most important problem facing women today, job inequality ranked first.

506 The Roper Organization's . . . : Bickley Townsend and Kathleen O'Neil, "American Women Get Mad," *American Demographics*, Aug. 1990, p. 26.

506 When the *New York Times* . . . : Dionne, "Struggle for Work and Family," p. A14.

506 In the 1990 . . . : 1990 Virginia Slims Opinion Poll, pp. 29–30, 32.

506 In national polls . . . : Data from Roper Organization and Louis Harris polls. The 1990 Roper survey found most women reporting that things had "gotten worse" in the home and that men were more eager "to keep women down": See 1990 Virginia Slims Opinion Poll, pp. 18, 21, 54. The Gallup Organization polls charted an 8 percent increase in job discrimination complaints from women between 1975 and 1982. Mark Clements Research's 1987 Women's Views Survey (commissioned by *Glamour* magazine) found that on the matter of women's inequality, "more women feel there is a problem today." Reports of wage discrimination, the survey noted, had jumped from 76 percent in 1982 to 85 percent in 1988. (See "How Women's Minds Have Changed in the Last Five Years," *Glamour*, Jan. 1987, p. 168.) The annual surveys by Mark Clements Research also find huge and increasing majorities of women complaining of unequal treatment in hiring, advancement, and opportunities in both corporate and political life. (In 1987, only 30 percent of women believed they got equal treatment with men when being considered for financial credit.) A *Time* 1989 poll found 94 percent of women complaining of unequal pay, 82 percent of job discrimination.

506 Sex discrimination charges . . . : Statistics from U.S. Equal Employment Opportunity Commission, "National Database: Charge Receipt Listing," 1982–88; "Sexual Harassment," 1981–89.

507 At home, a much increased . . . : Townsend and O'Neil, "American Women Get Mad," p. 28.

507 And outside their . . . : 1990 Virginia Slims Opinion Poll, p. 38.

507 Government and private surveys . . . : Economic trends from U.S. Bureau of Labor Statistics, U.S. Equal Employment Opportunity Commission, Office of Federal Contract Compliance, National Committee on Pay Equity, National Commission on Working Women. See Chapter 12 for closer look at the deteriorating status of women in the work force.

507 The status of women . . . : In the first six years of the Reagan administration, $50 billion was cut from these social programs, while at the same time defense spending rose $142 billion. See "Inequality of Sacrifice: The Impact of the Reagan Budget on Women," Coalition on Women and the Budget, Washington, D.C., 1986, pp. 5, 7; Sara E. Rix and Anne J. Stone, "Reductions and Realities: How the Federal Budget Affects Women," Women's Research and Education Institute, Washington, D.C., 1983, pp. 4–5.

507 In national politics . . . : Data from Center for the American Woman and Politics, Eagleton Institute of Politics. See Chapter 9 on women in politics.

507 In private life, the average . . . : Philip Robins, "Why Are Child Support Award Amounts Declining?" June 1989, Institute for Research on Poverty Discussion Paper No. 885–89, pp. 6–7.

507 Domestic-violence shelters . . . : "Unlocking the Door," p. 8.

507 Reported rapes more than . . . : Statistics are from the U.S. Department of Justice's Bureau of Justice Statistics; the Sourcebook of Criminal Justice Statistics, 1984, p. 380; Uniform Crime Reports, FBI, "Crime in the United States," 1986; "Sexual Assault: An Overview," National Victims Resource Center, Nov. 1987, p. 1. While rape rates between 1960 and 1970 rose 95 percent, this increase—unlike that of the '80s—was part of a 126 percent increase in violent crime in that era. (Crime statisticians have widely rejected the argument that the increase in the '80s might simply be the result of an increasing tendency for women to report sexual assaults. The National Crime Survey found no significant change in the percentage of rapes reported to police in the periods between 1973–77 and 1978–82.) Scattered indicators suggest a sharp rise in the rate of rapes committed by young men, too. Between 1983 and 1987, rape arrests of boys under 18 years old rose 15 percent. In New York City between 1987 and 1989, according to data from the district attorney's office, rape arrests of boys under the age of 13 rose 200 percent. In Alaska, according to the state Division of Youth and Family Services, sexual abuse and assaults from young men increased ninefold in the course of the '80s, the fastest growing juvenile problem in the state. See Larry Campbell, "Sexually Abusive Juveniles," *Anchorage Daily News*, Jan. 9, 1981, p. 1.

508 They believed they were facing . . . : 1990 Virginia Slims Opinion Poll, p. 16.

508 In the 1989 *New York Times* . . . : Lisa Belkin, "Bars to Equality of Sexes Seen as Eroding, Slowly," *New York Times*, Aug. 20, 1989, p. 16.

509 Just when women . . . : "Inequality of Sacrifice," p. 23.

509 Just when record numbers . . . : A 1986 Gallup poll conducted for *Newsweek* found a majority of women described themselves as feminists and only 4 percent said they were "antifeminists." While large majorities of women throughout the '80s kept on favoring the full feminist agenda (from the ERA to legal abortion), the proportion of women who were willing publicly to call themselves feminists dropped off suddenly in the

late '80s, after the mass media declared feminism the "F-word." By 1989, only one in three women were calling themselves feminists in the polls. Nonetheless, the pattern of younger women espousing the most pro-feminist sentiments continued throughout the decade. In the 1989 Yankelovich poll for *Time*/CNN, for example, 76 percent of women in their teens and 71 percent of women in their twenties said they believed feminists spoke for the average American woman, compared with 59 percent of women in their thirties. Asked the same question about the National Organization for Women, the gap appeared again: 83 percent of women in their teens and 72 percent of women in their twenties said NOW was in touch with the average woman, compared with 65 percent of women in their thirties. See Downie, "Decade of Achievement," p. 1; 1986 Gallup/*Newsweek* poll; 1989 Yankelovich/*Time*/CNN poll.

510   "A backlash may be an indication that . . .": Dr. Jean Baker Miller, *Toward a New Psychology of Women* (Boston: Beacon Press, 1976) pp. xv–xvi.

510   Some women now . . . : Kate Michelman, "20 Years Defending Choice, 1969–1988," National Abortion Rights Action League, p. 4.

510   Some women can now . . . : "Employment and Earnings," Current Population Survey, Table 22, Bureau of Labor Statistics, U.S. Department of Labor.

510   (Contrary to popular myth . . .): Cheryl Russell, *100 Predictions for the Baby Boom* (New York: Plenum Press, 1987), p. 64.

510   While a very few . . . : "A New Kind of Love Match," *Newsweek*, Sept. 4, 1989, p. 73; Barbara Hetzer, "Superwoman Goes Home," *Fortune*, Aug. 18, 1986, p. 20; "Facts on Working Women," Aug. 1989, Women's Bureau, U.S. Department of Labor, no. 89–2; and data from the Coalition of Labor Union Women and Amalgamated Clothing and Textile Workers Union. The surge of women joining unions in the late '80s was so great that it single-handedly halted the ten-year decline in union membership. Black women joined unions at the greatest rate. Women led strikes around the country, from the Yale University administrative staff to the Daughters of Mother Jones in Virginia (who were instrumental in the Pittston coal labor battle) to the Delta Pride catfish plant processors in Mississippi (where women organized the largest strike by black workers ever in the state, lodging a protest against a plant that paid its mostly female employees poverty wages, punished them if they skinned less than 24,000 fish a day, and limited them to six timed bathroom breaks a week). See Tony Freemantle, "Weary Strikers Hold Out in Battle of Pay Principle," *Houston Chronicle*, Dec. 2, 1990, p. 1A; Peter T. Kilborn, "Labor Fight on a Catfish 'Plantation,'" *The News and Observer*, Dec. 16, 1990, p. J2.

510   In 1986, while . . . : 1986 Gallup Poll; Barbara Ehrenreich, "The Next Wave," *Ms.*, July/August 1987, p. 166; Sarah Harder, "Flourishing in the Mainstream: The U.S. Women's Movement Today," *The American Woman 1990–91*, p. 281. Also see 1989 Yankelovich Poll: 71 percent of black women said feminists have been helpful to women, compared with 61 percent of white women. A 1987 poll by the National Women's Conference Commission found that 65 percent of black women called themselves feminists, compared with 56 percent of white women.

511   Other signs of . . . : For increase in violent pornography, see, for example, April 1986 study in the Attorney General's Commission on Pornography, Final Report, pp. 1402–3.

511   More subtle indicators . . . : Sally Steenland, "Women Out of View: An Analysis of Female Characters on 1987–88 TV Programs," National Commission on Working

Women, November 1987. Mystery fiction survey was conducted by Sisters In Crime and presented at the 1988 Mystery Writers of America conference; additional information comes from personal interview in May 1988 with the group's director, mystery writer Sara Paretsky. On popular music: Alice Kahn, "Macho—the Second Wave," *San Francisco Chronicle*, Sept. 16, 1990, Sunday Punch section, p. 2. On Andrew Dice Clay: Craig MacInnis, "Comedians Only a Mother Could Love," *Toronto Star*, May 20, 1990, p. C6; Valerie Scher, "Clay's Idea of a Punch Line Is a Belch After a Beer," *San Diego Union and Tribune*, Aug. 17, 1990, p. C1. On Rush Limbaugh: Dave Matheny, "Morning Rush Is a Gas," *San Francisco Examiner*, Jan. 2, 1991, p. C1. On American Women in Radio & TV: Betsy Sharkey, "The Invisible Woman," *Adweek*, July 6, 1987, p. 4.

512   The backlash line claims . . . : Data from Children's Defense Fund. See also Ellen Wojahm, "Who's Minding the Kids?" *Savvy*, Oct. 1987, p. 16; "Child Care: The Time is Now," Children's Defense Fund, 1987, pp. 8–10.

513   "I myself . . .": Rebecca West, *The Clarion*, Nov. 14, 1913, cited in Cheris Kramarae and Paula A. Treichler, *A Feminist Dictionary* (London: Pandora Press, 1985) p. 160.

513   The meaning of the word "feminist" . . . : *The Feminist Papers: From Adams to de Beauvoir*, ed. by Alice S. Rossi (New York: Bantam Books, 1973) p. xiii. For discussion of historical origins of term feminism, see Karen Offen, "Defining Feminism: A Comparative Historical Approach," in *Signs: Journal of Women in Culture and Society*, 1988, 14, no. 1, pp. 119–57.

513   I AM NOT A BARBIE DOLL . . . : Carol Hymowitz and Michaele Weissman, *A History of Women in America* (New York: Bantam Books, 1978) p. 34.

Acknowledgments

The editors wish to thank:

Ellen Chesler
Kara Clark
Diane Gelon
Carol Giardina
Zoe Gutenplan
Temma Kaplan
Emily Katz
Robert Leleux
Charlotte Sheedy
Barbara Smith
Barbara Winslow

and

Jenny Gotwal and the Arthur and Elizabeth Schlesinger Library of Women's History, Harvard University.

Kirsten Grimstad and Susan Rennie and their New Woman's Survival Catalog/Sourcebook archives.

Laura Micham and the Sallie Bingham Center, Duke University.

Kathie Sarachild and the Redstockings Women's Liberation Archives for Action.

Holly Smith and the Women's Resource and Research Center, Spelman College.

Laura X and her now digitized International Women's Movement Archive.

To Library of America, gratitude for the invitation to edit this volume and for their guidance and hard work: Stefanie Peters, Max Rudin, Brian McCarthy, and Jennifer Didik.

List of Sources

Betty Friedan, from *The Feminine Mystique* (New York: W. W. Norton & Company, 1963), pp. 15–32. Copyright © 1963 by Betty Friedan. Reprinted by permission of Curtis Brown, Ltd., and The Orion Publishing Group. All rights reserved.

Casey Hayden and Mary King, "Sex and Caste: A Kind of Memo," *Liberation* (April 1966), pp. 35–36. Copyright © Casey Hayden and Mary King. Reprinted by permission of the authors.

Pauli Murray and Mary O. Eastwood, from "Jane Crow and the Law: Sex Discrimination and Title VII," 34 George Washington Law review. 232 (1965), pp. 233–35, 256. Reprinted by permission.

Valerie Solanas, from *SCUM Manifesto* (New York: Olympia Press, 1968), pp. 3–14, 36–45. Copyright © 1967, renewed 1997 by Judith A. Martinez.

Beverly Jones and Judith Brown, from "Toward a Female Liberation Movement, Part I," *Toward a Female Liberation Movement* (Gainesville, FL: Redstockings of the Women's Liberation Movement, 1968), pp. 9–13. Copyright © 1968 by Beverly Jones and Judith Brown. Reprinted by permission of Redstockings of the Women's Liberation Movement, www.redstockings.org.

New York Radical Women, "No More Miss America!" *Sisterhood Is Powerful*, ed. Robin Morgan (New York: Vintage, 1970), pp. 521–24. Copyright © 1970 by Robin Morgan. Reprinted by permission.

Black Women's Liberation Group of Mt. Vernon, New York, "Statement on Birth Control," *Lilith*, no. 1 (December 1968), pp. 8–9. Copyright © 1970 by Robin Morgan. Reprinted by permission.

Dana Densmore, "On Celibacy," *No More Fun and Games: A Journal of Female Liberation*, no. 1 (October 1968), pp. 23–26. Copyright © 1968 by Dana Densmore. Reprinted by permission of the author.

Anne Koedt, "The Myth of the Vaginal Orgasm," *Radical Feminism*, ed. Anne Koedt, Ellen Levine, and Anita Rapone (New York: Quadrangle/The New York Times Book Co., 1973), pp. 198–207. Copyright © Anne Koedt. Reprinted by permission of the author.

(New York: William Morrow and Company, 1970), pp. 146–55. Reprinted by permission of Farrar, Straus & Giroux and Verso Books.

Kate Millett, from *Sexual Politics* (Garden City, NY: Doubleday, 1970), pp. 24–26, 54–56. Copyright © 1969, 1970, 1990, 2000 by Kate Millett. Reprinted by permission of Georges Borchardt, Inc., on behalf of the author.

Shirley Chisholm, from "The 51% Minority," speech delivered at the Conference on Women's Employment. Hearings before the Special Subcommittee on Education of the Committee on Education and Labor, House of Representatives, 91st Congress, 2d session (Washington, D.C.: Government Printing Office, 1970), pp. 909–15.

Lucinda Cisler, "Abortion Law Repeal (Sort of): A Warning to Women," *Notes from the Second Year: Women's Liberation, Major Writings of the Radical Feminists* (New York: n.p., 1970), pp. 89–93. Copyright © by Lucinda Cisler. Reprinted by permission of the author.

Radicalesbians, "The Woman Identified Woman," *Notes from the Third Year: Women's Liberation* (New York: n.p., 1971), pp. 81–84. Reprinted by permission of Radicalesbians.

Gene Boyer, from "Are Women Equal Under the Law?" *Discrimination Against Women*, ed. Dr. Catherine R. Stimpson (New York: R. R. Bowker Company, 1973), pp. 385–89.

Doris Wright, from "Angry Notes from a Black Feminist," mimeographed position paper distributed by FEM, New York (1970), pp. 1–4.

Young Lords Party, from "Position Paper on Women," *Palante*, Vol. 2, no. 12 (1970), pp. 11–13.

Judy Syfers, "Why I Want A Wife," *Notes from the Third Year: Women's Liberation* (New York: n.p., 1971), pp. 13–14. Copyright © Judy Syfers. Reprinted by permission of *Ms.* magazine.

Robin Morgan, "A Brief Elegy for Four Women," *Going Too Far* (New York: Random House, 1977), pp. 147–48. Copyright © 1968, 1970, 1973, 1975, 1977 by Robin Morgan. Reprinted by permission of the author.

Marcia Sprinkle and Norma Allen Lesser, from "The Children's House," *off our backs*, Vol. 1, no. 17 (February 12, 1971), pp. 8–9. Copyright © 1970 by Off Our Backs. Reprinted by permission of the authors.

Susan Griffin, from "Rape: The All-American Crime," *Ramparts Magazine* (September 1971), pp. 29–33. Copyright © by Susan Griffin. Reprinted by permission of the author.

Mirta Vidal, from "New Voice of La Raza: Chicanas Speak Out," *International Socialist Review* (October 1971), pp. 8ff. Copyright © 1971 by Pathfinder Press. Reprinted by permission.

Catharine R. Stimpson, from "The New Feminism and Women's Studies," *Change* (September 1973), pp. 46–48. Copyright © by Catharine R. Stimpson. Reprinted by permission of the author.

Alice Walker, "In Search of Our Mothers' Gardens," *Ms.* magazine (May 1974), pp. 64ff. Copyright © by Alice Walker. Reprinted by permission of *Ms.* magazine.

Silvia Federici, "Wages against Housework," pamphlet distributed by the Power of Women Collective and the Falling Wall Press (1975). Reprinted by permission of the author.

Lolly Hirsch, "Practicing Health Without a License," *New Women's Survival Sourcebook*, ed. Kristen Grimstad and Susan Rennie (New York: Alfred A. Knopf, 1975), pp. 33–34. Copyright © by Lolly Hirsch.

Anne Forer, "Sex And Women's Liberation," in Redstockings, *Feminist Revolution: An Abridged Edition with Additional Writings* (New York: Random House, 1978), pp. 141–42. Reprinted by permission of Redstockings of the Women's Liberation Movement, www.redstockings.org.

Angela Davis, from "Joan Little: The Dialectics of Rape," *Ms.* magazine (June 1975), pp. 74–77. Copyright © by Angela Davis. Reprinted by permission of *Ms.* magazine.

Susan Brownmiller, from *Against Our Will: Men, Women and Rape* (New York: Simon & Schuster, 1975), pp. 31–33, 78–81. Copyright © 1975, renewed 2003 by Susan Brownmiller. Reprinted by permission of Simon & Schuster, Inc. All rights reserved.

Michele Wallace, from "A Black Feminist's Search for Sisterhood," *Village Voice* (July 28, 1975), pp. 6–7. Copyright © Michele Wallace. Reprinted by permission of the author.

Maxine Hong Kingston, from *The Woman Warrior: Memoirs of a Girlhood Among Ghosts* (New York: Alfred A. Knopf, Inc., 1975), pp. 9–16. Copyright © 1975, 1976 by Maxine Hong Kingston. Used by permission of Alfred A. Knopf, an imprint of the Knopf Doubleday Group, a division of Penguin Random House LLC and reproduced with permission of Pan Macmillan through PLSClear. All rights reserved.

Judy Chicago, from *Through the Flower: My Struggle as a Woman Artist* (Garden City, NY: Doubleday & Company, Inc., 1975), pp. 59–67. Copyright © 1975, 2006 by Judy Chicago. Reprinted by permission of the author.

Adrienne Rich, from *Of Woman Born: Motherhood as Experience and Institution* (New York: W. W. Norton & Company, 1976), pp. 29–40. Copyright © 1976, 1986 by W. W. Norton & Company, Inc. Used by permission of W. W. Norton & Company, Inc.

Jo Freeman, from "Trashing: The Dark Side of Sisterhood," *Ms.* magazine

(April 1976), pp. 49ff. Copyright © by Jo Freeman. Reprinted by permission of Jo Freeman.

Del Martin, "A Letter from a Battered Wife," *Battered Wives* (New York: Pocket Books, 1983), pp. 1–5. Copyright © 1978, 1983 by Del Martin. Reprinted by permission of the Estate of Del Martin.

Barbara Ehrenreich, "What Is Socialist Feminism?" *WIN Magazine* (June 3, 1976), pp. 4–7. Copyright © by Barbara Ehrenreich. Reprinted by permission.

Gerda Lerner, "The Majority Finds Its Past," *The Majority Finds Its Past: Placing Women in History* (New York: Oxford University Press, 1979), pp. 160–67. Copyright © 1979 by Gerda Lerner. Reprinted by permission of University of North Carolina Press.

The Combahee River Collective (Barbara Smith, Beverly Smith, and Demita Frazier), "A Black Feminist Statement," *Capitalist Patriarchy and the Case for Socialist Feminism*, ed. Zillah R. Eisenstein (New York: Monthly Review Press, 1979), pp. 362–72. Copyright © 1979 by Zillah R. Eisenstein. Reprinted by permission.

Suzanne Lacy and Leslie Labowitz, from "In Mourning and In Rage . . ." *Frontiers: A Journal of Women Studies*, Vol. 3, no. 1 (Spring 1978), pp. 52–54. Published by University of Nebraska Press. Copyright © 1978 by Women's Studies Program, University of Colorado. Reprinted by permission of University of Nebraska Press.

Mary Daly, from *Gyn/Ecology: The Metaethics of Radical Feminism* (Boston: Beacon Press, 1978), pp. 1–9. Copyright © 1978, 1990 by Mary Daly. Republished by permission of Beacon Press; permission conveyed through Copyright Clearance Center, Inc.

Susan Jacoby, "Notes from a Free-Speech Junkie," *The Possible She* (New York: Farrar, Straus & Giroux, 1979), pp. 31–35. Copyright © 1973, 1974, 1976, 1977, 1978, 1979 by Susan Jacoby. Originally appeared in *The New York Times* (January 1978). Reprinted by permission of Georges Borchardt, Inc., on behalf of the author.

Lin Farley, "Eleven Ways to Fight Sexual Harassment," *Sexual Shakedown: The Sexual Harassment of Women on the Job* (New York: Warner Books, 1978), pp. 266–69. Copyright © Lin Farley. Reprinted by permission of the author.

Audre Lorde, from "Uses of the Erotic: The Erotics of Power," *Sister Outsider: Essays and Speeches*, 2nd edition (Freedom, CA: The Crossing Press, 2007), pp. 53–56. Copyright © 1984, 2007 by Audre Lorde. Reprinted by permission of Charlotte Sheedy Literary Agency.

Barbara Smith, "Racism and Women's Studies," *The Truth That Never Hurts:*

Writings on Race, Gender, and Freedom (New Brunswick, NJ: Rutgers University Press, 1998), pp. 95–98. Copyright © 1998 by Barbara Smith. Reprinted by permission of Rutgers University Press.

Rosario Morales, "We're All in the Same Boat," *This Bridge Called My Back: Writings by Radical Women of Color*, ed. Cherríe Moraga and Gloria Anzaldúa (Watertown, MA: Persephone Press, 1981), pp. 91–93. Copyright © 1981, 1983 by Rosario Morales. Reprinted with the permission of The Permissions Company, LLC on behalf of Aurora Levins Morales, aurora levinsmorales.com.

Gloria Anzaldúa, from "Speaking In Tongues: A Letter to 3rd World Women Writers," *This Bridge Called My Back: Writings by Radical Women of Color*, ed. Cherríe Moraga and Gloria Anzaldúa (Watertown, MA: Persephone Press, 1981; reprinted by SUNY Press, 2015), pp. 165–69. Reprinted in *The Gloria Anzaldúa Reader* (Duke University Press, 2009). Copyright © 1981 by Gloria E. Anzaldúa. Reprinted by permission of Stuart Bernstein Representation for Artists, New York, NY, and protected by the Copyright Laws of the United States. All rights reserved.

Catharine MacKinnon, "To Change the World for Women," *Butterfly Politics* (Cambridge, MA: Belknap Press, 2017), pp. 11–22. Copyright © 2017 by Catharine A. MacKinnon. Reprinted by permission of the author.

Andrea Dworkin, from *Pornography: Men Possessing Women* (New York: Putnam, 1981), pp. 199–202. Copyright © 1979, 1980, 1981 by Andrea Dworkin. Reprinted by permission of Elaine Markson Literary Agency.

Paula Webster, "Pornography and Pleasure," *Heresies: A Feminist Publication on Art and Politics*, Vol. 3, no. 4 (1981), pp. 48–51. Copyright © by Paula Webster. Reprinted by permission of the author.

Joan Nestle, "My Mother Liked to Fuck," *Womanews*, Vol. 3, no. 1 (December–January 1982), p. 14. Copyright © 1981 by Joan Nestle. Reprinted by permission of the author.

Cherríe Moraga, from "La Güera," *This Bridge Called My Back: Writings by Radical Women of Color*, es. Cherríe Moraga and Gloria Anzaldúa (Watertown, MA: Persephone Press, 1981; reprinted by SUNY Press, 2015), pp. 28–30. Copyright © 1981 by Cherríe L. Moraga. Reprinted by permission of Stuart Bernstein Representation of Artists, New York, NY, and protected by the Copyright Laws of the United States. All rights reserved.

Mitsuye Yamada, from "Invisibility Is an Unnatural Disaster: Reflections of an Asian American Woman," *This Bridge Called My Back: Writings by Radical Women of Color*, ed. Cherríe Moraga and Gloria Anzaldúa (Watertown, MA: Persephone Press, 1981; reprinted by SUNY Press, 2015), pp. 36–40. Copyright © 1979 by *Bridge: An Asian American Perspective*. Reprinted

List of Illustrations

Bettye Lane, courtesy of the Bettye Lane Estate and Schlesinger Library on the History of Women in America, Radcliffe Institute.

26. "The Liberation of Aunt Jemima" by Betye Saar. © Betye Saar. Photo by Benjamin Blackwell, courtesy of the artist and Roberts Projects, Los Angeles, California.

27. Artist Faith Ringgold in her studio with her painting "Soul Sister," 1971. Photo by George Hopkins, courtesy of Michele Wallace.

28. "You're Seeing Less Than Half the Picture," 1989 poster by the Guerrilla Girls. © Guerrilla Girls. Digital image © Whitney Museum of American Art. Licensed by Scala, courtesy of Art Resource, NY.

29. "In Mourning and in Rage . . . ," 1977 performance by Suzanne Lacy and Leslie Labowitz. Courtesy of Suzanne Lacy and Leslie Labowitz. Photo by Maria Karas, courtesy of Suzanne Lacy and Leslie Labowitz.

30. Judy Chicago, ad in October 1970 issue of *Artforum*. Courtesy of Judy Chicago.

31. Democratic congresswomen marching up the Capitol steps to demand a delay of the Senate's vote to confirm Clarence Thomas to the Supreme Court, October 1991. Photo by Paul Hosefros, *The New York Times*, courtesy of Redux Pictures.

Index

law, 131, 151–58; and prostitution, 488–89; and sexual happiness, 59, 442; and sexual harassment, 395; social and political, 240; traditional versus radical feminism on, 80

Equal pay for equal work, 156, 189, 200, 479, 481, 484, 504

Equal protection, 152

Equal Rights Amendment (ERA), 131, 237, 366, 424, 489, 500, 505, 509, 516, 518

Erikson, Erik, 204

Erotica, 368, 407, 411, 439

Eroticism, 51, 58, 124, 436; and erotomania, 123; and male supremacy, 123; and pornography, 374–75, 398–99, 402–3, 407; as power, 179, 373–76; and romanticism, 118–19; and sex roles, 180

Essence, 479

Estrogen, 224, 228

Evil, and women, 358–59

Exorcist, The (film), 359

Exploitation, 78, 89, 112; of black women, 97–99; economic, 96, 98, 103, 165, 484; of homosexuals, 467, 470; of housewives, 267–68; of prostitutes, 486, 488–89; racial, 100–103; sexual, 48, 55, 123, 181, 436–37, 439, 464–65, 486, 488–89; of women as caste/class, 20, 121; of working class, 188, 332; of working women, 410

Faggot, 34, 146

Fair employment practices, 156

Faking orgasm, 278–79

Faludi, Susan: *Backlash*, 500–520; "Death of a Revolutionary," 500

Family: black, 94–95, 161–62, 479–85; patriarchal, 117, 119, 161–62, 433, 482

Family Assistance Plan (FAP), 221–23

Family Circle, 45

Family law, 153–55

Fancher, Edwin, 107

Fantasies, sexual, 279–80, 406–11, 434

Farley, Lin: "Eleven Ways to Fight Sexual Harassment," 370–72; *Sexual Shakedown*, 370

Fatal Attraction (film), 502

Fatherhood, 32–33, 447–48

"Father tongue," 472–76

Fauquier County, Va., 100

Federal Communications Commission, 368

Federici, Silvia: *Wages against Housework*, 262–70

Female chauvinism, 252

Female homosexuals. *See* Lesbians/lesbianism

Femininity, 5–8, 14–15, 18–19, 34, 52, 60–61, 63–72, 95, 123, 148–49, 185, 196, 205, 266, 268, 411, 466

Feminism, 5, 28, 136–37, 240, 250, 323–24, 441, 468; and abortion, 136–39, 144; backlash to, 131, 501–3, 509, 511–13; basic divisions in, 494–99; as ideology of equality, 425; as political movement, 469–70; socialist, 330–37. *See also* Moderate feminism; Radical feminism

Feminist Anti-Censorship Taskforce (FACT), 402, 494

Feminist divide, 494–99

Feminist Party, 233

Feminists: moderate, 80, 109, 145, 192, 320–25, 461–62; radical, 20, 28, 50, 75, 79–82, 92, 104, 109–10, 136, 145, 148, 159, 163, 192, 194, 198, 238–41, 249–50, 295, 310, 320, 324, 330, 333, 345, 358, 366, 385, 411, 416, 418, 433, 435–36, 438, 467–68, 494, 503

Feminists, The, 28, 79, 437–38; "Women: Do You Know the Facts about Marriage?," 92–93

Feminist Studio Workshop, 304

Feminist Women's Health Center, 271–73

Fertility, 6, 224, 226, 314, 436, 463, 503, 508

Fetal deformity, 137, 139, 143

Field, Sally, 502

Firebrand Books, 451

Firestone, Shulamith, 45, 110, 500; *The Dialectic of Sex*, 117–24, 436; "Women Rap about Sex," 279

First Amendment, 366–69, 391, 399

Judith (biblical figure), 179
Jung, Carl G., 205
Jury duty, 152

Kali, 313
Kansas City, Mo., 237
Karina, Anna, 278
Kauffmann, Stanley, 64
Kelly, G. Lombard: *Sexual Feelings in Married Men and Women*, 57–58, 62
Kennedy, Florynce R., 296; "The Verbal Karate of Florynce R. Kennedy, Esq.," 233–37
Kentucky, 155
Keres, 456–57
Kinder, Melvyn: *Smart Women, Foolish Choices*, 502
King, Martin Luther, Jr., 78, 89
King, Mary: "Sex and Caste," 20–23
King, Stephen: *Misery*, 502
Kingston, Maxine Hong, 444; *The Woman Warrior*, 298–303
Kinsey, Alfred C., 17; *Sexual Behavior in the Human Female*, 57–58, 62
Kitchen Table: Women of Color Press, 377
Koedt, Anne, 278; "The Myth of the Vaginal Orgasm," 54–62
Ku Klux Klan, 237
Kumin, Maxine, 207

Labor Department, U.S., 98, 221, 447
Labor laws, 155–58
Labowitz, Leslie: "In Mourning and In Rage . . . ," 354–57
Lactation, 246
Lacy, Suzanne: "In Mourning and In Rage . . . ," 354–57
Ladies' Home Journal, 45, 69, 96
Laguna Pueblo, 455
Lakey, George, 466
Lakey, Judy, 466
Lakota, 457, 462
Language, 129, 349, 386–90, 472–76
La Raza Unida Party, 187–90
Larsen, Nella, 256, 258
Las Hijas de Cuahtemoc, 187

Latinas/Latinos, 134, 482–83. *See also* Chicanas/Chicanos; Puerto Ricans
Lavender Menace, 145
Lavender Woman, The, 191
Lavin, Mary, 207
League of Women Voters, 9
Leake, Priscilla, 49
Leduc, Violette, 71
Legal Action for Women, 493
Legal Defense and Education Fund (NOW), 151
Legal issues, 92–93, 151–58, 370–71, 391–401
Legal Momentum, 151
Legal residence, 152–53
Leghorn, Lisa: "The Man's Problem," 104–6
Le Guin, Ursula K.: *The Dispossessed*, 472; *The Left Hand of Darkness*, 472; "The Mother Tongue," 472–76
Lenin, V. I., 83
Lerner, Gerda: "The Majority Finds Its Past," 338–44
Lerner-Scott Prize, 338
Lesbian Herstory Archives, 413
Lesbians/lesbianism, 54, 84, 106, 242, 244, 296, 351–52, 368, 378, 386, 413–15, 451, 464; black, 191, 345, 348, 353, 373, 387; exploitation of, 467, 470; and female orgasm, 61; and heterosexism, 210, 345, 347, 418, 438, 462, 466, 468–69, 471; and homophobia, 210, 330, 380, 384; identity of, 211, 214; Latina, 387, 417–18; and male supremacy, 146, 210–15, 380; and patriarchy, 438; as political choice, 210–11, 215; radical, 145–50, 210–15, 358; rights of, 326; separatists, 50, 104, 210, 437–38; and "sexual revolution," 434–39
Lesser, Norma Allen: "The Children's House," 173–78
Lessing, Doris, 207
Levey, Michael: *Fifty Works of English Literature We Could Do Without*, 70
Levittown, N.J., 16
Lewis, Janet, 207
Liberalism, sexual, 441–42, 465

Marx, Karl/Marxism, 83, 213, 250, 262, 330–35, 348–49, 384

Maryland, 140, 142, 155

Masculinity, 34, 43, 60–61, 64–68, 71, 95, 180, 314, 411, 443, 466

Massachusetts, 142, 152, 155

Masters, William B.: *Human Sexual Response*, 54, 57, 62

Masturbation, 54, 57, 245–46, 278–80, 288, 411

"Maternity clinics," 100

Maternity leave, 481, 484, 505

Matisse, Amélie, 89

Matisse, Henri, 89

Matriarchy, 75–76, 126, 192, 195, 413, 456, 458

Matrilineal surnames, 238

McCall's, 69

McCarthy, Mary, 71–72, 207; *The Group*, 69–70

McCullers, Carson, 206

McFarland, Morgan, 429

McKellips, John, 514

McNamara, Robert, 37

Medea, 313

Media Workshop, 233

Memphis, Tenn., 366, 368

Men: and abortion, 157, 314, 448; art community dominated by, 304, 308; backlash from, 79–80; and battered wives, 326–29; black, 48–49, 60, 75, 77, 94–96, 103, 132–33, 159–64, 195, 292–96, 348, 350–51, 482; bodies of, 244–45; Chicano, 188–90; control of marriage by, 38–44, 92, 95; fatherhood, 32–33, 447–48; fears of, 105; feminization of, 194; and housework, 86–91; literary criticism by, 63–72; machismo, 163, 165, 187–90, 265, 383; masculinity, 34, 43, 60–61, 64–68, 71, 95, 180, 314, 411, 443, 466; orgasms of, 55, 57; and pornography, 398, 407, 410; predatory, 442–43, 477; and pregnancy, 448; and prostitution, 486; Puerto Rican, 163–65, 383; radical organizations led by, 38, 82, 159; and rape, 393–94; and *SCUM*

Manifesto, 28–37; sexual expectations of, 50–53, 57, 59–61; and sexual harassment, 396; sexuality, 29–30, 95, 181, 464–66; vasectomy for, 99, 226, 229, 272; virility, 95, 118; and "woman problem," 8–10, 17; and women's movement, 21–22, 46

Menopause, 19, 242, 244, 272, 318

Men's magazines. *See* Newspapers/ magazines

Menstruation, 19, 225, 242, 245, 247, 272–73, 310, 318, 368

Metapatriarchy, 363–64

Mexican Americans. *See* Chicanas/ Chicanos

Mexico, 295, 386, 456–57

Michelangelo Buonarroti: *Pietà*, 318

Michigan, 152

Middle Ages, 224, 272, 275, 287–88, 358

Middle class, 108, 217, 220, 388, 497; and abortion, 139, 141; apolitical women in, 419; black, 77, 160, 418; and capitalism, 265; feminist movement as white and, 102, 132, 244, 295, 351, 380; and psychotherapy, 230–32; and Puerto Rican feminists, 383–85; white, 48–49, 78, 97, 100, 102, 132, 244, 252, 295

Midwest Regional Women and the Law Conference, 391

Midwives, 272

Militant, The, 187

Militarism, 333

Military, 35, 287–91, 420–21

Military service, 152

Mill, John Stuart: *The Subjection of Women*, 86, 391

Miller, Alvin, 284

Miller, Jean Baker, 510

Millett, Kate, 205; *Flying*, 125; *The Prostitution Papers*, 403; *Sexual Politics*, 125–30

Mindoka War Relocation Center, 419–20

Minimum wage, 90, 155, 195, 484

Minneapolis, Minn., 391, 402

Minnesota, 155, 397

Minot, Susan, 514

Misogyny, 63, 68, 121, 326, 435, 509